BURNING BUSH

ALSO BY STEPHEN J. PYNE

Henry Holt and Company · New York

BURNING BUSH

A Fire History of Australia

Stephen J. Pyne

Published by Henry Holt and Company, Inc.,
115 West 18th Street, New York, New York 10011.
Published in Canada by Fitzhenry & Whiteside Limited,
195 Allstate Parkway, Markham, Ontario L3R 4T8.

Library of Congress Cataloging-in-Publication Data
Pyne, Stephen J.
Burning bush: a fire history of Australia/Stephen J. Pyne.
p.   cm.
Includes bibliographical references and index.
1. Man—Influence on nature—Australia.   2. Fire ecology—
Australia.   3. Natural history—Australia.   4. Shifting
cultivation—Australia.   5. Australian Aborigines—Agriculture.
I.   Title.
GF901.P96   1991
304.2'0994—dc20   90-25116
CIP

ISBN 0-8050-1472-1

Henry Holt books are available at special discounts
for bulk purchases for sales promotions, premiums,
fund-raising, or educational use. Special editions
or book excerpts can also be created to specification.
For details contact:
Special Sales Director, Henry Holt and Company, Inc.,
115 West 18th Street, New York, New York 10011.

First Edition

Designed by Lucy Albanese
Maps by Barbara Trapido

Printed in the United States of America
Recognizing the importance of preserving the written word,
Henry Holt and Company, Inc., by policy, prints all of its
first editions on acid-free paper. ∞

1   3   5   7   9   10   8   6   4   2

Frontispiece illustration: "Mr Phipps and Bowman engaging
the blacks who attempted to burn us out, March 15, 1856,
Depot Creek, Victoria River," by Thomas Baines.
[Courtesy Royal Geographical Society]

TO SONJA, LYDIA, MOLLY—

tolerant pynes who made room for gums

Contents

x   **Contents**

Preface

Firestick History

Australian history is almost always picturesque; indeed, it is so curious and strange, that it is itself the chiefest novelty the country has to offer, and so it pushes the other novelties into second and third place. It does not read like history, but like the most beautiful lies.

—MARK TWAIN,
Following the Equator (1897)

SOMETIME—or rather at several critical junctures—in the saga of Australia, the island continent opted for fire. A sequence of environmental events made fire possible as soils deteriorated, aridity became seasonal and drought common, ancestral rainforest broke up into a suite of tough, woody weeds, and storm tracks hurled fierce winds from interior deserts. Fires kindled and spread, and they interacted with the emergent biota in often extraordinary ways. Fire acquired a signatory rhythm and power that indelibly identified it with the bush it shaped. And then *Homo* arrived.

Humans brought chronic fire, inextinguishable fire; they were a uniquely fire creature for whom fire was a universal tool. They all—Aborigines, Europeans, Australians—applied it universally in every conceivable landscape and for every conceivable purpose. They exploited fire to extract from an often forbidding environment the critical elements of their existence. Their fires reinforced tendencies already encoded in the natural environment. The ability to tolerate fire evolved into a preference for it; a biotic preference for fire became a near addiction; Australia's natural history moved irreversibly toward fire-proneness. Bushfire became inexpungable, compelling, pervasive.

The relationships mediated by anthropogenic fire were reciprocal: they restructured natural fire regimes even as they remade human societies. Anthropogenic fire shaped Australian geography and informed Australian history. It penetrated the Australian consciousness in special ways. In return, Australians have profoundly reworked the historical geography of fire. To celebrate their bicentenary Australians even encircled their continent with a ring of bonfires.

AN ENVIRONMENTAL EPIC pleads for an epic style. Instead I offer a cautious alternative. In studying the Aborigines of Arnhemland, Rhys Jones coined the expression "fire-stick farmers" to describe their relationship to their land. Through their skillful manipulation of fire, Aborigines fashioned an analogue of farming, a means by which to massage the indigenous environment into serving their particular needs. By analogy, I propose a kind of firestick history, an alternative genre in which fire is both a means and an end.

What follows is not merely a history of fires, fire regimes, and fire practices—all fascinating in their own way. Rather, this fire history proposes, in addition, to use fire as a means of historical understanding. By studying fire one can extract information from the historical record that is otherwise inaccessible or overlooked, much as burning often flushes infertile biotas with nutrients and cooking renders palatable many otherwise inedible foodstuffs. Fire can reconfigure historical landscapes and remake raw materials into humanly usable history. Thus, fire history introduces new data into Australian history; it provides new means by which to explore historical events; and, like fire—which integrates innumerable environmental conditions into a coherent flame—it offers a synthesis. In the end, it describes as few phenomena can the interplay between humans and landscape, which is to say it illuminates the character of each.

Burning Bush is thus several histories for several audiences. Like an ellipse, it has two foci—one in fire history and the other in Australian history. Likewise it has two national audiences, Australian and American, and two sets of data, one from the natural sciences and one from sources more traditional to historical scholarship. They combine into inherently unstable compounds, at times bonding like epoxy and on other occasions becoming as volatile as nitroglycerin, ready to explode with the first stumble. Though it ranges widely through the scientific literature, this examination is not science. Rather, it seeks to use fire to elicit new insights from existing scholarship and archives, and to establish a context for understanding the global status of Australian fire. Free-burning fire is a catalyst, an accelerant, a magnifier, and its history inevitably an exaggeration. That is especially true in Australia, and pyrophilia can infect historians as it has so much of Australian life. Obsession can replace narrative, recalling Gaston Bachelard's belief that fire-induced reverie renders impossible the rational study of fire. Herman Melville warned: "Look not too long in the face of the fire, O man!" It's a risk worth taking.

In many ways, Australian fire history recapitulates the history of fire on all the vegetated continents. Its special character becomes apparent only through careful comparisons. That, at least, is my justification for the running contrast with North America and for the occasional contrasts with Britain and Greater Gondwana. However much Australians might lament their isolation, the tyranny of distance that segregates them physically and psychologically from cultural developments elsewhere, there is no such quarantine for fire. Australian fire history is an indispensable chapter in a global epic that began when early hominids captured combustion and changed forever the human and natural history of the planet.

THIS BOOK BEGAN many years ago when I decided that I would study in a serious way the cultural history of fire on Earth. I had just completed a fire history of the United States, started a general textbook on fire management, and was seriously researching a history of Antarctica. A symposium on Antarctic geoscience took me to Adelaide in 1982, from which I visited N. P. Cheney at the CSIRO Division of Forest Research and introduced my scheme to him. A National Science Foundation grant (Geography) paid for a nine-week tour of Australian archives and landscape in 1986. A conference on Australian science at the University of Melbourne in May 1988 brought me back for a few more weeks of miscellaneous library research. The breakthrough came when an Arizona State University Faculty Grant-in-Aid and a National Endowment for the Humanities Fellowship (1988–89) combined to give me the time to write the book. To all of these institutional sponsors, I am deeply grateful.

What made my time in Australia so productive were the Australians who hosted me. Very special thanks go to Phil Cheney, who never hesitated to make available to me whatever resources he could, not least of which was to organize an ad hoc fire-study tour of Australia. Despite his deep attachment to Alan McArthur, he never pressured me to write the story along any ideological track, believing that untrammeled scholarship would best serve McArthur's memory. He is an exceptional fire scientist—and a good friend. I hope the outcome merits his trust.

Others who contributed include Margaret Saville, Erika Leslie, Chris Trevitt, Colin Pierrehumbert, David Packham, Athol Hodgson, J. Barry Johnston, Noel Kemp, John Smart, Gordon Styles, Mark Dawson, Marcia Tommerup, A. B. Mount, D. R. Douglas, Athol Meyer, Wilfred Crane, Fred Kerr, Geoffrey Brown, Ross Smith, R. R. Richmond, Andrew Bond, Ross Hamwood, Bob Barchard, R. H. Burke, Neil Burrows, Jim Hickman, N. J. deMestre, Graham Medhurst, Neil Price, Ron Hooper, R. W. Home, Ian Knight, John Baxter, Peter Hutchins, R. W. Condon, and Andrew Wilson. From Oxford, I need to thank Miss Jasmine Howse and Michael Williams. Special thanks go to Harry Luke, who took me into his house for several days of delightful conversation, and to Jim Gould, a fellow North American (and to his children, Jane and Toby), who helped with housing and travel while I resided with them in Canberra. In addition, Roger Underwood, Roger Good, A. Malcolm Gill, and the unfailing Phil Cheney not only assisted while I traveled in Australia but read critically all or portions of the manuscript, a burden much greater than any of us anticipated. They spared me many errors, though even they could not save me from myself and a "poetic license" that, for all their goodwill, must have set their teeth on edge. While they certainly do not agree with everything I have written, I could have written nothing without their help. My debt to other Australian scientists and scholars on whom I have relied through the published record is obvious. Thanks, mates.

Special thanks go also to Bill Strachan for his encouragement, editorial strategy, and skill at piloting around the shoals of corporate publishing.

And of course I could never have undertaken this project without the support of my family. To Sonja, Lydia, and Molly—who gave me the time and, more important, the reason to continue—thanks.

BURNING BUSH

There an angel of the Lord appeared to him [Moses] in fire flaming out of a bush. As he looked on, he was surprised to see that the bush, though on fire, was not consumed.

—EXODUS 3:2

And the sun sank again on the grand Australian bush—the nurse and tutor of eccentric minds, the home of the weird, and of much that is different from things in other lands.

—HENRY LAWSON,
"The Bush Undertaker"

INDONESIA

PAPUA
NEW
GUINEA

SOLOMON IS.

0°

VANUATU

AUSTRALIA

Tropic of Capricorn

30° S

NEW
ZEALAND

120°   150°   180° E

TIMOR SEA

KIMBERLEY

GREAT SANDY DESERT

PILBARA

GIBSON DESERT

WESTERN

AUSTRALIA

GREAT VICTOR

GERALDTON

NULLARB

INDIAN

PERTH

DARLING RANGES

OCEAN

Rottnest
and
Garden
Islands

STIRLING
RANGE

ARCHIPELAGO
OF THE RECHERCHE

GRE

AUSTRAL

ALBANY

N

MILES

0   100   200   300   400   500

0   100 200 300 400 500

KILOMETERS

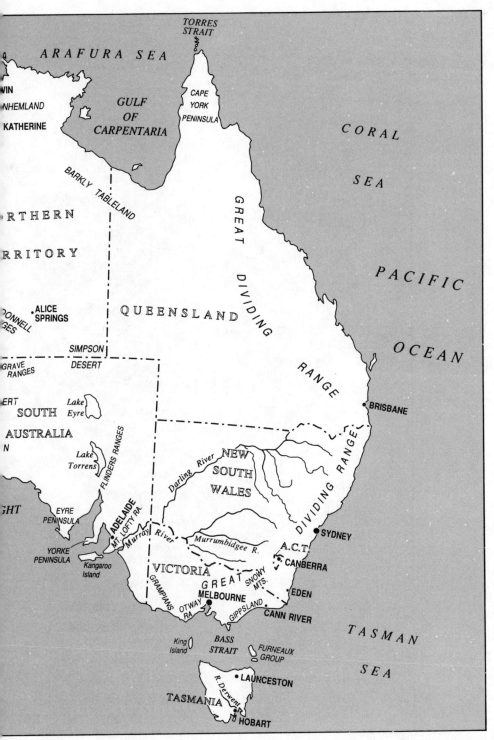

AUSTRALIA

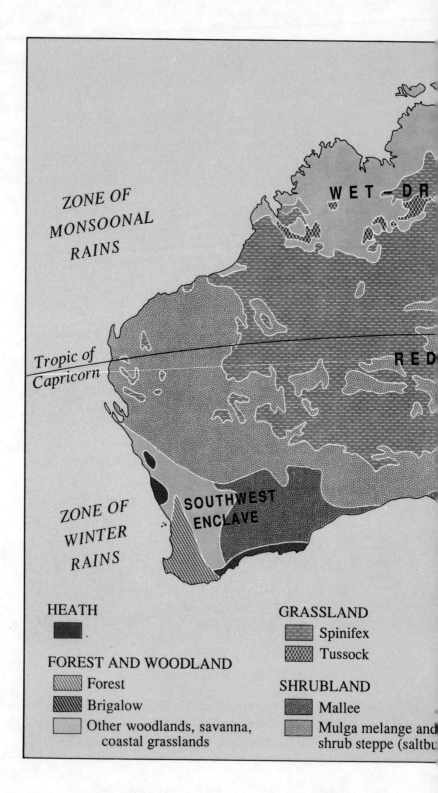

ZONE OF
MONSOONAL
RAINS

WET – DR

Tropic of
Capricorn

R E D

ZONE OF
WINTER
RAINS

SOUTHWEST
ENCLAVE

HEATH

GRASSLAND

Spinifex

Tussock

FOREST AND WOODLAND

Forest

Brigalow

Other woodlands, savanna,
coastal grasslands

SHRUBLAND

Mallee

Mulga melange and
shrub steppe (saltbu

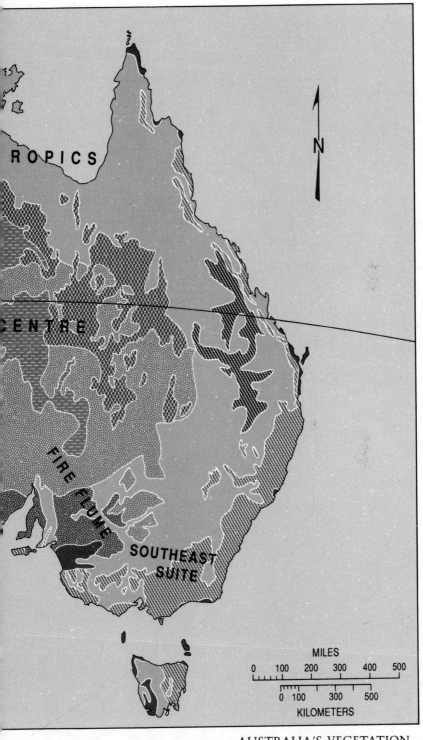

ROPICS

CENTRE

FIRE FLUME

SOUTHEAST
SUITE

N

MILES
0 100 200 300 400 500

0 100   300   500
KILOMETERS

AUSTRALIA'S VEGETATION

Prologue

Dust to Dust

> . . . *Flood, fire, and cyclone in successive motion*
> *Complete the work the pioneers began*
> *Of shifting all the soil into the ocean.*
>
> —JAMES MCAULEY,
> "The True Discovery of Australia"

GONDWANA GENESIS

In the beginning—even 250 million years ago—all lands were one. Then they began to break apart. Great rifts appeared that opened and closed uncertainly over a period of tens of millions of years, and when the final tear ceased, Pangaea had become two continents. One, Laurasia, drifted north. The other, now known as Gondwana, moved south.

Over the coming eons the continental masses migrated, fractured, grew, and reoriented themselves. They massed mountains to their flanks, fresh lands swelled out of submerged basins, volcanic eruptions piled new rock onto old crust. Laurasia broke cautiously into Old World and New, Eurasia and North America. Gondwana was more prolific. As it fissioned, it spawned continents, subcontinents, and microcontinents. New island arcs broke through Gondwana's peripheral oceans as colossal plates of crust grated, subducted, melted, and bubbled upward into chains of fiery volcanoes. Greater Australia, which included Papua New Guinea and Tasmania, moved northeast into an empty Pacific. By 80–60 million years ago, with the opening of the Tasman Sea, Australia segregated from New Zealand, the last of its Gondwana affiliates. In its travels it had rotated nearly 90 degrees, and it had rafted northward at roughly six or seven centimeters per year until it rammed into the submerged Pacific margins of Asia and helped raise the Sunda arc, punctuated by the towering mountains of New Guinea.

Australia's geology preserved a Gondwana core, a continental craton, in the enormous plateau that sprawled over the western and central thirds of the continent. Its odyssey, however, had raised mountains along its eastern flanks—the Flinders Range, the Tasmanian Alps, and the Great Dividing Range, a plateau eroded into dramatic escarpments. Continental warping had raised basins and bulged crust into domed, long-wasted mountains in the center. Associated with the eastern uplift, too, were local outpourings of volcanics, largely Tertiary in age, occasionally sputtering into the Holocene.

But overall the post-Gondwana history of Australia was one of geologic quiescence. Australian tectonics were muted; mountains were relatively low in elevation; the principal periods of vigorous activity were old and circumscribed. Australia became the most level of continents. Small rises in sea level resulted in massive incursions of ocean, while small recessions exposed vast regions of land with catastrophic suddenness. The geologic story of Australia required geologic time to record—the minuscule migration of the craton, the relentless leaching and the implacable erosion of its surface. The rejuvenation proposed by the first failed to match the degradation of the second.[1]

Where rainfall remained plentiful, deep weathering became the norm. Soils edged into acidity and deteriorated in those physical properties vital to groundwater. Laterization bound phosphorus to iron and aluminum complexes, chemically inaccessible to most organisms. Minerals once distributed more or less uniformly were reworked, concentrated, or removed from the scene. In some instances this led to localized lodes of gold, bauxite, and uranium, but overall the processes only encouraged the generic pauperization of soils, the loss of phosphorus and such critical trace elements as molybdenum, copper, cobalt, and boron. Without renewal by major tectonic forces, without intervention by some process like glaciation that could overturn or scrape away the surface debris or recharge lowlands with new minerals derived from mountain catchments, there was little chance to reverse the inexorable tread toward an entropy of emptiness. The process might be slowed, even locally defied, but it could not be resisted. In Western Australia, at Mount Narryer, weathering exposed zircon some 4.1–4.2 billion years old, incorporated into rocks formed 3.6 billion years ago. New landscapes emerged from the successive exfoliation, by erosion, of old landscapes. Australia's biologic renaissance had to rise out of a geologic decadence.[2]

THE BREAKUP OF GONDWANA freed Greater Australia to pursue a separate destiny. That burden fell to its biota: its curious flora and fauna would proclaim the unique character of the island continent. Old Australia's geology and its biology coexisted in weird counterpoint. Where one degraded and removed, the other exploded into a biotic efflorescence, a proliferation of species unlike those found anywhere else on Earth. Instead of much devolving into less, a relatively small Gondwanic inheritance evolved into more. Some components of green Gondwana not only accepted the geologic legacy—soil depletion and geographic isolation—but turned them to advantage.[3]

Its originating biota was one Old Australia shared with most of Gondwana. The ancestral forest was dominated by the gymnosperms—the southern conifers, the araucarias and podocarps—but just as Gondwana began to break up, and perhaps in partial response to the stimulus of that profound dislocation, the angiosperms—the flowering plants—proliferated. From a projected point of origin where Africa joined South America, the angiosperms spread throughout Gondwana. Their migration was selective, and the resulting geographies of the conifers and the flowering plants varied. Gondwana was too large, too unbroken a landmass for a single climate to characterize it everywhere, and as the giant continent fragmented, separate lines of biotic advance and exchange danced in slow choreography with geologic cratons. This meant that a single pan-Gondwanic biota did not exist everywhere in equal composition. What part of the ancestral forest the different continental fragments took with them depended on their relationship to Greater Gondwana and on the sequence of their fissioning, all played against the larger drama in which the angiosperms invaded and claimed greater proportions of the supercontinent.

It appears that Old Australia embarked with a solid complement of the ancestral rainforest, a Gondwanic ark. Among the dominant conifers were the araucarias and the podocarps; among the angiosperms, the dominant genus was *Nothofagus,* the Antarctic beech. Minor families included the myrtles, the grasses, casuarinas, chenopods, and xanthorrhoeas; important genera included *Banksia, Hakea, Melaleuca, Eucalyptus.* Much the same paleoflora characterized large portions of Antarctica, South America, and New Zealand. In all these lands the Gondwanic rainforest was sustained by a persistent, year-round moisture regime. The relentless rains leached and degraded soils, but the process occurred so slowly that the biota kept pace and adapted. The minor flora claimed special niches; many probably scavenged along the margins of rainforest, better adapted to disturbances, occasional dryness, a more fractured biotic environment.

When Old Australia broke away, about 30 million years ago, the rupture was remarkably final. There would be some late contamination along the north from Indo-Malayan biotas, though these would be restricted by the high mountains thrown up along the New Guinea border and by the deep waters, between islands, that only select species could cross. Together mountain and sea presented an effective biological filter. Greater Australia differentiated into the Australian mainland, New Guinea, and Tasmania, to be reconnected and sundered from time to time with the geologic tides of a rising and falling global ocean. Not until historical times would there be a further, significant contamination of the biota.

The move to the tropics, while slow, induced climatic change, a new biotic force. Aridity did to the Gondwanic rainforest what tectonic stress did to the Gondwanic supercontinent. The ancestral rainforest fractured and multiplied, cleaving along biotic planes of weakness that divided those species that required uniform moisture from those that could accommodate dryness and change. The onset of aridity did not simply replace one enduring condition with another; it made regular and sporadic change a fundamental part of the biological calendar.

Australian aridity was seasonal, episodic, and chronic. It became, in places, part of an annual cycle of wet and dry seasons. In the tropics, the seasons followed the monsoonal winds, wet in the summer and dry in the winter. In the Mediterranean-like climates of the southeast and southwest, aridity took the form of a prolonged, parching summer, with moisture mostly a product of winter storms. Elsewhere aridity manifested itself as drought, extending regionally over several years. In the enormous center of the continent, aridity became a relentless presence, crowding moisture regimes to the coastal fringe and assaulting the littoral with desiccating winds. The southeast trades and the Great Dividing Range combined to raise moisture along the eastern seaboard, but the interior deserts, like a stony ice sheet expanding and contracting, defined the frontier. At times, like a red giant exploding among the stars, the desert core threatened to engulf the continent.

This transformation—the Great Upheaval—occurred over the course of the Tertiary period. It commenced with Greater Australia's segregation from Gondwana during the Eocene epoch, and acquired a signature rhythm, long but emphatic, during the Oligocene. The Earth cooled and, overall, dried; Antarctica acquired an ice sheet; Australia continued its tread toward the equator; new circulation patterns established around the Southern Ocean and within and around the Australian continent; global changes in sea level catastrophically flooded then reexposed vast portions of the continental plains, reshaping the interactive meteorology of ocean and continent. By the Pliocene and Pleistocene epochs—over the past 5 million years—the trend became all but inevitable. Aridity became the norm and humidity the exception. The area of stony desert came roughly to equal the area of true forest. During the last glacial epochs, the transfiguration could be called irreversible. Australia's low latitudes and low relief confined glaciation to Tasmania; there were no loess plains blown downwind, no fresh rocks exposed to weathering, no transfer of nutrients and sediments from mountain to plain. Where rainforest taxa reemerged, they bloomed like ephemerals after a desert storm. The Great Upheaval ended with a Great Inversion of the Australian biota.

In this biotic revolution once-minor constituents, now hardened and shaped by drought and disturbance, became dominant. The survivors evolved into scleromorphs (or sclerophylls)—literally, "hard leaves," referring to the small, tough evergreen leaves that hoarded nutrients and resisted the transpiration of precious water. The scleromorphs adapted not only to soil impoverishment but to aridity—and, in fact, to disturbances of many kinds. By the mid-Miocene epoch (c. 15 million years ago), as the continental interior acquired its imperishable dryness, the relatively homogeneous biota of ancestral Australia began to differentiate.

What had been a more or less uniform cover of closed Gondwanic rainforest splintered into new, peculiarly Australian biotas. The hermetic forest became open; woodland surrendered to savanna, shrub and heathland, grasses, or outright sand and stony desert. The ancestral rainforest dominated by *Nothofagus* and *Podocarpus* gradually retreated before aridity like leaves before a blower. In its place emerged a scleroforest. Casuarinas succeeded araucarias. Tough grasses and scrubby scleromorphs seized understories formerly softened by fern, moss, and fungi. About 34 million years ago the eucalypts appeared, quiet and unannounced. Sometime around 25 million years ago acacias arrived, probably by sea from elsewhere in Gondwana. Thereafter the biotic isolation of the island continent was nearly total. By the time of European discovery the ancestral rainforest had retreated to minor enclaves in the Great Divide, where they occupied probably less than 1 percent of the total land surface of Australia.

The Great Upheaval had all but replaced a pan-Gondwanic biota with a marvelously endemic suite of biotas. About one-third of all Australian plant genera are endemic, nearly 90 percent of all plant species; Victoria alone has a flora twice as great as that of Britain. But such figures fail to convey the utter, continental-scale domination of the landscape by the scleromorphs. The revolution was comprehensive. With the new flora came new fauna and new patterns of interaction between sclerophyllous plants and sclerophyllous animals. Birds and mammals, not insects, typically pollinated the flowering scleromorphs. Placental mammals and reptiles repeated the radiation of specialized plants. Two genera, *Eucalyptus* and *Acacia*—gums and wattles—virtually tyrannized every forest and woodland biota, excepting only the relict rainforest. Two genera of grasses, *Triodia* and *Astrebla*—the hummocks and the tussocks—similarly dominated the grasslands. Scleromorphs invaded and reshaped forests, woodlands, grasslands, deserts. They penetrated every ecological niche—the canopy, the understory, the surface. They claimed relatively dry sites and relatively wet and those areas that were, on an annual cycle, both wet and dry. The rainforest eroded away like the plateaus of ancient Gondwana. What began as a Gondwanic ark ended as an island continent, Old Australia, that only remotely resembled anyplace else.[4]

The final expulsion of rainforest came relatively late. By the onset of the last glaciation (80,000 years ago) a rough balance still existed between forests consisting of scleromorphic angiosperms like the casuarinas and those composed of ancient gymnosperms like the araucarias. By 38,000 years ago, however, the araucarian forest had all but vanished. Aridity had decided the contest between rainforest and scleroforest, but as aridity settled in to an enduring presence, it became more complex and found new allies. During the final, near extinction of rainforest another biotic revolution broke out, this time within the scleroforest. Casuarinas receded, eucalypts advanced, and charcoal saturated the landscape. This second upheaval was decided by the renaissance of a new, vastly more complicated stress—fire.

WHAT ESCALATED THE GREAT UPHEAVAL was not the simple fact of aridity, but its rate of growth, the frequency of its oscillations, the way it introduced routine disturbances. Wet periods gave way to dry, and dry returned to wet, like a two-cycle engine. With the onset of the Quaternary era the frequency of oscillations increased. A gradual change could have been met with gradual adaptations, but rapid, frequent flux encouraged organisms that could respond with equal vigor and speed, that thrived amid disturbance. It encouraged the tough, the opportunistic. It promoted the weeds among the Gondwana greenery. What began as a tendency stiffened into a trend as Australia began to burn.[5]

There had been some fire in the past. Coal seams preserved, as pyrofusinite, the charcoal of Carboniferous- and Tertiary-era fires. Brown coals from the Yallourn-Morwell district of Victoria reveal ample evidence of burning, probably in the late Tertiary or early Pleistocene times. Where coal seams had been exposed as outcrops, they also ignited from surface fires. Burning Mountain in New South Wales, already smoldering when Europeans arrived, is a celebrated example. But smoldering coal and fiery basalt flows could not become a selective force of continental proportions. Lightning fire could—and did.[6]

What is required is not lightning per se, but the interaction of lightning with appropriate fuels properly cured and dried. The scleromorphs and grasses offered ideal fuels, and a pattern of seasonal aridity and lightning storms stirred the right mixture of fire and water. The storms had to arrive when the vegetation was cured, massed, and dried. Too much rain dampened the fuels; too few storms reduced the probability of ignition; and too prolonged aridity not only dried but killed the vegetation and starved the fire of fuel. During the Great Upheaval, however, the proper, improbable combination of conditions appeared and persisted.

Those circumstances are difficult to reconstruct in any detail. As scleromorphs emerged from the morass of rainforest taxa and as aridity evolved into seasonal or secular patterns, it is likely that fires appeared where they had not been present before, or became more active where they had gained footholds. For fire to be biologically effective, it need not occur annually, only at critical times within the life cycle of the prime species. For rainforest these cycles may involve decades, centuries, perhaps millennia. Elsewhere in what endures of Gondwana rainforest, there is evidence of fire. Thick lenses of charcoal of uncertain origin underly sites in Amazonia. The rainforest of East Kalimantan, Borneo, burns in long, relentless stringers from surface coal seams that act as a slow match, ready to kindle the surrounding terrain at times of severe drought. In the early phases of the Great Upheaval the fossil record suggests a pattern of swamp fires within a landscape of closed rainforest. The frontier between scleroforest and rainforest was almost certainly etched with fire.[7]

Current statistics furnish some insight into the potential power of lightning fire in Old Australia. A 1961 lightning barrage in the Australian Alps impressed fire professionals that "there is no doubt that if all the fires . . . had spread unhindered by firefighters, they would have burnt over most of the Snowy Mountains area before winter rain put them out." During the 1970s in Victoria lightning was responsible for 24 percent of all fire starts. In terms of area burned it accounted for 60 percent of the acreage. A single storm in 1972 ignited thirty-nine fires in rugged terrain. While most fires began in the eastern mountains, the largest fires raced through the more interior grasslands. Some 80 percent of fires in western Queensland, it is estimated, originate with lightning. About 20 percent of fires in southeastern Australia and perhaps 12 percent of fires in the forests of the southwest, plus potentially large fractions in the north and center begin, on the average, from lightning. Perhaps 60 percent of the fires in Victoria's Big Desert originate with lightning, as do about 12 percent of starts in the national parks of Western Australia. The onset of the tropical monsoon is a time of storm and sun, even of dry lightning—ideal conditions for fire starting. In the Mitchell grasslands of the subtropical north, where anthropogenic fire is infrequent, lightning remains an important cause. The capacity of lightning to kindle fires in the desert interior is largely limited by fuels, a product of rains. Many of the worst fire complexes of recent decades include multiple starts from lightning—the 1951–52 fires in New South Wales, the 1961 fires in Western Australia, the 1977 fires of the southeast, and the gargantuan fires of the central deserts in 1974–75. Perhaps 97 percent of the area burned in 1974–75—about 15 percent of all Australia—is attributed to lightning. (Lightning starts in Tasmania, however, appear to be negligible.) Such statistics, however, are allusive rather than conclusive. Millennia of human intervention have so distorted natural fire regimes that it is difficult to assign reasonable values. That lightning is most prominent where humans are least present is no accident. Yet the numbers do testify to the power of lightning to kindle fire in nearly every environment, and that is enough.[8]

Initially, fire reinforced the trend toward aridity. It is possible that fires dried out landscapes, further favoring scleromorphs and shaping microclimates that made future fires more likely: increases in fossil charcoal parallel increases in scleromorph pollen. Then, as its domain expanded and it established reciprocity with critical components of the biota, fire began to redirect the evolution of the Australian scene. Almost certainly fires are implicated in the emergence of sclerophylly, in the astonishing ascendancy of the scleromorphs from their obscurity within the ancestral rainforest, and in the rapidity of overall environmental change. It was no longer sufficient on the Australian ark to adapt to soil paupery and aridity; to thrive, organisms had to adapt also to a regimen of fire. Fire set to boil the whole biological billy that was Old Australia.

INFORMING FIRE

When it first appeared, fire was a minor phenomenon, and it supported minor elements of the biota. The rainforest thrived under a regimen of rain and stability. It adapted to soil degradation, tolerated minor disturbances, closely resembled its Gondwanic cognates. If fire infiltrated that environment, it did so marginally or episodically. With or without it the rainforest continued.

The advent of aridity expanded enormously fire's potential habitats. It made available new fuels and served new environments that mingled wet and dry, the rain that flushed the landscape with fuels and the spark that kindled them. Yet fire remained one process among many that rallied around aridity, that drove Gondwana greenery toward sclerophylly. It was a catalyst, an accelerant, not—until the complex triumph of scleroforest over rainforest —a driving force. Once established, however, it was difficult to extirpate. Fire created the conditions for more fire. So long as fire persisted, there could be no biological counterrevolution, no resurgent rainforest.[9]

Fire forced, fire stressed, fire quickened. Fire's dynamism made it, over the short term, the most powerful of the environmental determinants shaping Old Australia. Soils changed only over geologic eons; aridity was, likewise, a product of infinitesimal change—the migration of the Australian craton into the tropics, the reformation of climates, the restructuring of storm tracks. But fire was abrupt, vigorous. Fire responded to brief bouts of drought, as well as to prolonged aridity; to storms, lightning, and winds, not just climatic change; to rapid ecological successions, environmental selections, restructured habitats, and mobilized nutrients, not merely to ponderous evolutionary coadjustments. Compared with soil degradation and

climatic reform, fire was more mobile, more sensitive, more varied and malleable, more compelling. The dynamism of fire was inextricably bound to
the dynamism of life.

In the drive toward sclerophylly, fire had a paradoxical role. Often it
complemented aridity. It pushed biotas to greater sclerophylly as quickly as
they could, within their genetic reserves, tolerate the move. Equally, fire
released precious nutrients otherwise stockpiled in dead wood or cached in
forms inaccessible to biological agents. While the overall nutrient level of
average soils might be degraded, fire kept the existing stock in active circulation; it made nutrient caches into rapid nutrient cycles. It also recycled
organisms and whole communities. It favored those plants that were already
disposed to survive as scleromorphs and it burned maladapted competitors
into oblivion or herded them into fire-safe enclaves. What had existed as
generic adaptations to sclerophylly now often acquired more fire-specific sig-
natures.

Among the scleromorphs fire constantly fine-tuned composition and dynamics, the balance between those organisms that needed more light and
those that needed less, between those that reproduced by seed on mineral
soil and those that propagated by vegetative sprouting or suckering, between
those that needed access to surface water and those that reached deep into
the water table. In the face of pressures toward geologic uniformity, fire
helped inspire a biotic diversity. The many niches that had existed in the
ancestral rainforest because of long stability now had, within the scleroforest, dynamic analogues, niches made possible because of frequent disturbances by fire.

A remarkable reciprocity developed between the scleroforest and fire. If
fire helped differentiate the biota, so also that biota helped particularize fire.
Different communities revealed different patterns of fire starts, spread, frequency, timing, and intensity. If rainforest ecosystems could be differentiated largely on the basis of precipitation regimes, then scleroforest
ecosystems could be aptly characterized by fire regimes. Fire interacted with
the uniquely Australian biota in spectacular, sometimes special ways. Fire
created circumstances that promoted the spread of the scleromorphs, and the
scleromorphs reciprocated by promoting the spread of fire.

Australian fire acted on and redirected those trends toward sclerophylly
that preceded it. Those preadaptations gave fire an entree into Old Australia
that it exploited with brilliant effect. Fire swelled into continental dimensions, a selective force that flamed across nearly the whole spectrum of Australian biotas, one that exhibited a special relationship, a positive feedback,
with scleromorphs, grasses, and ephemerals—the most characteristic and
unique of Australian floras. As fire spread, it became something more than a
process; it assumed the character of a defining presence—or more, of an
informing principle. The second upheaval, the internal revolution within

the scleroforest, is unintelligible without reference to it. Bushfire became an inextricable part of Australian geography, history, and consciousness.

The history of Australia is not synonymous with the history of fire, but the history of neither can be told without reference to the other. Even as fire proliferated, the resistance to its spread was terrific; rainforest gave way grudgingly. But of all the environmental levers by which the landscape could be moved, fire was the most sensitive, subtle, and, in short spells, the most powerful. It was, more tellingly, the lever most accessible to humans. It thrived on instability, and humans destabilized. With each transformation, the pressures argued for more fire, not less.

WHEN GONDWANA BROKE UP, its rafting fragments had to search out new identities. They could no longer derive their meaning from the collective commonwealth of the supercontinent. With each passing eon their Gondwanic heritage faded, the imperative for a separate future became larger, and the possibility of new alliances among the continents and subcontinents more likely. India hurried to a violent union with Asia, massively deforming each in the process. South America rafted eastward toward an eventual, tenuous linkage with North America, part of a brave if wary New World. Africa reunited with Europe and Asia, suturing microplates in Asia Minor, warping borders into mountains and huge basins that filled to become separating seas. Along its great rift valley it nearly split, then halted—a place of origins, and a crossroads for the Old World. Madagascar, New Zealand, the Seychelles— all fragmented so badly that they became outright islands, too insular to share in continental history. That left Antarctica and Australia.

Antarctica drifted only slightly poleward. Its deteriorating climate, which culminated in its colossal ice field, was the product of its singular isolation around the South Pole. As the other Gondwanic plates deserted it, as its connections to other continental masses were removed, Antarctica acquired new patterns of circulation that made it not only cold, but wet. Precipitation fell in what had been a continental desert. Snow became ice, ice created more ice, and the entire continent evolved into a slab of glacial ice so immense that it deformed the shape of the planet. Its ice was ruthless, final, deathly. The ancestral biota it once shared with much of Gondwana failed, without replacement. In the ice of Antarctica, life all but vanished. Its ice, too, repelled humans.

Its Gondwanic twin, Australia, took an antithetical direction. Australia became steadily isolated because of its own positive plate motion, not merely the relative movement of the plates around it. Those travels, however, took Australia into the Pacific, away from the other continents; only to the north, where its edges ground against a submerged Asian plate, did it reestablish contact, and then with the upheaved islands of the Sunda arc; and as often as not even that land linkage was lost to deep channels and rising sea levels. As Australia entered the tropics, new circulation patterns not only raised its overall temperature but introduced aridity—seasonal, secular, selective. Aridity promoted the scleromorphs, and the scleromorphs brought fire. Where Antarctica was progressively informed by ice, Australia was increasingly shaped by fire. Rock had turned to dust, and dust to ash.

The Australian biota might have evolved in several directions. Sclerophylly encompassed a suite of traits that adapted organisms to a suite of environmental conditions; not every trait was specific to fire, and fire could hardly subsume the whole spectrum of adaptations. But among the dominant environmental pressures fire was the most active, and like Antarctic ice, Australian fire had self-reinforcing tendencies. It was as though the landscape had been gently tilted and its streams accorded a particular channel. Each subsequent event tilted the land further and the stream of fire history entrenched itself more deeply. The fire-proneness of the island continent ratcheted steadily upward, each event so tipping the balance that correction became impossible. Even before the arrival of humans, Old Australia had probably crossed a biotic threshold that bound it irreversibly to fire. The advent of humans, however, inexpungably committed Australia to the Pacific's ring of fire.

Like Antarctic ice, Australian fire became more frequent, more intense, more pervasive, more domineering a presence. But there the similarity ends. Ice is profoundly abiotic; fire is inextinguishably tied to life. Where ice reduces, removes, and buries, fire enhances, multiplies, stimulates, recycles, and animates, a plural not a singular process, massaging a varied, subtle biota. It is above all vital—at times awesome but also playful. Always it is associated with life. Life made fire possible—and fire, in return, dramatized Australia's life. Its history, natural or cultural, could not be understood without it. To invoke the lands that evolved from Old Australia is to conjure up a burning bush.

BOOK I

The Eucalypt

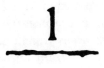

1

The Universal Australian

> . . . round the bases of the bark
> Were left the tracks of flying forest-fires,
> As you may see them on the lower bole
> Of every elder of the native woods.
>
> —HENRY KENDALL, "A Death in the Bush"

> The extreme uniformity of the vegetation is the most remarkable feature in the
> landscape of the greater part of New South Wales . . . In the whole country I
> scarcely saw a place without the marks of a fire; whether these had been more or
> less recent—whether the stumps were more or less black, was the greatest
> change which varied the uniformity, so wearisome to the traveller's eye.
>
> —CHARLES DARWIN,
> The Voyage of the Beagle (1845)

IT IS NOT CLEAR just when the first eucalypt emerged out of the welter of
ancient rainforest taxa. The earliest definite pollen appears in the Oligocene,
around 34 million years ago, long after Australia had separated from the bulk
of Gondwana. Nor is it obvious whether the genus developed from a single
protoeucalypt or from several related forms.[1]

What is incontestable is the degree to which the genus *Eucalyptus* is
endemic to Australia, the extent to which, by Holocene times, it came to
dominate the forest and woodland environments of Australia, and the peculiar attributes to which it owes its evolutionary triumph. Its successful coup
within the scleroforest, in particular, came from a powerful set of alliances, a
triumvirate that *Eucalyptus* formed with fire and the genus *Homo*. Found
virtually nowhere outside Australia, but within Australia found nearly everywhere, the eucalypt became the Universal Australian.

15

THE EUCALYPT AS COLONIZER

Amid the Great Upheaval, the family Myrtaceae—flowering trees and shrubs with fleshy or dry fruits—emerged as one of the scleromorphic winners. Although it probably originated in Australasia, Myrtaceae saturated all of Gondwana, a minor element in the ancestral rainforest. When Gondwana divided, so did Myrtaceae. Its fleshy-fruited genera concentrated in South (and Central) America, and its dry-fruited genera in the eastern cratons including Greater Australia. In Australasia the family Myrtaceae featured ninety-five genera, ninety-three of which were endemic. Australia contained sixty-nine genera, of which forty-five were endemic, among them *Leptospermum, Melaleuca, Callistemon, Baeckea, Verticordia,* and *Eucalyptus.* By the time *Eucalyptus* appeared in the fossil record, Myrtaceae had experienced perhaps 30 million years of evolutionary history.[2]

The Tertiary upheaval completely reformed the status of *Eucalyptus.* Its genetic inheritance included as a matter of course generalized Myrtaceaen traits and scleromorphic tendencies. Probably it appeared along the margins of rainforest, a weed searching out disturbed sites at least momentarily free of an obscuring canopy. Interbreeding was common; hybridization, frequent. As the Australian ark floated into the Pacific and experienced upheaval, a genus that thrived amid disturbance found itself on an increasingly disturbed continent. Quickly *Eucalyptus* began to diversify, to radiate into the new niches that blinked from a disintegrating rainforest, and to reshape those environments in its own image. Southeastern and southwestern Australia divided into biotic subcontinents, segregated first by intervening seas, then by different soils, and finally by endemic biotas. As the Australian plate threw up an arc of mountains to the north, a few eucalypts crossed the Torres Strait and found a marginal existence in drier, unsettled sites of New Guinea and beyond. The remaining genera discovered plenty of opportunity within Australia, first as scleroforest replaced rainforest and then as the proliferating eucalypts seized dominance over the scleroforest.[3]

The scleroforest revolution concluded between 38,000 and 26,000 years ago as the scleromorphs, led by *Casuarina,* completed their abrupt, all but catastrophic, expulsion of the araucarias. But almost as suddenly, between 20,000 and 7,500 years ago, *Eucalyptus* did the same to *Casuarina.* By the time of European discovery forests and woodlands comprised about 25 percent of the Australian land surface; perhaps 70 percent of those lands could be classified as pure eucalypt forest. Eucalypts claimed about 16 percent of the tropical eucalypt and paperbark biomes, and an estimated 11 percent of the cypress pine biome. Across Old Australia eucalypts comprised some 95 percent of the constituent tree species. They thrived almost everywhere—at the snow line of the Australian Alps, along the saltwater tide of tropical mangroves, along desert watercourses, on monadnocks; in relatively wet climates and in relatively dry, on impoverished sites and on more enriched; in Mediterranean climates, in true deserts, in wet-dry tropics, along the margins of rainforest and interpenetrating grasslands. They were absent only in the true, the relict rainforest. With minor exceptions, *Eucalyptus* dominated Australian forests. Every other organism had to accommodate that fact.[4]

"The remarkable plurality of the Eucalypts," as Ferdinand von Müller called it—what staggered Charles Darwin as the "never-failing Eucalyptus family"—prevailed over the Australian continent to an extent unrivaled by any other genus on any other continent. *Eucalyptus* had exploded so widely that it is considered by some authorities as less a genus than an alliance composed of three suballiances, ten subgenera, and over six hundred species. The plasticity of the genus is extraordinary. Hybrids are common within subgenera, juvenile habits persist into adulthood, and even phantom species (apparently hybrid populations that now exist in the vicinity of only one parent) have been identified.

The eucalypt conveyed to Australia a special character. Marcus Clarke gave it poetic expression as "Weird Melancholy." Here, where "flourishes a vegetation long dead in other lands," is found the "Grotesque, the Weird, the strange scribblings of nature learning how to write," a "phantasmagoria of that wild dreamland termed the Bush." Others described or cursed it in more prosaic language, but no one could deny that Australia was different and that the eucalypt was to a large extent both cause and symbol of that difference. But if the eucalypt animated the bush, fire animated the eucalypt. The abrupt, smothering rise in *Eucalyptus* pollen that accompanied the scleroforest revolution paralleled an equally sudden increase in charcoal.[5]

THE EUCALYPT AS SCLEROMORPH

Eucalyptus was first a scleromorph and then a pyrophyte. Of the three suballiances that comprise the genus, Monocalyptus shows the greatest adaptation to impoverished soils but displays limited tolerance for drought or hostile soil microorganisms. By contrast, Symphyomyrtus avoids the worst soils, but shows considerable tolerance toward drought and microbes. Corymbia falls somewhere in between, and was probably intermediate in the evolution of the alliance. But degraded soils were something to which most members of the Gondwanic rainforest had to adapt. *Eucalyptus*, however, elevated nutrient scavenging and hoarding to an art form.

The eucalypts typically developed extensive, deep roots, capable of foraging widely. Rather than target particular nutrient niches, rather than hone their search with exquisite refinement, the eucalypts processed soil catchments in volume, partially compensating for the relative poverty of soil at a restricted site. In addition, eucalypts evolved chemical and biological aids to improve access to those nutrient reservoirs, particularly phosphorus, that did exist. Through various biochemical mechanisms, probably involving phosphataze enzymes or organic exudates, eucalypts could extract phosphorus from iron and aluminum compounds. Similarly, it appears that leachates from leaves and litter of some eucalypt species can percolate into the soil and mobilize phosphorus compounds that are otherwise inaccessible. And then there are the biological allies of *Eucalyptus,* soil microbes and mycorrhizae, that evidently improve phosphorus uptake. The scavenging eucalypt can grow where other trees starve.

Getting scarce nutrients is only half the equation. Once absorbed, eucalypts carefully, obsessively retain and recycle them. Seedlings develop lignotubers—enlarged storage organs in the roots. Here nutrients can be collected and stashed until needed. If the shoot is killed, new shoots promptly emerge. Some eucalypts retain their lignotuber into adulthood, and some can send out from it multiple stems. A lignotuber ensures that, when conditions are right for growth, the seedling will have adequate reserves of the nutrients it needs. Likewise, eucalypts store nutrients selectively within their bole. A nutrient gradient exists between inner heartwood and outer sapwood such that phosphorus, in particular, is cached where it will be most useful. If branches are destroyed, new sprouts shoot out from beneath the bark, and the nutrient reserves in the sapwood ensure that this process will be rapid. Thus not only the roots but also the crown are buffered against erratic and ephemeral changes. The effective nutrient reserve shifts from the soil alone to the tree itself and the immediate environs under its biological control. Eucalypts can thus acquire nutrients far in excess of their immediate needs, and they can cache that surplus for years, perhaps as long as a decade. When young, eucalypts prefer mechanisms of internal cycling; when more mature, cycling between the soil and the tree.

Recycling occurs as well in the crown. A eucalypt canopy is dynamic: old branches become senescent and die back, while new branches immediately spring forth from epicormic sprouts lodged just under the protective bark. The crown is thus continually reshaped for maximum efficiency, and nutrients are reabsorbed before the branch is vulnerable to breakage and loss. As an evergreen, the eucalypt retains its leaves, shedding them as infrequently as possible, tenaciously hoarding their precious supply of nutrients. Instead, eucalypts shed their impoverished bark. When leaves do fall, they are drained of vital nutrients to the fullest extent possible before deposition. And once on the ground, leachates from the crown quickly return residual nutrients to the tree through the soil.

These adaptations served *Eucalyptus* well during the Great Upheaval. The particular mechanisms it favored for the foraging and cycling of nutrients did double duty for water. But there were greater variances in coping with aridity; the range of responses to water stress among eucalypts exceeded their range of responses to soil degradation. In fact, *Eucalyptus* is not a true drought evader. Eucalypts do not close their leaf stomata, go into seasonal hibernation, or shed their leaves. Instead they tolerate drought. They search out new water sources, hoard existing reserves, shut down nonessential processes. When drought comes, they tough it out.

Like all the scleromorphs, eucalypts have hardened leaves that reduce moisture loss. (The same is true for the operculum, from which derives the name *Eucalyptus*—from the Greek *eu*, meaning "well," and *kalyptos*, "covered.") Their canopy drapes downward, evading excessive leaf temperatures. Their vast, plunging root systems; their lignotubers; the capacity of seedlings to reside in apparent dormancy within lignotubers for years, even decades; their ability to shrink their leaf stomata to reduce transpiration and conserve water—all ensure the survival of the eucalypt within a land that is seasonally dry or episodically blasted by drought. But eucalypts have a harder time conserving water than nutrients. Their physical geography is thus limited, in some regions, by cold and in others by water. Where aridity becomes chronic and pronounced, eucalypts surrender to grasses, scleromorphic shrubs like saltbush, and that prolific rival, *Acacia*.

Its acquired traits were adequate to keep *Eucalyptus* alive during the eons of soil impoverishment, and they were enough, within the context of the Great Upheaval, to liberate eucalypts among the emergent scleroforest. The reformation in the physical environment meant a reformation in the biotic environment as well, and organisms had to accommodate to both circumstances. The eucalypts were supreme opportunists, infiltrating sites more and more frequently disturbed. As they broadened their domain, entire biotas had to reorganize around the defining properties of *Eucalyptus*. Eucalypts were too effective as scavengers and as hoarders of scarce nutrients and water to ignore. They were aggressive competitors—and a vital focus for grazing by insects, mammals, and birds. They concentrated bionutrients into particular forms; their hard gum nuts, for example, were accessible to some species and not to others. They created special niches and coevolved unique associations with koalas, termites, possums, and parrots; while eucalypts covered 25 percent of the surface of Australia, they harbored some 50 percent of its avifauna. The patterns of eucalypt forests defined the structure of critical habitats; the processes of eucalypt life determined the flow of nutrients and water.

If they wished to survive, other organisms had to seek out an accommodation with the Universal Australian. But the revolution did not end with the breakup of rainforest into scleroforest. The last 20,000 years—the epoch of the eucalypt revolution—have been marked by massive biotic realignments and extinctions. Each stress inspired others. Selective aridity encouraged fire, and fire fostered another suite of conditions, both abiotic and biotic. If they wished to survive, flora and fauna had to adapt not only to fire in the abstract but to the kinds of fire their scleromorphic neighbors supported. How their associates burned and reproduced determined in no small way the kind of fire they confronted. Amid fire the eucalypts flourished.[6]

THE EUCALYPT AS PYROPHYTE

The spread of *Eucalyptus* traced the spread of fire. Charcoal and eucalypt pollen march side by side in the geologic record of the late Pleistocene and Holocene. Fire proliferated across the spectrum of Old Australian biotas—in scleroforest of course, but also in the grasslands, the acacia-splattered savannas, the heaths; it rolled back the rainforest into sharply bounded sanctuaries. The environments were varied, and so, not surprisingly, were the responses even among the prolific eucalypts.

Those inherited traits for contending with deteriorating soils and unreliable water preadapted the genus to survive fire. It knew how to cope with irregular nutrient fluxes, with an erratic tempo of too much and too little. Its quest for water already plunged roots safely out of the way of surface fires. Its weedy ancestry had groomed the eucalypt into an opportunist, ready to seize disturbed, opened sites. Eucalypts could capture nutrients released by fire, could store them until another release, could in emergencies live off internal caches in heartwood and lignotuber. Bark was thick, tough, and it shed as it burned like the ablation plate of a descending spacecraft. If branches were seared off, new ones could sprout from beneath the protected layer. If the bole burned, new trunks could spring from the buried lignotuber. A eucalypt could pour old nutrients into new growth, even as it scavenged liberated minerals from freshly burned ground. Fire could, for a couple of years, purge hostile microbes from the site; it might encourage better percolation of groundwater; it opened an area to sunlight, allowing the sun-worshiping eucalypt seedlings a chance to outgrow more shade-tolerant rivals. For most eucalypts, fire was not a destroyer but a liberator.

There were differences between fire and other pressures toward sclerophylly. Fire acted on a scale of minutes or hours, not over decades or millennia or eons. It was also interdependent with life in ways that leaching and drying were not. Soils degraded regardless of vegetative cover. Droughts arrived and departed whether there was anything on the surface or not; rocks or rainforest, it mattered little, for while organisms could alter the surface concentrations of minerals and water, while they could modulate the force of climate, they could not prevent rain or drought from appearing. But fire could only thrive in the presence of organic fuels. The character of those fuels profoundly influenced the character of the fires that resulted. And those fires, in turn, shaped the kind of biotas on which the fires fed. Fire and flora entered into a process of mutual selection, of positive reinforcement, that was far more rapid, intimate, and compelling than any of the relationships that preceded it.

Eucalyptus was excellent at extracting and hoarding precious nutrients; but so were most of the Australian flora. It was successful at persevering through dry seasons and episodic droughts; but so, again, were the other scleromorphs. Eucalypts, in fact, tended to occupy the relatively better sites of Old Australia—shunning the driest, the worst waterlogged, the most nutrient-degraded. In none of these attributes was there anything to account for its extraordinary ubiquity or its supremacy within the scleroforest. What made the eucalypt special was its extraordinary opportunism, a relationship reinforced by fire. Eucalypts accepted wretched soils and tolerated drought, but they thrived amid fire.

A eucalypt forest became a fire forest. The alliance between *Eucalyptus* and fire compelled other organisms to respond likewise to fire—and not just to any and every fire, but to fires occurring at certain seasons and across a specified range of frequencies and intensities, a fire ensemble to a considerable extent dictated by the burning properties of the eucalypt and its scleromorphic associates. No organism could survive in Quaternary Australia because of its fire-hardiness alone; but it became equally, increasingly true that generic sclerophyllous traits were by themselves inadequate. Fire was too sudden, too powerful. Fire could even allow the eucalypt, within limits, to defy climatic oscillations, to preserve a relatively dry environment against pressures to restore elements of rainforest or araucarian forest. This apparently explains the otherwise anomalous persistence of *Eucalyptus* and scleroforest pollen at Lake George on the Atherton Tableland during the wet cycle of the last glaciation. The growing prevalence of fire revolutionized the internal relations among the scleromorphs.[7]

As Pleistocene inflected into Holocene, *Eucalyptus* was primed for a biological explosion. Once torched, the burning bush resembled a spiral nebula, its fuels and fires like paired arms locked into an accelerating vortex. Anything that altered the bush altered the regime of fire. Any change in fire behavior, timing, or frequency rippled throughout the entire biota. One encouraged the other. Unlike many organisms—*Acacia*, for example —*Eucalyptus* did not mold microenvironments unfavorable to fire, or shape fuel complexes unlikely to burn routinely, or inhibit those environmental parameters that supported free-burning fire. It burned readily, greedily, and gratefully. A fire weed had discovered a fire continent.

The Universal Australian became the archetypal fire colonizer of Australia. Granted a certain abundance of water, its range was limited by fire, and fire, by the prevalence of ignition. The Pleistocene revolution dramatically expanded those sources of ignition. With fire the genus *Eucalyptus* and the genus *Homo* had common cause and shared a common future.

THE EUCALYPT AS EMIGRANT

Eucalyptus is almost, but not quite, confined to Australia, and the exceptions are revealing. A few eucalypts have crossed the Torres Strait (or its land bridge, the Sahul) northward, and an extraordinary quantity of eucalypts have, through human efforts, become established throughout the world. The contrast between the natural and the anthropogenic—the extra-Australian eucalypts and the emigrant eucalypts—is expressive.[8]

Some ten species of eucalypts have infiltrated northward, half of which belong to the Corymbia subgenus, and half to the Symphyomyrtus—the later branches of the grand *Eucalyptus* alliance to emerge. They represent, that is, Australian indigenes that have attempted to occupy extra-Australian sites. Some probably crossed the Sahul, the shallow plains that, from time to time, have joined northern Australia to Papua New Guinea. Others may have colonized afterward, a product of catastrophic windstorms that biologically bridged the strait. Of the ten, four are still found in Australia, and only two exist outside the provenance of Gondwanic Australia before it sutured with the Sunda arc.

The New Guinea eucalypts claim drier sites, outliers of rainforest. In effect, they have rediscovered more ancient niches, not unlike those that species of *Eucalyptus* occupied during the early tremors of the Great Upheaval. They are minor, marginal constituents of New Guinean rainforest. All but *E. deglupta* live in monsoonal climates where fire is seasonally important. Two species, however, continued their move away from Australia. *E. urophylla* entered Timor, the Lesser Sunda Islands, and New Caledonia. It claims seasonally dry or disturbed sites, but it shows few of the typical eucalypt traits, and it competes poorly with other scleromorphs of the Myrtaceae family such as *Melaleuca*.

By contrast, *E. deglupta* penetrated into New Britain, New Ireland, the Celebes, and the Philippines—the only eucalypt to cross the classic Wallace Line. In the process it shed most of its Australian traits and entered the rainforest, thronging gregariously onto wet, lowland sites. No longer did it seek out niches thrown up by disturbance or seasonal aridity; it chose another, alternative path. The farther it distanced itself from Australia, the further it sloughed off those attributes that accounted for the dominance of *Eucalyptus* within Australia. As a result, neither *E. urophylla* nor *E. deglupta* survived in Australia, and may, in fact, have emerged outside Australia altogether. *E. deglupta*, in particular, lost completely any affiliation for fire. Fire destroyed it.

Clearly the special status of *Eucalyptus* within Australia depended on its special circumstances—its isolation, its pattern of disturbance and aridity. Yet, paradoxically, this most indigenous of Australian flora has been successfully transplanted not only throughout ancient Gondwana but into Eurasia,

Africa, and North and South America. In the early years the French more than the British actively promoted eucalypts (most often *E. globulus*, the blue gum). It was hoped that gums would become a valuable hardwood, provide fuelwood, assist agriculture by establishing windbreaks and shelterwoods, and decorate the countryside with attractive ornamentals. Eucalypt oil was promoted for medicinal and commercial purposes, as an antimalarial agent and as a chemical base for perfumes. French explorers to Australia returned to Paris with seeds, and from the Jardin des Plantes eucalypts were propagated throughout the Mediterranean littoral. Britain soon followed suit, moving *Eucalyptus* out of the category of an ornamental for estate aboriculture and extending it through Kew Gardens into its African and Asian colonies. Italy, in turn, became another center for export, largely into North Africa. The Trappist monks of the Tre Fontane monastery inaugurated perhaps the most celebrated experiment when, in 1868, they planted thousands of eucalypts in the Pontine Marshes in the pious hope that the mysterious, aromatic "gums" would purge the miasmic swamps of malaria. Only with the accession of the indefatigable Ferdinand von Müller to the status of colonial botanist in Victoria did Australia become an active distributor.

About twenty to thirty species define the emigrant eucalypts. Their chief liability is their intolerance to extreme cold—a reason why their range in central and alpine Australia is restricted, and another legacy of their Gondwanic heritage in a rainforest and of Australia's migration toward the equator. But in Mediterranean climates, especially, *Eucalyptus* has proliferated. It thrives in Spain, Portugal, Italy, Turkey, Israel, and such islands as Corsica and Cyprus. It has been widely planted in Africa—the northern littoral of the Mediterranean, the southern and eastern veldt, the Ethiopian plateau, the Congo basin. Eucalypt plantations are extensive in Brazil, and they have reclaimed otherwise denuded plains in Chile, Ecuador, and Argentina. Gums are grown in China and India, where they are praised as fast-growing fuelwood and cursed as thirsty aliens. Eucalypts clothe patches of the Coast Ranges of California, where they were promoted by various interests (including the Southern Pacific Railroad), often as a surrogate for that enduring California passion, real-estate speculation. *Eucalyptus* has successfully transplanted to a panoply of islands from Madagascar to Mauritius, from Sri Lanka to the Seychelles, from Easter Island to Alcatraz. Eucalypts grace the royal palaces at Katmandu and Addis Ababa. Where Australian soldiers have fallen on foreign battlefields, local gravesites are framed with eucalypts. (Poignantly, they refuse to grow on the cold flanks of Gallipoli.)[9]

The reasons for the success of the emigrant eucalypts are several. They flourish in climates similar to those they knew in Australia. They were often unpalatable to local browsers (even goats). No less, there exists a strong fertility gradient between Australia and most other lands such that it is often easier to export indigenous plants from Australia than to import exotics into it. Only a special suite of organisms could thrive under Australian conditions, and then primarily if the native biotas were upset beyond their normal tolerances. But transplanting flora like eucalypts that had evolved in a nutrient-deprived and droughty environment into relatively rich, well-water sites was a formula for successful colonization. The outcome could be extraordinary. Between 1950 and 1974, for example, eucalypt plantations increased worldwide (including China) from 0.7 million to 3.7 million hectares—and continue to rise.

It is probable, too, that its alliance with humans explains the ubiquity of eucalypts in Australia. They moved overseas because humans took them into compatible environments. They did not have to transcend endless oceans or navigate through rainforest, a biota they had abandoned during their evolutionary history: they could appear directly on suitable sites. In most cases, those sites could not offer worse conditions of soil and aridity than they had known in Australia. Native organisms were kept off balance, the site chronically manipulated, by human intervention. With a few exceptions, free-burning fires were less pervasive, and when they came, they inflicted less damage than on native trees.

Its enlarged dominion has had a cost, however. The eucalypts' interdependence with humans could not eliminate their more ancient interdependence with fire. They continued to behave as though fire were still a principal ally, persisted in littering fuels as though surface fires routinely passed over them, acted as though fire would remain instrumental in purging the biota of competitors, in restoring conditions for regeneration, in recycling scarce nutrients. Those environmental conditions that allowed emigrant eucalypts to prosper so gloriously also encouraged an excess of unchecked fuels. Interestingly, other fire-hardened scleromorphs from Australia like *Casuarina* and *Melaleuca* have also become major fireweeds in such exotic landscapes as south Florida. But these were weeds, unwanted escapees, not assisted emigrants.[10]

The environments that encourage eucalypt plantations also encourage eucalypt-dominated fire regimes. Not only commercial plantations, but other environments receptive to eucalypts have witnessed a rise in fire hazard. The transported eucalypts shed fuel as though they expected to burn. The Berkeley fire of 1923, which consumed about a fourth of the city and entered the University of California campus, was propelled in part by windfall and litter from extensive eucalypt plantings. The scene had little improved when an Australian fire specialist visited the Bay Area in the 1960s. Familiar with the intensity of eucalypt fires in their native setting, he gasped at the specter that greeted him—the intermixture of houses and giant eucalypts, branches and bark piled deep, a surreal scleroforest composed equally of *Eucalyptus* and houses. Shaken, he abandoned the conference tour and retired to his motel room, his head spinning with visions of holocaust.[11]

THE EUCALYPT AS AUSTRALIAN

The Australian bush owes its peculiarity, more than anything else, to *Eucalyptus*. No other continental forest or woodland is so dominated by a single genus. Other biomes on Earth have scleromorphs, most have grasses, and few are spared wholly from fire, but none has the combination that exists in Australia and has given the bush its indelible character. *Eucalyptus* is not only the Universal Australian, it is the ideal Australian—versatile, tough, sardonic, contrary, self-mocking, with a deceptive complexity amid the appearance of massive homogeneity; an occupier of disturbed environments; a fire creature.

But the ideal Australian is also the typical Australian. Its peculiar strengths delineate as well its weaknesses. The hostile environmental conditions that pushed the biota toward sclerophylly, the chronic disturbances that at once simplified and complicated the biotic ensemble, the alliance with fire that allowed a single genus to overrun a continent—all these were enormous strengths so long as those informing circumstances remained more or less in force. While the domain of fire in Australia had expanded, it ruled within an evolved order. If, however, those pressures were removed, if new biotic elements were introduced or significant portions extirpated, if the fire regime were reconstituted by new fuels or new sources of ignition, then those special traits could become liabilities.[12]

The bush was perhaps too dominated by *Eucalyptus*, and *Eucalyptus* perhaps too closely reliant on fire and, through fire, on *Homo*. The eucalypt was less a pyrophyte than a pyrophiliac: fire became a near addiction with its own peculiar perils. The tendency was to create more fire, as though the biotas linked by eucalypt and fire were a kind of chain letter, a leveraged biotic buyout sustained by ever-increasing infusions of fire. Any reform in the fire regime would upset not only the status of *Eucalyptus* but the entire bush. And in this complex biotic chemistry lies the colossal significance of the genus *Homo*, advancing on Pleistocene Australia with bold firesticks.

2

Unimaginable Freaks of Fire: Profile of a Pyrophyte

> . . . But enough!
> Where are the words to paint the million shapes
> And unimaginable freaks of Fire,
> When holding thus its monster carnival
> In the primeval Forest all night long?
>
> —CHARLES HARPUR, "The Bush Fire" (1853)

> . . . I had a full opportunity of examining this, one of the finest sights which
> tropical countries display . . . Above us the sky was gloomy and still; all round
> us the far-stretching forests exposed a strange and varied pageant of darkness and
> fire, accompanied by the crackling of flames and the crash of falling trees.
>
> —"AN EMIGRANT MECHANIC,"
> Settlers and Convicts (1849)

WITH GATHERING SPEED, like a flaming maelstrom, Australia spun to its destiny as a fire continent. Proliferating fires pushed scleroforest and grassland across a biotic threshold. Bushfire became a reality with which almost—but not quite—every landscape of Old Australia had to contend. Since the Pleistocene it has generally been the case that, where biotas have changed, they have moved toward a state of more fire, not less. Some species were swept aside, while some accommodated, adapted, and learned to tolerate fire. Others thrived.

The eucalypts flourished overall. Their evolutionary history, its peculiar genetic makeup, had conditioned *Eucalyptus* to exploit those unsettled times. Nutrient scavengers of ravenous dimensions, woody weeds ready to colonize disturbed sites, evergreens that could adopt many growth habits and that wrapped protective coverings around critical tissues so that they could thrive in strong heat and sunlight—the eucalypt alliance amalgamated hundreds of species which were ideally predisposed to survive in an environment of increasing fire. Their scleromorphic traits were even better pre-adapted to fire than to drought, and the rising tide of fire soon swept them before it. Generic adaptations evolved into more fire-specific traits.

No other genus that had so far survived the voyage from Gondwana could compete with *Eucalyptus* for dominance within Australian forests. Yet there remained areas from which they were excluded: eucalypts shunned the frost-ridden subalpine terrain; on chronically dry sites eucalypts gave way to spinifex, mulga, and gibber desert; on perennially wet sites, eucalypts were crowded out by rainforest or were challenged by paperbark *Melaleuca*. But everywhere else—wherever fire was routinely possible, even over a span of centuries—eucalypts flourished and shaped whole communities of pyrophytes. The scleroforest it dominated bloomed when burned. Without fire its biophysical engines cooled, and its biotic dynamics decayed.

FRIENDLY FIRE

Most eucalypts can accommodate most fires. But they do so in ways both common and diverse.

Their defenses begin with their bark. What kills is a kind of thermal ring-barking caused by a very high temperature or a long duration of lower heating. But bark is thick, it is densest at the base where the fire burns, and it conducts heat poorly. Surface fires pass by, charring the exterior but not killing the living cambium beneath it. While it is common for heat to concentrate preferentially on one side or the other, either because fuels pile up on the uphill side of a trunk or because winds form eddies on the lee side, at worst this wounds only one side and explains why most basal cavities develop uphill or downwind.[1]

The thick bark, too, protects epicormic buds buried beneath it. When branches die, new buds are liberated and shoot out. Even if fire torches the crown, a new canopy rapidly emerges and clumps of epicormic sprouts clothe the bole and major branches like moss. Canopy-depleting fires, however, are abnormal in most scleroforests. Once past a juvenile stage, eucalypts shed their lower branches. Between the forest litter, which sustains the fire, and the living canopy, which maintains the tree, there is a considerable gap in fuels that is difficult to bridge by flame unless the surface fire burns with extraordinary intensity, a pilot light in a forest furnace. Even if the canopy is burned off or irredeemably scorched, the fatal fire is only a flash burn. It does not consume the live tissue or the woody fruits encased in tough, nutty caps. Eventually some sprouts become dominant and shape a renewed canopy, and seeds rain down to the waiting ashes.[2]

Something analogous happens below the surface as well. All but twelve or fifteen eucalypts develop a lignotuber. In place of bark, these subsurface tissues are protected by soil and the simple physics of heat transfer. Probably 95 percent (or more) of the heat released by a fire dissipates upward through radiation and convection; the remainder enters the soil, but it cannot penetrate far since soil is a poor conductor of heat and a few centimeters is ample to shield roots and microbes. An intense surface fire could well consume or lethally scorch a seedling; but if a young tree existed in an environment that burned—if, that is, adequate litter was piled around it—then it was probably not thriving anyway. Regardless, the seedling had already stored in its lignotuber most of the critical nutrients it required. A new shoot, or multiple shoots, punches through the ashy crust; within a few years one stem becomes dominant and rapidly evolves into a new tree; the lignotuber matures. In many species, even if the entire bole is destroyed, new sprouts appear. In the mallee habit, the process is so well developed that *Eucalyptus* grows naturally as a coppice.

The lignotuber is particularly important because eucalypt seed is not long-lived. A tree holds its seeds for one or two years and in exceptional cases for as many as four. After a fire, seed predation is heavy. Germination is typically poor unless the seed is buried in mineral soil or in an environment free from competition for scarce water and nutrients in the critical first years. But a fire, paradoxically, can produce ideal circumstances for germination. Seed virtually rains down from the charred canopy, overwhelming the capacity of those invertebrate animals that normally feed upon it. The fluffy ash accepts the falling seed, buries it, encases it in an environment full of mineralized biochemicals and temporarily purged of antagonistic microorganisms.

The ashbed effect is multiple, complex. The fire temporarily sweeps competition away. It sterilizes the soil of microflora and microfauna, most of which resided in the combustible litter. It may burn away or cripple other woody species, thus permitting greater access to the site resources by the phoenix eucalypts. It mobilizes vital trace nutrients like molybdenum that are never more accessible for biological intake than in their disintegrated forms after a fire. It volatilizes leachates in the litter, some of which are packed with inhibitory chemicals. A moderate or severe fire restructures the canopies of forest and scrub to permit greater sunlight and to restrict toxic leaching from rain drip. A burn scours out fuels, permitting a few years of fire-free existence. Although the biochemical details are not altogether understood, the outcome for most eucalypts is incontestable: it is essentially only in such a context that new seedlings emerge, and it is through successive burns that the resprouting lignotuber allows eucalypt seedlings to triumph over less vigorous competitors. While various scenarios exist for regeneration, almost all depend, at some stage, on an intense fire.[3]

These are generic traits, common to most eucalypts, and it is important to recognize that an extraordinary variation exists within the alliance. *Eucalyptus* had, over its evolutionary history, acquired a suite of traits to cope with a suite of environmental stresses. Particular adaptations to fire were, after a fashion, grafted on to already existing traits. Defoliation by fire might differ little from defoliation by insects; the decapitation of a seedling by burning, from decapitation by browsing; branch loss by fire, from branch failure by wind; temporary nutrient losses by fire, from soil paupery or drought. Some eucalypts favor seed production; others, vegetative propagation. Some have enormous lignotubers, while others feature lignotubers that seem almost vestigial or persist only through certain stages in their life cycle. Some eucalypt forests tolerate surface fires; others thrive on stand-replacing fires. *E. regnans*, the mountain ash, is highly sensitive to surface fires but seeds prolifically after a conflagration with the result that the towering mountain ash forests are even-aged. Even within one species, there are variations according to the pattern of fire to which they are subjected.

It is important to realize that not every fire is identical to every other fire. Fires vary in their physical properties—their intensity, their rate of spread, their frequency, their flame heights, and their size. Different fires act on the same biota with different outcomes. Even two fires with similar physical parameters will yield different ecological outcomes as a function of their timing. If one fire burns in the summer and another in the winter; if one succeeds an initial fire after four years and the other after forty or four hundred; if one eliminates certain species from the site and another permits enough to survive to recolonize; if one occurs amid exotics and another does not; if one burns around a seedling, another around a juvenile pole tree, and another around an adult of the same species, the biological consequences may well differ.

Thus it is not enough to say that *Eucalyptus* is adapted to fire. Rather, particular eucalypts are adapted to fires of particular sorts, to fire regimes. Different species of *Eucalyptus* require different fires. In wet forests, severe fires, even if infrequent, are more important than mild fires. Wet eucalypt forests tend to be even-aged, triggered by episodic holocausts that prescribe the proportion of eucalypts to invading rainforest taxa. In dry forests, fires tend to be more frequent and less intense, and conflagrations, while less likely to incinerate whole stands, may cause shifts within the existing population of eucalypts.[4]

Nor is fire a singular event. Typically, fires occur as geographic complexes and historical cycles. Once some part of a biota burns, it influences the other parts of an ecosystem. With long-range firebrands, a fire in one site may propagate into others, and by shaping new patterns of fuels it may propagate into the future as well. Real fires do not occur in strict cycles, like returning comets; they burn in eccentric rhythms. They integrate not only seasonal and phenological cycles, but events that are unexpected, stochastic, irrepeatable, and irreversible. A site's history is rarely wiped clean; almost always the past lingers in ways that bias the future. Once fire insinuated itself into the eucalypt environment, it was not easily expunged. Instead it spread, like a drop of acid etching new and indelible patterns on whatever it touched.

SUPPORTING SCLEROMORPHS:
FIRE BY SYNERGY

Even where the eucalypts dominate as trees and control the canopy, they share the surface with other organisms, a cast of supporting scleromorphs. Within the scleroforest, all must interact—sometimes as competitors, sometimes as complements. No organism can afford to establish a special relationship to fire one-to-one in biotic isolation. Rather, its success will depend on how it responds to the spectrum of fires to which the site is subjected and which it helps to shape. If few organisms can survive without regard to the eucalypt, neither can the eucalypt ignore those scleromorphs with which it shares a site and with which it often develops a special fire synergy. In broad terms, these include grasses, shrubs, other scleromorphic trees, and a few Australian exotica such as the grass tree *(Xanthorrhoea)*.

Gramineae—the grasses—are the most extensive fuels in Australia. They interpenetrate with most scleromorphic biotas, and they claim for themselves a great concentric ring between the central deserts and the coastal forests. In woodlands they sustain understory burning; in many drier forests they often replace eucalypt litter as a driving fuel; in deserts, they appear in the form of ephemerals after heavy rains, promoting widespread if episodic fire. Yet grasslands display few adaptations unique to fire. Their fire-hardiness derives from their adaptations to drought and grazing; grasses that survive under arid conditions and heavy browsing also survive burning. Conversely, grasses that are not palatable, that are not grazed heavily, are available as fuel for fire. Fire acts on mixed grasslands much as drought and grazing do, by shifting the floristic composition from certain species to others. Grasslands that are not grazed or burned rapidly decay in productivity.[5]

Other organisms show more specialized adaptations to fire in which burning stimulates reproductive success. Nearly a score of Australian vascular plants, for example, flower after a fire. The grass tree *(Xanthorrhoea australis)* not only floresces profusely following burning but rarely flowers without it. (Fire so stimulates the plant that a blowtorch is often applied to specimens sold at nurseries in order to improve growth and sustain them through the shock of transplanting.) A number of scleromorphic shrubs also respond to fire by flowering, though the onset of florescence may be deferred a year; in the absence of fire, the size of the flowering crops in subsequent years diminishes. Australian orchids, too, flower following burning, and in the aftermath of the Ash Wednesday fires of 1983, rare orchids carpeted whole hillsides. Whatever the proximate causes, florescence after fire leads promptly to seeding.[6]

Flora that rely on seed for reproduction must either protect that seed from fire or use burning as a means to stimulate germination. Some species, by means of tough coverings, shield seeds from flash fires by storing them in the crown or in the soil, where they are sheltered from fire. Others rely on intense, fast-moving fires to inaugurate seeding—to instigate seed fall or to stimulate germination. Thus many heath shrubs rely on fire to activate seed or to liberate seed from protective follicles. *Banksia ornata*, for example, has a dry wood fruit that fails to open unless it is scorched by flame. *Hakea teretifolia* initiates reproduction upon the desiccation of a parent branch, an instance in which fire replaces drought as an active agent. Those eucalypts without lignotubers—the mountain ash is probably the best known—rely on massive seed release following infrequent but intense fires to sustain their presence. Other species litter the ground with seeds over the course of many years until conditions favor their release. Among many leguminous species hard seeds are the norm and must be softened, scarified, or stripped away before germination can occur. This is true for both *Acacia* and *Melaleuca*, which compete aggressively with eucalypts in the desert and tropics, respectively. The proportion of hard to soft seed among species of *Acacia* seems to be related to the frequency of fire.[7]

Other species seem well adapted to disturbance—opportunists ready to claim niches newly shaped by a fire. A fire volatilizes organic nitrogen, so nitrogen fixers like the Leguminae are ideally positioned to seize the ashy floor. It is, for example, in this capacity that viney acacias enter into the eucalypt forests. Where *Casuarina* survives, it does so in part because it, unlike the eucalypts, can fix nitrogen. Some Australian species respond to fire as other species do to rain. After a fire, particularly after an intense fire, ephemerals that have not been seen since the last burn appear and flower. There are instances of species, thought extinct, that fire freed from a near-fatal dormancy.[8]

Accommodations by Australian flora force accommodations by Australian fauna as well. Only a few fauna show specific adaptations to fire itself, like a fly *(Microsania australis)* attracted to smoke, and a beetle *(Melanophila acuminata)* apparently steered to heat by means of infrared sensors. Equally, only the most severe fire panics animals. More common is the tendency for a fire to collect an entire food chain, from invertebrates herded in advance of the flames, to small mammals, reptiles, and insectivorous birds foraging on them and other fauna flushed out by the flames, to raptors like kites and wedge-tailed eagles who hunt in swirls through the smoke. Far from killing the ecosystem, such fires bring it to life.[9]

Nor does the effect end when the flames expire. Whole populations of organisms—from microbes to macropods—adjust to the new opportunities presented by fire. Fire's immediate impact is to reduce the numbers of most species and to shift the relative proportions of those constituents which remain. Old foods and old habitats are consumed by fire; and no less than organic nitrogen, some old relationships are vaporized. But that is only half the equation. It is equally true that fire mobilizes nutrients, fashions new niches, reorganizes habitats, liberates species that were formerly suppressed, animates biochemical cycles, and recharges biophysical batteries. The site is recolonized—sometimes within as little as three to five years. What results from this sort of burning is a kind of natural swidden, a shifting mosaic of biotas that enormously enriches the species diversity of a regime.

This capacity of fire to animate and diversify is particularly critical in sluggish, apparently run-down ecosystems—heaths, tropical biotas on laterized soils, arid environments where ephemerals lie dormant until rain or fire release them. And it is particularly vital to the cavalcade of indigenous species that need the disturbed, refreshed landscapes that routine fire replenishes. Kangaroos, wallabies, and wombats—the grazers need the nutritious new growth that springs up after a burn. Termites may proliferate into cavities carved by fire in eucalypts. Koalas need fire to prevent other trees from crowding out eucalypt regeneration. Certain species of ground parrots (like *Pezoporus wallicus*) require heath of a certain height in which to nest and reproduce; a possum like *Burramys parvus* exists only in dense stands of even-aged snow gums; the rat kangaroo *(Bettongia penicillata)* prefers thickets of *Casuarina* for shelter—all habitats that can perpetuate themselves only through some regimen of burning.[10]

A pattern of fire, like a pattern of rainfall, has become an expected norm for many Australian biotas. Some species have made the expectation of fire an essential part of their strategy for reproduction and survival; and a few, within the parameters of their genetic resources and the dynamics of their resident ecosystems, have shaped themselves in ways that sustain advantageous fire patterns. The linkage between life and fire is the biomass they share—for one, part of a cycle of nutrients and habitats; for the other, fuel. But what fire considers fuel is the residue and living tissue of organisms and is subject to ecological dynamics and evolutionary selection. The kind of fuel available determines the kind of fire that burns, and the character of the fire helps shape the character of the fuel that reburns—a brilliant dialectic of fire and life. Once started, once pushed by climate and genetic predisposition, once confirmed by isolation, fire could propagate beyond its prime movers into a pervasive presence from which few residents of Old Australia were exempt.

FUELING THE FIRE

The dynamics of bushfires are thus intimately interdependent with the dynamics of their fuels. Fuel chemistry and physics determine whether fire is possible; fuel availability sets important parameters for fire frequency and intensity. Fuel links fire with biotas, for, in the broadest sense, fire and organisms compete for litter. In environments that are uniformly warm and humid, such as tropical rainforest, productivity is high but organic decomposition is equally aggressive and little litter remains as potential fuel; there are few natural fires. In cold, dry environments like the boreal forest productivity is low, but decomposition by biological agents is even more retarded; fuels build up relentlessly over long years until a fire, or cycle of fires, sweeps through. In temperate regions, the interplay between biological and physical decomposition is complex and irregular. What really matters is its mobile fraction of the fuelbed, the surface litter. Where soils are poor and the climate dry—where, that is, biological agents are few—fire becomes increasingly obligatory if that litter is to be recycled. If fire fails to decompose it, the system slows, its nutrients sitting in worthless caches, a natural economy in which scarce hard currency is stuffed into mattresses or buried in backyards.[11]

In natural systems, all these fuel attributes vary. There are variations within a single biota and, of course, variations between biotas. Over time fuels build up in quantity; they are rearranged; they show seasonal changes in chemistry and structure; they interact not only with fire but with storms, insects, diseases, and organic decomposers. Different biotas exhibit very different patterns of fuels, and the same biota may show radically different patterns of fuel availability according to seasons and moisture content. The rhythms of fuel availability, however, define the boundaries for fire frequency and fire intensity. Grasslands may burn annually; wet scleroforest, on a cycle of several hundred years.

It is a simple fact, often overlooked, that not all biomass is available as fuel. Here, again, natural biotas differ dramatically in how much of their above-surface biomass they offer as fuel. In grassland, this includes virtually everything; in heath, approximately 93 percent of its biomass; in eucalypt forest, less than 5 percent; in brigalow (Acacia aneura), barely 0.1 percent. These proportions reflect not only the relative frequency of burning within the respective biotas but something of the biological significance of fire to them. The forest figures are especially low because so much biomass is locked into the living trunks and branches of trees, which may char but will not be consumed by even the most intense fire.

Nor is all the potentially available fuel always accessible to a fire. What drives a fire are its surface fuels, and what drives a surface fire are its fine fuels with their large surface-to-volume ratios that render leaves, needles, and bark stringers so receptive to radiant heat and so sensitive to wetting and drying. In eucalypt forests, surface fuels vary along a gamut that runs from open grasses to dense scrub. Eucalypts influence the understory by regulating sunlight, by dripping leachates from their crown, by depositing litter in the form of leaves, bark, and branchwood that is at once both nutrient and fuel. This influence varies considerably according to the supporting sclermorphs with which eucalypts share the biota.

Where grass dominates—such as in semiarid savannas, the wet-dry tropics, blade-grass coastal forests—bushfires are really grass fires. Eucalypts contribute litter and shade beneath the thinning woodland, but the dynamics of fire follow the dynamics of the primary fine fuel, grass. Such biotas typically burn annually or biennially. Without fire, the grasses become decadent, some species after only one or two seasons. Fires are frequent, and if intense, fast moving.

Dry scleroforests, while they feature some grasses, obey the dynamics of eucalypt litter. On the average, it takes about three to five years for litter to build up sufficiently in quantity and coverage to sustain a fire, and somewhat longer for litter accumulation to reach a steady state through organic decomposition. Depending on forest type, 34 to 84 percent of the litter consists of leaves. Eucalypts shed perhaps a third to half of their leaves annually, with a peak drop during late spring and summer when new growth flushes the canopy. Other contributors to the litter are twigs and branches, and of course there is the celebrated eucalypt bark, also dry and nutrient-poor and prone to endless shedding.

These fuels burn well when dry, and on the open, sun-immersed floor they dry quickly. Interestingly, eucalypt leaves are flammable in the canopy because of their high heat content (due to their oils) but are flammable in the litter because of their low mineral content, which allows combustion to flame vigorously. The phenological cycle is thus perfect for fire. Dry scleroforests burn on a three-to-twelve-year rhythm. The lower limit is set by minimum fuel needs; the upper, by the opportunity for ignition. In addition, about 150 species of *Eucalyptus* feature stringybark or candlebark, filigree strips that not only add to litter but carry fire up the bole and, during intense burning, can break free as firebrands and ignite new fires as far as ten to thirty kilometers away. A fire in a eucalypt forest is rarely self-limiting—or put differently, eucalypts help to enlarge their sphere of fire influence far beyond the sites they inhabit.[12]

Wet scleroforests are more efficient at biological decomposition, but they compensate by supporting scleromorphic shrubs that effectively enlarge the surface layer available for burning. The litter layer proper needs only to support enough fire to ignite the shrubs, nearly all of which are available as fuel. The combined combustion of litter and shrubs enormously inflates the flaming zone and multiplies—"accelerates," in Australian parlance—the heat output of the advancing front. The shrubs are a fuel threshold that, once crossed, powers a fire to a state of uncontrollable fury. If the litter and shrub zone is large—if they have not burned for many years, if the moisture content of the fuelbeds is low—the flaming zone may expand further to include the canopy. In the oil-rich canopy, a crown fire is a flash fire.

Actual fuel accumulation is complex. Surface fuels increase rapidly then approach a quasi-steady state. Grasses slow their growth after a few years unless cropped or burned. Eucalypt litter mechanically breaks down into smaller, more compact portions; some biological agents support outright decomposition; and growth rates, after the postfire flush, decay. What controls the variability of the fuel load is the low layer of shrubs, grasses, and herbs, entangled with tree-shed litter, that extends up to thirty centimeters above the forest floor. Its size and arrangement vary widely, but the time since the last fire is a critical parameter. In scrub-prone environments, the longer the interval between fires, the more fuel builds up and the more vigorous a subsequent fire; and the more intense the surface fire, the more likely it is to involve the canopy. While there exists in some scleroforests a scenario by which a maturing, fire-free forest will suppress by shade and leachates a scrubby understory, this assumes a condition of stability that is almost unknown in contemporary Australia. Besides, episodic and sometimes catastrophic events—windstorms, insect invasions, major infestations of diseases —can quickly superimpose enormous quantities of fuel onto a site. The best means to counter massive fuel deposition is by equally massive decomposition—fire.

Not all of the fuels can burn all of the time. A fuel complex's true availability depends on the moisture content of the dead and living components. Fine dead fuels like grass require only a few hours to dry adequately enough to burn. Large-diameter fuels such as logs demand a season, perhaps a drought. Intermediary-sized fuels dry out and wet at different rates, and a single large-diameter fuel particle will likely have imbalances within itself— a dry surface and a moist interior at the start of summer after a wet winter, or a moist surface and a dry interior as a result of light rain at the end of a blistering summer. Thus the fuel complex is far from uniform; fires reflect this heterogeneity.

Burning is patchy, combustion incomplete, and the more complex the fuel, the more complicated the fire. Under normal circumstances fires will burn more fiercely in summer than in winter, along exposed ridges better than within sheltered ravines, in open forests more vigorously than in closed. Only during times of severe drought—when all fuels, living and dead, small and large, are drained of moisture—can a fire burn with relative disregard for local nuances of fuel moisture. Under such conditions everything burns, and fire intensity correlates closely with fuel quantity. Where the climate makes fire routinely possible, where ignition is abundant and reliable, fire history follows fuel history.

This was almost certainly the case with Old Australia. Fires followed from fuels, but fuels reflected, in part, a history of past fires. Fire worked on selective species, tilting the biotic balance, priming the scleromorphs. A source of new ignition could result in an explosion; new fuels could expand or contract the realm of that detonation. Then intruders violated the isolation of Old Australia. With firestick and later with new biological allies— weeds and domesticated fauna—*Homo* could break down and reorganize the boundaries imposed on Australian fire regimes by climate and genetic inheritance. Humans could attack the surface litter, alter the frequency and timing of fire, and restructure fire regimes. By revising fuel history, humans could rewrite fire history.

FIRE WINDS, FIRE FLUME

Combustion chemistry requires oxygen as well as fuel, and combustion physics makes fire a flaming boundary between a fuel array and its surrounding air mass. The fires of Old Australia inscribed patterns that balanced biotas with winds. Old Australia's fire regimes integrated not only the variability of fuels but the variability of air flows. Each, however, had been disciplined over eons into certain patterns and they interacted in predictable forms. Together they defined a typology of Australian fires.[13]

In the absence of wind a fire would assume a shape according to the available fuels. A perfect distribution of fuels would result in a perfect circle of expanding flame. If fire burned on a hillside, the flames that burned upslope would be closer to fresh fuel than flames backing down the hill, and the upslope fire would spread more rapidly. Exactly the same principles govern the interaction of flame and wind. A wind-driven fire acquires a head; the stronger the wind (or steeper the slope) the more rapid the spread; the more rapid the rate of spread, the narrower is the ellipse that traces the flaming front. The combustion properties of the heading fire differ from those of the backing fire. Where fuels are light, the backing fire may be simply snuffed out.

The flaming part of the fire is its perimeter, and it assumes a shape that integrates the combined effects of both fuel and wind. The more fuel, the more vigorous the fire; the more wind, the more rapid its spread; and the two in combination define the fireline intensity, a measurement that correlates roughly with flame height. These interactions are complicated, however, by terrain, by the fuelbed, and by the flaming front itself. Terrain directs and deflects general air flow. Fuelbeds, particularly in the case of forests, greatly modify the flow of air across the fire. It is normal for wind speed to be far less at the surface than at the canopy. The fire itself, by generating gases as a result of pyrolysis and combustion, produces a convective flow upward. This gaseous outflow interacts with the ambient winds and can engender special phenomena during high-intensity fires.

Horizontal vortices may roll alongside the flanks of fast-moving fires like mobile levees. If eddies develop within the combustion zone, firewhirls may appear. Perhaps no less dramatic is the phenomenon of long-distance spotting. Particles of burning fuel are lofted above the canopy—perhaps through a torching tree, or by a firewhirl, or simply by the overall convective vigor of the flaming front—and then enter the main winds to be carried away and ultimately deposited, still burning, far from the fire. Through long-distance spotting, a single ignition multiplies into many; a chain reaction begins that scatters fire like broadcast seed through a host of environments. If the convective flow is stronger than the ambient winds, then the fire may collapse its spread and intensify its burning rates into a mass fire, but this is rare in nature, and probably rarer still in Australia. The great fires of Australia are the product of great winds.

Those winds are patterned, roughly predictable as to place and time. They are the product of local airflows between valley and mountain, land and sea, and of large-scale weather systems expressed as monsoons or fronts. They flow at particular seasons and in particular directions. Exposed ridges rich in fine fuels can develop into "fire paths," preferential routes for fast-moving fires, while complex terrain may exhibit "fire shadows" in which fires are commonly confined to the windward side of slopes. Frontal weather systems complicate that scenario with accelerations and wind shifts, but again winds must interact with curing, drying, and ignition sources to mold particular fire behaviors and fire regimes. The geography of wind helps to shape a geography of fire.

There is one pattern, however, that dominates the typology of Australian fires as much as *Eucalyptus* dominates the composition of Australian forests. It transforms the southeastern quadrant of the island continent into a veritable fire flume. Here the climate is broadly Mediterranean, culminating in a prolonged summer drought. Gradually, storm tracks migrate northward and cold fronts, sweeping west to east, brush the southern border of Australia. Ahead, they draft air from the north, and from the Nullarbor Plain to Tasmania this means desert air from the interior—hot air, dry as tinder, violent as a dust storm. No Mediterranean Sea mitigates this Australian sirocco. What it passes over it parches. Clouds may roll ahead of it, a squall line of dust and, often, of ash.

As the front approaches a site, the northerly winds accelerate. Air streams out of the Red Centre in violent gusts, a dusty avalanche. If a high-pressure cell stagnates over the Tasman Sea, frontal progress may slow and desiccation, by desert winds, prolong. But once the front passes, there is an equally violent shift in wind direction from north and northwest to south and south-

west. What had been blistered by hot winds is now swept by equally fero-
cious cold winds. It is a deadly one-two punch, calculated to knock down by
fire anything still standing after drought. As often as not flames ride the
winds like froth on a surf. When the wind shift comes, it instantly punches
new heads out of what had been a fire flank. Fires double, triple in size.
Renewed, they rage on with irrepressible vigor.[14]

This combination—desert blast followed by southerly burster—concentrates in the southeastern quadrant, the fertile crescent of Australia, where
the best soils, the best-watered landscapes, the greatest fuel loads are found,
where the continent gathers itself together into a great funnel with its spout
at Tasmania. Here reside the fires that give Australia its special notoriety, not
merely as a continent of fire but as a place of vicious, unquenchable conflagrations. In the fire flume lurk the great, the irresistible fires of Australia.

PYRIC DOUBLES:
MALLEE AND BRIGALOW

It was not inevitable that the eucalypts should dominate Australian woodlands or that fire should pervade Australia with the singularity it has enjoyed. There were alternative biotic candidates and alternative fire histories.
Isolation and aridity explain only part of the mystery; other fragments of
Gondwana, outfitted with a similar biotic stock, moved into the tropics,
seasonal drought, and fire, yet did not come so ruthlessly under the spell of
one genus or one process. *Acacia*, not *Eucalyptus*, was the great arid woodland species of the Gondwana commonwealth. Yet to compare these two
genera in Australia is to trace a contrapuntal history. In particular, the mallee (a eucalypt) and the brigalow (an acacia)—outwardly similar in their
multistemmed growth habits—record fire histories so different that they
may be considered as biotic doubles, the one a pyrophyte, the other a
pyrophobe.

In Old Australia neither accepted fire on an annual basis. But mallee
assumed that fire would repeat according to some quasi-regular rhythm, and
brigalow, that if fire happened once it might never occur again. The mallee
withstood fire, even defied it. It managed to thrive across the maw of the
southeastern fire flume; probably it needed fire to favor it against those potential competitors, hovering around it like raptors, whose powers of postfire
recuperation were far less vigorous. Brigalow ignored fire, shunned fire, created an environment in which fire was, under natural conditions, almost
impossible. It squeezed out the eucalypts. Their different fire regimes reflect
not only diverse biologies, but different wind regimes and vastly different
fuel histories.

The expression "mallee" describes a place, a growth habit, and the conglomeration of eucalypt species which exhibit that habit—multiple stems and relatively short canopies (three to nine meters) that make mallee woodlands resemble a large woody shrubland. Geographically, mallee claims the most inland and arid of the eucalypt-dominated woodlands, clustering in both the southeast and the southwest quadrants of Australia. More than a hundred eucalypts are mallees, of which seventy-one are endemic to Western Australia and another twenty-one are shared between southeast and southwest. What makes this coppicelike growth possible is an enormous lignotuber, some of which actually hold free water. (The largest on record has measured ten meters across, out of which branched 301 stems.) But what makes the mallee so flammable is the complex of associated pyrophytes.[15]

Mallee eucalypts share a diverse understory with grasses like *Stipa* and spinifex *(Triodia)*, with scleromorphs like the shrubby chenopods and the casuarinas, and with ephemerals that blossom after major storms. Between them the mallee complex can generate fuel loads for which only fire appears competent to decompose. Mallee litter reaches a quasi-steady state at 10 tons/hectare^{-1}, and further flammability depends on a rain-flushed understory. Thus, under routine conditions, lightning fires fail to spread beyond a clump or two; under exceptional conditions, however, the outcome is a conflagration. One by one, the pieces come together, like an old cannon readied to fire—heavy winter rains, which cause bare ground to burst with ephemeral grasses and forbs; an outbreak of desert winds, washing over the landscape like blown sand across a dune; the steady, year-by-year growth of resinous spinifex and of eucalypt litter, which hangs in seductive streamers from the branching stems, ready to fly like flaming chaff to new sites. Fuels are continuous, deep, crackling with a pyric chemistry that requires only a spark to explode.

No such fire could occur more than once unless the biota that sustained it could recover. In fact, it appears that episodic fires are essential to the perpetuation of the mallee community, especially in the southeast. Seeds germinate poorly, almost always confined to burned sites. But the primary mechanism of regeneration is resprouting from the giant lignotubers. Within six months after a fire as many as seventy shoots may be present; after seven years, some twenty to thirty may remain; and after a century, somewhat fewer than ten. The capacity to resprout after a fire is astonishing, though sensitive to seasonal timing. Studies suggest that two or three successive autumn fires may prove fatal, but that a twelve- to eighteen-month-old eucalypt mallee can be completely defoliated twenty-six times before exhaustion culminates in death. At less frequent rates, fire stimulates productivity. Mallee eucalypts can continue to increase biomass production in the canopy at a rate of 6 to 9 percent per year for up to thirty-five years following a burn. By favoring vegetative regrowth over seeds, fire is actually a conservative event, perpetuating the existing over the experimental, promoting the inevitable return of fuel and fire.

What is true for the mallee eucalypts holds equally for their understory. Where spinifex underlies mallee, species diversity after a fire can, in places, increase from eighteen species of vascular plants to sixty-three species, of which twenty-six are annuals. The shrubs experience an efflorescence in species and an acceleration in growth rates. Fire prunes back and stimulates spinifex, assuring a spectrum of habitats as the hummocks grow back over many years to their prefire dimensions. Overall productivity does not peak in the mallee biota for probably fifteen years, with a plateau for canopy fuels at thirty years. Without fire the understory lapses into decadence. Once established, so long as ignition and winds persist, fire assumes the status of a normal event, like earthquakes rupturing episodically along a fault line.

The contrast with brigalow is profound, rendered more enigmatic by the overall success of *Acacia* within the commonwealth of Gondwana. Outside Australia many acacias thrive in seasonally arid grasslands that burn routinely, even annually. A canopy well above the flame heights of grass fires, bark sufficiently insulating to survive the brief spurt of flame, hard seeds that must be stripped of their coat in order to germinate—these generic traits help make *Acacia* the great tree of the Gondwana savannas. Within Australia *Acacia* copes with water stress better than *Eucalyptus*, its many species challenge the eucalypts in truly arid landscapes, and it successfully interpenetrates with them in wetter environs. As a legume it can fix nitrogen, whereas the eucalypt cannot. In sheer variety it outnumbers *Eucalyptus* by more than a hundred species. What most differentiates their geography is their response to fire.[16]

The brigalow belt spans mostly the interior flank of the Great Dividing Range where it crosses the Tropic of Capricorn. It amounts to a dead zone of fire. In its penumbra what *Acacia* species dominate and what growth habits predominate depend largely on rainfall. Brigalow proper is the domain of *A. harpophylla*, which grades from shrubland to woodland as rainfall improves. Following a disturbance, root suckering leads to a relatively low, branching expression not unlike mallee. The associated flora—wilga, bottlebrush, yellow wood—have more in common with rainforest than with scleroforest. Where conditions grade into further aridity, brigalow degenerates into a shrubland characterized by gidgee *(A. cambagei)*. Regardless, the *Acacia* dominants suppress grasses and forbs.

Fuel chemistry is marginal for burning, and fuel loads, feeble. The shape of acacia leaves makes for flat, poorly aerated fuelbeds. The leaves themselves are barely flammable. Bark is not shed. Associated species like yellow wood *(Terminalia oblongata)* burn only under protest, a heat sink. Although the biomass may total over 250 tons/hectare, without shrubs, without grasses, its surface fuelbed limited to leaf litter, the available fuel for combustion is less than 0.1 percent of the biomass, or under 1 ton/hectare. Leaf fall, moreover, is keyed to intermittent rains rather than to seasons, complicating the timing of kindling to spark routine fire. The microclimate of the forest floor discourages drying and promotes biological decomposition. For practical purposes, combustible litter does not exist.[17]

There is little to compel the brigalow belt to accept fire. The dominant acacias are not by and large capable of long-distance dispersal; they do not demand disturbance to perpetuate themselves; they do not require fire. Except where they share sites with eucalypts and grasses, there are no associated scleromorphs. The belt resides outside the major fire tracks—south of the monsoonal winds, north of the temperate storms, inland and on the mountain lee from the Pacific trades. It lies outside the fire flume. Its fuel dynamics made natural fire improbable in much the same way that mallee made fire all but inevitable. Whatever ecological tilting the biota received in the past, here it could right itself without catalyzing a future of endless fire cycles, without committing to an evolutionary path down which the pyrophytes like the mallee were forcibly marched, then seized as their own.

Like the relict rainforest, the brigalow persisted as a kind of stubborn refugia—or more correctly, as a kind of alternative future, a path not taken generally in Old Australia. Along the fringes of the brigalow belt, and occasionally interpenetrating with it, are scleromorphs like *Casuarina* and several species of *Eucalyptus*; spinifex crowds the margins, and, where severe disturbances have temporarily destroyed the acacias, grasses carpet the surface. A greater frequency of catastrophic disturbance, more fire under extreme conditions, a different local history during the eucalypt revolution— and the brigalow belt might have evolved toward something like the mallee. But it did not. Disturbance was irregular. Fire did not lead to more fire. Along with rainforest, brigalow became instead the only real forest type not dominated or codominated by eucalypts, the only one for which fire does not appear to be essential. Like the eye of a hurricane, the brigalow belt flourished in the skewed calm center of a fiery vortex.

3

Red Centre: Fire Regimes of Old Australia

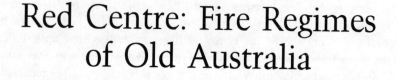

"There's different kinds of bushfires. There's grass fires, like you seen. They don't mean much at all, just burn off your fodder, maybe catch your stock if you don't move 'em fast enough. Then you can have slow scrub fires, ones where there ain't no wind and the fire don't get up above the bush. You can belt that out easy. And then there's a scrub fire that gets along at a pretty good lick. You get that when things are as dry as this."

"Yes?" said Venneker. "There's another one. That's the one you're scared of."

—JON CLEARY, *The Sundowners* (1952)

THE NATURAL FIRE REGIMES of Old Australia can only be guessed at. Too much happened at the transition to the Holocene for relict biotas to have survived intact. There were wild oscillations in climate and oceanic transgressions. There were wholesale extinctions and repopulations of which the eucalypt revolution is the most dramatic expression. And there was the introduction of a limited number of floral and faunal exotics, among them the fire-brandishing *Homo.* The revolution was rapid and almost universal. The ancien régime collapsed, utterly reformed or driven into remote refuges.

Yet coarse patterns endured and prescribed then, as now, the parameters of the continent's fire regimes. Each complex had to integrate fuel, spark, and wind. As a general rule, each of these phenomena increased from the center outward, a kind of centrifugal outflow. The farther from the center, the greater the fuels, the more vigorous the winds, the larger the interaction with humans. Old Australia resembled a centrifugal pump, with its axis at its desert core and its discharge in the southeast, pointing toward Tasmania.

Along with those increases there followed an increase in the intensity of resident fires. Beyond the arid core, moisture improved and became more regular, thus amplifying fuels. With consistent storms came consistent outbursts of lightning, timed to kindle cured grasses, drought-blasted scrub, or desiccated litter. The great wind systems, too, flowed from desert interior to watered littoral. Across the northern third of the continent, the Asian monsoon powered a seasonal tide of winds, southerly in the summer, northerly in the winter. Across the southern perimeter frontal systems smashed cold air masses into warm, a migrating whirlpool of winds that hurled desert dust across coastal biotas. The particulars of each circumstance converged into patterns by which life and fire shaped distinctive regimes. But all in some way referred back to the dry core of the continent, its fabled Red Centre.

MULGA MÉLANGE

Like a fat boomerang, Australia arcs northward far enough to share the monsoonal rains and dips its pendulous ends sufficiently southward to capture the belt of temperate storms. Between these two zones—summer rains and winter rains—precipitation is less reliable. Fuels are sparse, scattered, typically confined to swales, peaks, and ephemeral watercourses that can augment, even marginally, a precarious supply of water or are restricted to those exceptional times and places in which storms penetrate in force. Terrain mixes relentless plains with mountains that bubble upward like lithic mud geysers—the Hamersley Range, the Macdonnell and Musgrave Ranges, and of course the coast-spanning Great Dividing Range. But the added rainfall the mountains attract is countered by a broken landscape of rocky ridges and canyons. The interior deserts are a source for fire winds, not a recipient of them. In the Red Centre fires dance to an atonal beat.

The characteristic trees are acacias. From the perspective of fire dynamics, one part can stand for the whole, however, so consider the representative case of *Acacia aneura*, the mulga, whose visibility lends a certain unity to what is otherwise a mélange of biotas, starved by wretched soils, choked by aridity, and largely uninformed by fire. The mulga is typical of the constituent species—dispersed or strung into intergroved strips, suppressing grasses around it, contributing indifferently to fuel loads. It cannot by itself sustain a fire nor propagate flame beyond isolated patches. Large fires require surface fuels in continuous carpets, but among the mulga mélange, those fuels sprout in sufficient profusion only after extraordinary rains. When that happens perennial grasses and shrubs put forth extra growth; ephemerals fill up the interstitial spaces; the mélange acquires a fuelbed capable of supporting fire. Its fires follow its rains.[1]

The irregular rhythm of rainfall and drought determines the tempo of bushfire. Normal years are dry, with a growing season restricted to a period of less than five weeks. To this comes drought, roughly one year in four. If rains materialize, they cluster around high peaks or accompany outbreaks of exceptional weather that send the moist monsoons deep into the interior or that warp storm tracks and fling cold fronts, like stray asteroids, far to the north. It is estimated that for the moister eastern environs large wildfires occur between two and five times a century. In the drier center and west, incomplete records suggest major fires every fifty years or so, with known outbreaks documented for 1921 and 1974–75. The 1974–75 fires consumed an estimated 117 million hectares in a colossal swath through central Australia. Here lightning is a competent source of ignition. It kindled most of the 1974–75 fires, and in 1984–85 a lightning storm in Cobar Shire (western New South Wales) burned some 620,000 hectares in December and another 770,000 hectares in January; one fire alone burned 101,290 hectares.[2]

But while enormous, such fires are too infrequent to drive a biota. What rain and fire momentarily unite disintegrates after the emergency passes; the fires are sustained by exceptional, not normal, flora; when those annuals and ephemerals no longer bind the rest of the biota together, the separate species return to their prior existence. Mulga is a type case. Easily killed by fire, it seeds profusely after a burn with seed that can remain viable for over sixty years, or until sufficient rains germinate it. If, however, one burn rapidly succeeds another, if one wet year and its fires follow hard on the heels of another, the fires may consume mulga seedlings and destroy the prospects for replenishment. There is, however, no other tree to claim the niche vacated by the mulga. Granted enough undisturbed decades, the mulga will eventually return. Fire is not so much essential as tolerated, accommodated rather than encouraged.

The point is reinforced by considering the chenopod shrublands like saltbush *(Atriplex)* with which mulga sometimes collates in drier environments. Fire devastates saltbush with incomparable thoroughness; recovery is painful and tedious. It is likely that the shrubs originally evolved in a littoral environment for which fire occurred as an exceedingly rare event that did not really rejuvenate the biota but simply restarted a replacement cycle. In response, *Atriplex* makes fire as unlikely as possible. Shrubs grow in strongly patterned clumps; interstitial grasses and forbs are normally suppressed so that bare ground prevents fire spread; leaves are both succulent and rich in salts, a fire retardant. As an individual fuel particle and as a fuelbed both, saltbush burns poorly, rendering it an ideal understory for mulga. Only when abnormal precipitation carpets the landscape with ephemerals and annuals does the scene carry fire. *Atriplex* restoration is possible because the site lacks alternative colonizers. The salty shrubs complement mulga well.[3]

The mulga environs are not informed by fire, and this perhaps helps to explain why, in contrast to so many other Australian biotas, they constitute a mélange rather than a fire regime, strictly speaking. No Australian pyrophyte has taken over the habitat. Conditions are too arid for tropical grasses, spinifex, or eucalypts to grow, and ignition is too unpredictable to force a selective pattern of fire. In fact, the primary inhabitants like mulga and saltbush inhibit rather than promote fire. In its eastern terrain, mulga merges into the unburnable brigalow.

Pyrophytes are most effective in those environments that are capable of supporting any one of several biotas. In such a context, fire can be a selective, driving process; it can perpetuate one species over another, direct the energy dynamics of an ecosystem, or restructure habitats. In return, the pyrophytes assure that fire has adequate fuels, both in amount and in arrangement, and that such fuels are available at times when ignition is probable. In a biological sense they make fire predictable and undeniable. Only in selected places, however, do eucalypts and spinifex interpenetrate with the mulga. Instead the mulga mélange hosts a biotic corroboree, a massing of multiple species that dance around a central fire which illuminates but does not inform.

THE CENTRAL FIRES

The enduring central fires follow the perennial grasses—the hummocks called spinifex. Collectively, they comprise the dominant flora for 22 percent of the continent; for arid Australia, their prevalence is even greater (41 percent). They crowd the mulga mélange and in places interpenetrate with it as rain and fire allow. Classically, uniquely Australian plants, they claim as their special dominion the infertile soils of the ancient craton; they flourish on the interior steppes, even those devoid of surface waters; and they burn, regularly and hugely. In their breadth and interdependence with fire, they resemble grassy equivalents of the eucalypt.[4]

The provenance of spinifex spans the tropical savanna to the north and the stony deserts and acacia-fringed mountains of the south. Monsoon rains are too scant to support a subtropical biota, yet too abundant to allow the mulga mélange or gibber deserts to thrive without competition. The ragged boundary of the monsoon rains—like the berm thrown up by storm waves—defines its flexible frontier. The consistent rains assure consistent growth, which assures a consistency of fire.

To a remarkable extent, fuels follow the life cycle of the principal spinifex grasses, *Triodia* and *Plechtrechne*. Perennials, they grow in spiny bunches—known, when young, as tussocks; when mature, as hummocks; and in some local vernaculars, as porcupine grass. Each tuft grows outward, sometimes assuming the shape of a living ring around a dead center. In the better-watered north, maturity may come within ten years; in the less reliable south, in perhaps twice that. In most environments, spinifex requires three to five years to develop sufficiently to support fire, but its distinctive growth habit demands that fire propagate from one hummock to the next. One solution is to combine large clumps and high winds, the one to flare into huge flames and the other to drive those flames across bare ground to a receptive hummock. The other solution is to flood the interstitial voids with grasses and forbs, and this requires exceptional rains. Fire history thus synthesizes two rhythms—the regular beat of spinifex growth and the irregular rainstorm or rainy season. Too many wet seasons encourage too many fires, which prevents the spinifex from recovering as an important fuel. Too many dry seasons prevent the eruption of ephemerals that carry fire from one coughing hummock to the next.

Still, spinifex makes an extraordinary fuel. For three years after burning, spinifex sprouts are palatable and nutritious, with up to 6 percent crude protein. Then its dietary value collapses and, with less than 3 percent protein, it becomes all but inedible. Its decomposition becomes almost wholly restricted to fire; virtually all new growth is available fuel. The hummocks do what they can to encourage combustion: live stems are rich in resins that burn fiercely, dead stems are typically dry, and all of the hummock is thoroughly ventilated. Spinifex and its associated flora weave a powerful fuelbed; a mature community may groan under a load of 3–8 tons/hectare in available fuels. Once begun, there is little in the steppe lands that spinifex favors to break down a major conflagration. Only changes in winds or surges of moisture or the past history of fires, as recorded in large-scale fuel mosaics, can modulate a free-burning blaze.

The fire history of spinifex shapes the biodiversity of the entire ecosystem. Spinifex pervades 20 to 80 percent of the total ground cover, and it erects a structural matrix for the remaining flora and fauna. In the Simpson Desert hummock grasslands support 180 species of plants; in the central Australian sandplain, 154 species. Combustion releases species—fire ephemerals—that lie otherwise dormant. In regions of little variability, spinifex's peculiar growth habits thus provide a diversity of habitats. Its microniches testify to a history of disturbance, which is largely a history of fire. Without fire the hummocks become decadent, the landscape uniform, and the cycling of nutrients feeble. Even the hardest-seed ephemerals spoil.

Remove fire and watch mulga, *Callitris*, and other fire-sensitive refugees timidly reconquer a site. But, paradoxically, remove reliable rains, even precipitation as meager as that in the spinifex, and watch fire retreat before stony desert or a renewed mulga mélange. Free-burning fire requires a full-flushed biota. What powers fire in the spinifex is the mingling of seasonal rains with seasonal drought. That pattern makes spinifex into a kind of central fire, and a model for the two-cycle engines that drove the centrifugal pump that was Old Australia.

THE WET AND THE DRY

Northward, a hesitant, spotty monsoon—its southern fringe brushing against deserts—hardens with grim finality into summer and winter, the Wet and the Dry. Spinifex grades into savanna, hummock grasses into tropical swards; the Australian tropics ripen into a voluminous grassland studded with trees. Sorghums dominate the north, kangaroo grass *(Themeda)* the eastern steppes, and black spear grass *(Heterogon)* the coastal woodlands. Eucalypts are universal. On wetter sites, they share dominance with *Melaleuca;* in more arid lands, with *Acacia.* Where they can be shielded from fire, mangrove swamps cling like barnacles to the tidewater streams, enclaves of *Callitris* blossom, and patchy rainforests endure. But there is little protection from fire.[5]

The climate of the wet-dry tropics makes routine fire possible; its biology makes it inevitable. Soils are heavily laterized, and even by Australian standards, nutrient-drained. The monsoon and the biochemical cycles it brings to life give the nutrient flow a strongly seasonal dimension—captured into biomass during the Wet, released by fire during the Dry. The expansive grasses focus the action.

Those dominant grasses are large in biomass but small in nutritional content. Their quality, not their quantity, limits their harvesting by consumers. With the onset of the Wet, grasses spring to life and by the end of the growing season yield standing biomass on the average of 375–625 tons/hectare in central Queensland or 227 tons/hectare around Katherine in the Northern Territory, the difference between the Australian llanos and the Australian sahel. But after an early flush, the protein content decays to an abyssmal 2.5–3.0 percent by the end of the season, and grasses typically transfer important nutrients, including organic nitrogen, to underground storage. Few fauna consume the dead stalks. Without removal, without recirculating the precious nutrients, future growth falls off rapidly. Seed regeneration falters, finer grasses supersede the coarse sorghums, and woody shrubs suppress the grasses altogether.

Thus the life cycle and the fire cycle of the tropical grasses converge with machined precision. Burning stimulates biomass production (5–10 percent over that of unburned sites) and enriches its crude protein content by a factor of four or five. Fire brings the biota to life. Whole food chains—from invertebrates to raptors—collect around a moving fire. Grazers rush to the green pick that pokes through the ashes soon afterward. Even termites preferentially invade trees on burned sites rather than members of the same species in rainforest. By the end of the Dry, fire has readied the savannas for new growth, and it has even burned lowlands that, at the height of the Wet, are flooded. Fresh rains act on cleared sites and mobilized nutrients to turn black to green.

Its grasses establish the fire regime. The wetter sites are burned annually; the drier, once every two or three years. The exceedingly low nutrient reservoir and high fire frequency affect everything in the system. Unlike *Eucalyptus* elsewhere, the tropical eucalypts do not thrive on this fire environment. They survive. They are stunted, marginal; they can barely capture sufficient nutrients to sustain themselves; they coexist in uneasy equilibrium between rainforest and savanna. Although fire rolled back the rainforest sufficiently for eucalypts to transgress into the region, it now promotes the tropical grasslands with a fire frequency that has left the eucalypts living on the margin. While the eucalypts and paperbarks can survive the fires, they cannot compete as aggressively for the liberated nutrients, for annual fires constantly short-circuit the cycles that the trees demand. Even minor changes in fire frequency and the scale of burning can shift the balance of power. Biennial firing leaves the mosaic of woods and grasses stable; annual firing pushes it toward the grasses. The biota is poised on a knife-edge, sensitive to any variation in fire frequency.

This sensitivity makes it difficult to reconstruct the fire history of Old Australia. In the interior, routine fire is impossible because of limited fuels, which reflect uncertain rains. Outside that barren core, however, fuels are generally ample, and the patterns of fire history reflect the patterns of ignition. In Old Australia the early storms of the Wet brought lightning, forking like a lizard's tongue. The old grasses—once tall, now laid low by monsoon winds—readily kindled. The drier sites burned first. A texture of burns resulted, a mosaic of black soot and yellow grass, as dry, unburned patches took fire. The Australian savanna—like those in tropical Africa and South America—formed a belt between rainforest and desert. As the monsoon transgressed and regressed, that savanna expanded and contracted, marched south and retreated north.

It is difficult to trace exactly these dimensions because, during the Pleistocene, a new ignition source appeared, the Aborigine. From that moment onward human uses, not natural sources, dictated fire frequency. The fire regime of the wet-dry tropics dates from that event as firesticks imposed new fire frequencies and timings onto different portions of the biota. Rainforest retired to special enclaves, more or less deliberately spared from fire. The anomalies that presently exist—such as the status of the eucalypts—date from changes in human fire use that accompanied European settlement. Thus, in this exfoliating geography of Australian fire, the increase in fire from the center outward reflects also an increase in human ignition. Humans sought out fire, added to it, and through it reshaped Old Australia.

THE SOUTHWEST ENCLAVE

In the southwest the pattern of seasonal wet and dry became Mediterranean, a cycle of winter rains followed by a long, thirsty summer. Its biotas are complex, syncretic; they form an easy enclave, the product of a double isolation—the first as Australia departed Gondwana, and the second as encroaching seas and later deserts divided the emerging Australian scleroforest into east and west. *Eucalyptus* rules the forest; scleromorphs fluff the understory. Toward the interior, woody savanna grades into spinifex, the mulga mélange, and unburned desert. On some sandplains heaths flourish, and on many arid ridges, mallee. Endemism is extraordinarily high, and fire is everywhere.[6]

But southwest fire, like its landscape, is syncretic, muted, balanced. No single fuel drives the regime; no single ignition source, no single wind, no single topographic feature, no singular climatic phenomenon imposes a domineering pattern onto the southwest ensemble. Instead a suite of biotas balances a suite of stresses, such that fire is one force among several, so routine as to be unexceptional. Fire is endemic, not demonic. It shapes and stirs the biotas rather than overturns them. If it is inexpungable, it is also less inclined to be catastrophic. It subjects the southwest to a low-intensity simmering, not a violent boiling; while there are seasons for fire, they are broad and accommodating. While there are few sites notorious for their fires, neither are there many refugia spared fire.[7]

The major terrain feature is a corrugated plateau, shallow yet sufficiently elevated to capture moisture enough to support scleroforest. The dry scleroforest is renowned for jarrah *(E. marginata)*, a tree of extraordinary tenacity, almost impervious to fire. Its counterpart in the wet scleroforest is karri *(E. diversicolor)*, a towering gum that resists fire and regenerates vigorously after even intense burns. Existing species tend to be self-perpetuating, immediately reclaiming their sites rather than emerging into dominance after a period of decades. The scleroforest suites appear secure, a stable compound of rain and fire; there is enough fire to ward off any resurgent rainforest, yet not so much (or so vicious) fire as to degrade scleroforest into grass or scrub. The regimes flourish amid abundant fire, yet can survive, within limits, in its absence.

Overall, the southwest represents an enclave of fire, a province small and a fire regime mild by Australian standards. Big fires do occur, of course; normally they accompany frontal passages as winds accelerate and shift, and as atmospheric instability encourages strong convection above burns. But storms approach from the Indian Ocean, with winds moderated by seas, not desiccated by deserts. Inland, on the lee side of the Darling Range, precipitation declines and desert winds stir. Here there is wind to drive fire but too little fuel to flame. Conversely, where ample fuel exists, winds are much less violent; only 5 percent of fires in the southwest, for example, have recorded winds that met or exceeded a strength of six on the Beaufort scale. (In Victoria and Tasmania, the percentage is 25; in South Australia, 30; in New South Wales, 35.) Moreover, during the summer fire season, high-pressure cells tend to be less intense. In the southwest enclave bushfires burn under more diverse conditions, few of which favor conflagrations.

There are two exceptions. One scenario requires that a stationary High draft desert air over the region, a kind of muted chinook splashing dry winds across the Darlings. The other involves infrequent hurricanes that churn out of the Indian Ocean. Monster storms not only hurl trees to the earth, piling abnormal fuels; they can, in the right circumstances, suck huge desert air masses into their vortex, like a black hole capturing streamers of stars from a passing galaxy. The fuel loads and fire winds of Cyclone Alby (1978) testified vividly to what, in Old Australia, must have been a rare but inevitable event.[8]

If so it was one the southwest enclave accepted and contained, even as it absorbed the cavalcade of Aboriginal firesticks that imprinted routine fire ever more firmly on the landscape. It is likely that the latter held the former in check. In recent years, lightning has accounted for approximately 12 percent of all fires in Western Australia, roughly equivalent to the frequency of lightning fire in the United States. In Old Australia the mountains would have experienced more starts; the open grasslands, the larger fires. All this only readied the southwest, however, for the profound reformation kindled by Aboriginal firesticks. Not every locale experienced those new fires with equal intensity, but where they burned more fires meant reduced fuels, which meant a smaller domain for natural burning. Anthropogenic fire branded the landscape with a seasonal regularity no less pronounced, and far more pervasive, than the meteorological minuet of lightning and cyclone. The firestick initiated the fissioning of Old Australia into New.[9]

FIRE FLUME: THE SOUTHEAST SUITE

Three points—Eyre Peninsula, Botany Bay, Port Phillip Bay—inscribe the great fire triangle of Australia. Here the centrifugal pump discharges all it has gathered up, as though every attribute that propels fire throughout the continent were hurled across this region, a running stream of fire. Everything within this colossal fire flume must accommodate big fires—not merely large in area or frequent in recurrence, but high-intensity holocaust, a fire possessed, vicious, unquenchable, final.[10]

Its geography prescribes an ideal formula for conflagrations. A Mediterranean climate reigns over a vast area, one of varied and elevated terrain that enriches the seasonal rains. Soils are newer overall, precipitation fuller, fuel loads abundant, ignition almost constant. Migrating storm tracks draft volumes of desiccating desert winds from the north, the desert interior, then shift abruptly to cold blasts from the south that drive fire flanks before them like a flaming blizzard. Those winds rush over the most rugged terrain in Australia, mountains that act less as baffles than as wings to accelerate and channel the most violent air on the continent. Over the course of the twentieth century, climatologists have noted that "potentially bad fire seasons" tend to occur in the southeast about once every three years, "bad fires" every six or seven years, and "very bad fires" every thirteen years. While these figures reflect ignition patterns (a largely human product), they do outline a rough proportion of fire severity relative to fire frequency.[11]

That severity is something with which every component of the southeast suite must live. Its fuels are varied—interior savannas, scleroforests, heaths, mallee, buttongrass moor, and rainforest. Each biota modifies the coarse geography set by mountains, climate, and winds into distinctive regimes with their own frequency and typology of fires. There are fires of all sorts, a kind of background count of chronic combustion, but each landscape must in some way also survive the holocaust that rushes down the fire flume, for that is the trying, the distinctively Australian fire.[12]

Fortunately, the Australian sirocco must interact with fuels readied by drought and kindled by a well-timed spark. Considered in this way, those varied regimes are out of sync. The ideal formula for grass fires calls for an exceptionally wet winter followed by an exceptionally dry summer—the one builds up fuel loads beyond what fauna can consume, the other cures and desiccates it. For scleroforest, however, a dry summer may not be sufficient. The larger fuels and deeper taproots drain only after true drought, or following several seasons of cumulative water deficits. Thus, the circumstances that favor grass-driven fires do not promote equally vigorous fires in scleroforest fuels, while, conversely, the prolonged drought necessary to prepare scleroforest strangles the heavy growth necessary to propel grassy fires. In any year large fires affect either the lowland savannas or the mountain forests but not both simultaneously. The intermediate scleroforest varies between those extremes in timing, fire frequency, and fire intensity, its fuels meshing with its biology in rough, sometimes uncanny synchronization.

In dry scleroforest eucalypt litter sets the fuel loads (65–70 percent of the total), with minor contributions from herbs and grasses. Fires are frequent, light, syncopated with fuel buildup. Surface fuels can reach levels of 15 tons/hectare within ten years, 22 tons/hectare after twenty years, and 27 tons/hectare after thirty. But fires typically burn between three and twelve years, between the time at which fuels are adequate to support sustained combustion and the time beyond which it is unlikely that a site can escape ignition. For several years after a burn, a dry scleroforest lacks the fuel to reburn, and this pause allows the woody scleromorphs to maintain their position. More rapid burning would degrade the biota to pyrophytic grasses, if any are present, or choke the forest with coppicing eucalypts and sclero-morphic scrub.[13]

By contrast, wet scleroforest cultivates an understory rich in shrubs, a higher overall productivity, and a greater proportion of available fuels. Where dry scleroforest encourages easy ignition and spread, however, wet scleroforest discourages it with a microclimate that inhibits drying and a dense canopy that shelters the surface from wind. It claims niches protected from desert winds, sites often swathed in maritime moisture. Within their understory are often found the flora of an embryonic rainforest. Short-rhythm fires are unlikely, yet long-rhythm fires essential. When they come they burn with catastrophic fury, the fuels thick and kiln-dried by intemper-ate drought; fire razes whole forests, from standing eucalypts to lush under-story. In what has been described as a near miracle of timing, fire even rejuvenates the mountain ash *(E. regnans).*[14]

When surrounded by parched litter and shrubs, mountain ash not only burns vigorously but carries fire briskly to the canopy and hurls smoldering bark far in advance of the flaming front. Unusually thin-barked, lacking a lignotuber, even a modest fire will kill the bole. Its canopy fire, however, scarifies and liberates seeds stored in the crown—as many as 14 million seeds per hectare by some estimates. The tough tissues around the seeds can just hold off, and in fact need, the explosive heat created by a torching canopy. The thick ash left by the surface burn creates an ideal seedbed. After a fierce fire at Noojee, Victoria, nearly 2.5 million seedlings per hectare carpeted the burned lands. Patiently, the wet scleroforest begins its rejuvenation, a re-newal dependent on a holocaust fire every two or three centuries. The ages of the wet scleroforests chronicle the ages of their great fires.

Too many fires—the rapid, forced succession of a holocaust by repeated surface burns—and the site will degrade to scrub, perhaps to heath. Too few fires and the rainforest taxa latent in fire-sheltered niches will mature, stran-gle the scleroforest like parasitic vines, and restore a lost world of green Gondwana. The fire flume ensures that the reconquest is improbable. Only in sodden gulleys, on leeward ridges flanked by castellated rocks, in isolated mountain fire shadows can the relict rainforest persist. Elsewhere the fire flume sweeps it away in floods of flame.

SCLEROSCRUB:
OLD AUSTRALIA IN MINIATURE

For nearly all the major Australian biotas there exists a type of heath. There are tropical heaths, alpine heaths, mallee heaths, temperate heaths, dry heaths, and wet heaths. The kwongan—the heath of the sandplain—claims sites intermediate between the mulga and the mallee. The wallum—the heath of the Queensland coast—is a diminutive wet scleroforest. Large swaths of heath dot the Kimberleys and Arnhemland, a distilled rainforest. Patches of heath on the Cape York Peninsula concentrate the flora of the tropical savanna. Throughout the southeast a kaleidoscope of heaths compresses the biomes of the scleroforest. Its heaths form a kind of scleroscrub, Old Australia in miniature.[15]

If their distribution distills the biogeography of Australian life, their history recapitulates its evolution. Heaths claim sites with wretchedly impauperate soils. Even slight alterations in the nutrient flux—a sudden surge, a steady loss—can destroy the delicate balances that sustain the heath flora. Next, they accommodate water stress. Too much or too little, waterlogged or desiccated—either way, the imbalance can lead to scleroscrub, a wet heath in one case, a dry heath in the other. But these conditions only intensify circumstances to which Old Australia had long adapted in its transformation from rainforest to scleroforest. The final stress was fire.

As fire regimes, heaths resemble the dynamics of those biotas that surround them and of which they are distillations—they concentrate those properties. Their propensity for burning is extraordinary. Leaves are rich in oils, low in moisture, lean in mineral content—particularly in phosphorus—all of which makes for brilliant, flaming combustion. Fuel loads build rapidly. For three to five years surface fuels increase quickly, then taper off while shrubs proliferate, their growth rates peaking between five and ten years but never really ceasing. Biomass can reach 10 tons/hectare within five years. In *Banksia*-rich heath at Jervis Bay, fuels measured 50 tons/hectare after fourteen years. Virtually all the new biomass is available as fuel. On average, fuel loads in mature heath range between 20 and 35 tons/hectare, values comparable to wet scleroforest. Its open nature, its chronic aridity, its sweeping winds—all make heath fuels ideally available for burning. A heath requires only a few years of recovery from one fire to prepare for another.

Not only fuels but ignition dictates the frequency of fire and the relative proportion of high- to low-intensity burns. Most heaths reflect the fire frequency of their adjacent regimes, and, claiming less than 1 percent of Australia's land surface, many fires necessarily enter heath from the outside. They accept such fires readily and with tremendous resilience. They accommodate a range of fires, and while those fires influence the internal dynamics of the heath, they do not alter its status relative to surrounding biotas. Fire neither perpetuates nor destroys: nothing else can claim the site. With or without fire, the heath will persist.

If not obligatory, fire is nevertheless frequent, welcome, useful, and inescapable. It modulates the scleroscrub, miniaturizing and intensifying the impacts it makes on scleroforest. Overall, heath fires are conservative; they can recycle and release precious nutrients, seeds, and access to water, but they cannot by themselves augment or diminish the total quantity of those minerals or waters present. Still, there is much to influence, for the floristic richness of heath is legendary. Australian heaths admit about 3,700 typical species, embracing representatives from nearly every prominent Australian family including many of the more flamboyant floras—the grass trees *(Xanthorrhea)*, the ground orchids, the nectar-rich *Banksia*, the stilt plants *Dryandra* and *Hakea.* The kwongan contains 70 percent of the species found in the southwest enclave. This variety is fundamental. Not a dominant species, but their scrubby growth habit is what defines heathland.

There is, accordingly, plenty of flex in the system by which to accommodate fires. Because of their fuel history, even high-intensity fires can occur at almost any time, and floristic composition reflects shifts in fire frequency and seasonal timing. More-frequent fire favors those flora that propagate by sprouting; less-frequent fire, those that reproduce by seed or that aspire to control the canopy. Too frequent fire can remove some flora by not allowing them to mature into seed-producing states. Too occasional fire pushes other flora into senescence, beyond their ability to regenerate from lignotubers or beyond the capacity of their seed to remain viable. Fire early in the summer selects some species; fire in the autumn, others. Fires twist the heath like a kind of biotic kaleidoscope, the pieces always there but constantly reorganized into new patterns. The heath, in turn, testifies to the universality, ease, and subtlety of fire in Old Australia.

RELICT RAINFOREST

That leaves the rainforest.

It endured—secure from swelling drought and blasts of wind from the desert core, preserved in sheltered grottos around the watered seaboard. Like heath it was multiple, a distillation of many biotas. Unlike scleroforest, it was a relict. It claimed only a fraction of the land surface it once held and which it was yet capable of reclaiming under existing conditions of soils and climate—except, that is, for fire. Bushfire surged against rainforest, etching its geographical and historical boundaries. Insinuating itself into a mixed flora, fire selected for and shaped scleroforest and scleroscrub. It crowded rainforest to the margin of the island continent until it resembled a chain of coral reefs, a biotic atoll subsiding in a sea of scleromorphs. Fire seized the Red Centre.

There were many rainforests. Tropical rainforest revolved around the araucarias, supported by a rich understory of vines. Temperate rainforests favored *Nothofagus* and an understory blanket of ferns and mosses. By stratifying into gallery forests these Gondwanic relicts packed an enormous number of species into small domains. In all their variants, they showed tolerance to degraded soils and often to the peculiarities of eccentric sites. Their tenacity derived from a stability of climate made possible by reliable rainfall, by a precipitation regime that was not simply high but consistent across the seasons; a biotic stability that left true rainforest almost empty of scleromorphs; a stability of nondisturbance, the relative freedom of a site from routine disruptions, or if disturbed, by the capability to repair itself without surrendering to another biota. Together they spared rainforest from fire.[16]

Australian rainforest shows some tolerance for aridity—it has to—but it does not accommodate prolonged drought or seasonal dryness. Its layered canopies and dense understories work avidly to conserve moisture and preserve a fetid microclimate; dry spells have to work against this powerful moisture gradient. Likewise, few Australian rainforest types exclude completely scleromorphic species. The tropical rainforest is the most successful, being virtually free of scleroforest elements—no pyrophytic grasses; no scleromorphic scrubs; no eucalypts, casuarinas, or melaleucas. The temperate rainforest shows some intermixing, and merges uneasily into wet scleroforest. Thus the border between rainforest and its competitors—savanna or scleroforest—is, in the tropics, sharply etched and, in more temperate climates, blurred. Inevitably, too, there are disturbances. Windstorms, for example, can level tracts of rainforest far in excess of what organic agents can decompose, a shifting cultivation of rainforest by the slashing of cyclones and the burning of lightning fires.

Its fire history sums up the rainforest's various stabilities. In tropical rainforest leaves make up probably 80 percent of the surface fuels and biological agents quickly decompose them. What persists is sparse, perennially wet, and sheltered from dry winds. When fires reach the rainforest border they flash against a green wall, gasp helplessly for fuel, and expire. If rainforest advances or retreats, it does so as a unit in response to broad shifts in climate. Changes in the dry season—greater moisture, fewer fires—allow the rainforest to advance into scleroforest and savanna. The reverse allows fire to eat a little farther into the frontier. Blowdowns along the border open the canopy, dry out surface fuels, and allow fires that normally flame out along the perimeter to enter into the interior according to a scenario that may become irreversible. The burn alters microclimates; fireweeds and pyrophytes invade the site; the new fuels carry additional fires over the burn and incinerate those slow-growing rainforest flora that demand shade and moisture.

In temperate regions, succession into and out of rainforest is less sharply defined. The borders blur; rainforest intercollates with wet scleroforest. Undisturbed, wet scleroforest will pass, over the course of several centuries, into rainforest. Disturbed—burned—it reverts to scleroforest or scleroscrub. What actually exists on any particular site reflects the unique sequencing of its past fires. Small sites are especially susceptible to irreversible change. Once initiated, a rhythm of frequent fire encourages soil erosion and the loss of nutrient capital. This encourages scleromorphs, which accept more fire. In such a scenario wet scleroforest degenerates into dry scleroforest, sclero-scrub, or savanna, and rainforest no longer possesses the means to reclaim the site. Without refugia, rainforest vanishes.[17]

If its heath miniaturizes Australia's fire geography, its rainforest minia-turizes its fire history. The uniformity of the Gondwana rainforest fractured under the impress of isolation, aridity, and disturbances. Increasingly, the principal disturbance and the great integrator of new conditions—fire— shaped those new regimes. The fragmentation continued, like rocks spalling off a heated cliff. From it came the unique species and unexampled biotas of Old Australia. With the relict rainforest, the story comes full circle. The flames licking at the wet flanks of tropical vine forest or overturning wet scleroforest on a rhythm of centuries are recapitulating a cycle of fire begun with the Great Upheaval.

4

Land of Contrarities

Drought, dry seasons, and, more than all—that deadliest weapon of the tyrant—the bush-fire, reduces and selects the life of the country.

—W.H.L. RANKEN,
The Dominion of Australia (1874)

The aspect of the country was fearful. Brown, burnt-up, and sweltering under a broiling sun! . . . Imagine all the trees and scrub high above your head blazing —all the ranges, as far as the eye can reach, one mass of smoke and fire.

—MARCUS CLARKE, letters

IN ITS ORIGINS, ancestral Australia was all but indistinguishable from the rest of Gondwana. Its biota was similar, if not identical; its climate was mild and wet; its seasons, invariant. But the breakup of the supercontinent had led, inevitably, to changes that demanded, and forged, new identities. Leaching, drying, and burning, each in turn and with cumulative impact, worked over Australia's Gondwanic legacy. The tempo of disturbance quickened and beat to irregular rhythms. Isolation ensured that recolonization was negligible, that new biotas would have to evolve from the inherited stocks. The Great Upheaval installed to dominance a dramatically different biota. A second revolution within the emergent scleroforest furthered and confirmed that transformation. After *Homo* infiltrated the continent, the process was irreversible. Out of Gondwana rainforest emerged, through these trials, Australian bush.

By the time Europeans arrived, the bush presented an inverted world, a parallel universe. It was as if a second ark had escaped the Flood, as though a whole continent had passed through an enchanted looking glass. Compared to northern Europe, Australia exuded the alien, the hostile, the sterile, the bizarre. François Peron alluded to "whimsical freaks of Nature" that defied

57

attempts at scientific understanding. James O'Hara disparaged a Nature that apparently "indulged in whim," such that nothing—neither animal nor vegetable—resembled anything anywhere else. Charles Darwin mused that here at the antipodes "an unbeliever in everything beyond his own reason might exclaim, 'surely two distinct Creators must have been at work.' " Marcus Clarke invoked a "Weird Melancholy" to conjure the spirit of the bush, later softening that cry with an appeal to "read the hieroglyphs of haggard gum-trees." Perhaps the most famous denunciation, already couched in sardonic tones, was the declaration of an anonymous colonial poet of the 1850s:

> There is a land in distant seas
> Full of all contrarities.[1]

The nature of Australian exceptionalism was difficult to identify precisely. It was there in the bush, certainly, though the bush echoed bits and pieces of other Gondwanic lands. It meant coming to grips with miserable soils, aridity, desert winds. And, everyone agreed, it involved bushfire. Whatever elements led to the bush, fire integrated and accelerated, like a flask of chemicals held over a Bunsen burner. By geologic standards, the bush was a sudden invention, kindled almost instantaneously from drying Gondwanic tinder and the flint of *Homo* sharply striking the continent. However the bush defined Australia, so fire defined the bush. In ways both obvious and obscure, the land of contrarities was a land of fire.

AN EVER-LIVING FIRE

The geographical border that so sharply segregates rainforest from scleroforest has a temporal analogue in the veritable explosion of fire that raged across Australia during the Holocene. Fire was abrupt, ubiquitous, grasping. It insinuated itself into malleable biotas. It welded the biotic pieces into a dynamic whole. Not fire alone but its versatility—its ability to interact with the other elements of the bush—established its importance. Fire dominated the dynamics of the Australian bush as fully as *Eucalyptus* dominated the composition of its forests and woodlands.

This was not inevitable. Had Australia rafted into the tropics at a different rate, had its initial floristic composition not included so many scleromorphs, had *Acacia* replaced the ancestral *Eucalyptus* as part of the original Gondwanic ark, had Australian soils experienced more general rejuvenation, had other species leaked across its borders, the story might have turned out differently. Instead fire seized the core, not merely recycling habitats and nutrients but diverting the whole biota into new evolutionary pathways from which recovery might be impossible. Fire integrated the elements of the bush, and anything that affected the presence of fire ramified throughout the bush. Above all, fire bonded the bush to humans. The bush could not be understood without its distinctive, singular fires.

But fire did not by itself render Australia a land of contrarities: fire is everywhere on the planet. The evolution of the Earth into a fire planet has paralleled the evolution of life. Marine life gave it an oxygenated atmosphere; terrestrial life packed its surface with fuels accessible to oxygen; lightning supplied spark to both life and fire. Since the time these elements first came together, the Earth has burned. Terrestrial life has evolved in the presence of fire. The earliest coal beds are laced with fusinite, the charcoal of ancient fires. Heracleitus was right, "This world . . . was ever, is now, and ever shall be an ever-living fire, with measures of it kindling, and measures going out."[2]

Fire has been everywhere on the Earth's lands. Huge conflagrations have swept the boreal forest on a cycle of centuries. Temperate forests burn on more irregular rhythms, with greater variations in intensity. Conifer forests throng like chemical kindling, ready to erupt into fire. Thick lenses of charcoal underlie the Amazon Basin. Fire on the order of 4 million hectares gutted the normally dripping jungles of Borneo after several years of drought. Tropical savannas burn almost annually. Fire invades temperate grasslands routinely, sometimes yearly. The grasses of wetlands burn. Tundra burns. Peat burns. Swamps drained by drought burn. Deserts, suddenly flush with life after rains, burn. Cropping out from the ice of Antarctica are coal seams charged with pyrofusinite. The fires in each of Australia's climates can be matched, and often exceeded, by fires elsewhere or in the past.[3]

Likewise, the adaptations to fire regimes that Australian organisms display, while marvelous, have analogues among the flora and fauna of other continents. Warm-season grasses everywhere show a similar suite of traits to protect against grazing, drought, and fire. The longleaf pine of the American South experiences a "grassy" stage in its early life cycle that makes it susceptible to burning; if not burned, it is vulnerable to the fatal blue spot fungus as an adult. The seeds of *Sequoia* germinate best in warm, ashy soil, exactly the conditions that prevail after an intense fire. Several North American pines—lodgepole and jack, among them—feature serotinous cones that open only when heated; a flash fire through the canopy exactly serves this purpose, and the exposed mineral soil is quickly saturated with descending seeds; the forest recovers as an even-aged stand. Other organisms rally around these patterns—the endangered Kirkland warbler thrives only in jack pine of a certain age class. Evergreen sclerophylls exist in all Mediterranean-climate sites. The chamise of California, for example, prepares itself to burn as it ages. By age twenty it steadily increases the proportion of dead wood to live in its crown; virtually all new growth is available as fuel; a woody understory begins to form; the oily leaves, drained of moisture by seasonal or secular drying, blaze like blow torches.

The list goes on. And on. Combustion is too much a part of the biological fabric of the Earth for Australia to have created a monstrous incongruity of fire. The fire regimes of ancient Australia echoed those found elsewhere among its Gondwana cognates. In the deserts fire followed episodes of unusual rainfall. In a pattern that mimicked the central Australian fires of 1974–75 extensive fires swept the Kahalari in the early 1980s after a bout of exceptional precipitation. The border between grassland and desert has ebbed and flowed with the movement of storm tracks and monsoonal winds. Fires have crept into the Sahara with the encroachment of grasses; in Pleistocene times, when the region was much wetter than at present, fires burned grasslands in what is now sanddune and stone. The border of rainforest in eastern India, equatorial Africa, and Amazonia is all but universally inscribed by fire. Tropical savannas burn almost annually. More temperate grasslands burn only slightly less often, a shifting cultivation by fire of scattered trees, shrubs, and grass. The Mediterranean-climate regions of modern Gondwana are notorious as fire environments, fluffed with scleromorphic vegetation, kiln-dried under a baking sun, and subject to outbreaks of foehn and sirocco winds that drive fire before them like a flaming avalanche. Fire is everywhere, differentiated into regimes but never truly absent.

Yet Australia *was* incontestably different, and fire served as a catalyst for that difference. By the end of the last glacial epoch the island continent moved from the triumvirate that had governed Old Australia—impauperate soils, aridity, lightning fire—to the triumvirate that would shape its succeeding Australias—eucalypts, humans, anthropogenic fire. Old Australia felt that impact first in those regimes where the new elements most intersected, its savannas and its Mediterranean-climate lands. Its ever-living fire was a means of transition, the point through which, like a crystal lens reversing everything within its field of vision, the landscape inverted.

FIRE FUSE: THE AUSTRALIAN SAVANNA

Australia's savannas link it with a global biogeography. Tropical savannas are extensive in Africa, South America, Mesoamerica, India, and Southeast Asia; temperate savannas, often enormous, border the pampas, veldt, steppes, and prairies of the major continents. The essential ingredients are grasses, a seasonal cycle that brings sufficient moisture to grow fuels yet passes through a dry phase, and fire. In the tropics and subtropics, the border between savanna and rainforest is abrupt and, except in droughts, unbridgeable by fire. In more temperate lands, wooded enclaves thrive in wet river bottoms or on the lee side of rocky outcrops, wherever fires cannot routinely penetrate. When fires are excluded, forest reclaims grassland. Apart from these generic traits, however, the Earth's savannas reflect local biotic materials and their history.[4]

It is not clear how the savannas originated. Grasses first appear in the geologic record during the Eocene (50 million years ago). Associated forbs and composites materialize in the Miocene, roughly coincident in Australia with the onset of the Great Upheaval. To what extent this grass mélange constituted a grassland is difficult to determine; almost always there is a concurrent record of trees, either conifer or hardwood. Probably the associated grasses were elements of a forest understory. Then, as climates dried, as drought appeared in seasonal rhythm, as fire increased in prominence, grasses replaced trees as a dominant flora, and forests evolved into savannas. In some places grassy fuels massed; elsewhere they fingered outward into surrounding biotas. Regardless, they became an enormous fuse that carried fire throughout Old Australia.

What complicates this simple scenario is the origin of that critical fire. In historic and prehistoric times, the vast proportion of ignitions has been anthropogenic—so much so that many observers have even doubted the competence of natural sources. In part this reflects how massive human intervention has been: humans have preempted natural fire, or through their fire practices have restructured its vital core. In part, however, contemporary observations speak to a biota that now exists under a climate different from that under which it was created.

The savanna exists in dynamic equilibrium between a tidal climate that drives it alternately to grassland or forest. Lightning fire assisted, and anthropogenic fire arrested, those natural oscillations. The contemporary savanna is likely a human artifact, a biotic edifice sculpted by anthropogenic burning. Fire is not merely something that occurs in a savanna: it is a prime mover of savanna dynamics. To be effective, the burning must be regular and at short intervals for which, as Carl Sauer asserts, "man is the competent agent." [5]

Yet where humans are removed, where the climate is sufficiently ambiguous to support either regime in the absence of hominids, natural ignitions are evident and often potent. Lightning at the onset of the wet season can be effective at kindling large fires. When combined with drought, grass-fueled fires may break through the microclimatic barrier that segregates grassland from forest and raze even rainforest into prairie. The rhythms, however, are irregular. The geography of a natural savanna is a swale of patches, of lands lost and reclaimed as drought and rain alternately flame and quench grassy and woody fuels. What humans do is to overwhelm, redirect, and regularize that fire regime; and particularly where fire is used with other forms of land use such as herding or swidden agriculture, to extend their mutual dominion. Human firesticks can reorganize the geography of fire much as irrigation can reorganize the natural geography of water and extend the realm of agriculture. With routine anthropogenic burning, savanna can even defy climatic changes that, if left untrammeled, would push the biota into forest. [6]

Its fire bond with humans made the Australian savanna more than one biota among many. It opened Old Australia to *Homo.* It seems likely that hominids emerged on an African savanna swept by lightning-caused and volcanic fires. Alone among organisms humans learned to use fire actively, and they learned those practices on grasslands. It is likely that humans entered Old Australia when the Sahul was a grassy plain that not only defined a physical corridor by which to travel but gave entree into the critical dynamics of the emerging Australian ecosystems—a biotic corridor, a fuse for anthropogenic fire. Fire created conditions attractive to humans, and humans reciprocated by introducing more fire.

CONCENTRATED FIRE: AUSTRALIA'S MEDITERRANEAN LANDS

Its Mediterranean landscapes are Australia's other special environment. Like its savannas, they are local expressions of a global feature. They come and go with climatic oscillations. They are recent, dating from the Pleistocene. And they are at least partially anthropogenic, their histories inextricably tied to humans and their biological allies. Unlike the savanna, Mediterranean lands are not corridors but collecting basins. They are less a frontier, advancing and receding, than a crossroads where many biotas converge, claim distinctive niches, and settle into a complex caste system of subbiotas. If savannas are fuses, the Mediterranean landscapes are the explosives to which they lead. Australia's Mediterranean and peri-Mediterranean regions contain its most heavily stocked biotas, the densest populations of humans, the fullest congregation of fire practices, and the most violent fires.

By area less than 5 percent of the Earth's land surface, the Mediterranean-climate lands fall into five terrains—the Mediterranean Basin proper, South Africa, northern Chile, Southern California, and the southern perimeter of continental Australia. Each terrain exhibits mild wet winters and long dry summers. Their common geographies include a littoral, a seasonal pattern of cold offshore currents, mountains, and recurring disturbances. Interestingly, four of the terrains border fragments of Gondwana. Mediterranean California (ever the exception) overlies a sliver of the Pacific plate that is only coincidentally, ephemerally attached to the North American plate. Their common Gondwanic heritage helps to account for the apparent dominance of evergreen scleromorphs that trace their evolutionary origins to tropical or subtropical floras; they mingle the moist with the arid, the tropical with the temperate. Their complex physical geography makes possible, in turn, a complex geography of life, the mosaic of microclimates sustaining a mosaic of microbiotas.[7]

Mediterranean ecosystems are chocked with new and relict species—a living palimpsest stuffed with biotic glosses and interlinear subtexts. The border between floral types is abrupt. A change in climate, land use, or fire patterns can deflect the system into any of several subbiotas. At their core are shrubby scleromorphs—chamise and chaparral in California; maquis, garrigue, macchia, and phrygana in the Mediterranean; renosterveldt and fynbos in South Africa; matorral in Chile; mallee in Australia. Each label subsumes a host of species. If precipitation increases, scrub matures into mountain forests of evergreen scleromorphs or, if they front Laurasian lands, of drought-toughened conifers. If precipitation decreases, scrub surrenders to a subdesert of low, dispersed shrubs. If soil fertility improves, grasses thrive. If fertility degenerates, heath flourishes. Each terrain pieces together a mosaic that balances, on small sites, these competing pressures.

All share, too, a history of human manipulation. Humans are intimately implicated in the maintenance, if not the origins, of the Mediterranean lands, all of which emerged during the Pleistocene under the combined impact of climate, biotic revolutions, and humans. Mediterranean soils are either impauperate or prone to degradation; their constituent species are survivors—tough, weedy, thriving on disturbance, perfect associates for humans; and microclimates are ideal for fire. Burning can occur over a long dry season, droughts blanch the land frequently, and while large burns are possible, the rugged terrain compartmentalizes fire, giving it a specificity not unlike the fuels upon which it fed. Such an environment humans found congenial—as they cut, grazed, and fired and so altered biotic composition, induced soil erosion, and upset water regimes.

Anthropogenic fire was everywhere present and everywhere absorbed. Yet, while formative, it was not always mandatory. In Chile, for example, lightning fire is infrequent (less than 2 percent of all starts), and it appears that the scleromorphs took over the landscape without fire driving them into ascendancy. But because these environments were so susceptible to fire, they were especially susceptible to human manipulation, and once colonized, humans indelibly branded them with anthropogenic fire, typically associated with other practices such as hunting, grazing, clearing, farming, and war. So ubiquitous has anthropogenic fire become that it is difficult to reconstruct what a fire regime without human influence might look like.[8]

There were of course differences among the Mediterranean environments. Chile lacks the violent winds that power large fires in the cognate lands—the bora, mistral, and sirocco that sweep the Mediterranean Basin; the Santa Ana and Mono of Southern California; the desert winds and southerly burster of southeastern Australia. But large or small, fires were in Chile, as they were in the other sites. The Mediterranean Basin was notorious as a tinderbox, constantly burned in association with human land practices. The west Mediterranean and islands like Corsica and Sardinia continue to be known, because of their fires, as the "red belt." Southern California was fired until it resembled a burnt-out case. Veldt and fynbos fires greeted the first settlers of Cape Town. The Chilean landscape continued a pattern of burning that extended from the lowland llanos to the lofty altiplano. Australia was rimmed with smoke, seared with episodic conflagrations. Whatever the natural state, the condition of the Mediterranean terrains from the time of human colonization has been one of chronic fire.

Australia's Mediterranean terrains possess some distinctive features. They are more influenced by intermittent summer rains, less controlled by a weaker ocean current. Their soils are among the oldest and most degraded, constantly pushing the system toward heath and scrub. With fewer mountains, the terrains display fewer niches. Their shrub component—mallee—is high, between half and three-quarters of all the biomes assimilated. They have experienced a far more intense isolation because they have been severed from large continents that could restock the site with new species. Instead they have been exceptionally dependent on flora and fauna introduced by humans, often from other Mediterranean terrains. While the number of eucalypts included among the mallee is comparable to the total number of woody species found in cognate terrains, the mallee all derive from a single genus, and its genetic variability is inherently less than the others.

As with its savannas, however, the decisive difference between Australia's Mediterranean terrains and those elsewhere derive from their human history. In the southeast, particularly, fire practices congregated. The Aboriginal occupation of Australia subjected the Mediterranean terrain to elaborate foraging and burning, but without farming, land clearing, herding, and the massive introduction of exotic flora and fauna that grossly complicated and magnified the effects of anthropogenic fire elsewhere. That came with European colonization. Europeans, in fact, arrived already long experienced in the settlement of Mediterranean-type terrains, and with remarkable persistence they sought out one Mediterranean landscape after another.

And with good reason. It was in the Mediterranean Basin that Western civilization honed its agricultural techniques, selected its preferred species of plants and animals, accumulated the experience that would make possible the colonization of the remaining Earth's Mediterranean terrains, all prime sites for human habitation in part because of the ancient bonds developed in the model region. Thus Australia quickly established important ties with South Africa, Chile, and California, and through Britain with the Mediterranean Basin as a source of crops, livestock, irrigation expertise, and human immigrants. In return, Australia exported eucalypts.

As with savannas, so also Mediterranean lands became points of entry for human colonizers. If the Aboriginal march through Sahulian savannas recapitulated the origins of *Homo*, European colonization into Australia's Mediterranean terrains recapitulated the origins of Western civilization. In both instances, those biotas influenced Earth history far beyond what their minuscule land areas suggested was possible. It was no accident that both streams of colonists sought out exactly those Australian lands most amendable to anthropogenic fire. Landscapes that had known fire apart from humans now found themselves ruled, in good measure, by human fire.

"A FIRE HUGE IN IMAGINATION AS THE WORLD"

The Australian bush was far from completed when the first humans arrived, and its antipodean qualities only partially confirmed. It shared ancestral origins with other Gondwana flora. Its biotas and subbiotas had analogues elsewhere. Other Gondwanic shields had leached soils, some on a massive scale. Seasonal drought afflicted every continent and most islands. The Sahara and the Kalahari deserts in Africa, the Atacama in South America, the Thar in India—all developed on Gondwana cratons in roughly the same latitudes as Australia's Red Centre. Excluding only the ice sheets, free-burning fire was universal. Everywhere fire performed similar functions and obeyed the same laws of physics. In Mediterranean terrains fire was routine, sometimes explosive.

Yet the landscape of Old Australia was different, too. It contained some unique elements, combined in unique ways, and animated by fire into a unique presence. The universality of *Eucalyptus* is a striking phenomenon. Other lands had evergreen scleromorphs that dominated a biota, many such genera of ancient tropical or subtropical origins and all inured to fire. But nowhere else did one genus dominate across nearly all the wooded environments of a continent. In Australia gums define the character of the bush from tropical savanna to Mediterranean shrubland to mountain forest. Eucalypts tyrannize the entire spectrum of wooded lands, excepting only the mulga mélange. It is as though, in North America, chamise *(Adenostoma)* grew not only as a shrub but as a tree, as though it were supreme not only in Southern California but in the Everglades and the Rocky Mountains and along the watercourses of the High Plains, as though forests of pine, spruce, fir, oak, and hickory were all banished or shrunk into vestigial relicts and replaced by species of chamise. While the variety within the *Eucalyptus* alliance is staggering, there remains a commonality of history and behavior that has indelibly equated the bush with the eucalypt and stamped that bush with a distinctive monotony. When the explorer John Oxley despaired that "one tree, one soil, one water, and one description of bird, fish, or animal prevails alike for ten miles and for one hundred," he was hardly accurate, but Australia did show a remarkable singularity for which its singular addiction to fire is partly accountable.[9]

The pieces that made up the bush came together in a unique context. Australia combined unusual size with extraordinary isolation. Until humans arrived, there were few exchanges with other lands. Australia imported little and exported less. Environmental stresses acted wholly on indigenous materials. Particularly in the southeast, winds, soils, precipitation, and biotic reserves concentrated the bush into a dense, volatile mosaic boiled down into a distillate by periodic fire. By Pleistocene times—as climatic and biotic disturbances became more violent and routine—*Homo* arrived with flickering firesticks to impose a complex economy of hunting, foraging, and gathering. For this task fire was an indispensable and universal tool. Initially it affected those landscapes that were especially susceptible to anthropogenic fire, then spread like an oil slick into every niche it could find.

In the process fire became more than a phenomenon: it asserted a presence. In Australia fire had a relentless intensity and a continental scale. It was pervasive, persistent, singular. It magnified, telescoped, and simplified the bush. Fire had touched other continents, but it branded Australia. The contrast with New Guinea, once joined to Australia across the Sahul plain, is instructive. Here soils were remade or freshened by volcanism; the climate was spared aridity, except in a few sites that were seasonally dry; and fire loads were vastly reduced, almost wholly anthropogenic. The environment resisted fire. Only constant attention by swidden agriculturalists and hunters, only on sites prepared by humans into slash or prairie, could fire persist. The island overflowed with cornucopic diversity—a continental flora in miniature; a fifth of known human languages. By contrast, Australian fires burned over long periods and large areas, anthropogenic and natural ignition complemented each other, and once installed fire became inexpungable.[10]

The greater the commitment to fire, however, the greater the difficulty of removing it. Pyrophilia had its perils. Fire could become a kind of biotic addiction, seemingly relieved only by more fire. It opened Old Australia to fire-hardy species and denied it to others. It imposed a special character on the bush, and committed it to a special vulnerability. Any change in the frequency, intensity, or timing of fire would ramify throughout the continent. Species that shaped Australian fire would be, in turn, shaped by it. If humans used fire to reorder the bush, it was equally true that the bush, through fire, would reorder human society. What it granted as power, fire also took away as weakness. Fire, for humans, meant both access and danger.

Those conditions that made fire so universally powerful also placed it beyond total human control. Bushfires could burn independently of any human will or act. If fire was a universal solvent, bushfire was also a brooding, ineffable, sometimes fatal presence that from time to time could burst forth with terrifying effect, a psychological as much as a physical presence, a nightmare out of a Gondwana Dreamtime.

> When, with the dreams of Egremont, a strange
> And momently approaching roar began

To mingle, and insinuate through them more
And more of its own import—till a Fire
Huge in imagination as the world
Was their sole theme: then, as arising wild,
His spirit fled before its visioned fear . . .
　　　　　—CHARLES HARPUR, "The Bush Fire"

BOOK II

The Aborigine

5

Flaming Front

To clear the forest's dark impervious maze
The half-starv'd Indian [Aborigine] lights a hasty blaze
Then lifts the Torch, and rushing o'er the Strand
High o'er his head he waves the flaming Brand
From Bush to Bush with rapid steps he flies
Till the whole forest blazes to the skies . . .

—THOMAS MUIR, *"The Telegraph:*
Consolatory Epistle" (c. 1790s)

Our cots we fence with firing
and slumber when we can
To keep the wolves and tigers from us
in Van Diemen's Land.

—ANONYMOUS BUSH BALLAD,
"Van Diemen's Land"

THE REVOLUTION THAT SHOOK Pleistocene Australia was part of a global reformation. The world ocean rose and fell. Ice sheets on the scale of continents
formed and disintegrated. Climates reversed from glacial to interglacial and
back to glacial again in rapid order as though the Earth were being swept by
slow-moving planetary storms. A massive wave of extinctions—the most
comprehensive since the great Cretaceous extermination—visited the world
biota. It was within this context, within the biotic center of the Pleistocene,
that the genus *Homo* emerged. With the arrival of humans, the eccentric,
the protective isolation of Old Australia broke down. Well before humans
brought other, allied species to the island continent, they carried and distributed fire.

Even for a fire planet like Earth, humans are special. For the first—and
probably the only—time an organism seized control over ignition itself. That

71

moment was unique, unprecedented, and it is unlikely that *Homo* will ever allow another species that experience. Thus the elaborate rituals by which human societies preserve fire have an allegorical dimension. Once acquired, humans would never allow fire to be extinguished. Fire remained as part of *Homo*'s biological heritage, and around it much of human culture has evolved. Take fire away from a human society and its technological base would be devastated.

The onset of domestication and the acquisition of fire were reciprocal processes: if *Homo* domesticated fire, it was equally true that the nurturing of fire advanced the domestication of *Homo*. The hearth fire became the practical and symbolic center of human society; it defined family, group, nation. The hearth expanded to become a ring of fire that shielded humans from the dangers of the night. It divided the world of the human from that of the nonhuman. As the ring moved outward, it projected human will and imprinted a human touch. Humans advanced like a flaming front, steadily expanding their protective, transforming, magical ring of fire.[1]

RING OF FIRE

Again and again, as conditions waxed and waned, new species of *Homo* incubated in Africa, then dispersed to all the contiguous lands accessible to them. The critical range was apparently the chronically disturbed rift valley of eastern Africa. Near here the other great primates flourished; here the fossil record, though always tenuous, is best preserved; here climate and biological potential carved savanna from forest on a landscape abundantly fired by lightning and volcanics. Here it appears *Homo* emerged as a distinct genus some 2 million years ago.

The event was long in coming. During the Miocene anthropoids had colonized the Gondwana tropics in Africa, Eurasia, and South America. The ancestral great apes, Pongidae, thrived only in Africa and Eurasia, however, appearing about 15 million years ago. Hominidae arrived probably 5–4 million years ago. The hominid alliance included *Australopithecus* and, perhaps 2 million years later, *Homo;* some specialists would accept also *Ramapithecus,* which is ancestral to the australopithecines, and the closest of the great apes, the chimpanzee and the gorilla. While the precise evolutionary relationships between the major members of the alliance are unclear, a reasonable guess is that the earliest hominid, *Homo habilis,* broke free of *Australopithecus* around 2 million years ago. Within a few hundred thousand years—that is, by 1.7–1.5 million years ago—it was replaced as the dominant hominid by *Homo erectus. H. erectus* thrived until 200,000 years ago, and perhaps as recently as 100,000 years ago, when *Homo sapiens* claimed supremacy.[2]

Among the critical differences between *H. habilis* and *H. erectus* were a dramatic growth in brain size, more sophisticated stone tools, and the acquisition of fire. With firemaking, the new hominids merged two evolutionary trends, one trend common to many genera and one specific to *Homo*. To the fire adaptations among Earth's flora and fauna, hominids added others. To the human capacity to make and use tools, they contributed a new implement. Toolmaking was a necessary preadaptation to fire, for without the capacity to grasp tools, humans could not apply or remove firebrands. Likewise, the capacity to start fires by percussion or drilling, as distinct from the much older ability to preserve fire, surely derived from experiments in tool manufacture with flints, bone, and wood.

Yet fire was not mandatory to hominids. *Australopithecus* apparently wandered widely throughout Africa and southern Eurasia without fire, as did *Homo habilis*, who possessed some stone tools but lacked fire. Few flora are utterly helpless before fire; few fauna recoil in terror from flames. Domesticated dogs and livestock will lie or stand beside humans as they, too, stare into flames. The Philippine tarsier, it is reported, will gather around a quiet fire and even pick up coals (from which practice comes its scientific name, *Tarsius carbonarius*). Full-blown flight occurs only before rare conflagrations, a reasonable response. When early hominids used fire, they mimicked processes in nature—hunting along fire fronts as did other predators and raptors, scavenging among burned areas, slashing and burning not unlike winds and lightning. But once established, *Homo*'s fire practices revolutionized human society and its relationship to the natural world.

Homo erectus became a fire creature. The hearth granted heat, light, power. Cooking redefined the availability of foods, rendering edible many seeds, meats, and roots otherwise too tough, poisonous, or unpalatable to consume; anthropogenic fire began to slow cook the Earth. The reformation of diet made possible a reformation in dentition, which allowed new patterns of facial muscles and a loftier skull. A controlled flame fire-hardened wooden spears and gave flint a stony tempering. Later, fire made possible a primitive metallurgy and ceramics. Humans used fire to fell trees, to carve trunks into dugout canoes, even to mine. The hearth fire expanded the realms of climate accessible to human existence. The controlled flame was a technology of incredible, almost universal power.

The warming hearth similarly reconstituted society as it drew together bands of hominids and restructured domestic relationships. It defined a family or a group; it defined *Homo*. Yet it was a precarious presence, in need of constant attention. Humans knew how to capture and preserve fire long before they knew how to make it. Even when the skills and equipment were present to ignite fire almost at will, fire was preserved in slow matches or coals. The hearth fire acquired ceremonial, sacred properties, and was never to be allowed to extinguish; the role of fire keeper was among the earliest of human roles and institutions. The preservation of fire, in turn, demanded shelter, which fire often helped provide. If windbreaks shielded flames, so too could fire hollow large trees into habitable cavities, and smoke could drive off bears, sloths, and saber-toothed tigers that would otherwise compete for caves. Even without roofs and sides, fire itself made a kind of cave of light and heat. Fire's brilliance prolonged the day, extended the realm of human activity, even apparently altered the circadian rhythms that governed sleep cycles. With fire, humans—hunted by so many nocturnal predators—could quell some of their fears of the night. Within their protective ring of fire they could work, eat, talk, and sleep.[3]

That fire ring segregated their cultural world from the natural environment around them. For such creatures there could be no innate fear of fire. Any member who instinctively pulled back from flame would be automatically excluded from the human group. To pass through the ring of fire—to live within it—was, in practice and symbol, the mark of humanity. Around their evening fires they told stories, related myths, danced to rites; fire induced a kind of hypnotic, contemplative reverie. Though sacred, fire remained peculiarly human—a gift (or theft) from the gods, but not often a god itself. Still, the ability of humans to use firebrands and the capacity of so many lands to receive fire expanded the ring of fire from hearth, cave, and hollowed bole outward. It remade the natural world into a humanized world.

Broadcast fire was important for hunting and habitat, for foraging and the early domestication of flora and fauna. Fire could drive game—and most birds and mammals valued as game by humans thrive in fire-prone biotas. Smoke flushed game out of nests and caves. Burned areas were prime sites for scavenging and tracking; the sour odor of charcoal even suppressed most smells, an advantage for humans whose sense of smell was crude. Burning maintained such preferred habitats as savannas and forest-grassland ecotones. Broadcast burns temporarily swept away cover and made travel easier. With torches humans could hunt fish and wildlife at night. Burning favored many of the tubers, nut trees, forbs, and other plants useful to a diet of foragers and exposed them to harvest. By hunting large browsers and grazers, hominids upset fuel complexes, and had they not fired sites, those fodder-rich biotas would have shifted toward scrub and woodlands.

Early hominids answered a wanderlust that urged even *Australopithecus* as far as Java by 2 million years ago, *H. habilis* throughout Africa and possibly into Southeast Asia, and *H. erectus* from an African hearth to Europe, China, and Java along what was becoming a virtual pilgrimage route for peripatetic hominids. But this time hominids had fire, and their progress through mountains and plains resembled a flaming front, a broadening ring of fire, feeling its way into grasses, brush, bog, and forest, here flaring and there dampening, but always widening like fiery ripples spreading from a central ignition in Africa.

Not surprisingly, much of the confirming evidence for *erectus* is fire. There is a hearth in east Africa dated at 1.7–1.5 million years before the present. Cave fires sustained by *H. erectus* have been dated at over a million years old in France (Escale Cave), Spain (Torralba-Ambrona), and perhaps Hungary (Vértesszöllös); at Choukoutien, China, charcoal remains date from approximately 450,000 years ago; in Sangiran, Java, from perhaps 1 million years ago. The site at Torralba is particularly interesting because the distribution of charcoal and mastodon bones suggests that fire may have been used actively in the hunt, not merely for cooking afterward. While bones and charcoal give somewhat different dates, some older and some younger, they appear together, hand with brand.[4]

The pace accelerated with the appearance of *Homo sapiens*. Fossil records suggest an emergence between 200,000 and 100,000 years ago. Genetic records, encoded in DNA, recommend a more recent appearance, perhaps less than 100,000 years ago. Again, the source is Africa, and again another ring of fire radiated outward, a rhythm of anthropogenic burning that added to the other disturbances of the Pleistocene. The timing of its appearance, however, involves sparse evidence and complicated calculations. Migrations occurred not once but several times; new arrivals likely interbred with old residents; fire had to interact with other environmental parameters, particularly with a climate that often dramatically reversed itself within a span of centuries, a transformer that charged biotas into a kind of alternating current. That human procession, however, marched by torchlight.

By 40,000 years ago, *H. sapiens* had spread anthropogenic fire across Eurasia and the great land bridges—the Sunda and the Sahul—that joined Indonesia and Greater Australia to Southeast Asia. The colonization of the New World followed, synchronized with the ebb and flow of northern ice sheets that elevated Beringia from the seas and kept open a steppe corridor through central Alaska and along the eastern flank of the Rockies. Although some artifacts suggest an entry around 30,000–25,000 years ago, the substantive, confirmatory caches document another wave, or waves, that arrived in the New World with the waning of the Wisconsin glaciation around 11,000 years ago. Within 1,500 years, these new pioneers—big-game hunters—reached the southern tip of the Americas, Tierra del Fuego; the land of fire. The colonization of more remote islands occurred later, in historic times and by boat rather than by land: Greenland, by Inuit and Norse; the Atlantic islands, by Europeans from the tenth to sixteenth century; the Pacific Islands by Melanesians and Polynesians, from 1300 B.C. to around A.D. 900. Anthropogenic fire reached Antarctica only on the eve of the twentieth century. By then *Homo*'s ring of fire had encircled the Earth many times over.

CARRYING THE FIRE

Just when anthropogenic fire appeared in Australia is unclear. There is evidence for an abrupt, dramatic surge in burning around 40,000 years ago, coincident with the first documented fossils of *Homo*. But there are tantalizing suggestions that humans and their fires may have arrived much earlier. *Homo erectus* reached Java more than a million years ago; *Homo sapiens* swarmed over Asia about 100,000–70,000 years ago. Whether the venerable Wallace Line was as effective a barrier to humans as to other Asian mammals is unknown. For 50 million years Wallacea—a cluster of volcanic islands and deep-water channels—had segregated Southeast Asia from Greater Australia. Only mice, rats, and humans made the passage. One other migrant, the dingo, almost certainly traveled with humans, along a route that avoided Wallacea proper.[5]

The strength of the Wallace barrier flickered inconstantly. Over geologic time, it depended on systems of volcanic arcs, which varied according to plate mechanics. Over the span of the Pleistocene, its geography rose and fell with glacial tides. During glacial maxima, as ice sheets abstracted more and more of the world ocean, sea level fell, and what had been broad seas became channels. Even at its minima, however, a journey across Wallacea demanded at least eight voyages, and never fewer than fifty kilometers of sea had to be spanned. Two major routes seem probable, a southern route through Java and Timor and a northern route through Borneo.

Evidence for early human presence, however, is indirect. During the glacial epoch of 150,000–100,000 years ago, there is a geologic record of deposition, debris flooding, and vegetation change—from rainforest to scleroforest—and charcoal that has been interpreted as a possible consequence of human activity. There is, it appears, a pulse of change that subsequently settles into a more routine, but altered landscape. During this initial outburst, burning increased fourfold. It is suggested that early humans might have followed the Sahul savannas, then gradually encroached by fire into more heavily forested lands as seasonal and secular drought permitted. Once established, they could have used fire to keep open major corridors and hunting sites against reclamation by rainforest.[6]

Another line of evidence concerns the Pleistocene remains of hominid skulls. While the skulls all differ from those typical of contemporary Aborigines, they fall into two distinct groups, "robust" and "gracile." The robust shape is the more ancient, as close to *H. erectus* as to *H. sapiens*. One speculation is that it represents a hybrid or intermediate type such as *Homo soloensis*, which flourished in Java between 300,000 and 100,000 years ago. Or it may represent an earlier subspecies of *H. sapiens*, analogous to the Neanderthal of Europe. Either way the hominid possessed fire, and if the geologic record prior to the last glacial epoch expresses a pulse of anthropogenic activity, then the robust Australian was the likely agent. There are, however, no sites that directly date *Homo* to these early times.[7]

The gracile Australian arrived later, probably crossing into the Sahul during the last glacial maximum, around 55,000 years ago. By 40,000 years ago this hominid had spread to both southwestern and southeastern Australia. From then onward the archaeological record is firm. Both robust and gracile skulls coexist, and probably there was interbreeding. Eventually the gracile form predominated. The modern Aborigine—remarkably varied in physical traits—is the evident outcome. By 20,000 years ago the Aborigine had colonized the perimeter of Australia, including Tasmania (then joined to the mainland), and had penetrated up rivers to the freshwater lakes of the interior. The climate overall was wetter, colder, and probably less intensely seasonal than today. Only the most arid core, small offshore islands, and the higher mountains of the southeast were not fully settled. As the last of the Pleistocene glaciations (c. 30,000–12,000 years ago) waned, sea level rose. At its minimum (roughly 16,000 years ago) sea level had plummeted 150 meters below current values. As the world glaciers receded, however, the seas returned. By 14,000 years ago the resurgent ocean submerged most of the Arafura plains that bonded Australia to New Guinea. By 12,000 years ago, the relentlessly rising seas permanently separated Tasmania from the mainland. By 8,000 years ago, Australia and New Guinea became separate islands. Two millennia later, the sea level stabilized and the littorals claimed approximately their present positions.[8]

The rising seas did not end all human migration to Australia. The earliest migrants had depended on watercraft; but these were primitive affairs, little more than log rafts, probably of Asian bamboo. With time the seas to the north, west, and east of Australia became the scene of maritime cultures, and Australia was visited many times, intentionally or accidentally. Around 4,000 years ago, a new stone toolkit of delicate flakes arrived; so did the dingo, macrozamia cultivation, and new styles of hearths. The likely origins are the Indian subcontinent, whose inhabitants exploited the new technology of seacraft and monsoonal winds to bypass the Wallace barrier. The introductions quickly spread across Australia. The eastern mountains, in particular, experienced an order-of-magnitude increase in human activity. Polynesians must have visited the Australian coast during their voyages. In the seventeenth century Malaccan traders and trepang gatherers began routine visits to the northern coastline of Australia, a practice that continued, intermittently, until the twentieth century. The impact of Malaccans and Polynesians, however, was minor: the patterns of Aboriginal life had been laid down over the preceding millennia, an existence that more or less bypassed the Neolithic revolution which was, on other continents, transforming foragers and hunters into herders, farmers, and urbanites. The phenomenal isolation of Australia continued until European colonization in the eighteenth century, and when it again broke down, the rate and magnitude of change proved almost catastrophic.[9]

If it is not clear just when *Homo* first arrived in Australia, neither is it obvious what routes early humans used to disperse throughout the continent. One theory argues for a coastal colonization. Watercraft were essential to make it to the Sahul, and rafts could continue to carry humans around the resource-rich perimeter. Movement inland followed rivers and clustered around the many lakes that splashed across Pleistocene Australia. Another theory suggests a more interior route, exploiting the watered savannas that wound between the desert core and the more heavily wooded coasts. In this instance, the rivers would lead to the well-lardered coasts and lakes; and from the grassy plains humans could gradually claim the forested bush and mountains. Obviously both patterns could coexist. What seems indisputable is that by 40,000 years ago humans had colonized the major landscapes of Australia. The more inhospitable environments—cold glaciated mountains, arid stony deserts—did not come under year-round human influence until the past few millennia. Whether or not other humans were on the scene, the newcomers wrote a separate record, one preserved not only in fossil bones and campsites but in the environment. Their primary tool was fire.

Erectus or *sapiens*, robust or gracile, one variable population or two (or more) distinct groups—regardless, *Homo* brought fire with him and picked up fire from the new lands he entered. His techniques for preserving fire were adequate to survive short sea voyages. It may have been, as in historic times, that fires were simply maintained on the craft in dishes of clay and sand. It may well have been the case that foraging parties were alerted to the new islands and eventually to the Sahul by bushfires. Even small fires with columns on the order of 1,000 meters can be seen from distances of up to 110 kilometers, which would readily render the Sahul coastline visible from Timor; more intense fires are common in heavier fuels. At night the light from fires carries brilliantly, a beacon. It is habitual for voyaging peoples to identify fire with humans, so it is possible that the smoke not only alerted early parties that land existed but promised human society as well. Once humans did arrive, their own ignitions made that promise a reality.[10]

The record of early hominids is, by and large, a record of fire. Fossil sites are universally associated with fire—with open hearths, with stony ovens, with charred bones, including cremations. Charcoal both preserves and makes possible dating by carbon-14 methods. It is obvious that the abrupt dispersal of humans around 40,000 years ago brought with it an unprecedented wave of burning that reinforced, if it did not catalyze, the internal revolution within the scleroforest that assured the dominance of *Eucalyptus*. Hearth fire contended with wildfire, broadcast fire with bushfire.

While fire practices varied in detail, they showed a remarkable uniformity in intent and effect. By the time Europeans arrived, the structure of the forest reflected tens of millennia of Aboriginal fire, a profound modifier of climate and a selector of biotic stocks. Virtually the entire landscape of Australia was itself, as Josephine Flood concludes, "an artefact created by Aborigines with their fire-sticks." Even forested bush often resembed an open woodland or savanna, astonishingly like the oak woodlands and champion fields of England. Large grassy corridors were carved by fire for access to prime foraging and hunting sites.[11]

Of course fire had its limitations. It could not roll back glaciers in the Tasmanian Alps, alter the patterns of the seasons, stay the rising seas, or, unaided, wipe out rainforest. Fire was a catalyst, a shaper, a multiplier of other effects and other practices. It was subtle, intimately tied to local sites and local practices. Without drought, fire could not invade rainforest, and anthropogenic burning could not indefinitely hold out against a wet climate intent on restoring rainforest over scleroforest. Fire could not promote thirsty flora in a dry climate. Fire interacted differently in various environments, affecting savanna in ways distinct from its effect on a Mediterranean terrain or a subalpine forest. Likewise, fire practices acted differently when used in concert with other human practices. Broadcast burning by one group would not be identical with burning by another group, or by similar groups at different times in their history.

Still, of all the implements in the toolkit of the Aborigine, fire was the most powerful because it went to the dynamic heart of Australian life. As Norman Tindale expressed it, "for at least fifty millennia during the Late Pleistocene, and subsequently, man has ranked with climate as the arbiter of change in Australia." The Pleistocene revolution was a human revolution. Gently, insistently, violently, the Aborigine put Old Australia to the torch.[12]

FIRES OF REVOLUTION

The tempo of environmental reform intensified as the Pleistocene approached the last of its glacial epochs. Global changes revised, then rewrote over and again the physical geography of Australia. Temperature and precipitation regimes fluctuated, storm tracks migrated, seasonality became more pronounced—and less so. During glacial maxima conditions cooled, dried, and spread uniformly over season and place, sea level fell, and increased moisture made otherwise inhospitable sites in the interior habitable. During the interglacial periods, the climate was warmer, often wetter, and more seasonal and regional in distribution; sea level rose such that as much as 25 percent of the Sahul flooded. Rapid change became itself an inexpungable feature of Old Australia.

This climatic revolution paralleled a biotic revolution. The Pleistocene was a time of major extinctions and recolonizations. Extinction was a global phenomenon, but it affected different continents at somewhat different times and with different intensities. It was felt with special keenness in Australia. Among flora, scleroforest completed its accession over rainforest, and *Eucalyptus* claimed primacy among the scleromorphs. Among animals, megafauna were preferentially devastated. About a third of Australian megafauna—mostly giant marsupials like *Sthenurus*, a huge browser, and *Thylacoleo*, a lionlike carnivore—vanished between 50,000 and 15,000 years ago. The major extinctions, affecting the largest megafauna, occurred between 40,000 and 20,000 years ago. A slower rate of extinction, acting on somewhat smaller megafauna, continued for a few thousands years after than time. A third wave of extinction swept away two marsupial carnivores on the mainland—*Thylacinus* and *Sarcophilus* (the Tasmanian tiger and devil, respectively)—between 5,000 and 3,000 years ago. The magnitude of the Australian extinctions is comparable only to those in the Americas. Unlike the Americas, however, the species were not replaced, except by *Homo* and his sometime associate, the dingo.[13]

These coincidences—the advent of humans, the disappearance of a rich megafauna, the sudden ascendancy of the eucalypt—have argued for a causal linkage. Clearly massive extinctions have occurred in the geologic record without human assistance. Equally, the record of human colonization in prehistoric times is a register of selective biotic extinctions, and megafaunal extinctions, in particular, have tended to trail human migrations. In Pleistocene Africa, where humans and megafauna evolved in collaboration, few species were exterminated; in Eurasia, there were more; in Australia and the Americas, extinctions were apparently rapid and extensive. The historical record is especially telling with regard to islands, whether invaded by Siberians, Europeans, Madagascans, or Polynesians. Because of their isolation from human migration routes, both the Americas and Australia were effectively vast islands. Humans exploded into them almost without control.

Thus the Australian scene could be considered two ways: it was a climatic phenomenon, the last in a rhythm of Pleistocene extinctions from natural causes; or it was an anthropogenic artifact, among the first of the historic extinctions by marauding humans outfitted with spear and torch. The evidence is not unequivocal for either position. But it does appear that the extinctions occurred across all climate zones, that they preceded the onset of major aridity during the glacial maximum, and that the timing of migration and extinction is uncannily close.

What is apparent is that the Aborigine moved into an environment which was undergoing dramatic, perhaps irreversible change. These were circumstances to which *Homo*—an ambulatory weed, a species nurtured in the Pleistocene, a torch-carrying pyrophile—was well adapted. Of all creatures humans were prepared to survive in a disturbed environment, and humans became in turn a contributing disturbance. Whether the Aborigine hunted megafauna to extinction, or whether he burned away critical environments, or whether he favored some species who subsequently outcompeted rivals, or whether he only hastened an irrevocable decline driven by distant sunspots and Milankovitch wobbles in the Earth's orbit, he was an important, an unprecedented presence. While his hunting mimicked other carnivores and his torch mimicked lightning fire, the rapidity, the purposes, and the scale of those actions made his abrupt arrival new and troubling. The Aborigine did not move passively into niches vacated by climatic extinction: some of those niches he created and others he actively sustained. As Josephine Flood argues, "the weight of circumstantial evidence favors human hunters as the decisive factor" in the revolution that was Pleistocene Australia.[14]

The interpretation of prehistoric fire history is anchored by two deep sediment cores. One comes from Lynch's Crater on the eastern coast of Cape York Peninsula; the other, from Lake George in the tablelands of New South Wales. The Lynch's Crater sequence dates back 140,000 years. During glacial maxima, scleroforest advanced somewhat on rainforest and charcoal lightly laced the preserved pollen. Then, around 40,000 years ago, the charcoal content abruptly increased tenfold and rainforest elements melted away before scleroforest. Thereafter, the charcoal content shrank to a lower, steadier level, then peaked after the last glacial maximum (c. 20,000 years ago). It disappeared when, after relentlessly wet conditions were reestablished, rainforest reclaimed the site around 8,000 years ago.[15]

The Lake George core dates back 350,000 years. Steppe grassland typified the glacial maxima, while *Casuarina* woodland characterized the interglacials. There is some charcoal preserved in the interglacial sediments, but around 130,000 years ago the oscillation ends; charcoal content quadruples; scleroforest, with a heavy eucalypt component, dominates the biota, resisting the climatic pressures to submerge the site under rainforest. A steady rhythm of burning persists unchanged into the Holocene. The overall quantity of preserved charcoal rises slightly. It is clear that ignition is now chronic, that the large amplitudes in the preserved charcoal contents signify droughts that allowed average fires to become extensive. It is suggested that the sudden magnification of burning prior to the last interglacial represents anthropogenic firing. If so, it is the earliest record of human presence in Australia—and an isolated artifact. More reasonable is the persistence of burning throughout the last glacial epoch, through wet and dry periods both, a regularity for which natural causes are an unlikely explanation.[16]

Other evidence testifies to remarkable changes around the whole continent at about 40,000 years ago. There are preserved hearths at Devil's Lair in the southwest, at Lake Mungo in western New South Wales, and at Keilor in Victoria—all of which date from 38,000 to 32,000 years ago. Many hearth sites from around the continent date to around 20,000 years ago. Among indirect, geomorphic evidence there are charcoal-laden deposits ("red alluvium") laid down by streams along the Darling Scarp that date to 37,000–

28,000 years ago; charcoal lenses washed into the Koonalda Cave of the Nullarbor Plain, probably around 30,000–20,000 years ago; charcoal, silt, even charred wood deposited along the Darling and Lachlan drainages of the southeast around 21,000 years ago. In Tasmania even uplands were occupied and fired by 20,000 years ago and held in partial defiance of a returning interglacial climate. A major resurgence of burning and destabilized soils materializes around 7,000 ago; it is speculated that new lands, more heavily forested, were being opened to exploitation and burning. With the onset of roughly contemporary climate conditions around 6,000 years ago, that pattern of chronic firing, broken occasionally by drought-borne conflagrations, continues. Whatever else happened in Old Australia—whatever processes contributed to the extermination of its megafauna—anthropogenic fire was on the scene. If it did not contribute to the wave of extinction, it did reshape the environment in ways that made a megafaunal reconquest unlikely.

The subtlety and universality of anthropogenic fire makes it difficult to evaluate. There is no way to avoid its presence in Pleistocene Australia, yet there is no way to assess its full impact. Perhaps it is enough to say that anthropogenic fire was there, that it was ubiquitous, that it was capable of interacting with the rest of the Australian environment in ways that no other human implement could. It made the environment after the arrival of *Homo* fundamentally different from that which existed prior to *Homo*. Whether or not Aborigines actively destroyed megafauna or the megafaunal habitat through the use of fire, they certainly changed the conditions by which that environment could be repopulated. They changed the rules of the game. They made it impossible for the old species to regroup and reclaim their old niches. The Aboriginal firestick may well have been the smoking gun of Pleistocene extinctions.

It has often been observed that in Australia, unlike its closest analogue, America, no new megafauna replaced those that were lost. But this is not quite true: the versatile, omnivorous *Homo* seized those niches—not in one locale, but across the whole spectrum of Old Australia; not a single biota, but all of them. A variety of human cultures replaced the variety of Pleistocene creatures. Some forty species of megafauna were lost, but some seven hundred tribes of Aborigines, organized into perhaps two hundred linguistic groups, took their place. The specificity of their differences was fantastic; it is said that a tribe on one side of Sydney Harbor could not communicate with a tribe on the other. Once humans moved in, once anthropogenic fire was established, they were difficult to dislodge. In the new regime some creatures would thrive, and some would suffer. Their relationship to *Homo* —and to anthropogenic fire—would determine much of their relative standing. "The land the English settled was not as God made it," archaeologist Sylvia Hallam concluded. "It was as the Aborigines made it."[17]

Increasingly, as climate stabilized to roughly its present conditions around 6,000 years ago, human history drove natural history. The isolation of Australia discouraged other biotic invaders. Some new anthropogenic elements apparently intruded around 4,000 years ago, but otherwise Aboriginal existence was remarkably stable. Only other humans could dislodge what humans had fashioned. That did not occur until European colonization, which set in motion a biotic revolution that swept across Aboriginal Australia as the Pleistocene had Old Australia. Apart from outright extinctions, there was a profound restructuring of habitats such that indigenes, including the Aborigine, found it all but impossible to reoccupy old sites. Inevitably, fire was a vital catalyst. Once more it became for humans a point of entry, a tool of landscape modification, a weapon of interspecific (and intercultural) warfare. The history of this second invasion, as of the first, is one equally illuminated by fire and obscured by smoke.

"THIS THEIR PLACE OF DWELLING WAS ONLY A FIRE"

With uncanny mimicry, the genus *Homo* recapitulated the experience of the genus *Eucalyptus*. From an origin in other environments, humans adapted to the unique circumstances of Old Australia. Their total numbers were never extraordinary, but the specificity of their adaptations was astonishing. Societies of small endogamous clans favored genetic drift; their physical variability remained high. In effect, they became sclermorphs, discovering cultural equivalents to sclerophylly. With language the Aborigine possessed a means by which information and experience could be stored outside genetic codes. With nomadism, Aborigines could exploit the various resources made available at different places and at different times, overcoming the nutrient impoverishment or aridity of particular sites. With fire, the Aborigine could manipulate the dynamics of entire biotas.[18]

Like the eucalypts, Aborigines were uniquely indigenous to Australia. Genetic marker studies suggest that Aborigines have no close affinities with other human groups. The closest affinities—and they are based on traits that date back to very early origins—are to Southeast Asian and Melanesian peoples. Rather, the Australians developed in Australia. If they did not receive fresh genetic stock from outside sources, neither did they export their own. Until Europeans arrived, the isolation of Aboriginal Australia was almost total: nothing came in, and nothing left. Early colonization by the Aborigines and their subsequent isolation, however, meant that an entire continent bypassed the Neolithic revolution which had spread domesticated flora and fauna—agriculture—to the Old World. Unlike the Americas, no autonomous agricultural centers developed in Australia. None was necessary. Population remained light, and resources ample. The landscape could be "farmed" to an adequate degree by fire.

Within Aboriginal society fire was pervasive. It assured Aboriginal dominance over megafaunal Australia much as it confirmed eucalypt dominance over megafloral Australia. Fire and Aborigine were never far apart; on this the hottest and the driest of the vegetated continents, Aborigines habitually walked across the landscape armed with smoldering firesticks. Of fire's role at the nuclear core of Aboriginal life, perhaps William Dampier put it best: "This their place of Dwelling was only a Fire, with a few Boughs before it, set up on that side the Winds was of." Their shelter existed for the fire, not for themselves. The hearth, as Robert Hughes has observed, was for the nomadic Aborigine "of far greater significance than the home." They carried their hearth—the society that it created and symbolized—with them.[19]

Yet the Aborigine had forged, as had the eucalypt before him, a Faustian bargain with fire. The dependence on fire was perhaps too total; the reliance on fire, for all the subtlety of its usage, too singular. Once committed to a fire-dependent society, anything that altered the status of fire or fuels would ripple catastrophically throughout the social and ecological system. Add new ignitions, remove old flora, alter the seasonal timing of fires—such changes would selectively reorder a biota. Tease apart the fuel structure and a whole ecosystem could unravel. While their reliance on the firestick made Aborigines a power in Old Australia, the society that lived by the firestick could also die by it. A landscape shaped by fire could be seized by more powerful fire.

When that moment occurred—when European fire arrived—it set into motion a biotic revolution that rivaled that of the Pleistocene. With breathtaking speed Europeans destabilized and restructured the fire regimes of Aboriginal Australia on a scale that had not been experienced for tens of millennia. Repeatedly, instinctively, Aborigines turned to fire to drive off the invaders. But the Europeans had even more assertive fire arms, and with domesticated biological allies they could attack the fuel structure of Australian fire regimes. A wave of extinction and of humanly dictated repopulations followed.

The pillars of smoke by day and of flames by night that likely beckoned the first humans across the waterways to Australia were a kind of siren song. They suggested that other humans were present, that humans could thrive in this environment because it could be manipulated by fire. Yet once in Australia there was apparently no means to depart and few alternatives to the widespread use of fire for survival. The rafts that brought early migrants to the Sahul could not be rebuilt with Australian materials. The route to Australia was a one-way journey, and once committed to a fire-intoxicated society, there were few opportunities to escape the firestick. The Aborigine, and Aboriginal Australia, became vulnerable to anything that distorted ignition, fuels, or the health of Aboriginal society. With palpable irony the smokes of Aboriginal Australia beckoned the Europeans, as the smokes of Old Australia had once called the Aborigines.[20]

6

Firestick Farmer:
Profile of a Pyrophile

*The natives were about, burning, burning, ever burning; one would think they
. . . lived on fire instead of water.*

          —ERNEST GILES, *Australia Twice Traversed*
           (1889)

*. . . [Burning was] the alpha and omega of their simple notion of "doing their
duty by their land."*

          —ROBERT LOGAN JACK, *Report on
           Explorations on Cape York Peninsula
           1879–80*

IN THE ABORIGINE, Australian fire had discovered an extraordinary ally. Not
only did ignition sources multiply and spread, but fire itself persisted
through wet season and dry, across grassland and forest, in desert and on
mountain. Lightning was a highly seasonal, episodic ignition source; the
Aboriginal firestick was an eternal flame. The domain of fire expanded, not
only geographically but temporally, for this inextinguishable spark obliterated even the seasons. But "if fire was maintained by the Aborigines, it is
also true," as Phyllis Nicholson notes, "that the Aborigines were maintained
by fire." The relationship between them was reciprocal, symbiotic. "The
evidence that fire was the indispensable agent by which Aboriginal man
extracted many of his resources from the environment is irrefutable." [1]

    Those means—and their remarkable consequences—were pervasive, var-
ied, and subtle. A flaming front does not advance with the crushing finality
of a glacier. Rather it progresses like the exploratory probe of a surgeon,
responsive to an environment of landforms, local and regional winds, micro-

climates, and fuels. It establishes feedback with its sustaining biota. It acts in concert with climatic and biotic changes, a catalyst: in some cases, creating; in others, maintaining. It can leverage one process into larger dimensions. It interacts with and magnifies other human practices. In Aboriginal Australia it hardened wooden spears and it drove game onto those spears. It tempered the flint used for cutting flakes and cooked the meat those flakes carved. It helped shape stone adzes and burned the wood the adzes cut. It promoted the growth of yams, cycads, bracken, and then cooked the harvest. It mediated between a Pleistocene Australia populated with marsupial tigers and giant wombats and a Dreamtime crowded with mythological beings. Its ring of fire transformed Old Australia into Aboriginal Australia.

BLACK LIGHTNING

The Aborigines of Van Diemen's Land, reported James Backhouse in the early 1830s, had "no artificial method of obtaining fire, before their acquaintance with Europeans: they say, they obtained it first from the sky—probably meaning lightning." George Robinson reported from his informers that, should a fire expire, they had "to walk about and look for another mob and get fire from them." The reference to lightning as an ultimate source has both environmental and mythological backing, as does the need to beg, barter, or steal fire from other humans; but the rest is hearsay. Even the maligned Tasmanians could ignite fire with the proper materials. It was an act, however, rarely witnessed by Europeans.[2]

Firemaking required controlled friction, tinder, and a degree of skill in putting the two together. For tinder Aborigines resorted to fur, feathers, shredded kangaroo dung, dried fungi, grass, and other finely disassembled organic matter like dried seed heads or powdered flowers. Friction resulted from rubbing or drilling. Worldwide, there are three types of implements used —the saw, the drill, and the plow. Another strategy, stone percussion, creates a spark by striking flint with steel or iron pyrite. While few cultures have employed more than one technique, it is "notable," as D. S. Davidson remarks, that Australia contained "not only the presence of all four for the continent at large, but the knowledge of at least three in certain localities.[3]

Commonly a woomera (spear thrower) was rubbed against a wooden shield or a log or another woomera. Sand in the groove increased resistance, which added to the heat produced. The fire maker would then add tinder, blow, and transfer the glowing matter to larger fuels. By contrast, the firedrill relied on rapidly spinning a rod in a cavity for the frictional heat of ignition. The most common material was the stalk of the grass tree. Depending on local materials, there were variants of drills, saws, plows, and tinders. There is some suggestion that percussion was used in South Australia, Tasmania, and elsewhere, but the documentation is sparse. Tindale suggests that an

Aboriginal expression for pyrite near Nairne was "fire-stone." It appears that the drill is the most ancient device, a likely part of the toolkit of the ancestral Australians. The woomera-saw technique probably represents a later introduction, which apparently entered Australia at its northwest quadrant. It may thus belong with the special toolkits, also originating in south or southeast Asia, that appeared around 4,000 years ago, a technique universally employed in Polynesia.[4]

The ability to generate fire by hand was clearly part of Aboriginal lore and must have been practiced frequently to maintain the level of skill that seems to have existed. The anthropologist Baldwin Spencer, documenting practitioners during the 1920s, thought that "any native will make fire in, at most, a minute and a half by either of these methods." That observant Victorian squatter, Edward Curr, snapped that "any blackfellow with the proper materials would make fire in this way in a few minutes."[5]

The operative phrase is "proper materials." For a nomadic people, it was inconvenient to transport the paraphernalia of firemaking. The advantage of the woomera-and-shield apparatus was precisely that these were objects which were necessarily carried quite apart from their utility as fire starters. Its disadvantage was that it required at least two participants. The firedrill made from grass-tree stalks was widespread because the grass tree was widespread. But this still meant that abundant, dry tinder had to be present as needed or be carried, yet the conditions that would likely extinguish an existing fire were precisely those that made it unlikely to find a ready cache of dry tinder. In brief, before firemaking could commence, the proper materials had to be gathered. As nearly every observer of the Aborigine has commented, it was far simpler to keep an existing fire going than to start a new one.

It was easier to carry a firestick. Anything that could be grasped and could glow could serve the purpose. The choice of implement varied by season, place, and purpose. The stalk of a grass tree, a slab of smoldering mulga bark, ironbark, a decayed branch of eucalypt, a *Banksia* cone—all were employed. To early European observers, the native and the firestick were inseparable. Shortly after landing, Captain Arthur Phillip wrote Viscount Sydney that the natives "are seldom seen without a fire, or a piece of wood on fire, which they carry with them from place to place, and in their canoes . . ." On the western coast Scott Nind in 1831 reported the same phenomenon: "Every individual of the tribe when travelling or going to a distance from their encampment, carries a fire-stick for the purpose of kindling fires . . ." In South Australia Richard Helms confirmed that "they are always careful, to carry a piece of burning bark with them on their day's march, or whenever they go any distance away from camp; this is partly for the purpose of setting the spinifex-grass on fire, but principally to have fire ready when about to settle down again." In Queensland Tom Petrie described fire starting, but quickly qualified his observation: "it was only on rare occasions that the natives needed to do this, for they took care always to carry lighted firesticks with them wherever they went." In his meticulous journals about life in Aboriginal Tasmania, Robinson casually reiterates what every observer of Van Diemen's Land witnessed, that the association of Aborigine and firestick was indissoluble.[6]

There appears to have been a division of labor by gender. Men made fire; women principally transported it. Men employed fire for hunting; women, for the harvesting of vegetable staples and small game. The bushfire belonged to the male universe; the hearth fire to the female. In cold weather, however, everyone seized a firestick as a matter of warmth. Children freely played with fire, to the astonishment of Europeans. It is said that by the age of three they displayed a familiarity that was unimaginable to a society trained to other fire practices and educated to very different perceptions of fire.

Some skill was required to carry a brand without burning the body and without allowing the embers to die. From time to time, the firestick would be waved, fanning the coals to life, or plunged into scrub or spinifex, which in flaring would rekindle the main stalk. A sympathetic European claimed that, by unburdening women from firesticks, the "tinder-box," along with tobacco and iron tomahawks, were the "three boons which the Blacks received from the Whites in compensation for their endless disadvantages." By lining their craft with clay, Aborigines even transported fire in their canoes. Each firestick ended in a campfire, which ended with the ignition of a new firestick, and so the cycle continued, waxing and waning with opportunities and seasons, but never ceasing—a dynamic chain of fire. Almost never did Aborigines deliberately extinguish a fire.[7]

The constant interaction between firestick and landscape replenished both. The liberal distribution of fire also meant that, if lost, fire could be more readily reclaimed from the land. The banking of fires in large tree boles, the lighting of heavy scrub, the ignition of larger trees directly or indirectly, all littered the scene with fire caches, not unlike food caches or waterholes—temporary sources of an essential element. Everywhere smoke marked the presence of Aborigines, whose wanderings traced storm tracks of black lightning.

ITS OWN FIRESIDE

Whenever Aborigines stopped, however briefly, they habitually ignited a small fire. The act had practical consequences: it replenished firesticks, warmed travelers on cold days, and served to cook whatever had been collected, which was often the reason for stopping. But, even on the hottest days, a hearth fire was kindled because it promoted fellowship and solidarity. Each family, Baldwin Spencer reported, "lives as a separate unit within the camp but the essential thing is that its life is centred around its own fireside." Writing in the early 1840s Robert Austin stated that each family in the tribe had "its own territorial division, its own ka-la or 'fire-place' . . ." At night, as James Bonwick remarked, fire "kept the bad spirits away." Around the fireside were conducted the important rituals and ceremonies of spiritual existence. In symbolic, no less than technological terms, fire prescribed the conditions of domestic life.[8]

The hearth took many forms. Cooking fires suited the food to be prepared. Hot stones were ample to fry Bogong moths; small banks of coals suited marsupial rodents; somewhat larger, specially shaped hearths baked cakes, cooked tubers, and leached toxins from various foodstuffs. Kangaroos —usually cooked where killed—required larger, temporary fires, and proceeded in stages. The carcass would be singed on one side, then turned and singed on the other, then removed and scraped clear of fur, gutted, and thrown back on the coals for deep roasting. Fish were cooked in canoes, which carried fire in clay-lined niches. Cockles—consumed by the tens of millions—were prepared for eating by heaping the shells into piles, then topping the mound with a small fire, which heated the valves sufficiently to pop them open without the need for breakage. The ever-handy firestick ensured that cooking fires could be manufactured on demand. With the exception of the larger game, hunted by men and prepared on site, the domestic fire was the province of Aboriginal women.[9]

More permanent ovens were made, as Edward Eyre described in 1845, by "digging a circular hole in the ground," lining it with stones or clay balls, and building a hot fire that dried the cavity and heated the stones (often splitting them in the process). Some hot stones were then placed into the gutted animal, the bottom of the oven lined with leaves or grass, and the carcass placed into the oven. The top was sealed with more grass or leaves and a dressing of dirt. The ground oven could be reused. Hot stones were employed to crack open hard fruits and *Acacia* seeds. In canoes, Aboriginal fishermen used seaweed in place of leaves and dirt, and searched out branches of "false sandalwood," often at some cost, to burn as fuel. The aromatic wood burned virtually smoke-free.[10]

Constructed ovens, in particular, warranted protection. The ideal site was a cave. Here fires were located near flat rock walls that could better reflect the heat. In more open areas Aborigines might erect a bark windbreak, the origin of semipermanent dwellings. In areas infested with mosquitoes and other insects, they could enclose the windbreak in a hut that trapped a fumigating smoke. Again, it was "the business of the women . . . to build the hut and also to fetch wood for the fire." But perhaps the most intriguing variant was the use of large eucalypts, whose trunks were shaped by Aboriginal burning into ovens and fire depots.[11]

Pilot-Major Francoys Jacobsz described such trees in Tasmania; John Lhotsky cited examples from the Australian Alps; and others noted them as well, from South Australia where red gums were used, to Westralia where the jarrah was preferred. Governor Phillip observed that "the natives always put their fire, if not before their own huts, at the foot of a gum tree, which burns very freely, and they never put a fire out when they leave the place." The process began by using large trunks as reflectors for campfires. The fire naturally ate into the green bole, and the more the site was revisited, the larger the fire-excavated cavity. In places, such hearths showed signs of digging, sometimes of lining by clay. The larger cavities could even shelter Aborigines. But the primary side benefit was that, as the hollowing process continued, possums and other creatures took up residence in the upper cavities. The Aborigine could then return and hunt those creatures by smoking them out with a fire at the base. Either way a long-glowing fire became, for days, a public utility at which faltering firesticks could be renewed.[12]

The hearth warmed sleeping areas. At night, J. B. Cleland noted, the Aborigine "sleeps behind a breakwind with a little fire on each side of him and another at his feet." It was not uncommon for burns—sometimes disfiguring—to result. To prevent the hearth fire from escaping, camp sites were cleared of fuel, often by preburning it. To maintain a fire through the night involved constant tending, which broke an evening's sleep into a chain of lighter naps.[13]

Preferred camping sites—links in an annual cycle—were fired when first revisited. Ludwig Leichhardt observed that "the natives seem to have burned the grass systematically along every watercourse and round every waterhole" so, he thought, that they would be surrounded by new growth. More recently, Richard Gould described how, "back at Pukara, the man with the firestick uses it to ignite the dry brush surrounding the waterhole. In a few minutes all the brush and thorns that have accumulated since the place was last visited are burned off." Fire was the modus operandi by which Aborigines reclaimed a site; it was so common that astute explorers in the desert quickly learned to identify smoke with Aborigines and waterholes. The likely reason was not only to attract game to fresh herbage in a few weeks, but to clean up the site—to purge it of overgrowth, evil spirits, and noxious creatures such as ants, spiders, and especially snakes. Over and again in Aboriginal legends a hunter is killed by a poisonous snake at a waterhole, and a quick fire was a simple prophylactic. Sites dense with mosquitoes could be fumigated, at least temporarily, by burning.[14]

The domestic fire interacted with other tools. Careful charring hardened digging sticks and spears. Heated waxes and resins made a useful glue for hafting. Warming a spear shaft could help in straightening it. Heating bark in ashes made it easier to mold into a canoe. Fire was probably used in preparing flint, perhaps even in quarrying it. Ashes served as a poultice for wounds and snakebites, for body decoration, for disguising the human odor. Fire cauterized wounds and assisted with the healing of ritual incisions. Fire applied to the base of trees replaced the axe, generating fuel for more hearths and firesticks. And fire made light. It gave humans the nighttime for story, ceremony, and companionship.

The hearth fire defined the human world, for through it Aborigines remade Old Australia. Thus, while Aboriginal vocabularies contained many words for fire, they carefully distinguished the hearth fire from the bushfire. The hearth fire was the origin of all other anthropogenic fires; without it human society was unthinkable. Europeans often marveled that, during in-clement weather, Aborigines would huddle around a fire rather than forage or hunt, that they would rather go without food than without fire. No less marvelous was the fact that Aborigines would kindle multiple hearth fires on even the hottest days. "Whatever the weather . . . ," Bonwick con-cluded emphatically, "a fire was essential." During the height of the Black War, Aboriginal Tasmanians listed the prohibition against fire—essential to avoid detection by marauding Europeans—as among the worst of the priva-tions forced upon them. Without fire life was too hard, too cruel, too fright-ening to be endured.[15]

"THE WHOLE COUNTRY IS SHORTLY IN A BLAZE"

The constant rubbing of nomadic tribes against a tindered Australia was itself an environmental firedrill that littered the landscape with smoldering ignitions. A semipermanent campsite could be insulated from accidental fire by a preparatory burn; but those sites were only a fraction of the chronic fire setting that occurred, and even those burns typically ranged far beyond the actual site of occupation. When traveling, Aborigines rarely extinguished their ephemeral fires after they served their purpose. The fires simmered, their domain restricted only by the vagaries of the weather and the patterns of previous burning that limited their access to fuels.

To the casual eye this habitual unconcern with secondary consequences seemed careless. His interest "often aroused" by bushfires, Leichhardt pon-dered the Aborigines of Queensland "who light fires all over the place to cook their food but leave them unextinguished." In the early days of the Swan River colony a reporter for the *Perth Gazette* was "persuaded" that "the origin of these fires is not at all to be attributed to any malicious intent at all on the part of the natives; they resort to their accustomed practice of lighting a fire in the bush, for the purpose of cooking and from the bush, being highly inflammable at this season, it extends with resistless violence." In addition to their cooking fires and signaling fires, George Moore noted that Aborigines tossed aside individual firesticks when they no longer needed them. "The half-clad native starts with the lighted bark; as the day advances the warmth of the sun renders artificial heat unnecessary; the bark is discarded . . . A breeze comes . . . and the whole country is shortly in a blaze."[16]

Signal fires were no less common and no less likely to be abandoned. Explorers rarely advanced into lands unwatched. Many of the smokes that announced the presence of natives to them were in fact announcements by Aborigines of the presence of the exploring party. Thus as Robert Logan Jack "approached the site of the old diggings, signal fires broke out on the Twelve Apostles, in advance of us in such a manner as to leave no doubt in our minds, that the ABORIGINALS (themselves unseen) were honouring our progress with their serious attention." Some observers noted how a person "entering another clan's territory lit a fire and placed green branches on it" so the smoke would alert the local Aborigines that the party was on a peaceful mission. Captain Hamelin reported from Tasmania how "one man was walking in front and carrying a brand with which he set fire to everything as they went along," an act Hamelin understood as "customary when they want to stave off or begin a war among themselves . . ."[17]

With the firestick and combustibles usually handy, signal fires became a bush telegraph. The techniques were again continental. On Cape York Jack McLaren related how the Aborigines would overlay a flaming fire with green boughs, which proceeded to smoke heavily, then controlled the output with sheets of bark. In the Kimberleys A. B. Facey, lost and prostrate with illness, watched as three Aborigines "piled all the green bushes and scrub onto the fire which made a thick white smoke. Then one of them took the saddle cloth from Dinnie and kept putting it on and off the fire." Although Europeans puzzled over the complex messages that such simple acts conveyed, the explanation is probably that the smoke only confirmed texts that were agreed upon in advance. In areas barren of distinguishing landmarks, a smoke column imposed a geodetic order to which foraging parties could orient themselves. Flames from coastal fires—pandamus palms made a favorite torch—similarly guided fishing canoes at night.[18]

While special smokes could convey special messages, the Aborigines themselves were a traveling smoke. Smokes blazed their trails, and to the fires that they abandoned Aborigines added others in a deliberate strategy of broadcast burning to assist travel through tall grass or dense scrub, to flush out game, and to sustain a preferred habitat. The great corridors of Aboriginal transit were broad paths of fire. And since humans need water frequently, those paths tended to follow watercourses or connected waterholes. "A great party of natives appeared to be travelling up the creek," A. C. Gregory jotted into his diary, "as fresh fires are constantly seen to the northeast along its course." Charles Sturt wrote that "although the river line was lost in the distance, it was as truly pointed out by the fires of the natives, which rose in upright columns into the sky, as if it had been marked by the trees upon its banks." In his interminable journals Robinson reported open thoroughfares through otherwise dense Tasmanian scrub, the vegetation change corresponding to frequent transit and burning by Aborigines. His companions shunned unburned areas, on one occasion warning Robinson that he would never emerge from an almost impenetrable, unburned thicket. Elsewhere, even when "the country was a succession of hills covered with thick forest," it was "rendered tolerable easy travelling by the recent burning of the bush by the natives." In this way throughout Australia broadcast burning, by intent or accident, coincided with regions of travel. For a continent inhabited by a congeries of nomadic tribes, that realm was enormous.[19]

In Australia, as Geoffrey Blainey has imagined, "every day for millions of days countless fires had been lit or enlarged for countless purposes, and many of those fires had unintended effects." Rhys Jones has estimated that in the better populated areas of Australia, an area of thirty square kilometers would have supported a band of roughly forty people. "Assuming that on average, three foraging parties of various types left camp per day, that each lit ten bushfires and that this happened on only half of the days of the year, then within that area, no less than 5,000 separate bush fires would be lit each year." And this, he considered, is "a highly conservative estimate." [20]

Their kindling multiplied by several orders of magnitude the frequency of natural ignitions, and they imposed, even as they obeyed, new rhythms and new patterns. Increasingly, the geography of humans defined the geography of fire: the more humans, the more fire. Their traveling fires laid down a matrix within which lightning fire had to function. Fire seasons tended to follow the seasonal migrations of Aboriginal firesticks.

"TILLED HIS LAND AND CULTIVATED . . . WITH FIRE"

Other sites—neither camps nor corridors of travel—demanded additional fire practices. These included areas in which local plants were subjected to semicultivation, a spectacle that in part led Rhys Jones to refer to Aboriginal economies as "fire-stick farming." Broadcast burning assisted foraging, as Captain John Hunter speculated, after watching "large fires" set by Aborigines in the apparent ambition of "clearing the ground of the shrubs and underwood, by which means they might with greater ease get at those roots which appear to be a great part of their subsistence during the winter." But other natural products assumed a more conscious status as protocultivars, among them such environmentally inconspicuous but dietarily important foodstuffs as bracken, macrozamia nuts, cycads, yams, and others. In each case, the prescriptions for growing, harvesting, and cooking included prescriptions for fire. As Edward Curr shrewdly noted, "living principally on wild roots and animals," the Aborigine "tilled his land and cultivated his pastures with fire."[21]

Sir George Grey observed in the southwest that "the natives must be admitted to bestow a sort of cultivation upon this root [flag, a species of *Typha*] as they frequently burn the leaves of the plant in dry seasons, in order to improve it." Others related how, during the dry seasons, the "swamps" and *warran* were fired to expose and cure the edible roots. "The root is in season in April and May," wrote George Moore, "when the broad leaves will have been burned by the summer fires, by which the taste, according to native ideas, is improved." In the southeast the daisy yam (*Microseris*) was a major foodstuff, whose range could be extended by suitable firing. "In order to get more easily at the roots amongst the underwood and scrub," George Angas observed, "the natives set fire to the 'bush' in many places; when the fire is extinguished, they dig up the roots." Doubtless, burning was also part of general site preparation, as it is throughout southeast Asia, New Guinea, and Polynesia.[22]

Bracken—an Australian indigene (*Pteridium*)—supplied another palatable root. That the fern was a fireweed, an aggressive colonizer of recently burned sites, made it a perfect complement to routine broadcast burning for other purposes. The roots were roasted in ash and preferably served with kangaroo. In Victoria Edward Curr witnessed "bags full" of mallee manna in almost every camp. He "understood the Blacks to say that they used to set fire to a portion of the mallee every year and gather the manna the next season from the young growth." Broadcast burns assisted the harvest of bunya seeds by exposing the cones and keeping the woodlands open. Other edibles emerged from the fire regimes as useful by-products. Recolonization of recently burned spinifex, for example, increased the abundance of wild tomatoes (*Solanum*) and the wild banana, a vine that sought out burned trees. Not every edible plant thrived in such a regime, as the Europeans quickly discovered; but once committed to broadcast burning, Aborigines learned how to shape the enduring and fire-adapted elements of the biota to their advantage.[23]

In some cases, this meant intervening in the life cycle of native grains. The Bagundji who inhabited the semiarid basin of the Darling River harvested wild millet (*Panicum*) by gathering the cereals when the seed was full but the grass was yet green. They then allowed the stacks to ripen simultaneously; this pattern also ensured that the grains would not be burned accidentally prior to collection. Surveyor-General Thomas L. Mitchell was shocked to see "ricks, or hay-cocks, extending for miles" along the Darling in 1835. The uncut stalks were almost certainly fired after harvest, caught up in an annual conflagration of the countryside.[24]

Even more spectacular was the manipulation of cycads like *Cycas media* and especially *Macrozamia* or burrawang. This palmlike species features a huge and highly nutritive, but highly toxic, seed, which must be leached and heated before it can be consumed. It appears that *Macrozamia* cultivation belongs with those other introductions to Australia that arrived around 4,000 years ago. Fire attended all stages of cycad production: it cleared the site of competing vegetation, apparently increased the output of kernels (up to eight times that of unburned plots), and caused the seeds to ripen more or less simultaneously. The latter was important because the nuts served as "communion food," a preferred foodstuff for large ceremonial gatherings. The extensive stands of cycads that existed at the time of European discovery, it is suggested, may be "the result of Aboriginal manipulation of the woodland ecosystem," principally through fire.[25]

Equally, there was a time and a place for fire exclusion. A grass fire through a yam (*Dioscorea*) patch, responding to the curing cycle of grass, not that of yams or flag, could injure the valued plants and disguise their tops, which made harvesting more difficult. D. F. Thompson reported that Aborigines in Arnhemland kept their broadcast burning under control for fear that indiscriminate burning might injure yam *warran*. Hunting fires were not lit until the roots were collected, "after which everything was burned." There are several reports—J. L. Stokes near Albany, George Robinson in Tasmania—of Aborigines actively swatting out fires with boughs to encourage special sites of copse or to keep fire from spreading in some undesired direction. Active intervention of this kind was, however, limited in scope.[26]

More extensive were prohibitions against burning particular subbiotas. The best-known expressions are protected "jungles" in the tropics, vine thickets that harbor foodstuffs not well adapted to fire. But similar sites have been documented for the interior deserts, and probably they existed throughout Aboriginal Australia. In each case, the site claimed totemic protection. In Arnhemland, it was believed that spirits in the sacred thicket would blind with smoke anyone who allowed a fire to burn into it. Instead, firebreaks as much as a kilometer wide were burned around the thickets as soon as possible after the Wet, so that the sites would be spared from the free-ranging fires that plague the Dry.[27]

There is, again, a curious reciprocity at work. As the protected thickets demonstrate, not every potential foodstuff demanded that Aborigines arm themselves with firesticks or that they loose broadcast fire wherever they tread. But once committed to broadcast fire—in large measure for hunting— the resultant fire regimes selected the assortment of roots, fruits, and nuts that would be available for consumption. It is no surprise that these plants would be manipulated, at least at critical times, by fire. It is especially revealing of Aboriginal Australia, however, that the exclusion of fire called for special attention. Fire was a norm; its restriction an exception that demanded human intervention.

If there is a cameo of the fire-driven Aboriginal plant economy, it is surely *Xanthorrhoea,* the fire-florescing grass tree. *Xanthorrhoea* absorbed the cycles of fire around it, both natural and Aboriginal. It supplied the essential components of the firedrill, it served as a firestick, it flowered after burning and thrived in fire-frequented environments, it was harvested and eaten after roasting over a hearth fire it probably started. Even its appearance pointed to the fundamental circumstances of this fire economy. Known colloquially as the "blackboy," its shape mimicked that of an Aboriginal hunter standing cannily in the bush, wooden spear thrust boldly upward, as though in unconscious recognition that the pattern of harvesting fires followed a pattern of hunting fires.

"THEIR SPORT, THEIR SPECTACLE, AND THEIR MEAT-GETTING, ALL IN ONE"

"These interesting Downs," Allan Cunningham wrote of land through which he trekked in the early 1820s near present-day Canberra, made a "striking contrast." Those portions that had been "burnt in patches two months since" had greened brilliantly. Those that had escaped burning had a "deadened appearance." The agency for the burns was the Aborigine, whose "common practice" it was to "fire the country in dry seasons where it was wooded and brushy." Cunningham immediately recognized two causes for these fires. They assisted with the hunt, flushing kangaroos in particular from cover; and these "extensive . . . conflagrations" also attracted kangaroos and emus to mass on the nutritious new grass which soon accompanied the rains. In both cases, the grazers were exposed to native spears.[28]

These observations built on those of earlier European explorers, and they were repeated, in one way or another, by virtually every commentator on Aboriginal life and for virtually every environment of Aboriginal Australia. Fire was employed in all aspects of hunting and on a variety of scales. That Aborigines everywhere in Australia hunted meant that hunting fires—fires used to drive or flush game, fires used to shape desired habitats—were everywhere implicated in shaping the biotas of the continent.

Some uses were almost laughably small. The bush possum and pademelon (a wallaby) frequented the large gums hollowed out by the hearth fires that Aborigines constructed at their bases. By igniting another small fire at the base, the possum would be forced out of the hole, often through cavities at the top of the tree. Either the possum then fell or a hunter would climb after him. Torches assisted the operation, as they did night fishing from canoes. "They frequently go fishing during the night,"

Angas recalled, "each man carrying a torch, which is replenished by a bunch of inflammable wood slung across his shoulders; the light attracts the fish, which, as they rise, are struck with the *wodna* or the spear."[29]

Other fires were applied to brush that harbored game, from bandicoots to lizards to kangaroos. The magnitude of the fire varied accordingly. Since the object was to flush out small creatures, the technique called for a relatively controlled fire, specific to a particular site. This practice was commonly conducted by women and assisted by children. Scott Nind reported that the women, "who also kindle fires," would search through the ashes for lizards, snakes, and bandicoots. Where fire exposed burrows, Aborigines smoked out small marsupials. Fire flushed euros from spinifex and smothered pied geese rooting in paperbark trees. "The natives in summer set fire to the grass and dry herbage for the purpose of hunting," George Moore noted, "and after the fire has passed over the ground, you could hardly find as much green food as would feed a rabbit, till the herbage has time to grow again. Over the hills the grants in that locality are less burned, being less frequented by white or black people." Special sites for hunting were identified and sustained by regular burning. Rock cliffs, box canyons, rivers—any barrier could serve to help concentrate the hunted animals. What is evident is that such fires were the faunal equivalent of the fires used in "gardening" the Australian flora.[30]

An uncontrolled fire was wasted, even hazardous. J. L. Stokes of the *Beagle*, upon meeting "a party of natives engaged in burning the bush," noted that they distributed fire "in sections every year," that the "duty" was "specially entrusted" to particular members, and that they used "large green boughs to beat out flames" that moved in an errant direction. In Tasmania George Robinson related how the Aborigines not only exploited a landscape of grass and wooded copse—firing the wooded clusters, one after another, to flush out game—but shaped that very landscape. "When burning the underwood," the Aboriginal hunters "beat out the fire in order to form these clumps." The "whole range for miles," he concluded, formed "a beautiful picturesque" scene. Near Perth George Grey outlined "another very ingenious mode of taking wallaby and the smaller kinds of kangaroos." The Aborigines encircled a "thick bushy place," broke down the scrub all around it into a tangle of debris, then fired the site and speared the "frightened animals" as they attempted to flee. Tribes in riverine environments routinely fired the adjacent lands as part of their annual treks. Sturt, for example, described how the "natives continued to fire the great marshes . . . to procure food, by seizing whatsoever might issue from the flame." John Wollaston noted how the "margin of some river or swamp" could serve as a trap; once driven to the water or the water's edge, "animals and reptiles . . . become easy prey." Obviously, to be effective, the same sites would be repeatedly burned, or the same techniques would be applied to newly visited sites in the process of being incorporated into an annual regimen. In this way, too, Aboriginal hunters could exert some control over the fire by controlling the fuels on which they depended. While the prospects for escaped conflagrations were, as Nind put it, "very great," the Aborigines "generally guarded against [it] by their burning . . . in consecutive portions" or according to some secular calendar. Control also had social dimensions, as Moore described when "some trespassers went upon this ground [near Perth], lighted their fires, and chased the wallabees," and were themselves chased out after a "general row" with the local Aborigines.[31]

When conducted by whole tribes, hunting operations could themselves be far-flung, as Captain John Hunter observed. The Aborigines, "when in considerable numbers, set the country on fire for several miles extent, this, we have generally understood is for the purpose of disturbing such animals as may be within reach of the conflagration and hereby they have an opportunity of killing many." In Western Australia Richard Dale recorded similar sights, "the natives having at that season set fire to the country round for many miles" for the purpose "of driving objects of chase from their fastnesses . . ." Families, "who through the winter have been dispersed over the country," reassembled, commenced to fire the country, and procured "the greatest abundance of game." On such occasions, Nind concluded, "vast numbers of animals are destroyed."[32]

The most daring expression of fire hunting involved the use of free-burning fire to drive game in open country. Such an operation could succeed only with the skill and patience that Hedley Herbert Finlayson detailed for a maala drive conducted in central Australia in the early 1930s. The maala (Lagorchestes hirsutus) inhabited spinifex, "on which it thrives exceedingly and grows fat." Where burning is impossible, it is necessary for someone to leap into the tussock—its "spines like a darning-needle"—and try to flush the maala out into the waiting spears or clubs. For two becalmed days Finlayson's party tried this technique without success. "But the third day was ideal, a scorcher with a hot north-west wind." The party left camp "for the ground," a site not randomly selected but chosen for its abundance of maala tracks and its mature stands of spinifex. "The blacks were in great spirits, chanting a little song to themselves, twirling their fire-sticks and at intervals giving instructions to the two weeis, who had not seen a maala drive before." Their confidence was fully warranted, for "event followed event to a final success, with the precision of a ritual."

The "whole procedure" appears to have "become standardized and perfected by age-long repetitions." The first step was to send runners outfitted with firesticks "into the wind" along two lines inscribing a flaming horseshoe. Spinifex tussocks were fired about every fifty yards. While the size of the burn depended "of course, on the size of the party operating," Finlayson estimated that the arms of the horseshoe were nearly two miles long and the open end approximately a mile wide. This effectively enclosed the area of densest tracks, which equally defined a patch of spinifex of a certain age. The strong winds meant that the flames advanced primarily away from the hunting party, that the open area burned toward them much more slowly, that they were themselves safe. "The country outside the horseshoe is left to its fate."

Finlayson identified three distinct phases to the hunt itself. While it backed into the wind, the fire steadily concentrated all the creatures into a narrowing island of unburned fuels. Aborigines crowded the successively igniting spinifex, "keenly watching for a breakaway" maala that they could club with a throwing stick. This operation took all morning. It concluded when the "wings of flame" finally met. The unburned middle was now surrounded by flame, and the formerly open side of the horseshoe, now sealed with fire, could run with the wind.

The action quickened. What had been a backing fire now became a heading fire, and with a "steady roar" it raced to engulf the interior fuels. The small band heard crashes, "as some isolated patch of mulga or corkwood is engulfed, and swept out of existence in a second." The Aborigines gathered their spoils and hurried to their starting point, by now burned over, and waited to receive the wildlife flushed out by the renewed wall of flame. "Every living thing which has remained above ground must come within range of their throw." Finlayson, too, shared in this "time of most stirring appeal."

The world seems full of flame and smoke and huge sounds; and though the heat is terrific, yet one is scarcely conscious of it. In the few tense moments that remain before they break into frenzied action and frenzied sound, I watch the line of blacks. The boys can scarcely control their movements in their excitement; the three men, muscled like greyhounds, are breathing short and quick; they swing their weight from foot to foot, twirling their throwing-sticks in their palms, and as they scan the advancing flames their great eyes glow and sparkle as the climax of the day draws near. It is their sport, their spectacle, and their meat-getting, all in one; and in it they taste a simple intensity of joy which is beyond the range of our feeling.

When the flames expired, the party retired to camp to wait for the ashes to cool. For the rest of that day and part of the next—the third phase—they scavenged through the fire. The shallow "pop hole" of the maala made it an easy victim for digging sticks. Had the party been larger, women and children would have eagerly joined the search. The ash disguised human scent, traced the movements of lizards, snakes, and rodents, and exposed burrows. It made human travel through the prickly site easy. Finlayson noted that such a fire, which to the uninitiated "might be thought" to "wipe out every living thing in its path," was selective. In effect, it largely claimed those creatures that depended on a certain age-class of spinifex, a habitat that was temporarily destroyed by the fire and was integral to the natural and human history of the region. This "whole business has been carried out systematically for untold generations and over enormous areas of country."[33]

What Finlayson related was a paradigm of fire hunting. With minor inflections, it could describe the spectacle witnessed by J. L. Stokes of the *Beagle,* who noted the "astonishing" dexterity of an Aboriginal fire drive that disgorged "various snakes, lizards, and small kangaroos, called wallaby, which with shouts and yells they thus force from their covert, to be dispatched by spears or throwing-sticks . . ." Anticipating Finlayson, Stokes could "conceive of no finer subject for a picture," the whole scene being "most animated," the "eager savage, every muscle in action and every faculty called forth, then appears to the utmost advantage, and is indeed almost another being." A century later in Arnhemland D. F. Thompson reported that, as the grass begins to dry, "the people start to burn it systematically in conjunction with organized fire drives." Burning was not random: they fired grasslands and spared viney jungles. The harvest included "wallabies, bandicoots, native cats, 'goanna'—monitor lizards, and large snakes and their eggs, both Pythons and Rock Pythons being taken in numbers." Daisy Utemara of the Mowanjum tribe reported, in steps identical to those outlined by Finlayson, how her tribe burned for kangaroos. "This was," she concluded simply, "my life which I lived." [34]

Fire hunting was a marvelously effective device, but as with any technology it had its dangers and its limitations. It was restricted by its fuels. In perennial grasslands or savannas a fire drive could be used at most once a year—another incentive to confine fires to relatively small areas, so that the overall burning could be staggered over the course of several weeks. In spinifex its frequency depended on the capacity of the tussocks to rebuild. Equally, by removing many grazers, fire hunting granted a small reprieve to the burned grasses in their rush to recover. Because it was essentially a once-a-year event, the fire hunt had to maximize returns, and this argued for a communal enterprise. It made little sense to sweep up large numbers of animals when there was no means of preserving the meat. It had to be eaten quickly.

It is abundantly true, as well, that hunting fires escaped. Once ignited there was little chance of stopping such a fire, unless the surrounding fuels were sparse or the fire burned into a river or a cliff. If the weather dried and the winds rose, the fires could range widely. A stiff wind was of course essential to the prescription. Grass fires in particular could burn extensively —as any European explorer of the interior would readily testify. Other fuels, however, could carry fire as well. In Tasmania, John Wedge told of a hunting fire that spread "to a range of hills five to six miles in extent." Outside Adelaide ship-borne observers watched as a "fire on one of the hills"—set by Aboriginal hunters—"seemed to spread from hill to hill with amazing speed . . . as if the whole land was a mass of flame." It is remarkable how many reports tell of fire hunts during the dry season or high winds. Captain John Hunter spoke for many early witnesses when he "observed that they [Aborigines] generally took advantage of windy weather for making such fires, which would of course occasion their spreading over a greater extent of ground." More recently, Richard Gould told how a fire hunt conducted for three feral cats swept across twenty-three square kilometers. Fire was far from being a precision instrument. The principal control the Aborigine exercised over fire, apart from the original decision to burn, was the distribution of fuels, which was a reflection of past burning history. The process was circular: fire controlled fuel which controlled fire.[35]

In many such cases—and there are numerous such reports—the object was probably not fire hunting per se but other purposes, among them a purging of woody shrubs and the desire to drive off encroaching Europeans. What made such fires tolerable was the nomadism of the Aborigine and the millennia of burning that shaped the fuels. Without a fixed habitat, the Aborigines could accommodate an unusually large fire. They could move from site to site, from resource to resource as each in its proper season became available. They could wait years for spinifex to recover and restock with maala. They could move to new grass, new mallee, new heath to burn. Once established, patch burns created a mosaic of fuels that were, except under the worst conditions, self-limiting. What was problematic was the initial establishment of such a regime.

And what made broadcast burning effective in the end was not its direct effects but its indirect ones, not the fire hunt but the fire habitat. By regenerating preferred environments, fire hunting evolved into a renewable resource. Within limits Aborigines controlled the productivity and geography of the grazers they hunted. They favored some creatures and some environments over others. This was clearly recognized by European visitors. After describing "the extensive burning by the natives, a work of considerable labor," Surveyor-General T. L. Mitchell documented how the burns "left tracts in the open forest which had become as green as an emerald with the young crop of grass." Leichhardt echoed that observation. The burning, he speculated, "is no doubt connected with a systematic management of their run to attract game to particular spots in the same way that stockholders burn parts of theirs in the proper season." The burning was far from random or promiscuous, or applied without regard to consequences. Rather it played upon the pyric patterns inherent in the Australia biota, even as it confirmed that dependence on fire. It exploited the nomadism of the Aborigine even as it compelled that trait. It reinforced the special capacity of humans to wield a firestick, even as it committed humans to an ever greater reliance on that implement.[36]

Fire fused Aborigine and bush into a special weld. After nearly a century and a half, the celebrated commentary of Mitchell still speaks with astonishing clarity:

> Fire, grass, and kangaroos, and human inhabitants, seem all dependent on each other for existence in Australia; for any one of these being wanting, the others could no longer continue. Fire is necessary to burn the grass, and form those open forests, in which we find the large forest-kangaroo; the native applies that fire to the grass at certain seasons, in order that a young green crop may subsequently spring up, and so attract and enable him to kill or take the kangaroo with nets. In summer, the burning of long grass also discloses vermin, birds' nests, etc., on which the females and children, who chiefly burn the grass, feed. But for this simple process, the Australia woods had probably contained as thick a jungle as those of New Zealand or America, instead of the open forests in which the white men now find grass for their cattle, to the exclusion of the kangaroo . . .

As further proof, Mitchell cited the melancholy consequences that followed the expungement of Aboriginal fire. "Kangaroos are no longer to be seen there [Sydney]; the grass is choked by underwood; neither are there natives to burn the grass . . ." Extinguishing Aboriginal fire extinguished as well the Aborigine and the peculiar biotas of Aboriginal Australia.[37]

CLEANING UP THE COUNTRY

Dutch, British, French—all the European explorers of coastal Australia witnessed fire by night and smoke by day. Each understood those phenomena as emblematic of human settlements. Captain James Cook summarized their collective experience when he wrote that his crew "saw upon all the Adjacent Lands and Islands a great number of smokes—a certain sign that they are inhabited—and we have daily seen smokes on every part of the Coast we have lately been upon." When Philip King extended that domain to the interior, he also spoke for many: "Very distant smokes were distinguished inland, proving the existence of natives removed from the shores." Fires deep in the mountains convinced Governor Arthur Phillip that Aborigines inhabited them. Leichhardt, Sturt, Stuart, Mitchell, Eyre, Gregory, Giles—one could pick almost at random among the classic exploring parties around and across the continent for the identification of smoke and fire with Aborigines. Even those who considered lightning as a possible cause, as did First Fleeters Arthur Phillip and George White, soon agreed that the Aborigine was by far the most powerful agent. Whatever the natural pattern of fire, the fire regimes of Aboriginal Australia were shaped by the firestick.[38]

Over and again astonishment at the extent of burning punctuated initial reports. Hooker DeNyptang in 1697 saw, "after sun-set," a "great number of fires burning the whole length of the coast of the mainland." Soon after landing Governor Phillip wrote to Viscount Sydney that "in all the country thro' which I have passed I have seldom observed a quarter of a mile without seeing trees which appear to have been destroyed by fire." Exploring the Derwent River in 1802, François Peron marveled that "wherever we turned our eyes, we beheld the forests on fire." William Edward Parry exclaimed that "I never saw anything like the state of the country with the fires— literally as black as charcoal for miles together." At Port Essington in Arnhemland, it was reported that "the natives set fire to the grass which is abundant everywhere, and at that time quite dry . . . The conflagration spreads until the whole country as far as the eye can reach, is in a grand and brilliant illumination." The peripetic George Robinson routinely noted in Tasmania that "the country as far as we had come was all burnt off and there was fires in all directions." Near King George Sound Archibald Menzies, with Vancouver's expedition, found "but few places I travelled over this day but what bore evident marks of having been on fire." There were "frequent marks of fire and general burnt state of the country everywhere." George Vancouver himself spoke of "the very extraordinary devastation by fire which the vegetable productions had suffered throughout the whole country we had traversed." At the Swan River colony John Wollaston entered into his journal how "for 50 miles through the forest a tree is hardly to be found which has not the mark of fire upon it"—a mark that prevails "so universally in Australia." T. L. Mitchell concluded that "conflagrations take place so frequently and extensively in the woods during summer as to leave very little vegetable matter to return to earth. On the highest mountains, and in places the most remote and desolate, I have always found on every trunk on the ground, and living tree of any magnitude also, the marks of fire; and thus it appeared that these annual conflagrations extend to every place." And so it went, in virtually every environment of Australia.[39]

Commentators not only catalogued bushfires among the exotica of this land of contrarities, but soon implicated fire as a cause of its singular peculiarities. The careful Charles Sturt, as knowledgeable as any explorer of his age, concluded that "there is no part of the world in which fires create such havoc as in New South Wales, and indeed in Australia generally. The climate, on the one hand, which dries up vegetation, and the wandering habits of the natives on the other, which induce them to clear the country before them by conflagration, operate equally against the growth of timber and underwood." The "general sterility" of New South Wales he ascribed to "the ravages of fire." Edward Curr thought that it would be difficult to "overestimate" the consequences of the Aboriginal firestick. "We shall not, perhaps, be far from the truth if we conclude that almost every part of New Holland was swept over by a fierce fire, on an average, once in every five years. That such constant and extensive conflagrations could have occurred without something more than temporary consequences seems impossible, and I am disposed to attribute to them many important features of Nature here." Curr "doubted" whether any other group of humans "has exercised a greater influence on the physical condition of any large portion of the globe than the wandering savages of Australia." To the ubiquitous bushfires Europeans even attributed the blistering winds from the interior that scorched coastal settlements.[40]

The interplay between natural and Aboriginal ignitions, the subtle synergism of varied fires and varied biotas, the actual pattern of fire regimes—all have to be understood within the context of particular places and times. But there can be little doubt that the firestick brought anthropogenic fire everywhere to Australia, that Aborigines used fire consciously and systematically, that they powerfully, perhaps irreversibly, reinforced the trends by which fire pervaded Old Australia. But just as the ecological consequences of fire involve more than the sum of its separate effects on individual flora and fauna, so the character of Aboriginal burning appears to embrace more than the sum of its separate instrumental uses.

In describing the cycle of contemporary burning by the Gidjingali of Arnhemland, Rhys Jones lists among the reasons for fire their desire—their understood obligation—to "clean up the country." Other observers have echoed the sense with which Aborigines consider the role of fire as a restorative, and their use of broadcast burning, a moral imperative. C. D. Haynes even concluded that this impulse "dominates all other reasons" for Aboriginal burning. Thus, while there were purposes for burning, each independently reasonable and justifiable as contributing to a livable habitat, overriding each was an ensemble effect, a perception that land unburned or burned badly was land unmanaged. Land rumpled with litter was "dirty" and disgraceful. What Aborigines typically did to prepare a site for occupation—to burn it over—they thus projected across the entire inhabited regions of Old Australia. That relationship was reciprocal: if fire made the land fit for humans, humans in return accepted an obligation to use fire to sustain the land.[41]

It is an old drama, this replacement of the bushfire by the hearth fire. But it has been replayed in Australia in special ways. Aboriginal fire was not identical with any fire. It owed its character as much to Aboriginal culture as to Australian nature. It bound the material life to the moral life. It bridged technology to ritual, environmental manipulation to social myth. The revolutionary fires that raged during the Pleistocene raged also in the minds of men.

7

Fires of the Dreaming

Goorda then led the men away from the blackened area and showed them the secrets of fire . . . "This is fire," he said. "Guard it carefully so it will serve you and not devour you."

— *RECORDED BY LOUIS A. ALLEN,*
"The Coming of Fire: the Goorda Myth"

. . . the actual fire ceremony, the torch fight, seemed to be regarded as a kind of "clearing" ceremony . . . Whatever else it was or was not, it was extremely wild and picturesque from start to finish.

— *BALDWIN SPENCER,*
Wanderings in Wild Australia (1928)

FIRE WAS AS INTEGRAL to the mental as to the material existence of the Aborigine. It was a universal accompaniment to Aboriginal ritual, and it became itself on occasion an object of ceremony. Storytellers frequently incorporated fire into legends as a routine participant in the mythological life of the Dreamtime, as a common vehicle for the explanation of natural and spiritual phenomena, and as a presence that cried out for explication, for fire both divided and brought together. It differentiated the human world from the nonhuman, yet it bridged the mental world with the material. It made possible a cognitive corroboree of Aboriginal culture.[1]

Remove fire and that spiritual universe would collapse. Spiritual invention depended on a material context of heat and light; the social life that sustained cognition pivoted around a fire. Without campfires, there would be no evening storytelling. Without torches and bonfires, there could be no ceremonial community after dark. Without the protective radiance of the hearth fire, Aborigines were defenseless against the evil spirits that marauded the night in search of souls to devour. Fire was ubiquitous in Aboriginal ritual and myth because it was ubiquitous in Aboriginal life.

Yet those experiences and practices were only a beginning because the human revolution that fire helped make possible was ambivalent. Humans were not genetically programmed to start, preserve, use, explain, or otherwise live with fire, whose prevalence and power made it a profoundly variegated and even contradictory phenomenon, ideally positioned to explain and exemplify the specialness and ambivalence of human existence. So clearly, among the animals, was fire a uniquely human possession that its origins could be related to the origins of humans, and its exercise to the special duties and responsibilities incumbent upon humans. The possession of fire —at once both an extraordinary power and an exceptional danger—was an archetype for all human behavior.

Humans had to explain fire and to define its proper usage. They had to substitute cultural codes for genetic codes. They had to record their knowledge and experience in stories, songs, ceremonies, paintings, rituals. They had to construct and populate a moral universe that would both prescribe and proscribe behavior. Accordingly, Aboriginal societies evolved an elaborate mythology to explain creation out of an inchoate Dreamtime, to legitimate contemporary beliefs and behaviors, and to vivify the important rites of passage in the life of individual Aborigines, and for this endeavor fire was ubiquitous, both a means and an end of inquiry. In this way fire established new, symbolic relationships, its behavior following the fuels of metaphor, the litter of the subconscious. Old Australia and its fires entered a symbolic world whose ecology was vastly different from that which it knew in the bush, but one that also placed fire at its core.

ORIGINS

The ancestral Dreamtime was at least partially conceived and animated by fire. As a context, fire invited contemplation, and as an object, it demanded explanation. The reverie induced by fire helped transport narrators back to the Dreamtime; staring into flame brought magicians to a trance from which they could communicate with the spirit world; the vital stories of creation and existence were almost always retold or reenacted around a fire. It is too much to argue, as Bachelard has for humans in general, that fire was the originating phenomenon of mental activity, "the *first phenomenon,* on which the human mind *reflected.*" But one could agree with him that the "mind in its primitive state, together with its poetry and its knowledge, had been developed in meditation before a fire." The Dreaming was likely illuminated, if not inspired, by fire.[2]

The pervasiveness of fire in Aboriginal Dreaming reflects the pervasiveness of fire in Aboriginal life. Fire practices created a repertoire of actions and effects that could be transfigured into stories and symbols. But once in this cognitive realm humans could reassemble the pieces according to other kinds of logic. They could establish new patterns that relied on emotional or symbolic associations, without analogues in actual life; like a collage, they could alter the individual parts to make a larger truth, a new register of meanings. From this register came a cognitive universe that told the Aborigine who he was, and a moral universe that informed him how he should behave. Through its metamorphosis into a parallel mental universe, the significance of fire in Aboriginal Australia expanded far beyond its presence in the landscape. "Fire, and its benefits," Ainslie Roberts concluded, "was possibly the richest Dreamtime heritage of all."[3]

Common fire practices become common features of Dreamtime stories. Hunting fires, for example, appear frequently. In the tale of Wirroowaa, a mob of giant kangaroos (perhaps an echo of remembered monsters that populated the Pleistocene bestiary) attacks humans until fire drives them off. Thereafter humans keep fire in the hollowed base of old gums. Lungkata the blue-tongue lizard puts his firestick to spinifex to drive out his defiant sons. After Wyungare, the hunter, keeps the two wives of Nepele, Nepele avenges himself by igniting a magic fire outside their shelter, a fire that subsequently pursues them to the waters of Lake Alexandrina. Bullabogabun fires an enormous tree in which Karambil has taken refuge. The carpet-snake people, angered at the selfishness of Lunkana, the sleepy lizard man, set fire to his shelter and he dies in flames. Women, in particular, use fires to burn out anthills and to flush out bandicoots and other creatures from cover. Often they attempt to hide their fire, even from their husbands, and are killed for their selfishness. When Wildu, the eagle, seeks revenge, he causes a rainstorm to drive the offending creatures into a cave, then blocks the entrance with grass and branches and sets the pyre alight. Though most animals escape, the crows and magpies emerge with black plumage. Two women destroy Thardid Jimbo, the "enemy of man," by luring him into a cave, then plastering the entrance with fire. When Thardid Jimbo tries to flee, he is consumed in the flames.[4]

The most interesting motif among the fire myths—one again associated with hunting—is the identification of fire with birds. In some cases, fire is invoked to explain unusual plumage such as the ebony feathers of crows, magpies, and black swans, or the red tail-feathers of the finch and red crest of the cockatoo. But the major raptors, the eagles and kites (and sometimes the crow), are envisioned themselves as fire preservers and fire users. As often as not it is a bird that first knows how to make fire or that captures fire for humans or saves fire from some sinister creature determined to extinguish it. The image clearly originates from the frequent appearance of such raptors at savanna fires, where they scavenge for meals. Often the fire-clutching eagle or hawk of myth drops his firestick into grass, which carries fire everywhere.[5]

Such escaped fires are common, and their practical moral obvious. They testify, first, to the danger of fire. In one of the most fully developed fire myths, Goorda the fire spirit abandons the heavens and descends to earth like a meteor or lightning flash. But as soon as Goorda touches the grass, it flames, and the fires sweep the horizon and kill a group of boys, waiting to be circumcised, who have crowded into a bark hut. Both Goorda and his human friends have to work out a protocol so that fire may be used, not feared. Once the secret is transmitted, Goorda returns to the stars.[6]

Escaped fires explain also how fire became so prevalent in the landscape and among people. In this case a stolen fire or a hastily dropped firestick engulfs the countryside, and what had been jealously hoarded now becomes widely available to everyone. Fire enters the trees, which absorb its spirit and rerelease it when properly rubbed. If a firestick fails, a new fire can be extracted from nature. Another variant is to insinuate fire into the basal cavities of large trees, where it is sheltered from the rains. Similarly, digging sticks and spears—capable of spouting fire from their broken ends—act as surrogate firesticks. It is as though, having once been hardened by fire, they have assimilated a fire spirit and can regurgitate it later. The story of Kondole tells how this selfish man hid his firestick rather than share it at a corroboree. After he was changed into a whale, the fire escaped and entered into the grass tree, whose glow advertised its presence. The firedrill made from the grass tree recovers that hidden fire.[7]

But not all creatures know how to get fire or how to keep it. In most origin myths, the possession of fire is the guarded secret of a creature who does not deserve it—a reptile like a lizard or a crocodile or, if a mammal, an aquatic dweller such as a water rat—a character hopelessly, recklessly selfish who refuses to share his fire and who lives in a nonflammable environment. Through the cunning and daring of his rivals, or his own carelessness, the fire hoarder loses his fire—but not before a final defiance in which he attempts to extinguish fire once and for all by tossing it into water. Thus Kanaula tries to end a corroboree by leaping into the sea with the fire, until Unwala impales his hand temporarily with a spear and Mulara flies to the scene and retrieves the firestick. Mulara then drops the firestick into pandamus, which flares and saves fire from extinction. An analogous version has Kunmanggur, the Rainbow Serpent, attempt to punish humans for their wickedness by retiring to the waters with the final firestick. At the last second Kartpur seizes the subsiding firestick and sets the grass alight, and fire is broadcast throughout creation. When the fire of Goodah, an evil magician, is pirated away, he attempts a retaliation by causing rain, and only the storage of fire in the basal cavities of large gums prevents a total loss. Birik-birik, the plover, acts quickly to rescue fire from Gumangan, the crocodile, who in a temper tantrum seeks to extinguish his firesticks in a river. The stories not only reestablish the proper relationship between human and non-human, but that between fire and water.[8]

The ritual uses of fire in caves, at night, and around gloomy waterholes—not every waterhole, only a select group—originate in the value of fire for illumination. Fear of ambush, alarm over poisonous snakes that might be trod upon accidentally, difficult footing in unburned vegetation all made a torch an act of prudence. But these fears attached to others, to a generic apprehension of darkness as a place of evil spirits who could be held at bay only by torches or fire. While Eyre noted that "all tribes of natives appear to dread evil spirits . . . [that] fly about at nights," fire "appears to have a considerable effect in keeping these monsters away, and a native will rarely stir a yard at night . . . without carrying a firestick." Grey reported that "if they are obliged to move away from the fire after dark," they will "carry a light with them and set fire to dry bushes as they go along." Angas observed that "their belief in spirits is universal; hence their dread of moving at night, unless provided with a firestick or torch." More recently Gould observed the matter-of-fact way in which "women going out for firewood or water at dusk usually set fire to the vegetation along the way to illuminate their way to and from camp." By such means cognitive and behavioral fire practices converged.[9]

Other legends identify the heat and light of fire with the sun and sometimes with the stars. In some, earthly fire leads to heavenly fire. Thus the sun and moon are the firesticks of Wuriupranill, the sun-woman, and Japara, the moon-man, each cycling the world in their own time. The first man, Purukupali, discovers fire accidentally and gives it to others with the instructions that they never allow it to expire. An emu egg hurled against a pyre built by Gnawdenoorte, the Great Man's Son, kindles the light of day. The firestick of Koolulla, before he drowns, scatters embers skyward to make the stars. In most myths, this celestial fire is returned to an Earth—or at least to humans—that lacks it. Spears, boomerangs, and throwing sticks capture fire, a symbolic variant on fire hunting. From the Murrumbidgee region, an origin myth, closely following real conditions, relates how the magician Goodah captures lightning as it strikes a dead tree, then uses the captive lightning as a kind of personal firestick. When his selfishness becomes intolerable, a whirlwind sweeps Goodah's fire and scatters it around the countryside where it quickly becomes common property.[10]

More important than joining the lights of heaven and earth, fire myths and fire rituals joined the spiritual and the physical; they married the great moieties of Aboriginal existence. Much as it made the world habitable, so fire made it understandable. Fire helped explain the colors of animals, the heat and light of celestial objects, the distribution of species, the warmth of the human body, the wondrous process by which fire may be extracted from wood. Fire's power made it useful as a dramatic plot device. Even more, fire helped explain motives; it exposed character. By their relationship to fire, creatures are revealed as brave or pusillanimous, generous or selfish, obedient or defiant. By their use of fire, humans reveal themselves as either responsible or evil.

A reciprocity existed between the two worlds. What was abstracted into myth returns, rereified in practice. But in this fire cycle, the end is different from the beginning. When humans took fire out of the landscape, they passed it through a mental—a spiritual—world before returning it to the land. Anthropogenic fire had to reconcile both universes. Those myths and rites helped guide the proper use of fire by shaping fire practices around waterholes, campsites, hunting grounds, and along the corridors of the Dreamtime. As nomadic Aborigines traced and retraced the ancestral pathways of their Dreamtime totems, the legendary paths etched on their stone *churingas* took on a material existence in the Australian landscape by trails of fire and smoke. As they told and retold the saga of creation, each tribe holding a fragment of the master myth cycle in the form of a bushfire song, the rhythms of Australian fire took on a new cadence. If fire transported Aborigines into the Dreamtime, it also superimposed elements of the Dreamtime onto Australia. Fire ecology acquired symbolic dimensions; fire history, new depth of metaphor; fire practices, new codes of behavior. A fiery land became a burning bush.

MYTHIC FIRE

In the early Dreamtime the creatures of the world did not look as they do today. These disordered animals eventually gathered in the country of the Rembarrngas, where Nagorgo, the Father, examined them and proclaimed, "You are not proper people and not proper animals. We must change this." With his firestick he lit a ceremonial fire that spread and spread until it encompassed the world. It swept over all the creatures. It burned the earth and the stones. After the fire passed, the creatures and the humans assumed their present forms and characters.[11]

In Aboriginal myths fire, once freed, spreads widely and impregnates woody flora and other phenomena. The fire spirit is not an exclusive possession of humans, but only humans have the capacity to invoke it and the necessary knowledge to preserve it, and only humans need to explain fire and to incorporate it into ritual. This special attribute, however, is enough to cause the natural world and the human world to diverge. Humans cannot renounce fire and still remain human, yet they must reconcile fire practices with both realms of existence. Because the possession of fire fundamentally changed the world, the behavior of humans toward fire becomes a moral paradigm for the behavior of humans toward one another and toward the rest of the natural world.

The crocodile possessed firesticks. The rainbow bird would ask for fire, but was knocked back every time. The rainbow bird was without fire: he had no light, slept without a camp fire, ate his food (fish, goanna lizards, mussels) raw.

The rainbow bird could not get fire because the crocodile was "boss" for fire and would knock him back.

"You can't take fire!"

"What am I to do for men? Are they to eat raw?"

"They can eat raw. I won't give you firesticks!"

The crocodile had fire. No man made it. The crocodile had had fire from a long time ago. Then the rainbow bird put fire everywhere. Every tree has fire inside now. It was the rainbow bird who put the fire inside.

The rainbow bird spoke. *"Wirid, wirid, wirid!"* He climbed into a tree, a dry place, a dry tree. Down he came, like a jet plane, to snatch the firesticks, but the crocodile had them clutched to his breast. Again and again the rainbow bird tried.

"You eat raw," the crocodile told him. "I'm not giving you fire."

"I want fire. You are too mean. If I had had fire I would have given it to you.

"Wirid, wirid, wirid, wirid!" Down he came. He missed. He flew up.

"Wirid, wirid, wirid!" They argued again.

"I'm not giving you fire. You are only a little man. Me, I'm a big man. You eat raw!" That is the way we had been going to eat.

The rainbow bird was angry. "Why do you knock me back all the time?"

The crocodile turned about. Snatch! The rainbow bird had the firesticks! *Wirid, wirid, wirid!* Away he flew. The crocodile could do nothing. He has no wings. The rainbow bird was above. "You can go down into the water," he called. "I'm going to give fire to men!"

The rainbow bird put fire everywhere—in every country, in every kind of tree (except the pandamus). He made light, he burned, he cooked fish, crocodile, tortoise.

The crocodile had gone down into the water. The two had spread out.

"I'll be a bird. I'll go into dry places," the rainbow bird called out. "You can go down into the water. If you go in dry places you might die. I'll stay on top."

The rainbow bird put the firesticks in his behind. They stick out from there now.

That was a long time ago.[12]

In attempting to reconstruct an ancestral supermyth from recorded fragments, Kenneth Maddock uses the above story as a myth of reference. With its allusion to jet planes, the story has obviously acquired recent embellishments, and with its reliance on crocodiles and a division of the world into wet and dry, it clearly identifies itself with the Australian tropics. But its themes and story line are ancient, with strong parallels in myths told throughout the region, and with fainter, metastructural echoes in fire origin myths told elsewhere in Australia and throughout the globe.

The fundamental concern of such stories is what the possession of fire means to humans. Fire differentiates humans from other creatures, and it demands that a moral code be prescribed to guide its usage among humans. Fire brings power. If misused, if not shared, fire must be removed from its possessors and given to others. Once shorn of fire, a creature descends to a lower scale of existence. It occupies earth or water, while the fire possessor climbs to the sky; it lives a more debased life, while that of the fire keeper aspires to a nobler code. For humans, the first necessity is to acquire fire, and then to distribute it among themselves.

For these stories, too, there is a practical basis. The extinction of fire is such a catastrophic, dehumanizing loss that people must be willing to share their fire with those who need it. In wet times, a fire once extinguished may be difficult to rekindle. Robinson, for example, described how he carefully put out the native fires he found so that dispirited Tasmanians would have to approach his band for new fire and, one presumes, a lesson in Christian theology.[13]

Two women were cutting a tree for the purpose of getting ants' eggs, when they were attacked by several snakes. The women fought stoutly, but could not kill the snakes. At last one of the women broke her fighting-stick, and immediately fire came forth from it. The crow picked up the fire and flew away with it. Two very good young men, named Toordt and Trrar, ran after the crow and caught him. In a fright the crow let fall the fire, and a great conflagration followed. The blacks were sore afraid when they saw it, and the good Toordt and Trrar disappeared. Pund-jel himself came down from the sky and said to the blacks, "Now you have fire, do not lose it." He let them see Toordt and Trrar for a moment, and then he took them away with him, and set them in the sky, where they now shine as stars. By and by the blacks lost the fire. Winter came on. They were very cold. They had no place where they could cook their food. They had to eat their food cold and raw like the dogs. Snakes also multiplied. At length Palyang, who had brought forth women from the water, sent down Karakarook from the sky to guard the women. She was a sister of Palyang . . . a very fine and very big woman, and she had a very, very long stick, with which she went about the country killing a multitude of snakes, but leaving a few here and there. In striking one snake she broke her big stick, and fire came out of it. The crow again flew away with the fire, and for a while the blacks were in great distress. However, one night Toordt and Trrar came down from the sky and mingled with the blacks. They told the blacks that the crow had hidden the fire on a mountain named Num-ner-woon. Then Toordt and Trrar flew upwards. Soon Trrar returned safely with the fire wrapt up in bark, which he had stripped from the trees . . . Toordt returned to his home in the sky and never came back to the blacks. They say he was burnt to death on a mountain named Mun-ni-o, where he had kindled a fire to keep alive the small quantity he had procured. But some of the sorcerers deny that he was burnt to death on that mountain; they maintain that for his good deeds Pund-jel changed him into the fiery star which white men call the planet Mars. Now the good Karakarook had told the women to examine well the stick which she had broken, and from which had come forth smoke and fire; the women were never to lose the precious gift. Yet this was not enough. The amiable Trrar took the men to a mountain where grows the particular kind of wood called *djel-wuk* out of which firesticks are made; and he showed them how to fashion and use these implements, so that they might always have the means at hand to light a fire. Then he flew away upwards and was seen no more.[14]

Set in Victoria, this myth has shed many of its Arnhemland characters and its sharp contrast between wet and dry. There are emotive surrogates—the snake, for example, replaces the crocodile—and other elements of Aboriginal life are explained, principally the division of labor by which women maintain fire and men make it. Overall, the story is a rich mythopoeic ensemble, a register of codes and symbols, that recommends it as a myth of reference for southern, drier Australia. Other variants have the women attempt to hide their discovered fire, a deed for which they are punished.

The dissolution of Aboriginal Australia meant as well the disassembling of the Dreaming. The old dialectics disintegrated. What they had bonded together broke; what they had separated merged. Fires that should have burned expired, and fires that should have traced the corridors of the Dreamtime ran wild. The Dreamtime fire became a nightmare.

RITUAL FIRE

Nearly every rite had its fire. Campfires, torches, smoking fires, even bushfires accompanied virtually every ritual just as they accompanied virtually every aspect of Aboriginal material existence. Often they were a practical necessity, essential to provide the heat and light without which ceremonies could not proceed at night or to help heal ritual cuts or to prepare food or other implements. The principal colors used for ritual decoration mimicked the colors of fire—white (ash), ocher (flame), and black (charcoal). Occasionally fire was itself the object of ceremony. But regardless, fire rites helped shape the social world as fire practices did the natural world. Between the spiritual and the material world, between the Dreamtime and the present, fire was alternately weld and barrier. As individuals and as tribes retold their history, fire was there.

The retelling began at birth. Often a woman in labor would squat over a small fire to facilitate birthing. After birth she would hold a baby over a smoking fire. The smoke helped dry the mucous membrane and sealed into the body the life spirit. Similar rites of purification by fire and sealing by smoke were repeated at each important life passage, in a sense signifying a rebirth into each new status.[15]

As males came of age, they underwent a sequence of rites which concluded with circumcision and often subincision. After ritual cutting and bleeding they stood over a fire, which putatively helped the healing. At other critical stages the boys had to stand over a smoking fire or on hot coals in the expectation that the steam—arising from soaked lily leaves or dampened grass on heated stones—would pass from anus to mouth and cleanse the inner self. The act recapitulated the birthing fire. After its purification and sealing, the initiates learned the first of the sacred songs and saw some of the sacred totems, including the bushfire song and the fire totem. Among desert tribes participants threw firesticks into the night prior to circumcision.[16]

When initiation was complete, the young male could marry. In the simplest ceremony the bride came to her husband's campfire. Other ceremonies could be more elaborate, with differing roles for fire. Ramsey Smith described a marriage ceremony celebrated at midnight that centered around a huge campfire. A procession, in which each family member carried a firestick, brought the bride to the bonfire. The two families converged at a point where they placed their firesticks together—literally joining the two family fires. The respective uncles of bride and groom addressed them. "Children, the fire is symbolical of the severity of the law . . . As fire consumes, so will the law of your fathers destroy all who dishonour the marriage-bond." [17]

Adult ceremonial life was rarely without fire in some form. Corroborees —manifest by large congregations of Aborigines at night—danced and sang around enormous fires. The reverie of fire assisted communication by shamans with the spirit world. Cleansing ceremonies, at which participants were brushed with or passed through smoke, were common to prevent illness and to prepare for the acceptance of foods. In ritual dances fire could stand for a variety of totems, from the wild turkey Nganuti to the rock python Muit. Many reenacted totemic myths and often incorporated fire practices, such as a fire drive, within an elaborate choreography that could last for days. Thus there were ritual fires to hunt kangaroos, brush turkeys, even quail, sometimes in company with hawk totems. The fire drive lends itself, much like smoke and steam, to a symbolism of purging. Typically, participants sublimated the drive into torches, although Smith documents a case in which the bush was fired all around.[18]

Perhaps the most famous of fire-related ceremonies was the one performed by the Warramunga, photographed and recorded by Baldwin Spencer —a scene "most grotesque and, at the same time, picturesque." The dances and preparations went on for days, but the culminating scenes involved two furious episodes of active fire. The first incident occurred as a group placed torches against a giant wurley in which a company of men sat. The men fled; the entire congregation danced; and then another group picked up lighted branches and scattered burning embers from them over themselves and the rest of the company. One moiety, the Kingilli, draped itself in bundles of eucalypt twigs, then formed a procession and encircled the other moiety, the Uluuru. The Uluuru stripped those branches off and tossed them into large fires.[19]

The second episode came at the climax. After the men coated themselves with mud and white pipe clay they ignited a dozen giant torches of eucalypt branches (each perhaps four meters tall), and a "general mellee" ensued. What the first incident had restricted to a petite rain of embers now became a downpour. "The smoke, the blazing torches, the showers of sparks falling in all directions and the mass of howling, dancing men, with their bodies grotesquely bedaubed, formed a scene that was little short of fiendish." It was not possible, Spencer admitted, "to find out exactly what it all meant," but it seemed to be regarded as a general "clearing" ceremony, a ritual cleansing of enmity among the tribal members, a rebirth from an immersion in smoke and fire.

This sense of fire as a protector and purifier was rife in Aboriginal life and legend. The world teemed with evil spirits that caused nightmares, infested the living with illness and death, and snatched away the life spirits. The prime evil took many forms—the dingo Mamu, the spiny Nadubi, and the enormous serpent known variously as Gumba, Jinga, Waugal, Moulack. Humans were most vulnerable when alone or in dark places like caves or waterholes or, of course, at night. But fire repelled the spirits. Grey reported the belief that one could fight off a nightmare by waving a firestick and reciting appropriate chants. Stokes told how fires warded off the malevolent spirits of the night. There were abundant myths to describe the consequences for those without fire.[20]

The winds were under the power of Wurramugwa, the night spirit. Without them the monsoon rains did not come and the people faced famine. The woman Dagiwa consulted the magician Barunda who instructed her how to reach the great rock that is the home of Wurramugwa. The journey was dangerous, and Dagiwa was warned never to leave the light cast by her fire or Wurramugwa would kill and eat both her and her child. That night the voice of Wurramugwa sang out from the darkness. It insisted that the woman lie with him. She paused, lingering in the shadow line between fire and night, before the leaves on the bloodwood tree warned her to return. They explained that if she would cut the tree, the monsoon wind, which was in them, will be released. But there was danger everywhere—in the river, from the crocodile and the jellyfish; in the darkness, from Wurramugwa. She could not leave her fire. Dagiwa stoked her fire with grass. The smoke drove away the evil spirits. Then she carried her protective firestick home. The next day her husband returned and cut the tree and liberated the monsoon winds.[21]

Death completes the ritual cycle. Mortuary fires both treated the dead and protected the living. The function of the funerary fire is to segregate the living and the dead. Thus both bright and smoky fires are lit—in some cases to drive away the lingering spirit of the recently dead and prevent its reinvasion of the body; in other instances, to propitiate the dead, which lack fire; and in other cases, for reasons that the participants themselves hardly understand or decline to divulge. Thus Lloyd Warner describes a funeral ceremony in which the mourners, with firesticks, march in two lines, containing the departed spirit between them. The leader then seizes a firestick and displays the fire, an act intended to drive the spirit of the dead away from the living. "It is thought by some that this is for the good soul and by other informants that this is for the bad soul, and by some it is not believed at all."[22]

The last rites involved more than a symbolic exorcism, however. Funerary fire practices included burning graves prior to disposal of the body, burning after the body had been placed into the grave, firing reeds that had been laid into special designs, and maintaining fires around the gravesite "for the special use of the departed." The latter practice was intended to discourage the spirit of the dead from returning to the hearth fires of the living. William Buckley, however, told of a burial he saw in which "a ring" was made "by clearing away, and lighting fire." The ashes were scraped over the grave, and "whenever they pass near these graves they re-light the fires" in the belief that when they "come to life again," they will need the fire. Mourners often built fires and brushed their bodies with smoking branches in an apparent act of ritual cleansing; failure would leave the dead to haunt the region and scare off game. In some instances a wife would rub her body with charcoal, both as a sign of death and as a symbol of spiritual sanitizing.[23]

Burial usually meant cremation, most widely practiced in the southeast and Tasmania, where several Europeans witnessed it. The Baudin expedition to Tasmania discovered recent cremations, and some of the Aboriginal mounds the English found around Sydney Cove were crematoria; Moore described the practice around the Swan River colony; Angas reported it in South Australia, where "the natives . . . burn their dead by placing them in hollow trees in an erect position, and covering them with leaves and dry sticks," they set "fire to the whole." Backhouse described how a pyre was constructed and the tribal sick were gathered around it. The resulting fire not only burned away the body and prevented reinfection by the departed spirit, but the dead woman would return to "take the devil out of" the assembled sick. The ashes of the dead were collected, a portion to be smeared on the faces of the mourners each morning. Others reported a similar practice among the Tasmanians in which the ashes would be worn as an amulet to ward off evil spirits. At Mount Gambier tribes deposited ashes in a tree hollow. And Bennelong, that infamous experiment in European-Aboriginal relationships, cremated his wife, then interred her ashes in a grave.[24]

Such funeral fires complete a life cycle of rites that began with birthing fires. The spirit that the one sealed in, the other now sealed out. They bring full circle, too, the life saga of Aboriginal Australia. The oldest human fossils on the continent are the interments at Lake Mungo. The first to be uncovered, and the most ancient—Mungo I, the remains of a slender woman—bear the unmistakable signs of cremation. The remains had been burned, the bones broken, and the ashes and crushed bone deposited in a grave near the pyre. The charcoal is a convenient dating horizon, and the preserved remains a cross-cultural linkage between the Dreaming and modern science. That the earliest presence of Aborigines is a hearth and the earliest human skeleton a ritual cremation—that fire should bridge two alien societies—is something the Aborigine would have instinctively understood. As amulet and artifact, those ancient ashes continue to join, even as they divide, the living and the dead.[25]

TWILIGHT OF THE DREAMTIME

All peoples have fire myths and fire rituals, and neither in structure nor in theme are the fire legends and rites of Aboriginal Australia unique. What makes the fires of the Dreaming special is what makes the fire regimes of

Australia special, their context—their pervasiveness, the unusual combinations they concoct, the singularity of their presence. In the sacred as in the secular realms fire was at once subtle, varied, and prominent. Reviewing the cognitive role of fire among Aborigines in southwestern Australia, Hallam identified a "complex of ideas" that included "sky-sun-moon-stars-crystals-fire-birds-tree-earth-cave-womb-blood-red-firestick-serpent-water-fertility." A natural response is to ask what is *not* included. The catalogue may be best understood, however, as testifying to the symbolic as well as to the practical prevalence of fire.[26]

There is one master myth of great antiquity and power, however, that highlights how the natural conditions of Australia could combine with the Aboriginal imagination to explain fire and its meaning to humans. This is the myth of the Rainbow Serpent. Variants are found everywhere in Australia, but it may be no accident that the two points of entry into the Sahul—through New Guinea and through the western deserts—pass through regions unusually abundant in reptilian fauna. Snakes, in particular—large pythons and poisonous vipers—were both food and enemy, at once both fascinating and hideous. They appear in the mythology of most cultures, and much of their symbolic potency may trace back to the genetic memory of mammals. What is unusual about Australia is how the serpent and fire came to be associated.

In the Dreamtime when the earth was young and people had not yet come to be lived Kunmanggur, the first ancestor. He had the form of a python. His home was in a deep pool on top of the mountain, Wagura. By day he rose from the depths of the waterhole and lay coiled in the sunshine, his scales glowing with all the colors of the rainbow. Then one day he decided to create people.

He fashioned a *didjeridu* and when he blew on it, out came creatures and a boy and a girl. He changed himself into a man and instructed the children how to behave and sent them out to populate the land. Kunmanggur decided to live among his people. He took a wife and fathered two daughters and a son. He instructed the two daughters in the power songs but his son, Jinamin, who displeased him, he taught nothing.

When the daughters had grown, they set out to the camp of their mother to find husbands. Though it was forbidden, Jinamin desired them for himself, intercepted them in their journey, and forced himself upon the younger, Ngolpi. The two sisters try to drive Jinamin away with magic and watch him plunge over a cliff to the rocks below. They report what had happened to Kunmanggur. Jinamin, however, did not die, and when he returned to camp, Kunmanggur welcomed him and warned him to stay away from his sisters. Then he arranged a corroboree.

Kunmanggur blew his *didjeridu*. The people danced around a great bonfire. After the last dance, the fire dance, Jinamin thrust his spear into Kunmanggur. Before he fell to the ground, Kunmanggur smashed his magical *didjeridu*. Jinamin leaped into the sky and became a bat. Kunmanggur recovered, though the wound did not heal and he weakened daily. He taught the sacred songs. Then at a place called Toitbur, a deep pool, he announced that he would leave and take with him fire, "so that the people will know they have done wrong." But before the firestick disappeared under the waves, Kartpur snatched it and set the countryside ablaze so that fire could not be removed again.

Kunmanggur sank into the water and became again the Rainbow Serpent. He fashioned stones into spirit children. Thereafter, when women wanted children, they would journey to the pool, set bushes on fire, and strike the stone figures.[27]

It is an archetypal myth, only one of whose themes is the permanent acquisition of fire by the earth and humans. What is perhaps most interesting is less its narrative line or its moral prescriptions for intrafamilial behavior than its symbolic division of the universe into two realms. It is as though the mythological world, like Aboriginal society, were segregated into two great moieties whose interactions had to proceed according to a carefully ordained protocol justified in myth and encoded in ritual. On one side was fire, and on the other the serpent. Though antagonistic, incompatible, they remain symbolically and emotionally linked in a dialectic of life and death. Evil lurked in the wet and the dark, the hidden waterhole and the sinister cave. Good went with the dry, the light, the open landscape. Where the great serpent is unwanted, fire is used to drive him off; and where the intent is to propitiate the serpent, fire is withheld. In many Aboriginal paintings the same iconography, a wavy line, applies equally to serpent and to fire.

The use of the serpent captures other archetypal images and symbolic meanings that are not evident in the fire origin myths of other peoples with their appeal to birds and bunnies, clever coyotes, and defiant Titans chained to Mount Caucasus. That dialectic endowed the mythology of Aboriginal fire with a special power. It divided the universe into the burned and the unburned, and it granted to humans alone the power to shape that universe guided by their ancestral totems and songlines. Through fire they projected their power, recreating an ancestral Dreamtime; with fire, they protected themselves from the terrors beyond. But this intellectual pyrophilia also had its fatal flaw. The secular was not divided cleanly into two moieties, and fire was not the exclusive property of the Aborigine.

When the white invaders appeared, they too had fire. They used it not against the Rainbow Serpent but against the Aborigine. Their firesticks imposed a new dialectic and defined a new geography. The power of Aboriginal fire apparently lost its potency. *This* nightmare of death and loss could not be dispelled by a waving firestick. Fire—the defining technology of humanity, the great shield against the terrors of evil—became a weapon of destruction against Aboriginal society. The Dreamtime ended, as it began, in a world-consuming flame.

8

Smokes by Day, Fires by Night: Fire Regimes of Aboriginal Australia

We perceived, that much pains had been taken by the natives to spread the fire, from its burning in separate places.

—*T. L. MITCHELL,* Three Expeditions into the Interior of Eastern Australia *(1839)*

That such constant and extensive conflagrations could have occurred without something more than temporary consequences seems impossible, and I am disposed to attribute to them many important features of Nature here . . . it may perhaps be doubted whether any section of the human race has exercised a greater influence on the physical condition of any large portion of the globe than the wandering savages of Australia.

—*EDWARD CURR,* Recollections of Squatting in Victoria *(1883)*

FEW OBSERVERS OF ABORIGINAL LIFE doubted the power of Aboriginal fire. Wherever explorers sailed along the coast, wherever they journeyed to the interior, they saw evidence of Aboriginal burning all around them. Their Aboriginal guides carried firesticks. They tracked Aboriginal bands by their trails of smoke. But it was difficult in this land of contrarities to identify just how Aboriginal burning shaped the continent, and it is difficult in retrospect to reconstruct, in creditable detail, the particulars of Aboriginal fire regimes. Native fire practices were best preserved in those areas that were least populated. The full impact of Aboriginal burning is best conveyed by comparison with those lands that Aborigines did not occupy or with the dramatic changes that European settlement inspired.[1]

The Aboriginal colonization of Australia revolutionized the pattern of ignitions. Everywhere Aborigines traveled, fires proliferated. Anthropogenic fire occurred in seasons for which natural fire was rare or unknown. They burned year-round, their propagation restricted only by larger environmental circumstances. By holding ignition constant, large fires became more likely. Many sources record how Aborigines burned scrub under the most severe conditions, at the end of a summer, with high winds. Only a history of prior burning, which suppressed fuels, prevented a general holocaust. In forested areas, however, large fires became inevitable after droughts; and in deserts, after rains.

Lightning fire persisted of course, just as it persists today. But it most influenced those environments in which Aborigines were a transient presence or in which the fuel cycle dictated the fire cycle. In areas like the wet-dry tropics, there was always abundant fuel at the end of the Wet. In the central deserts, there was never enough fuel except after unusual rains. Either way anthropogenic fire could not by itself control the fuel complex; the patterns of Aboriginal burning laid down a matrix within which lightning fire had to operate. Millennia of Aboriginal burning restricted fuels to certain arrangements and loadings, and Aboriginal fire practices imposed a new order on the fire regimes of Old Australia.

ARNHEMLAND: AN ABORIGINAL PARADIGM

The Gunei tribe of Arnhemland burns according to a meticulous prescription of place and time. Burning commences on special sites while the rainy season is still in progress. It escalates as drying spreads, searching out with fiery fingers for newly cured fuels, and it culminates at the end of the Dry with a conflagration of those places destined for burning but not yet fired. Lightning fires must seize those sites spared from Aboriginal firesticks. Protective early burning shields rainforest enclaves from late-season fires. Lowland sites tend to burn annually; upland sites on a cycle of two, three, or even four years. In a landscape in which several fire regimes are imaginable, Aborigines imposed one that suited their purposes. The Gunei are representative of Arnhemland tribes, and the Arnhemland Aborigines are a probable paradigm of fire practices throughout Aboriginal Australia.[2]

The Gunei calendar of burning begins during the waning wet season; specially targeted are camping sites. Some upland locales cure early, and some may have escaped burning during the previous year or two, so as bouts of dry weather break the gloom they can be torched. Their scale is small, but their value important. On such sites the life of the land tends to throng, a sometimes fatal congestion of humans and snakes. Those blackened patches redefine, year by year, the reclaimed dominion of humans.

The early fires test out the land's receptivity to burning, defining the actual onset of fire season. The monsoon rains cease. Thunderstorms continue to flatten the tall grasses. *Munwag*—the open fire, as distinct from the hearth fire, *gunrag*—spreads from campsites to the general landscape. Along the margins of the floodplains, the receding waters expose grass and sedge, and these are fired. Around the borders of the closed forest—the rainforest, the paperbark swamps—fires etch a protective perimeter. As sward after sward of dead grass cures, fires crop them. The successive availability of fuels leads to a succession of fires. The early burns inscribe the landscape with fuelbreaks.

More land cures, the last storms depart, and burning expands. Fire sweeps the floodplains. Portions may burn twice—fired once if they cured early, and again after a second growth. Typically, the fires expire in the afternoon humidity or end when they run into prior burns or the waters of drying swamps. The patches and strings of burning continue. Macropods crowd into the burned sites to taste the green pick; waterfowl (magpie geese, in particular) thrive in the rejuvenated sedges; snakes are unable to surprise hunters in matted grass and become themselves the hunted. As Aborigines enlarge their realm of foraging, fires mark their travels. The same routes burn year after year. Fire moves from the grasses into the woodlands.

It is a blustery season, cool and swept by southeasterly winds. No longer is the afternoon humidity sufficient to strangle fires, only the more prolonged dampness of the evening. Gunei now set their fires at midday and let them run before the winds, which, paradoxically, improve control because they dictate where the fires will burn. By bending the flames, a strong breeze protects the flowering tree crowns from scorch. Drying is irregular, however, and fires feel their way through the available fuels largely under the lash of the winds. The process continues. Day after day, week after week, the Gunei kindle more fires. The patches grow, interlock, and blanket both floodplain and woodland. The dry season advances from cool to hot.

Fuels become uniformly dry, winds are constant, and fires burn freely. The Gunei extract fewer specialty resources from the woodlands and upland savannas and they burn broader patches. They conduct fire drives for kangaroo and wallaby and forage through the ash with digging-sticks for goannas and snakes. They hunt macropods who, even before the fresh growth appears, swarm onto the burned sites. They set fires at the base of stream-cut gorges and let the flames drive game before them. They exercise control by timing the fires with diurnal wind shifts, by relying on the evening humidity, and by exploiting topographic features like cliffs and streams and old burns. They burn patches that escaped fire in previous years. Some sites burn with terrific fury. Some fires escape. Whatever remains to burn is burned. Speaking of the neighboring Gidjingali tribe, Rhys Jones notes that "barely a day passed without the passage of some foraging group being marked by a series of plumes of black smoke." The firing ceases when the evening humidity no longer extinguishes the free-burning blazes.[3]

The fires were sequential, and burning a composite of practices in a mosaic of environments that extended over nine to ten months. Most of the grasslands and savannas burned; portions of the floodplains burned twice; the woodlands and forests burned on the order of a fourth to a half their area. Few sites would escape fire on a three- or four-year cycle. Even rainforest sanctuaries, it appears, may burn with a cool fire kindled in dry but not fully cured fuels perhaps once or twice a decade. Overall the regime is remarkably stable, and the Arnhemland reported by European explorers was its product.[4]

The pattern of Gunei burning, however, is only one of several that this environment can accommodate. The Wet begins and ends with thunderstorms. At its conclusion, lightning has to compete with Aboriginal firesticks for scarce fuels. At the onset of the Wet, indigenous fire can burn only within the matrix of burned and unburned lands laid down by Aboriginal fire. At the height of the Dry, when Aboriginal burning achieves its greatest extent, there is no lightning.

When Europeans finally penetrated the tropics they installed a different regime of broadcast burning. Concerned with a single resource—fodder for cattle—they kindled large, rolling fires at the end of the Dry. The Aborigines hired at the stations assisted with the transition. As one Darwin pastoralist put it, "Aboriginal stockmen didn't have to be taught to burn; they grew up with it . . . and that's the way we learned about burning this country." Another, with considerable hyperbole, observed simply that "for Abos the change from hunting and burning for roos to hunting and burning for cattle was easy. It just meant that they had to deal with one animal instead of a hundred-and-one other damn things." But those fires were not the same. The change in culture was as profound as a change in climate, and together they restructed the ecosystem.[5]

What distinguished the Aboriginal regime was the amount of burning that occurred in midseason, the regularity of the annual burning cycle, the biological timing of the fires, the insistence that some areas never be fired and that others be fired as often as possible. All this had immense biological significance. It is doubtful, for example, that *Callitris* could have survived a pattern of late-season burns, or that most woodlands could have endured a relentless late burning on an annual basis, or that rainforest enclaves could have thrived without protective early burning. What emerges from Arnhemland is a routine of anthropogenic fire—of regular burning, of sequential burning, of variable burning, of a geography that staggers the burned with the unburned. That complexity captures the essence of Aboriginal fire practices. The landscape it fashioned was one the Aborigines recapitulated wherever it was possible to do so.

BURNING DESERTS

When Aborigines colonized the lands of Old Australia outside the tropics, they marched with firesticks and imposed related fire practices. They burned campsites routinely, and fired their main corridors of travel. They returned fire, on some cyclic basis, to favored hunting and foraging grounds. They used topography, wind, and old burns to control fire size, and they burned patches of various dimensions. Campfires, signal fires, hunting fires all escaped on occasion. Beyond the more frequented sites, lightning fires alternately sputtered and raged.[6]

But however similar the template, the landscape could look vastly different as a result of local materials. In tropical savannas, fire could burn annually. In deserts, it beat to longer rhythms, syncopated to the growth cycle of spinifex and episodic outbursts of rainfall. In wet scleroforest fire burned according to perhaps even longer rhythms, with fuel limited by drought, not moisture. In dry scleroforest and scleroscrub fire came frequently; not quite annually, but every few years. In all the inhabited landscapes there was a common, a signatory mosaic. But the coarseness of that pattern, the history by which its patches were fired, the competition between anthropogenic fire and lightning fire—all varied according to particular places and times.

Aborigines occupied the central deserts relatively late. They claimed interior lands during wet cycles, when savanna and scleroforest advanced to the Red Centre. When continental drought parched those biotas into dust, the Aborigines retreated. By the time of European exploration, the central deserts were lightly populated with tribes that traveled extensively and imposed their signatory mosaic on the land. Instead of sorghums, they burned spinifex. Instead of protected rainforest enclaves, Aborigines maintained other fire-free sanctuaries—sacred sites typically around waterholes. Instead of fitting an annual monsoon cycle, their fires had to balance sudden episodes of drought and downpour. Strips and patches of spinifex—all at different stages of recovery from the last fire—traced routes of travel, framed preferred hunting grounds, and defined the principal sites for foraging. To contain fires, Aborigines exploited natural features such as rocky cliffs, sand dunes, and old burns, for it took several years for a patch of spinifex to restore itself to the point at which it could be burned again. What occurred over the course of a few weeks in Arnhemland could require many years in the central deserts.

What makes the scene really different and not just slower, however, is that anthropogenic fire is not everywhere and that exceptional rains can override fuel mosaics built up over decades, if not centuries. There were not enough resources to sustain large human populations, so tribes were restricted to particular waterholes and particular foodstuffs that could be harvested according to some calendar of travel. Not visiting substantial portions of the land, Aborigines did not burn it routinely. Very large burns, instead, followed unusual rains that blanketed the scene with ephemeral fuels. At such times, Aboriginal fire could burn very widely.

But so could lightning. In the Red Centre the competition between lightning and firestick is keener, yet less closely synchronized. In most years anthropogenic fire cannot propagate widely beyond areas of human visitation; lightning is free to start fires outside the belts of routine human travel. Yet its fires cannot spread far either, and lightning fires dominated particularly those mountainous regions not frequented by Aborigines. Thus a split geography resulted, though one given shape by the fire practices of the Aborigines. Sites critical to Aboriginal life and economy were protected, by Aboriginal fire, from wildfire. This division broke down during those extraordinary years when the desert swelled with continuous fuels. Then fire from any source could spread widely, and these very large events could override the pattern built up from many small events.

The longevity and significance of Aboriginal fire practices became fully apparent only after they ceased. As tribes were alienated from their lands and relocated to missions, stations, and reserves during the 1920s and 1930s, the entire biota had to readjust. Fuels stacked up, stockpiled for conflagration; habitat deformed; many fauna were no longer hunted, and no longer cared for; the biotas homogenized; and eventually very large wildfires broke out in the 1920s, the 1950s, and the 1970s, kindled by lightning. These fires had no competition from the firestick, no abatement on their spread. Fifty years of very large fires had shredded the old patchwork quilt of fuels, and they attended a massive extinction of mesoscale mammals, those with body weights between forty-five grams and five kilograms.

The decline coincided with the removal of the Aborigines. Where Aborigines maintained traditional lives, as did the Pintupi of the Gibson Desert, the endangered mammals survived. It appears that these animals had coexisted with a particular fire regime, that they were in a sense husbanded by Aboriginal fire practices. With the firestick removed, lightning fire reasserted itself as an ignition source; old fuels metastasized uncontrollably; and European flora and fauna began to intervene in the fuel complex—tentatively in most places, emphatically in select sites. The combination was fatal. What had happened to the Pleistocene megafauna as Aboriginal fire was introduced was now repeated with Holocene mesofauna as that fire was removed.

ISLAND CAMEO: TASMANIA

In Tasmania climatic pressures and anthropogenic pressures confronted each other along a sharply etched frontier. The island is a geographic condensation—crowded with varied terrains, redolent with moisture, fertile soils, a rich flora, and fires. It is also a historical cameo of the competition between rainforest and scleroforest. Lightning fire is, at present, a trivial force, contributing between 0.01 and 0.09 percent of the total burned area, and it claims a well-circumscribed geography. Instead, nearly all observers agree that "the incidence of fire in Tasmania has been virtually determined by human agency for the last 20,000 years." Tasmania condenses the saga of Aboriginal fire.[7]

Early explorers, beginning with Abel Janszoon Tasman in 1642, were unanimous in reporting smoke and flame along the coast. Its littoral was a popular habitat, chocked with mussels and other foods. Aboriginal fires so ringed Tasmania that Tobias Furneaux, who visited in 1773, assumed the country was "very thickly inhabited, as there was a continual fire along-shore as we sailed." Most of these smokes emanated from coastal campsites, but the Tasmanians habitually carried firesticks—were notorious for never being far removed from one—and it is clear that they applied fire extensively beyond their windbreaks and throughout the interior. The Baudin expedition observed that "the natives" had lit many fires, and witnessed "five of them on the nearest shore, each one holding a firebrand and setting fire to everything." As they advanced up the Derwent, it seemed "that the country along the river had been nearly all burnt." François Peron reported that, from the D'Entrecasteaux Channel, "in every direction, immense columns of flame and smoke arose, all the opposite sides of the mountains . . . [were] burning . . . for the extent of several leagues." Advancing farther upstream, they witnessed bushfires "wherever we turned our eyes," and near Mount Wellington a "new" conflagration made the countryside appear to be "only a large desert, ravaged by fire." Along the northeast coast in 1831, George Robinson noted matter-of-factly that "all the country fifteen miles inland from the coast had been burnt" by the "natives."[8]

The Tasmanians fired their lands much like other Australians. Their heaviest burning corresponded with their heaviest populations, which were (at least seasonally) coastal. They burned around areas of settlement, carried fire along major corridors of travel into the interior, burned favored hunting and foraging grounds, and of course had fires escape. The incentives and techniques of Aboriginal fire in Tasmania were essentially identical to those throughout Australia. Robinson recorded fires set whenever conditions permitted, which amounted to some fire in some areas on a nearly year-round basis. But the peculiar environment of Tasmania gave those common fire practices a different expression. If the Australian tropics compressed a fire regime into an annual cycle of burning, if the interior deserts extenuated that regime into a pattern of decades, then Tasmania spoke for a cycle over centuries. Its isolation also meant that, once extinguished, Aboriginal fire could not be rekindled.

Climatic pressures confined Aboriginal fire to special areas, and biotic pressures sharpened the boundary between scleroforest and rainforest. If the desert burned extensively only after heavy rains, Tasmania burned broadly only after drought, and drought tended to be local rather than island-wide. Areas once opened by fire could be maintained by fire, however. And only constant fire resisted the pressures to replace savanna, sedge, scleroscrub, and scleroforest with rainforest. Biotic competition did not pit pyrophyte against pyrophyte, but scleromorph against rainforest. The frontier between them was narrow, its historic shape largely attributable to Aboriginal burning.

Aboriginal fire could preserve existing grasslands and scleroforest in defiance of a rainforest climate, and it could, during droughts, roll back rainforest into scleroforest and revert scleroforest to grasses or heath. Once installed, grassy parks acted as fuses to propagate fire into other environs; routine burning nibbled back the encroaching wet scrub and rainforest. This still left large tracts unburned, except on very long cycles. Many remote lands escaped anthropogenic burning because they were inaccessible and unusable, but they were so, in part, because they could not be easily burned.

As on the mainland, the full power of Aboriginal fire became boldly apparent once it was removed. All environments felt the loss. Grasses and sedgelands thickened into scrub, scrub into scleroforest, scleroforest into rainforest. What had been open downs became forest, and what had thrived as a eucalypt forest trended into wetter scleroforest and, when time allowed, into *Nothofagus*-dominated rainforest. In the northwest, what Henry Hellyer described in 1827 as grassy plains of *Poa* had by 1835—with Aborigines removed—degenerated into a tangle of scrub and sour grass. Formerly open corridors through wet forest closed. Along the west coast, a narrow biotic littoral of heath and sedge slowly succumbed before an encroaching rainforest. Louisa Meredith wrote in the early 1850s how dense scrub and dead debris spread through the forested bush. In the east, along the Midland Valley and elsewhere, extensive plains of *Poa* grassland and open savanna were apparently maintained "by a long history of firing by the Tasmanian natives." Almost everywhere, however, territory early explorers recorded as open or grassy had, as James Walker asserted for the north, become "overgrown with forest through the discontinuance of these annual burnings." On elevated plateaus and across highlands, in the north and the southwest, on sites where soils are marginal, the geography of sedge, scrub, scleroforest and rainforest reflect a long history of fire. Except on soils so badly impauperate that rainforest could not flourish or even establish itself over the span of a century or two, the geography of rainforest followed a geography of fire. So overpowering is the evidence for Aboriginal fire that some researchers have speculated that the scleromorphic flora of Aboriginal Tasmania was a colossal example of biotic drift, a distortion induced by extensive burning.[9]

Whether those distortions primed Tasmania for extinctions is an open question. Whatever extinctions may have accompanied the introduction of Aboriginal fire, a massive one followed its extinguishment. Its ultimate victim was the Aborigine. During the Black War, Aborigines dreaded as much as anything the loss of their fire, especially at night; what they deemed essential to ward off evil spirits became a beacon inviting the white ghosts to their destruction. But the suppression went beyond hearth fires and firesticks to free-burning fires and the land they shaped. The quenching of Aboriginal fire led to an environment that was literally unlivable to the Tasmanians.

With considerable irony, it became increasingly problematic to the Europeans who replaced them. When Lieutenant Henry Bunbury argued for the linkage between broadcast fire and the grassy downs that made possible the pastoral settlement of Australia, he referenced Tasmania where "this has already been proved." There the elimination of the natives and "the consequent absence of extensive periodical fires" allowed the bush to grow up "to a most important degree, spoiling the sheep runs and open pasture and affording harbourage to snakes and other reptiles which are becoming yearly more numerous." Clearly, it was in the interests of the interlopers to burn. But "we could never do it with the same judgment and good effect as the natives, who keep the fire within due bounds, only burning those parts they wish when the scrub becomes too thick or when they have another object to gain by it." The new Tasmanians are uncertain yet about the objects to gain, or the fires by which to gain them.[10]

COUNTEREXAMPLES: ISLANDS AROUND
THE ISLAND CONTINENT

Among the islands that fringed Aboriginal Australia, Tasmania was exceptional for its size and its permanent population. Together they made Tasmania into a cameo of mainland fire history. But there were other islands around the island continent with very different histories, some of which Aborigines inhabited permanently and some seasonally, and a few of which they once inhabited then abandoned; some they never reached. Collectively, these offshore arks suggest the different histories that were open to Old Australia—counterexamples to what appears, in retrospect, an inevitable evolution.

Islands in which Aborigines resided full-time or which they visited seasonally were fired in traditional ways. The Tiwi of Melville Island used fire drives to hunt kangaroo and cultivate select plants. Matthew Flinders and

George Bass, tacking around the Maatsuyker island group off Van Diemen's Land in 1799, "saw with some surprise, for it is three miles from the main, that its grassy vegetation had been burnt"—in this instance by transient foragers who traveled to the islands by raft. Allowing for the peculiarities of island biogeography, these fire practices wrought consequences similar to those on the mainland; the islands remained as recognizable fragments of Aboriginal Australia. The really fascinating stories belong with the other islands—those in which Aboriginal fire never arrived or once thrived and vanished—because they point to alternative biotic histories.[11]

Until 10,000 years ago Kangaroo Island joined the mainland and supported an Aboriginal society whose artifacts are among the very oldest discovered in Australia. Then the rising seas marooned a resident population too small to absorb the environmental shocks delivered to it and too remote to receive new infusions. The dingo and microlithic toolkit never arrived. Climatic warming propelled the scleromorphic revolution onward. Since Aborigines never developed watercraft designed for much more than coastal spearfishing, the islanders could not leave and reinforcements could not arrive. When the first Europeans sailed the coast of Kangaroo, they sighted no smokes, an anomaly on what, following the example of Captain Cook, had become known as "a continent of smoke." But long before that time the mainland Aborigines knew the place as Kartan, the island of the dead.[12]

Sediments laid down at Lashmar's Lagoon, at the far eastern point of the island, record a rough history of vegetation and, through charcoal, of fire. From 7,000 to 6,400 years ago, the biota was more open than at any other time in its prehistory. Then the plains thickened into a scleroforest of *Casuarina* with an understory of scrub and *Poa* grass. Between 5,300 and 4,800 years ago, the island steadily dried. Lenses of buried charcoal testify to major outbreaks of fire, probably correlated with drought. Then, delayed, came the eucalypt revolution. *Eucalyptus* usurped *Casuarina;* scleroscrub, including mallee, weeded out most of the grasses. Charcoal continued as a powdery background, only infrequently thickening or washing out.

Around 2,500 years ago, however, the fire regime changed. Charcoal increased and became irregular, and *Casuarina* began a counterrevolution. Fires became more intense, infrequent, episodic. The fire rhythm that had ruled the island for millennia—a pattern of abundant, low-intensity fires—surrendered to a more violent, atonal beat. Clearly, ignition was less routine, and fuels more profuse. It is believed that the change coincides with the final extinction of the Kartan Aborigines, and in their absence lightning fire burned according to its own, distinctive logic. *Casuarina* undertook its reconquest of the island. When the Europeans arrived early in the nineteenth century, they found the eucalypts still dominant but in rapid recession. Casuarinas thickened the forests; woodlands blanketed the central plateau, and dense scrub covered the coast—both formerly grasslands. The absence of grasslands and their impermeable cover severely retarded European settlement, which could proceed only by felling and burning.

By contrast, Middle Island (Recherche Archipelago) never experienced Aboriginal colonization after its isolation around 7,000 years ago. While it shared a common flora with the mainland—plants forged in Australian fire—it removed them from routine burning. There is some evidence for lightning fire on Flinders Peak, and apparently natural ignition ensured enough fire on the island to keep the biota from losing entirely its pyrophytic elements. But while the floral composition between island and mainland was similar, their expression was dramatically different. On Middle Island cover became dense. Mature forests and woodlands featured understories of grass or fern, not scrub. Acacias grew to old age. Three eucalypt-dominated subbiotas displayed habits of growth and group structure dramatically different from their counterparts across the sound. *E. angulosa,* a mallee on the mainland, grew as a tree on Middle Island.

The reason appears to lie in their different fire histories. The mainland burned more often. Not only did Middle Island lack Aboriginal firesticks, but it could not accept, as mainland sites could, fires that burned into it from surrounding lands. Regardless, lightning was apparently adequate to keep the flora from major extinctions. Evidence suggests a major burn around the time of European discovery (c. A.D. 1800), likely set by explorers, whalers, or sealers, a common practice. The next significant fire swept half the island between December 1972 and January 1973. Plants not witnessed for a century bloomed amid the postburn regeneration. It is clear that Middle Island had preserved a fire-inspired biota which had, in a sense, become lax under a flaccid regimen of fire sufficient to prevent a total atrophy but not enough to tone it into fire-hardiness.[13]

Rottnest and Garden Islands (near Perth), on the contrary, never possessed a biota truly preadapted to fire, never experienced Aboriginal colonization, never knew fire. When the ascending Indian Ocean separated them from Western Australia about 7,000 years ago, they possessed scleromorphs like acacias, cypress pines, and melaleucas, none of which regenerated by sprouting. They had no eucalypts. They were not subjected, as both Middle Island and Kangaroo Island were, to the dry winds of the interior. They simply did not burn. When Europeans arrived, the colonists conducted a fascinating ecological experiment, for they attacked Rottnest Island with clearing and firing but left Garden Island alone. When, in 1956, accidental fires swept both islands, their biological response differed dramatically. On Rottnest, acacia and melaleuca failed to regenerate. On Garden, they recovered.[14]

One explanation is the past century of different fire histories. By putting the scrub of Rottnest to the torch, Europeans approximated the Aboriginal colonization of the mainland. Had the biotic reserves of Rottnest better matched those of the littoral—had it possessed *Eucalyptus* and *Xanthor-rhoea*— it might have evolved into something very like its coastal cousin. But fire alone accounted for only part of the difference. A century of clearing and burning on Rottnest had greatly multiplied the population of quokkas. The quokkas, in turn, grazed away the seed-regenerated scleromorphs and promoted tussock grasses, better suited for fire and quokka. Garden Island lacked quokkas, and its resident wallabies could not overwhelm the woody regeneration. Even though Garden Island suffered more severely from its fire, it could recover. The fire was a freak. It would not lead to another fire. There were no organisms, including humans, poised to exploit it. There were no mechanisms to redirect the biota into the complex dynamics of a new fire regime. On Rottnest Island fire had become a more or less permanent feature, and all of the biota adjusted accordingly.

There were limits to Aboriginal fire, and limits to what can be extrapolated from island experiments. Anthropogenic fire could not concoct new species out of whole cloth; it had to work with the existent genetic stocks and within the parameters of the prevailing climate. Yet those islands do bear witness to alternative biotic histories that were potentially available to Old Australia. They are roads not taken. They could not be taken in good measure because Aboriginal fire became a pervasive pressure, not a catastrophe so much as a chronic stress to which whole ecosystems had to readjust, piece by piece, century by century. Those island counterexamples suggest how Aboriginal fire made its presence felt, how it sculpted one regime out of the many that were possible, how it "must have wrought on the mainland during the last tens of thousands of years, and particularly over the last few thousand," a new environment.[15]

RESTITUTION

Over and again, in almost every environment of Australia, Europeans reported rapid ecological changes with settlement. It was not simply that one group of humans replaced another, but that each encouraged the reconstruction of whole ecosystems. Some of the reforms were deliberate; many, accidental. In some places that transition was brief; in others much delayed. But everywhere fire remained the most sensitive of the biotic barometers that recorded the transfiguration of Aboriginal Australia.

Shortly after settlement British observers cited a thickening of scrub on lands they had initially likened to English parks. The suppression of Aboriginal fire and an infestation by exotic grazers, which attacked the grassy fuels, had stimulated woody growth, and unless cut or burned the blossoming scrub threatened to close off open forests. Typically a period of years, sometimes decades, passed between the Aboriginal and the European regimes, with the result that European firing acted on a far greater accumulation of fuel than was possible in Aboriginal times, a process repeated with remarkable singularity throughout Australia. Bald hills in Queensland revegetated with forests, and formerly open forests choked with understory. In New South Wales Murray pine grew like weeds until the dense scrub forced the abandonment of runs along the Lachlan River; in the Pillaga Scrub nearly twenty-five years passed between regular burnings, and the woods reached unprecedented dimensions; near Cobar the suppression of periodic fire promoted a cancerous explosion of *Callitris,* a species otherwise "easily destroyed by fire," but which now took "complete possession of the soil, to the exclusion of other plants." Something similar occurred in the southwest—in the jarrah and karri forests, in the Kimberleys, along grassy plains, subtropical savannas, and heaths. It was clear to early observers like Stokes that "native fires" seemed "readily to account for this." Bunbury concluded that through Aboriginal fires "the country is kept comparatively free from under wood and other obstructions, having the character of an open forest through most parts of which one can ride freely; otherwise, in all probability, it would soon become impenetrably thick . . ." Around Sydney, where Cook, Joseph Banks, Hawkesworth, Parkinson, Hunter, and Elizabeth Macarthur spoke of a country swept clean of underwood, "like an English park," similar processes were at work such that T. L. Mitchell could write that "the omission of the annual periodical burning by natives, of the grass and young saplings, has already produced in the open forest lands nearest to Sydney, thick forests of young trees, where, formerly, a man might gallop without impediment, and see whole miles before him." On Beecroft Peninsula rainforest encroached into scleroforest. D. A. Herbert cited Aboriginal fire as the principal reason for the distribution of upland savannas and the "great areas in coastal Queensland, formerly savannah, [that] have, following protection from fire, become re-clothed with trees." And so it went. By the 1890s the consequences of removing Aboriginal fire became inescapable. By the 1980s, they required restitution.[16]

Some reintroduction of fire became essential. How this was accomplished is a complicated story, and with two exceptions it is a tale that resides outside the fire history of the dispossessed Aborigines. The exceptions derive from recent, profound changes in land usage by contemporary Australia, in particular the establishment of effective reserves for both Aborigines and native biotas. For each to be preserved in something like its pre-European state, an approximation of their ancient fire regimes had to be reinstated. In both instances, however, reinstatement had to proceed within the context of the political and environmental realities of New Australia. Much as the Aborigines had laid down a matrix within which natural fire had to operate, so European settlement had blocked out the boundaries within which a reinvigorated Aboriginal fire must survive.

The outstation movement has sent bands of Aborigines away from strongly Europeanized settlements and into their old territories or new reserves. The outstations are themselves a halfway house, a syncretic blend of the old and the acquired. Early reports suggest that broadcast fire is not being exploited in what is understood as traditional ways. In part this may reflect a loss of tradition and, in part, the altered environmental conditions within which anthropogenic fire must function. But it also derives from the fact that the new settlements tend to revolve around the outstation rather than cycle through the landscape. Broadcast fire and nomadism are ancient allies. Whenever humans settle more or less permanently, the domain of broadcast burning begins to shrink. To the extent that outstation Aborigines attempt to recapture their old ways, they will have to reacquire, at least in compromised form, the practice of broadcast burning. There is some evidence that patch burning around outstations has begun.[17]

In nature reserves, the need to abate typical European fire and to substitute for it some form of patch burning is driving managers into programs of controlled burning. For some areas, like Uluru National Park, this has meant a reconstruction of Aboriginal fire history with the idea of progressively restoring the kind of fire regime that characterized the pre-European epoch. The great fires of 1974–75 burned 80 percent of the park, an event unlikely in Aboriginal times. Recurring fires subject mulga groves to intense, sequential fires that could lead to their extirpation. Preservation of the old biotas will require the preservation—by restitution—of old fire practices. For Kakadu National Park, reform has even led to the employment of Aborigines as technicians to assist with burning. For nearly all reserves, the recognition grows that a diverse flora and fauna demand a diversity of fires, that the character of native biotas, so valued by New Australia, had been sustained or created by Aboriginal burning practices.[18]

Yet it is not possible to restore completely that ancient mosaic. Too much has changed, and for too long. The exotic flora and fauna that swept over Australia in wave after wave of European colonization cannot be expelled. A nomadic society demands lands on an order that is difficult for an industrial society to meet; no single fire regime or set of fire practices can satisfy all purposes. Nature reserves and Aboriginal reserves, while complementary, are not identical; they cater to different clienteles and express different purposes; they must enact different fire practices. Australia exists within a global economy and a global ecology and can neither deny nor defy that reality. Any new fire practices must compromise old techniques with new needs.

The Aboriginal contribution to Australian fire history, while nearly extinguished, never expired completely. When A. W. Howitt contemplated the role of Aboriginal fire, he remarked that "more than is generally surmised" is owed the Aborigines "for having unintentionally prepared it [the land], by their annual burnings, for our occupation." That debt continues, and it extends far beyond the establishment of bush paddocks readied for English sheep and cattle. It even goes beyond the resurrection of the firestick as an implement for the administration of natural landscapes. It was the mind, not only the land, that Aboriginal firesticks prepared. The perceived pervasiveness of Aboriginal fire helped inspire an Australian system of fire protection—unique in the world—that emerged during the 1950s. And in its symbolic ashbeds, philosophical and political questions struggle upward like seedlings—questions about what is natural; questions about the relationship of Australians to their land and to one another; questions about just which Australia, and which fire regimes, it is that the parks want to preserve. The torch was passed, not extinguished.[19]

9

This Wonderful Depository of Fire

Fires moulding the landscape? It [antipodean Australia] is indeed a strange world but who knows which is the obverse of which?

—RHYS JONES

. . . as if bent upon putting the whole earth into a state of conflagration. As that earth and its works are one day to be burnt up, when the awful event takes place this wonderful depository of fire, so tremendous in effect, will surely be one instrument in the hands of its Almighty for bringing it about.

—REVEREND JOHN WOLLASTON, Journals and Diaries of Archdeacon of Western Australia, Rev. John Ramsden Wollaston (1842)

ABORIGINAL AUSTRALIA WAS IN TRUTH a "wonderful depository of fire." Fire left no part of Australia untouched, and where Aborigines congregated, in seasonal gatherings or for more durable residence, free-burning fire proliferated. "It seems impossible," Eric Rolls concluded, "to exaggerate the amount of burning in Aboriginal Australia." The coastal resources of Australia sustained an almost circumcontinental settlement; Aboriginal fires ringed the island continent. The most influential of the European explorers, Captain James Cook, referred matter-of-factly to "this continent of smoke." As he sailed its eastern shores, he entered in his journal time and again that "we saw smokes by day and fires by night upon the Main . . ." [1]

It is, on consideration, a bizarre spectacle that on this, the hottest and driest of the vegetated continents, its prehistoric peoples—nomads all—habitually walked through their annual cycles of hunting and foraging armed with a smoldering firestick. Yet the firestick was everywhere. It was, notes Josephine Flood, "one of the very few artifacts used all over prehistoric Australia at the time of contact with Europeans." For the Aborigine, fire was a universal solvent of ecological existence, and the firestick, a universal implement. "If the hundreds of small independent aboriginal societies which once occupied Australia had adopted a coat of arms," Geoffrey Blainey comments, "an appropriate emblem would have been a firestick." [2]

That Aborigines burned, and burned extensively, cannot be disputed. What is unclear is how those fires interacted with Old Australia, and how, if at all, such fire practices made Australian Aborigines distinctive. Native peoples used fire throughout the Pacific Islands, all across the landscapes of Greater Gondwana, on savannas and in Mediterranean terrains wherever they occurred or could, through fire, be shaped. Around the globe European explorers recorded coastal smokes and fires with numbing regularity, and European colonists almost universally discovered in fire a sensitive barometer of their relationship to new lands and new peoples. Not anthropogenic fire itself, but its idiosyncratic interplay with human and natural history made the fire histories of various lands distinctive. What seems to have distinguished fire in Australia was its combination of singularity with universality. It was almost everywhere and it was almost everywhere intensely felt.

A CERTAIN SIGN THAT THE
COUNTRY IS INHABITED

Its fires shaped not only the landscapes of Aboriginal Australia but the European encounter with those lands and its native peoples. Aboriginal fires were a means of discovery and a medium of engagement. Seaborne European explorers often interrogated Australia indirectly through its smoke and flame; smoke documented the movements and habits of natives too cautious to display themselves; fires traced the dimensions of a coastline too formidable to inspect except by telescope. The plenitude of fires testified to the character of the new land. They were, as the incomparable James Cook observed, "a Certain sign that the Country is inhabited." They intimated that the country could also be habitable to Europeans. Encounters between Europeans and Aborigines almost always involved an exchange of fire.[3]

All this can be found in the voyage of the *Endeavour*. Not only did this, Cook's first voyage of discovery, lead years later to the first English settlement, but the *Endeavour'* s fires introduced Europeans to a full spectrum of Aboriginal fire practices and they imprinted, with an indelible stamp, the character and irony with which European and Aborigine met. Throughout the Australian journals of Cook and his august naturalist, Sir Joseph Banks, fire glows constantly in the background, occasionally flaring into prominence. When Cook sailed to Van Diemen's Land from New Zealand, he followed Tasman's journal from 1642. The departing Tasman had watched the coastline "the whole day through" immersed in "much smoke arising from fires." [4]

A storm pushed the *Endeavour* north, and its crew sighted the Australian mainland on April 19, 1770. As they cruised north, Banks began a routine catalogue of fires. "At noon a smoak was seen a little way inland and in the Evening several more." The landscape resembled "in my imagination," Banks recorded, "the back of a lean Cow," a mottled hide of hairy forest and bare skin. Even with winter approaching, fires were abundant—some obviously campfires, others more immense and perplexing, including some larger "than any we have seen before." At night fires were all that could be viewed of the shadowed continent. During the day smokes "directed our glasses" to promising views and led ultimately to the much anticipated rendezvous with the Aborigines. By the twenty-first, fire became a common entry in Cook's journal as well. "We saw the smoke of fire in several places." Thereafter he recorded fires along with azimuths and latitudes. On May 12 the captain reported the first large fire "upon the Top of a hill." The following day he named a headland obscured by fires "Smokey Cape." [5]

But already the English had encountered those fires more directly, a painful paradigm of Aboriginal and European relationships. The night prior to landing at Botany Bay, the *Endeavour'* s crew witnessed "many fires," obviously the work of Aborigines. Anxious to inspect, Banks directed his landing party to "a small smoak arising from a very barren place." When the English finally made contact with the natives—an "old woman followed by three children"—she ignored them and instead "lighted a fire." There followed a hostile encounter with nearby Aborigines, all of which led to an exchange— guns from the one, lances from the other. The hours passed in wary watch. The Aborigines lit their cooking fires and filled their canoes with fire. The next morning they went "into the woods," Banks wrote, "where they lighted fires about a mile from us." Another shore party, this one with grass cutters, proceeded inland. There, as a sergeant of marines reported, they were approached by "14 or 15 Indians having in their hands sticks that shone . . . like a musquet." The English fled. The Aborigines pursued, halfheartedly. Firearms and firesticks—a new dialectic had come to Australia, and brought with it a new irony. [6]

The *Endeavour* continued its exploration from the sea, gradually coasting northward. The chronicle of fire and smoke continues—cooking and fishing fires along the coast, larger fires farther inland. Direct contacts were difficult. "In neither morning nor evening," Banks remarked, "were there any traces of inhabitants ever having been where we were, except that here and there trees had been burnt down." Aborigines vanished before the encroaching Europeans, leaving only campfires and towering smokes inland as emblems of their flight. Some of the coastal fires were surely signal fires by which Aborigines marked the passage of the ship. The English understood only a fraction of their intent, however, and a baffled Banks reported that "fires were made upon the hills and we saw 4 Indians through our glasses who went away along shore, in going along which they made two more fires for what purpose we could not guess." [7]

This pattern of discreet fire ended after the *Endeavour*, having foundered on the Great Barrier Reef, wrenched free and beached at the Endeavour River in Queensland for repairs. Avoidance became more difficult. Banks, for his part, eagerly searched out the natives and eventually established some peaceful contacts and exchanged gifts—welcome additions to his artifact collections. He pondered the fire practices of the "Indians" and the fire-proneness of Australia. He marveled how the natives could use a firedrill—"just as Europeans do a chocolate mill"—and get a fire "in less than 2 minutes." He expressed admiration for the spectacle of a man running on the shore outfitted with a tiny firestick who "as he ran along, just stooping down every 50 or 100 yards," would kindle "smoake and fire . . . among the drift wood and at that place almost the instant he had left it." He noted the promiscuous campfires and the use of smoke to drive off mosquitoes and the glowering smokes from deep in the hills. He "guessed," too, that "the fires which we saw so frequently as we passd alongshore, extending over a large tract of countrey and by which we could constantly trace the passage of the Indians we went from us in Endeavours river up into the countrey, were intended in some way or other for the taking of the animal calld by them *Kanguru* . . ." [8]

And, while on shore during the overhaul of the *Endeavour*, he learned about the potency of Australian fire when—taking advantage of tall grass and offshore winds—frustrated Aborigines surrounded their encampment with fire and drove the intruders to their boats in a frenzy. The episode frightened and infuriated the English, who returned fire. It staggered Banks, who had perhaps grown complacent about the ubiquitous "smoaks." It put the Europeans on notice that this land was different from those they had come to know. To cope with Australia they had to cope with Aboriginal fire. Thus with knowledge, irony, power, terror, and sublimity—with bushfire—began the Australian education of the European.

WHEREVER WE CAME:
GONDWANA'S FIRE

If the fires of Aboriginal Australia were somehow different, they were also much the same as elsewhere. Wherever Europeans voyaged, wherever they found people, they found fire. Except on ice sheets, sand deserts, and the most impenetrable rainforests, explorers witnessed anthropogenic fire. Except for lands subjected to intensive agriculture, they encountered a passionate, seemingly casual use of free-burning fire. The cooking fires, the evening fishing fires, the varieties of broadcast burning, the capacity to ignite fire by drill—all were similar to fire practices the *Endeavour* had witnessed throughout the Pacific and those fragments of Greater Gondwana it had visited. *Endeavour'*s fire was a part of Gondwana's fire. At the Isle of Pines, Cook put the matter simply: "We saw either smoke by day, or fires by night, wherever we came." [9]

Both Cook and Banks compared Aboriginal Australia with the islands of Polynesia. Of Arag Island, Cook observed "great columns of smoke" that rose "out of the woods in such parts of the island as came within . . . our sight." In the New Hebrides, the "country was illuminated with fires, from the sea-shore to the summits of the mountains"; the crews witnessed "columns of smoke . . . by day, and the fires by night." At New Caledonia, after descending the central mountains, "the first thing I observed they [the natives] did, was to set fire to the grass, etc., which had over-run the surface." It was common practice, "observed by all the nations in this sea," to let the land lie fallow after cropping, then fire it. The outcome was a curiously humanized landscape, with alternating fields and fallows, the "woods being without underwood," the country overall bearing "great resemblance to some parts of New Holland." [10]

But Banks quickly seized on an essential difference. He had not, he remarked, "observd those large fires which we so frequently saw in the Islands and New Zealand made by the Natives in order to clear the ground for cultivation . . ." The fire practices of the Australian Aborigines were special not because they used fire but because they did not use fire for agriculture. Everywhere around them elements of agriculture—more advanced gardening or sedentary farming, pastoralism with beasts that fed upon grass or cultivated fodder—created a fundamentally different pattern of fire use that boasted of fire regimes allied to active land clearing, exotic cultigens, and domesticated animals. In some respects these practices graded into or complemented Aboriginal fire usage. The herding of livestock clearly evolved out of hunting, and arable farming out of the close management of indigenous grasses and tubers. In important ways, however, fire practices differed. Agricultural fires tended to confine themselves to specific places and times, they supported an alien biota, and they compounded fire as an ecological event with other phenomena and created very different fire regimes. [11]

Within the lands of Greater Gondwana, there were other aboriginal peoples who resembled the Australians in their fire practices—the Bushmen of southern Africa, the Fuegans of South America, perhaps tribes in the wilder regions of southern India, all marginal to an expanding frontier of agriculture. Everywhere outside Australia such peoples were being driven back and compressed, like creatures trapped in a hunting surround, to lands that were inhospitable to herding and cultigens or that were otherwise unknown. By the time of European settlement the Aborigines of Australia were encircled by gardeners, farmers, and herders—fire practitioners of alternative means and ends. Throughout the islands of the Pacific, from New Zealand to New Guinea, swidden agriculture became the norm. Where large grasslands were possible, where indigenous grazers or browsers were hunted, where domesticated grazers could be introduced—there herding and hunting became common. In many places swidden led to a herding economy. Lands once cleared could be kept in grass or browse, perhaps indefinitely, by periodic burning.

But the island continent escaped. Australia was least hospitable to agriculture on its west and north shores, where the Gondwana agriculturalists were most likely to encounter it. Its soils required fertilizer. Its droughts punished cultigens. Its tropical grasses lacked sustained nutrition. The eucalypt revolution pushed Australia beyond the common stock of Gondwana flora. Its fires were too ravenous. Some of these features agriculturalists had faced and overcome elsewhere; some they had not. When agriculture succeeded, it did so with Mediterranean-derived plants and animals brought to the Mediterranean terrains of Australia. Still, there is little reason why horticulture could not have crossed the Torres Strait. It did not, however, and agriculturalists streamed around Aboriginal Australia like the waters of a creek around a large boulder.

The swidden cycle required cutting, burning, planting, and fallowing. After a few seasons, soils lay exhausted, weeds invaded, and the site had to be abandoned. After a period of many years, often decades, the swidden farmers would return to old sites and begin the cycle over again. The first clearing was the most difficult. Special slashing clubs cleaned out the understory and trimmed branches to add to the fuel and to structure the proper mixture of light and shade demanded by cultigens, particularly tubers like yams and taro. Horticulturalists felled large trees by burning through their base. Second growth was easier to prepare and reinforced the tendency to return to the same sites. Among the Polynesians, the Melanesians, the polyglot New Guineans, the peoples of Borneo and Indonesia, and—to range more widely across Greater Gondwana—the tribes of India, Madagascar, sub-Saharan Africa, forested South America, Southeast Asia, this same pattern played out. Often it supplemented an economy that continued to forage and hunt seasonally on other sites and to fire them accordingly. It was common, for example, to harvest native bracken.[12]

Introduced species had to interact with native species. If there were pyrophytes among either, the new fire regime promoted them. Pyrophytic grasses, in particular, invaded sites even as they were planted. Fire-hardy species like *Imperata* became universal weeds, reluctant to surrender a landscape once claimed. What had been forest opened into grassland or savanna. Something similar happened throughout Greater Gondwana. In Australia anthropogenic fire involved an interplay among the native scleromorphs, and it accompanied the hunting of native grazers. But elsewhere burning involved introduced livestock. Especially when combined with swidden, pastoralism forced a biotic revolution, for it attacked not only the pattern of ignition but the fuel complex itself.[13]

Again, there were important cultural and environmental differences. Tubers and pigs favored the perpetuation of woodlands; grain and cattle pushed the landscape toward grassland. The Polynesian colonization of the Pacific with taro, yams, pigs, dogs, and rats produced different consequences than the colonization of Madagascar by cattle and cultigens. Livestock filtered only slowly through the Indonesian archipelago, the Wallace Line still holding firm. In Africa and India pastoralists from the Mediterranean Basin and central Asia advanced across the landscape with dramatic effects. When combined with swidden, forest evolved into savanna. Only the Southeast Asian dog successfully entered Aboriginal Australia, where it became the dingo.

Across Greater Gondwana the combinations were many, the fire practices varied, and the new environments striking. In New Caledonia increased clearing and burning encouraged *Melaleuca* to spread to the interior. While Australia confined the genus to wetter sites, New Caledonia lacked a woody pyrophyte like *Eucalyptus* with which to compete, so *Melaleuca* moved into the ecological void. On Vanua Levu, Fiji, the swiddens became "densely covered with wild sugar canes, reeds, grass, and such hardy kinds of trees and shrubs as can best resist the fires which periodically burn up the dry herbage"—fires "that break out annually among the grass." Among the cannibals of New Britain, grasslands were fired to prevent ambush and to hunt cassowaries and wallabies. The Caroline Islanders maintained the productivity of their coconut palms by spreading out fronds around the base, far enough from the trunk to avoid scorching, then firing them. In New Zealand the Maori invasion around A.D. 1000 resulted in widespread deforestation on North Island and on the eastern half of South Island, a more or less permanent conversion of podocarp forest to tussock grass and browse; the moa, a large flightless bird, was hunted and harried to extinction. The invasion of Madagascar during the first centuries A.D. by Asian horticulturalists on the east and by African herders on the west set in motion a similar but more devastating process of land clearing, savanna spreading, and faunal extinctions such that an unburned piece of land was exceptional. Even New Guinea, rank with rainforest, witnessed a conversion to savannas within its mountains by means of swidden, the introduced grass *Imperata*, and broadcast burning. In lands that experienced at least seasonal aridity open forests as well as savannas were fired annually. During the dry monsoon, India burned. "Jungle" fires were an annual occurrence; most grasslands not converted to arable fields, particularly those in tropical climates, were shaped by human firing; the great timber trees of the subcontinent—chir *(Pinus)*, sal

(Shorea), and teak *(Tectonis)*— were all maintained by anthropogenic fire practices. The African veldt burned on a nearly annual basis. Some such practices were ancient, no doubt continuous since the days of *Homo erectus.* But swidden and pastoralism added new synergy; swidden leveled forests and broadcast fire preserved the sites in grass or savanna. The Mediterranean-climate lands around the Cape of Good Hope were stocked with pyrophytes that often erupted into fire. Throughout Greater Gondwana, fires etched the border of rainforest. Like Atlas shouldering the globe, anthropogenic fire held up the new world that humans had fashioned.[14]

And so it went. Fire and axe, fire and hoof—all around Australia in a great vault of lands, Gondwana fragments and volcanic additions, agriculturalists insinuated fire nearly everywhere it could go. They carried fire into areas for which it had, under natural conditions, been a rare and alien event. Elsewhere they competed with the fire practices of other human groups, and they restructured fire regimes in the contested territories. Where the farmers and herders could not thrive, or had not yet penetrated, hunters and foragers exploited fire practices much like those that flourished in Australia. Fire rituals, fire myths, torches to ward off threatening creatures of the dark— tigers in India, cobras in Borneo, lions in tall-veldt Africa—all were a common heritage of the fire-spangled societies that arced around Aboriginal Australia. Those beliefs, those practices extended in fact to most of the inhabited world beyond.

CALIFORNIA COGNATE: ABORIGINAL AMERICA

Similarities do not end with Greater Gondwana: Aboriginal Australia has a close cognate in aboriginal America. California, in particular, matches nicely with the southeast suite; both are Mediterranean terrains, both span a similar range of environments, both concentrate the human populations of their continents. Desert winds sweep California from time to time, driving devastating fires before them, as they do Australia. Californian tribes consisted of small bands, linguistically and historically unrelated, with the poorest groups pushed toward the interior deserts. Among the subbiotas pyrophytes flourished in abundance. While lightning fire remained prominent in remote areas, the mountains and deserts, it was submerged by anthropogenic burning in those lands most amenable to humans. Aboriginal fires—applied for broadly analogous purposes and with roughly comparable dimensions— showed remarkable parallelisms. "Our kind of people," explained a Karok informant, "never used to plow, they never used to grub up the ground, they never used to sow anything, except tobacco. All that they used to do was to burn the brush at various places, so that some good things will grow up." [15]

With minor exceptions, the Californian cultural amalgam never adopted the agriculture that had emerged in Mesoamerica and spread into much of North America. Rather, with great sophistication, local bands persisted in a foraging economy, supplemented along the coast with marine resources from fishing and shellfish and in the mountains by seasonal hunting and harvesting. Fire hunting was nearly universal, and fire was all but ubiquitous in manipulating the seeds, roots, and wild crops that were harvested out of the indigenous biota. So powerful, in fact, was the acorn economy in California oak savannas that it probably excluded the penetration of Mesoamerican-style farming. The lands outside the oak savannas—coniferous mountains, chaparral brushlands, and desert—excluded any form of agriculture except pastoralism, and that was never part of Mesoamerican economies. Along the coast grassland intercalated with other flora, a sensitive fuel easily manipulated by anthropogenic fire. Like Australian Aborigines, Californian indigenes thrived in a foraging and hunting economy for which fire was a comprehensive tool.[16]

All, or at least several, tribes exploited broadcast fire to hunt grazers like deer, antelope, rabbits, wood rats, squirrels, and grasshoppers. Burning was part of a fall hunt, and it was apparently applied preferentially to special locales. Techniques varied, of course. Some tribes or locations favored a surround by fire; others, a drive. Some preferred a mixture of fires, and a few, that they might concentrate insects and rodents, dug pits to collect the creatures steadily compressed by an encircling, shrinking ring of fire. By day hunters signaled their presence through smokes ignited on hilltops or ridges. At night they hunted by torchlight for birds and fish. Understories were accordingly open, which facilitated the movement of beasts and hunters. Sites that were burned annually graded into prairies. The succulent grasses that sprouted with the winter rains were recognized as an essential consequence of fire hunting, without which hunting would be nonrenewable. Sometimes the grasses, forbs, and avid sprouters that forced their way through the burn and fed wildlife sustained humans directly. In 1792 the naturalist José Longinos Martínez wrote that "in all of New California from Fronteras northward the gentiles have the custom of burning the brush, for two purposes; one, for hunting rabbits and hares (because they burn the brush for hunting); second, so that with the first light rain or dew the shoots will come up which they call *pelillo* and upon which they feed like cattle when the weather does not permit them to seek other food." [17]

The heaviest firing fell upon the grasses, and one outcome was to expand grasslands and to sustain oak savannas through those landscapes most thoroughly exploited by humans. An acorn economy supported the heaviest populations of aboriginal Californians and concentrated them along the coasts, lowlands, and mountain foothills. Broadcast underburning exposed fallen acorns and prevented trees other than the fire-hardy oak from invading the "fields." Exploring the Sacramento River in 1837, Captain Edward

Belcher observed that during the dry season the local tribes burned annually, "and probably such means destroy many oak plantations that otherwise would flourish." Reviewing the outcome in the early twentieth century, W. L. Jepson concluded that "it is clear that the singular spacing of the trees is a result of the periodic firing of the country—an aboriginal practice for which there is ample historical evidence."

Why are the plains treeless, is a question repeatedly asked. An understanding of the problem can only be had historically, by a consideration of the former annual vegetation and the habits of the California Indians. The herbaceous vegetation in aboriginal days grew with the utmost rankness, so rank as to excite the wonderment of the first whites . . . This dense growth was usually burned each year by the native tribes . . . The presence, therefore, of groves of oaks is rather to be explained than their absence.

The oak *(Quercus)* is an evergreen scleromorph.[18]

In the oak savanna grass seed complemented acorns. Grasses were tended in what can only be described as semicultivation by a cycle of harvesting and burning, often followed apparently by some kind of hand sowing. Clearly these practices brought selective pressures to bear on grasses that did not, as in Eurasia, have to confront overgrazing by domestic livestock. Field fires purged the sites of many fungi and pests. But the fields and harvestings were not restricted to mast and grass. Aboriginal Californians burned to improve weaving grasses and the hazel sprouts used in baskets. They burned to stimulate favored herbs, a wild sweet potato root, and seed-bearing annuals. From burned grasslands in natural salt pans they collected salt. They burned rosebud to stimulate budding, the ends of which were harvested. They fired berries and certain fruiting trees and shrubs to prune and promote flowering. They flash-burned the chaff of rice grass and cattail *(Typha)* to assist processing. They used smoke to gather insects and retard pests, like mistletoe, that might infect mast trees. They used fumigant fire for mesquite, whose beans were collected, and they applied fire to desert palms, otherwise susceptible to fungi. They burned to drive off rattlesnakes. They burned plots of native tobacco annually to prepare the site; usually this was followed by seeding. There are reports that in selected areas brush was allowed to increase so that it could be burned before planting tobacco—if so, the practice represents a close approximation to swidden. Some sites they sought to protect from fire and then hand-cleared of debris. Where they desired manzanita or sought to protect sensitive fruiting trees, they tried to exclude fire. But overall it was the selective introduction of fire, not its selective exclusion, that characterized this economy. Aboriginal Californians were, in effect, fire farmers.

Through such cultivations the dominant environments of California resembled a near simile to classic rural landscapes. The critical distinction was that California, like Australia, lacked the essential trait of true agriculture, the substitution of domesticated flora and fauna for native species. Instead the scene evolved out of indigenous biotic stocks—from oak and mesquite, not fruit or imported nut trees; out of local grasses, not Eurasian cereals; with deer and rabbits, not cattle, horses, and sheep. So, too, aboriginal Californians exploited, with subtlety and variety, their indigenous fire practices as surrogates to imported implements like plows and scythes and fertilizers. Broadcast fire was incorporated within an evolving matrix of peoples and biotas; it was not used, as purely agricultural economies use it, to convert the native flora to ash as a stimulant for exotic cultigens. Though powerful, it could only massage the indigenous biota. It remains an interesting question whether aboriginal peoples resorted to fire because it favored the species they desired or whether those species became prominent because of a human preference for fire as an environmental tool. Regardless, the analogy between aboriginal America and Aboriginal Australia is phenomenally close.

The similarity encompasses whole suites of fire practices. Californians set campfires at the base of large oaks, which after many years toppled the trees to the ground. While traveling they ignited campfires and signal fires, which they rarely extinguished. They burned around villages to control snakes and pests and to prevent ambush. They fired along major thoroughfares. They burned around heavily used springs. They cremated their dead. Where humans were most dense, fires were most abundant. Aboriginal Californians, too, projected anthropogenic fire far beyond their own daily presence by means of distant sites visited as part of an annual cycle and fired to render accessible foodstuffs only seasonally abundant.[19]

No less than in Australia, this florescence of fires created a dynamic matrix within which natural and accidental ignitions had to coexist. Sedimentary varves laced with charcoal in the Santa Barbara Channel and other depositories suggest a preaboriginal fire cycle of roughly sixty years. But this "pattern" was episodic, largely the outcome of intense fires powered by offshore desert winds. Aboriginal burning restructured this regime by reshaping some landscapes, particularly those amenable to grasses, and by encouraging the remainder to burn whenever its fuels prepared it to receive fire. When anthropogenic fire was removed the landscape quickly reverted to woody species—to chaparral in the foothills and coast ranges, to conifers in the mountains, to choking thickets where open vistas had formerly prevailed.[20]

European explorers along the coast of California referred often to fire and smoke. Sailing along the coast in 1542, Juan Cabrillo sighted numerous shore fires and "great smokes" farther inland. At San Diego he witnessed "many valleys and plains and many smokes and mountains in the interior" and named the harbor the Bay of Smokes. Sebastián Vizcaíno reported in 1602 that the Indians "made so many columns of smoke on the mainland that at night it looked like a procession and in the daytime the sky was overcast." Vancouver thought a volcano must have erupted in the interior, so voluminous was the pall of smoke. Traveling in central California, Deflot de Mofras dismissed as "ordinary spectacles" fires that "smolder for months and spread from one end of the province to the other," occasionally astonishing an observer by sweeping the sky "with black and copper clouds," inflicting "stifling heat," and raining a "cloud of ashes." [21]

The conflicts between aborigines and Europeans was complicated here, as in Australia, by the introduction of agriculture. It is a shared, sad irony in the history of both lands that aboriginal firing prepared the landscape perfectly for European pastoralism, for once established, pastoralism demanded a different regimen of fire. Early land-use conflicts between Californians and Spaniards often focused on fire practices. In October 1774 a distraught Captain Moncada of Monterey related how he led soldiers and settlers out to battle aboriginal fires "to preserve the grass for our animals." The "heathens," he explained, "are wont to cause these fires because they have the bad habit, once having harvested their seeds, and not having any other animals to look after except their stomachs, they set fire to the brush so that new weeds may grow to produce more seeds, also to catch the rabbits that get confused and overcome by the smoke." Twenty years later Governor Arrillaga complained to the mission president about "widespread damage which results to the public from the burning of the fields, customary up to now among both Christian and Gentile Indians in this country, whose childishness has been unduly tolerated . . ." [22]

Like the fire practices evident throughout Greater Gondwana, the California comparison complicates a simple assessment of Aboriginal fire. It both clarifies and confuses. It makes the reports of Australian explorers and settlers more understandable and the claims for major Aboriginal influence on the land more reasonable; considered by themselves, there is nothing peculiar about Aboriginal fire practices. To observe that the Australian Aborigine incorporated fire into the technology and mythology of daily life is only to declare him human.

At the same time, the comparison confutes the meaning of Aboriginal fire within the Australian context. Aboriginal fire practices appear far less special, or rather their distinctiveness must be understood as deriving not from themselves alone but from the peculiar synergism that developed between fire and the other components of the Australian scene. The Californian environment possessed richer soils, a more active geology, and fuller biotic diversity; lightning was denser; desert winds tended to channel into specific topographic flumes, like avalanches, not sweep the whole landscape like a tsunami, as in Australia; no single species in California dominated as the eucalypts did in Australia. New species, new peoples repeatedly infiltrated into California, which was far less isolated than Old Australia. The Californian biota showed more resilience; fire was one dynamic process among several.

In Australia fire went beyond the status of an ecological process or a human practice and became something like an informing principle. No account of California can disregard its phenomenal fire history, but fire alone can explain only so much. It goes further in Australia, and no comparison, however close, can explain away totally the peculiar status of bushfire in the Australian landscape or banish satisfactorily its specter from Australian history. Burning California added another voice, if a powerful one, to a chorus of commentators. But Australia's burning bush remained a savage, enigmatic oracle for Australian identity.

"TO BURN EVERY THING ROUND US BEFORE WE BEGIN"

Old Australia and Aboriginal fire worked on one another with uncommon vigor, with almost cunning insight into the special strengths and weaknesses of each party. The susceptibility of Old Australia to fire encouraged Aborigines to burn widely, and pervasive burning pushed the scleromorphs and pyrophytes into further prominence. Its special environment gave fire a special status. Those fires, in turn, bestowed on Aboriginal Australia a unique character.

Compared with the fire practices of agriculturalists, Aboriginal fire was more subtle, more allied to a natural biota. When farmers burned, they used fire to dispose of native vegetation, to prepare a site to receive exotic cultigens; pastoralists, to encourage forage for alien livestock, or to sow alien grasses. But Australia's Aborigines burned to select from among indigenous flora, and their fires had to conform to the rhythms and flows of those fuels, droughts, and winds.

Compared to other hunting and foraging societies, Australia's Aborigines used fire with singular ruthlessness. Many societies carried embers with them on their journeys, and all could make fire; but perhaps no other people routinely walked through the landscape with firesticks ceaselessly dripping embers. That habit made fire a ready implement for almost any purpose. By tying up one hand, it almost commanded Aborigines to use fire in preference to other options. That Old Australia was primed for fire made its use effective. Aboriginal fire and native biotas readjusted, one to the other, and set in motion a process of mutual, positive reinforcement that rendered the firestick much more than a slow match or a blazing fetish. It became a flaming lever that, suitably placed, moved a continent.

Ark Australia had transported a heavy consignment of pyrophytes from

Gondwana. The degeneration of its soils, its northerly drift to aridity, its fantastic isolation as the island continent—all established special conditions that rendered Australia singularly susceptible to scleromorphs, and readied its scleromorphs for fire. When ignition became both abundant and constant through the arrival of *Homo,* a positive feedback welded eucalypts, humans, and fire into a ruling triumvirate. Elsewhere fire remained a seasonal or episodic phenomenon, and human fire practices part of a set of tools, one exploited in phase with a complex calendar. In Australia, Aborigines used fire whenever and wherever they could. Fire became a sublime and terrible obsession, a biotic and cultural addiction.

It is to be expected then that, in some fashion, new arrivals had to interact with Aboriginal Australia through fire. Australia fronts the East Indies, which were connected with major maritime civilizations, and time and again exploring parties or vessels driven by storms must have reached its shores. Most probably sailors saw the low-lying coast because of towering smoke columns. A routine traffic in trepang (sea slugs) and possibly slaves developed between northern Australia and Indonesia. Beginning in the seventeenth century annual trade and trepanging voyages flourished between Arnhemland and Macassar, by then under Dutch control. There were annual visits by prau, and Macassans erected structures, planted tamarind trees and other cultigens, and kept kettle fires boiling.[23]

There is a legend in Arnhemland about a Macassan who established a homestead complete with garden and later conversed with a dog (surely a dingo). The Macassan gave the dog some matches, and the dog reciprocated with firesticks. While they sat some distance away, smoke appeared near the man's dwelling. The Macassan rushed to his house, now fully ablaze. Immediately, he announced in despair and anger that he was going back to sea, to his distant home. Fire had driven him away. Where the posts to the house rested, shell middens rose skyward.[24]

The Macassans departed permanently around the time the Europeans began to seriously explore the eastern flank of Australia, but these latest visitors would not pass with the seasons. They, too, saw the Australian littoral through smoke and fire. In circumnavigating the continent Flinders observed how Aboriginal fires served as beacons for coasting at night, and Parkinson reported that the *Endeavour* "saw several fires along the coast lit up one after another, which might have been designed as signals to us." Ironically, the signal fires ignited to warn others about the intruders only assisted their travels. That the first encounters between European and Aborigine should involve an exchange of fire should surprise no one. A shore party at Botany Bay mistook firesticks for a kind of musket. The stay at the Endeavour River brought Aboriginal fire to bear on the English, which the English returned in (altered) kind.[25]

For Australian fire history, that latter episode holds special symbolism.

The incident began when Cook beached the *Endeavour* for repairs and set up an encampment. Relations between natives and sailors were cautious but appeared cordial. When Aborigines insisted on taking a portion of the turtles collected by the crew and the crew refused, however, trouble boiled over. The Aborigines tried to carry away the carcass. The crew forcibly resisted. Confused and angry, the Aborigines retired to shore, seized fire "from under a pitch kettle," and ignited the windward grass, which burned, as a horrified Banks recalled, with "vast fury." The shore party fled to their boat, beaten off by fire. The English returned, and "with the greatest obstinacy," Cook observed, the natives fired more grasses, waving away the white ghosts and threatening to burn other goods still left on shore. The imperturbable Cook fired his musket, hit one Aborigine (not critically), and the pack fled to the scrub. The Europeans attacked the bushfire, rescued their equipment, and resolved to take future precautions.

For the Aborigines the incident was a defiant, hopeless, misplaced vale-dictory to a way of life. The hoarding of turtles, the strange clothes, the confusion of belligerence and friendliness, the natural history collections, the animals on ship—all signified that the new hominids held odd mores, defined their relationship to nature in unusual terms, and possessed curious biological allies. The firearms testified to new fire technologies. The perma-nent goods stockpiled in the tent told of new food chains to which they had access, of values attributed to material property, of principles of fixed owner-ship, all of them hostile to broadcast fire. Collectively, if powerful enough, the Europeans could circumscribe the dominion of Aboriginal fire as Aborigi-nes had the domain of natural fire. The Aborigines retired to the woods and ignited the land on all sides. "All the hills about us for many miles were on fire," gushed Banks, already hedging into romanticism, "and at night made the most beautifull appearance imaginable." [26]

For the Europeans, the incident was a fitting initiation to their settlement of a new and alien environment. Even Banks, the resident savant, had "little Idea of the fury with which the grass burnt in this hot climate, nor of the difficulty of extinguishing it when once lighted." Obviously, Australia's spe-cial hazards required special preparations. With ominous resolve Banks de-termined the next time "to burn Every thing round us before we begin." [27]

BOOK III

The European

10

Entwining Fire

But as they have been passing from creation they [Aborigines] have performed their allotted task; and the fires of the dark child of the forest have cleared the soil, the hills and the valleys of the super-abundant scrub and timber that covered the country and presented a bar to its occupation.

—J. C. BYRNE, *Twelve Years' Wanderings in the British Colonies . . . (1848)*

From what I have seen, in this country, of the effects of sodburning, I am more and more convinced, that . . . it forms a valuable part of British husbandry; and may become an instrument of real improvement, in places where it is not, at present, known; especially in bringing the WASTE LANDS of the Island into a proper course of cultivation.

—WILLIAM MARSHALL, *The Rural Economy of the West of England (1796)*

IN THE OPENING to *The Tree of Man* Patrick White sketches a stringybark Garden of Eden into which intrudes an unnamed "man." This Australian Adam, amid an "immense" silence, strikes a tree several times with his axe, then builds a fire. "He sighed at last, because the lighting of his small fire had kindled in him the first warmth of content. Of being somewhere. That particular part of the bush had been made his by the entwining fire. It licked at and swallowed the loneliness." [1]

The European settlement of Australia was a complex affair. It was both calculated and reckless. It began under one set of purposes and suppositions and propagated beyond any control or expectation. It was sometimes heroic and endlessly ironic. What began as a prison quickly swelled into a broad biotic invasion that utterly reconstructed the environment of the island continent. The haste of settlement was breathtaking, and everywhere accented with fire.

153

Fire catalyzed the violence of colonization and accelerated the rate of its biotic reactions. It was agent, expression, tool, and symbol. Between Aborigine and European, fire was both a point of contention and a medium of exchange. Between Australia and European, fire illuminated and obscured. It highlighted the coast and hid the interior. George Evans complained that it burned off "Marks in the Trees" cut by surveying parties. Mitchell lamented that it obscured distant landscapes in flame and smoke, blocked off the horizon, and so darkened the sky at night that it prevented him "from ascertaining our latitude." Mostly, the fires were just there. Help or hindrance, they had to be accepted.[2]

The character of Australian fire is not easy to assess. Natural fire preceded both Aboriginal and European, and anthropogenic fire accompanied their every move. Eventually, for the European settlers, as for the Aborigines, there were two antithetical fires—the anthropogenic and the natural, the domesticated and the wild, the fire in the bush and the bushfire. The hearth fire echoed a familiar past. It linked immigrant with "Home," not unlike those torches carried by colonists in the ancient world by which they transported the sacred fire of the mother city to new environs. The hearth fire could be distributed to the bush and help remake it into a usable land. To a large extent Europeans had exploited agricultural burning, ultimately derived from the hearth fire, to remake Europe.

The bushfire, however, pointed to an alien, threatening, often incomprehensible future. It lurked in the dense scrub and waving grasslands; it could appear suddenly and uncontrollably; it could sweep away in minutes a society painfully transplanted over years and decades. Fanned by desert winds from a forbidding interior, it represented everything terrible and inscrutable about the bush. Explorers and settlers confronted bushfire as a constant, unpredictable hazard. "The Mountains have been fired," Evans wrote on his travels across the Great Dividing Range, and "had we been on them we could not have escaped." At Frew's waterhole John Stuart found "the plain burnt for ten miles." They were fortunate to have escaped, Stuart wrote, for "nothing could have lived in such a fire, and had we been caught in it we must have perished." Because they had prudently preburned around their campsite, King's party felt unconcerned when Aborigines fired the countryside about them, and his men soon joined in, "for amusement," increasing the "conflagration . . . so that the whole surface was a blaze." Then came the surprise—a shift of wind, a pocket of heavy fuels, a burst of furious burning—as the fire stunned the explorers and sent them packing their tents and gear to the water's edge. The line between controlled fire and wildfire was a fine one.[3]

The Australian bushfire was to fire what the eucalypt was to trees and the kangaroo to grazers. It had taken a separate evolution. Australia had progressed relentlessly toward status as a fire continent, increasing the importance of fire, while Europe had steadily expelled wildfire, pushing it out of the core and toward the perimeter. This contrast magnified the encounter between European and Australian fire. There was no single attitude toward fire, any more than there was any one set of fire practices. Rather, the interaction between a European legacy and an Australian environment was multiple; one practice often overlaid others, new practices were invented, curious (often incomplete) transfers occurred from Aborigine to European, and at least some Aboriginal practices persisted in selected environments. Lessons once learned had to be relearned. In the end the European bushman, like the Aborigine, became a nomad, a scleromorph—attacking with new tools the soil impoverishment, the aridity, and the fire that had shaped Australia and was equally shaping him. Like Patrick White's Adamic archetype, the newcomers found themselves entwined with Australia by fire.

IT WAS ALL A PLANTED GARDEN

There was little doubt among European explorers and colonists that Australia was different from Britain. But the antipodes had their analogues. Some scenes resembled, with eerie fidelity, those from the home islands. At Botany Bay an excited Captain Cook journeyed into the "Country, which we found diversified with Woods, Lawns, and Marshes. The woods are free from underwood of every kind, and the trees are at such a distance from one another that the whole Country, or at least great part of it, might be Cultivated without being obliged to cut down a single tree." The soils, "except in the Marshes," produced a quantity of "good Grass." The exploring party sighted a small animal "something like a Rabbit," found the dung of an animal which, they determined, "could not be less than a Deer," and discovered the "Track of a Dog, or some such like Animal." The trees showed marks of cutting and bark-stripping. Ever eager for nature's novelties, Banks added some curiosities such as "Loryquets" and "Cocatoos" and a tree that yielded gum "much like *sanguis draconis.* " But he also reported a small animal whose feet were "like those of a polecat or weesel," quails "much resembling our English ones," and sandy country that looked like "our Moors in England, as no trees grow upon it but every thing is coverd with a thin brush of plants about as high as the knees." If many of the pieces seemed strange, the assembled puzzle looked uncannily familiar. The scene encouraged those who determined to remake Australia into the largest of the British Isles.[4]

Those impressions were not without substance. Britain had edged into a wet climate rather than a dry one—its climate deteriorated by becoming waterlogged rather than droughtridden. Yet much of its lands were covered with marginal or infertile soils, and it exhibited a history of anthropogenic changes from the earliest times. Britons had cleared, burned, hunted species

to extinction, and introduced exotic flora and fauna with devastating consequences. The Pleistocene revolutionized Britain more thoroughly than it
had Australia, and when that fantastic epoch concluded, its events exaggerated the fire consciousness of each island. In Britain, fire consciousness was
lower than history supported, and in Australia, perhaps higher than circumstances warranted.

Climatic oscillations affected nearly all of Britain. Glacial episodes submerged most of the island under ice sheets; even the climate of the spared
southern rim became periglacial under the influence of the ice sheets. Interglacials witnessed rising seas that severed land connections to the continent
and flooded lowlands, principally those in the southeast. Although it is possible that pockets of settlement persevered throughout these cycles, so comprehensive was each shock wave of Pleistocene ice and ocean that most of
the island had to be recolonized after every recession. Compared to Pleistocene Australia, the natural and human history of Pleistocene Britain was
far more concentrated in time and space. The human occupation of Britain
was more recent, and once begun—despite a permanent channel separating
it from the continent—the islands were subjected to repeated, comprehensive invasions from Europe. The revolution was more profound because,
from early times, it was agricultural.

There are records of Paleolithic hunters at scattered sites in the south of
England that date back through several glaciations. But it appears that the
last major episode, the Devensian glaciation (c. 18,000–15,000 years ago),
effectively depopulated the island, and the modern history of human usage
must date from the recovery that attended the receding ice and rising seas.
Rapid climatic changes encouraged considerable erosion; glaciation scoured
soil profiles; an upheaval in island flora and fauna followed. A succession of
forest species reclaimed former ice fields and periglacial steppes. Elk, horse,
reindeer, and red deer arrived along with human hunters, while lion, mammoth, and woolly rhinoceros vanished. Preferred sites included the banks of
major rivers and lakes. Paleolithic settlers exploited the littoral. Everywhere
they claimed caves.[5]

The real tremors of revolution arrived with the Mesolithic, roughly the
period between 10,000 and 5,000 years ago. The climate ameliorated and
stabilized; sea level reached its modern equilibrium (c. 7,500 years ago),
achieving the final isolation of Britain from the European mainland; and an
influx of primitive farmers and pastoralists broke the landscape like punc-
ture wounds and abrasions, a source of spreading infection. By 5,500 years
ago a mixed deciduous forest dominated by oak and elm replaced conifers
and birches. But even as this biota matured, it was attacked by local land
clearing and almost certainly subjected to broadcast burning. Clearing encouraged soil degeneration. On wet sites, lowland or upland both, deforestation led to peat; on drier sites, to heath and moor. Its trees had functioned

like biotic pumps, draining the subsurface waters and venting them by transpiration to the air. Felling them affected Britain as destroying its windmills would Holland; the soils slowly flooded with excess water. Continued burning and grazing, moreover, prevented forest regeneration, so that sites once propelled into peat could not easily be restored without major climatic change or human intervention. Local sites enlarged, and through centuries of repeated clearing, burning, and grazing impauperate soils—leached and flooded—matured, spreading like some floral leprosy across extensive areas. It has been estimated that, through such means, as much as five-eighths of England and Wales experienced soil acidification and disrupted nutrient cycles.[6]

The economy of the Mesolithic was mixed and transitional. Hunting complemented herding, and foraging, agriculture. The case of the dog is a cameo of what occurred—first a competitor for wild game, then a domesticated partner for hunting, later an assistant to herd flocks. The flora shifted from dense woods to more sun-tolerant trees and to browse-rich understories that demanded light. The association between clearance and hunting is reinforced when Britain is compared to Ireland. There isolation prevented repopulation by major ungulates and Mesolithic records show little evidence of land clearing. For Britain a likely scenario is that sites once cleared were kept open as hunting grounds by broadcast burning.

From the Paleolithic to the Neolithic (c. 3,000 years ago) humans expanded their influence with relentless pressure, like a stone slowly sinking into paraffin. They roamed more widely and affected lands more intensely. Disturbers by nature, they thrived amid the climatic and biotic disruptions. When those disequilibrations acted in concert, they rewrote the landscape of Britain. The revision became a revolution, however, with the arrival of Neolithic peoples more heavily dependent on livestock and cereal cultivation. Britain crossed a threshold that set its biotic evolution on a nearly irreversible course. Blanket peat spread across highlands. The biotic future of Britain belonged with its humans; they determined what grew and what perished, what lands degenerated and what would be reclaimed.

For reasons not entirely understood, the advent of the Neolithic throughout northern Europe coincided with a dramatic decline in elm. The agencies involved are complicated, but the recession of the "high forest" symbolized by elm correlates with remarkable fidelity to the advent of an agricultural economy associated with aggressive land clearing. Farmers felled and burned forests, planted plots to cereals, then abandoned the sites to weeds and eventually to reforestation. In stratigraphic profiles, the catastrophic loss of elm pollen corresponds to thickening layers of charcoal. It was a classic slash-and-burn regime, now known by the Danish word *landnam* ("land taking"). (Ironically, the original English word for the process, *swidden*, which derives from the Old Norse *svithinn* [related to the verb "to singe"] has become a generic expression to describe this pattern of farming everywhere except at its linguistic point of origin.)[7]

Low population pressures kept a balance among the subbiotas. Long fallow times locally restored a semblance of the original forest, while continued burning and grazing pushed abandoned fields into grasses and browse. The peoples migrating across Europe from Asia Minor or Central Asia were, after all, trying to recreate the environments of origin for their cultigens and livestock, which meant the steppes and shrublands of Asia Minor. It is likely that they used fire accordingly. The clearings that dappled Britain were more a cameo of a pastoral landscape than a miniature of a landscape dedicated to arable cultivation. The Neolithic farmers and herders used the native trees to support an exotic flora of cereal crops and a parade of alien browsers. The trees they burned to create ash and promote sunlight; the understories they kept in preferred berries, forbs, and browse; elm and alder bark they exploited as cattle fodder.

The *landnam* phase in Britain lasted for centuries. It expanded Mesolithic precedents enormously, and it persisted through waves of new invaders—the Beaker peoples from the Rhine basin, the Celts, the Romans, the Angles and Saxons, the Vikings, and the Normans. None of the newcomers imposed a dramatically different regime. Rather, if warriors, they seized political control over existing practices or, if settlers, accentuated trends that were already operating. They expanded the realm of agriculture, accelerated land clearing, and introduced greater numbers of exotics, both as crops and cereals, livestock and faunal pests. A critical moment came with the gradual promotion of sheep over cattle because sheep could not be easily fed in the woods, as cattle and swine could; they required pastures, which meant greater deforestation and the cultivation of special pasture grasses, and they could not coexist with deer, which further prevented their agistment in forests. They demanded, too, the extirpation of predators, the substitution of the domesticated dog for the wild wolf. Since Britain lacked a wild equivalent for sheep, their wholesale introduction required a wholesale reconstruction of the British biota.

As the climate deteriorated, which for Britain meant an increase in moisture—the enlargement of oceanic over continental influences—these anthropogenic practices wove a tapestry of cultivated and degenerated landscapes. The arable lands became more intensively farmed and hedgerows encased the open fields. Wastelands served as seasonal pasturage, though in places like the Fens agriculturalists began converting waste to field. Elsewhere, particularly in the uplands, clearing, grazing, and firing initiated more blanket peat, the onset of empty moors. As farming became more sedentary, villages and towns were platted out. And, interestingly, nearly every people preserved some sacred groves or woods. With the consolidation of the Norman hegemony, the basic structure of the British landscape was complete. A final surge of reclamation by monasteries (the Cistercians, in particular) and a bustling peasantry even carried agriculture into lands previously shunned as barren.

There were modifications over the next few centuries. The Normans im-. posed an immense system of "forests," which meant land subject to forest law and dedicated to the king's hunting. At one point, forests officially enclosed nearly a quarter of England, but claims of this magnitude could not resist a growing population and the peasantry never lost completely their rights of access to the lands for traditional usage. Forest courts severely punished crimes against vert and venison—destruction of the habitat and poaching of deer. Yet forest law also provided for the agistment of livestock on a seasonal basis and for gathering other products. Most forests included some woods, often disguised as "covert," or cover for deer; other "forests" consisted largely of heath, grass, or other flora. As the lands were sold off or otherwise disafforested, the woods receded. It is reported, too, that the Normans introduced rabbits to Britain, with predictable devastation.[8]

The Black Death depopulated vast stretches of rural Britain and forced abandonment of much marginal land and many villages. As population rebuilt from the plague, reclamation revived. More marginal land was reworked into fields or paddocks, and arable land was converted to pasture for sheep. The rage for "improvement," a kind of agricultural Enlightenment, drove landowners to still more intensive cultivation and husbandry throughout the seventeenth and eighteenth centuries, an agricultural revolution that reworked old lands and reclaimed new. Reports poured out from Parliament and local improvement societies that urged systematic reform—fertilization with marl as well as with manure, new field crops like turnips, crop rotations to sustain fertility, new implements, new winter fodder for livestock, and new techniques by which to cultivate former wastelands.

Sheep, of course, posed special problems, and the passion for wool pervaded land use as the agricultural revolution metamorphosed into an industrial revolution. One response was the notorious parliamentary enclosures that continued into the middle of the nineteenth century. But enclosure was itself symptomatic of an interlocking chain of desires and demands: improved wool required improved breeds of sheep, which required superior pasturage, which required more land and more intensive cultivation of existing land. It was during this period that white clover, imported from the Low Countries, became widely planted for its nitrogen-fixing properties as well as its palatability as sheep fodder. Britain was becoming a sheep run. The need for more land pushed the technology of soil improvement into sites previously written off as hopelessly barren.

By the time the *Endeavour* surveyed Botany Bay, the British countryside was a land of minute manipulation and intensive consumption. Woods were confined to almost ceremonial groves, or otherwise coppiced or pollarded.

The underbrush had been disciplined into hedges or driven into remote moors. Grasslands had evolved into manured paddocks or manicured lawns. Herding became husbandry; specially bred flocks fed on specially cultivated grasses or field fodder. Grasses that thrived on browsing and trampling replaced those that thrived on burning. Everywhere the human hand shaped, pruned, felled, drained, plowed, planted, replaced. Even in the 1720s Daniel Defoe reported with approval the observations of two "Foreign Gentlemen" who remarked of the scene from Bushey Heath that "England was not like other Country's, but it was all a planted Garden." [9]

That James Cook could perceive an equivalent landscape in Australia testifies in part to the extraordinary accomplishments of the Aborigine and his cultivating firestick. What Defoe wrote of Britain was also true of Australia, "In a Word, it was all Nature, and yet look'd all Art." The Aboriginal achievement was ironic, however. The British intruders were British "improvers" ready to exploit the environments of Aboriginal Australia much as the Neolithic invaders of Britain had reworked the lands shaped by the sophisticated hunters and foragers and protoagriculturalists who had preceded them. Once begun in earnest, the reclamation of Australia attempted to recapitulate the reclamation of Britain. British settlers had the example of their own past, the vast preparations of the Aborigines, and the vigor of their concurrent agricultural revolution, for the Second Reclamation of Britain was approaching a climax. There was little reason for them to be intimidated by sandy or moorlike or boggy soils along coastal Australia, or to fret over water imbalances—or to shirk from fire as a vehicle of land reform. That, too, was a venerable part of British history.[10]

HOME FIRES:
A FIRE HISTORY OF BRITAIN

Probably no fire practice in Australia—or throughout all of Gondwana— lacked an antecedent in British history.

Almost certainly natural fires flickered across the landscape. They burned with special vigor during the drier episodes of Pleistocene and Holocene history when the British Isles assumed a more continental climate. Spring fires burned prior to green-up; fall fires after curing; and summer fires, even in peat, during times of drought. The biota that recolonized Britain during the interglacials brought with it a heritage born of disturbance and often forged in fire. Moors degenerate unless fired; grasslands and heath recede before advancing forests, particularly Scots pine, unless they are burned or heavily browsed. Even-aged stands of conifers probably reflect a natural swidden of windfall and fire, a potential never completely lost. A Glengarry pine forest that burned from an escaped moor fire in 1740 regenerated spontane-

ously, for example, in what was surely an echo of natural processes. A great
fire in the Duack Valley that reportedly destroyed 2.5 million trees in 1746
reforested itself with "a new crop of excellent timber." A fire in 1948 incinerated over seven hundred acres of standing conifer forest in two hours.
So thoroughly have humans reworked the fuels of the island, however,
that contemporary statistics on lightning fire are a poor guide to past frequencies. Lacking dry lightning storms, savage droughts, or desert winds, the
amount of fire prevalent in Britain has been almost wholly determined by
humans.[11]

Paleolithic hunters carried anthropogenic fire—fire of hearth and field—
across the Channel. They gave Old Britain a background count of routine
burning, recorded by a shift in understory composition and a persistence of
grasslands on selected sites. Waves of new migrants from the continent introduced livestock and crops, and they adjusted their fire practices accordingly.
It was easy to adapt burning for hunting to burning for herding, somewhat
more complex to adapt foraging fires to the cultivation of alien crops, for the
problem was not simply to extract resources from the indigenous flora but to
replace that biota with an alien flora. But there could be no slashing without
burning, so swidden fires merged with broadcast burns; sites once felled
could be maintained in grass or browse through free-burning fire. Overall,
fire became more common and more regular. "Even though Mesolithic societies were technologically simple," a group of British archaeologists has concluded, "their usage of fire seems to have conferred on them the ability to
alter their surroundings in a purposeful way." Some of those environmental
changes became more or less permanent.[12]

The full revolution came with fire and axe. Fires multiplied, and their
geography swelled as *landnam* and livestock—as Neolithic agriculture—
seeped through Britain. Fire made possible the clearance of felled deciduous
forest; it prepared ground for cereal crops of wheat, flax, and barley, and for
pulse crops like the bean, lentil, and domestic pea. It expanded the domain
of forage, within the woods and beyond them, greening up the island for
pastoralists. It assisted in the gathering of wild foodstuffs and in the hunting
of wildlife. Even in historic times, there are records of fires used to smoke
out fowl in Scottish caves and of torches used to fish illicitly for salmon.[13]

Fire practices restructured, often in irreversible ways, the environments
of Britain; not fire alone, but fire associated with felling, grazing, and exotic
plants. Along with axe and beast, fire cleared pine-birch uplands, extended
heathlands, and set into motion a biotic conversion that included a chain of
soil impoverishment. Alien weeds replaced native flora. On many marginal
sites fire helped tip the biotic balance from nutrient sufficiency to degener-
acy, from forest to upland moor and lowland mire. Once established, those
waving heaths and mossy mats, during droughts, became vast fuses to carry
fire through the wastelands. And as with ancient Australia, fire preserved

that Neolithic record and made possible its interpretation by charring protected artifacts and leaving residual charcoal for dating by stratigraphy and carbon-14.[14]

In most of Britain, land clearing was a multiple, not a singular event; it was repeated over and again through several centuries. Burning accompanied each episode and persisted long after the initial bout of forest land clearing such that successive waves of farmers and pastoralists steadily brought the landscape under a different regimen of fire, one tied to the rhythms of crops and domesticated beasts. The great surge of Cistercian-led land clearing saw gangs slashing and burning across the countryside, and fighting escaped fires with brooms, rakes, and axes. Farmers burned straw after harvest and fired their fallow to fertilize and to purge fields of pests. Where pastoralists exploited native grasslands or the woods range, they often burned, particularly sites remote from permanent settlement or on lands unsuitable for farming. Without burning the principal grasses and shrubs became decadent and unpalatable. Thus moor (or muir) burning became routine, and herders burned gorse on hill pastures and fired the poorer grasses on downs. Where the range was used seasonally, it was often fired; Welsh shepherds, for example, burned in the fall as part of their cycle of transhumance. The southern Pennine moors, and others, were apparently pyrogenic, the outcome of firing and grazing. [15]

In one of the best-known examples, villagers regularly burned the ling swaying over Yorkshire moors, the origin of the term "swiddening." Yorkshiremen fired the swiddens in patches according to an agricultural calendar that spanned seasons and years. Mostly they burned in the spring, and in theory they fired only the older, decadent heath (*Calluna*) on a roughly ten-year cycle. Pastoralists recognized that such practices introduced variety to the landscape and ensured vigorous growth. "Burning the ling" was also the preliminary stage in turf graving, the harvesting of flaughts and peats from drier moors.[16]

The agricultural revolution of the eighteenth century inaugurated a whole new round of agricultural fires. Some targeted untouched or regrown forests—classic slash-and-burn cultivation. Thus, as the Reverend Arthur Young prescribed for Sussex, "if the forest be broken up for the first time, the furze, ling, broom, heath, with all other rubbish covering the surface, should be burnt as it stands, and then pared and burnt" preparatory to planting. Something analogous occurred where moss had advanced over formerly felled forests, the onset of peat formation. An observer from Aberdeen and Banff noted that such sites featured "firm and fertile land, which, no doubt, is unfit for the plough unless it is burned, and then the crops luxuriate wonderfully with ashes. After a year or two new ashes must be made with new fires." As farmers exploited these immense organic soils, the deep layers disclosed "huge trunks of trees" buried "and in many places de-

stroyed by fires." Where surface fuels were too light to support deep burning, wood ashes (potash) were added and ploughed into the soil.[17]

The reclamation of impoverished or organic soils—the farming of moor,
heath, peat, and sod—was a major thrust of the agricultural revolution. In
this Second Reclamation agriculturalists mimicked the practices of the original *landnam*, except that they cut and burned soils instead of forests. In
dense peat or loam, the practice evolved into sod burning (also known as
burn baiting, beat burning, or burn baking) in which the organic mat was
pared, heaped, and fired. A specified sequence of annual crops followed, at
the end of which the process was repeated. In his compendium of West
Country agriculture, William Marshall (1796) concluded that "sodburning
is essential to success." The practice spread northward to Scotland and acquired the sobriquet "denshiring" ("Devonshiring") as one of its many
names. In shallow heathland soils, it converted waste to arable. In the Fens
the Reverend Young observed that "it is scarcely possible, profitably, to bring
boggy, mossy, peat soils, from a state of nature into cultivation, without the
assistance of fire." In Sussex he declaimed that paring and burning was "one
of the greatest improvements which land is susceptible of receiving." The
farmer knows that, having slashed and burned the turf, he is "in possession
of a dunghill," and selects his crops accordingly. After four years of cropping, the land was rested, the turf rebuilt and readied for another cycle.[18]

The spread of sheep and herding to new lands encouraged broadcast fire
on nonarable lands. An observer to the Highlands in 1790 spoke of the
"liberality, worthy of imitation" with which a lord "suffered the heath to be
burnt," a "useful practice." Others witnessed muir burning "practiced with
advantage, by the sheep-farmers in the south country" and imitated them.
The coming of the English sheep to the Highlands inaugurated the notorious
Clearances, but the Year of the Burnings had its environmental symbolism as
well. Fires filled the dead heathlands vacated by retreating snows, and acquired new dimensions; patch burning gave way to broadcast burning on a
colossal scale. As sheep multiplied across the landscape, more waste was
burned and more woodlands felled and fired to support them. Under the
impress of fire and grazing, woods became heath and heather became grass.
In order to improve sheep pasture, it is reported that pastoralists kindled a
great fire in "Glen Strath-Farrer" that burned "twelve miles of pine, birch
and oak woods." The clearing of the Highland clans went hand-in-glove
with the clearing of the Highland flora. Once put under a regimen of intensive grazing by sheep there was little forest regeneration. Small-scale firing
evolved into vast burnings; subsistence herding escalated into market pastoralism; hordes of sheep trampled, plucked, and browsed a new pasture out of
former woods and waste. Since sheep required protection from predators as
well as special feed, additional woods were destroyed by axe and fire to
exterminate wolves.[19]

More firings meant more wildfires, of course. Some were accidental burns; some incendiary; and some the product of conflicting purposes. That different fire practices supported different land uses was an old theme. The quarrel between royal forests and the rights of commoners to agist their stock brought the herders' desire for fire and the verders' fear of it into conflict. In thirteenth-century Sherwood Forest, where heather and fern were considered "covert" for the king's deer, authorities inquired who "burnt them to get pasture for his animals." When in 1638 a John Harton was arraigned for burning in the Forest of Exmoor, he protested that the overgrown heather improperly entangled his sheep, which limited his right of passage, and he argued that the lands had become so rank with old heath that it was fit browse for neither cattle nor deer, that the land ought to be burnt to restore it, a method sure to work, "as is found by daily experience of burning commons not far from the forest." Manwood's treatise on forest law, from the sixteenth century on, recorded prohibitions on underburning and on the burning of "dry Oaks." Instead, the debris that would otherwise have fed free-burning fire went to feed agisted stock, large herds of deer, or to stoke the hearth fires and cottage industries of local villages.[20]

Even where allowed, moor burns often escaped, and in drought years they could range widely, by British standards, through field and woods. In 1762 it was said that "everything burnt up, and the moors being on fire from Ewden to this [Broomhead] common and consumed several hundred acres. Cowel was for the most part on fire and almost all the moors in England and Wales." While moor fires were a common nuisance, they enraged landlords intent on establishing forest plantations, whose young conifers were particularly vulnerable to fires that raced out of the heather. This, too, was an old conflict. Laws passed to prohibit malicious or careless burning were largely unenforceable. Queen Mary protested in 1566 that in the counties of Nairn and Moray the "diuers of the inhabitants" were "making mureburne and raisis fyre . . . to the great hurt and destruction of policie within our realms." In 1685 Parliament passed an act that prohibited muir burning after the end of March, thus regulating a tool rather than eliminating a nuisance. Other statutes followed. In 1693 three men accused of a heather fire that destroyed fir woods on the Craigmore of Abernethy had their ears nailed to the gallows on the Moor of Belintomb.[21]

But the practice was too entrenched to extirpate easily. As the rage for sheep put more and more of the countryside into browse and grass, fires were common, and where not encased by arable lands, they readily escaped into waste or woods during dry years. The earl of Fife almost despaired of eliminating fire in the woods, whose danger was "scarce to be conceived." A single cotter in the woods was capable of enormous harm, since around his few open acres everything was "exposed to be totally destroyed, either by wilful Fire-raising or by Neglect, or even by Accident." The earl cited one such fire that had taken "the whole country under Invercauld" to contain it. A fire in Glen Urquhart in 1770 was halted only after gangs cut a fuelbreak some 500 yards wide. In 1790 the Reverend James Headrick wrote of "several instances" of widespread heath burning in the Highlands, and recalled especially "an extensive forest of native firs, which had been burnt by a fire kindled at the distance of many miles. The flame, urged by an impetuous wind, and acting upon the withered grass, and heath, in early spring, soon spread itself over many hills; until it caught this forest, when the blaze became tremendous." William Schlich's monumental *Manual of Forestry* confirmed that "forest fires are of frequent occurrence in the heathlands of Berkshire, Surrey, and Hampshire." In 1636, the lord chamberlain wrote the high sheriff of Staffordshire to explain that His Majesty knew of the "opinion entertained" there that "the burning of Ferne [bracken] doth draw downe rain," and that since he planned to travel to that part of the realm, he "hath commanded me to write unto you, to cause all burning of Ferne to bee forborne, until his Majesty be passed the country." In the eighteenth century, Gilbert White fumed over the persistence of folk burning in Selborne.

Though (by statute 4 and 5 W. and Mary, c. 23) "to burn on any waste, between Candlemas and Midsummer, any grig, ling, heath and furze, goss or fern, is punishable with whipping and confinement in the house of correction"; yet, in this forest, about March and April, according to the dryness of the season, such vast heath-fires are lighted up, that they often get to a masterless head, and, catching the hedges, have sometimes been communicated to the underwoods, woods, and coppices, where great damage has ensured. The plea for these burnings is, that, when the old coat of heath, etc., is consumed, young will sprout up, and afford much tender browse for cattle; but, where there is large furze, the fire, following the roots, consumes the very ground; so that for hundreds of acres nothing is to be seen but smother and desolation, the whole circuit round looking like the cinders of a volcano; and, the soil being quite exhausted, no traces of vegetation are to be found for years. These conflagrations, as they take place usually with a north-east or east wind, much annoy this village with their smoke, and often alarm the country; and, once in particular, I remember that a gentleman, who lives beyond Andover, coming to my house, when he got on the downs between that town and Winchester, at twenty-five miles distance, was surprised much with smoke and a hot smell of fire; and concluded that Alresford was in flames; but, when he came to that town, he then had apprehensions for the next village, and so on to the end of his journey.[22]

There was no doubt, however, that under the proper circumstances fire could assist that branch of forestry conceived as tree farming. This, too, became part of the reclamation of wasteland, and trendy landowners—aware that in wood-poor Britain the economics of plantation forestry could be favorable—planted to conifers lands not arable or really suitable for pasture. Preparations called for an initial site burn, a form of swidden adapted to forestry. Particularly in heath, the treatment of choice was to burn "a year or so before the trees are planted." This practice continued, "irrespective of the nature of the site," even after the Forestry Commission had been established in the twentieth century.[23]

But if the new wave of reclamation restored fire to wasteland, it expunged it elsewhere. What had been the most ubiquitous source of prehistoric anthropogenic fire—hunting—became at best a source of accidental fire. Although Shakespeare has King Lear proclaim that he will flush out his enemies by seizing a brand and then "drive them hence like foxes," fire hunting had long since vanished from Britain. Royal forests and chases, in particular, had become rigorously managed, with carefully prescribed rights of access. Foresters sought just the right mix of browse and shelter, and as pressures for use mounted, they maintained that habitat through control over cutting, grazing, harvesting, and other semicultivations rather than through fire. The forest laws of 1662 proscribed muir-burning within a quarter mile of young woods, and restricted burning to what would provide a year's fuel—the understory was more valuable as coppice for fuelwood than as habitat, as Gilbert White recognized.

> Such forests and wastes, when their allurements to irregularities are removed, are of considerable service to neighborhoods that verge upon them, by furnishing them with peat and turf for their firing; with fuel for the burning of their lime; and with ashes for their grasses . . .

Natural fuels, that is, were more likely to be combusted at special sites or furnaces than burned in situ. Dogs replaced fire as a means of flushing game.[24]

Only on more remote sites, inaccessible to agriculture, did broadcast burning persist, and then it was regulated as to season. John Evelyn reported in his *Sylva* (1664) that legislation prohibited moor and marsh burning between April and September because of the hazard of escape fires, the obnoxious smoke, and the harm to preferred species of wildlife. For their part hunters, most of them transients, contributed accidental fires from abandoned camps and smoldering wadding. In 1801, for example, a Mr. Adam prohibited shooting on his moors because of "the great danger which his Woods run, last year, by the Heath having caught fire, from the Wadding of Fowling pieces or the carelessness of those who accompanied the Sportsmen . . ." By the nineteenth century hunting had become a ritualized sport, and it was subjected to the same micromanagement as the rest of the British landscape.[25]

Something similar happened with Britain's other firebrands. Fire and sword swept Britain less frequently. The long period of invasions had witnessed an outburst of burning—some in the fields, some in the villages (which, constructed of wattle and thatch, were really reconstituted woods and moors), and some in the wastes. Whether as an accident of record or a reflection of fact, the Vikings stand out as notable incendiaries, often firing upwind from a village and letting the flames drive the villagers from their cover, burning towns and fields, felling and firing the woods to prevent ambush and to deny sanctuary to enemies. It was an old Norse custom to establish title to land by burning it or, where more care was required, to carry a symbolic brand around the tract; in a sense, this is what the raiders did, but with the frenzy of a berserker. In 1006 the *Anglo-Saxon Chronicle* recorded that "every shire in Wessex [was] sadly marked by burning and by plundering." The devastation increased during the long Norman war of conquest, and fire helped put many demenses into "waste." Border wars were fought with torch as well as pike. It was common practice for English marcher lords to fell and burn Scottish woods; it is said that John of Gaunt had his troops cut enormous quantities of trees which they gave "as fodder to the fire." The Scots reciprocated. After defeating the earl of Buchan, Robert the Bruce put the district to the torch and the "marks of the fire," Archibald Geikie noted six centuries later, "are said to be visible on the trees in the neighbouring peatbogs." The civil war burned across much of England and Scotland. When a house inhabited by Jacobite rebels was torched in 1746, "some sparks catched hold of the young wood, and did irreparable mischief before it could be extinguished." Apart from war itself, fire was an expression of a chronic unsettledness that afflicted the less-developed regions of Britain, a violence that was only partially sublimated into rick burning and was never lost entirely. It was not enough to domesticate the landscape: the people had to be disciplined as well.[26]

By the time the First Fleet sailed for Australia, Britain had experienced a full and varied fire history. A Briton might well echo a couplet from Arthur Johnston's "Newcastle" :

Why seek you fire in some exalted sphere?
Earth's fruitful bosom will supply you here.[27]

There was fire aplenty, but it was increasingly confined, sublimated, restricted in place and season. On newly reclaimed lands, agriculture advanced under a cover of smoke, and during droughts fires could escape and rage through lands that were lightly managed. On the increasing domains of arable lands, however, the agricultural revolution all but strangled fire out of the countryside. Instead peat was cut and burned as fuel; the woods were coppiced for fuelwood or converted to charcoal; underwood was carefully manicured; grass and browse replaced domestic crops or were cropped by domestic livestock. Excess growth was cut and burned in hearths or piles. Fire fertilized lands indirectly by preparing lime or readying heaps of rich ash to be ploughed into spring furrows. Underwood, furze, and bracken were harvested for "hop-poles, hoops and cordwood" or rendered into charcoal. Villagers gathered small branches into faggots for hearth fires or to kindle the heartier fires that burned lime and brick. Coal replaced wood as a critical open fuel. So intensively was the land used that there was increasingly little opportunity for fire. Human pruning and harvesting, rigorous browsing and grazing, the planting of new species of pasture grasses, field crops, and trees —all substituted in specific detail for the generic power of free-burning fire. Broadcast burns became debris fires, an implement of gardening like spades and rakes. As Robert Louis Stevenson put it in "Autumn Fires":

> Sing a song of seasons!
> Something bright in all!
> Flowers in the summer,
> Fires in the fall!

So, too, were human firebrands restricted. Authorities eager to protect property strengthened the laws against arson and careless fire. Rick burners were transported to Australia. The home fires burned feebly, more symbol than fact.[28]

Yet it had all gone too far. Even among European nations Britain was exceptional, most closely approximated by the Low Countries. Around the perimeter of Western Europe free-burning fire continued—with pastoral burning endemic through the Mediterranean Basin, swidden cultivation widespread in Scandinavia and Russia, and assorted fires elsewhere. Agricultural fires burned in field and forest; wildfires soared in the steppes, the taiga, and other remote lands. And everywhere in their overseas possessions, colonial powers encountered scenes full of fire and firesticks. But by meticulous control over fuels and peoples, by intensive cultivation and land use, fires became increasingly alien in the newly industrialized heartland. When William Brereton lamented in seventeenth-century Berwickshire that "here is a mighty want of fire in these moors," he referred to domestic fuels, but two centuries later his words could have applied to free-burning heath fires. Only along the frontier was organized fire protection essential.[29]

Certainly by the nineteenth century British fire history had moved to the empire's overseas dominions. Britain's own expulsion and containment of fire perhaps made all the more intense the shock of rediscovering free-burning fire as an endemic and universal phenomenon. To travel to India, America, Canada, or Australia was to step back into British history to the early centuries of *landnam* and to engage environments where nature could escalate bonfires into holocaust. So ill-equipped were the British that they lacked even foresters, and had to import German professionals—a remarkable company of intellectuals and adventurers—to spearhead the administration and industrialization of their colonial wildlands.

Gradually the home fires rekindled, however. Railroads distributed fires wherever they traveled, and the receptivity of the adjacent lands to burning suggested possibilities for fire that had generally been forgotten. As Britain slowed its Second Reclamation, as it accumulated surplus straw and stored up marginal pastures, as it retained lands for purposes somewhat resembling their ancient uses, as it restored forests and hunted wildlife and grazed hardy hill sheep and preserved moors for their natural beauty and habitat, Britons found that they needed ancient fire practices as well. They had to restore fire.

Perhaps the most startling revelation came from sport hunters in the Highlands. The agricultural revolution had tolerated muir burning as a means of expanding pasture but denigrated it as a means of continual cultivation. "Enlightened" lairds suppressed those fires, however, seeking more cover for grouse and more income from sport than from sheep. The fires faded; the heather *(Calluna)* became decadent, disease swelled to plague proportions, and the population of red grouse spiraled into collapse. By the twentieth century it was necessary to restore burning to salvage the plantations. Likewise, the value of "hill sheep" for crossbreeding reinstated the value of native pasture, which senesced without fire. The old alliance between hunting and herding found new vigor as inquiries revealed that hill sheep and grouse required similar moors and extracted a similar fire tithe. Almost every environmental ill could be traced, so a parliamentary inquiry concluded, to inadequate burning.[30]

Elsewhere a relaxation of usage liberated more straw; and burning the fields after harvest, an ancient practice, revived in scope. Everywhere the countryfolk burned the year's rank growth in bonfires of spring and fall. Often "commoners" agitated for more burning on forest lands to retard the encroachment of scrub and woods on protected heaths and to make "pasturage more plentiful." By the 1870s crown officials adopted controlled burning as a regular practice, though its dimensions were never as great as the commoners wished. Incendiary fires—a popular attempt to redress that imbalance—became increasingly frequent. In 1926 a critic lamented the legal and illegal fires on Exmoor, which the commoners demand "to improve the feed for their cattle and ponies," fires that "during the dry weather of the spring can be seen burning day and night."[31]

Something analogous happened as Britain attempted, after World War I, to reforest: fire proved a far graver threat than anyone had imagined. While natural ignition was negligible, agricultural burning and accidental fires from tourists and railroads combined with dry spells to require an aggressive strategy of fire protection in young plantations and on those sites where mature trees had been killed by disease or insects, or uprooted by winds. Ancient tools—fire beaters, brooms of birch—were stored at important locations. Authorities laid down fire traces, fire belts, and fire rides to interrupt spreading flames. Some breaks were maintained by regular burning; others by planting to a more incombustible flora. Guards patrolled for fire at critically dry times. Articles about fire protection salted British forestry periodicals. The Forestry Commission devoted nearly an entire issue of its *Journal* to the subject of the drought-driven 1933 fires. Having drained moors to plant pine, a Northumberland forester was shocked to discover that "fire in the spring months is an appalling risk in such a huge forest of conifers." In 1936 heavy rains prevented the burning of firebreaks, a hard frost cured fuels, dry winds drained them of moisture, and fires broke out—one from an "Indian peddlar" who tossed out matches as he walked; the fires propagated everywhere from "papery masses of dry molinia blowing about and lodging against banks and in holes," a "facility for forest fires which could hardly be surpassed." As public usage increased, one stunned forester proclaimed that "we have had almost completely to remodel our system of fire control . . ." Forest fires became prominent again because, for the first time in centuries, forests had become at least locally prominent again.[32]

The restoration of fire surprised nearly everyone. Fire came to Britain largely through human agency, and human agents had removed it by converting the island from a wildland to a garden. As new ignition sources appeared, so did fires. As more land was put into less intensive cultivation, fire found fuel with which to expand its domain. And there remained, within the genetic memory of its indigenous biota, the record of a more fire-conscious past—heath was only the most prominent expression of that heritage because it was the most extensive. It took German firebombings during World War II to revive that buried history. Amid the wreckage, bursting through the ash, there appeared species of plants rarely seen—fireweeds, biotic relicts from a more fire-rich antiquity.[33]

NEED FIRE:
BURNING THE GOLDEN BOUGH

What happened to fire in the British environment happened also to fire in British cognition. Britons had fire rites, fire ceremonies, and fire myths to which they added a fire science and an industrial fire lore. Fire simmered and flared, brightened and blackened the cultural world of Britons as it did their natural landscape. The syncretic symbolism of fire reflected, in fact, the multiple conversions—the successive reclamations—of the British countryside.[34]

The core, the eternal flame, was the hearth fire. It appears that ancestral Indo-European peoples had a fire cult centered on Atar, the god of the hearth. In India, Atar became Agni (Latin cognate, *igne*), who along with Indus reigned over the Hindu pantheon. In Persia, Zoroaster reworked the cult into one of the first monotheisms. Vestiges of the Atar cult appear among Celtic and Teutonic tribes, manifest in special fire ceremonies of which the Yule log is a relic. Fire accompanied sacrifice and divination. In Greece and Rome the hearth evolved into the temples of Hestia and Vesta, respectively, sacred emblems of family, city, state. A family were those who shared a fireside; the family god, the god of that hearth. But special symbolism adumbrated the village fire, unlike the village well, beyond the status of public utility. Colonists and armies carried fire from their polis or nation with them in their travels. The vestal fire, nurtured by priests and virgins, represented the Roman state, never to be extinguished. The ever-burning fire testified to enduring institutions of learning and technology. From it, as Aeschylus has Prometheus proclaim, came "all the arts of men." By it humans distinguished themselves from other creatures. With fire they, or their gods, made and remade the universe. Once kindled, the sacred, the informing fire could never be allowed to expire. That inextinguishable fire stood for civilization.

The fundamental fire ritual of Western civilization, from which springs all its other fire ceremonies and myths, reenacts the capture of fire by humans. "Whatever their origin," Sir James Frazer concluded, the fire ceremonies "prevailed all over this quarter of the globe, from Ireland on the west to Russia on the east, and from Norway and Sweden on the north to Spain and Greece on the south." The originating rite involved the "need-fire," sometimes known as the "wild fire" or "living fire." Its prescriptions required that all fires in the surrounding land be extinguished, that a new fire be kindled from the friction of rubbing wood, and that hearth fires be reignited from this renewed fire. Sometimes there were sacrifices associated with the new fire. Always its effects were distributed among society and land, both in fact and in symbol. Participants passed over or through its coals and smoke, tossed its ashes to the land, or painted them on faces, a charm to ensure fertility. They carried its charred brands to fields or homes, a purgative and prophylactic against lightning, plague, murrain, vermin, evil spirits, and wildfire.[35]

Through the need-fire ceremony, tribes and villagers recreated the origins of their indispensable flame. By spreading it from hearth to hearth, from field to field, from mountain top to mountain top, they symbolically recreated their identity, reaffirmed their shared society, and reclaimed their landscape from disease, witchcraft, blight, and terror. The practical value of broadcast fire as a fumigator and fertilizer here found sublimated, symbolic expression. The ceremony occurred as needed, typically during times of stress, famine, or plague; cattle diseases were a common motive. But as nomadic bands became more settled, as they organized their lives under the rhythms of herding, the need-fire ceremony became part of an annual cycle and evolved into special fire ceremonies of spring and fall.

The best documented examples are Celtic. The Beltane fires (May Day) and the Halloween fires (October 31) were ceremonial elaborations of the need-fire rite. They correspond to the calendar of the European herdsman, the opening of summer pasture and fall pasture (or, where winter was harsher, the drive back to the barn)—the traditional seasons for broadcast burning. For the Celts, they correspond to the onset of a new year (Halloween) and the year's halfway mark (Beltane). The ceremonies testify to the pastoralist's obsession with his herds, as participants applied its cleansing flame and smoke first to cattle, then to other livestock, passing their herds between the sacred flames, over its coals, or through its roiling smoke. Those animals that were sick should be healed; those who were healthy would be inoculated. And what was good for the herds was also good for the herders. Children, in particular, passed through the cleansing fire. But the rites became increasingly ceremonial and abstracted. Where herders once burned the fields, they now scattered ashes and cold brands from the ceremonial bonfires to encourage fertility and eliminate pests. Where they once burnt human victims, they now burnt effigies.

The two ceremonies corresponded, for pagan worshipers, to the two nights when the spirit world erupted, when a chasm opened between the world of the living and the world of the dead. In the spring, it was Walpurgis Night; in the fall, All Hallow's Eve, the festival of the dead. Then witches ride the night; fairies, trolls, hobgoblins, dragons, and bewitched creatures of all kinds boldly pour forth; the dead roam the land, haunted and haunting; and these spirits, both good and bad, have to be appeased and expelled. Fire does both. Significantly, both the Beltane and Halloween fire ceremonies were known colloquially as "burning the witches." In many cases, the ritual fires consumed effigies of straw or live animals (cats, preferably)—the brood of witches and warlocks. In ancient times, these lurid fires probably included sacrificial humans as well. Condemned criminals were the first choice, then prisoners of war, then victims chosen by lot. Many rites associated with the fires were, in fact, a means of selecting a victim. By the eighteenth century practitioners had sublimated that sacrifice into symbolism, but the appeasement of evil spirits, the destruction of witches, the rekindling and dissemination of a sacred fire to drive off death and darkness remained a fundamental purpose of the great fires that informed the Celtic calendar. In ancient times, for example, all the fires of Ireland were kindled from the sacred, originating fire of Halloween.

As mixed agriculture spread and remade the English landscape, as husbandry replaced nomadic herding and sedentary farming supplanted *landnam,* the ancient fire ceremony accommodated itself to new chronometers, an annual rhythm of seasons important to farmers. To the fire ceremonies of Beltane and Halloween were added ceremonies at Midsummer and Midwinter, signs that a society organized its life less around the migrations of its herds than around the solar cycle that directed sowing and harvesting. The rites expanded accordingly, as village after village raised great fires on hilltops, passed their livestock (and themselves) through coals and smoke, and "burned the witches."

But this time they also carried torches through their fields and orchards. Here they applied, in symbolic form, the recognized powers of free-burning fire to fumigate and fertilize. In some instances, they lit huge bonfires upwind of fields and allowed the smoke to pour over the reclaimed land. The height of the bonfire determined, it was believed, the height of the crops. At one time the fields themselves had been felled and fired, and many are still burned after harvest or when fallow; but no farmer torched them at Midsummer or Midwinter. To reconcile an agricultural calendar with the solstice meant that these fires were ceremonial, mere vestiges of once-real fire practices. As land use intensified, the opportunities for nonintensive fire diminished as well. At Midsummer Eve, the festival concluded with a great wheel of straw set on fire and trundled down the hill by young men. At Midwinter, fire had to burn in the hearth, where it became the Yule log—a talisman against domestic harm, an oaken charm whose ashes strewn across the fields during the Twelve Nights promoted their health and vigor. Around the fires revelers danced and sang, a peasant corroboree.

"The custom of kindling great bonfires, leaping over them, and driving cattle through or around them would seem to have been practically universal throughout Europe," Frazer concluded, "and the same can be said of the procession or races with blazing torches round fields, orchards, pastures, or cattle-stalls." Similarly,

> as the ceremonies themselves resemble each other, so do the benefits which the people expect to reap from them. Whether applied in the form of bonfires blazing at fixed points, or of torches carried about from place to place, or of embers and ashes taken from the smouldering heap of fuel, the fire is believed to promote the growth of the crops and the welfare of man and beast, either positively by stimulating

them, or negatively by averting the dangers and calamities which threaten them from such causes as thunder and lightning, conflagration, blight, mildew, vermin, sterility, disease, and not least of all witchcraft.[36]

The fire ceremonies originated in antiquity and they persisted with extraordinary tenacity. Much as they accommodated agriculture, so they survived Christianity. The earliest written records of the ceremonies, in fact, emanate from the eighth century, when missionaries—revolted by heathen rites—reviled them. In the twelfth century, the Church Militant fought the fires as it battled stubborn pockets of paganism. Instead of abolishing the ceremonies, however, the church co-opted them: the Midwinter fire—the Yule fire—it grafted to Christmas. Halloween became the Feast of All Souls; the Easter fires supplanted the Beltane fires as the great celebration of spring. On Easter Eve churches extinguished their lights, then rekindled them from a "new" (need) fire, the Paschal or Easter candle. The Midsummer fire became an innocuous secular festival. Where it desired new ceremonies, the church adopted variants on the basic rite. Its Lenten fires even retained the custom of brushing ashes on the body, baptizing pagan custom with a cross on the forehead and absorbing Ash Wednesday into the church's liturgical calendar just as peasants had absorbed the preagricultural need fire into the secular calendar of herding and farming. Instead of burning witches, communicants burned "Judas" (or those possessed by the devil; later, "Luther," heretics, and others). In some form, fire accompanied virtually every ceremony of public life, both sacred and secular. At night and indoors it was essential.

All this was folklore. But Western civilization had also evolved a written language, and intellectuals too grappled with fire. Writers—philosophers, dramatists, theologians, litterateurs—reworked folk stories into formal myths about the origin of fire. Hesiod and Aeschylus told the saga of Prometheus, one of the Titans overthrown by the Zeus-championed Olympians. While there are many versions, each retelling with its own concluding moral, the essence is that Prometheus stole fire from the gods and gave it to humans. Perhaps the fundamental perception is that fire was the essential human attribute; the basic lesson, that fire was power. The horrible punishment inflicted on Prometheus became a synonym for defiance, and "Promethean" became, for the Romantics, a code word for the hero who sought to burst the bounds of fate and experience. In the *Protagorus* Plato told how the gods fashioned mortals from compounds of earth and fire and explained how humans came to be so poorly endowed with natural gifts and how Prometheus reasoned that the possession of fire could correct that imbalance and thus stole fire for them. In *The Republic* Plato again appealed to fire, this time as a metaphor for human understanding. The Allegory of the Cave portrays humans as living in a darkness illuminated only by fire, a world in which they can only know what fire's lights and shadows reveal. Christianity retained some elements of ancient myths and metaphors, like the concept of a world-ending conflagration, and it adopted others after exorcising the fire ceremonies of their heathen spirits. Through such stories fire myths entered Western literature and Western religion.

It also entered Western science. Early natural philosophers accepted fire as a fundamental phenomenon. Heracleitus thought the world itself was a fire. "All things," he pontificated, "are an exchange for fire, and fire for all things." Whether or not fire was somehow inherent in everything, it certainly symbolized the sea of reactions that kept the universe in ceaseless flux. Other intellectuals, like Empedocles, considered fire as one of the basic elements, of which most philosophers identified four (air, earth, water, fire). Stoics like Epicurus accepted a natural history of world cycles, each creation begun and destroyed in a global conflagration. Theophrastus devoted an entire book to combustion, *De Igne*. Fire remained both an object of scrutiny and a means of scrutiny. *Philosophus per ignem*— knowledge through fire, asserted the alchemists. As late as 1720 Hermann Boerhaave affirmed that "if you make a mistake in your exposition of the Nature of Fire, your error will spread to all the branches of physics, and this is because, in all natural production, Fire . . . is always the chief agent." Fire was as much a part of Western science as of Western literature.[37]

But the agricultural revolution that was in full flush at the time of the First Fleet coincided with an intellectual revolution that would remake the cultural landscape of Britain as fully as its economic revolutions did the island's natural landscape. Alongside the one's reformation in fire practices there marched a concurrent reformation in ideas about fire. Much as Enlightenment skeptics criticized folk fire practices as degenerate, so they dismissed fire ceremonies and fire beliefs as superstition. Increasingly, too, industrial fire uses challenged agricultural fire uses. Mechanics captured burning within machines, and these new "fire engines" powered an economic and social revolution that helped evoke a new landscape for which ancient fire ceremonies were not only archaic but irrelevant. Inflamed by the new sciences, natural philosophers reinterpreted fire as a chemical reaction, not as an informing principle, an element, or a universal constituent (as the phlogiston theory made of it); Antoine-Laurent Lavoisier announced the discovery of oxygen and a new catalogue of elements as the First Fleet completed its first year.

All this complicated the transport of British fire to Australia. The British were seldom far from fire: it was in their heritage, their minds, their toolkits. They even constructed special hearths to carry fire within their blue-water ships. Some of their fire practices associated with land clearing, pastoralism, and agriculture could transfer to Australia. Others, long forgotten, they had to relearn or acquire from Aborigines. For European settlers to be without fire in Australia was as curious a sight as for Aborigines to go on a walkabout in England with glowering firesticks.

But the same could not be said of their beliefs and practices. The cognitive universe of British fire did not survive the passage, and precious little (if anything) was borrowed from the Aboriginal Dreamtime. By the end of the eighteenth century ceremonial folk fires had died out along with the way of life they explained, receding into Britain's Celtic fringe, and then, with further enclosure and clearances, into a fanciful Celtic twilight. Practitioners died out; dispossessed Highlanders went to cities or to Canada, not to Australia; the urbanites who made up the bulk of convicts were neither folk practitioners nor intellectuals but the "surplus" population simultaneously squeezed by the ongoing agricultural and industrial revolutions. Where fire ceremonies persisted they survived as secular holidays shorn of their formative significance; they had increasingly less meaning in Britain and almost none in Australia. Fire imagery and symbolism became literary conventions, a clichéd rhetoric. Fire rites embedded within agricultural and liturgical calendars had little meaning in antipodean Australia, where the seasons were reversed; it made little sense to burn a roaring Yule log in a land without oak and at the summer solstice, when the land's heat was oppressive.

As the transplanted Europeans struggled to remake the land, so they had to reinterpret the place of fire within it—and within the cognitive and moral universes they constructed in tandem with that landscape. Without that effort, their settlement had little meaning and less legitimacy. It proved easier, however, to adapt and acquire fire practices than to understand them. In Australia, bushfire was no vestigial flame. In ways that had not been true for centuries, perhaps millennia in Britain, fire was a formative environmental power and a presence equally beyond ancient folklore and modern science. What fire as a literary convention lost in the transfer, it regained as a powerful and autonomous symbol of Australian life.

"FIT FOR NO PURPOSE . . . BUT THE FIRE"

The Neolithic colonizers of Britain did not live wholly off the land they found. They journeyed to this new world outfitted with what Alfred Crosby in another context has termed a "portmanteau biota"—a mob of interdependent organisms, a mobile biota that swarmed like an undisciplined flock across the landscape. Their success came by replacing the indigenous biota with their organic allies or by so altering the native scene that it better suited their affiliated species. The Neolithic Britons replaced wildlife with swine, cattle, horses, goats, fowl, and sheep. They substituted cereal grains for native grasses and woods. Where the indigenous flora could be shaped to provide fodder or a favorable habitat, they felled and fired the forests. And of course they brought their familiar weeds and pests. A slow, biotic shock wave passed over Britain, not once but time and again. Then they traveled to Australia. The island continent forced some inevitable inversions.[38]

Incredibly, the First Fleet of this proudly agricultural nation lacked farmers. The closure of America to convicts had precipitated a crisis, and British authorities wanted little more than to transform their rotting prison hulks into self-supporting gardens. But the architects of European Australia did ship with its convicts a complement of British flora and fauna, an improbable ecological transportation. The early convict fleets were a latter-day Noah's Ark of an agricultural civilization that had, for many millennia, become accustomed to moving into new lands and adapting to new circumstances their entourage of grains, tubers, weeds, livestock, diseases, and vermin. The reclamation of Australia paralleled in time, if not entirely in practice, the Second Reclamation of Britain.

The First Fleet contained 736 convicts, a company of guards, assorted vegetable and grain seeds, and a floating farm of fauna—2 bulls and 5 cows, 29 sheep, 19 goats, 74 hogs and sows, 18 turkeys, 35 ducks, 35 geese, 209 chickens, and 5 rabbits. Thus the settlers brought their own food, or pretended that they would cultivate in Australia what they needed from seed and stock shipped from Europe. As Botany Bay evolved from the status of a beached hulk into an embryonic neo-Europe, authorities transported further biotic reinforcements. Successive voyages added to the growing menagerie. Ships brought cattle from Britain, Spain, Madagascar, South Africa (vaderlanders), and even Bengal (zebus); horses from Britain, India, and the Cape; sheep—fat-tails and crossed merinos—from the Cape and Bengal. Both South Africa and India—cratons of Greater Gondwana—supplied important organisms, either natives or European species naturalized to their new homes. Both helped British immigrants make the transition to Mediterranean terrains and drought-blasted landscapes. Governor Phillip noted that "all the plants and fruit-trees brought from Brazil and the Cape that did not die in the passage thrive exceedingly well." By May Andrew Miller recorded that the colony had 1 stallion, 3 mares, 3 colts, 2 bulls, 5 cows, 29 sheep, 190 goats, 49 hogs, 25 pigs, 5 rabbits, 18 turkeys, 29 geese, 35 ducks, 122 fowls, and 87 chickens. In time, free settlers and a small but growing number of convicts arrived with at least some knowledge of English farming. Yet the process of reconciling this imported biota with indigenous lands was arduous and unpredictable.[39]

The British precedent was of mixed value. Infertile soils blanketed much of Britain—many critics, in fact, believed that Britain had the sorriest natural soils in Western Europe. Even the worst wild and waste lands, however, agriculturalists had eventually tamed. Skirmishers first broke the land by shifting cultivation, cutting and burning, then reworked it into a mixed landscape of pasture and plow. But the settlers at Sydney Cove needed to do in months or years what had taken millennia in Britain. When climate deteriorated in Australia, it signified drought; not, as in Britain, a spell of cold and wet. Unlike America, once joined to Eurasia, Australia knew a different geologic and biologic evolution. It resisted an easy union. Surgeon-General George White denounced Australia as a "country and place so forbidding and so hateful as to merit only execration and curses," utterly worthless to the commercial world. What from ship resembled an oak park on close inspection revealed coarse grass, and wood "fit for no purpose . . . but the fire." "I do not scruple to pronounce that in the whole world there is not a worse country," wrote an appalled First Fleeter, Lieutenant-Governor Robert Ross. "All that is contiguous to us is so very barren and forbidding that it may with truth be said that *here nature is reversed;* and if not so, she is nearly worn out." The land, Ross concluded, was not only unfit for European settlement, it was almost beyond the capacity of European language to depict.[40]

Others, too, had difficulty finding words for what they saw, with the result that they described Australia with a calculated babel of transferred, borrowed, corrupted, and invented words. Their language for the bush became a microcosm for their dealings with it. *Bush* itself derived from the Dutch *bosch*, probably acquired at Cape Colony and already generalized from its original meaning as "woods" into a generic descriptor of unreclaimed land; it quickly bred an infinite number of compounds. *Gum* as an expression for *Eucalyptus* dates from a misperception of Governor Phillip, first recorded in May 1788. Other words reached back to older English, as though moving into a preagricultural environment relocated the language back in time as well. *Scrub* harked to Viking origins, from the Danish *skrub* (brushwood) and the Norse *skrubba* (dwarf cornel tree). Words that had fallen out of usage in colloquial English found new life in Australia, much as did ancient fire practices. Colonists resurrected *wattle,* referring to the daub-and-wattle construction of Saxon and Viking houses, to apply to the vinelike species of *Acacia* found along the eastern shore. The other common word for the acacias, *mulga,* they picked up from the Aborigines.[41]

It was one of many such borrowings. Aborigines contributed *mallee, humpy* (a corruption of *oompi), brigalow, wallum, coolibah, jarrah, gidgee, karri, marri, billabong, bunyip, boomerang, kookaburra, euro, kangaroo, wallaby, wombat, joey, taipan.* They also supplied numerous place names. Interestingly none of the Australian words for fire needed help from Aboriginal or other sources but came out of basic English. If refinements were needed, it was enough, as with *bushfire,* to compound the English word with a newly acquired expression. In that sense the story of how English adapted linguistically to Australia parallels the story of how they adapted to Australian fire.

From its very beginnings the British encounter with Australia had been edged with fire. Some saw the fire-sculpted landscape as an asset. Forests were generally clear of underbrush, and there were grassy fields ready to receive sheep, cattle, and horses or to accept crops. The scene appeared to them, as it had to James Cook, as one of semicultivation. What Britain had accomplished by intensive farming and grazing—by biotic means—Aborigines had done with fire. In exploring the Swan River in 1827 Captain James Stirling described a "Tongue of Land" flanked by streams of good soil where "the ground had been cleared by fire a few weeks before and was ready to receive seed . . ." W. C. Wentworth glowingly informed prospective immigrants that "the colonist has no expense to incur in clearing his farm . . . he has only to set fire to the grass, to prepare his land for the immediate reception of the ploughshare . . ." Others, including a long stream of pastoral explorers, declared the grasslands—Australia's unbounded downs—as immediately ready to receive cattle. Repeatedly, the British sought out exactly those sites—the parklike forests and champion fields—that had been fashioned and shaped by Aboriginal fire.[42]

The product was one thing, however, and the process another. It was quickly apparent that a recreated Britain could not thrive amid Aboriginal fire regimes. The financier behind the Swan River colony, Thomas Peel, arrived in time to witness his chosen lands consumed by a bushfire. Governor Phillip wrote Viscount Sydney a year after settlement to explain how his "intention of turning swine into the woods to breed have been prevented by the natives so frequently setting fire to the country." The surest observation, however, perhaps belongs to Captain William Bligh. In August 1788 he coasted Australia and began planting fruit trees that he had brought from the Cape—apple, vines, plantain trees, oranges, lemons, cherry stones, plum, peach, apricot, and pear. His crew also sowed pumpkins, onions, cabbages, potatoes, and "two sorts of Indian corn." Bligh expressed "great hopes" that some of his experiments would thrive. But he noted "a circumstance much against any thing succeeding here." The endless "fires made by the natives are apt to communicate to the dried grass and underwood, and to spread in such a manner as to endanger every thing that cannot bear a severe scorching." If the new settlements were to succeed, they had to cope with fire as a routine, ubiquitous presence, and they had to do so without centuries of relentless reclamation by agricultural agents.[43]

The solution was, like the evolving language, a mélange of the borrowed, the corrupted, the invented, and the retained. Like the Neolithic conquest of Britain, agricultural reclamation began with the pastoral, then advanced into the arable. Settlers seeped through an environment in which fire was abundant and in which, they soon learned, fire promised quick returns even as it posed immediate threats.

Their first charge was to protect themselves from bushfires. Then, partly out of self-protection and partly out of opportunism, they turned to fire as an implement. They used it everywhere and for every purpose. The fires that had first repelled them, they soon realized also gave them access to a problematic land. They broadcast burned to green up stubborn pastures, to tease out scarce nutrients, and to protect themselves against wildfire. They slashed and burned for shifting cultivation. Wherever they wandered, whenever they halted, they set fires to boil their billies. As the Australian reclamation progressed, they restructured the fuel complexes, introduced new ignitions and removed some old ones, and redefined suitable fire practices. Their burning patterns created a matrix for Aboriginal fire much like that which Aboriginal burning had laid down for natural fire. They became scleromorphs, nomads, pyrophiles. Their new regimes bore an uncanny resemblance to the old. It was the European, not fire, that was reversed.

In 1927 E.H.F. Swain, Conservator of Forests in Queensland, surveyed the panorama of rural fire. The "firestick habit in Australia," he noted, began with the Aborigine. The white pioneer quickly discovered that "by using the aboriginal method" he could improve his cattle; the new selector found fire "to be a settler's blessing"; and since then "Australia has been burned and grazed, and burned and grazed as it never was burned and grazed before." A good forester, Swain worried about the effects of all this fire on soils and trees, particularly on exotic conifers. Where graziers and selectors saw assets, he saw liabilities. But he realized that "there can be no question of trying to prohibit the practice of rural firing." It was too firmly entrenched in the daily life of rural Australians. "At this stage the rural population is so enamored of the use of fire that wherever he now goes, and in the periods of highest fire hazard . . . the bushman blithely distributes his matches, and the schoolboy is learning to follow in father's footsteps." [44]

"BECAUSE THEY LOOKED INTO THE FIRE"

Australian fire assumed dimensions on the island continent that fire had never known in the British Isles. Britain had domesticated both its land and its people, and fire could flourish only where the British populace chose to have it. With the landing of the First Fleet, however, Australia witnessed a clash between two peoples and two biotas. The friction between them kept the bush constantly rekindled with fire. In the end one pyrophile replaced another. Australian conditions liberated European fire practices much as Aboriginal fire had liberated the eucalypt. In ways that had not been true for Britain for millennia, if ever, fire—both the bushfire and the anthropogenic fire in the bush—became an inexpungable presence, a defining fact of Australian life.

Fire accentuated whatever emotions the bush elicited in an observer, which meant a mix of horror, appreciation, and amusement. Thus Sturt, depressed by endless plains, found that a bushfire rendered the scene black and smoldering and "as dreary as can be imagined." Louisa Meredith considered the tall gum forests of the Great Dividing Range as "a deformity" due to a bushfire that had charred everything and stripped the woods of even the means to cast shadows. Pioneers spoke of natural terror and human heroism. D. H. Lawrence indelibly identified the "horrid spirit of the place"—its searing emptiness—with its scorched forests. "And the vast, uninhabited land frightened him. It seemed so hoary and lost, so unapproachable. The sky was pure . . . But the bush, the grey, charred bush. It scared him . . . It was so phantom-like, so ghostly, with its tall pale trees and many dead trees, like corpses, partly charred by bush fires . . ." [45]

Others perceived a wild romance to the panorama. "A sublime view," thought René Lesson in 1824, as he scanned the ridges and "desolate heights that appear on the horizon." Smoke cast a bluish veil over all from "the columns of smoke billowing in the burning forests which the carelessness of the aborigines has very often set alight." Sophia Stanger was "amused" when her party's campfire roared "to a considerable extent" in the bush. Later in the century, however, strangeness sometimes gave way to appreciation. Sidney Long painted "the spirit of the bushfire" an an art nouveau nymph. More accepting of the ephemerally blackened scene, the Reverend R. Collie reflected on popular misconceptions of bushfires. [46]

"When we read of a bush fire," he wrote, most observers conjure up images of "square miles of trees and shrubs destroyed" along with precious fencing and a "selector's barn." They imagine a landscape scorched into submission. But bushfires "must have had a most important influence in the distribution of species in Australia," Collie realized, which meant that much which the newcomers found attractive about the Australian scene they ought to attribute to fire. "If we should visit the district a few years later, the scene will be completely changed. The grass is richer and more abundant, the wild flowers more numerous, and new shrubs and trees have taken the place of those destroyed by the fire." The bushfire was both scourge and savior. "I am not aware that any one has called attention to what is going on before our eyes every summer in Australia, when at the expense of a certain number of forest trees, and scrub bushes, space is given for a hundred species of plants and flowers, which gladden our hearts as we walk abroad and make our lives all the happier because of their existence." [47]

Good or bad, ally or enemy, hopelessly alien or terrifyingly familiar—the fire was always there, and the new immigrants found their lives entwined to Australia by it. At a climactic moment in *The Tree of Man* Patrick White subjects his settlement to flood, then flame, a baptism of water followed by a judgment of fire. As the smoke approaches, the community rallies, discovering in their land "an austere beauty that they now loved with a sad love."

Some prepared to meet the fire; others to deny it, futilely. But its arrival was inevitable and inescapable.

"So they waited for the fire, and had been waiting many years of their lives. And nights." They attacked the fire, fled from it, stood hollow-eyed and slack-jawed before it. Some perished in the flames while others were redeemed by them. The experience tested, shaped, and revealed their character. The community could never be the same again. "The fact was, the fighters had become not only exhausted but fascinated by the fire," White explains in words that could stand as a signature to the fire history of European Australia. "There were very few who did not succumb to the spell of the fire. They were swayed by it, instead of it by them. . . . Because they had looked into the fire, and seen what you do see, they could rearrange their lives. So they felt."[48]

11

Reconnaissance by Fire: Education of a Pyrophile

In all the country through which I have passed, I have seldom gone a mile without seeing trees which appear to have been destroyed by fire.

—GOVERNOR ARTHUR PHILLIP *(1788)*

These bush fires are a very great nuisance for the time, though they ultimately do good.

—REVEREND JOHN WOLLASTON,
Picton Journal (1842)

ALMOST EVERYWHERE and at almost every occasion in the European encounter with Australia, there was fire. Fire exposed the land, illuminated the biota, blotted the sky, reformed ecosystems, watersheds, and soils, and defined relationships among human inhabitants. Europeans saw fire, learned fire, and applied fire. They discovered novel fire regimes and they destabilized those regimes with novel fire practices, biotic allies, and exotic fuels. Their fire practices gave them access to Australia while denying it to the Aborigines. Their relationship to fire was, by synecdoche, their relationship to the land.

The encounters mediated by fire were multiple and often violent. There was the conflict between European and Australia, between European and Aborigine, and among the disparate Europeans themselves. The clash between Australia and European was perhaps the most fundamental, and the dramatic fight by settlers against a demonic bushfire quickly became a set piece of Australian literature. The dramatic alarm, the wild ride of warning, the sudden appearance of flame and the hail of embers; furious struggles with beaters, boughs, and brands; the camaraderie of the fight and the social solidarity of its aftermath; the terror and sublimity of a bush burning like a galaxy in self-immolation—all became a recurring metaphor for the Australian frontier, its brutality, stoic resolve, and alienness. Bushfire was inevitably hostile; but European fire, a means of transplanting a European civilization. The British, unlike the Aborigines, used fire principally as a means by which to replace the native bush with an imported landscape.

The encounter between Aborigine and European was also played out with fire. Sturt spoke for scores of explorers when he recounted how natives observed his passage with a great fire, which "was answered from every point; for in less than ten minutes afterwards, we counted no fewer than fourteen different fires . . ." Signal fires were, however, only a prelude to fire and spear. Aborigines ceaselessly harassed parties of traveling Europeans with hostile fire, until the "new chums" learned to camp in protected sites or to burn out the tall grasses around them. Firesticks were hurled against bark humpies, wheat stocks, paddocks; broadcast fire disguised the trail of retiring raiders; distraction fires allowed the plundering of houses, barns, and flocks. The British retaliated with firearms, and their ruthless pursuit of hostile natives deprived the Aborigines of their own fires, an unspeakable hardship.[1]

But these were only direct encounters. Equally influential were indirect exchanges of fire, the irreconcilability of different fire practices. From Darling Downs to Adelaide, from Sydney Harbor to the Swan River, traditional Aboriginal burning conflicted with the requirements for European-type settlement. Pioneers attributed to routine bush burning an antagonism that was not so much personal as it was intrinsic to the conflict between very different cultures. In an event no less symbolic for being commonplace, an Aborigine named Willamy was arrested outside Adelaide in 1839 for "wilfully and maliciously setting fire to the grass," then publicly flogged for an act that, for tens of millennia, had been as traditional as walking or sleeping. Aboriginal fires, however, had lost their sustaining context.[2]

Yet European fire practices were no less disruptive to Aboriginal geography. In areas that cried for fire, the European often withheld it, and in areas that had been spared routine burning, it was often applied. Alfred Searcy described, for example, how on the McArthur River in 1886 he discovered a "patch of jungle." The country adjacent had not burned for years, "for there seemed to be feet of dry undergrowth. The temptation was too great, so a match went into it and we cleared. It was a truly wonderful sight." Searcy expressed his delight in igniting such sites because "we were too far away from anywhere for the fire to do damage." In all likelihood that "jungle" had been an Aboriginal garden, carefully spared from fire; what the European considered good sport was probably to the Aborigine an act of vandalism. But Europeans routinely deposited fire at their landfalls as they did goats, rats, and seeds. Either by accident or design, Flinders's crew fired

Mondrain Island (Recherche Archipelago) in 1802 so effectively that the entire island burned. Only within a certain tolerance were the fire practices of the two cultures compatible. The frontier between was commonly in flame.[3]

Even among the Europeans there were incompatibilities. The fire practices of the grazier did not synchronize with those of the farmer, and both challenged the fire expectations of the forester. The miner burned everyone's lands indiscriminately. The urbanite understood only the terror of the bushfire. Each of these groups so evolved, moreover, that practices suitable for one time and place were unacceptable at a later time. The "white blackfellow" hunting kangaroo and loosely herding semiwild ponies—a vanguard of early settlement—became anathema as farming matured and as forestry claimed jurisdiction over the wooded bush. The pastoralist burning his snow lease became anachronistic in an age of pasture improvement with "sub and super." The selector waiting for a blistering northerly before lighting up his few acres of new slash amid a forest thick with ring-barked tinder menaced the wheat fields and paddocks of more settled farmers.[4]

Yet fire was there for all, as inexpungable as the bush. With the axe it preceded and prepared the lands for a transplanted European biota. With sublime indifference, it could roar out of the bush and raze the foundations of a transplanted European civilization. Fire destroyed the foundations of Sydney Cathedral and the notorious model prison at Port Arthur, preceded the major mineral discoveries in South Australia and New South Wales, accompanied explorers and surveying parties, announced the independence of Victoria as a Crown colony and the advent of World War II. In the metachemistry of Australian settlement, fire was both a catalyst for change and an expression of change, the fiery outcome of a reaction that was poorly controlled, that brought unrelated elements together into a volatile new compound. It both built and destroyed, but it could not be denied or eliminated.

**BY FIRE'S LIGHT:
EXPLORATION BY FIRE**

The exploration of coastal Australia followed pillars of smoke by day and fires by night. In the interior, explorers requisitioned native guides who pointed out the landscape with their firesticks. Shrewd explorers knew that Aboriginal fires clustered around waterholes and used those smoke columns as beacons. They sought out pastures greening up after fires and shunned recently burned landscapes that lacked fodder for their horses. They encountered indigenous fires for which they had little preparation, and they struggled to learn how to transfer European fire to Australia without being burned in the process. In the process of European discovery, bushfire was a means, an object, and an outcome.

"All the country from where we started is all burned, and in every direction the bush is on fire," wrote Captain Hovell in 1824. With suitable allowances that observation could be repeated for nearly all the early treks into Aboriginal Australia; the bushfire was as common as gums and spinifex. One reason is that European explorers had Aboriginal guides and traveled to areas frequented by them and were accordingly constantly immersed in an environment shaped by Aboriginal fire. But it is also true that the colonists had access to such places because Aboriginal burning had readied it for them.[5]

An interesting example is the journal of Allan Cunningham, surgeon on John Oxley's 1817 expedition to the Lachlan River. While it lacks the classic insights on Aborigines and fire found in the published memoirs of Mitchell, Sturt, or Leichhardt, the journal records a routine of fire that conveys authenticity and recommends itself as a miniature of the fires that explorers saw and exploited.

The exploring party departed Parramatta on March 1, 1817. On the twenty-fourth, more than sixty miles west of Bathurst, they passed "a fine, rich, grassy tract of country, which, however, has at this period rather a bare and naked aspect, having been fired by natives." The next day they discovered that "the whole of the vegetation on this rocky hill has been lately burnt by the natives in search of game." On May 15 they inspected Mount Melville and learned that "the timber upon it is small and stunted: its surface had been recently fired by natives, and it has that self-same aspect of sterility as Mount Cunningham." The expedition abandoned its boats and set out toward Mount Flinders. Desperate for water, Cunningham recorded on the nineteenth that they "managed 2 miles farther and encamped among some burnt grass which had been fired by the natives." Two days later they came to a "burnt grass tract" that induced them to halt and look for water before proceeding further. Later, on June 3, they "came upon a patch of burnt grass" about four miles from Mount Cayley. On the fifth, while camped for the night, they observed that "the country at the verge of the horizon southerly is in flames, being fired by natives." In the vicinity of Peel's Range on the nineteenth they found that "the hills bounding the valley have been lately fired by the natives." Closing on the hills, they discovered an "extensive tract of burnt grass," where they chased a flock of twenty emus; the eastern side of Good's Peak, they saw, had been "lately burnt by natives, whose fires we could distinctly see at the base of a hill a few miles to the eastward of us." They passed through the burned flats and came the next day "to an elevated open but burnt country full of gullies and watercourses." On their left they marched past a "mount that has been fired" and continued over "a flat of burnt grass and scrubby spots alternately" in the vicinity of Barrow's Hill. When he ascended Mount Flinders on June 22, Cunningham found that its whole eastern and southern sides had been "recently fired by the natives, consequently it afforded me nothing, the whole being burnt to the ground"—the voice of the collecting botanist, frustrated by the timing of the fires. On the twenty-seventh, having explored lakes and swamps, they marched to the northeast where they "passed some land that had been fired by the natives." They forded the Lachlan, entered thickets of mallee and acacia, and discovered "some patches of land that had been formerly fired by the natives producing some good tufts of grass [which]induced us to turn out of our course in the scrub and halt upon it." This scene continued for "some miles." By July 7 Cunningham noted that "the land continues of the forest description with slight risings for upwards of 6 miles to a considerable tract of burnt grass, where was good pasturage for our horses." They moved on, hoping to intersect the Macquarie River. On the twelfth, after miles of travel through "a very sterile scrubby district," the party pitched tents "near some holes of water, where was burnt grass for the horses." The following day, in the vicinity of Mount Johnston, Cunningham noted that "the hills on this side were fired by the natives, the flames making rapid progress in the dry high grass." The plants, unfortunately, "now became exceedingly uninteresting." On the eighteenth they crossed a deep dry creek and "passed a flat burnt track" in their ascent to a range of rocky hills "which there is no avoiding." On the twenty-first they engaged in extensive surveys down the river—near Molle's Rivulet—and discovered that "the country has been burnt at no distant period, and the grass that has grown from the old clumps is exceedingly strong and luxuriant." Exposed limestone outcrops, "half burnt by the natives having fired the grassy hills," had changed to lime by the action of rainwater. On the twenty-fifth they departed the Macquarie and passed "over some gentle hills that had been very recently burnt by the natives." Short of provisions, their return to Bathurst ended in a series of forced marches.[6]

Other expeditions experienced more dramatic encounters. In 1838 a surveying party in South Australia, under a Mr. McLaren, was running lines through scrubby ground (probably mallee) when James Hawker "saw that the tremendous high grass in the head of the valley was on fire." The sight was "grand" and the observer, "not at all realizing the fearful position we were in," ran to tell his friend Darke so that he, too, could enjoy the "splendid sight." But Darke had known bushfires in Tasmania and realized the danger to the party; he shouted for the men to instantly abandon their tools and race for their lives to the southern end of the valley where the road passed, the ground was open, and the grass short. The flames "rose to a fearful height, and the heat and smoke were awful," but the party—"pretty well blown"—reached safety. Recovered, they dashed back to their camp where, in lighter fuels, they were able to beat the flames. Then they hurried to other threatened locales—to Major O'Halloran's homestead, to a camp set up by "passengers of the Surry ship," to other neighbors. Chief-of-Party McLaren himself barely escaped with his life when he found himself completely surrounded by fire. He spied a weakness in the flames, covered his panicked horse's eyes with a hankerchief, dug his spurs into its flanks, and rode through the flames, his clothes and whiskers singed, his hat lost, and on a horse that "required no clipping." [7]

The whole question of how fire behaved in Australia had to be learned empirically. Fires could not be lit as casually as in Britain. If the violent encounter with a bushfire was one side of discovery, the other was the endless record of campfires that escaped. Until they took strict precautions, until they learned the true vigor of Australian fire-proneness, virtually every expedition lost fires and sometimes gear. Casual travelers and indifferent bushmen were notorious for their carelessness around fire. George Cayley described how, from afar, he observed a fire rage around his camp and "began to be afraid the men has set the place on fire and what heightened my apprehensions was their never having been accustomed of making fires in the woods." With the "greatest difficulty," the camp was saved and a lesson learned. But even veteran bushmen had campfires flare out of control. On his second expedition, Ernest Giles recorded how Jimmy Andrews set fire to the spinifex close to their packs and saddles and "the fire raged around us in a terrific manner." The party ran and shouted and turned back, and frantically threw anything "we could catch hold of onto the ground already burnt." The "instant a thing was lifted" the grass beneath it seemed to burst into fire spontaneously. "I was on fire, Jimmy was on fire, my brains were in a fiery, whirling blaze; and what with the heat, dust, smoke, ashes and wind I thought I must be suddenly translated into pandemonium." [8]

The accepted solution was to camp on sites of light or green fuels, or, as Joseph Banks had early resolved, to burn out the grasses before pitching camp. An alternative was to imitate the Aborigines—techniques no doubt learned from native guides. The Reverend John Lhotsky quickly appreciated the value of fires banked in the hollow cavities of large gums, although combustion could spread throughout the excavated interior and flames spurt out of open branches "like a Bengal fire." The branches could then burn through, fall to the ground, and ignite the surrounding bush. It was a hazard readily accepted by most travelers in exchange for not having to stoke a fire through the night. [9]

Even precautions could be frustrated. Backhouse explained how he prepared a camp "under the shelter of a wood" in Tasmania. Carefully, he burned off the grass, swept the site, and kindled a fire against a log. The log, however, was rotten; it ignited, and threw sparks into nearby grass, which communicated the flames to a forest full of "brushwood, that did not appear to have been burnt for many years." The outcome was an "exceedingly grand" conflagration, though one that cost the party considerable labor in beating the flames and burning out the grass around their camp and not a little anxiety as hollowed trees burned through and thundered to the ground throughout the night.[10]

The newcomers soon made accommodations. Often they adjusted to fire by using fire. In his 1802 survey of Port Phillip, for example, Charles Grimes recorded how the party shot a kangaroo and proceeded to broil it and soon set the bush ablaze. Without great fuss, however, the group moved "a little further where we made another fire." In the early afternoon the captain "set fire to the bush, and we marched on towards the marquee." Bushfires became normal, and anthropogenic fires expected. The exodus of Aboriginal fire created a vacuum into which moved European fire. Not surprisingly, Grimes noted that "the country in general is newly burnt." [11]

FIREPOWER: FIRE WAR
ON THE FRONTIER

The European reconnaissance was frequently violent, and the friction between cultures, no less than that between invader and land, found expression in fire. The experience of Cook and Banks, while symbolic, was far from unique. When his French counterpart, Captain Marion, landed in Tasmania in 1771, an Aborigine handed the curious captain a firestick, "that he might set light to a pile of wood heaped up on the flat shore." Marion accepted in the belief that he was inspiring confidence, that he was participating in a savage formality. But once he set the pile alight, the Aborigines retired to a small height and hurled stones; the French retaliated with muskets; and the encounter dispersed in confusion and death. Between them the two episodes announced the terms of a curious fire war.[12]

Exploring expeditions knew well—or soon learned—the hazards of an unprotected campsite. Leading a party along the coast to Broken Bay, Governor Phillip ordered the long grass around the camp to be fired all around, "for fear the natives should surprise us in the night by doing the same, a custom for which they seem always happy to indulge themselves." Mitchell noted with satisfaction that the grass around his proposed camp "had been assiduously burned by the natives"; had grass remained, it could be fired, "which, in case of hostility, on the part of the natives, is usually the first thing they do." Others described a scorched earth strategy by which Aborigines apparently burned vast tracts in advance of the expedition to deprive its horses of food and to inconvenience or frighten the men. Baudin, for example, related how in Tasmania the Aborigines systematically applied fire to scare off the exploring expedition, then covered their retreat up the slopes of a mountain by trailing fire.[13]

Later expeditions routinely echoed those experiences. Crossing the plains of the Macquarie, Sturt witnessed some Aboriginal burning with consternation, for "we knew that the natives never made such extensive conflagration, unless they had some mischievous object in view . . ." In another encounter, the Aborigines fled before the explorers. "Their huts were in a moment in flames, and each with a fire-brand ran to and fro with hideous yells, thrusting them into every bush they passed." Leichhardt surprised an Aboriginal camp occupied chiefly by women and a few old men, "who immediately ran off, but set the grass on fire as they went to prevent the approach of the horsemen." Gregory complained about Aborigines who made frequent attempts to burn the camp and disperse the horses by setting fire to the grass as a prelude to more open hostilities. Giles related how a band of Aborigines appeared with an "emission of several howls, yells, gesticulations and indecent actions" before encircling the whites with fire "to frighten us out, or roast us to death." The small band rode through the flaming spinifex and away to safety. E. B. Kennedy's expeditions of 1847 barely escaped bushfires on several occasions. In one instance the natives allowed the explorers to enter a large grassy plain, then ignited the dense grasses to the windward; the party barely gained some burned ground (which they remembered from previous travels) before the flames were upon them. When Aborigines chose to assault the McKinlay party, a grass fire masked a force of some 150 warriors. Stuart found his marches constantly flanked and harassed by hostile Aboriginal fire. On the Finke River natives repeatedly fired the scrub to windward "so that the blinding smoke blew across, providing an effective screen for an attack at close quarters with spears and boomerangs." Broadcast burning— perhaps for multiple reasons—encircled their camp as fires "came rolling and roaring along in one immense street of flame and smoke, destroying everything before it." Along the Mary River bands of Aborigines "set fire to the grass all around us to try and burn us out. Two of them came again close to camp under the pretence of looking for game before the fire, at the same time setting fire to the grass closer to us." Finally Stuart vowed to use preventive means, for "I can stand it no longer." [14]

Settlements were even more vulnerable precisely because they were settled. Until the bush was cleared back, until Aboriginal firesticks were swept from the scene, fire was a constant fear. In the early years many of the fires were simply a product of traditional burning, now—to white eyes—grossly out of context. Native fires annually threatened the countryside, and as settlers installed new combustibles like humpies, wheat fields, slash, and ring-barked gums they only aggravated the situation. Thus George Moore voiced common folk experience when he wrote from the fledgling settlements in Western Australia that "the country has been fired by the natives and we have been obliged to use great efforts to save ourselves and our property." The vulnerability of these embryonic neo-Europes was immediately apparent to Aborigines, and when they wished to attack, they freely resorted to fire. Writing from Ripon Shire, Mrs. Kirkland noted that "the fires in the bush are often the work of the natives, to frighten away white men." Mary Gilmore, after quoting an Aboriginal chief on the carelessness of white fire practices, related how he then applied fire "miles wide" to burn out "him and his." Shepherds were easy targets for spear and fire. In their journals of life on the Glenelg Plains (1837), the Hentys describe how they were watched by a band of Aborigines, who "fired the hills when they left," then returned to ignite more area around the hut before the whites discharged a warning shot, at which point the Aborigines returned to encircle the graziers with fire. The fires "spoiled our day's shearing," Frank Henty wrote in his diary, "in consequence of being obliged to put the fires out." On Kangaroo Island a Dr. Leigh recalled how in 1837 "some of the wretches" hurried down upon their encampment at midnight with firesticks and set fire in an enormous circle of three miles. The conflagration, the hour, "the uproar caused by the capture of some of the ringleaders, the shouts of the men, and screams of women and children, formed a scene which I wish never to again witness." [15]

"It was in their power," George Cayley explained to Joseph Banks, to have "done us almost an irreparable injury by fire." While fire enhanced Aboriginal hunting and foraging, it had equal capacity to obliterate the European transplants. Governor Phillip wrote London that Aborigines might "attempt to burn our crops, of which I am apprehensive." In 1800 Governor Hunter pondered how "fire in the hands of a body of irritated and hostile natives may with little trouble to them ruin our prospects of an abundant harvest." The early fields had, in fact, been repeatedly threatened by bushfires and occasionally damaged by them. This the Aborigines understood, and Hunter realized that "they are not ignorant of having that power in their hands." Around Melbourne in 1840 a large assembly of Aborigines, outfitted with muskets, threatened to burn down the settlement. Where border warfare intensified into genocide, as in Tasmania, burning became more systematic. Alarmed settlers petitioned the governor in 1830 to warn that broadcast burning threatened "the extinction of the Colony itself by firing our Crops and Dwellings." [16]

The notorious Black War that raged across Tasmania during the 1820s saw fire used freely by both sides. For all its horror, the situation was not without paradox. Aborigines applied fire to fields and houses, while Europeans erected signal fires on the hills, flushed out hiding Aborigines by burning scrub, and strung out miles of broadcast burns in an approximation of a fire drive. Bonwick described a firefight at Eaglehawk Neck. "The enemy sought to gain the barbican by fire. Soon the flames were seen penetrating the dark gorges, and climbing the rocky steeps. The colonial force . . . kept up the vast fires for observation and destruction." [17]

Aboriginal tactics clearly derived from hunting precedents. They fired houses as they did hollow eucalypts, ready to kill the creatures that the smoke and heat flushed out. They fired wheat shocks as they did tussocks. They hurled firesticks as though they were warding off night demons escaped from the Dreamtime. Fields and paddocks they burned like favored hunting grounds. They set decoy fires to distract settlers, then plundered their homesteads and barns for food. Attaching firesticks to spears, they ignited thatched roofs from a distance. Even when the battle had to be fought subliminally, by sorcery, they resorted to fire, as in the apocryphal story of Old Billy who worked his revenge by unleashing his lightning totem and burned the house of his white boss to the ground. In brief, the Aborigine brought fire where the Europeanized environment could not accept it.[18]

The European reciprocated with firearms and a devastating deprivation of fire. Their campfires revealed the location of Aboriginal bands to European forces; Aborigines complained bitterly that they had to live in darkness, travel cold, and eat uncooked food or else face surprise attack. Cattle and sheep cropped the native grasses to the point at which they could no longer carry fire or feed kangaroos. Scrub flourished on former grasslands. Prime hunting grounds, made accessible by fire, became fields planted to unburnable tubers or flushed with domestic grasses protected by firebreaks and firearms. Where the British burned, they did so for different purposes and at different times, and they yielded different effects. To each, the other's was a hostile fire.

TRANSPORTED FIRE: WHILE ALL
AROUND THE CONFLAGRATION RAGES

The contrasts and conflicts intensified where Europeans erected towns. Permanent settlement—whether as a penal state or a Wakefield-inspired planned colony—was incompatible with broadcast fire, which always favored some kind of nomadism. If European settlement was to spread, it had either to convert the whole Australian biota or to adopt forms of burning and a transient existence. It did both.

British settlement clustered around intensely urban cores, a conglomerate of city-states. Yet it also dispersed as vagrant mobs of diggers, graziers, swagmen, explorers, and adventurers swarmed across those landscapes that resisted easy conversion to agriculture or city. Until they were cast in stone, the cities—made of wattles, gum bark, and thatch—were little more than a reconstituted bush and were highly vulnerable to bushfires. The problem was not merely with Aboriginal fires but with those fires transported from Britain, temporarily disciplined fires that authorities could not indefinitely keep in prison. Once loosed, they ran wild.

The first years of settlement at Sydney coincided with a wet weather cycle, and the colony suffered more from misplanning, poor lines of supply, ignorance of farming, and the wretched infertility of the Hawkesbury sandstone than from fire. All this changed as the weather gradually dried. In 1790 a grass fire bore down on the settlement, though it was controlled without major distress. By 1792, however, drought scorched the land and fires raged. David Collins reported how, in December of that year, the country "was everywhere on fire." The dampened burning of the past few years was now recouped with vengeance.[19]

In the outlying areas, where bush intermingled with farm, the fires were fought with the tools at hand. A Mr. Arndell suffered "greatly"; the fires spread to his farm, where his laborers and neighbors fought it down, until an "unlucky spark" from a flaming tree flew to his thatched roof before destroying his hut, outbuildings, and wheat harvest. Elsewhere the fires destroyed gardens and fences. The "whole face of the hill" on the west side of the cove was ablaze, jeopardizing every thatched dwelling and stack of wheat. The settlers fought back, the New South Wales Corps joined in, and the fires were gradually beaten down. Only two days previously had farmers harvested the wheat at Toongabbie; now the stubbled field burned, and terrified officials contemplated how narrowly the fledgling colony had averted disaster. Immediately, Collins reported, the settlement took precautions against a similar accident "by clearing the timber for a certain distance around the cultivated land"—a *cordon sanitaire* between the two Australias.[20]

The next outbreak came in 1797. Governor Hunter marveled at the power of the fires. "Trains of gunpowder cou'd scarcely have been more rapid," he exclaimed. The fires ravaged stacked wheat, huts, and livestock, and ruined some settlers. At Toongabbie they consumed some eight hundred bushels of precious wheat. The governor himself was called out abruptly one night to a government field at Parramatta to which "a vast fire was quickly approaching." It was a sublime, wonderfully Australian scene. "The night was dark, the wind high, and the fire, from its extent, and the noise it made thro' lofty blazing woods, was truly terrible," Hunter wrote to the duke of Portland. No effort was too great to save the precious wheat; in desperation the embattled governor ordered out a convict chain gang and promised them a pardon if they could beat back the flames. All night they fought, in linked shackles, with eucalypt boughs, silhouetted against the blazing bush, and in the morning, as the fires retreated away from the fields, they were freed.[21]

The episode impressed the governor, who promulgated edicts to protect critical property. The people in general had been careless and indifferent in shielding their farms from "those vast and tremendous blazes to which this country in its present state is so liable." Public orders followed to secure wheat stacks from fire. But drought and fire persisted into the next year, and Hunter had, again, to report serious losses sustained from fires "set by the natives." The governor urged that firebreaks be plowed, or trenches or ditches dug, a kind of earthworks fortification. The summer of 1798–99 was little better. The "whole country has been in a blaze of fire, our pasturage for a time destroyed." Rumors flew that some of the most damaging fires had been set by debt-plagued farmers hoping to inflate the value of their surviving crops. The governor knew, however, that wildfires would vanish as the press of settlement advanced. Bushfires were a phenomenon of a frontier that advanced slowly and incompletely. In 1826 the Reverend John Lang could stand on the Sydney Rocks and watch conflagrations roar through the surrounding bush.

> Fearful I stood on the moss-covered rock . . .
> The forest blazed around, volumes of smoke
>   Towering to heaven obscured the face of day:
>   And as the red sun shot his parting ray
> Through the dense atmosphere, the lurid sky
>   Glowed with a fiercer flame—spreading dismay—
> As if the dread day of doom were nigh!
> . . . O then to stand upon the Rock of Ages,
> While all around the conflagration rages![22]

Similar scenes characterized the settlement of all the new cities. The first land and survey offices of central Adelaide were constructed of reeds, thatched roofs, and slabs of eucalypt bark—amid grasses. In January 1839 they burned and took with them thirty years of Colonel William Light's journals. The settlement of the plains, a prime scene for Aboriginal burning, demanded fire protection, and once the strictures compelling close settlement were lifted, pioneers still hesitated to leap too far ahead of neighbors, in part for fear of bushfires. The suppression of wild bushfires came only with the suppression of the wild bush.[23]

At the Swan River colony settlement patterns were more diffuse, native burning abundant, and damaging fires common. The *Perth Gazette* reported in February 1833 that "the fires, kindled by the natives, in different parts of the country, have spread with alarming rapidity and presented a grand and interesting spectacle." The country was "one continuous blaze." Some fires were fought by isolated families on the fringe of settlement; some by a congeries of neighbors; and some by the military. George Webb described with breathless detail how at Perth the detachment of King's Light Infantry rushed off "double quick" to fires at Mount Eliza in 1841. "There were many native fires burning," and at night the distant conflagrations were "very beautiful at this season of the year." But when they bore down on farms, they had all the traits of an enemy invasion. "It is wonderful what can be done under the influence of excitement," Webb gushed. He himself suffered the soles of his boots to be burnt through, and at one point he passed out from heat and smoke and had to be rescued from the flames.

But it was all a night of business-as-usual for the largely Irish 51st.[24]

Yet Australia could not be remade completely into another Europe. Biotic transfers were unpredictable and important cultigens were often slow to transplant. Settlement would show extremes—densely urban in a handful of sites, extensively rural and wild elsewhere. Episodic drought, desert winds, old and new pyrophytes all assured a continued existence for fire. The founding purpose of European Australia as a closed prison was inadequate, flawed as a social vision and untenable as an environmental reality. The newcomers could not extirpate the bush, and with the bush there would exist the bushman, whose storied mobility made him the antithesis of the convict. It is with considerable poetic justice, in fact, that the constructed exemplars of that penal world, the model prison and penitentiary at Port Arthur, should end their existence in a bushfire.

The particular fire that gutted the hated vestige of the "system" was first observed on land outside the town around two o'clock on January 1, 1898, part of a complex of conflagrations that afflicted most of Tasmania and that on the mainland devoured large chunks of Gippsland. Within two hours the fire had rushed through the town with the malevolent, selective cunning of a tornado. Untouched were buildings to the flanks of its narrow perimeter. Instead the fire raced directly into the penitentiary, then to the police office, then through other miscellaneous structures. The penal establishment burned first and longest. After forty-eight hours it was a ruin. This—the third fire to strike the town—was the final blow for the haunted buildings. The model prison, the hospital, the lunatic asylum, and the church had all been consumed in the earlier burnings. It seemed, wrote a reporter for the *Tasmanian Mail,* that fire is "to be the destiny of Port Arthur."

There was a bitter irony to the scene. "The fire and tempest had a method in its work, and it was of a merciful kind." There were many, the reporter continued, "who will make no concealment of their satisfaction at the destruction of the Penitentiary," and if any old crawlers yet lived, they no doubt rejoiced at the avenging fire. But there was also a singular symbolism to the scene. Transported fire ranged free in Australia, and no settlement could endure which, like the prison, could not suffer fire. Although the European immigrants could not live as Aborigines, neither could they live as English villagers. They needed a different relationship to fire.[25]

FOSSICKING BY FIRESTICK

Although most British colonists had lived in cities, their Australian identity was paradoxically with the bush. The European became an Australian when he took to the bush. The bushranger, though easily romanticized, was flawed by his own lawlessness and his predatory dependence on urban settlement. Instead the torch passed, literally, to the squatter, the selector, and the digger. The agriculturalists enjoyed a complex relationship with fire because they had complex relationships to the biota that constituted its fuels. But the digger cared for none of that. His purposes were extractive, and he used fire against the Australian flora as he would a pick against a reef of Australian quartz. Between his boiling billy and his matches, the prospector burned a trail across and around the continent. In the heyday of the Victorian gold rushes an outraged William Howitt contrasted the serenity of Mount Buffalo with "this fire-scattering race of rude men" who burned the forests around it.[26]

Broadcast fire often prepared the landscape for mineral discovery. In 1841 two Cornish miners four miles outside Adelaide systematically fired the rank grass to expose outcrops and discovered galena. The "smoke from burning grass," Geoffrey Blainey has written, "signalled the birth of Australian metal mining." Six days after Black Thursday, February 6, 1851, in which a fourth of Victoria burned, Edward Hargraves revealed nuggets of gold that he had discovered west of Bathurst. The revelation started a rush that quickly spilled into Victoria, largely over those very regions that had been swept by the fires. Dispatched by Sir Roderick Murchison from the British Geological Survey, Charles Gould opened up the western Tasmanian fields by "setting the scrub ablaze as he went." In February 1862 his party of bushmen fired out the Linda Valley, and blustery winds compelled Gould and company to light protective backfires; the fires burned out the valley and up the slopes of Mount Lyell. While Gould missed the signs of mineral wealth, others followed, and by repeating his tactics uncovered one of the great mines of Australia.[27]

Actually the new diggers didn't need such examples to encourage them. Broadcast burning was an ancient ally of prospecting, as common in Mesoamerica as in the Mediterranean. But Australia was so easily put to the torch that burning assumed new standards of recklessness. Miners swarmed like flocks of galahs, and as mobs roamed from one site to another their exploratory burns cleared the land and their campfires set the horizon aglow. Around Australia the prospectors ranged, ringing the island continent with fossicking fire. Baron von Müller observed in Western Australia during the 1870s that the "miner ignites the underwood" to better uncover quartz reefs, and in so doing "really sets the whole forest on fire." Howitt, describing the scene near the Buckland River in 1855, noted that "the grass and scrub were nearly all burnt up by the diggers, who burn up the country wherever they go, as they say, to get rid of snakes." Their profligacy with fire —not only from outright burning but by flattening and uprooting the flora into slash—required them to send their horses to the plains for keep since no fodder remained near their camps. Prospectors in the upper Hume catchment burned off the cover so that they might more easily trace the line of gold-bearing reefs and carry on "loaming." Claim jumpers set fires to the windward of camps to drive off competitors. In Tasmania it became "quite an ordinary custom for the prospector to set fire to the timber and let the flames spread at will over as much of the surrounding country as they can reach." It was, most agreed, a "miner's right," though one dismayed forester, contemplating that "this course is adopted by hundreds of men scattered far and wide over extensive districts," shuddered at the cost in timber. The mining towns of the west coast, another reported, were breeding grounds for "intentional and unintentional incendiarists." The untended billy fire was as common a source as a deliberate torching, and both were tolerated—applauded—as contributions to "clearing up the country." The *Tasmanian Mail* assured readers that even the horrendous fires of 1898 had their redeeming points. "They have cleared away miles of almost impenetrable bush and scrub, so that the prospector may now carry out his work with a tithe of the toil and trouble" he knew before.[28]

As prospecting gave way to mining, however, free-burning fires became a menace. The slashed bush and marauding swagmen made summer fires as common as spring floods. In Queenstown, Tasmania, for example, bushfires over the course of five summers destroyed four hundred huts and houses; some homeowners were burned out three times. Some mining leases had been fired so often—as many as fifteen times—that cynics suggested sulphur coated the bush. If mobile diggers were incendiarists, sedentary miners became firefighters. Fire even invaded the timbered mineshafts. Fire gutted the North Lyell mine in 1912, the Great Coban in 1920, Mount Morgan in 1925. The Proprietary mine at Broken Hill, kindled in 1895, burned for years. Gradually, like the diggers themselves, however, fire lost its mobility and was relegated to furnaces of forges and smelters.[29]

The consequences of the mining booms for fire did not end with the domestication of the torch. Mining profoundly disturbed fuels over large areas. The landscape was not only repeatedly burned, but cut, dug up, rearranged. The bush was slashed, the soils disturbed, the streams deranged. Smelting demanded enormous quantities of wood and charcoal, and these came initially from the surrounding countryside. When plastered with the toxic fumes from smelters, the biota never recovered. Where Queenstown had once witnessed recurring bushfires through its hills, by the mid-twentieth century it resembled a toxic moonscape. There were no longer fires because there was no longer anything left to burn.

By stimulating a population boom, moreover, mining changed the entire character of European settlement, and this also hastened the restructuring of Australian fire regimes. Population would not be contained within close-settled cities; land would not be monopolized by the crown or by squatters; European Australia would not endure as a self-subsisting folk society but would be integrated into a global economy that imposed its own striking dynamism. Fire followed the flag. Capitalist mining—epitomized by the gold rush—was by nature hyperbolic, exaggerating everything it touched. Yet its fire practices had a prophetic commonness about them, too. It put fire into folk hands.

Mining brought fire where fire had been at best an infrequent presence, and it removed fire entirely from sites that had routinely burned. It accelerated, magnified, and warped the fire history of Australia in ways that made it a distorted allegory for European settlement at large, a scene viewed through shimmering heat waves. Yet if the "fire-scattering" digger was a harbinger of what was to come, he was, equally, too indiscriminate to survive. He came, he cut, dug, and burned, and then he left. His extractive industry was destructive not only of land but of itself. What the fossicking fire revealed, later fires smelted away. But the grazier, the farmer, and the forester stayed. They required the bush. They had to coexist with bushfire. They had to use fire as a recurring tool in a renewing flora.

12

Red Steers and
Green Pick

The introduction of sheep, cattle and horses from Europe . . . has in effect constituted the engine by which the Englishman has, to some extent, insensibly modified a few of the great features of nature in Australia.

—EDWARD CURR, *Recollections of Squatting in Victoria (1883)*

Is the grazier right to regard, as he frequently tells me, a box of wax matches as the best grass seed he can sow?

—C. E. LANE-POOLE, *Testimony before the Royal Commission (1939)*

IN PONDERING THE CHARACTER OF 1870S AUSTRALIA, W.H.L. Ranken noted in particular the power of fire to clear the land of all but eucalypts. "Hence," he concluded, "the open forest of Australia; hence grazing and squatters and land-laws; hence wool and meat-growing are before everything else." Its graziers were indeed the great pioneers of Australia, and pastoralism the economic and ecological engine of European settlement. Explorers sought out new pasture lands; diggers, otherwise impervious to nuances of biotas, created local markets for meat; improved transport and a sequence of immense stimulants—British industrialization, the Napoleonic wars, and the subsequent Pax Britannica—bound Australia to global markets for wool. The Australian economy rode on a sheep's back.[1]

Its pastoral age announced an explosion of capitalism and colonization, a fever that ravaged every niche in Australia. The Reverend Lang summed up its spirit:

The *sheep and cattle mania* . . . seized on all ranks and classes of its inhabitants . . . barristers and attorneys; military officers of every rank, and civilians of every department; clergymen and medical men; merchants, settlers, and dealers in general, were there seen promiscuously mingled together . . . and outbidding each other in the most determined manner . . . for the purchase of every scabbed sheep or scarecrow horse or buffalo-cow that was offered for sale in the colony . . .[2]

Graziers openly defied colonial governors and creaking land laws promulgated in distant London and quickly invaded the expansive grasslands of the interior. Those marauding flocks and herds became a shock wave that transformed the Australian landscape, redistributing fire and fuels. The pastoral explosion not only destabilized indigenous biotas but restructured them in ways that made restoration impossible.

For all this there was ample precedent. A mixed farming economy had become the norm in northern Europe, and the First Fleet brought livestock. Since the great Renaissance voyages of discovery, European explorers had routinely deposited goats and sheep (and, by accident, rats) on uninhabited islands, where they could multiply and feed future exploring parties. But Australia was an enormous island, and with human assistance livestock exploded in population, the foremost of the Holocene pests to infest the landscape. European livestock soon penetrated every biota of Australia, and in each European graziers had to work out a new relationship to fire.

What made livestock herding different from kangaroo hunting, however, was the self-destructive character of "domesticated" grazing. Grazing became, in places, almost as extractive as mining, and early fire practices by graziers often resembled those of diggers, using fires to expose the biotic potential of this strange landscape. The exotic fauna compacted the soil with hard hoofs, something unknown in Australian natural history. They selected some grasses and forbs over others, upsetting the floral composition of native pastures. By close cropping, by ruthless overgrazing, the alien herds devoured the fine fuels that could carry fire and allow the ecosystem to recycle itself; only in years of exceptional rainfall was fire even possible. Consequently, scrub invaded some grasslands and other ranges turned to sand, eroded into gulleys, or flooded with noxious weeds. On badly disturbed sites, burning often entered into a furious spiral in which broadcast fires became essential not only to flush out ever-scarcer nutrients but to dampen fuels that threatened wildfire. Without fire Europeans could never have opened up the Australian biota for exploitation on the scale they did, but it is equally true that without fire's association with axe and hoof, it is likely that the Australian scene could have absorbed a shift in fire practices without irreversible consequences. Australian grasses, for example, were resilient to fire but not to grazing; Australian soil could accept fire and drought, but not compaction from hooves.

If, as Lang despaired, pastoralism came before all else, it is also true that it usually came with fire. If, as Mitchell had observed, fire, grass, kangaroos, and Aborigines formed an interdependent ensemble, that was no less true of fire, livestock, and pastoralists. To reform one part was to reform the others.

KEEP IT WELL UNDER, BUT LET IT RUN:
FIRE PRACTICES OF AUSTRALIAN PASTORALISTS

As Ranken realized, Aboriginal fire had prepared many sites for European occupation. It was a simple matter for domesticated stock to replace wild grazers and browsers. Fire stimulated the indigenous grasses and pruned the restless scrub; allied with metal axes, it could transform forest bush to bush paddocks. Long British experience suggested how fire could force infertile lands to yield, at least temporarily, their hoarded nutrients. Graziers knew that stock would naturally gravitate to the more palatable grasses thrusting up through the ash; they soon learned that fire could, momentarily, transform marginal bush into pasture; they believed fire reduced weeds, checked pests, and stalled reinvasion by scrub. They wanted the "green pick" of fire, but they did not want the "red steer," as they called bushfire, to produce it.

Over and again explorers reported that freshly burned sites yielded succulent grass, and time and again pastoralists witnessed the power of fire to improve yields. Within limits fire could overcome some of the nutrient deficiencies that debilitated stock with "cripples" and "coasties" and other ailments. Leichhardt observed that Aborigines used fire "in the same way that stockholders burn parts of their [range] in the proper seasons. At least those who are not influenced by erroneous notion, that burning the grass injures the richness and density of the natural turf." A number of surveyors—Mitchell in New South Wales, Wedge in Tasmania, for example—advocated burning as a method of improving pasturage. Mitchell ridiculed as coarse ignorance an order by the "Imperial Government" that sought to prohibit firing. Peter Cunningham noted that the old grasses were customarily "burnt off in the spring, and often at other periods of the year if you have an extensive run for your stock." The effects were astounding—rich feed and banished insects. In the early days of Yea Shire, John Cotton affirmed that it was "a great benefit to have a portion of the run burnt off ocassionally," since it flushed the grass and cleared the scrub. Around Adelaide it was observed that "every year our grass is partly burnt, and every year it has become more closely planted." In Victoria the flocks that fed "on the succulent feed of the burnt hills" enjoyed a "very perceptible change" for the better. Around the Port Phillip settlement the country that had been "all burnt by bushfires during the previous summer" now had grasses flourishing "as green and luxuriant as if it had been a field of grain." [3]

William Moodie probably spoke for the majority of pastoralists when he wrote that fires were "severe" in the early settlement of the country, but that they had "their good side in keeping the country free from plagues even to the latest, the blowfly"; that there is "no doubt the country is much sweetened by a good heavy fire"; that pastoralists had found out "by dearly-bought experience" that it was desirable to have "some burnt country." He cited the case of a man named Willis who had some of his pasture burned and some spared. He put his best wethers on the unburned grass, and although there was grass enough for "double the number," they languished, while those he put on the burned land flourished and the lambs were "the finest lot I had ever seen or since." A bushfire damaged the woolshed, an economic hardship, but the improvement in sheep and lambs produced by feeding on the burn "would make full compensation in one year." As the country thickened with settlers, however, it was "not so easy to get all you would wish done" toward burning. Newcomers liked the results but objected to the burning itself, which they claimed made "for a dangerous place to live." The result, Moodie wryly noted, was an abundance of "unaccountable fires." [4]

Most fires, however, were expected. That oracle of Victorian squatting, Edward Curr, described the process at length. It cost him some trouble every year to burn off portions of the run on which he had few sheep. February was the preferred month because it produced a hot fire, though March or April, Curr believed, were better because they were more likely to be followed by rain. His gang would set fire to the windward of the paddock "on some hot windy day at about eleven o'clock." They would often get an Aborigine to lead their horses while they fired dry branches (or bark torches) and dragged them across the tussocks. In this way a "fire was set a-going in a line of from one to five miles, and then left to chance." Sometimes the fire burned poorly, a "very troublesome job." On other occasions, "the flames went merrily ahead in every direction, now rushing up the tall stems of a thousand eucalypts, the leaves of which it shrivelled like old parchment." [5]

K. C. Rogers recalled burning off in the tablelands around Black Mountain in 1902. Before his family arrived, "it had been the accepted thing to burn the bush," and as soon as Rogers and his brothers were old enough, "we were keen to do the burning." The practice called for firing the country as often as possible, approximately every three to four years as conditions allowed. Wanting a clean burn—"the hotter the fire, the sweeter and better the feed"—they waited for the summer sun of January and February. To enhance effectiveness, they lit along the valley bottoms so that fire could "roar up the steep slopes on either side, making a terrific inferno and sweeping all before it." Of course not every site could support a fire, but to the extent that conditions were uniform—or could be made uniform by drought —the country burned roughly every three years from graziers and whenever wildfire could propagate among the fuels that remained.[6]

As settlement aged, burning became more difficult. Fuels changed, livestock changed, neighbors changed. Unless pastoralists adopted controlled burning, they could suffer wildfire, which could destroy dwellings and take all of their pastures at once. But broadcast fire worked best when it was rotated among extensive fields, and this required very large holdings or a pattern of seasonal nomadism—both conditions possible in the early glory years of squatting, but more difficult as settlement matured. Thus the Reverend Wollaston, surveying the annual burns in Western Australia, observed how readily it could be "imagined that a great extent of country is absolutely required for grazing, poor as it is at best." From Victorian experiences A. W. Howitt argued that as settlement intensified and as grazing lessened the standing grass, it was to the interest of pioneers "to lessen and keep within bounds bush fires which might otherwise be very destructive to their improvement." Alexander Hamilton concurred, noting that the settlers burned off the grass ("and still more in older days") for the new growth, "yet on the whole it has been their aim to fight the fires and keep them down." [7]

And fight them they did. A large bushfire could consume most of a squatter's paddocks, leaving his sheep to starve over the winter. Or it could drive the herds before it, overtaking them by sheer velocity or after they had crowded helplessly against a fence. It could even burn down dwellings. One precaution taken at Murnday, "as everywhere," was "to plough a double furrow alongside long strips, and then burn off the strips in the early summer, on the principle as iron ships are protected against foundering by isolated watertight compartments." Rolf Boldrewood recalled how the Henty estate at Muntham included "light wagons, with an adequate number of horses, called the fire-horses, kept ready to start at a moment's notice for the warning smoke column." Overseers sent riders—"mounted sentinels"—out to watch for smoke. Once spotted, the word spread quickly through the mulga telegraph; every homestead and station readied for the fire. Farmers could fire the land outside their plow lines to starve the approaching bushfire; squatters, however, needed that fuel as fodder, and sent horsemen and sometimes wagons to gather the flocks and attack against the fire directly. In light fuels, they would fight the flaming front with bags and boughs, or pinch off the racing front by advancing along the lightly burning flanks. In heavy fuels, they would retire to a stream or a road and burn out, or in desperate circumstances they could simply begin a line of fire, lighting with one hand and swatting out the back side of the fire with the other.[8]

A large fire was an extraordinary and dangerous scene. "The sun is livid and shines as through a fog," James Bonwick recalled. "The roar, of distant stormy waves, booms upon the ear, increasing hastily and violently in sound. Dark masses of smoke come flying on with the fury and speed of a whirlwind. Breaks in the cloudy wall disclose to view the leaping flames." The whole bush community rushed to wherever they could do the most good. "All the Duntroon employees," Samuel Shumack wrote of the 1858 bushfire near Canberra, "were out fighting the fire for forty hours." Social distinctions vanished. If the winds shifted, as they usually did, firefighters who regarded themselves as protected could suddenly discover that they were vulnerable. Thus a "Mr. Burke and a number of men," wrote the Reverend James Hassall, found themselves galloping for their lives; Burke's horse stumbled; another stockman hoisted the dazed Burke up on his own mount until the fire overtook them, Burke fell to a fiery death, and the stockman, staggering from his horse, ran into a swamp seconds before the main flaming front. John Bull recalled how, surrounded by fire with a mob of cattle, he drove them furiously through the "hedge of fire" to safety. The spectacle so awed Anthony Trollope, visiting his son at a Queensland station, that he made fire—its threat and reality—the central plot device of his novel *Harry Heathcote of Gangoil* (1874). "Keep it well under, but let it run," he has the young squatter command, as Heathcote's heroes string out a line of backfires to stave off an arsonist's burn. "A ticklish thing," the gentrified Heathcote mutters, "to think that a spark of fire anywhere about the place might ruin me," when swagmen, station hands, and hostile neighbors all "have matches in their pockets." [9]

Bushfires were a fact of life, an environmental hazard along with drought, flood, unsuitable land laws, and unstable prices. They trapped the pastoralist in a classic bind. In a dry year feed was at a premium, so fire was unwanted and, to the extent that the pastures were grazed heavily, unlikely. In a wet year, it was impossible to stock quickly enough to remove the surplus grasses. The unconsumable grass would, as one grazier from Bourke remarked sardonically, "just lie down and cause fires." Until the countryside was settled bushfires were a chronic nuisance, though one that could be abated by selective burning. But once settled, not only routine bushfires but controlled burning faded from the scene; fires, when they came, were far more damaging. Yet without fires, the native grasses degenerated, brush encroached on the site, and conditions worsened for a horrific bushfire. [10]

Either way, from drought or fire, from too-frequent bushfire or too-infrequent burning, the squatter faced ruin. For all its terror, however, the bushfire was a sublime spectacle, integral to the haunting rhythms of Australian natural history and fundamental to an evolving cultural identity. Fighting a bushfire evolved into one of the great moral dramas of the Australian frontier. The sight of mortal enemies like squatters and cocky farmers, constables and felons, townsfolk and swagmen all rallying to repel an invading bushfire became, in the hands of Australian writers like Henry Lawson, a tableau of bush life, an epitome of the ideal of mateship, a vision that out of an improbable origin in an implacable environment there might emerge an Australian social and political ideal.

It was otherwise, however, with the colonial fire dictated by the cycles of a global economy. The only fire practices left were directed at the destroyed stock. Carcasses were boiled down into tallow or burned in situ to prevent blowfly infestations. During the drought and depression of the 1840s, "oil smoke stinking of charred mutton," recalled one survivor, "hung heavy" over the Goulbourn Valley. The pall spread throughout Australia.[11]

THE BUSH PADDOCK

The woods range—in Australia, the bush paddock—was a practice with ancient European antecedents that supplemented grassy downs and sown pastures as a critical source of food. For this, fire was essential. Aboriginal burning has to be credited with maintaining that grassy understory, and Europeans followed local practice as well as those of their own past in perpetuating the burnings. Fire teased vital nutrients out of a hoarding biota, encouraged grasses over scrub, and prolonged the growing season. Its association with the axe, with hoofed grazers, and with an exotic flora all multiplied its effects. Examples span the forests of Australia.

In Tasmania a longtime resident named Wainwright described the burning practices of the 1920s and 1930s, which were "typical of the northwestern region from the 1830s to about 1950." All the country, he recalled, was kept "well burnt." Pastoralists fired the higher plains country in September as soon as it was dry enough. The lower country and swamps they fired in summer while the peat was still too wet to carry flame. If the country was not burned, it reverted to scrub—and this occurred as routine firing came under regulation during the 1950s. Moreover, in the early days, firing allowed bushmen to extract native foods, especially marsupials, a transitional harvest between the economy of the departing Aborigine and the establishment of a full-blown European agriculture. Wainwright noted that early settlers snared brush possums and the red-bellied pademelon for skin and meat, and that both creatures gravitated to freshly burned sites.[12]

In Westralia it was asserted "as a literally correct statement" by Conservator of Forests Stephen Kessell that "prior to 1920 the whole Jarrah forest was burnt over by surface fires every three years." This reflected the coalescence of a number of fire practices, not only those of pastoralists. But the bush paddock was central, and outraged foresters urged special action against the "white blackfellows," so hostile to property and so ready with fire. On one occasion, a forester recalled, "kangaroo-hunters" lit a series of twelve fires along a six-mile front "at the bottom of a big gully just before noon on a particularly hot Sunday in March." Without chronic underburning it was impossible to run cattle in the forest bush; but when heavy overgrazing combined with innumerable clearings by small farmers and with slash heaps the size of cities left by industrial logging, the effects were catastrophic.[13]

The issue reached a crescendo in the southeast, where the forested bush had its greatest domain. In 1926 foresters again repeated the charge. "The noted fire-raiser by selfish design," thundered the forestry commissioner of Victoria, is the grazier, the "scourge of the forest." He fired for "grass and muster"; his methods were "many and subtle"; prosecution was virtually impossible because of sparse settlement, community sympathy, and, not infrequently, intimidation. An informant might find his own property torched. The image, repeated endlessly by official sources, is of a slovenly outlaw, an incendiary bully who replaces industry with the torch. A bushranger with a brand.[14]

A royal commission impaneled to investigate forest grazing in 1946 showed a greater depth of understanding. While admitting that widespread firing by pastoralists was "true beyond the barest possibility of doubt," the commission recognized that the grazier was not the only offender. Fire and grazing were not some bizarre Australian aberration. They typified pastoralism in Africa and the Americas as well, and graziers rightly justified their practice "by long usage." What was "good enough (and profitable enough)" for their fathers was good enough for them. The graziers advocated burning, too, for protection against wildfire.[15]

In this the commission, headed by Judge Stretton, concurred. The commissioners argued, additionally, against overgeneralization. The strong impression existed that "the breeder causes fewer fires than the dealer; that the permitted grazier of long standing behaves somewhat better than the newcomer; and that those whose cattle graze upon the high plains and in high places are to be preferred to those of the lowland country." The most dangerous class was "the small dealer of insufficient financial stability" who must seek a quick profit or face ruin and who turns to the torch as an addict would a needle. Yet the commission believed somewhat improbably that "the relationship between grazing and forest fires can be bettered to the point of the almost complete prevention of grazing fires." This would not eliminate fire or the value of underburning, but it would remove the torch from graziers and give it to foresters.[16]

These insights are elaborated in a remarkable thesis written by D. M. Thompson in 1952 about the fire practices of East Gippsland's Cann Valley. Here the forester assumed the role of an anthropologist who had discovered a valley that time seemingly forgot, an Australian Appalachia where "they have a tradition of fire handed down over three, and in places four, generations." Otherwise conservative folk openly ignored fire regulations and insisted that "patch burns [were] necessary to their very existence." Sequestered in deep valleys, enveloped by dense forest, remote from roads and markets, the early settlers were graziers because cattle could be walked to market. As farmers infiltrated into the Cann Valley, settlers discovered that cattle could thrive in the forest provided that the "rough feed" was fired for green pick. The forests were open and visibility was excellent. The flat bottom lands were cleared and the slashed scrub burned in hot summer fires; the mountains provided bush paddocks for cattle. For a time the kangaroo hunter and wallaby shooter added to the mélange. But even as farming concentrated more and more on the arable fields and less on the bush, and as some herders converted to dairy farms, the old fire practices persisted and so did the community sympathies that sustained burning.[17]

Firing was pervasive but far from indiscriminate. It had two purposes—first, to improve bush feed and, second, to protect settled areas from wildfire. In each instance, graziers adjusted their burning to landscape features, fuels, seasons, even the peculiar nutrient deficiencies (calcium, phosphorus) that caused "cripples" in young calves and pregnant cows. Burning was selective—not all sites produced equally flush growth, and not all sites were equally important as fuelbreaks. Burns balanced the need to exploit grass with the need to protect the settlement. These forest graziers were, in brief, residents, not transients. While their practices were far from husbandry, their herding did represent a careful modus vivendi between a small human enclave and a large and hostile bush.

Burning commenced in the spring, concentrated on ridgetops clothed with silvertop eucalypts. The high-hazard areas most in need of annual firing were those, like the ridges, that could expect strong winds, particularly winds from the northwest that raged from the interior deserts and drove off coastal moisture. The men walked or rode along the windward side of the ridge, somewhat down the slope, and torched fires during the heat of the day. So early in the year, the fires typically crept over the crest and down the other side before dying out. Later, around Christmastime, it was not uncommon to light long stretches of slopes in the hopes that the fires would spread out from the protected sites and expand the zone of reduced fuel—a trickle-down theory of hazard burning. Next came the spear-grass plains, even sword-grass swamps. These were burned during mid- to late-summer at those times when the wind was ample to carry flame. A burned plain made an efficient fuelbreak for two summers. Conversely, a "very real fear exists, and tension mounts when dense growth is present in the valley" in such fuels. Between them the burned ridgetops and spear-grass plains established a matrix of fuelbreaks that doubled as bush paddocks. Fires ignited along these corridors were allowed to spread into the surrounding environs as far as conditions permitted.

Those circumstances prevented fire from entering, except at unusual times, such sites as the east-aspect slopes and the "jungles" of impenetrable scrub. But some burning did occur, and drought and desert wind transformed these infrequently burned sites into fearsome propagators of wildfire. When conditions allowed, some slopes were fired and, given fuels and winds, burned as patches. Otherwise, to the minds of settlers, only the routine burning of graziers offered a modicum of protection against catastrophic bushfire.

Inevitably, there were accidents and disagreements. "Store cattlemen" favored small patch burns near ranches and broadacre burning farther away. Dairymen desired the close management of milkers and thus argued for larger proximate burns, with more remote bush paddocks relegated to winter use. Disputes sometimes resulted in spite fires. Other fires spun off from sport, rationalized with a shrug and the observation that the scrub needed a good burn anyway. Lightning fires, fires from transients, accidental burns— all were feared because they occurred outside the predictable rhythms of routine burning and perhaps outside those sites where fuels rendered them harmless. Residents responded to a major wildfire with protective backfires such that a single uncontrolled ignition quickly multiplied into many.

Without fire, forest grazing was impossible, and settlement, lived under the constant shadow of bushfires, treacherous. But when encoded in traditions learned over generations, fire could be a remarkably supple and precise instrument. Far from being condemned as wanton incendiarists, the graziers —"specifically those who habitually use the bush runs"—were regarded kindly by the local inhabitants. They were the men whose burning protected the settled valleys; they were more likely to be cursed for not burning enough than for burning too much. Yet, even as the empathic Thompson documented this fascinating tribe, he recognized the limitations of their means. For all its abundance, the existing fire load was incompetent to suppress the brush. Vistas that had once looked through eight hundred yards of open forest were now choked off at ten yards of scrub. Abuses of grazing privileges had created "terrible fire hazards now far beyond their creator's control." Only more fire could, in the interim, resolve that imbalance. This, in turn, led to a final paradox.

Only constant burning kept the fuel hazards sufficiently under check to allow settlement. But more fire only encouraged the flammable scrub that served as fuel, which demanded control by more fire. The burners, moreover, had to ignite under conditions that were filled with "uncertainty" due to weather. Their "extensive use of fire"—their reliance on fire as a dominant relationship to the Australian bush—was thus a double-edged sword. It made the valley habitable, yet it compelled still more fire, which stimulated flammable fuels, which made it likely that, on some gusty day, a fire would inevitably escape. After its pioneering phase, after settlement matured beyond nomadism, the community lived in constant peril, a metastable equilibrium mediated by fire. It was as though the residents lived amid growing stocks of nitroglycerin, and they reduced the hazard by constantly tipping out the flasks. But more was produced than could be removed; tipping only stimulated further production; and every reduction, however skillfully done, risked an explosion that could obliterate the community.

THE IMPLACABLE TROPICS

There were other marginal environments for pastoralism to penetrate, and tropical Australia was among the most interesting. Throughout the era of European colonization attempts to recreate European agriculture in the wet-dry tropics failed with dismaying regularity. Mixed farms failed, plantation agriculture failed, and Aboriginal economies were hardly suitable for absorption into European political empires as were those in Java or India. No large cities flourished, either as service centers for a surrounding hinterland or as a commercial entrepôt. Dreams of a second Singapore in Arnhemland disappeared into a miasma of boredom and decay, aggravated by few export products, poor harbors and treacherous navigation in the Torres Strait, and wretched markets. Stokes's "Plains of Promise" south of the Gulf of Carpentaria became an economic tar pit. Mining offered only temporary prosperity. The one permanent basis for European settlement was grazing.[18]

Explorers encouraged pastoralism with their extravagant praise for the savanna grasses. They also persistently and completely misread the tropical soils. An exodus of squatters to the gulf region became a rush in 1865, powered by the peculiar dynamics of pastoral expansion, a speculative boom in livestock instead of bonds. The mobbing of the new grasslands far outstripped the infrastructure needed to support the industry; drought and depression chastened enthusiasms; the absence of transport and markets; hard-won knowledge about the true nature of tropical grasses; savage diseases that attacked both settlers and stock; and the vital necessity for permanent water —all disciplined a wild rush into something like a steady-state settlement. By the 1880s the basic elements of pastoralism in the gulf region had been laid down. The chronology in Arnhemland followed a somewhat different rhythm, stimulated by the cross-continental telegraph, the emergence of Darwin as a port, and changing political alignments as control passed from South Australia to the Commonwealth in 1910.[19]

It became apparent that cattle, not sheep, had to be the basis for pastoralism. Cattle could thrive on the rank grasses, they could walk to market, they could better endure the boggy wet season, and they could be tended with far less labor. The long, irrepressible belief that pasturage could be controlled by grazing alone—a legacy of English husbandry—died slowly. Not grazing but fire dominated the dynamics of the savanna. Intensive sheep management required the intensive management of flocks through shepherds and the intensive management of pasture, ultimately through the introduction of special pasture grasses and fertilizers. But pastoralism in the tropical savannas had to exploit native pastures and to rely on native herders. It could change but not expunge the dynamics of the wet-dry grasslands. It had to accommodate fire.

What developed was a fascinating amalgam of Aboriginal and European fire practices, administered by a mixed population of Aboriginal station hands and European squatters. Domesticated livestock could adapt only with special human manipulation of the savanna. (Only a few European imports, particularly those like pigs and water buffalo that originated in tropical environments, became successful ferals.) Pastoralists were accustomed to burning; they only needed to adjust their burning to the new circumstances. In the drier inland stations, spinifex plains were burned as often they could carry a fire, usually about once every four or five years. On the cattle ranges of northern Queensland, Charles Davis observed in the 1950s, "men ride through the grass throwing lighted matches into the tussocks and go away only when they are certain that the fire has a good start." This "diffuse pioneer economy," he continued, preserved practices that had occurred a century before in the south of Australia.[20]

Everyone used fire as a routine tool, and all were adamant that their business would collapse without it. There were two principal periods of burning—early and late. Pastoralists conducted early burns as soon as possible after curing. These were cool fires, set in large patches, that relied on residual soil moisture to stimulate a "second crop" of grass. If the dry season arrived in stormy pulses rather than a prolonged drought, then different burnt patches could flush up for several weeks beyond the normal season. In complement, pastoralists conducted late burns at the conclusion of the dry season. Late burns were hot and extensive, and their timing was critical. If too late, the rains prevented a burn; if too early, forage—however marginal in nutrition—was lost. Graziers accordingly adopted a strategy of firing in strips and patches, a speculative minuet with the uncertain rains. Unburned strips were kept as "insurance against a late season" and were not fired until the end of the next wet season. This "natural spelling system" meant that cattle grazed grass less than a year old, too green to burn. The practice perpetuated the kangaroo grass that graziers esteemed.[21]

Burners adjusted plans to accommodate fuels, moisture, winds, and terrain, and they considered their knowledge of local fire behavior an adequate form of control. They relied on natural features and old burns for firebreaks, and calculated when morning dews would suppress running fires. They first burned firebreaks around station property. Ridges were typically fired in June and July, the flatlands in November and December. No one willingly burned all his land in any one year, but none allowed an area to escape burning for more than two years. Left unburned the grass degenerated, ticks infested the thickets, and wildfires became more likely. For ignition graziers simply dropped wax matches into tussocks.[22]

In Arnhemland, Henry Lewis has detailed a similar pattern of pastoral burning. Early burning in the Dry targets the grasses and shrubs of the eucalypt woodlands, which cure faster than fuels elsewhere. The first fires serve as fuelbreaks to protect stations and corrals. Fenced paddocks of native grasses are next, and the alluring green pick assists the mustering of cattle. As new areas dry, they are fired—the hills and ridgetops, the open forests, the flats. Each adds to a matrix of protective burns. By mid-June, after which soil moisture can no longer support green pick, probably 40–60 percent of the savanna has burned. Most of the remainder is fired during the rush of late burning at the end of the Dry, or after a preliminary rain or two assures new growth and some control over running fires. There are exceptions, however. The burning of floodplains ("flats"), of swamps and the grassy fringe of rivers, of rainforest "jungles"—all vary among pastoralists according to felt need to stimulate growth, control ticks, or drive cattle out of thickets.[23]

They differ, too, from the fire practices of the Aborigines. The pastoralist directed all his burning to the maximum production of cattle; the Aborigine had to extract from that same environment an immense variety of foodstuffs. European burning was thus less subtle and more uniform, more given to large rolling fires at the end of the Dry. The grazier could sell cattle for other foods and goods, the nutrients of the wet-dry tropics he cycled through a national and global economy. His fires, considered in that scale, were small. But the Aborigine lived within a far smaller natural economy, and his fires reflected that difference.

Pastoralists' reliance on Aboriginal station hands, however, assured a degree of continuity in anthropogenic burning. Most graziers brought with them ample experience with Australian fire, yet there is reason to believe that the Aborigine greatly assisted the transformation from a hunting to a herding economy. "That's the way we learned about burning this country," one pioneer pastoralist recalled. "All we had to do was give them a few boxes of matches and they went off and burned the places that they were supposed to and left the rest alone." [24]

The patterns of pastoral burning in the Australian savanna broadly resembled those in the bush paddocks of Gippsland. Fire alone made the savanna habitable to the Aborigine, and fire alone made settlement by European graziers possible. Their reliance on fire also confirmed a similar paradox. Burning and grazing together pushed the biotas toward the marginal grasses, the kind most prone to burn. Spear grass *(Heterogon)* proliferated and extended its range; Mitchell grass, the most productive native, survived only if not regularly burned. To break this cycle of fire and pyrophyte, more of the native grasses had to be eaten or other, more nutrious, grasses had to be introduced or the land devoted to other purposes. With superphosphate fertilizers, there has been some success in larding spear grass with Townsville stylo *(Stylothanses)*, a leguminous subclover. Even the stylos, however, are established with the assistance of fire and can, within limits, tolerate burning. In brief, without fire, grazing cannot thrive; with it, grazing productivity cannot improve.[25]

THE SNOW LEASES

Graziers also used fire to enter the high catchments of the Australian Alps. A region of mountain forest—of alpine and subalpine steppes and woodlands—its biota was low in productivity, marginal for livestock, and amenable only to seasonal exploitation. It was an ideal setting for transhumance—and for pastoral fire.[26]

Aborigines traveled to the mountains in the summer to harvest the fatty Bogong moth, but there are few solid references to routine Aboriginal burning. Citing the Gippsland Plains, W. A. Brodribb remarks that the "natives had burnt all the grass at Gippsland late in the summer." George Clarke, writing in 1851, states that Aborigines had recently visited the Snowy Mountains where they obtained moths by lighting "large fires, and the consequences was, the country through the whole survey was burnt." Drawing on earlier (unspecified) sources, Andrews stated that "the natives were accustomed to burn it [kangaroo grass] off almost every year and thereby prevented the heavy growth of young trees." While this may well have been true for selected grasslands in the lower elevations favored by kangaroos, it is doubtful that the high country experienced systematic burning.[27]

Rather, the preponderance of evidence suggests a pattern dominated by infrequent but high-intensity burns probably keyed to droughts. The landscape is normally damp, such that burning can require considerable labor; early loggers did not report the butt scars that regular burning on slopes would produce; apart from moths, there was little forage and prey for Aboriginal hunters; and the biotas could not have perpetuated themselves in the condition Europeans found them had they burned on a fixed schedule. There are reports from early settlers that European burning, in fact, alarmed the Aborigines. Yet very large fires were not only possible but a historic fact. Escaped Aboriginal campfires and broadcast firing could merge with lightning during times of intense drought to unleash horrific, episodic fires.[28]

The first Europeans rode into the country seeking pasture and drought relief during the 1830s. By the late 1850s a number of squatters had claimed runs. Not until the 1870s or so—after a gold rush and after the Land Act of 1869 opened crown lands to free selection—did settlement thicken sufficiently to drive graziers from the open steppes to the "despised and feared" forests and high country. Fire was not, at first, a routine tool. The 1851 fires had frightened many settlers, and diggers, eager to strip the land of impediments to "loaming," had burned widely in ways that threatened settlers. In the early years, moreover, the pressure on perennial grasslands was insufficient to require forcing by fire. When an accidental fire surged through the Omeo-Cobungra area in the early 1880s, graziers reportedly flocked to the scene in amazement as cattle crowded the green pick. Pushed by lowland drought and pulled by lush highlands, transhumance became common, however, and in 1889 "snow leases" on crown lands acquired statutory sanction. Then came the hard times—depression, drought, rabbits, overgrazed paddocks. With them came fire.

Graziers first burned the swamps to liberate more pasture. Next they moved into the poorer lands, particularly the crown lands, with the torch as a guide. They mustered on the forested slopes and along the tree line. Revealingly, they refused to burn richly productive sites such as the Bogong high plains. Even with fire the land was marginal; without it, the land was useless.

Accordingly, graziers evolved a system of burning to ensure maximum summer and winter feed. They burned winter pastures in the spring after mustering the cattle and moving them to the high country; this meant that fresh feed would await their return. Likewise, after removing the cattle from the high country in the autumn, the typical grazier would burn those sites too. The autumn fires served several purposes. They kept access open and readied a site for future burning; they discouraged livestock from migrating back up the slopes once a drover had removed them; and they rewarded the burner with a lush green pick in the spring.

Winter burning was tricky, however. Until years of firing opened up and dried out the country, its normal dampness retarded fires. Under average conditions, high-country scrub and steppe burned poorly. This forced graziers into a kind of shifting cultivation. After a patch was burned it would support good feed for only three or four years, each time forced by fire. This compelled the grazier to advance to another patch and repeat the cycle until, patch by patch, slope by slope, valley by valley, the grazier "succeeded in burning all the country." After three to five years, the old patches could be fired again. Every biota burned—wet scleroforest, subalpine woodland, steppe and tundra, snowgum and snowgrass.[29]

As the economy degenerated and the rabbit invasion worsened, the cycle of firing intensified and it acquired additional justifications. A "clean" run became a badge of pride. Light fires, it was held, prevented large ones and were, after a fashion, a form of community service. This, of course, only restated the classic paradox of pastoral fire. The introduction of routine burning had shifted the floristic balance in favor of pyrophytes. The microclimate had dried and accepted winds more easily. Flammable scrub flourished. Despite broadcast burning on a short cycle, the flammability of the high country had increased, and burning became mandatory as a fire protection measure. Defying legislation (beginning in 1889), summer fires became necessary. They could not always be contained, however, in their avatar as light, creeping surface burns.

In 1932 the celebrated bushwalker B. U. Byles summarized the situation in the Murray catchment, a reconnaissance that became a blow-by-blow account of how fire and grazing had restructured the high country. "I am told by men who worked on this block over 30 years ago," he wrote, "that their first job was to burn and keep on burning the woody shrubs and snow gum," not only for new feed but to dry out the swampy ground to the point that horses and cattle could travel over it. The only areas spared were those that were too rocky or lightly fueled to sustain a fire. Again and again, Byles documented the shift to pyrophytes—the flammable scrub that took over the mountain ash, the perennial bracken that alone retarded erosion but at the cost of almost annual fires, the insidious soil losses that further lowered the water table and swept nutrients away and thus further encouraged the scleromorphs.[30]

Yet Byles sympathized with the locals. Grazing in the mountain pastures, he recognized, was "still in a very primitive state." It was all based on folk wisdom, in which "old ideas and practices are accepted without question." The one vital fact that the graziers knew "for certain" was "which areas produce fat stock and which areas produce stock not so fat." He argued against the outright removal of graziers, suggesting with stunning counterintuitiveness that the mountain pastures "are actually understocked." And he appreciated, even as he distrusted, the critical role of fire. Pastoral burning, he argued, had inaugurated a "retrograde movement" that would not cease until the pastoral fires were abolished. It was not obvious, however, how to eliminate burning after decades of fire use and grazing had restructured the landscape into a fire regime of chronic high hazard. One approach, Byles believed, was for more intensive grazing on the European model. But a steady restoration to pre-European conditions or to one analogous to rural Britain demanded a long period free from fire. Neither was likely.

The 1939 holocaust demonstrated just how difficult the situation had become. The fires terrified everyone. For a while grazier fires disappeared—their fuels vaporized by the 1939 burns, the will to fire temporarily smoked out of habitual burners. Instead there existed "confusion in the minds of the graziers," S. G. Fawcett reported, as they confronted their mounting dilemma. Only more intense burning could subdue the ever-encroaching scrub, yet the fires did not offer the degree of protection they once did or their advocates continued to assume. The 1939 fires had burned everything: they were driven by climatic factors, not by fuels.[31]

Despite decades of burning, the fire hazard had actually increased. Graziers recalled how, in the early days, as boys, they had watched fires set by their fathers smolder for weeks and had been dispatched to swat them out when they approached fences or dwellings. Now the fires burned more vigorously, and protective burning was no longer optional but mandatory. Without fire grazing in the high country would be impossible. But with or without grazing fire had acquired a life of its own whose threats could, it appeared, be abated only by more fire or by the removal of European settlement.

FIREWEEDS

The introduction of livestock set in motion an ecological chain reaction that led to an explosion of alien flora. Native grasses were, on the whole, inadequate—too nutrient-poor, too susceptible to trampling, too diffuse in their tussocks. The exotic fauna demanded an exotic flora; they would thrive best in association with those plants with which they had coevolved. But new plants demanded new soils and new moisture regimes; they had to be fertilized, watered, tended. This is what had occurred, over centuries, in Britain, but Australia was not Britain writ large.

Some of the exotic flora died out, some went wild, some thrived only under human husbandry, and some naturalized. The line between useful domesticate and wild weed was a narrow one—all were alien, wheat and corn no less than blackberry and burr grass. Basically, if the flora depended on humans for propagation, then it was useful; if it propagated beyond human control, then it was a weed. Floral introductions, moreover, were calculated, accidental, misguided, and systematic. Contamination of seed stocks from Europe was rampant. When the Federal Quarantine Act passed in 1908, an inspection of white-clover seed discovered 37,440 seeds of impurities to each pound of clover. Explorers and settlers distributed exotic seeds with wanton abandon. Mark Twain observed that Australia "has levied tribute upon the flora of the rest of the world; and wherever one goes the results appear, in gardens private and public, in the woodsy walls of the highway, and in even the forests." Acclimatization societies experimented freely with aliens, with plenty of precedent and generally obnoxious consequences. "Never," concluded Eric Rolls, "was a body of eminent men so foolishly, so vigorously, and so disastrously wrong." [32]

The exotics interacted not only with the native flora but among themselves and with the exotic fauna. In a land subject to chronic, often violent disturbances, new niches multiplied, harrowing the landscape for weeds. Alien birds and livestock, feeding on allied plants, spread their seeds. Rabbits hid in blackberry thickets. Eurasian grazers and the European graziers who oversaw them introduced a new array of selective pressures and a host of new competitors. In places, the exotic flora displaced the native; in other places, the native flora shifted its composition. Elsewhere an eco-ensemble emerged that amalgamated weeds, naturalized aliens, and an altered array of native flora and fauna. Exotics demanded additional exotics—some to feed them, others to control them. A contagion of prickly pear required the *Cactoblastis* moth to control it. The rabbit plague led to the introduction of myxomatosis virus. Land clearing, heavy grazing, trampling, a medley of new and old fire practices, a cascade of alien organisms—the outcome was nothing less than the reconstruction of whole ecosystems.

In this process fire was both a means and an end. The fire regimes of Australia changed in fundamental ways. Not all the new parts fit, many interactions were unpredictable, and the transition from Aboriginal Australia to European Australia was, for many areas, indefinitely incomplete. Some sites became more fire-prone, some less. But for the whole period of transition, when fire practices were out of sync with fuels, fire loads tended to increase, fireweeds proliferated, and the fires became more violent. Beyond this no single generalization seems appropriate.

Grasses were among the first elements to feel the impact of colonization. Livestock promoted a shift in composition from *Themeda* and *Poa* to tougher, less palatable grasses, to native colonizers and exotic pyrophytes. Their lower protein and higher fiber content required fire to flush up their nutritional reserve. Graziers burned; the weeds spread. But, as if to protect themselves, their spearlike heads penetrated into the hides of sheep and cattle and caused weight loss. Burning and grazing together propagated another spear grass *(Heterogon)* like a creeping ground fire. Precious native legumes like the Darling pea *(Swainsonia)*, which had shielded themselves from native grazers by containing poison, moved vigorously into sites ravaged by overgrazing. This led to a surplus of nitrogen, which promoted annuals at the expenses of perennials, which crowded out the Darling pea and created ideal conditions for Eurasian exotics. Everywhere that fire persisted annuals replaced perennials because they could seed before the onset of the dry season and fire. In places where heavy grazing, trampling, and close cropping had prevented bushfires, Curr observed, many tussock grasslands had converted to swards.[33]

Overall it was the destruction of native grasses by intense use that interrupted the prior rhythms of fire. There was insufficient fuel to carry flame. Scrub blossomed: fire could no longer fight it back. Even as gangs of Chinese and Russians and mobs of rabbits and untold swarms of selectors and squatters slashed and ringbarked the Australia forest, trees proliferated on former grasslands. In the western districts of Victoria and New South Wales, the forest became a plague. By the early 1870s, after twenty-five years of de facto fire exclusion, herders turned to fire. They burned in the winter to destroy spear grasses, and in the summer to reduce scrub. But it was evidently too late. Sheep had driven out the kangaroo rats that ate *Acacia* and *Callistris* seeds, and unless burning could proceed with enough vigor, year after year, tree seedlings were stimulated. Hampered by weather and the poor cover left after grazing, fire alone was incompetent. By the time rabbits assumed the role of the kangaroo rats the forest had established itself.[34]

All over Australia, on sites that could support trees, the flora told a similar story. Settlers cleared and restored trees simultaneously such that the forest itself was not so much destroyed as rearranged. "Australia's dense forests," Rolls concludes, "are not the remnants of two hundred years of energetic clearing, they are the product of one hundred years of energetic growth." The details of that reconquest are particular to each site, full of serendipity and the bizarre synergisms of climate, the timing of introductions, and the interactions between native and alien organisms. But the shared engine of growth was the advent of European livestock.[35]

Where native grasses failed to survive, Eurasian grasses often filled the vacuum. Some resulted from calculated introductions; some from accidental contamination. If the Eurasian aliens proliferated uncontrollably, they became weeds. But if they stabilized their spread, if they furnished adequate feed, then they became naturalized and their origins were often forgotten. To newer stockmen paddocks of barley grass and burr medic made unbeatable "natural" pasture. Elsewhere, pasture was simply sown. Paddocks were farmed by "sub and super"—leguminous subterranean clovers and superphosphate fertilizers. Improved yield required improved grasses, for most Australian grasses responded to fire, not fertilizer. Other pastures larded native and naturalized pastures with introduced legumes like stylo. The grasses ceased to roam.[36]

The herds followed suit. With fixed, improved paddocks came sedentary, improved herds. Breeding replaced an emphasis on sheer numbers. Herding became husbandry. But the logic of the process did not stop with the livestock. What happened to the herds happened also to the herders, and for this, too, there were English precedents. A demand for improved wool had led to improved sheep, which led to improved pastures through imported grasses and fertilizers, which led to a more intensive farming of herds—the enclosure of common fields, a redistribution of wealth and land; the restructuring of English society, the transformation of herders into farmers.

In Australia what began as a change of flora and fauna concluded with a broad social reformation, the domestication and naturalization of the European from the status of self-destructive weed. The fire practices of Australia changed accordingly. Where stations practiced extensive management, there weedy pyrophytes flourished, fire promoted annuals over perennials, and selective burning assisted in the control of certain noxious weeds. Where pastoralists practiced a more intensive husbandry, they circumscribed and disciplined the role of fire. Paddocks planted to lucerne—drought-tough and poorly designed for burning—resisted fire. Other Eurasian pasture grasses survived trampling and heavy grazing but not fire, which had to be ex-

cluded. Over most of Australia, mixed pastures of native, alien, and naturalized grasses transformed fire without banishing it.[37]

August, and black centres expand on the afternoon paddock.
Dilating on a match in widening margins, they lift
a splintering murmur; they fume out of used-up grass
That's been walked, since summer, in to infinite swirled licks.

The man imposing spring here swats with his branch, controlling it:
only small things may come to a head, in this settlement pattern.
                                        —Les Murray, "The Grassfire Stanzas"

FAUNAL FIRE: THE CURIOUS CASES OF
THE RABBIT AND THE EURO

The spectrum of fauna introduced into Australia by the Europeans is staggering. Virtually every domesticated species found in Britain, and many species
hunted for game, sooner or later arrived. Some went wild from the start;
some spread only with vigorous assistance from humans; others survived as
little more than pets. Hares, foxes, deer, sparrows, mynahs, starlings, trout,
carp, redfin, blackbirds, robins, pheasants, partridges—individuals transported some, and acclimatization societies encouraged "the introduction,
acclimatization and domestication of all innoxious animals, birds, fishes,
insects and vegetables whether useful or ornamental." But it was not obvious what was "innoxious." Ticket-of-leave species transported against their
will to Australia remained after serving their time with humans. Domesti-
cates from Eurasia that became feral in Australia include camels, water buffa-
loes, donkeys, horses, pigs, cows, and dogs. Pests like the rat—and other
camp followers of European expansionism—arrived in short order. And settlers repeated the mistakes of other lands—including Britain.[38]

The introduction of livestock had revolutionized the British landscape.
The principal differences between Britain and Australia lay in climate, the
biotic context of the introductions, and the speed of their consequences.
Transplants often propagated in Australia on a huge scale and at rapid rates,
shocking observers. The classic example, of course, is the rabbit.[39]

The Normans apparently introduced the rabbit ("cony") to England and
it spread steadily and deliberately, a welcome source of fur, meat, and sport.
Warrens were actively cultivated, particularly in wasteland. Until established at a new site, rabbits were often protected. Improvers aggressively
transplanted new colonies throughout the island and even onto the offshore
islands of Scotland. Agriculture supplemented the rabbit's wild foods, further encouraging their propagation. Hunters destroyed potential predators
by restricting weasels, hawks, and foxes to sport hunting. Harsh game laws

prevented popular harvesting of rabbits. Even in the early nineteenth century Scots were actively establishing new colonies. The consequences were soon felt: the rabbit revealed itself as a pest. Particularly as former wastelands fell under more intense cultivation, rabbit and agriculturalist became competitors.

There was then a certain historical if distorted logic to the introduction of rabbits into Australia. The earliest experiments, beginning with the First Fleet, involved domesticated rabbits. But serious propagation started under Thomas Austin near Geelong in 1859, who wanted sport and so introduced wild rabbits from England. The land was well prepared: predators had already been hunted or poisoned into near oblivion, livestock were busy destabilizing biota after biota, land clearing was vigorous, wombat and bilby-possum burrows were available for squatting, and native grazers (potential competitors for grass) receded in advance of settlement. By the early 1870s five breeding centers were active between Sydney and Adelaide. A little population spread resulted from natural dispersion, but the image of the rabbit plague as a furry wildfire racing across the countryside is inaccurate; most of the new warrens were deliberate transplantings. By the time settlers appreciated the magnitude of the disaster, the rabbits were unstoppable. Paying a bounty on rabbit scalps only worsened the situation. It gave rabbiters incentive to leave some rabbits in each warren to serve as the nucleus for rebreeding. And it rewarded the unscrupulous for establishing new colonies where none previously existed.

The full impact became apparent during the 1890s when the rabbit plague interacted with drought and depression—when rabbits became a full-fledged competitor with livestock for scarce grass. The remedies were often as catastrophic as the disease. Rabbits, moreover, were big business; they had evolved into a quasi-naturalized form of herding. They even inspired their own surreal fire practices. It was a bushfire that, by burning the wooden fence around Austin's property, made possible the first release of rabbits into the wild. The growing absence of fire—or its transformation under the pressure of grazing from primarily grass fire to scrub fire—provided shelter for the early escapees. When efforts at control became serious, officials burned off logs, thickets, and other sheltering scrub. Rabbiters boiled billies, burned carcasses, employed fire lanterns for night hunting, prepared poisons with campfires, fumigated warrens with smoke from fire boxes, and distributed phosphorus bait widely and loosely, a common source of delayed ignition. Rabbiters' fires littered the landscape; official reports they burned as rubbish; in 1890 they burned the minister of lands in effigy. Not until the myxomatosis virus asserted its merit after World War II did the rabbit plague abate. Its success, however, was a product of new social attitudes as much as cumulative environmental degradation. It was the rabbiter, not the rabbit, that had been uncontrolled. He spread fire as liberally as the herders he mimicked. The era of the rabbit squatter, like that of other herders, had to end. Until then the rabbit profoundly rewrote the composition of fine fuels that powered Australian fire regimes south of the Tropic of Capricorn.

Elsewhere, exotic fauna paradoxically promoted an explosion in the population of native grazers. As Europeans transformed many landscapes into paddocks, as they multiplied watering holes, as they purged the bush of natural predators, they sometimes encouraged population eruptions among the native grazers. The kangaroo, in particular, assumed pestilential proportions, its numbers far in excess of pre-European populations. Perhaps the most intriguing example concerns the hills kangaroo, or euro, of the Pilbara region in northwest Australia. The long-term outcome has been to reduce the numbers of sheep and increase those of the euro.[40]

The chronology is a complex one. Sheep arrived in 1866. At first they were confined to watercourses and waterholes. These they soon grazed to nubbin, and only artificial wells allowed these flocks to radiate throughout the district. They fed on grasses and salt brush and some palatable species of spinifex *(Triodia)*. There were no predators. The Aborigines, thought to have been numerous, faded away or were co-opted as shepherds. Sheep multiplied exponentially, approaching a climax in the 1920s. Overgrazing reached catastrophic proportions. Winter burning to encourage green pick in the spring became routine over very large areas, and signal fires in spinifex were exploited during mustering to keep track of droving. This dramatically restructured the presumed pattern of Aboriginal firing, which had ranged more widely through the calendar year and had concentrated around waterholes, hunting grounds, and corridors of travel. Now the waterholes and grassy fields no longer supported fuels adequate to carry a fire. The intense mosaic of small patch burns eliminated summer fires.

Simultaneously, the primary kangaroos—the red and the euro—stabilized at low numbers. After mining collapsed (c. 1910), prospectors no longer substituted for the Aborigines as hunters, such that human predation on euros ceased at approximately the same time that sheep populations reached a maximum, thanks to a proliferation of waterholes and a shift in the floral composition of the range. Intense grazing had put the grasses into recession and eliminated saltbush, while regular firing promoted toxic forbs or spinifex, particularly those species that were unpalatable to sheep but suitable for kangaroos. The stage was set for a dramatic role reversal with the droughts and depression of the 1930s.

Eager for wool rather than mutton, pastoralists stocked their degraded wild pastures with more sheep. The heavier grazing forced the graziers into more burning, which drove the system toward the pyrophytes that only kangaroos, not sheep, could consume and thrive upon. (The low nutritional content of the spinifex could not support lactation among breeding sheep.) When drought came in 1934–35, both sheep and kangaroos declined precipitously. But the kangaroos, ever opportunistic, soon recovered. A second drought in 1944–45 selected from among the kangaroos—the euro over the red. The sheep continued to withdraw and the euro to expand. Another drought in 1953–54 decimated the euro population, but it rebounded while, again, the red kangaroos and sheep faltered. In 1955 it was estimated that there were four euros for every sheep.

When intervention came it required control over both euro and sheep populations and over what remained of the range. Pastoralists learned to regulate sheep numbers, in part through fenced paddocks and "set stocking." Hunting and poisoning brought down euro numbers. Burning was shifted from winter to summer, from cool to hot fires. If grazing pressures were removed after burning, then perennial grasses of much higher palatability could be restored and some naturalized tussocks encouraged. By the 1970s the ecosystem was edging toward a relative equilibrium.

BLACK THURSDAY

On the morning of February 6, 1851, James Fenton's wife told him of a dream she had had. It sketched a "dreadful scene" of terror and universal anxiety, acted out amid death and darkness. A pall so oppressed the world that candles were needed day and night. Fenton dismissed the specter until, by early afternoon, that premonition had become reality. Black clouds rolled across the sky. A marbled sky swirled with lurid glare and dense obscurity. A preternatural stillness gripped the land. Animals behaved weirdly. Then from the clouds there fell burned debris and leaves charred to ash but with their veins yet visible. By midafternoon "the whole face of Nature was enveloped in utter darkness." Neighbors lit candles and stood in mute amazement. Some believed that the Great Day of Wrath was at hand. The smoke and ash, Fenton realized, were the portents of some "terrible catastrophe." He rushed to the shore. The fires—for only a bushfire could instigate such phenomena—were not on Tasmania. The smoke, the blight of ash, the bizarre atmospherics, the miasma of enveloping terror had spanned the Bass Strait from the mainland. Bushfires of immense size were burning Victoria.[41]

Black Thursday was the first of the great holocausts that flash across Australian history with the coming of European settlement. Its dimensions are not known exactly, the country being lightly settled, but all accounts declare that the conflagration was enormous. Rolf Boldrewood thought that the "whole colony of Port Phillip was on fire at the same time, from the western coast to the Australian Alps, from the Snowy River to the Murray." Garryowen recalled that the "whole countryside" was transformed into a "billowy ocean of fire" from flames that "glided swift as lightning." Everywhere the dead and dying carcasses of horses, sheep, cattle, birds, kangaroos, and wallabies littered tracks and waterways. "No quarter of the district escaped, for the fires might be said to be general from Gippsland to the Murray, and from the Plenty to the Glenelg." The Pyrenees, the Loddon country, the Wimmera, Colac, the "far West," the Portland country, Mount Gambier, the country between Geelong and Ballarat—the fires blasted all. The Dandenongs were so devastated that "every vestige of tillage or verdure was burnt off the ground." Not one house in ten survived in the Barrabool Hills. Only a few areas were spared, like "islets in an ocean of flame." And though they escaped burning, Kilmore, Seymour and Honeysuckle, and the dense heart of the Gippsland mountains were nonetheless sealed off by a smoke pall "denser than a total eclipse." Save for an abrupt change in winds, towns like Portland might well have been incinerated. The Reverend J.H.L. Zillman wrote how "the flames leaped from tree to tree, across creeks, hills, and gullies, and swept everything away. Teams of bullocks in the yoke, mobs of cattle and horses, and even whole families of human beings in their bush huts were completely destroyed, and the charred bones alone found after the wind and fire had subsided." William Howitt believed

> that the fire destroyed the face of the whole colony over a space of 300 miles, by 150, with farms, flocks, and herds, by tens of thousands, and numbers of people. So rapidly did it travel that men on horseback galloped before it till their horses fell dead. Herds of cattle were seen running over the country in a frantic state, and birds, in whole flocks, fell suffocated into the flames. We have since travelled over much of this ground and seen everywhere the traces of the conflagration remaining; while the people tell you how they had to run and sink themselves in rivers and fords, the very hair or skin being singed off if it appeared above water. The whole country, for a time, was a furious furnace; and, what was most singular, *the greatest part of the mischief was done in a single day.*

Surprisingly, only ten settlers died. Perhaps a quarter of Victoria burned.[42]

The details of the fires—their behavior and dimensions—are lost in the breathless rush of original accounts. The fires exceeded anything the colonists had experienced; they were too great for existing knowledge or institutions to absorb. It is obvious, however, that the fires conformed to the classic scenario for large fires in the southeast: a wet winter had inflated grassy fuels, a powerful summer drought dried them to tinder, a slow-moving low-pressure system drafted desert air in advance of a cold front. At Melbourne thermometers on that fateful day recorded temperatures of 112–117 degrees Fahrenheit. Morning opened with a "heavily vapourous sky," filled with an awful stillness. Later, searing winds from the northwest tore through the streets in terrifying gusts. The air choked with red dust and smoke. Nearer the fire, survivors reported a strangling canopy of smoke, a drizzle of ash and brands, a horrifying silence followed by an instantaneous roar of flame. The fire appeared to fall upon them. The countryside seemed to erupt spontaneously in sheets of flame. It was, James Bonwick wrote, a "perfect tempest of fire." [43]

This "mysterious," but peculiarly Australian, "convulsion of Nature" set up a serious of aftershocks. Estimates of stock losses vary wildly, but squatters such as Niel Black and Company each lost as many as 4,000 sheep. The destruction of fodder resulted in the subsequent destruction of perhaps 500,000 lambs. Exports of wool were cut in half. In an age without insurance, small selectors and herders faced financial ruin, and the fledgling colony, destitution. The greatest loss of life occurred at Diamond Creek, but the fire maimed and physically injured many people.

Equally, the experience "left a haunting sense of danger" among the survivors. Bushfires had been more or less expected, but the magnitude and suddenness of this conflagration stunned all who saw it. Black Thursday—bushfire—became an indelible part of the Australian experience. Those who rebuilt never forgot their "peculiar sensations of terror and hopeless helplessness." Others fled to "the town to labour at perhaps less congenial but also less risky avocations." In Melbourne relief subscriptions generated over £3,000, but good feeling dissipated when it was learned that not all the money was needed and that indifferent accounting or outright fraud had drained away the difference.[44]

Yet even amid devastation on this scale there were lessons learned and a recovery predicted. A bushfire, Boldrewood noted, was "not so bad as a drought." Rains followed the holocaust and the burned pastures turned "emerald-green"; survivors sold mobs of "fat cattle" at good prices. Settlers learned to take precautions. The progress of settlement itself, it was argued, would eventually abolish such outbursts by eliminating bush fuels, by regulating the burning off of grass and scrub, and by improving skills at bushfire fighting. In a letter to the editor of the *Argus*, an irate "Macedonian" demanded an inquiry into the carelessness of the pastoralists. "It will not do for every man who has more grass on his run than he has stock to use it, to put a fire stick in, merely because he may wish for something green for a lambing flock." There were conflicts among the fire practices of the various settlers. The time was approaching when the colonizers would truly *settle.* [45]

The 1851 fires were the emblem of an earlier period when European wildfire joined European livestock and weeds as an environmental plague. The most volatile periods for wildfire are the transitional phases between fire regimes; so long as the European onslaught destabilized Australian biotas, catastrophic outbreaks of fire could be expected. When, three months earlier, Victoria had gained status as an independent colony, her citizens celebrated with hilltop fires. Black Thursday announced that same newness in bolder lights. And events quickly accelerated. Within a week of Black Thursday reports of gold set in motion a mob of half-mad transients. Even before new grass pushed up through the ashes, even as eucalypts bravely sent out new shoots, diggers crashed through the fire-scoured landscape in a frenzied search for gold.

"SUCH EXTENSIVE CHANGES IN AUSTRALIA AS NEVER ENTERED INTO THE CONTEMPLATION OF THE LOCAL AUTHORITIES"

As he scanned the Australian scene, Surveyor-General Mitchell pondered the ripple effect of livestock. The "intrusion" of cattle, he observed, set in motion "such extensive changes in Australia as never entered into the contemplation of the local authorities." His biotic tinkering was the most profound of the European's affects on Australia, and the complex infestation by livestock—not only the beasts themselves but their allied flora, their impact on soils and catchments, on forests and fire practices—was the most pervasive and relentless of those uncontrolled experiments. The herds went everywhere. The need for pasture drove exploration and frontier settlement. The economics of pastoralism financed colonization and shaped politics. Pastoralism destablized biota after biota after biota. Nothing fully escaped.[46]

Some of the ecological consequences were direct; some indirect. Grazers altered the floral composition of many ecosystems. By selecting for some species over others, they encouraged additional floral exotics. By influencing soils, they modified the hydrology of marginal biotas. By attacking the fine fuels and by helping eliminate the Aborigines, they rewrote the dynamics of fire regimes. The herds were by themselves, Mitchell thought, "sufficient to produce the extirpation of the native race." Pastoralists cleared forests, planted pastures, fought back scrub, applied and withheld fire—all to encourage palatable grass. In some regimes they changed the timing of fire; in some they introduced fire where it had not previously existed; in others, by consuming the fine fuels, they denied routine fire. Everywhere, during their initial passage, they inadvertently promoted larger, more unpredictable bushfires. Brigalow they felled, burned, and planted to Eurasian grasses; then fired to prune back brigalow sprouts. The mountain forests they underburned. Coastal scrub they fired down to the beaches, and set in motion an unstoppable chain of erosion. When fire was suppressed "thick forests of young trees" sprang up around settlements like Sydney "where, formerly, a man might gallop without impediment, and see whole miles before him."[47]

Once destabilized, many biotas underwent irreversible change. The newcomers could be regulated but not expelled; they could not be herded back into their Eurasian ark and shipped away; there was no return to the *status quo ante.* What is ironic is that the new regime could not survive as it began. It exhausted its sustaining grasses and to the classic scourges of Australia, drought and bushfire, it added others from its lifeline to a global economy, speculation and depression. What Yeh-lü Ch'u-ts'ai, his Chinese counselor, told Genghis Khan—that he could conquer an empire from the saddle but he could not rule it from one—applied also to Australian pastoralists. By the onset of World War II, the invasive period had reached its limits. After the war, a complex period of reformation began that had to reconcile not only Australian and Eurasian biotas but the emerging, often conflicting society of Australians.

There were reforms in fire practices, particularly after the 1939 Black Friday holocaust. Tougher fire codes sought to regulate burning, rural fire brigades emerged to orchestrate firefighting, and a fire community, building on a program of scientific research, labored to rationalize fire use with fire control. As late as 1986, a workshop sponsored by the Commonwealth Scientific and Industrial Research Organization (CSIRO) concluded that, in the woodlands of southeastern Australia, "prescribed burning is the only economic method of restoring the balance between woody and herbaceous vegetation and ensuring continued pastoral production." In northern Australia burning was the only feasible basis for a pastoral economy. Equally, broadcast fire was the most widely adaptable instrument for the manipulation of fuels. What changed was the use of fire from an implement of extraction into a tool by which to shape biotas from within, an old means to new ends.[48]

These changes in fire practices occurred within a broader social context in which Australians deliberated over appropriate land use. Most graziers had leased crown lands, though the state often exercised nominal control. Now society found other uses for those lands and they were converted to forests, parks, protected catchments for reclamation projects, and reserves for nature conservation and for the Aborigines. So long as herding remained nomadic or transhumant, so long as it expanded into new domains, it could survive off the native flora, particularly if marginal sites were enhanced by burning. But when the range closed, when the marginal paddocks had degraded into powder, scrub, or weed, when global markets put a premium on quality, when Australian society demanded other uses from its public lands than as cattle runs and sheep walks, then pastoralists had to change both their grazing practices and their fire practices. Everything had to be "improved." Prime lands converted to sown pastures, for which fire had a circumscribed role. Lucerne replaced fire-induced green pick. Crossbreeding made the red steer into a prescribed burn. Herding evolved into husbandry; the herder into a farmer. Graziers ceased to be nomads. The European ceased to be an exotic.

The reformation of the landscape by pastoralists ended in the reformation of the pastoralists themselves. Where they survived, they did so as naturalized citizens of Australian biotas. Where they were removed, they were replaced by a new transhumant, the tourist. In the end, the relationship had proved to be reciprocal: Australia had shaped pastoralism as much as pastoralism had Australia. Reforms in land use, economics, and pastoralism broke apart the unstable compound that had presided over the transitional era of settlement. In all this, fire had an inextinguishable role. If Europeans had changed the character of Australian fire, it is no less true that Australian fire had helped change the character of the Europeans who came to reside there.

13

Beyond the Black Stump

Be theirs the task to lay with lusty blow
The ancient giants of the forest low,
With frequent fires the cumbered plain to clear,
To tame the steed, and yoke the stubborn steer . . .

—WILLIAM CHARLES WENTWORTH,
"Australasia" (1823)

THE INSTRUCTIONS from George III to Arthur Phillip informed the governor-designate that it was the "will and pleasure" of the crown that, after securing themselves from any attacks, the company of the First Fleet should "proceed to the cultivation of the land." Agricultural reclamation was enjoying a revival in Europe, a final rush into previously infertile, remote, and hostile environments. To political economists, agriculture was the primary industry, and farmers the essential component of the physiocratic state. For an isolated penal settlement, whose supply lines to Europe were tenuous, self-sufficiency in foodstuffs was a sine qua non of survival. Although more remote—and valued for that reason—it was possible to dismiss Australia as another example of the heaths, mountains, and dune-grass fields rapidly reduced to cultivation in Europe or the many islands that felt the tread of Eurasian livestock and waved with transplanted cereal grain and sugar cane. Australia would be farmed. Revealingly, ominously, the orders from George III that instructed Phillip to report on the means of cultivating and improving soil said nothing of appropriate fire practices.[1]

RECLAIMING AUSTRALIA

The difficulties in transplanting European agriculture were staggering. Australia posited a natural resistance more stubborn than any known in Europe and for which recent experiences in expanding reclamation into infertile sites offered only a partial analogue. In Europe the agricultural expansion of the seventeenth and especially eighteenth centuries built on the experience of several millennia of farming in and around these sites, and on experimentation with cultigens that originated in Eurasia or along the Mediterranean margins of the continent. Europe offered a degree of social continuity and environmental contiguity that was completely absent from Australia. Relying on stocks from India or Cape Colony was only a partial palliative. Eurasian cultigens encountered new kinds of soils, unused to compaction by hoof or ripping by plow, and new varieties of soil infertility, such as deficiencies in boron and molybdenum. They had to survive seasonal and secular droughts on an order unprecedented in northern Europe. They had to cope with routine fire. Where lands were fertile, they often flooded. Beyond floodplains, they burned. Phillip described how fires frustrated his desire to turn pigs out to browse in the bush. Bligh wondered if any of his fire-sensitive cultigens could survive the annual bushfires. Leichhardt—wandering beyond the Peaks Range, planting his last "peach-stand"—feared that the annual burning would overrun his saplings.[2]

But there was also social resistance to agriculture. Neither guards nor convicts were, for many years, trained as farmers. Before a major influx of farmers could enter the settlement Britain had to cultivate a different vision of New South Wales than that of penal colony; the official interest in agriculture sprang initially from the wish that the colony not be a drain on the British exchequer, not that it contribute to the global economy in foodstuffs. Markets were poor and transport wretched. Despite endless tinkering, land legislation frustrated mixed farming. Close settlement put farmers near markets but limited their geographic expansion. Instead livestock, not cultigens, became the basis for land wealth, and not until serious land reform in the 1860s did selectors begin to compete vigorously with squatters; not until wheat challenged hay for commodity production did farming become pervasive. Land reform, drought and rabbits, superphosphate fertilizers—all converged to quadruple farmland from 2.2 million hectares in 1890 to 8.9 million hectares by 1930. The farmer replaced the herder or forced the pastoralist into the husbandry of livestock such as milk cows. The fraction of the Australian landmass under cultivation was small, but it figured large within those regions made dense with European settlement.[3]

Fire practices were an amalgam of techniques intended, alternatively, to exterminate and to enhance the Australian bush. Unlike the Aborigine, the European did not cultivate Australia; he cultivated *in* Australia. If the Aborigines "farmed" with their firesticks, then the Europeans farmed with axe, plow, and match. What the Aborigines claimed, the Europeans reclaimed. Farmers used fire to convert the old and to catalyze the new. They cleared and burned across much of the wooded bush. They used fire to help pump nutrients into select cultigens and to purge old fields of pests and disease. They fired the surrounding bush to flush it with green pick suitable for a few head of cattle or sheep; they burned uncultivated lands to protect their sedentary properties against wildfire. As pioneers opened tough new lands—the mallee, the brigalow—old practices were constantly refined, for European colonization was a mixed and mobile affair. Agriculture changed, and fire practices changed with it.

Ultimately agricultural fire was less a means by which to live within Australia as to replace Australia. With fire and axe it was possible to clear a site of its native biota and replace it with alien cultigens, and then to jump start that exotic growth with a flush of mineralized ash temporarily free of pathogens and native competitors. If productivity could not be sustained, then the site was abandoned, perhaps to be burned again after years of fallow. If, however, productivity continued, then fire had a shrinking role. Grazing, fertilizing, tilling, pesticides—all could substitute specifically for the generic power of broadcast fire. Intensive farming pushed fire to the perimeter where the bush still presided. On those marginal sites where it was essential to compromise between the native and the alien, fire persisted. To the degree that the Australian bush could not be erased or replaced, then fire endured. Until then the black stump served as the signpost of a farming frontier.

"ANYWHERE, EVERYWHERE, NOTHING BUT SMOKE"

From the earliest days Europeans had to protect themselves from bushfires. Early bush houses were firetraps, assembled out of eucalypt slabs, forest debris, and plated with bark, and fields and paddocks intermingled with bush. Governors admonished farmers to shield their properties, especially their wheat, from the ubiquitous fires. Regulations abjured them to dig trenches around harvested stacks and burn "a considerable circle of ground" as a precaution against fires lurking within the bush. Proclamations prohibited anyone from lighting fires or even smoking pipes near "wheat stacks, public or private." Pioneering farmers in the South Australian scrub often hesitated to go beyond the lines of contiguous survey "into the open country" for fear of bushfires. Urban centers converted to stone and brick, but it was years before settlement in the bush could follow suit. Instead, they cleared around their fields and paddocks as best they could, heavily grazed the open grasses around their humpies, burned the surrounding bush as a prophylactic measure, and fought fire. Military guards, convicts, and free settlers quickly learned the techniques of bush firefighting.[4]

Conflict with the Aborigine added some fire, or rather redirected Aboriginal burning, but its ultimate consequence was the near extinction of the

Aborigine and with him a prominent source of ignition. There were some exceptions, however. In the southwest, where Aboriginal burning coincided with European harvesting, farmers visited annual corroborees with bribes of sugar, rice, and blankets to forestall broadcast fires until the harvest was in. In Tasmania a farmer reported how Aboriginal campfires blew into the bush and threatened a field of standing corn. "We were doing our best to extinguish it by beating the flames out with green boughs," the farmer recalled, but their efforts would have failed "had not the whole tribe of Blacks all at once come forward to assist me." Another episode that "threatened the destruction of the Settlement" brought out Aborigines who "shewed great dexterity" in beating out the flames with green gum-tree boughs.[5]

The real need was less to protect settlers from Australia than from themselves. The encounter with the fires of Aboriginal Australia lasted only a few years; the truly disastrous fires were set by the Europeans. "Burning off" was a universal prescription for establishing farms and a persistent practice for insulating the farm from the bush. Escape fires were common. To ensure a clean burn, settlers ignited clearing fires under the most intense conditions from which fires not only escaped but often raged throughout the surrounding lands. The more the land was being cleared the worse the fires. In the early days, fires fled into a more or less untrammeled bush which could absorb them. Thus in early Tasmania a fire near the Don bridge leaped into barns and stacks of grain, "ran on with increasing fury" to other farms and consumed "everything in its course, stopping only where the belts of uncleared land stayed its progress." But as more land was cleared, as debris piled like haystacks, as hillside after hillside bristled with ring-barked forests of dead timber, as the native bush slid into instability, escape fires could devastate whole landscapes. The sparse settlement magnified the terror. The only response possible for a settler was to fire the bush around his own farm. "But this," as Wollaston despaired, "only makes more fires in another direction." [6]

Settlers responded with similar techniques throughout Australia. In a footnote to *An Emigrant Family*, Alexander Harris remarked on the practice of burning around "fences, &c." prior to fire season. Settlers hemmed in by forested bush cleared and burned around their property. "If they do not, they are soon taught." Protective burning proceeded cautiously, with small portions burned and swatted out after the fire "has done just enough." Once faced with a bushfire, settlers hurried either to burn out or sometimes to wait, depending on their perception of the threat. The "Emigrant Mechanic" who visited Australia in the mid-nineteenth century thus "heard the people talking of the fire that was burning in the bush, and saw numbers of them assembled in groups, pointing out to each other its progress across the adjacent country." Wollaston echoed similar sentiments, writing into his journal that "John came to tell me the fire of yesterday was creeping up to our pilings, so I have been to help whip it out with boughs." With fuels light, this was easy, but the fire would soon enter "high grass, scrub, old decayed wood and grass trees . . . impossible to stop," and he resolved to "burn about our premises tomorrow." In Victoria John Cotton noted casually that "it is a general plan for settlers to burn the scrub during the dry weather," for it both removed hazardous fuels and encouraged "the grass to grow and be available for cattle." In South Australia George Angas found "the settlers busy beating out a fire that was running furiously along the dry stubble of a corn-field, and had threatened to extend to the fences and buildings of a neighboring farm . . . a strange, wild scene, viewed with the storm and the darkness of the night." [7]

Bushfires became accepted, even expected, as part of the price of progress. If explorers could track the Aborigine by his fires, so visitors could trace the line of European settlement by its burnings. Thus in 1850, in addition to the normal burning off that surrounded Adelaide, an arsonist attacked ricks, wheat fields, and paddocks, and even ignited the parklands around Government House. But "these fires were petty compared to the ones which were raging in the Adelaide Hills . . . the entire countryside from Mount Lofty to Crofters' Inn was ablaze." While bushfires were "a very real hazard in those early days," a chronicler of Wagga Wagga reported, in the long run "they must have cleared a great amount of timber from the land and this would be of great advantage to the settlers." While fatigued by firefighting duties, and depressed by the fact that "the whole country round us has been in a burning state"—"nothing could exceed the wretchedness of the appearance of the burnt country," its ascending smoke reminiscent "of the scene Abraham witnessed on looking toward Sodom and Gomorrah"—Wollaston admitted that the bushfires "ultimately do good." They even "prepare the way for the wind, which continually levels the half-burnt trees." [8]

However treacherous the instrument, settlers refused to deny themselves access to fire. Without fire European-style agriculture could not be established. James Ruse, the first successful farmer in New South Wales—a man who had learned farming in Cornwall—cleared his lands by burning and plowed and dug in the ashes as a source of fertilizer. When James Atkinson reported on the state of Australian agriculture in the early 1820s, he had, first, to fight back his disgust and outrage at the "rude and miserable" practices he witnessed at the hands of a slothful and indigent populace. He could barely persuade himself that British and Australians were "derived from the same stock." Yet what he was really witnessing was a recapitulation of early British agriculture, the advent of the Neolithic revolution into Australia. [9]

Australia's *landlam* commenced with a small clearing, sufficient for a first crop. The woody debris a farmer assembled for burning, often piling it against large logs. Plantings proceeded amid the stumps. Meanwhile more land was felled and fired for other crops. The stumps were burned by various methods. Particularly in the mallee, the later firing of stumps was considered a useful source of ash, a secondary fertilizing; sprouting trunks from the stump became a kind of ashy coppice, allowing for swidden on a four- or five-year cycle. Wheat stubble was burned; corn stalks were "pulled up and burnt"; Moore wrote that he even had "two men out grubbing grass trees at £2 20s an acre. These I burn and spread." To support small herds of livestock, the grassy woodlands surrounding the fields were burned on the same system used by "the Natives." "In dry seasons these periodical burnings sometimes assume a truly awful appearance; the country seems on fire in all directions, and if the weather is calm, is enveloped in dense smoke." A believer in improvement, Atkinson condemned the practice but admitted that it was "unavoidable" under Australian circumstances. Cattle refused to eat except on the burned sites.[10]

The improvidence of this "miserable" system became quickly apparent. The land succumbed to exhaustion, became "a nursery for rank and noxious weeds of every description," and forced the settler to relocate and repeat the cycle. Farmers became nomadic. They distributed broadcast fire as they migrated, their bushfires easily merging with those of pastoralists. The "quantity of dead wood" littering the landscape was "a great disfigurement," thought Atkinson. Gradually, fire removed it. Attempts to intensify farming, particularly to fertilize, also led to more burning. Atkinson even experimented with "paring and burning," with modest success for turnips. But as a source of "valuable and forcing manure," ash from woods easily exceeded ash from the negligible Australian turf.[11]

What really frustrated improvement, however, were social conditions. Farmers were part of the *un*settling of Australia. Abandoned sites bred pyrophytic weeds and scrub. Fenton related how Scots thistle invaded disturbed lands in Tasmania and in the autumn generated fires that "no human power could abate." Flashy weeds became fuses from roads to fields. The proliferation of scrub forced farmers to burn the surrounding environs to cleanse them of exotics. In South Australia broom and gorse posed "a much greater fire menace than the less dense indigenous scrub." Like graziers, farmers were drawn into a vicious cycle of protective burning. At Illawarra it is said that settlers lived in "absolute dread" of bushfires until the Forests Department inaugurated controlled burning to clear the bush of its understory. Rural migrants, nomadic swidden farmers, cow cockies, absentee owners of small farmsteads—"who visit their properties periodically in the summer months, when energies are devoted to clearing and burning scrub, blackberries, and other noxious weeds"—all relied on fire.[12]

The only way to control fire was to control settlement. Until then fire was ubiquitous along the frontier, endemic in lands marginal to sedentary agriculture and at times of rapid transition in land use. Where and when farming matured, the role of fire subsided and the domain of burning became more circumscribed. With security "the need for the use of fire gradually becomes less and less," observed a royal commission, "and, by the time his land is largely under crop and pasture, the agriculturist no longer relishes the use of fire, except under the strictest control.[13]

That more stable era came slowly, if ever. It is symptomatic that some of the most innovative Australian farming machines were, like the stump-jump plows that enabled early planting in partially cleared fields, implements for use in unsettled conditions. Agriculture, moreover, responded to an increasingly global economy whose cycles of price inflation and depression were as uncontrolled as the mob of homesteaders; agricultural fire in the mallee and the Riverina reflected wheat harvests in Russia and Canada as much as Australian climate and soils. It reflected, too, beliefs about the relative merit of farming not only to the economy of Australia but to the composition of its society. So long as the farmer enjoyed an aura of moral superiority, so long as pioneering was valued as a patriotic and ennobling activity, there was an incentive for agricultural fire, and until Australia was truly settled there was ample opportunity for it. What the *Yorke Peninsula Advertiser* wrote after a new Scrub Act encouraged movement into the mallee could be said of the continent: "Smoke! smoke! smoke! anywhere, everywhere, nothing but smoke.[14]

A GOOD BURN

"The work in this new country is of the most laborious description—" Thomas Potter Macqueen wrote in the 1820s, "cutting down trees . . . making these trees into fires, and attending them, with the thermometer usually ranging in the middle of the day from 80 to 100 deg. for eight months in the year . . ." Compared with farming in England, this was rugged work. Everywhere that agriculture went in Australia land clearing preceded it, but not everywhere did pioneers attend that chore with prudence or skill. Often care was not required: it was to remove, not to reshape, the flora that the vegetation was slashed and the residue burned.[15]

In open woodlands, a broadcast fire without much felling could prepare a site for a mixed farming economy of livestock and cereals. Backhouse described how, in Tasmania, he "set fire to some dead grass and fern, which burnt rapidly, and ignited some of the dead logs with which the ground was encumbered." This cleared off "unproductive vegetable matter," but it usually required a sequence of burns to dispose of the logs entirely and a lack of persistence left charred logs "scattered in all directions over this Island." A disgusted James Fenton described the method of clearing the denser underwood as "truly stupid." Settlers grubbed up, cut, and burned the scrub, "usually against the trunk of a fallen tree." Such labor-intensive methods, even with access to convicts, was uncalled for. But then there were "no weeds to hoe up in those days." [16]

Large trees were felled and burned or ringbarked and allowed to dry for subsequent burning. In places acre upon acre, hillside after hillside, bristled with ringbarked gums, "a veritable necropolis of eucalypti," one appalled critic wrote, "a forest if not a city of the dead." Clearing gangs stacked light debris around the base of the standing trees, ignited the piles, and allowed the basal fire to fell the trunks. Once on the ground the logs were gradually dissolved by annual broadcast burns or systematically nurtured into ash by rolling them into pyres. To be effective the logs had to be dry; this meant burning at the height of summer. Stumps were problematic and were burned in situ or, in extreme cases, were extracted and burned in subsequent years. The ashy residues industrious farmers spread and plowed into the soil before planting. [17]

These practices galloped across Australia like a plague of bark beetles. At the Swan River colony, farmers immersed the coastal plain in smoke throughout the summer months. Canberra pioneer Samuel Shumack explained that "when the ploughing season arrived we had ten acres ready for the plough and six acres ready to be burnt off. From Monday to Saturday we never went to bed before midnight as we were busy burning off." Francis Ratcliffe wrote in the 1930s that he would "always associate the Tableland with smoke. A thin veil of it seemed to hang perpetually in the air, if not from the burning clearings, then from the trash fires of the cane lands on the coast . . ." From the Swan River colony a settler wrote that there were "fires in all directions." Under the circumstances, it is easy to understand how escape fires became common. Houses and fields burned as well as stumps. "I was setting fire to some stumps of trees today," wrote George Moore, "when a spark, communicating with the grass, in a few minutes the whole scene appeared one sheet of living flame. It was in the heat of the day." [18]

A. B. Facey described with detail, and gusto, how farmers readied Western Australia for wheat prior to the Great War. "Now Dick and I started to get some land ready for cropping. This was hard manual work—we chopped down small trees and burned down the big ones. The timber was then left, as on the other farms where I had worked, to dry out ready for burning season starting in February. . . . We completed one hundred and forty acres of felling in eleven weeks . . ." He then wrote down instructions for Dick to follow after his departure.

> During the summer months, that is December and January, get as much ring-barking done as you can. That will kill the trees and give the natural grass a better chance to grow freely, increase the feed for the stock and also make the trees easier to burn later . . .
>
> Now you must be ready to start burning off the land we have

chopped down, in February. You will want two or three men to help you do this, so each time you go to town try and make arrangements for them to start, or—if you can manage the finance—get a man just after Christmas. He can work on the ring-barking and post-cutting as well as helping with the burning—it would be money well spent . . .

Now, when burning off, first of all burn all the stumps down to ground level and be careful that you don't burn all the other wood up before you finish this—otherwise you will have to cart more wood to finish burning the stumps. A good idea is to mark out an area, then go all over it and pack wood on all the stumps. When all the loose wood burns shovel the burnt coal off and pack more wood in. Keep doing this until all the stumps are burnt to the ground level, then you can pack whatever wood is left onto the fires and clear it all up.

Plow "fire-breaks" around the felled timber, Facey advised. Light the slash around its outside perimeter and let the fire move inward. Pick up small pieces of unburnt wood and stack them against unburnt stumps for continued burning. Fill in the stumps before ploughing. Get four horses, a stump-jump plow, and a sixteen-run drill. Write the agricultural department for books on wheat growing. "I told Dick that when he had done all of these things he would be well on the way to having a real wheat farm." [19]

In South Gippsland, "the burn" was the "all-important event of the year to the selector," recalled W.H.C. Holmes. Everyone waited for exceptional dry spells before burning, which meant that everyone lived in constant anxiety about a bushfire that might, without prior notice, get into the slash. Rather than risk a bad burn, selectors would carry the slash through another year until conditions were more favorable. It was an "unwritten law" that a selector would notify his neighbors about his intent to burn. The fire was typically set at midday on the hottest, windiest day possible, which made lighting "an exciting operation."

If it was of any size, the burn required the assistance of neighbors. The gang would ignite all the sides simultaneously, and the flames would coalesce inward into a mass fire. At this point, "nothing more could be done," so "all hands settled down to watch, drink tea and speculate on the possibilities—and the progress of a scrub-fire in South Gippsland is a spectacle that for awful grandeur beggars description." The spreading fire flushed a cavalcade of animals from the cut scrub, including the enormous tarantulas that were Holmes's "pet aversion." The effect was eerie, unearthly—suggesting "to the uninitiated that the last days were at hand."

But here the excitement ended and the tedium set in. "Picking-up and burning off" continued. Gangs moved through the charcoal and ash to chop down standing spars, stack them, and burn the piles on a windy day. They shoveled live coals to caches of resting logs and reduced them to ash. "Picking up and sowing should be finished by the end of April," Holmes advised. "If you cannot do it by then, stack the timber and sow the seed, and burn off the timber next year." [20]

Edward Sorensen recalled how small trees could be merely "nicked" by the axe and large trees cut only partly through; when half an acre or so was prepared in this fashion, a giant tree would be felled that would carry "the lot crashing to earth in one tangled mass." As soon as one patch was down, work began on another with a "green wall" between the sites. These acted as firebreaks, and Holmes, too, remarked on the value of such a perimeter to prevent fires from spreading wantonly through the bush. Under prolonged drought conditions, however, such measures were incompetent. That selectors habitually relied on green swathes and area ignition to control fires infuriated foresters who fumed about fires on a "roasting hot day with a strong wind" that incinerated the selector's slash then advanced "on to other areas." Besides, some underburning in the surrounding bush could be valuable in stimulating green pick for a selector's herds.[21]

Meanwhile, the site of the huge patch drying in the sun inspired the "new settler" to greater labors. Where large trees were involved, the burning lasted for weeks; and where stumps were concerned, often for years. Thereafter the axe "figured no more in the farm work." Weeds invaded the site, particularly after the corn was pulled; these were scythed with brush hooks and fired. The weeds, in fact, became an essential part of the planting cycle, a source of quick fertilizer. "Occasionally, in dry seasons, we had to suspend operations until the weeds grew sufficiently for a good burn-off, without which we could not plant.[22]

In the mallee districts crushing supplemented slashing as a prelude to burning, a process known as "mullenizing." In 1868 a farmer named Mullen discovered that if the trees were felled low to the ground, then burned, a heavy log with spikes could "plow" the site sufficiently to sow seed. The burn was enhanced if the mallee stems were flattened and the roots exposed. This inspired a host of "farm-made rollers constructed from old steam boilers, huge logs, or with light logs bolted to a metal framework." The mallee suckered miserably, but if the woody debris and stubble were fired annually, the suckers could be controlled. In fact, some farmers encouraged the regrowth because it allowed for a kind of low-intensity swidden, making the scrub farmer "independent of fallowing and manures." [23]

When, after World War II, serious clearing began in the brigalow country, the techniques were essentially those pioneered in the mallee. By this time, however, herbicides supplemented fire as a means to control unwanted regrowth, and industrial fertilizers replaced ash as a source of nutrients. This was sedentary farming, not shifting cultivation. The fallen trees were residue; they could as well be ground into woodchips as burned. If some of the violence vanished from the scene, so did its magnificence. "I have never yet seen anything to equal the warring of the elements of fire and wind as has so often been seen by the pioneers of South Gippsland," Holmes recalled. The conversion of Australia by axe and fire had a heroic quality that its conversion by machine and herbicide lacked. There was, in the early years, a shared risk. Fire threatened the farmer as much as the land. Burning off touched both pioneer and bush.[24]

STRAW TO THE FLAMES

When René Lesson traveled to the Bathurst plains in 1824, he found "immense pastures" and "fields . . . rich in wheat and maize." Settlers had completed their harvest, and Lesson's party "often saw flames rising on different points of the surrounding country." They saw clearing fires, pasturage fires, and what particularly piqued Lesson's curiosity, field fires. The "gleanings," he observed, "are generally burnt and serve to enrich the soil." [25]

Burning straw—unconsumed hay, wheat and corn stubble, weedy fallow —was a fundamental practice of Australian farming from its origins. There were ample precedents in British history of course, but the drive toward "improvement" had by the time of Australian settlement found organic means to decompose residual straw or discovered in it social values as fuel or household material; Britons harvested standing straw as hay, fed it to sheep and cattle, or plowed it into the soil as compost. Farmers used stubble as thatch or fuel, or incorporated it into household uses as stuffing and brooms. This extreme utilization had little value in Australia; and even in Britain it soon gave way to a restored practice of straw burning after harvest. Burned straw eased plowing, stimulated new growth, sterilized wet fields of diseases and pests, and shielded high-yield paddocks from wildfire. All this was true also for Australia, whose impoverished soils made decomposition by organic means even less promising.

Plowing straw into soil encourages its decomposition by microorganisms. But the practice also drains the nutrient reservoir and promotes pests as straw becomes fodder for smut, rust, and other microbial flora and fauna that subsequently infect cereal crops. Hostile or innocuous, however, the microfauna demand nutrients to supplement those they extract from the stalky residue, and this comes from the soil. Scarce nutrients like organic nitrogen, in particular, thus sustain the decomposition of residue rather than the growth of new grains. Adding nitrogen fertilizer only stimulates the decomposers or encourages Eurasian weeds like Wimmera rye grass. Without fire Australian wheat yields steadily diminish. While some farmers stocked sheep and cattle on stubble—"folding the flock"—the low palatability of the stalks made them unacceptable as feed. Besides, the burning of fallow and stubble in Australia easily merged with other fire practices.[26]

Throughout the 1920s and 1930s stubble burning remained common practice. But gradually it fell out of favor. Intellectuals, in particular—ever distrustful of open fire in all its varieties—now railed against stubble burning as another indiscriminate abuse, as indistinguishable from indigent practices of burning off. Soil erosion, soil exhaustion, declining productivity were all blamed on routine agricultural burning. The declines were real, but their cause lay with drought, with overgrazing and competition from rabbits, with monoculture cropping—with the cumulative abuse of the land—not with fire. As farmers regained control over the true contributing causes, they reinstated burning. Over and again, the alternatives, both mechanical and organic, were found to be worse than fire. Problems that had been attributed to fire belonged not with fire per se but with fire in conjunction with poor cropping, careless plowing, indifferent fertilizing. The fact was that fire did not make for slovenly farming: slovenly farming made for slovenly fire practices. Where fire failed as a tool, the reasons often included serious deficiencies in soil moisture or insufficient fuel to make an effective burn.[27]

On many sites farmers reincorporated fire as they once did residue. Now, however, they managed fire intensively. They tested soil moisture, ensured adequate levels of fuel, prevented escapes, balanced fire with other techniques, adjusted fertilizers. They relied on the differential moisture contents of stubble and surrounding pasture grasses to program for evening burns, such that fire could burn the residue and nothing else. Stubble burning became part of the husbandry of fire.

FIRING THE CANE

The first cuttings of sugar cane were acquired by the First Fleet at Cape Colony. Plantation cane fields, however, did not emerge until the 1860s, when they expanded along classic tropical models that included imported labor (South Sea *kanakas)* before legislation and mechanization combined to end the practice. Assured of protection by tariffs, sugar cane emerged as an important crop along the North Coast of New South Wales and most of coastal Queensland. Its history became increasingly interdependent with fire.

Land clearing was laborious and proceeded in stages; so did crops. Between burns settlers typically planted maize. Even after cane assumed status as a monoculture, burning continued. That farmers ran a fire through fields after harvest comes as no surprise, but that they burned immediately in advance of cutting does. At issue was the enormous volume of leaves or "trash" that surrounded the cane. It made cutting onerous, and after prohibitions against kanakas acquired bite, the huge labor required for harvest could no longer be pawned off on a class of imported serfs. Migratory gangs assisted with the trashing, then harvested the cane. But it was soon learned that a preburn—the hotter, the better—instantly cleansed the fields of debris, readied the cane stalks, and drove off snakes and other pests. Companies refused to sanction "trash burning," but fires were frequent. Narrow-gauge trains in the fields, pastoralists and farmers around the fields, and of course "accidental" ignitions all put fire through the cane. So long as the cane was cut quickly afterward, there was no damage to the crop.[28]

Perhaps the real problem with cane fires was that they looked bad. They burned fiercely; trash strips ("fliers") could torch spot fires downwind, in fields not yet ready for harvest or in the paddocks of neighboring pastoralists; it was difficult to believe that they did not injure the sappy cane. Intellectuals again—agronomists this time—protested the practice, as they did stubble burning and the preharvest firing of forests. The *Australian Sugar Journal* reported in 1910 that the practice of burning before cutting was sweeping Hawaii. Experiments showed, however, that cane lost weight and purity if it was not harvested within forty-eight hours. Australian field trials over the next few years confirmed the dramatic losses, and the *Australian Sugar Journal* was led to editorialize that "every effort should be made to put a stop to so ruinous a practice." [29]

Nothing of the sort happened. For several decades, burning persisted as a sub-rosa folk practice, widespread but officially condemned. With World War II, however, labor shortages demanded aids to expedite harvesting, and public health regulations for areas subject to Weil's disease (leptospirosis) insisted on the sanitation of fields. Instead of removing fire, which was useful and endemic, sugar growers rapidly incorporated it.

Burning became an informing principle. Growers selected cane varieties in part for their combustibility. Drought-hardy and frost-resistant varieties tended to clutter their stalks with leafy trash, making fire both possible and mandatory. Growers took advantage of regular sea breezes and topographic winds and oriented their fields so that they could be burned accordingly. The burns established the rhythms of the harvest: each night the grower burned the patches that were to be harvested the following day. If a field had insufficient trash to carry a hot fire, it would be left to "stand-over" another year and burned then. If a field were flooded to the point that silt inhibited burning, the stalks might be chemically sprayed to enhance burning. In a remarkable reversal, factories penalized growers for "dirty," unburned cane.[30]

Fire even dominates the relationship between the cane growers and their neighbors along the coast because cane burning was out of sync with other agricultural burning. As the cane harvest wanes, the fire danger in bush and paddock waxes, and an escape fire from cane fields can seriously damage forest and field. Conversely, graziers, foresters, railways, and road departments all tend to burn during the winter months when the cane is vulnerable. A fire escaping into the cane under such circumstances would mean that the cane could not be harvested in time, and the crop would deteriorate.

There are persistent moves to abolish cane burning. To date, by allowing larger areas to be harvested at one time, mechanization has encouraged burning by promoting larger daily burns, thus reducing the prospects for escape. For many, however, the spectacle of fire is embarrassing and unwanted. They demand machinery that can harvest cane green and eliminate for once and all an appeal to fire with its low-tech, folklorish image. But for others, there is something especially appealing about cane burning and its reversal of contemporary trends. Here fire is no longer merely a tool of convenience, a device for rude extraction, or a necessity of climatic survival. Firing the cane has become an art form. Besides, its reliance on fire helps render sugar cane, if not quite Australian, at least somehow less alien.

RED TUESDAY

It was "the year of the Great Fires," T. J. Coverdale recalled in a memorial volume, the year from which Gippsland pioneers effectively dated their lives. The fires appeared early in the winter, reached nuisance proportions by late December, simmered and erupted like migrating fumaroles across the south Victorian landscape before reaching a crescendo of fury on February 1, 1898, "Red Tuesday," then alternately flared up and smoldered into extinction over the course of the following fortnight. When they ended, most of Gippsland and Cape Otway was a smoking wreckage. Distant Tasmania also felt the aftershocks, and officials there warned that unless such outbreaks could be prevented in the future, the fires would "extinguish, for all practical purposes, any hope" that Tasmania could develop a robust economy or even satisfy the demands of its own markets. In Victoria the fires destroyed, for a time, a frontier society.[31]

The Great Fires were, as the pioneers appreciated, intimately interdependent with settlement. Selectors and squatters had rendered the countryside into a medley of cleared, partially cleared, and uncleared lands. There were bush humpies insinuated amid dense gallery forest, shaded by trees reaching more than 150 feet in height; bush farms, surrounded with desiccated ring-barked forests, small paddocks, and cultivated fields; mature farms, the product of more than twenty years of relentless clearing, plowing, sowing, and road making. All were parched by drought, and all burned, but the marginal sites experienced the greatest fury. The density of the original forest had stalled outright land clearing, which proceeded slowly. Instead small clearings expanded into bush pasture by burning off the scrub and understory, and abandoning the towering, ring-barked mountain trees to a slow dry rot. Settlers transformed timber to tinder; old forests stood like stacked cordwood. And since the pioneers never completed their final slashing and burning, the enveloping forests accumulated a fuel and fire debt totalling twenty years. That, in retrospect, the Great Fires recouped in a single summer. Burning off—the desire for a final, "good burn"—was a prominent source of ignition.

Settlers anticipated a difficult bushfire season. Night after night, day by day, they watched distant fires flare across field and forest, unable or unwilling to do much until the fires approached their immediate environs. Those distant from the flames lived, A. W. Elms recalled, in a chronic state of "suspense." Those nearer found their lives dominated by the rhythm of the fires as flames raced forward into fresh fuels or receded into smoldering debris piles, as winds alternately blew desert and marine air across the flaming front.

The Great Fires were more terrible than any that the Gippslanders—accustomed as they were to intense clearing fires—had ever witnessed. Once started, they were uncontrollable. The sky eroded into a black pall, strangely shaded into a purple "tinged with blood" or domed into burnished copper that variously glowed and paled. Flames burned steel blue, and refused to emanate light. Long streamers of fire and sparks snaked across the pall "like fiery serpents." Winds thundered. Embers rained down upon the scene like snowflakes, sparkling silver, igniting everything they touched. Gusts whipped clouds of sparks into a blizzard of firebrands. Flames ignited the standing timber like stockpiled torches; they ripped bark and loose wood from the trunks and turned trees into flaming catapults. Fire raged through the canopy. It invaded cultivated fields, burned paddocks, ravaged the surrounding bush, devastated homesteads by the hundreds. Fire did not so much spread as leap across the landscape; settlers convinced that the fires were elsewhere suddenly discovered that fire had descended upon them. It was, as A. W. Elms recalled, "a spectacle that, once seen, could never be forgotten." [32]

As the fires ebbed and advanced, settlers faced the daily choice whether to fight or to flee. In the end, most did both. Those whose humpies nestled in dense forest could not hope to fight off the fires, though some tried. When falling trees cut off their narrow escape routes, they took refuge where they could—in small gardens, in waterholes (standing up to their necks), under wet blankets in small depressions, in root holes churned up by fallen trees. Those whose homesteads were more developed and more distanced from the bush had some room for maneuvering. They stacked valuables in potato fields and on dirt roads, mustered stock onto old burns or closely cropped fields, cut down fuelbreaks around their houses and fields. All hands, "including the girls," were pressed into service. Settlers organized into gangs, swatted the advancing flames with wet sacks and green eucalypt boughs, and set backfires. "We fell back," J. Western despaired, "on the Indians' device of fighting fire with fire." Neighbors moved from farm to farm, but unless the fuels were light or anomalously green, success was indifferent, almost random. Settlers told of fighting the fires not once but over and again, as flames outflanked them and approached from new directions, or as firebrand showers descended thirstily onto unburned fuels. At Jundivick one selector fought back the fire twice over three weeks before being overpowered in a third assault "that swept off the dwelling house and other buildings." In the Strzelecki district, scarcely a house survived. Homesteads by the hundreds lay in ruins, marked only by their chimneys "like tombstones in a cemetery." [33]

Again those from the more settled, cleared areas had a better chance for survival. By the time many backblockers realized their predicament, fires surrounded them. Older settlers had roads and relatively fire-free corridors by which to escape. But here, too, the suddenness of the fire, the unexpected intensity of the burns, desperation to protect the hard-won homestead, held too many back until it was too late. One selector readied a horse and dray for rapid flight, but the abrupt heat drove the horse into the fence to which it was secured and there the dray burned until nothing remained but "tyres and bolts." Others fled their homesteads only to encounter more fire. One family near Warragul abandoned their flaming humpy at the last instant. They placed their younger children on a horse, which they led to a neighbor's house half a mile away. The fire bore down on them, and the two families retreated to another neighbor a mile distant. They made their way through horrible heat and suffocating ash, the children half-blinded and screaming in terror. Again the fire roared out of the bush, and this time three families rallied and retired. The women stripped off their skirts to beat down the avid flames; the panicked children were again mounted; the men, "more dead than alive," guided their horde to a fourth farm. There the scene was repeated. Four families—twenty-four children in all—now set off once more beneath the pall and through the roar to still another dwelling. Yet again the "persecuting" fire approached like a malevolent harpy baring its flaming claws. Miraculously, this time the wind shifted, and the fire was unable to beat against it. The thirty-five refugees sank into exhaustion. They were lucky; others perished. Many settlers were unable to do more than endure. At 4:30 A.M. on Red Tuesday a woman gave birth to her first child while outside the trees torched and sparks showered the "homestead and its outbuildings." [34]

Red Tuesday's immediate aftermath appeared absolute in its devastation. Essentially the entire frontier was a smoking ruin. The Great Fires burned homes by the hundreds, gutted entire districts, consumed crops, and put every shred of grass to the torch. Livestock perished in vast numbers—burned to death when trapped against fences or slowly starved by the absence of surviving feed. Roads clogged with dead and dying fauna, a "plague spot." Fallen timber so jackstrawed the backcountry that it was impassable. South Gippsland, a reporter wrote, "is red eyed and heart-broken. There is not a man, woman or child in the whole forest country who is not, more or less, blinded by the smoke, and there are hundreds who are homeless." Aging homesteaders saw their life's work vanish in smoke. One of the original selectors, it was reported, was found by neighbors "in a nearly nude state standing below a burning tree near where his hut had been. Force had to be used to drag him from below the tree, as he said he would stay there till it fell on him as he had lost all he had in the world." [35]

But to stay was the exception. The greatest impact of the Great Fires was that they set the region in motion. Liberated herds roamed free from fencing; families, homeless and destitute, likewise wandered across the countryside in huge numbers. Throughout the frontier there was, another reporter affirmed, "nothing but want and misery." [36]

The story of the Great Fires did not end there. Red Tuesday was not so much an unprecedented aberration as it was a macabre, reckless parody of frontier land clearing, transience, and violence. It crowded into days and weeks what had been occurring over years and decades. Even as they tallied the pain and loss, careful observers realized that the frontier would quickly revive. Paradoxically, those settlers "with well improved properties," W. J. Williams recalled, "lost heavily through the fires, while properties which had been badly handled were improved." By burning the indigent sites more virulently than the diligent, the Great Fires actually accelerated the pace of settlement. By forcing graziers to find other pastures, the fires established a pattern of transhumance that sent herds seasonally to the plains. New, better houses sprouted from the ashes like stems from a lignotuber. In Melbourne private subscription undertook relief; clothing—including evening dresses, top hats, and "claw-hammer coats"—poured into the destitute areas; government extended seed, tools, and tents, another expression of its long commitment to assisted settlement. "Without any hesitation," A. W. Elms wrote admiringly, the Gippsland pioneers "set to work at once to repair the damage done by this overwhelming disaster." [37]

"What a change met our eyes!" exclaimed J. Western in the aftermath of Red Tuesday. "Instead of the forest of dry trees, there were great, clear spaces." It took no prophet, he concluded, "to discover the beginnings of a more prosperous future, as much of the timber which had before seemed to be the work of generations to clear had vanished in the night." On many burned sites dogwood came back in dog-hair thickets, logs littered the landscape in miserable tangles, scrub resprouted; but once cleared the "country looked better than before." Hard-eyed men saw in the smoldering wreckage the means by which to finish off the endless labor of "picking up and burning off." All that was needed was some good fire. Constables marveled that they were unable to secure "any definite information or evidence from settlers as to the origin of the fires"—even those "due to the grossest carelessness, if not to an even worse cause." Pioneers could tolerate no diminution in their access to fire. Without the torch there could be no settlement. For all its terror Red Tuesday was, after all, that great desideratum of frontier life, the "good burn." [38]

"THE SNAKE HIDDEN UNDER MY HOUSE, THE BREATH OF THE BUSHFIRE"

Fire was everywhere on the Australian frontier, and it was everywhere viewed with ambivalence. Without fire pioneering would cease; rather than suppress fire, settlers wanted ready access to it to extract precious resources from a stubborn continent, to manipulate native biotas to new purposes, and to convert the indigenous into the alien and the alien into the naturalized. Burning off was an exhilarating event, a dramatic ritual of colonization, the Beltane fire of the selector. Yet with relentless regularity fires placed those settlements in jeopardy, and bushfires rallied settlers against a common enemy, enforcing a solidarity of the flame; they baptized a community with fire. The European Australian became as much a pyrophiliac as the Aboriginal Australian.

It was generally assumed that the need for burning would pass as settlement matured. That did not occur. Not all the bush could be converted. Where settlement proceeded slowly, cultivated lands and wild bush intermingled for decades, like two volatiles needing only a spark to explode. Where settlement halted, or advanced and retreated, a palimpsest of alien and indigenous biotas emerged, also prone to fire. Where settlement existed on the margin, where it needed a compound of native and exotic biotas to subsist, there wildfire was pandemic. During the unsettling of Australia, fire loads multiplied manyfold. Throughout the island continent a transplanted European fire and Australian bushfire coexisted—the one supplementing settlement, the other threatening it. It was easy for the first to become the second. And in the process, the bushfire became more than a tool or a propagating chemical pestilence. It became a symbol of wild Australia—fearsome, alien, brooding. It was an association Judith Wright captured in her poem "Fire at Murdering Hut."

> You who were the snake hidden under my house,
> The breath of the bushfire—

No one captured the hostility of bushfire, its psychological as well as physical terrors, as well as Henry Lawson. In "The Bush-Fire" and "The Fire at Ross's Farm"—two poems that gallop to a climax of mateship—settlers battle against invading bushfires. One roars out of the Dingo Scrub, impenetrable and inscrutable, a place of "drought, and ruin, and death." The other burns through lands uneasily claimed by both squatters and selectors. Here the bushfires had "started in the north / And travelled south for weeks."

The scene at night was "grand and strange." In both instances, bushfire makes unlikely alliances out of a disparate society. Boozing Bill, Constable Dunn of the Mounted Police, and Flash Jim ride to rescue the family of Pat Murphy, "the cocky." And Black, the embittered squatter, with a dozen brawny men comes "racing through the smoke" to fight for Ross's farm at the last possible moment, when hissing flames had driven off all hope. Their human squabbling vanishes in the fire. "Two grimy hands in friendship" join on Christmas Day.

But Lawson also captured the other quality of the bushfire. In "A Child in the Dark, and a Foreign Father" bushfires set the stage for the gloom, ultimately spiritual, that oppresses the child with all the alienness of Australia.

A hot night in midsummer in the drought. It was so dark—with a smothering darkness—that even the low loom of the scrub-covered ridges, close at hand across the creek, was not to be seen. The sky was not clouded for rain, but with drought haze and the smoke of distant bush fires.

In Lawson's oeuvre there is nothing glamorous about bushfires. They emerge from a landscape that is cruel, vast, imponderable, morose, weird. They lurk like dingos in dense scrub and hiss like "angry snakes" through tall grass. They spring, too, from the hands of bush larrikins, brutalized and ignorant and spiritless. Because of them the "respectable farmer" in the backblocks lived in terror of the torch. "The crime of arson," Lawson lectured, "used to be very, very common in Australia." It expressed a malice "terrifying to those who have seen what it is capable of. You never know when you are safe." [39]

In "Water Them Geraniums" and "The Drover's Wife"—both studies in alienation, in the dark side of bush life that drove everyone more or less mad in the end—women have to battle against bushfires that rush against their homesteads. That they succeed, that neighbors come in the end to their aid, testifies to their endurance, a stoicism that brutalizes rather than ennobles. Here European and Australia have fought to a standstill, each degraded, exhausted, dangerous.

But the most powerful imagery belongs with "The Drover's Wife." Here Lawson symbolizes the bush in the form of an unspecified black snake, undoubtedly poisonous, that disappears through the chinks of a slab hut. The husband, an ex-squatter fallen on hard times, has gone a-droving. The woman must endure alone the hardships of bush life with her four children. That night she puts them to bed, lights candles and stokes a large hearth fire, and sits with a club to guard against the snake. The family dog, Alligator, shares her vigil. While a thunderstorm rains down lightning, a litany of her life in the bush swarms through her mind. The first of the terrors raised is the memory of a bushfire that very nearly destroyed the homestead had not "four excited bushmen" arrived in time to help her. The fire so blackened her that her own children could no longer recognize her, a cruel parody of the ashes painted or crossed over participants in European fire ceremonies. In such ways did the bush transform her.

Before dawn, while the "room is very close and hot because of the fire," the snake appears, glistening with an "evil pair of small, bright, bead-like eyes." Dog and woman attack and kill the reptile—this time. The woman knows that all snake dogs are eventually bitten and die. The bush does the same with those who live in its bleak remoteness. The woman carries the broken body of the snake to the fire and throws it in, piles up more wood, and watches the snake burn. It is a small victory, this triumph of the hearth over the bush, as the snake burns and the woman's young son vows never to go a-droving, because there will be more snakes and more bushfires.

In the end, the pioneer went the way of the bush, both a menace. The selectors, the cockies, the bushies, the backblockers—all vanished from the scene, either transfigured into sedentary farmers and shopkeepers or crowded into remnant pockets, historical relicts to be viewed with amazement, outrage, and empathy. The great fires of colonization had required both the fire-promiscuous European and the fire-prone bush. When either departed, so did the fires. Yet as the bush lost its terror, so its subjugation lost its grandeur. Farmers confined burning off to stubble and debris or well-defined paddocks. Australia moved beyond the world of the black stump.

14

Fire Conservancy

*Of the many problems which have to be dealt with by the forester, there is none
which is so constantly with him as that of fire. Its shadow is always over him:
the dread possibilities are ever present in his mind.*

—C. E. LANE-POOLE, Notes on the Forests . . .
of Western Australia (1920)

*If there were no Forestry in Australia, beyond mere fire-prevention, the benefit to
the country would be incalculable. This is almost a truism to anyone who has
travelled far through the forests of Australia; but, on the other hand, few Australians will admit that the fire-protection of the forest is practicable.*

—SIR D. E. HUTCHINS, A Discussion of
Australian Forestry (1916)

THE BRITISH SOON RECOGNIZED that fire and eucalypts were the warp and woof
of Australian forests. That the Aborigines were "so frequently setting the
country on fire is I apprehend," concluded Governor Phillip, "the reason we
find so little timber is sound." As European colonization upset one part of
that interdependency, they upset the other as well. A few places that had no
forests under Aboriginal fire practices sometimes acquired them when subjected to intensive grazing and fire exclusion. Elsewhere, established forests
disintegrated under the impact of axe, hoof, and fire. Even where Europeans
mimicked Aboriginal fire, they did so within a new biotic and economic
context that placed most forests in jeopardy. After decades of European colonization, Ferdinand von Müller wrote from Westralia that "I now can see no
means or system employed, no method adopted or followed to prevent this
waste; nothing but fire is used for the wholesale destruction of our best
timber." The future of Australian forests depended on the future of Australian fire. Foresters instantly identified bushfire as their great antagonist.[1]

Everywhere foresters went, they recorded an appalling devastation by fire

—big fires, surface fires, intentional and accidental fires, fires of every description and purpose, a record of casual burning so universal and pervasive that it deadened the senses even as it inflamed moral indignation. "There is," wrote a forestry commission from Tasmania, "a wholesale and reckless destruction of the forest growth, young and old, by bush fires in all directions during many months of the year." In Western Australia the Conservator of Forests concluded that "it may be accepted as a literally correct statement that prior to 1920 the whole Jarrah forest was burnt over by surface fires every three years." From Victoria Frederick Vincent, a forester on tour from Madras, believed that "all forests appear to be swept by a fire whenever there is sufficient undergrowth to burn, which is every second or third year." Victoria's Conservator of Forests thought that, "on the average," the reserved forests were fired "once in six or seven years." Settlers not only accepted bushfires but demanded access to fire as they did land, loans, and railroads. "Only a few years ago the general public," observed Stephen Kessell, "felt no compunction about setting the wild and untended forest alight whenever opportunity presented itself." [2]

Under such conditions forestry was impossible and foresters' accounts of Australian fire took on epic proportions, a lament almost Homeric in its scale and intensity. Their response was no less epic. If fire dominated Australian forestry, it was no less true that, in time, foresters came to dominate Australian fire. [3]

"SOLELY A MATTER OF ORGANIZATION"

No part of Australian forestry was immune from fire. It informed working plans, defined practical relationships with settlers, directed field operations. Fire was a subject "on which any Australian could talk for a week," explained Owen Jones to a British Imperial Forestry Conference. It was "undoubtedly the forester's greatest enemy." Chronic burning explained the damaged state of Australian eucalypts, the low productivity of Australian forests, the degraded soils, and rendered "sharp and unmistakable" the dividing line between worthless scrub and cultivated woods. The ravages of fire, Sir D. E. Hutchins wrote with breathless outrage, "is the first thing that strikes the Forester on seeing the Australian forest." Relentlessly Hutchins attacked the Australian "fatalism" which held that fire could not be extirpated from Australia, that the only practical response to fire was more fire. He scorned as misplaced Australian chauvinism the assertion that eucalypt forests could not be protected from fire. [4]

In the early years, however, foresters shared with other settlers a common environment, and they resorted to common fire practices. The practical bushmen who often doubled as working foresters frequently exploited fire in ways that were functionally indistinguishable from the fire practices of pioneers, pastoralists, and farmers. Foresters slashed and burned to prepare sites for planting or to stimulate the regeneration of native flora; they sent fire through woods after harvesting and sometimes before; they relied on protective burning around valued sites; they fought wildfires with boughs and backburns. They underburned to reduce fuels, to protect mature trees, and to prompt green pick. They installed firebreaks to shield planted forests of exotic conifers as farmers did wheat fields and sown pastures. Europeans showed an unquenchable restlessness that afflicted protected forests with transient fire as it did on other sedentary sites. Even within forests, one professional forester lamented, "Frequent bush fires were looked upon as inevitable and rather to be encouraged in that a fire every two or three years was much less of a menace than a raging conflagration in a forest which had escaped burning for a long period of years." Victoria's Conservator of Forests argued in 1890 that "it is entirely owing to the fact that the innumerable small bush fires which take place at various times all over the colony and which apparently die out in the night-time, rage furiously during the day— that immense conflagrations of the Black Thursday type are prevented." [5]

But foresters were not simply bushmen, and the professional forester feared, hated, and respected fire as other settlers did not. Alone among colonists, the forester demanded a systematic program of fire protection that would culminate, hypothetically, in the exclusion of fire. Foresters could not rely, as pioneer philosophers did, on laissez-faire settlement to create a fire-free landscape. They could not eliminate forest fires, as pastoralists and farmers could, by eliminating the forest. They could substitute controlled grazing for controlled burning only sparingly. Besides their pine plantations, they had to accept and live with the native woods, which meant they had to accept a fire load that was heavy and regular. They could not satisfy their needs by accelerating the tempo of burning; on the contrary, the first response of educated professionals was almost always to restrict fire. When he used fire, the forester did so apologetically. "Fire conservancy," he called it —conservation by fire control.

Foresters made an odd—and oddly influential—group. Unlike most settlers, they had the intellectual's distrust of free-burning fire. Unlike other educated critics, however, they had a mandate to manage considerable tracts of land. As professionals, foresters belonged with a transnational and in some respects a transcultural corps that by the latter half of the nineteenth century spanned the globe. They proposed a special kind of administration that made them blood brothers with colonial proconsuls, and they shared with engineers a peculiar ethos that bonded them to that rationalization of resource use known as conservation. England, they appreciated, was a wretched model, or rather a negative exemplar of what happened when a nation ignored its forested heritage. Instead they trained under French and German mentors at Nancy or at Cooper's Hill (later, Oxford). If British, they served field apprenticeships elsewhere in the Empire—India, Cape Colony, East Africa—before arriving in Australia. If their training made them suspicious of fire, it also endowed them with the means by which to examine fire rigorously. They made fire an object of academic and scientific study. Their education equipped them with precepts about land management and fire practices, inspired them with a genius for creating institutions, and inflamed them with a moral energy to address the problems of fire use and fire control. To the question of free-burning fire foresters brought discipline, expertise, and fervor.

But all this was premised on a more fundamental enthusiasm that can only be described as an ethical imperative to plant and preserve forests. In Australia successful forestry demanded fire control and it meant reconciliation with those social processes that scattered fire across the landscape like sparks off a grindstone. Here the idealism—the mental intensity of the intellectual—came into play in complex ways, for their understanding of fire divided foresters even among themselves. Practical, self-taught field men wanted rapprochement with fire; professionals with formal training, with international apprenticeship at Oxford and throughout the empire, urged its expulsion. In Australia the two coexisted in uneasy equilibrium.

The transnational professional invoked global examples of fire protection that had been successfully executed in environments as rigorous as any in Australia. Hutchins, for example, dismissed Australian protests that fire exclusion was impossible: "There is not a shadow of doubt that they [forests of gum and wattle] can be as completely protected against fire as the average house in a city." The fundamental issue was, he insisted, "solely a matter of organization." Field men thought otherwise. They doubted, in particular, the pertinence of European exemplars—French models of firefighting in *garrigue,* German clean-floor silviculture as a surrogate for burning. As late as 1937 Max Jacobs still found it necessary to refute the "popular fallacy (which is not yet dead in many foresters) that without periodic burning so much litter would accumulate in the bush that 'it would not be possible to hear a dingo bark.' " In truth, Hutchins's was a preposterous claim. But it was one that he could advance because animating his technical and organizational analysis of fire exclusion was something of which his forester audience needed no reminder, a sense of right purpose. Moral intensity was a powerful tool, and one that very nearly matched the physical intensity of the bushfires it opposed.[6]

EXOTIC FIRE:
THE PROBLEM OF PLANTATION FORESTRY

Farming—its techniques, its ethos—could subsume some of forestry. "Trees must be looked upon by the forester," explained J. Ednie Brown, "in many respects the same as the farmer views a cereal crop." E.H.F. Swain considered forestry as "that nationalized form of farming for which Governments are held peculiarly responsible." There was certainly plenty of European precedent; silviculture meant the cultivation of trees. Modern forestry emerged as part of the agricultural revolution that had swept over preindustrial Europe, and, no less than white clover and turnips, conifers were a means by which to reclaim lands otherwise dismissed as "waste." The strategy closest to farming was plantation forestry, but much as pastoralists used modified native pastures, so foresters sought to rework, rationalize, and exploit native woodlands.[7]

European forestry, however, was no easier in Australia than was European farming. Native eucalypt forests resisted British axes, made poor lumber by European standards, and refused to submit to chemical treatments for pulp and raw material. The ideal solution was to convert unruly native woodlands to plantations of exotic conifers. Plantation forestry thus mimicked, in its early stages, shifting cultivation. The native forests existed in order to be cleared, to make ash and charcoal, to be burned. Foresters slashed and burned new sites; they recycled their tree crop by firing the residue and replanting. Ashbeds forced growth in exotic trees as they did for wheat, rye, or cane. Temporarily they purged the site of competitors, and stimulated nutrient flow in often-poor soils; the baked soil behaved "as if it were the long-sought slow-acting nitrogenous (and phosphatic) fertilizer which is the ideal looked for" in Australian agriculture. This stimulant was ephemeral, however. As with successive crops of cultigens, successive crops of trees exhausted soils unless they were fertilized. Site preparation required new fallow and further burning.[8]

Protecting exotic conifers from fire commenced with the design of the plantations. South Australia led the way in planning, adopting an active program in the 1870s. The principles were essentially those evolved in Europe, and the techniques virtually indistinguishable from those practiced on surrounding agricultural lands in Australia. Foresters plowed and burned fuelbreaks—"fire-breaks"—around the site. These served to insulate young plantations in particular from fires that raged through the surrounding bush and fields. The exotics were notoriously vulnerable during the first decade of life or until their trunks could mature to the point where they removed the canopy from ground contact, shaded the understory, and replaced grass with needles, all of which abated the immediate fire environment. Quickly, too, foresters installed internal fuelbreaks to help compartmentalize fires; these sometimes absorbed 10 to 20 percent of the total area of the plantation, making fire protection a considerable investment. Internal or external, fuelbreaks were burned annually, or occasionally controlled by intensive grazing.

As the forest plantation matured, so did its fire problems and practices. If grass fires principally threatened plantations in their seedling stages, then crown fires devastated them in their closely stocked adult state, a competent fire capable of vaporizing an entire site in an afternoon. Thus it was not enough to protect the perimeter or subdivide a forest into smaller units. It was also essential to lessen the critical fuels that allowed a surface fire to escalate into a crown fire. Grazing was one means, though often limited by timing. In young plantations grazing harmed seedlings, while in mature forests pine litter replaced grass. Active fire control by on-site foresters helped beat back encroaching fires, but it was economically impossible to staff scores of small plantations with firefighting forces. Conifer plantations were timbered islands in a sea of grass and eucalypt litter, and the landscape burned too frequently and too diffusely to ward off all fires. Instead, with considerable apprehension, foresters experimented with controlled burning.

Here the analogy with agriculture broke down completely. No farmer tried to finesse a fire through a field of growing wheat or maize; cane patches burned as a part of harvesting. But foresters had, in the end, to accept a degree of fire. Some exotic softwoods were better adapted to fire than others —southern pine better than Monterey pine *(Pinus radiata)*, for example. Some climates were more forgiving of burning, and allowed greater tolerance and ranges of fire. With its pine plantations and treacherous weather, South Australia practiced burning reluctantly and on a small scale. Queensland sent fire through slash pine *(Pinus ellioti)* with good effects. Western Australia learned to burn pine in the winter and to operate within narrow windows of opportunity. An added benefit was that underburning in litter could encourage grass, which then allowed for some control of fuels by grazing.

These were late reforms, accepted only after it became apparent that Australia would not be domesticated as Britain had, that bushfires would continue to simmer around guarded forests, either planted or native. The realization came slowly, steadily opposed by old visions, resisted by the conviction that reclamation could somehow expunge fire from the landscape. In his novel *The Red Bull* (1959), H. A. Lindsay narrated the hardscrabble life of a Victorian selector who lived in annual dread of bushfires, those that emanated from an inscrutable nature and those set by unscrupulous settlers. " 'Only one way to block them big fires,' the stranger went on. 'Get in first by burnin' yer own country—and get it goin' again every time it'll carry a fire.' " But Tom Reeford disagreed. Somehow the cycle of fire—of fire used to control fire—had to be broken. To his daughter, a forestry student, he confided, "There's your cure for bushfires in these hills, Allie. Nature meant this country to grow trees. Trouble is, what's grown now is mostly useless stuff. You'd want to pull it down with tractors, then plant trees that won't burn." Plant English oak and ash. Plant American hickory. Then fires could no more run through the forest than through lucerne. Plantations of exotic hardwoods would blossom into incombustible green-

belts that would break the back of Australian bushfires. The way to eliminate bushfires was to eliminate the bush.[9]

It was a marvelous vision, the ultimate triumph of agriculture and the
moral order of the yeoman farmer. Farming would absorb forestry as it did
herding. Instead of the native bush devastating the exotic flora by fire, the
exotics would redeem the degraded Australian bush by abolishing fire. This
had been the history of much of Western Europe, and it was the chimera
accepted by most European foresters for Australia. What they could not
reclaim by plantations, they would reform by semidomestication, by the
systematic manipulation of native woodlands. Hutchins laughed away Australian objections that fire could never be removed from eucalypts—that
eucalypts could never be disciplined or domesticated—by citing examples
from southern Africa in which "close-packed" stands of planted eucalypts
guarded the more flammable pine plantations. There was no need, Hutchins
argued, for "the irregular forest in Australia." Still, as one character in *The
Red Bull* remarked, "Some nature lovers take exception to our ideas." But
these objections he dismissed as "absurd." [10]

Of course nothing like this could happen on the scale projected. Native
forest and exotic forest had to coexist. Increasingly conifer plantations replaced worn-out farms, not wild bush. The valued exotics were softwoods,
not hardwoods; conifer plantations were, if anything, more flammable than
the indigenous woods. New technologies, meanwhile, found unexpected
value in eucalypt sawtimber and pulp, and native forests acquired values as
protected catchments, nature reserves, recreational sites, and nationalist
symbols that greatly exceeded their role as a supplier of raw materials. The
future of Australian forestry resided principally in the Australian forest.
Farming could not subsume forestry. Forestry could not abolish fire.

"SOLDIER OF THE STATE AND SOMETHING MORE": FIRE PRACTICES IN NATIVE FORESTS

Reducing an indigenous forest to a cultivated forest was a laborious process.
Virtually all the forests of Western Europe had been cleared at least once and
either replanted or allowed to regrow under more or less controlled circumstances. Even Germany's famed Black Forest had largely rebounded through
active plantings and obsessive husbandry. Woodlands were tended for fuel,
almost gardened for their lignin. Intense cultivation extended even to the
litter on the forest floor, which peasants swept up and used for livestock
bedding; fallen branches went to hearths; farmers pruned lower branches for
firewood or for burning over fields. There was little free-running fire. In
Australia, by contrast, foresters confronted wild bush, a forest profoundly
disturbed by European settlement, a landscape chronically ablaze.

The process of reduction proceeded in stages. First came the politics of demarcation. The land had to be reserved for forestry, with jurisdiction over it granted to professional foresters. Control over trees was impossible without control over settlers; if graziers and farmers were allowed access to reserved forests, it had to take the form of latter-day agistments, rights granted for particular functions under the supervision of a forester. A forestry department, argued Hutchins, *"must have undivided autocratic control over all the operations"* under its dominion. It was not enough for forestry to subdue the bush: it had also to subdue the bushman.[11]

Once granted jurisdiction, at least by statute, the next stage was fire protection. This was an awkward affair: if virtually every act of forest trespass or destruction involved fire in some way, so did nearly every variety of resource exploitation. To deny access to fire was to deny access to the native woods, yet to tolerate bushfires was to risk losing all on a windy afternoon. Thus, in the early years, fire protection dominated the working plans developed for forest management and the working lives of field foresters. Fire—"the scourge of our forests and everything they mean to our existence," thundered the Forestry Commissioner of Victoria—is "the greatest enemy we have to combat." An empire forester versed in the scattered woodlands of Greater Gondwana insisted that "there are hardly any measures too stringent or precautions too great for foresters or forest authorities to take" to eliminate loss by fire. Without fire control nothing foresters could do would endure. Until assured of adequate fire protection, argued the Conservator for Western Australia, "all efforts at forestry must be puny and spasmodic." [12]

Empire foresters brought to this charge an élan that went beyond the spirit of the practical woodsman or the resident technician. The forester was a colonial officer gazetted to foreign duty; his profession ranked honorably; he was, thought one knight of the British empire, "a soldier of the State and something more." The military analogy was apt. In many European states (most spectacularly, Prussia) firefighting had been a duty of the military or state militia until society strangled fire out of its environment. In India the early experiments at fire control devolved on officers of the British Army. In America the first attempt at fire control by the federal government occurred when the U.S. Cavalry assumed the administration of Yellowstone National Park and spent their first summer suppressing sixty fires. Whether, as William James argued, war was the romance of history, firefighting was surely the romance of colonial forestry. It combined policy and field operations with an esprit de corps, an ardor, that made fire season into a quasi-military campaign and forestry an exercise in biotic counterinsurgency. The forester was like a naval captain, Hutchins argued. "A captain cannot lose many ships. A Forester cannot have many fires . . . That is the unwritten law." [13]

Pacification was arduous, but once achieved—once past the shock encounter between fire practices—fire control would release the woods from its tyranny under fire. Intensive silviculture would eliminate the extravagant fuels that fed bushfires. A stable society would abolish the promiscuous ignitions that kept fire simmering in the bush. Bushfires would become a nuisance rather than a menace; detailed working plans would expel wildfire from the core of producing forests as it would patches of weeds; slash would be burned as one would burn debris pruned from an orchard. For this evolution there were ample exemplars. Foresters pointed not only to the cultivated landscape of Western Europe, but to its rougher fringes like the *garrigue* of southern France. They cited French forestry in north Africa; British forestry in India, Cape Colony, East Africa, Cyprus; even the tainted experience of North American foresters, wrestling with a vast backcountry of resinous conifers and a restless surge of immigrants. All that was required was "system"—and the political will to apply it.

In Australia, however, everything seemed inverted. Forest demarcations were porous rather than absolute; fire could not be controlled except with the aid of fire; and extensive management of woodlands amid shifting populations was more often the norm than was an intensive silviculture practiced amid a society of nestled villages. Fire protection would not end. The appropriate analogue was less that of a single campaign of subjugation than of an ongoing guerrilla war. Instead of silviculture supplanting fire protection, fire practices would shape Australian silviculture. "System" smacked of a hated, haunted past of forced colonization through penal transportation.

By the early twentieth century, British Empire foresters had codified the fundamental elements of fire protection into a "trinity" that included fuelbreaks and fire paths, extra firefighters during fire season, and watchtowers staffed by a "resident, Hill-top Forester." Fuelbreaks reduced the hazard, provided access to firefighting forces, and served as holding lines from which to backfire. Extra guards brought manpower up to requisite levels as the fire danger increased and served to spot fires at early stages of development. The hilltop forester surveyed his domains and responded quickly to any fire, for which he needed force, communications, access, and control. "This central control," explained Hutchins to his Australian audience, "is necessary, as necessary, in fact, to the man in charge of the fire-work of the forest as to the general of an army in the field." (Invaluable, too, was an "active, healthy Forester's wife," for "she has often saved the situation when a fire has broken out in the Forester's absence . . .") But all this was worthless without the guiding "system" enforced by working plans. By such means the civilizing force of European ideas and institutions could reduce wild lands and wild peoples.[14]

There was little chance, in Australia, to install such a system overnight. Instead foresters adapted and "made do" with whatever elements of such a program they found handy. "Well," Owen Jones reiterated to the Second British Empire Forestry Conference, "there are quite a lot of things a forester can do—every forester knows them only too well, fire-breaks, lines, watch-towers, telephones, fire patrols, and so on." A conference of Western Australian foresters in 1923 debated some grimy details. They argued the relative merits of fighting fires during the day versus fighting at night, of grubbing out firebreaks versus burning them, of stopping a running fire at its head versus along its flanks. Although "Yankee forestry books" advocated attacking a headfire, a Mr. Smith profoundly disagreed and thought "Yankees must be hardier chaps than he." A vigorous discussion ensued on the best method of "beating" a fire with eucalypt boughs. Advocates of the single stroke technique argued with advocates of the sweeping stroke until Forester Mackay informed the assembly that if Westralia had "such forest fires as he had seen at Gippsland, neither the downward stroke, upward stroke, sweeping stroke nor the back swing would put the fire out, either in the daytime or at night time." [15]

Against such primitive circumstances, the breathtaking vision proposed by empire foresters had elements of parody. Yet gradually, improbably, the components of a system came into place. As control over the reserves improved, so did fire protection. Lookout towers sprouted on hilltops. Telephones and heliographs relayed smoke sightings and firefighting orders. Victoria even negotiated with the Royal Australian Air Force to jointly field a program of fire reconnaissance. But on one issue Australians felt isolated, off-key, unique. That was the way, as Jones told a conference of empire foresters in 1923, in which "we use fire to prevent fire." He had no doubt that "it seems a very wrong and a very dangerous thing to do," but in Australia—at this time—it was necessary and successful. [16]

If the appeal of fire to Australian foresters was predictable, so perhaps was their apologetic stance toward it. Yet the facts were that very few forestry programs argued seriously for total fire exclusion. What they demanded was fire protection, the elimination of random, chronic, promiscuous burning. For all his ridicule of Australian chauvinism, Hutchins never proposed to eliminate instantly all forms of fire use or to transplant a purely European model. On the contrary, he argued that an utterly European forester would be worthless in "extra-tropical countries" like Australia, and in elaborating the "four stages" by which to implement a working plan, he allowed for a postharvest burn. What he objected to was repeated burning—like "burning the carpets to save the house!"—and the fatalism of Australian foresters that systematic fire protection was impossible, that fire was healthy for eucalypts, that only by accepting fire could they control fire. [17]

The implications were serious, for if systematic fire protection was impossible, then so, in Australia, was systematic forestry. However useful it might be for fledgling Australian nationalism to emphasize Australian exceptionalism, the Australian emphasis on burning off was potentially devastating to forestry. What made the situation truly ironic was that Australian interest in controlled fire for forestry was not unique. Although Hutchins chose to understate the fact, by the 1920s foresters in other "extra-tropical" lands administered by Britain had come to base their fire protection schemes on forms of controlled, or "early," burning. Other foresters did not hesitate to explain burning in India or Cape Colony. Australians heard such tales but never quite believed them. Native-born foresters insisted emphatically that Australian fire was as uniquely distinctive as Australian forests.

IMPERIAL EXEMPLAR:
THE EMPIRE STRATEGY

When Sir D. E. Hutchins toured Australia in 1914 forestry in federated Australia was appallingly primitive. Most forestry departments still lacked organic acts, nowhere did he find a forester actually living on the forest, and bushfire legislation, where it existed at all, was void of enforcement mechanisms. There were even large numbers of "otherwise intelligent persons," he discovered, who held that the Australian bush could not be protected from fire. "In travelling through the Australian forests, I have met with quite a number of such persons." That folk wisdom he traced in part to Australian conditions, the pervasiveness of burning in the bush, and the extraordinary resilience of the eucalypt to fire.

But it derived too, Hutchins speculated, from the disastrous tendency to interpret the Australian bush as analogous to the "American backwoods," with its extravagance of waste and burning. Against that dark examplar Hutchins asserted a counterexample drawn from "a lifetime doing fire-work in India, in South Africa, and in British East Africa," as well as experience in the stubborn Mediterranean terrains of Cyprus and the south of France. That bionocular contrast—Europe and America—captured perfectly the status of Australian forest protection. European Australia was attracted to both, understood neither completely, and learned, ignored, or forgot the lessons of each. In its forestry, as in its forests, Australia remained an island continent.[18]

The novel element in Hutchins's treatise was his comparison of Australia to other British colonies in Greater Gondwana. The critical site was British India, where European foresters first learned what it meant to establish forestry outside the environmental and social context of Europe. In India forests were essential and fire ubiquitous. Its forests fueled the integration of British India into the world economy, supplying the "sleepers" (ties) and trestles upon which railway construction across the subcontinent depended as well as the firewood needed to power the locomotives. Soon after the mutiny, however, after Great Britain supplanted the East India Company as raj, the government of India began to set aside forest reserves to assure a perpetual source of timber and water, and it appointed Dietrich (later Sir

Dietrich) Brandis as Conservator of Forests. A botanist subsequently educated in forestry in the grand European manner, Brandis was the archetype of the transnational forester, an indefatigable agent of empire, a Clive of natural resource conservation in Greater India, a Humboldt of forestry who managed to combine precise technical knowledge with the kind of journey to exotic lands so fundamental to the literature of German Romanticism. Brandis quickly established the institutional and conceptual framework for forestry in Burma, India, and elsewhere in the empire.

Almost immediately free-burning fires threatened to overwhelm all plans for forest conservation. "Every forest that would burn," recalled E. O. Shebbeare, "was burnt almost every year." Fire littered the landscape almost year-round. Natives burned to drive game, improve grazing, render pathways safe for travel, ward off predators (notably tigers), and "to placate the local deities." As various portions of the biota cured, they carried fire. Where tropical grasses or other annual fuels dominated the environment, fierce fires yearly swept the "jungle," a term which served generically for India as "bush" did for Australia. Inspector-General Ribbentrop declared that the nearly annual "conflagrations are the chief reason of the barren character of so many of our Indian hill ranges, and are more closely connected with distress and famine than is usually supposed." This was matched by "a most marvellous, now almost incredible, apathy and disbelief in the destructiveness of forest fires." It was natural then, Shebbeare concluded, for the "pioneers" to see in "fire their chief, almost their only enemy." Eliminate fire and "perfect forests" would almost magically follow. No one, however, believed fire protection was possible. It was endemic, like malaria and venomous snakes. It was ineradicable.[19]

Thus when, in 1863, Brandis instructed Colonel Pearson of the Central Provinces to try to stop the burning, he advertised helplessness as much as hope. "Most Foresters and every Civil Officer in the country," Pearson observed, "scouted the idea." Edward Stebbing recalled matter-of-factly that "in every Province . . . the officers of the Department had to commence the work of introducing fire conservancy for the protection of the forests in the face of an actively hostile population more or less supported by the district officials, and especially by the Indian officials, who quite frankly regarded the new policy of fire conservancy as an oppression of the people." Even forest officers, Stebbing noted, "were openly sceptical" of the possibility of fire protection. Had his attempt failed, Pearson affirmed, "any progress in fire protection elsewhere would have been rendered immeasurably more difficult." Pearson laid out fuelbreaks, sent out patrols, exhorted locals to give up burning, and enjoyed a couple of exceptionally wet seasons. To everyone's astonishment, the experiment succeeded. The Bori Forest became a showcase of fire conservancy.[20]

Not completely, not without considerable debate and second-guessing—

but thanks to militant enthusiasm and patience and favorable weather, this improbable experiment in fire control evolved into a demonstration program, and then into a prototype suitable for dissemination throughout Greater India. The idea spread, promulgated from the top down. As with the native principalities, so with the native forests: more and more were reduced to British rule by fire protection. To control fire was to control the native populations; without fire they had no access to the resources of the reserves. By 1880–81 the Indian Forest Service had placed some 11,000 square miles under formal protection; by 1885–86, some 16,000 square miles. By 1900–01, fire protection incorporated an astonishing 32,000 square miles that spanned the spectrum of Indian fire regimes, from semiarid savanna to wet-dry tropical forest to montane conifers. It targeted, in particular, the great timber trees of the subcontinent—sal *(Shorea)*, teak *(Tectonis)*, and chir *(Pinus)*. What emerged was a robust exemplar of fire protection, an adaptation of European techniques to exotic wildlands and colonial politics. With modifications, empire foresters propagated it throughout Britain's Asian, African, and Australasian colonies.

But the empire strategy, while ideally honed for conquest, was less suited for settlement. Within twenty years field men voiced doubts about the wisdom of "too much fire protection." There had always been dissenters and skeptics, but now discontent bubbled publicly to the surface. In wet forests fire protection seemed to retard natural regeneration and it allowed fuels to accumulate that, once dried, exploded into all-consuming conflagrations. In drier forests, years of seemingly successful protection would be wiped out by massive fires during drought years. Exhortations and bribes with goats had not extinguished all the native firebrands. Villagers refused to resettle or remain in unburned sites for fear that tigers, hiding in the tall grasses, would seize child herders. Protected forests were fortified enclaves in a landscape that simmered annually with fire. In enigmatic India fire protection unsettled native forest and native society both.

Critics argued for a hybrid program in which controlled burning supplemented fire suppression. In 1897 Inspector-General Ribbentrop had to intervene. To protect regeneration and forest litter (the twin obsessions of European forestry)—to say nothing of saving imperial face—he ruled for the further expansion of systematic fire protection. Edicts, however, did not suppress doubts, and by 1902 the debate flared across the pages of the *Indian Forester* and the annual reports of conservators. In 1905 a compromise was proposed by which controlled burning could be brought into working plans. Sub-rosa burning in Bengal, Burma, and elsewhere scorched the landscape like a people's rebellion.[21]

The revolution finally boiled over in Burma in 1907. In the absence of underburning, teak simply refused to regenerate. Fire control drained away the lifeblood of the Asian monsoon forest; foresters had prescribed a cure where there had been no disease. Faced with a choice between excluding fire and excluding fire protection, the Inspector-General began withdrawing fire protection from prime teak forests. By 1914 conservators of sal forests recognized that regeneration "had ceased throughout the fire-protected forests of Assam and Bengal and that no amount of cleanings and weedings would put matters right." They tried to reintroduce fire, but fuels had so changed that it was no longer possible to run benign light fires through the understory; the *taungya* system by which swidden fields were restocked with planted timber trees evolved as a partial compromise. And nearly everywhere field foresters introduced some form of early—that is, spring—burning of grassy understories. Whatever the causes for the failure of natural regeneration, Shebbeare concluded for an audience of empire foresters, "fire appears to be the only real cure." [22]

By 1926 the cycle of fire practices had come full circle. Imperial resolve retreated before an unscorched earth, the passive disobedience of Indian silviculture. A conservators' conference amended the rules of the *Forest Manual* to make early burning the general practice and to extend complete protection only to special sites on a temporary basis. That new regime included the Central Provinces.

The legacy of British India rippled throughout the British Empire. Nearly all British foresters (or foresters in British employ) passed through a combination of formal schooling in European forestry and a field apprenticeship in Greater India. Inspectors-general retired to forestry teaching posts in England and Scotland. The Indian Forest Service published a dominant periodical of world forestry, the *Indian Forester*. From the experiences of British India came the magisterial tomes that lectured students from around the world on the management of native forests. From the shock encounter of Europe and India crystallized that hybrid program of fire protection, the empire strategy, much of whose rigor and moral intensity derived from the attempt to impose a set of expectations developed in one social and ecological environment onto another very different environment. Avatars appeared in Cape Colony, East Africa, Sierra Leone, Cyprus, and Canada. With misgivings, they appeared also in Australia. [23]

NO OTHER EXAMPLE:
THE AMERICAN STRATEGY

When the Australian colonies federated, India seemed remote and America close. "Where in the world," E.H.F. Swain asked, after a 1917 pilgrimage to North America, "is there another country which presents a parallel example, horrible or otherwise—an Anglo-Saxon democracy in the transitional phase between pioneering and waste, and Conservation and Efficiency?" The answer was the United States of America, from which Australia had "borrowed a constitution" and would soon draft an architect to lay out a capital city. America he regarded as "the elder sister of Australia." In forestry, as in politics, he concluded that "there is no other example." The American strategy, however, posed its own peculiar problems.[24]

Similarities included extensive histories of burning. There was no disputing the ubiquity of American fire. Lightning was a prominent source of ignition in the arid West, and burning was integral to American agriculture, pastoralism, land clearing, and other frontier economies; it was regarded as a folk right. Bernhard Fernow—a Prussian forester and naturalized American citizen—thought fire was the "bane of American forests" and dismissed its causes as a case of "bad habits and loose morals." [25]

Along the frontier fire was pandemic. Where associated with land clearing, it frequently got out of hand—a fatal eruption of frontier violence that incinerated forests, savaged fields and towns, and claimed an unconscionable number of lives. In the Lake States railroads opened up the big woods to markets, and settlers and timbermen poured in. Forests cleared by loggers were burned by farmers. During droughts and exceptional winds, fires raged on the order of hundreds of thousands of hectares, wiped out entire villages, and stripped the meager forest soils of all organic matter, rendering them unusable to agriculture. Most of the devastated forests were marginal to farming anyway; sites spared the worst holocausts quickly exhausted soil nutrients. But these were only the most spectacular flare-ups from what had become a rekindled landscape. In 1904 a surveyor laying out the Plumas Forest Reserve in northern California wrote that "the common type, and in fact almost the only type, of fire in the forest is a light surface burn. . . ." Accordingly,

> The people of the region regard forest fires with careless indifference . . . even to shrewd men . . . the fires seem to do little damage. The Indians were accustomed to burning the forest over long before the white man came, the object being to improve the hunting by keeping down the undergrowth, which would otherwise shelter the game. The white man has come to think that fire is a part of the forest, and a beneficial part at that. All classes share in this view, and all set fires, sheepmen and cattlemen on the open range, miners, lumbermen, ranchmen, sportsmen, and campers. Only when other property is likely to be endangered does the resident of or the visitor to the mountains become careful about fires, and seldom even then.[26]

On public lands and the larger private forests of America models of fire protection groped toward definition during the 1880s. In 1885 the state of New York adapted the administrative machinery of its rural fire warden network to accommodate the Adirondacks Preserve, and a year later the U.S.

Cavalry assumed responsibility for protecting Yellowstone National Park. In 1897 the General Land Office received a mandate for the administration of the burgeoning national forests. By the end of the century private timber protective associations staffed lookouts and paid for patrols on high-value lands. A National Academy of Sciences committee on forest policy alluded to British India as a possible model and recommended that, for the present, the forest reserves be turned over to the army and that forestry be taught at West Point.

Civilian foresters successfully protested, established forestry schools at major universities, and began the exhilarating, maddening task of transferring European models to American landscapes. It was a century of Germanic influence—Germans were the largest immigrant group to America in the nineteenth century—and forestry joined kindergartens, graduate education, and journals of Hegelian philosophy in reshaping American society. German foresters like Carl Schenk and Bernhard Fernow journeyed to America as their colleagues did to India. The charismatic Gifford Pinchot studied at Nancy under the tutelage of Brandis, and after the national forests were transferred to his control in 1905, he corresponded with Sir Dietrich about how to establish a national corps of foresters. His successor as Chief Forester, Henry Graves, formerly dean of forestry at Yale University (a school endowed by the Pinchot family), also passed through the classic curriculum of British colonial forestry. Clearly, forestry was a case of technology transfer. From that time onward American foresters interested in foreign models looked almost exclusively to Europe or, in more typically American fashion, let the world swirl into America. A contingent of forestry engineers sent to France during the Great War left with convictions that there was much to admire in European forestry. And after France, American foresters looked obsessively to Sweden rather than to India or Africa.

This pioneering generation shared a crusading ethos, a militant commitment to conservation, that brought a moral energy to the question of "forest devastation," sounded alarms over "timber famines," and advertised the horrors of wanton burning. Elers Koch marveled at what a wonderful thing it was to belong to an organization composed almost wholly of young men. Inman Eldridge wrote of those devotees that they believed Gifford Pinchot was a prophet, that he was "all-knowing and far-seeing." Coert duBois described his entry into forestry as head-down and tail up, animated by the cry *"Gifford Pinchot le vult!"* They grappled with fire as foresters in new lands everywhere did. As Americans they shared in that age of aggressive political and economic reform known as the Progressive Era.[27]

Then came 1910. That summer two crises simultaneously flared into public controversy. Parched by a vicious drought, the northern and western landscapes burned an estimated 5 million acres throughout the national forest system, more than 3 million in the Northern Rockies alone. The great fires traumatized the Forest Service, still reeling from Pinchot's dismissal earlier in the year. Some seventy-nine firefighters died in the line of duty. The Service sank into debt until Congress agreed to honor a deficit funding statute enacted two years earlier. It was the first great crisis for Henry Graves, Pinchot's hand-picked successor and another Brandis protégé. To add to the embarrassment, the same month (August) that the fires blew up, Graves finished publication in serial fashion of a treatise on fire control. Two future chiefs, William Greeley and Ferdinand Silcox, weathered the fires as regional officers. The fires were the Valley Forge—the Long March—of the Forest Service. Soon afterward Congress passed the Weeks Act (1911) which allowed for national forests to expand by purchase, for federal-state coopera-tive programs in fire control, and for interstate compacts in support of firefighting.[28]

Yet that same August *Sunset* magazine placed into public view a smolder-ing debate about fire policy. While professional foresters argued for fire pro-tection by means of aggressive fire suppression, others advocated a program of controlled "light burning" on the front country and "let burning" in the backcountry. The light burners were an unwieldy amalgam—the state engi-neer of California, sentimentalist poet Joaquin Miller, timber owners and stockmen, the Southern Pacific Railroad and novelist Stewart Edward White, the San Francisco newspapers, and Secretary of the Interior Richard Ballin-ger. They argued that fire protection only aggravated fuels, stoking uncon-trollable burns; that absolute fire control was technically impossible and fiscally irresponsible; that fire exclusion damaged forests, starved regenera-tion, and encouraged insect plagues. They proposed instead a rationalization of frontier fire practices organized around controlled burning, what Miller called "the Indian way."[29]

Thus the events of 1910–11 challenged the Forest Service as a fire agency across the board—the 1910 fires, its technical ability to control fire; the light-burning controversy, its capacity to formulate policy; the Weeks Act, its ability to establish a national policy, not just a national forest policy. The Forest Service responded with vigor and discipline. Former Chief Pinchot was already on the record as saying that "like slavery forest fires may be shelved for a time, at enormous cost in the end, but sooner or later they must be faced." Chief Forester Graves declared that fire protection was 90 percent of American forestry. Future Chief Greeley made "smoke in the woods" his yardstick of progress. The Service exploited the provisions of the Weeks Act to establish a federal-state cooperative fire program that allowed formal fire protection to extend well beyond the lands of the national forest system and the federal lands overall. Surveying the wreckage of 1910, German forestry professor Dr. Deckert noted that "devastating conflagrations of an extent elsewhere unheard of have always been the order of the day in the United States"—that, by contrast, its success with fire prevention constituted "a brilliant vindication of the forestry system of middle Europe"—and he expressed confidence that American foresters would follow their example. Within a decade after the 1910 holocaust, the U.S. Forest Service was trying to do exactly that.[30]

The light-burning controversy flared up throughout the Western states and across the South. In Florida and Arkansas new national forests were almost consumed by woods burning. But the ideological battleground was northern California. Here the Forest Service engaged light burning in what was less a dialogue than a dialectic. Against light burning, district forester Coert duBois proposed "systematic fire protection." In 1914, after "retiring to his cell like John Bunyan," he wrote a classic treatise on fire suppression that provided over the next two decades the basis for fire planning throughout the national forests. Essentially duBois adapted the industrial engineering of his day—Taylorism—to the problem of fire control. Each component he broke down into its atomic parts; measured, timed, assessed; then reassembled the lot into a machined whole. Its rigor made light burners appear like woolly-headed folk philosophers. The intensity of the controversy forced proponents to sharpen their concepts and lessened the opportunities for compromise. Except for allusions to Europe, there were no other counterexamples for critics to propose. Examples of fire protection from elsewhere in the world, with the exception of Canada, were ignored. America accepted what came to it but did not search out, on its own, new exemplars.[31]

Behind the logic, moreover, lay a fervor that had been burned into the Service by its 1910 trial by fire. No one who had weathered the Big Burn could seriously argue for more fire in the woods. It was a generation that was prepared for action, not contemplation—an era whose president, Theodore Roosevelt, advocated the life of "strenuous endeavor"; whose greatest philosopher, William James, argued for a "moral equivalent of war" to be waged against the threatening forces of nature; whose most popular author, Jack London, wrote novels and stories about struggle in the wilderness; and whose Eastern establishment was enamored of the Western experience as a place to test manhood. The peculiar circumstances that combined Harvard gentility with Oklahoma cowboys into Roosevelt's Rough Rider regiment now sent Yale foresters to battle forest fires in the Far West.

But like a fire in a damp log, light burning rekindled every few years. In the early 1920s a panel of foresters convened to compare the two philosophies and judge between them. They ruled for systematic fire protection. Light burning became heresy; controlled burning, anathema. The Service even suppressed research findings that contradicted what had now become an *ex cathedra* declaration. Here again, as in British India, chance intervened. The years designated for field experimentation were abnormally wet and the burns inconclusive; then, following the formal condemnation, drought returned and the 1924 season broke all records for wildfire. Only the means at hand prevented a universal extension of systematic fire protection. Subsequently, when, during the 1930s, the administration of Franklin Roosevelt, a gentleman forester, released enormous resources to the Forest Service, the Chief Forester announced a 10 A.M. policy, which ordered all fires to be controlled by 10 A.M. the day following their report, or failing that, by 10 A.M. the subsequent day until extinguished. The means at hand became so large that they determined the ends to which they could be put.

What had been possible now became mandatory. What was announced as an "experiment on a continental scale" became dogma. Controlled burning persisted only in scattered enclaves, without official sanction, condemned as the personal obsession of eccentric wildlife biologists, Indians on remote western reservations, and deranged southern arsonists. Year by year fire protection steadily assimilated new lands. The one exception was the South, where controlled burning to reduce fuels became accepted practice in the 1940s; but this was considered another manifestation of southern exceptionalism.

In America fire protection meant fire suppression.

BETWEEN GONDWANA AND AMERICA: AUSTRALIA'S ALMOST STRATEGY

If anything this diversity of counterexamples only added to the perplexity of Australian foresters. In the early years they followed the guidance of the empire and looked to India or its African echo, Cape Colony, for models. Both regions offered climatic cognates, and there were haunting similarities among the forests of Greater Gondwana; teak and sal, for example, resembled eucalypts in some important properties. The mobility of empire foresters and the transnational character of forestry conferences put experiences from Asia and Africa squarely before Australians. So did exchanges with North America. The light-burning controversy, one Australian noted with satisfaction, was so "practically similar" to what he confronted that he felt convinced that Australian circumstances "are not vital to the issues involved, nor do they affect the conclusions arrived at." [32]

The transfers, however, were never complete. While Greater Gondwana moved toward early burning and America hammered out the tenets of systematic fire protection, Australia muddled through without a coherent, autonomous strategy of its own. The establishment of Australian federation in 1901, which bound the separate colonies into a single commonwealth, made not the slightest difference. By the time Australia established schools of forestry in South Australia and Victoria (1910), British India had fought through the early-burning controversy and America was poised to begin its light-burning equivalent. By the time Australia established its national forestry school (1927), early burning had entered the *Indian Forest Manual* and light burning in America had suffered a humiliating condemnation.

Australians knew both histories—and others. During the Second British Empire Forestry Conference in 1923, for example, Australians listened to C. G. Trevor of the Indian Forest Service outline the history and precepts of fire protection, while Stephen Kessell reprinted, with approving comments, the findings of the forestry board that heard and ruled against light burning in California. A special concern of the conferees was "the forest fire problem in Canada." The Third British Empire Forestry Conference (1928), held in Australia and New Zealand, included a thorough airing of fire practices and policies throughout the colonies; and comparisons with Australia were frequent. Shebbeare noted that in Australia, unlike India, "bad fires can actually wipe out a whole forest." Jacobs commented that the fires in Bengal and Assam "did a tremendous amount of good and no harm at all." Then he observed, with irony, "that in a place [Australia] where you wanted to avoid having fires you cannot get the ordinary wooden matches," only wax vestas that light anywhere.[33]

As Australians endowed their own forestry schools, as they concentrated on the particular needs of Australian silviculture, their ties to British forestry faded. Between Australia and the rest of the empire, the exchange had gone one way—from India or Africa to Australia. Inspector-General of India Ribbentrop might visit Victoria, but Victorian foresters did not journey to India. This was even true of North America, to which Australians increasingly looked for inspiration and from which they returned with sometimes misplaced insights. His 1917 passage to America had shocked Swain with the ferocity of American crown fires—"bush fires, as a rule, do not attain the dimensions and intensity of the forest fires of America"—and by the time he departed, he did not, in comparison, "regard the Australian problem as difficult." A 1921 pamphlet from Western Australia condemned the "baseless belief" among Australians that fire did good by citing Canada and the United States where "it is generally recognized that forest fires are public calamities to be guarded against in every possible way"—an assertion that would have astonished American foresters then locked in mortal combat with light burners and let burners.[34]

American exuberance and extravagance fascinated Australians even as American violence and disorder repelled them. They were more comfortable with Canada, another dominion of the empire, whose political and economic history better resembled their own, and American precedents typically arrived through a Canadian filter. Increasingly, too, Canada dominated empire forestry conferences. But the overall outcome was oddly dissonant. At the very moment that British colonial forestry moved to accommodate controlled burning throughout Greater Gondwana, Australian forestry progressively looked to North America, where aggressive fire programs denounced controlled burning and sought, ultimately, the exclusion of fire from reserved forests. Australia found itself out of sync—its environment aligned one way, its social ambitions another.

From Australia there emerged nothing original, and the apology that Australian circumstances were unique lost much of its bite. Greater Gondwana and North America also experienced routine burning and frequent conflagrations, and they also sheltered populations accustomed to free access to fire and hostile to fire suppression. Foresters there also polarized around the proportional commitment to fire control and fire use. India's early-burning debate was virtually indistinguishable from America's light-burning controversy, and both strongly resembled Australia's debate about burning off. The peculiar attribute about Australia was not its choice one way or the other but its absence of choice.

This confusion was reflected in Australia's version of the early-burning and light-burning controversies. As Stephen Kessell, Conservator of Forests in Western Australia, summarized the issue in 1924, "two schools of thought" had emerged. One believed that the only solution to fire control was to clean up the forest floor and set frequent light fires to suppress fuels; the other, that "absolute control of all fires in and around the forests is the first and biggest step towards the establishment of Forestry." It was the "practical forester, of the woodsman type," A. H. Harris recalled, who "preached the need for controlled-burning." To professional foresters, particularly those from Oxford, "this was heresy"; they insisted that fire would vanish as better forestry came into practice. Once forests were "reasonably clean," Jones told his colleagues, "we hope then to be able to give up the use of fire which, of course, is in many ways very undesirable and very destructive of future growth." [35]

Each side had its dialectician. C. E. Lane-Poole—graduate of the École Nationale des Eaux et Forêts, forester in South Africa and Sierra Leone, Conservator for Western Australia and Inspector-General of Forests for the Australian Commonwealth, principal of the Australian Forestry School from 1927 to 1944 and held in awe by its graduates—attacked every tenet of the controlled-burning faction. The belief that "a fire through the bush is a good thing," he contended, has "no solid basis in fact." A "clean" forest was an unhealthy forest. A parklike forest was not a natural forest. There is, he admitted, "a specious contention which has become fairly universal in Australia and has even found official recognition" that the only way to control the bushfire is to underburn on a regular basis. France taught otherwise; so did other extratropical lands in the empire. There was perhaps a place for present-day compromise, but sound forestry would ultimately throttle fire from the woods. Fire protection was possible; and fire exclusion inevitable. [36]

More in his deeds than in his words, Stephen Kessell argued otherwise. Kessell conveyed perfectly the confused interplay between ideal with practice, between the desire for absolute fire control and the undoubted value of fire use as an aid not only to fuel reduction but to silviculture. "Complete fire prevention is impossible in practice," Kessell wrote in 1924, "and controlled fires play an important part in silvicultural operations." So long as controlled burning complemented, not replaced, fire control, it belonged in organized fire protection. Burning was not, however, "a cheap and easy method of solving or dodging the fire problem." Certainly Kessell did not argue that forestry should surrender to folkways. The belief that fire control created larger fires, he fumed, was the real "bogey" of organized fire protection. The only final solution was the conversion of the "present wilderness" into "tended forests." [37]

But like Colonel Pearson in the Bori Forest, Kessell had experimented with fire control in the jarrah belt and demonstrated, to his satisfaction, that "fire control is economically possible under conditions obtaining in this State." Relentlessly, enthusiastically, Kessell, a master administrator, extended the domain of organized fire protection. Westralia became a demonstration program for all of Australia. Kessell no longer hesitated to incorporate controlled burning.[38]

Different lands merited different fire programs, but in each working plan there was a role for controlled fire. Foresters fringed the "virgin forest" with fuelbreaks and burned its interior with low-intensity broadcast fires in the spring and autumn. Newly cut-over lands—expanding at roughly 20,000 hectares a year—were subjected to the classic techniques of systematic fire protection, adding as an Australian codicil that coupes were fired in advance of harvesting to reduce the likelihood of an accidental burn during cutting and hauling. Postharvest slash foresters fired in situ, though they took care to remove heavy debris around surviving seed trees. Once completed, they incorporated such lands under the regimen established for the virgin forest. The critical sites, however, were the vast acreages of untreated slash, a volatile inheritance that trailed decades of unregulated logging. Here, with fuelbreaks five chains wide, foresters subdivided unbroken fields of slash into compartments of roughly five hundred acres, which they burned about every three years. Within each compartment they encouraged regeneration by manual cutting. Then, when young growth reached heights that permitted a surface burn, they loosed broadcast fire through the coupe. Over time, however, foresters learned that a hot fire was the best stimulant to regeneration, and they replaced labor-intensive cutting with burning.[39]

Different colonies (later, different states) evolved different strategies and varied mixtures of practices. South Australia emphasized plantation forestry. Victoria, administering native forests in the great fire flume of the southeast, became a center for experimentation in fire suppression techniques. New South Wales did a little of everything. Tasmania did nothing. Calmly positioned outside the worst fire climates, Queensland observed and assimilated

Selector fighting a bushfire that threatens his bark humpy. [From E. E. Miller, ed., Cassell's Picturesque Australia *(1980)]*

The conversion of the Big Scrub, Gippsland. Note, initially, the heavy understory relative to human figures. Some clearing followed, but settlers mostly ringbarked, killed, and left standing vast domains of eucalypts. In the final stages, pasture replaces timber; a few groves of ringbarked gums endure, temporarily; and considerable evidence of fire persists. [Reproduced from South Gippsland Pioneer Association, The Land of the Lyre-Bird (1920)]

Fire hunting—using fire to flush prey out from cover—for kangaroo by Joseph Lycett. Lieutenant Stokes of the Beagle *concluded that he could "conceive no finer subject for a picture than a party of these swarthy beings engaged in kindling, moderating, and directing the destructive element, which under their care seems almost to change its nature, acquiring, as it were, complete docility, instead of the ungovernable fury we are accustomed to ascribe to it." [Reproduced from Lycett,* The Natives and Scenery of Tasmania and N. S. Wales *(1817)]*

ative Family of South
es, *by Philip King (later*
awn by William Blake).
produced from John
ter, Historical Journal of
Transactions at Port Jack-
and Norfolk Island *(1793)]*

king Out the Possum *by*
. Clark, engraved by
Dubourg. [Reproduced
n Field Sports of the Native
abitants of New South
es *(1813)]*

shfire Dreaming *(1982) by*
fford Possum Japaljarri.
e painting retells the story
Lungkarda, the Blue-
gued Lizard that unleashes
bushfire to punish two
others who have killed
acred kangaroo. [Courtesy
Art Gallery of South
stralia]

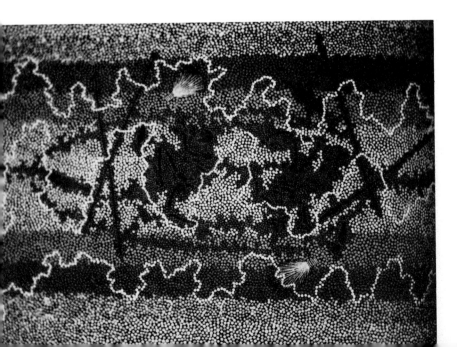

Bush Fire in the Lachlan District. *Note axe, beaters, boughs, and buckets.*
[Reproduced from Town and Country Journal 23, *(December 1871)]*

Fire brigade with wagon and tools—South Australia, c. 1910. [Courtesy Woods and
Forests Department, South Australia]

The bushman as firefighter—Western Australia. Metal pack known as an "Indian," after the tradename of its American manufacturer, holds water. [Courtesy of the J. S. Battye Library of West Australian History]

Early motorized fire truck—Western Australia, c. 1937. Mechanization brought significant improvements in response time and fireline power. [Courtesy of the Department of Conservation and Land Management, Western Australia]

Fury of the 1939 Black Friday fires demonstrated by burned and blown down eucalypt forest, Victoria. [Courtesy of the Forests Commission, Victoria]

Aerial ignition over Bemboka, New South Wales—1968. McArthur declared that "Instead of the Aboriginal firestick, we now use aircraft dropping incendiary capsules which light up the country in a grid pattern and produce a mosaic pattern of burnt and unburnt land." [Photo by A. Edwards, courtesy of CSIRO Division of Forest Research]

forestry with fire practices borrowed from agriculture. Kessell's successor in Western Australia, A. C. Harris, carried the Westralian system even further. "Without doubt," he argued, fire was the foremost problem of Australian forestry. But he urged his fellow foresters to "rethink their fire control problems and policies, and honestly assess whether a policy of virtually complete fire protection is practicable and economic." It had been his "bitter experience" and that of others that "fire exclusion and fire suppression were not so easy after all." Even among academic foresters, for whom controlled burning was anathema, "heretics appeared also in their own ranks." There was a reason, he thought; and he quoted G. K. Chesterton to the effect that Christianity had not been tried and found wanting—but found difficult and not properly tried. So it was with forestry's use of fire.[40]

Unlike their colleagues in Greater Gondwana or North America, Australian foresters hammered out no universal theory of fire protection. If anything, the contrast between their public declarations that fire exclusion was desirable and their practical applications of fire at nearly all stages of forest management compromised their identity as they mouthed British bromides but lived in the Australian bush. Max Jacobs captured the sentiment perfectly when he lectured that "complete fire-protection is not an impossible or impracticable, but an inevitable development" in Australia, while refusing to criticize broadacre burning by forestry departments. "As an administrative officer," he freely confessed, he had been himself "guilty of annually burning the poorer forests of the mountains" to protect the more valuable forests, and "with the present attitude of the Australian public towards fire he would do the same again." Whether as an expedient or as a goal, burning off was in Australia to stay.[41]

The controversy persisted, unresolved in practice or theory. While Australian foresters complained that their circumstances made them unique, they never proposed a uniquely Australian solution. Instead they soldiered on, adapting European and American theory and practice to Australian forests. Steadily they amassed more and more experience, and increasingly they made the problem of Australian bushfires their own. Commissions analyzed bushfires as forest fires. Foresters scrutinized, and sought control over, those forest-threatening fires set by graziers, farmers, kangaroo hunters, swagmen, rural migrants, rabbiters, and billy-boiling tourists, all of whom trespassed on forest lands or set fires that ignored the survey lines of legal demarcation. Of necessity foresters became the architects of more systematic bushfire protection on all lands, the arbiters of Australian fire practices.

Globally, Australian forestry shed much of its transnational character without substituting a robust nationalism. The island continent simply became more isolated and singular. Interstate conferences loomed larger than international congresses. Distinctions between jarrah and karri became more vital than contrasts with southern France or east Bengal. There remained considerable variance among the states and little pressure to concoct a commonwealth consensus. Western Australia most closely approximated the classic empire program. Victoria more resembled California. South Australia, its forestry all but monopolized by softwood plantations, could look to a reforesting England for guidance, in this as in other matters.

As much as graziers and farmers, diggers and merchants, foresters remained Europeans adrift in Australia, learning about the Australian bush and adapting to it in bits and pieces more out of necessity than from desire. The shared trauma that might inspire a nationalist system—the forestry equivalent to ANZAC at Gallipoli—had to wait for the 1939 fires.

BLACK SUNDAY

This time it was Black Sunday. And this time foresters bore the brunt of the fires.[42]

The conflagrations that climaxed on February 14, 1926, were a fiery cross section of European Australia. They raged in patches across the entire mountain region, from Gippsland to Canberra, from Healesville to Albury to the South Coast. The meteorological circumstances obeyed a classic formula: drought, brutal desert winds (over 75 kilometers per hour), a culminating heat wave that sent temperatures soaring on Black Sunday to 100 degrees Fahrenheit and relative humidities plummeting below 15 percent. The pattern of fire starts was completely predictable—in Victoria the product of graziers, settlers, and tourists, "in that order." Pioneers exploited the dry weather to ensure a good burn, an old practice made worse by the growing throngs of "absentee owners of small selections, farmlets or week-end blocks of land" who burned scrub, blackberries, and other noxious weeds according to their own schedule, without regard for neighbors. Sportsmen, campers, and tourists littered the landscape with abandoned billy fires. Steam tractors and harvesters, locomotives with defective spark arrestors and ash trays, road gangs, rabbiters with phosphorus bait, prospectors, lightning—all contributed to the total. There were reports of fires started by farmers in poor but overinsured croplands to collect premiums. There were fires set from malice. But forest graziers, all agreed, were the worst scourge, indifferent to everything save their green pick. Damages, too, followed a by-now-familiar pattern. The fires ravaged farms, fields, and forests; sixty persons died in Victoria, including isolated bands of bush sawmillers. In Gippsland the fires waxed and waned for six weeks, on a roughly seven-day cycle that saw fires survive light rains, burn through nights unabated, and erupt in an explosion that claimed thirty-one lives over the weekend of February 13–14. In New South Wales the 1926–27 season perpetuated the devastation, sweeping more than 2 million hectares and taking more lives.[43]

What is remarkable, however, is not the holocaust—which was distressingly common in all but scale—but the response given it. On the Black Sunday fires themselves there is scant literature; on the response to them there exists a small library. There was negligible interest in the fires as spectacle: instead they existed as a phenomenon to be understood and as a problem to be reduced. The reason is that they burned into reserved forests and they confronted, as previous conflagrations had not, the organized power of professional forestry. Within weeks of the last smoke, the first conference— an interstate convocation—convened at Sydney. New South Wales empanelled a royal commission of inquiry; Victoria staged a special bushfire conference; Queensland, alarmed by what it witnessed to the south, sponsored a summary commission to recommend reforms of state fire laws and institutions. The interstate conference included representatives from Western Australia and Tasmania. And it introduced into the debate a new consideration: that "the periodic recurrence of devastating fires is injurious to the prestige and credit of the country." [44]

Clearly more was at work than issues of practical settlement. The fires offended the pride of professional foresters, and the reckless burning challenged their recent, hard-won gains in forest protection. As much as anything the 1926 fires pushed foresters across a Rubicon, committing them to an inexorable expansion in their fire-protection schemes, for it was obvious that foresters could not protect their reserves without controlling fire, and that they could not halt fires magically along the boundaries that demarcated their forest reserves from surrounding crown and private lands. Fires originating outside the forest system accounted for 80–90 percent of the burned acreage within the reserved forests. Some 75–80 percent of these were deliberately set for traditional purposes but under circumstances that would never allow their control. Victorian bushfire acts prohibited fires only within a half mile of a forest boundary, a provision laughably inadequate under extreme conditions. One forest reported twenty fires burning under severe circumstances along a fifteen-mile horizon just beyond its territorial fire limits. To further complicate protection, haphazard settlement—more American than Australian in pattern—had insinuated itself into forest gulleys, strung out into indefensible ribbons, and broken up otherwise coherent forests. Settlement fires burned not only from the outside in, but the inside out. And then there were the forest graziers. Here the issue was one of confused, mixed jurisdiction. The Lands Department controlled grazing permits on reservations administered by forest departments. No matter how large or well-equipped, no army of firefighters could succeed under the conflicting orders of two bickering proconsuls.

Item by item the conferees analyzed each contributing element and made recommendations. They urged better public education. They wanted wax matches banned, spark arresters installed on machinery, and enforcement powers to break the back of malicious arson. They wanted bushfire legislation that would regulate—not abolish—traditional burning. They scoured the world for examples, and the interstate commission selected the fire code from the state of Minnesota, USA, "which is recognized as a world's model in rational fire legislation." They debated the value of firebreaks, patrols, lookout towers. They badgered the Meteorology Bureau into placing instruments by which to measure fire weather, particularly relative humidity. They resurrected interest in military aircraft for fire reconnaissance, like those conducted in North America. They issued findings of fact, conclusions, resolutions.[45]

Above all, Black Sunday burned into their consciousness the recognition that there were structural limitations in their capacity to cope with fire. They required what they did not now possess, complete control over fire practices within their own domains; and they sought a strong say in the fire practices of surrounding lands, without which they could not guarantee internal protection. Their appeal for a central fire authority in each state lapsed, predictably, for lack of political clout. Their desire to assume a commanding influence over neighboring firefighting forces foundered for lack of any coherent mechanism to organize such brigades. The 1926 fires were insufficient, by themselves, to catalyze reforms of this magnitude. But they did induce a reasonable consensus among foresters of the southeast, and they promoted public discussion about the larger necessities and ambitions of forest and fire protection. When those reforms arrived years later, they built on concepts and institutions crystallized in Black Sunday.

To measure the progress this represents it is only necessary to contrast the 1926 Royal Commission in New South Wales to that of the 1900 Royal Commission in Victoria impaneled to report on "fire protection in country districts." By 1926 the discovery of bushfire's power had been supplanted by the growing realization of how to counter it. Institutional conclusions had replaced individual narratives. The 1898 fires raged out of an ineffable bush, experienced through highly personalized encounters with terror and loss. The 1926 fires shortened the response time to disaster, formalized social understanding, and catalyzed bureaucracies and professional organizations into a program of reform. Instead of documenting the ways in which settlers fled the fires, reports outlined the countermeasures taken by the forestry agencies that principally fought them. Instead of alluding to hypothetical rural fire wardens, there now existed foresters capable of and intent upon orchestrating fire protection throughout whole regions. The American analogy had grown. The institutional capacity to generalize from one state to another almost hinted at a continental strategy.[46]

Not fires but fire conservancy informed the debate.

"THE BASIS OF ALL FORESTRY IN THE STATE MUST BE FIRE PROTECTION"

To its accumulating fire experiences Australia now added those of a militant forestry. Foresters rationalized fire practices, endowed them with purposeful rigor, and inflamed them with moral intensity. They found laissez-faire pandemonium and created system. Where folkways had guided practice, they imposed science. On lands ruled by faction, they brought uniformity. They built empires not by fire and sword but by overthrowing fire and axe. Like the ancient Romans, however, each victory—every new territory aggregated to the old—compelled them into further expansionism. They could not guarantee protection of their civilized enclaves so long as wild tribes roamed the surrounding lands and from time to time launched fiery raids against them. If they could not expel these marauders, if those lands could not also be absorbed within forest reserves, then at least foresters could control the most dangerous fire practices. Without fire protection forestry was impossible, but fire control restricted to reserved forests could not guarantee protection. The pervasiveness of fire argued for an equally pervasive system of fire protection.

Australian forestry and Australian fire shaped each other. If forestry rationalized fire practices, it was equally true that fire in Australia compelled forestry to change its precepts in ways that made "fire conservancy" an ironic expression. The dream of European forestry—that the domesticated would replace the wild—became, in Australia, a phantasm or a nightmare. Farm, field, and woodlot could not abolish bush. Bushfires would persist; a rationalization of Australian fire meant a rationalization of fire's presence, not its expulsion. Preserving the bush preserved fire. Fire protection meant the substitution of controlled fire for wildfire. Like the Romans again, foresters pacified their frontier by partially converting the barbarian tribes, by accepting some fire. The conservation of forests meant, in Australia, the conservation of fire.

Ideas were slow to catch up with practice, however. More than anyone else Kessell had been the architect of an Australian solution, and he captured perfectly the paradox. "The basis of all forestry in the state must be fire protection," he lectured. Those who disagreed were, "of course," wrong. But the meaning of "fire protection" changed in Australia. As he reprinted the conclusions of the American light-burning controversy, Kessell explained that "complete fire prevention is impossible in practice and controlled bush fires play an important part in silvicultural operations." To express this distinction the Forests Department of Western Australia had adopted the term "fire control" rather than "fire prevention." In ironic reversal, forestry operations even became a prime source of bushfires, mostly due to escapes from controlled burns. Fire conservancy did not extinguish the torch, but rather passed it from one group to another, from folk practitioners to forestry professionals.[47]

Their reliance on fire was a condition that Kessell expected to last for a long time, and it was a circumstance that Australian foresters explained to colleagues reluctantly and apologetically. Even as foresters elsewhere in the empire—with the important exception of Canada—elaborated on their conversion to some form of early burning, Australians were themselves unsure, unconvinced, unwilling to argue that their peculiar compromises had a significance beyond Australia or that they merited special chapters in forestry texts. They saw their work as a compromised ideal, not as a new creation. They insisted their problems were unique, yet proposed no unique solutions. Consequently, if Australian foresters looked increasingly toward North America, there were few North Americans who looked back. Australia became, once more, a remote place to which things migrated, changed, and stayed.[48]

15

Burning Off:
Fire Provinces of
European Australia

*Years ago we might have described fuel reduction as "burning off", "early burn-
ing" or something like that. The impression was that one had to burn the living
daylights out of everything at such frequent intervals that there was never anything left to burn in the bush. Of course there wasn't anything left to burn. The
forests were in a sorry plight. Neighbours fences had gone West. It was a case of
fight bush fires with bush fires. Which then was the worst bush fire?*

—R. H. LUKE *(c. 1950s)*

*"Uncle!" I shouted. "There's another bushfire coming straight for us from the
north!"*
    *I heard uncle's bed creak as he sat up with a muttered exclamation. He pulled
up his lowered blinds and looked out.*
    *"Aw, that!" he croaked in disgust. "That can't do no 'arm. That's just Sandy
Wallace burnin' arf!"*

—HELEN MEGGS, *"Burning Off"*

OUT OF THE WRECKAGE of destabilized biotas emerged the lines of a new order.
From broken, often disparate parts, Australians began to reconstruct new
patterns of fire behavior and fire effects that reflected their larger patterns of
colonial settlement. In particular, they established a geography of fire based
on arbitrary political boundaries. Initially as colonies, then (after 1900) as
states and territories, these political units helped shape the fire practices of
European Australians.
    The states oversaw much of this reconstruction. They exercised some
control over economic development and land use—that is, fuels. They en-

275

acted legislation to regulate the use of fire. They created institutions such as forestry departments that took active control over fire practices and they authorized shire councils to sponsor bushfire brigades. Political boundaries subsumed and reordered fire practices and sometimes consequences. They divided some regimes and recombined others. A single state had to cope with various fire problems on assorted regimes, and no single fire regime enjoyed uniform treatment among the various states. Instead, a political order amalgamated disturbed and fragmented fire regimes into rough patterns, a new geography of fire. Call those patterns "fire provinces." [1]

European settlement also revised the historical boundaries of Australian fire. From the first shock wave, they set to motion a cascade of instabilities that led to permanently altered conditions. It is difficult to identify a clearcut regimen because disturbance was relentless, idiographic, and dynamic; the landscape did not lie about like a shattered watch, its pieces inert and scattered, but like a deeply traumatized yet still living entity that somehow continued to function and that masked, often for decades, the full extent of its damages and infections. How the parts reconstructed themselves, moreover, depended on what pieces and processes had been added or lost.

But, if often irreversible, the process was not endless. Many of the destabilizing practices were self-regulating, and some self-destructive. The European era had to end, if only from its own exhaustion and excess. With remarkable uniformity, that conclusion came during World War II. In the two decades following the war, European Australia became a New Australia, a national system of bushfire practices emerged, and fire provinces reordered themselves into new patterns of fire and land use. Until then the European era was one of disequilibrium, and regardless of how they were institutionally defined, fire practices fell back on that ancient Australian stratagem, burning off.

A marvellous night, raving with moonlight—and somebody burning off the bush in a ring of sultry red fire under the moon in the distance, a slow ring of creeping red fire, like some ring of fireflies, upon the far-off darkness of the land's body, under the white blaze of the moon above.

—D. H. LAWRENCE, *Kangaroo* (1923)

COMPOSITE FIRE: NEW SOUTH WALES

The mother colony contains an environmental and social composite of Australia. It spans the major terrain features, captures the principal biotas, and samples most of the continent's fire regimes. Its pattern of fire starts approximates that of Australia as a whole. Among fire seasons probably 20 percent are serious, 40 percent moderate, and 40 percent mild. From time to time fires spill out of the southeast fire flume and wash over its mountainous south. Its frontier fire practices, too, typified European Australia. Fires in the forests—about 10 percent of New South Wales—were commonplace, a forester recalled. "The bush graziers, the bullock, the teamster and the sleeper, girder and log cutters were all united in a common policy that the forest floor should be kept clean so as not to impede their working and to promote grass for the feeding of their bullocks and horses." Fire protection consisted of intensive management on valued lands and broadcast burning on unsettled lands and commons. The interstitial landscape simmered and smoked, but the asynchronous timing of desert winds and floral curing spared most of the state from the specter of routine holocausts.[2]

Its composite nature was its strength and its weakness. Had a single fire problem involved all of the state, or had all terrains experienced fires at roughly the same time, New South Wales might have been compelled to evolve a coherent strategy of bushfire protection. Instead, different regimes experienced bad fire seasons at different times. Likewise, had a single institution committed itself to aggressive bushfire protection, it might have welded disparate social groups into a unified set of fire practices. But fire threats were too episodic and social incentives too ephemeral to enforce any sort of system. Instead, New South Wales became a political and environmental mosaic. It added new practices and institutions as the British constitution evolved new laws. Fire protection was flexible and accommodating without being particularly effective.

That evolution changed only slightly with the establishment of the Forestry Commission in 1916. The 1926–28 fire seasons, however, galvanized foresters into action—the fires of December 1927 alone probably involved over 2 million hectares. Other conflagrations raged around Sydney in 1929, the Western Division in 1931, the Blue Mountains in 1936. Beginning with a royal commission report in 1927, the Forestry Commission progressively strengthened its fire mission. The means at hand were, of course, primitive. Tools included the rake, hoe, axe, water bag, and box of matches. Roads were poor and vehicles scarce. Fuelbreaks doubled as means of access and as points from which small crews could backfire. Staff were few. Settlers were unorganized. "The fact that no organization has existed to cope with accidental outbreaks of fire in the forest," Kessell realized, "has given to graziers and others a chance to maintain, with some show of altruism, that it is better to set the forest alight as frequently as it will burn, rather than protect it for many years so that debris may be allowed to accumulate and then catch alight, with disastrous consequences for the whole countryside." Against folk burning off foresters proposed a systematic alternative.[3]

Fire protection was not easily done or easily sold to the public. It was, one forester recalled elliptically, "arduous, difficult, and primitive." In self-defense foresters themselves burned off: they burned in advance of harvesting, after logging, and around protected plantations and mature native forests. "Each Forester and Foreman" habitually carried "plenty of matches" on his person, and, when conditions were favourable, he used them. Their small numbers forced foresters to rely on their skills in using fire—backfiring during suppression, light burning for fuel reduction. Writing for the *Sydney Morning Herald* in 1932 Banjo Patterson described how "fire fighters in the mountains went to creeks, green areas and bare patches to burn back into the main fire." But gradually foresters reduced the fire frontier. From their forest citadels, they sent forth expeditions to pacify the surrounding landscape and subject them to a fealty of good-faith fire.[4]

In 1929 the Commission intensified its commitment to fire control. Until a better network of fuelbreaks and protective measures was installed, the Commission decided to shun any further investment in silviculture; there was no point in planting what they could not protect. In 1934 the Commission invited Kessell for a six-month tour of its forestry operations. Forest by forest, his report explained how the southeast could adapt the fire protection system developed in the southwest. In most forests he anticipated no particular difficulties or extraordinary expenses. With regard to conifer plantations, he reiterated that "plantation design is the basis of all fire protection measures." Secure the valuable forests first, he told them, then bring more and more of the wild commons under formal protection. What was needed was steady organization, and that depended on steady commitment.[5]

The following year Commissioner Hudson informed the British Empire Forestry Conference of the remarkable reforms wrought since the 1928 conference, which had followed quickly on the heels of a two-year bout of bushfires. "Measures in the last seven years," he intoned, "have resulted in a greatly reduced amount of fire damage." More than half of the annual expenditure of the Commission was going into fire protection, and supporting projects—particularly road construction—were possible due to emergency programs that sent gangs of the unemployed to work in state forests. Over the past two years, such measures had reduced fires by "something like 75% in the spread and extent to which they have occurred." The Commissioner assured his audience that their resolutions had made a definite contribution. He informed his South African colleagues that if they thought exotic Australian insects had made themselves insufferable pests, he could "introduce some of our Australian settlers" for some truly "astonishing results." But already the leading cause of fire in reserved forests was the Forestry Commission's own fire practices, its often loosely conducted burning off.[6]

Serious bushfires broke out the following year. It became painfully obvious that the reservation of forests could not, by itself, extend over enough of the unmanaged bush to protect the reserves from fire, that forestry had also to establish a fire protectorate over adjoining lands. One means was to extend the Careless Use of Fires Act of 1901; another, to exploit provisions in the Local Government Act of 1906 that authorized shire councils to form bushfire brigades. Since the statute denied any powers or responsibilities to those brigades, it was understandably little used. In 1937, however, concerned officials formed as a palliative the Bush Fires Advisory Committee—nonstatutory, advisory to the state government, dedicated to promoting fire prevention. In particular, it was hoped that the committee could influence the shire councils to apply for their districts to be brought under the provisions of bush fire acts. Meanwhile, the Forestry Commission reorganized and sought relief with "the more extensive utilisation of utility trucks specially designed for fire-fighting purposes." [7]

What New South Wales demonstrated was a pragmatic evolution of order —both of law and of practice—amid its composite of environments and social classes. The process might have continued indefinitely had not crisis, in the form of the great holocaust of 1939, intervened. New South Wales had lacked a coherent fire strategy or rigorous practices because, in part, it had lacked a coherent fire problem, but the 1939 fires and the continuing crisis of World War II dramatically changed that perception and gave decades of incremental institution building something to act upon. In that, too, New South Wales was a cameo of Australia.

LIFE IN THE FIRE FLUME: VICTORIA

The state of Victoria also spans a suite of environments, and its history surveys a spectrum of frontier fire practices. But its boundaries place it squarely, almost entirely, within the great fire flume of the southeast. Large fires explode with a frequency unknown in any other state, and they involve substantial portions of the state at one time. Serious fire seasons occur every two to three years, and major events, with a spasmodic rhythm of roughly eleven to thirteen years. While Victoria occupies about 3 percent of the Australian landmass, it claims roughly half the economic damage attributed to bushfires since European colonization. Bushfires have dominated its landscape history and the history of its forestry. They stripped away alternatives, concentrated attention on fire, made forestry a central institution (in good part because it assumed bushfire control as a central mission), and distilled fire programs into a near-obsession with fire suppression. This concentration of fire—this magnification of fire intensity, fire damages, fire consciousness —shaped the character of Victorian settlement and equally distorted the character of its fire programs. It makes Victoria at once the most and the least Australian of the continent's fire provinces. [8]

Bushfires greeted the earliest settlers to Port Phillip. The two great events of the settlement—its independence as a crown colony and the discovery of gold—virtually coincided with the 1851 fires, Black Thursday. Evidence of large fires in the decades that follow is limited only by the desire to search for it. Officials at Mount Macedon, for example, lamented in 1875 that "great as has been the consumption by sawmills and splitter, it has of late years been nearly equalled by the destruction caused by fire." The *Telegraph* reported in early 1877 that "nearly all the timber country from one end of the Colony to the other has been swept by fires or is burning now." In 1886 *The Age* cited reports of extensive bushfires "from all parts of the country." The era of the Long Drought is a chronicle of bushfires, held in check only by the lack of grasses (from aridity, rabbits, and livestock), for which the 1898 Red Tuesday fires are only a climactic midpoint. In exceptionally dry years, forests burned. After exceptionally wet years, grasslands and mallee burned as well.[9]

In 1887 the Governor, having served previously in India, invited the Deputy Conservator of the Indian Forest Service, F. D'A. Vincent, to report on Victoria. His conclusions—that "the useless waste and destruction defy all description"—were publicly suppressed. When finally released, Vincent's report noted with incredulity that "all forests appear to be swept by a fire whenever there is sufficient undergrowth to burn, which is every second or third year." Meanwhile G. S. Perrin was appointed to the generally power-less post of Conservator. His first report (1890) cited fire protection as the sine qua non of Victorian forestry. Fire, he asserted, was "the greatest enemy the forests have to encounter," and it was the "first duty of a forest officer to study the best means of fighting it." The Fire Act of Victoria was a "dead letter," Perrin wrote in disgust. "Police, selectors, tourists, sleeper hewers, and contractors generally look upon the notices with indifference." Team-sters tossed matches to the roadside, swagmen left billy fires aboil, boys burned to help muster cattle, sportsmen used paper for gun wadding and started fires "at almost every shot." [10]

Inspector-General Ribbentrop of the Indian Forest Service underscored the "extraordinarily backward state" of forestry when, by invitation, he toured Victoria in 1895. So far as he could tell, fire protection had "never even been attempted." That visit catalyzed a royal commission in 1897 whose reports extended over several years and in 1900 included a special volume on "Fire-Protection in Country Districts." That its release followed upon the disastrous Red Tuesday fires and coincided with a chronic, drought-inspired rash of serious burnings gave it some punch, however re-tarded the political response. In 1905 Acting Conservator A. W. Crooke despaired of ever corralling the menace. He cited as evidence that when a Melbourne newspaper reported on a recent burn, it concluded that there was little harm done because eucalypts recovered quickly and "the fire was con-fined to the State forest." Continued bush firing he attributed to "direct incendiarism or criminal negligence," acts intended to camouflage illicit be-

havior, folk protests against authority, or "sheer wantonness" by bush larrikins. Pioneers isolated into pockets of selected land within reserved forests
lusted after their "good burn." Forest graziers burned whenever and wherever they could. In the eastern division everyone pursued his firing in isolation since "no man trusts his neighbour when he is engaged on such a
delicate business as fire-raising." An outraged Hutchins, practically screaming his astonishment, declared that *Fire protection is the crux of Victorian
Forestry.* " He doubted the value of the Victorian commitment to patrols
and towers if unsupported by a comprehensive system of working plans and
fuelbreaks, and he questioned whether protection could come until all "the
accessible forests are organised in Victoria as they are in South Africa." But
field foresters had little choice except to make do and, where possible, redouble their vigilance. Fortunately, a succession of forestry statutes followed,
the first in 1907. The Forestry Act of 1918 established the Forests Commission, independent from other ministries, and gave foresters the mandate
they required.[11]

Fires continued through it all. Only in rare years did some portion of
Victoria fail to burn uncontrollably. In 1912 extensive fires swept from
Gippsland to the Grampians. Over 100,000 hectares burned in 1913–14.
What 1898 was to Gippsland, "1919 was to the Otway Ranges." Bad fires
broke out in late 1922 and in 1923. The Forests Commission held few illu-
sions about the magnitude of its fire mission. It recognized that there was
"one remedy, and one only" that could be truly effective—"the growth of
such a body of sound public opinion that wanton or grossly careless fire-
raising shall become a thing of the past." It was not something over which
they had more than marginal control.[12]

Like barons faced with insurrection around their lands, Victorian foresters erected watchtowers, laid down roads, sent out patrols, and steadily incorporated more lands into the realm. They campaigned for better fire codes,
and sought entente with the Lands Department that governed selection
around the reserves and grazing on lands within them. In addition, the
Forests Commission accepted the charge to control fires on many crown
lands outside forest reserves, but it had no control over fire starters; of necessity, this put a premium on fire suppression. Victoria moved toward a strategy of rapid detection and attack rather than protective burning—graziers
and others were still masters of the torch. Instead Victorians argued for a
mobilization as fast as its fires and speculated proudly that resettled soldiers
had adapted the tactics of tank brigades to motorized pumpers. Then came
the 1926 conflagrations, the worst since 1918 and "as far as loss of human
life is concerned . . . the most calamitous on record"; thirty-one people
died at Warburton on February 14 alone.[13]

The royal commission and conferences that followed reaffirmed the tenets of organized fire control. With dramatic flair the Commission bolstered

its fire suppression tools by promoting mountain fire trucks, by using wireless radio, and by signing agreements with the Royal Australian Air Force for assistance. It enacted a program of scientific research into fire behavior and effects. And with a shrewd sense of institutional power, it sought to establish "a network of volunteer fire fighters throughout the State." A departmental conference in 1929 standardized the construction and maintenance of fuelbreaks and restricted controlled burning, "including patch-burning and marginal burning," to lower-elevation eucalypt forests. Meanwhile the Conservator, Owen Jones, who had served with the RAF during the Great War, knew that in North America military biplanes otherwise destined for mothballing were being recycled into fire reconnaissance duties with brilliant success, and campaigned for similar arrangements with the Australian military. The first aerial patrols commenced in 1930. Two years later, admitting the limitations of its power, the Commission introduced a scheme of protective "dug-outs"—sites of refuge—for forest workers.[14]

There is something incongruous and symbolic about Victorian forestry's taking to the air at the same time it was digging into the ground. Airplane and bunker were images of the battlefield. While military metaphors came readily to this generation of foresters, nowhere else did they reify the metaphor quite so literally. In Victoria the emphasis was on fire*fighting.* Foresters practiced controlled burning in strips and patches, but to maintain lines of defense; if they used broadcast burning, they did not advertise that fact. To the Third British Empire Forestry Conference they explained apologetically that although "some properly controlled patch-burning in spring and autumn are regularly employed," this was a "drastic" and less-than-ideal technique that future progress would undoubtedly eliminate. The practice too closely resembled the firing of graziers and other incendiarists against whom the foresters campaigned. It looked suspiciously like simple burning off.[15]

Instead Victorian energies went into an alliance with volunteer fire brigades. The scheme was a masterstroke. Volunteer fire companies had sprung up on the goldfields manned by "enthusiasts, men of the good old British stock with a large sprinkling of Americans and Canadians." With some help from insurance companies, the brigades brought a level of protection to frontier towns highly vulnerable to fires. The Fire Brigades Act of 1890 instilled some rigor and state aid into the process. Within a year the Country Fire Brigades Board assumed the administration of volunteer urban brigades.[16]

What the Forests Commission proposed was to expand these beachheads to embrace the smaller towns and then orchestrate the lot of them into a network that could complement firefighting on reserved forests. If the Forests Commission fielded a regular army, its brigades constituted a militia on which it could call during emergencies. Between them the foresters and the brigades could dramatically shrink the realm of unprotected lands from which, like hordes spilling out of central Asia into Europe, bushfires came with devastating regularity and against which they now had common cause. After the 1926 fires the Forests Commission invited the police department and Country Fire Brigades Board to join it on a tour of Gippsland. Along the way they organized "31 brigades in 10 days." The Commission assisted with advice and "donations of equipment such as firebeaters, slashers, axes, water bags, rakes, &c." In 1928 the Minister of Forests called a conference of brigades to discuss further means of coordination. Out of this came the Victorian Bush Fire Brigades Association.[17]

The number of brigades steadily increased and a Melbourne Volunteer Bush Fire Brigade was organized to protect a sixty-mile radius around the capital city. By 1930 the number of brigades had swelled to 203, and the Forests Commission, to its regret, found itself unable to support them all. Between them the Commission and the association lobbied for state support and real statutory power for the brigades. After 200,000 hectares burned on nominally protected forests in 1931, authorization finally arrived in the form of the Bush Fire Brigades Act of 1933. The Forests Commission posted a secretary to the Bush Fire Brigades Association as a liaison. The association mounted a bushfire prevention campaign. By 1933 some 270 brigades had enrolled 10,000 rural Australians.

By the late 1930s there was reason for genuine satisfaction. Significant public lands still fell through the cracks, but no one could deny the dramatic improvement in the ratio of protected to unprotected lands. Each year strengthened the ligatures of formal fire protection. In 1937 the Commission appointed a senior forester as fire protection officer. In the Commission's annual report for 1937–38, the Conservator wrote with considerable gratification that, "despite hazards which prevailed over a long period" fire season, actual losses had been relatively minor, an indication that the "intensive fire protection organization now in operation is proving effective." [18]

The millennial fires of 1939 blasted that presumption. But while the fires raged, the Forests Commission found itself placed "in the position of being regarded as the fire warden for the State." It was a status the Commission derived less from legislative authority than from its own moral authority in the realm of fire protection. As the various agencies reconstructed after the holocaust, they had a considerable institutional foundation on which to build. Without hesitation they looked toward the Forests Commission for leadership.[19]

There was a thoroughness, a singularity, even a ruthlessness to Victorian fire protection—an unwillingness to compromise with folk fire practices— that was evident in no other state. In fact, Victoria looked less around Australia for counsel than it did overseas, particularly to California—long valued as a fellow traveler of the great gold-rush era, long perceived as a land similarly blessed and afflicted with a Mediterranean-type climate, desert winds, and extensive fires. To California Victoria sent eucalypts. From it, Victoria acquired the Monterey pine and lessons on frontier fire brigades, learned about systematic fire protection in the duBois mode, gazed in admiration at dazzling fire patrols by aircraft, found models for fire research, for fire weather forecasts by meteorological bureaus, and for mechanized firefighting "appliances." There, too, they discovered professional colleagues sympathetic to the Victorians' suspicion of broadcast burning as a tool for fire protection, for it was in California that American foresters had fought light burning to the death. Within their respective nations the two states became semiautonomous fire powers, and between them they became friendly rivals. Rather than comparing itself with other Australian states, Victoria more typically measured itself against California. It even became a matter of fervent if perverse pride for Victorians to proclaim that theirs, not California's, was the worst fire environment on Earth.[20]

FAITH, FORMULA, AND FIRE: SOUTH AUSTRALIA

South Australian fire history has a unity that reflects a concentrated geography of fuels and a relative homogeneity of European settlement. The state is arid—the driest in Australia. Ignition is almost always possible, but fuels can carry fire only sparingly except where topography concentrates rainfall and growth. The Flinders Range and an exposed coastline collect enough winter moisture to make the southeastern quad into a fire triangle, bonded to the Victoria fire flume. Scleroforest in the mountains, mallee and grasslands on the plains—all, under the proper circumstances, sustain large fires. The actual regime, however, depends upon ignition, and that follows from human colonization. The same features that encourage fuels also encourage settlement.

The earliest explorers sighted fires on the plains and peaks, and attributed most of them to Aborigines. From the coast explorers reported burning in the Mount Lofty Ranges in 1827. As Aborigines departed, pastoralists took their place as incendiarists. Where dense scrub, not native grasses, had to be converted, fierce fires from settlers roiled the skies. In the 1840s George Angas spoke breathlessly about the

> tall primeval trees . . . blackened in many places as high as fifteen or twenty feet from the ground, by the tremendous fires that sweep through these forests, and continue to blaze and roll along, day and night, for many miles, in one continuous chain of fire. These conflagrations usually take place during the dry heats of summer; and frequently at night, the hills, when viewed from Adelaide, present a singular and almost terrific appearance: being covered with long streaks of flame, so that one might fancy them a range of volcanoes.

In 1850 arson, provoked by thieves, plagued stations and even invaded Adelaide, burning the parklands between Government House and the Torrens "for a day and a night"; it was a petty scene, however, when compared with the great conflagration that set the "entire countryside from Mount Lofty to Crafters' Inn" ablaze. In January 1867 a reporter noted how "bushfires, the inevitable accompaniment of any hot windy day, were looked for early. They were not long in coming. A lull in the wind showed, through the dust, fires in the scrub to the W., N.W., and N.E. of Mount Gambier." Fires soon ringed the town, and "before the day was out there were heavy losses of stock, pasture, farm equipment, buildings, fences (post and rail) and people injured." [21]

But the relatively close, comparatively methodical settlement of the colony pushed bushfires to the margins of reclaimed lands. Bushfires were a phenomenon of the agricultural frontier, increasingly crowded to the fringe where wild lands and tamed lands intermingled. Year by year settlers reclaimed semiarid lands from bushfires as patiently as their English ancestors had reclaimed fens from the salty tides. Fuelbreaks assumed the role of canals and dikes, and in the form of roads, tracks, and plowed or burned strips the breaks segregated the wild from the domesticated, draining away the fuels that made bushfires endemic. As bushfires gave way to agricultural fires—the burning of stubble, the clearing of newly felled scrub, the firing of paddocks—sedentary agriculture created the prevailing matrix of fuels and fire practices. The completeness of agricultural reclamation determined the completeness of bushfire protection.

Even foresters behaved like farmers, and they laid out forest reservations in an almost Wakefieldian spirit. There was limited competition between farmers and foresters over native forests because those woodlands (except the mallee) were limited in area and soon largely cleared. Instead they competed over potential cropland, disputing whether a site should grow wheat or pines. South Australia planted plenty of both. The earliest acts to encourage forestry aimed at afforestation; foresters advanced aboriculture, stocked tree nurseries, and argued that extensive afforestation would augment rainfall and thereby enrich agriculture overall. Particularly in the early years, crops were sown amid the rows of trees. Foresters complained about grasshopper hordes that ate nurseries and succulent seedlings. Along with farmers, foresters shared a common enemy in pastoralists and transient incendiarists. With the Woods and Forests Act of 1882, South Australia confirmed in title, no less than prescriptions, its essentially English understanding of forestry.

Its fire practices reflected these values, its techniques of choice those of agriculturalists. Like croplands, forests suffered from bushfires that originated outside the fields; unlike wheat or maize, however, a forest needed protection over many decades. Accordingly, foresters built fire-control measures into the design of their plantations—a vastly simpler chore than installing them in a native forest. Fuelbreaks formed fire barriers around each plantation, and like fire walls they broke up the interior into small compartments; until 1924, guidelines called for fuelbreaks around every ten acres of plantation. Not surprisingly, foresters experimented avidly with green fuelbreaks of cereal crops or hay. They plowed rather than hand-clear weeds. They burned sites selected for planting, fired the debris left after harvest, and used fire to maintain fuelbreaks. They appealed to intensive grazing (by "agisted stock") to prune the understory into manageable fuel loads. The Interstate Forest Conference in 1915 was "favorably impressed with the thorough efficiency of the fire-break system by which the plantation areas are protected from fire." By the 1936–37 fire season, the Woods and Forests Department maintained some 1,450 miles of fuelbreaks. Statutes even mandated fuelbreaks throughout much of the selected lands.[22]

Its settler population, too, made South Australian forestry distinctive. In 1879 the Forests Board reported that posting fire notices had "a very salutary effect." The warnings had been read and largely obeyed—an event unimaginable elsewhere in Australia. The colony had promulgated its Bush Fires Act in 1854, primarily to regulate the use of agricultural fire. Elsewhere, statutory edicts were a dead letter because neighbors would never report violations or testify against one another, or because transients made for a chronically unsettled landscape. This was much less the case in South Australia. The colony had epitomized Wakefield's concepts of "planned colonization"; it had no convict heritage, no plague of bushrangers, no hordes of diggers uprooting the landscape. There were episodes of ignorant, negligent, and malicious firings, but the violations almost always occurred from agricultural burning and could be prosecuted. Two fires that threatened the Mount Brown Forest in 1889–90, for example, "arose through infringements of the Bush Fires Act, for which the perpetrators were prosecuted in due course and suitably punished." Foresters noted with dismay, however, the frequency with which damaging bushfires crossed the border from lawless Victoria. In South Australia bushfire statutes had the enforcement power not only of law but of popular opinion.[23]

As agriculture expanded it entered new environments, exposed new problems, and engendered new bushfire legislation. In 1885, for example, amendments to the Bush Fires Act extended coverage to the clearing of mallee scrub. In 1913 revisions empowered local councils to appoint fire control officers and to fund programs for fire prevention, thus inaugurating a network of rural bushfire brigades to which insurance companies contributed. By the mid-1920s, the councils in the penumbra of Adelaide began coordinating their efforts as the Northern Fire Fighting Association, which the Woods and Forests Department applauded as having "gone far towards ensuring the protection of the northern forest areas." In 1933 massive fires ripped the state from the Eyre Peninsula to the Adelaide Hills and beyond into much of the rural landscape. Quickly that alliance was strengthened by amendments to the Bush Fires Act that enjoined the councils to furnish equipment, not just legitimacy. Extensive fires persisted through the 1934 season. In response, first in Naracoorte, Millicent, and Penola, then elsewhere, district councils moved to establish volunteer fire services. The Woods and Forests Department actively campaigned to extend the Northern Fire Fighting Association and "the fine organisation" of the Adelaide Hills Councils to the southeast, "where forestry means much more in the economic life of the people.[24]

But if forestry in South Australia was less fanatical than elsewhere, it was also less powerful. It was one voice among several; its interests merged with a larger, less violent social consensus. Among state agencies, the Woods and Forests Department was the one most aggressively concerned with bushfires, but the larger matrix of fire protection belonged at the shire and district level where the department assisted but did not uniformly lead. Woods and Forests was prominent less because it housed foresters than because it was a major rural landholder whose actions affected those around it and which was, in turn, vulnerable to the practices of its neighbors. It was not subjected, as foresters in native forests were, to a guerrilla war of protest fire. It functioned not unlike the Forestry Commission in Great Britain, with one critical difference: afforestation in South Australia was a means of domesticating a wild landscape, of draining a fire fen, not, as in Britain, of inadvertently restoring fire to a landscape largely cleared of it.

Then came 1939. It was impossible for South Australia to escape the conflagrations. They devastated the fire triangle of the southeast and along with wartime needs they inspired important, evolutionary reforms. But the real work of wringing bushfire from the landscape had depended on classic, methodical reclamation for which the control of fires was an auxiliary task not unlike the control of weeds or vermin. Fire protection improved as settlement matured, as pioneers reduced more and more "waste" land to wheat or pine; Goyder's Line also segregated bushfire from agricultural fire. But even as the institutional context of bushfire protection improved, its environmental context altered.

Settlement changed, and with it changed fuels, patterns of ignition, and mechanisms for fire control. The worst bushfires of the postwar era tracked the new landscape fashioned by exotic flora and exurban homesteaders. Rural South Australia began to break up, hammered by a global economy and changing social values. On prime sites, farming intensified; on marginal sites, however, farming and pastoralism retreated; and elsewhere, other patterns of land use prevailed. A new wave of settlement washed over the Mount Lofty Range, in particular. Flushed with pyrophytic exotics like broom, a reinforced bush reclaimed lands previously converted to agriculture; suburbs invaded old farmlands and the newly exuberant flora; transients—tourists, weekend ruralites—failed to take protective measures even while they added negligent ignitions; and arson, not carelessness, became a dominant cause of conflagrations. As faith and formula receded, bushfires advanced.

UNDER THE VOLCANO: TASMANIA

No such integrating force organized the Tasmanian fire province—not the environment, not any element of European colonization. While lush with fuels, the landscape is fragmented. While rife with burning, Tasmanian bushfire disasters are relatively rare. The frequency of routine fire use and the infrequency of holocausts bred a fatalism of indifference. Tasmanians lived under a bushfire volcano.[25]

Its fascinating environment has inspired diversity rather than uniformity. Mountains divide Tasmania into a wetter west side and a drier east; they clutter its slopes and valleys with a profusion of microclimates and subbiotas. Scleroforest interpenetrates temperate rainforest, and both front moors and grasslands. On the average, precipitation is three times that of the mainland. Fuels are ever-ample, their availability limited only by their moisture content. Large fires thus follow droughts, and droughts, while intense, are localized and infrequent. Desert winds can strike the island, a detached outlet to the Australian fire flume. Once begun large fires in Tasmania reveal a fuel-driven intensity unusual in Australia. Since European settlement some seventeen fire seasons have flared into prominence; a half century of Forestry Commission records documents six disastrous seasons. They follow an arrhythmic beat.

Neither is there much human order. Colonization only compounded centrifugal tendencies. Tasmania acquired no effective center—urban, economic, political, or thematic. No metropolis so dominated the rural scene that it regularized human geography; no group, not even foresters, seized the bushfire problem as a preferred cause; no community sentiment campaigned to contain a scourge that, like cholera, would visit the colony then depart. After a bold start, Tasmania fragmented into multiple, squabbling settlements, a more dispersed rural landscape ravaged by open war between Aborigines and Europeans, by near civil war between authorities and bushrangers, by open hostilities between settlers and bush. Acre for acre, Tasmania probably had more fire than anywhere else in European Australia. Even in Aboriginal times the coastline had been fringed with smokes and the interior commonly smoldered with inscribed fire corridors that occasionally blew up into towering holocausts. Ironically, controlled burning in the big scrub was difficult; under normal conditions fires could not easily spread, while under exceptional conditions they could not be stopped. Tasmanians lived, with almost fatalistic resignation, atop a biotic fault line that ruptured from time to time into earthshaking fires.

To Tasmania's fire history there is no clear pattern, no integrative force of either nature or culture. First pastoralism then gold drained away capital and settlers to Victoria. Europeans protected themselves against fire in much the same way they warred against the Aborigines. There was state collusion without state control. Popular sentiment for reform rallied briefly after holocausts, then dissipated. The political tendency was toward faction rather than consensus; not only was Tasmania divided from Australia, it was divided within itself. Instead of concentrating Australian fire into a subcontinental island, Tasmania simply amassed every fire practice and every fuel without instilling a unity of purpose or plan. It was as though Australia had exported its worst problem fires, as it once did its problem convicts, to a Tasmanian exile but removed the guards. What a puzzled Flinders and Bass reported in 1798—"we saw . . . a man [Aborigine] who employed or amused himself by setting fire to the grass in different places"—could as aptly describe the European scene that succeeded it.[26]

Europeans employed the same fire practices in Tasmania that they exploited on the mainland. From time to time damaging fires erupted, though rarely were many parts of the Tasmanian mosaic involved simultaneously; rather, there were many eruptions, and their records are disynchronous. In 1854, for example, Frederick Mackie visited Mount Wellington outside Hobart and found it disappointing because it was being "rapidly cleared and the few large trees that remain are more or less charred with fire." In January he reported that the Huon district revealed "large volumes of smoke rising in various directions." As his party continued, they encountered denser smoke, oppressive heat, fireflakes of ash, and an opaque pall that sent them into retreat. Later they learned that between eight and fourteen lives had been lost to the fires, and Mackie thought that no such conflagration had afflicted the country before. Almost certainly European land clearing aggravated the fires by allowing much larger volumes of fuel to dry out, but had Mackie not recorded this fire there would be no evidence of it.[27]

"On many occasions," recalled James Fenton, "the farmers suffered loss from tremendous bush fires." Ring-barking became common practice in the 1840s, yet burning was ceaseless and careless; pioneers relied on the wet, unslashed bush to contain their promiscuous fires. The settlers, Fenton recalled, "burned indiscriminately when clearing the land." As weeds invaded disturbed sites, the fire problems multiplied; Scots thistle became a "plague" that, when burning, "spread with a fury that no human power could abate." James Backhouse described how easy it was for fires to escape and how difficult it was to cleanse a site of felled timber, for "it requires many burnings to destroy the logs, many of which, either partially consumed, or entire, are scattered in all directions over this Island." Farmers continued to burn them into oblivion. Graziers routinely fired the landscape. The Black War could have described the hostilities between settler and bush, no less than between European and Aborigine. Prospectors burned in the peaks and penetrated into the more moist environments of the west. After an initial diminution of fires, reflecting the recession of the Aborigines, the frequency and intensity of bushfires mounted, and protective burning reached epidemic proportions. The Bush Fires Act (1854) was a dead letter from the time of its enactment.[28]

Major outbreaks erupted in panoramic splendor. Spectacular bushfires raged in 1861. A conflagration that climaxed on Black Friday (December 31, 1897) anticipated the Red Tuesday fires in Gippsland and completed the destruction of the penal compound at Port Arthur. Severe fires seared wide swaths of Tasmanian countryside between 1912 and 1915. The Melbourne *Age* said of the February 1915 fires that they were the "most devastating bush fires ever known in Tasmania . . . the whole country for miles is one sea of flame." The Hobart Fire Brigade—reinforced by soldiers from the barracks and sailors from the HMAS *Australia*— battled to keep the fires from entering the suburbs. In the northwest, where the fires did particular damage, the Hobart *Mercury* told of settlers trapped by "an ever-increasing hail of fire," of women huddled in terror with children, of older children wrapped around the younger while the flames raged; a Mrs. Ryan saved her two children but at the cost of her own life, her clothes burned completely off her. To bring in her coffin rescue parties had to cut a hundred trees off forest tracks.[29]

Foresters did not—could not—intervene. Forestry reserves were pathetically ineffectual—their boundaries poorly demarcated, their staffs too thinly spread, their scattered fuelbreaks readily breached by high-intensity flames and spotting, their enforcement powers negated by the force of popular hostility. "The national Forestry in Tasmania," one spokesman shuddered in the early twentieth century, "is the worst in Australia." When Hutchins toured Tasmania in 1915, he was hopeful for this "the one all-forest State in Australia . . . the one State where the woodman can work in a bracing climate, and where Forestry can proceed so easily on European lines." Instead he saw burnt landscapes. "It was everywhere the same picture of utter neglect and wholesale destruction of forest by fire . . . ." The devastation was "indescribable." Even the government, to his incredulity, did "its best to cause fires!" The state refused to install spark arrestors on its locomotives, declined to commit to the organization necessary to stabilize the fire scene, and hired firefighters in "spasmodic attempts" to suppress wildfire, which only inspired new fires ignited by Tasmanians looking for employment.[30]

It was "futile to talk of preventing bush fires in Tasmania," the Surveyor-General concluded in 1915. Even the principal victims failed to agitate for reform. The Forestry Act of 1920 created the Forestry Department the following year, but the Conservator lacked resources to control even the fires on reserved forests and there was no movement for rural brigades. There was no legislative or practical means by which to protect reserves from fires on adjacent crown or rural lands. On the contrary, settlers "often regard the burning of the neighbouring forests as reducing the danger of fire on their own holdings." Instead the Forestry Department concentrated on protecting eucalypt regrowth. In 1926 "fire-rangers" were appointed to every district to patrol and maintain fuelbreaks. Meanwhile violent fires continued to break out from time to time even around cities. In February 1927 they came again to Hobart. "Fires could be seen to be raging practically on every hill top," the *Mercury* reported. "Everybody who could, got out of the city." The Hobart Fire Brigade, reinforced again from the Australian fleet at anchor, fought back; the northerly ("brick-fielder") winds died down; and the mob of fires migrated into the Midlands, Norfolk, Kingston, even Bruny Island, and elsewhere. More bad burns followed in 1931–32.[31]

Then came the 1933–34 fire season, widely regarded as the worst since 1897. The normal palette of rural fires simmered through December with "as usual, no importance attached to them." Then, over the next two months, a succession of dry cold fronts hurled northwest winds that fanned the flames into conflagrations. By mid-January the Forestry Department had fully mobilized to save its forests and render whatever assistance might be required to surrounding towns. The Conservator realized that it was "hopeless" to deal with the forest fires and concentrated on assisting the townships. But there was little with which to work. There was "neither organization nor equipment for effective fire-fighting—not even the nucleus of any organization." At the Conservator's request the Cabinet ordered the Forestry Department to assume overall command of the firefighting effort and to requisition men and equipment. After the danger passed, after a round of petitions to contain unrestricted burning off, public interest dissipated "because, for the time being, the danger is past." [32]

A new Bush Fires Act, enacted in 1935, empowered the Forestry Department to extend fire protection over all crown lands and, to a lesser degree, over lands adjacent to them. But its power of enforcement was negligible: the means by which to extend effective protection withheld. No bushfire brigades mobilized. In compensation, to each forest district the Department added "at least one motor fire-pump." It trained the volunteer fire brigades at Hobart and Launceston. When the great fires of 1939 struck Tasmania, the outcome was predictable. With few exceptions the holocaust scattered firefighting forces to the wind.

What was also predictable for Tasmania, but exceptional for Australia, was that the 1939 fires dissipated into a diffuse rural, oft-ravaged landscape. While almost everywhere else in Australia the great fires catalyzed a major overhaul in bushfire protection, in Tasmania they led to marginal reforms and yielded nothing distinctive. The 1939 fires became among the most intensely scrutinized in Australian history, but of the 160 fires reported in Tasmania, some 59 remained of "unknown" origin. The Bush Fires Act was again amended and nominally strengthened yet without the public support that could alone make it effective. The state forests stiffened their programs, schemes were proposed for bushfire districts, and systematic fire planning was urged. But the institutions, the experience, the means, the will to implement them—all were absent.

When Stephen Kessell reported on Tasmanian forestry in 1945 he indicted bushfires for their "heavy toll of Tasmanian forests." They had destroyed far more timber than the logging industry had cut and "evidence of this is to be seen on practically every timbered skyline in Tasmania . . ." Over the past fifteen years forestry had made, at most, "slow progress"; there was none in rural fire control. Providing protection when bad fires erupted "at intervals of five, ten, or fifteen years" was particularly problematic because what was adequate for normal years broke down under the exceptional year, precisely the time it was most needed. Although Kessell confidently predicted that the "Forestry Department can be relied upon to develop general measures for fire control as its work expands," in fact Tasmania apparently lacked both the means and the ends, unable to organize beyond the most narrow purpose and the most vocal interest group. The reforms that elsewhere in Australia followed the 1939 fires did not begin in Tasmania until bushfires once again savaged Hobart in 1967.[33]

FIRE SHADOW: QUIESCENT QUEENSLAND

Queensland has no declared fire season. Its topography is muted, its seasonal cycle wobbles weakly through the year, its fires and fuels derive largely from human artifice, and, while abundant, fires are rarely catastrophic. Serious bushfires lack the unpredictable viciousness characteristic of Tasmania or the driving intensity typical of Victoria. The elements that in the fire flume crowd together in metastable equilibrium are here disengaged, claiming different seasons or separate geographies. Natural fires follow a slow scenario of prehuman swidden—slashing windstorms, drought, and lightning. The cycle is long and recovery complete. Only along the hefty perimeter of the fire province does fire inform environments of spinifex, savanna, and scleroforest. At its center flourish the least pyrophytic of the Australian biotas, the greatest residue of Green Gondwana—Mitchell grasslands, the mulga mélange, brigalow, Gondwana softwoods like hoop pine, kauri, and bunya, and coastal enclaves of wallum and rainforest bathed by monsoon moisture and coastal trades and sheltered from fire. The core of quiescent Queensland lies in a continental fire shadow.

Its fires are anthropogenic. Humans create the necessary fuels, and humans apply the torch. Wildfire is less a visitation from an effable bush than an introduced pest like prickly pear or toads. Along the coastal zone, where 95 percent of humans reside, essentially all land management operations rely on open fire. Farmers burn for clearing; graziers, for green pick; cane raisers, as a tool of site preparation and harvest; foresters, at all stages of management; the Railway Commission, to clear tracks; protective burning is universal. So much smoke crowds the sky so often that it is difficult to distinguish wild fires from controlled ones, and compelled Francis Ratcliffe to always associate the Atherton Tableland with smoke. When Swain denounced the rural Australian for his wanton "fire-stick habit"—which he likened to the "Chinese method of roasting pork" by stuffing a skewered pig into a house and burning down the house—he was speaking of Queenslanders. He had expected in Queensland "to see a land of humid jungle," but discovered instead a "baked and burned" countryside. Somewhere, at almost any time, and everywhere, at some time, fires burn in the province.[34]

Yet, paradoxically, there has been much interest in fire protection. Fire destroys, not stimulates, the best grazing lands in the interior. Fuelbreaks account for substantial burning and not a few escapes. Outside the eucalypt woodlands, fires exist primarily where humans prepare a site to receive it. In *Harry Heathcote of Gangoil* Trollope described in condemnatory detail the terror and labor caused by arsonists on the great stations, and the near impossibility of obtaining a criminal judgment against them. "Every one around might be sure that some particular fire had been the work of an incendiary—might be able to name the culprit who had done the deed; and yet no jury could convict the miscreant." Landowners had to protect their own property. There existed no authority to regularize fire practices.[35]

That included foresters. Even after the Forests Act of 1906 state forestry was closely subordinated to the Lands Department. Officials regarded forestry as an adjunct to aggressive settlement, a manifestation of state-sponsored agriculture, and when it conflicted with other agricultural purposes or commercial logging, forestry usually lost out. Often the native softwoods—the hoop pine was the saddest example—were not even logged but simply felled and burned. To critics nurtured on high principles of professionalism and empire, forestry in Queensland seemed like a conspiracy to plunder, with more the character of a joint-stock company intent on raising British capital than an institution for the conservation of Australia's native softwoods. It is perhaps symbolic that what intrigued Queenslander Swain in his tour of American forestry in 1917 was its "hothouse" synthesis of "ruthless capitalism," "fierce competition," and "efficiency"—so unlike Australia's "feudal" forestry. A "fusion of the two philosophies of America and Australia," he concluded, "might lead to happy results—in other things besides forestry." While foresters around Australia also surveyed fire control across the Pacific, no one outside Queensland thought to merge so vigorously conservancy and capitalism. Revealingly, the chief of the Queensland Forest Service was titled "Director," not "Conservator." [36]

In their defense, foresters held little political power. For a few years, from 1924 to 1932, the administration of state forests reported directly to the Minister for Lands; but otherwise it was subordinated to a lascivious program of economic development governed largely by the disposition, not the conservation, of the forests under its protection. The destruction of native softwoods was relentless. In addition, Hutchins thought that the eucalypt woodland held "not a quarter of its normal timber," for which he blamed routine fires. The Director reaffirmed the official line: "that fire control pays is certain." But forestry enjoyed no special powers of regulation, nor could it claim much moral authority. Rather, it coexisted within a wonderfully diverse rural landscape that grew everything from bananas to sugar cane to maize to exotic pines and within a confining institutional matrix that keenly promoted rural development.[37]

With the spread of active land clearing, however, fires bubbled up like mud geysers; they infested disturbed sites like flaming weeds. In the interior there were large fires in 1917 and 1918; later, in 1922 and 1923. Along the coast there were serious fires in various locales in 1910, 1920, 1922, and 1923. Bad droughts often spared Queensland from fire due to "the very scantiness of the ground herbage." "Northern cyclones," however, compensated by pummeling the landscape into "trash." Then came 1926. The drought that readied the southeast suite for large fires spread into Queensland; fires that normally expired against the lushness of the uncut tropical biota this year propagated across it. For a while Brisbane itself seemed to be under siege. Queenslanders witnessed what was, for them, unusual fire behavior, even reports of intense burns "characterized by projections of flames from tree tops over wide spaces." The Minister for Lands appointed an Advisory Committee on Bush Fires to make a full inquiry. The chair was the Director of Marketing; other members included representatives from the United Graziers Association, the Bribane Timber Merchants Association, the Land Commission, and the Queensland Forest Service.[38]

The fires had rural causes, and the committee sought a rural solution. There was no question of denying access to fire, without which settlement would cease. What was required was regulation and organization to end a rampant individualism that employed fire indiscriminately. There was, the committee realized, "no organised method of operation in the legitimate use of fire." Moreover, malicious arson mocked any presumption of control on the strength of social consensus. Foresters could not protect state forests from fires originating on other crown lands. The reserves were in bad shape. Even the "whiff of smoke" was sufficient to lay low their Gondwanic softwoods; eucalypt woodlands thinned; and once-mature forests, blasted by fire and grazing, had transformed from grassy parks into a tangle of woody thickets that bred only white ants and more fire. The Careless Use of Fire Prevention Act of 1865 was of course incompetent. The core question was one Queensland particularly felt, the degree to which individuals could be restrained for the common good.[39]

The solution, the committee thought, was an oversight board, which the Rural Fires Act of 1927 quickly constituted. Its composition resembled that of the committee. Councils could proclaim rural fire districts to which a fire warden would be gazetted. Within two years the penumbral lands around Brisbane came under the board's protection. The fiscal crisis brought on by the Depression, however, caused the board to be dissolved by cabinet decree. The Forest Service, and later the Lands Administration, tried to carry the burden, but they had few resources and little effect. There were more serious fires in the west during 1932 and 1935. The Director reported that the 1936–37 season, when desert winds combined with regional drought, was "the worst fire year in the history of the Department." The Forest Service successfully prosecuted violators under the Rural Fires Act and recovered costs for damages and suppression. In November 1937 an area measuring fifty by one hundred miles reportedly burned near Charters Towers, but the critical fires arrived during the years of World War II. Reconstitution of the Rural Fires Board followed upon the conclusion of the war.[40]

Although, against the odds, forestry strengthened its status, it remained one landowner among many. Its fire practices resembled those of its more careful neighbors: it laid down fuelbreaks, erected towers, instigated controlled burning, and relied on the favorable weather, the rhythm of northern monsoon and southeast trades, that put most of Queensland outside the main natural fire belts of Australia. Its mission was not to suppress agricultural burning or to establish a fire protectorate over surrounding lands, but to synchronize its needs with those of its neighbors. In 1927 Swain apologized for the "compromise" by which foresters resorted to broadcast burning at night or in winter to reduce fuels. While better than the alternatives, no fire or wildfire, the practice still struck "at the gospel of the silviculturists." In small doses, fire—"like strychnine"—was a stimulant; in large doses, a poison.[41]

But like their rural neighbors, foresters, too, needed judicious fire to cultivate their plantations and nurture their native regrowth. In Queensland they were, as Swain said of them, farmers for the state. They were in special circumstances—outside the principal fire regimes, outside the fire flume, outside mainstream developments in forestry and fire protection. In all probability these conditions were interdependent. It was because they lacked a stronger fire mission that foresters lacked a stronger institutional presence. Over most of Australia foresters were ex officio fire wardens, leaders in fire control. Queensland, however, designated graziers and selectors as "honorary rangers," an institutional inversion as great as the biotic inversion that preserved the pyrophobes at the core.

FIRE AS SYSTEM: WESTERN AUSTRALIA

In Western Australia—the most isolated state, the biotic enclave richest in endemism—Australian fire came together into a coherent system. Here the environment effervesced with fire, chronic rather than catastrophic. Human history unfolded with an uncanny equilibrium of social interests in which forestry acted like a flywheel, helping to synchronize fire practices within an institutional order. Fire use balanced fire control. From this most secessionist of fire provinces came the paradigm for a national strategy of fire protection.

The southwest had persistent fire, not perverse fire. Lightning has been an effective source of ignition, and regimes display adaptations to frequent fire that are, even by Australian standards, remarkable. Its subdued topography, its prevailing maritime winds, the constant production of new fuels that otherwise refused to decompose—all promoted smoldering burns and a ceaseless rekindling that kept fire on the landscape for long months. In December 1930 the Conservator watched a fire in jarrah creep through virgin forest for fifteen miles over the course of three months in what he believed approximated the ancestral pattern of southwest forest fires. Occasionally, large fires erupt when a high-pressure cell stagnates to the south or a tropical cyclone pounds the north, in both cases spraying desert winds across coastal mountains. But, overall, the prevalence of low-density burning circumscribed high-intensity outbreaks. Fires were impossible to exclude from the landscape, difficult to extinguish completely, and essential to indigenous ecology.[42]

Anthropogenic fire built on this pattern. Aboriginal burning was, according to early accounts, extensive. Scott Nind noted in 1827, for example, that the violence of Aboriginal fires "is frequently very great and extends over many miles of country; but this is generally guarded against by their burning it in consecutive portions." This pattern the Europeans both upset and co-opted. Effective colonization came late to Westralia; the earliest settlements faltered and then attempted to revive by requesting convicts even after transportation had been abolished elsewhere in Australia. With poor markets farming developed slowly. Pastoralism—wary of poisonous forbs and the poorly grassed understory of most southwest scleroforests—veered northward. Graziers in the southwest trailed fire as they migrated from mountain to sea, but their practices apparently mimicked those of the Aborigines. So did those of the "white blackfellow," the hunter of kangaroos and herder of wild ponies. Around settlements fire was a nuisance, and where land clearing had progressed widely, sometimes a menace. "By 1927," G. C. Bolton and D. Hutchison concluded, "the native grasses were largely eaten out; attempts to introduce prairie grass, timothy, white clover, and other exotics had largely failed; the land was neither rested, ploughed, nor fertilized." Around Manjimup farmers believed that fire and clearing had promoted scrub and undergrowth, for which the only solution was more fire and more clearing.[43]

Visiting the region in 1879, Ferdinand von Müller recognized that "forest-fires are not so excessively destructive as in the eastern colonies" and that there would be "practically no great difficulty in stopping bush-fires." But he admitted as well that fire suppression would bring "no great advantage . . . sooner or later fires will come, and the advantages gained by fires more than counterbalance the disadvantages." He thought the timber country could be burnt every four or five years. Better yet, "allow the fires as a rule to take their course—if possible every two or three years." Attempts to flog an export economy into existence through logging concessions changed this situation, heaping the landscape with untreated slash. This set in motion a more intense cycle of fire: the opened canopy encouraged drying of slash and the growth of scrub, the mountainous fuels intensified the fire threat, which prodded loggers into heavier cutting, and so on. Still, prior to 1920, Kessell believed that it "may be accepted as a literally correct statement" that the jarrah forest burned every three years. By the time real population flowed into the colony with the gold rushes of the 1890s substantial stands of the original forests still remained, and foresters were on the scene to battle agricultural interests for prime timber lands.[44]

Of all the Australian states, forestry in Westralia most closely followed the classic precepts and prescriptions that emerged out of the empire. Hutchins undertook his Grand Tour of Australia at the instigation of the Western Australia ministry responsible for forestry. Forest fires in Westralia, he regarded, as "neither so bad in their effects nor so difficult to control as in the more fertile climates and soils of the Eastern States." The karri forest he considered "self-protective"; the drier jarrah as easily protected "at slight expense"; and the wetter jarrah, "the most valuable forest in Western Australia," as a rewarding site for systematic fire protection. With fire control the entire forest region could be regularized. The empire formula was taken to heart by the first important Conservator, C. E. Lane-Poole. Lane-Poole, however, had a prickly personality, fought political interests constantly, and was forced into resignation after five years, just as the Forests Act of 1918 was becoming effective. His successor, Stephen Kessell, seized the fire problem and matured into one of the great figures of Australian forestry.[45]

A native of New South Wales, Kessell had been educated at Oxford, served with the Field Engineers of the Australian Imperial Force (AIF), and assumed duties as Acting Conservator at the tender age of twenty-four. He quickly revealed exceptional administrative talents. In 1923 he became Conservator, a post he held until 1942. This extraordinary tenure brought stability to forestry. When combined with Kessell's keen interest in fire protection and an environment that had lots of fire but not so many conflagrations that it could overwhelm early programs, the result was the best-balanced and most comprehensive fire establishment of all the states. Among his first acts as Conservator, Kessell ordered to be reprinted the conclusions of the light-burning controversy in America, brought district officers together for a conference on fire protection, and fully integrated fire programs into working plans. Quickly, priorities were established for protecting the varied lands under the Department's jurisdiction and for reducing a staggering backlog of untreated logging slash that littered the forests like open cans of gasoline waiting to explode.

There was no doubt about his commitment to systematic fire protection. "Absolute control of all fires in and around the forests," he insisted, "is the first and biggest step towards the establishment of Forestry . . ." Reviewing the debate about fire use in both America and Australia, he left no doubt that while he distrusted controlled fire he was enough of a pragmatist to use it extensively so long as the practice remained within the parameters of systematic forestry. He recognized, too, the value of burning for eucalypt regeneration. As experience with controlled burning grew, and as the context of controlled burning changed, such that it became an integral part of forestry, Kessell tolerated, then accepted, and finally encouraged burning as a legitimate practice of fire protection and silviculture. "Bush fire," he noted, was a generic term; and what he found objectionable about bush firing was its generic, indiscriminate application. "The fact that no organization has existed to cope with accidental outbreaks of fire in the forest" granted to graziers and others the chance to argue, "with some show of altruism," that their broadcast burnings were a public service. Kessell's reply to that claim was to instill organization.[46]

Everything that was done by way of fire protection elsewhere in Australia was done in Western Australia, but nowhere else did the array of practices show such consistency and coherence. Fuelbreaks, lookout towers, heliographs and telephone lines, resident foresters, pumps, motorized fire vehicles brought order to an archipelago of especially valued sites, while controlled burning kept down the bushfire threat posed by outside lands. As Lane-Poole recognized, the conditions for firefighting in Western Australia were remarkably "favorable," once organization was applied. By 1929 Kessell reported considerable progress, and fire protection went stride for stride with the expansion of working plans. When unemployment relief schemes made camps of laborers available for forestry projects, the Forests Department was ready for them.[47]

The measures came none too soon. The legacy of unregulated logging and unwise attempts at group settlement in undeveloped lands, which added land-clearing fires, kept the southwest enclave aboil. Almost annually bushfires raged around towns somewhere; not infrequently, they crowded the Perth suburbs. European settlement had transformed the relatively benign simmering of fire in the southwest enclave into a lethal cauldron such that fires attacked rural and forest lands alike. In 1917, a year not recognized in the literature as a bad season, Lane-Poole lectured about "serious forest fires," warning that there was "no doubt that fires are a more serious enemy than uncontrolled exploitation by sawmillers and timber hewers." There were bad fires in 1923–24, which confirmed the newly appointed Kessell in his belief that "successful fire control cannot be based on a strenuous personal effort only"; it required organization. The prime causes were railroads, "bee robbers," and general burning off. During the 1933–34 season, a fire weather station was established at Dwellingup to measure "fire hazards." [48]

But what made Westralia really distinctive was its organization of controlled burning. The kind of system foresters here brought to fire control they extended also to fire use. They insisted that burning off was not a simple remedy for inadequate protection. While it "must always play an important part in fire protection work," by 1927 Kessell admitted that "evidence is accumulating to show that systematic controlled burning is a difficult and expensive operation." What was required was organization: fire use had to be as systematic as fire control. The Westralian solution made burning and firefighting complementary, reinforcing practices of a single, rigorous system. It did not allow burning off to substitute for aggressive fire control, and it did not permit suppression to abolish the legitimate purpose of controlled burning. If the means were still inadequate, the ends to which they were applied were clear.[49]

The 1936–37 season—a fire rampage—broke apart any comfortable assumptions of steady progress. The Minister of Lands appointed the Rural Fire Prevention Advisory Committee to make inquiries and recommendations. It was obvious to the committee that the protected lands of all categories had suffered far less than the rural countryside and the unprotected forests. One outcome was the Bush Fires Act of 1937 which provided for bushfire brigades. The frightening fires confirmed Kessell in his conviction that fire protection was at the foundation of forestry and that the conversion of irregular to regular forests had to continue with all due speed. For that foresters needed control over fire in the surrounding lands.

The two needs coevolved. Increasingly, the community looked to foresters, as fire officers, for leadership in the fight against bushfires, and their firefighting mission strengthened their influence, as foresters, over public land use. Kessell summarized departmental wisdom into a practical yet comprehensive handbook of fire protection that could serve foresters and farmers equally. Chapters on prevention, fire control officers, brigade formation and management, and "fire prevention on the farm" brought to the problem of rural bushfires the same "organization" that had served the Forests Department so well. By now, too, the Forests Department was sponsoring programs of public education and had gained considerable experience in the outfitting and training of "fire gangs." Its dedication to systematic fire protection had committed the Forests Department to systematic forestry, and its commitment to the organization of the state forests granted it a commanding role in the organization of all the public lands of the state. It brought system to fire practice and, through fire, to land management.[50]

But the Westralian exemplar, thanks to Kessell, traveled farther. He took it to interstate conferences, to British Empire forestry conferences, to commissions empaneled to investigate great fires in the southeast, to the forestry inspection tours he conducted in New South Wales and Tasmania. It was Kessell who addressed the Third British Empire Forestry Conference in 1928 on the subject of fire protection in Australia, and it was to Kessell that Victoria, after the 1939 holocaust, dispatched a delegation to investigate how to reorganize its own fire protection programs. When Kessell served as Controller of Timber for the Commonwealth during World War II, it was, as Leslie Carron has written, probably the closest Australia has ever come to a "national forest policy."[51]

What happened with Kessell personally happened as well with the fire protection system he and his staff had nurtured for so many years. The essence of the Westralian system became the essence of an Australian system. When, following the 1939 holocaust and a global war, a new generation of foresters sought to restructure bushfire protection and to infuse it with Australian nationalism, they turned to Western Australia for inspiration. If the southeast posed the problem, the southwest advertised a solution.

16

When the Billy Boiled

But couldn't find a stick o'wood
To bile his billy by,
So stuck a match into the grass
Which then was pretty dry . . .
Five miles across that flamin' plain
He raced that fire did he,
But when at last the billy biled,
He 'ad forgot the tea!

—T. RANKEN, *"Mickey Mulga"*

"The fire?" exclaimed Bony innocently. "Ah, yes! . . . People will never learn.
You can conduct 'Safety First' campaigns till you're blue in the face, and they
won't learn. Heard a statesman talking on the radio, urging listeners to 'put out
that match.' One moron talking to a million."

—DETECTIVE-INSPECTOR NAPOLEON BONAPARTE,
in Arthur Upfield, The Battling Prophet

THE ERA OF EUROPEAN AUSTRALIA lasted roughly from the advent of the First Fleet to the conclusion of World War II. For a century and a half colonizing Britons had subjected Australia to disturbances on a scale, of a variety, and at a tempo the continent had never before experienced. Whether there was direction to that change—whether it was progress or vandalism—was unclear. What was undeniable was that the European swarm had invaded and disassembled the Australian landscape in apparently irreversible ways; that of all the disturbing elements the Europeans were the vital agents, the worst of the exotics, the one to which all the others related; that motion itself, whether as searching or restlessness, had become a fundamental attribute of the colonizers. Instructively, the era concluded, as it began, with a new wave of colonization from Europe.

301

The exploration and settlement of Australia were part of a global saga in which tens of millions of Europeans relocated to other continents; in many they became the dominant society. The ecological and social dislocations of that transfer were profound. Emigrants had to reconstitute their natural environment and redefine their cultural identity, the remaking of the one being integral to the reworking of the other, a dialectic of nature and culture. Australians shared in this larger epic, yet they encountered special circumstances and contributed special leitmotifs.

Their passage was an exile, often unwanted, from Europe. They confronted an environment without obvious precedent in the British Isles, an antipodean universe. It was difficult to transplant a European ethos, and problematic to invent a distinctive creation myth based on such singular principles of settlement in such a singular landscape. North America, of course, had sprouted penal colonies and practiced indentured servitude, but they were one group and one theme among many. Other groups, like the Puritan colonies, could, however implausibly, believe that they would ultimately reform England. Immigrants arrived out of promise, not from punishment. They chose to come. However overflowing their wanderlust, they wanted to settle or resettle.

That sentiment was harder to cultivate in Australia, even after free colonists replaced transported felons. Emigrants defined themselves less by what they hoped to create than by what they had left. Too often they unsettled, then moved on. Lacking a creation myth for Australian society, they often lacked a sense of legitimacy in the Australian landscape. What made Australia unique was its bush, and what made Australians unique among the peoples of the world was their encounter with that bush; so it comes as no surprise that when Australians fashioned a viable identity, it was that of bushman. Increasingly, however, they realized how profoundly the bush was something they themselves had created—or destroyed. That made the question of identity a cultural conundrum, as restless and unsettled as their bush stations, a walkabout without songlines. Inevitably, that quest, too, often ended as it began, with fire.

AUSTRALIAN DIALECTIC:
BUSH AND BUSHMAN

Australian immigrants were remarkably British, and they transplanted—almost by the phylum—the flora and fauna of the British Isles to the island continent. A British society required a British environment. But this ambition was difficult under Australian conditions. Only in hothouse urban enclaves could Australians recreate British society, and only on special sites could water, fertilizer, and constant tending remake the English countryside.

The resulting dissonance set up a new dialectic. In their amorphous bush Australians discovered the source for a new identity; in their encounter with that bush, a new creation myth; in the society that came into equilibrium with it, a new moral order. The bush created the great Australian type, the bushman.

The process was difficult, and the reconciliation prolonged. There were few environments that framed so stark a contrast as that between the island continent and the British Isles. Emigrants to North America found plenty of novelty, but with minor adjustments the old biotas could be approximated. Australia resisted that environmental transformation with an obstinant, baffling, defiant differentness. It frustrated attempts to reestablish sedentary agriculture, the conditions for English country life. The great sheep runs of interior Australia were almost a parody of British herding, one part of settlement allowed to overrun all the others. There was little prospect that English hamlets would nestle somnolently in stringybark backblocks. The one dimension of British society that Australians could reasonably approximate was the exaggerated metropolis, so the Australian colonies became city-states, echoes of London. Elsewhere environmental conditions frustrated a simple recreation of English social patterns.

What sharpened the disparity was the remarkable homogeneity of European immigration. Almost all of it derived from the United Kingdom. "It was English life over again: nothing strange, nothing exotic, nothing new or original, save perhaps in greater animation of spirits," observed J. A. Froude in the 1880s. Australian society was another branch of the English oak. The "Australian swarm is like the hive it sprang from." Unlike America, Australia did not attract wholesale immigration from Eurasia and Africa. And unlike America, it issued no declarations of autonomy and experienced no political or cultural revolution. Its outstanding political act, federation, kept it firmly within the British Empire. Australia retained the royal family of the United Kingdom as the royal family of Australia. Australia was Britain at the antipodes.[1]

But that self-image was never really accurate. Immigration had been a selective process, and transportion more so. Whatever their desires, emigrants could not recreate England from Australian materials without dissonance or parody. Manjimup would never become a Lincoln, or Bourke a Canterbury. Acclimatization societies were as disastrously misguided in their ambitions as in their deeds. Australia's exclusive origins initially as a penal colony complicated further the search for identity. That Australia might become "another America" was plausible, but not through the means that Americans had used. Moreover, while the American exemplar promised legitimacy, it only substituted one borrowed identity for another, one empire for a successor. That left the bush, the unique Australia, and cultural nationalists sought to turn that apparent liability into an asset. From the dialectic of bush and bushman, Australia could evolve a distinctive national creation myth that would explain, celebrate, and legitimize Australian society.

There were precedents for the bushman in Britain and analogues in America. Economic revolution had literally mobilized British society, leaving it increasingly footloose and dislocated. Convicts transported to Australia often belonged to what some historians have termed the "nomadic tribes of urban Britain," a land bustling with transients. There was the "habitual vagrant—half-beggar, half-thief—sleeping in barns, tents, and casual wards"; the "mechanic or tramp," on his way to seek work, a kind of industrial transhumance; the "urban and suburban wanderers, or those who follow some itinerant occupation in and round about the large towns . . ." Enclosure, urbanization, and industrialization produced swarms of British workers no longer bound to villages and no longer born to clear identities. Many fled Britain for overseas colonies. Those who remained advertised a British blight, a society in rapid flux, incompetent to reabsorb its own peoples.[2]

In Australia, however, everyone was, as an emigrant, a transient by nature. Often he or she was an outcast—certainly the heroes of early Australia were. The bizarre and unsettled conditions of Australia made transience a near-permanent state; and by adapting to the most Australian of those circumstances, the bushman became a symbol of reconciliation, a point man for civilization. What in Britain had been an outcast became in Australia—a nation in exile, a land of outcasts—a source of celebration. A bush that, to British eyes, appeared to be alien, empty, melancholy, and ineffable could, to Australians, become a source of character. Those bushmen who bravely confronted the land as explorers, squatters, diggers, migrant shearers, and the lot were endowed by that experience with fortitude, robustness, resourcefulness, mateship. On such values could Australia build a society.

For this there were American analogues. Young America sought distinctiveness in its wilderness and chose for its national folk hero the frontiersman. In its majestic rivers and mountains America had a reply to European castles and museums. From its encounter with wilderness—from its experience in recreating European civilization in a new place and on new principles—it derived a moral legitimacy, even a manifest destiny. The frontier was the great saga of American nationalism. The same year that Francis Adams announced that the bushman was "the one powerful and unique national type yet produced in Australia," American historian Frederick Jackson Turner read his provocative essay on "The Significance of the Frontier in American History." The white blackfellow and the white Indian were blood brothers. The belief that kangaroo hunters and lean bushmen would stymie any invader, that they were better equipped than effete Pommies to fight off Boers and Turks, had its American counterpart in the naive belief that all America needed to beat the British or Spanish were a few companies of Kentucky rifles. If anything the Australian version was far more civilized—

more literate, less violent—than the American. The Australian bushman might take collective action; he might strike, for example. The American frontiersman fled, unable to marry or construct a society, prone toward atavism, profoundly antisocial. What D. H. Lawrence said of the American hero of the wild, that he was essentially "isolate, stoic, a killer," had no real equivalent in Australian literature. While Australia produced bush epics like Tom Collins's *Such Is Life,* Americans were writing naturalist mythologies of violence like Owen Wister's *The Virginian* and Jack London's *The Call of the Wild.* [3]

There could be no bushman, however, without the bush. But British colonization had set in motion a biotic revolution in Australia that was actively disassembling the valorized landscape. A noble bushman required a noble bush—it might be hard, but it could not be rotten. To see the bush distintegrating before their touch, however, compromised the character of the bushman and gave the pioneering experience a dark side—the anti-epic, which communicated a haunting sense of failure, skepticism, and insecurity; the empty outback, a place in which those who persevered were punished and those who endured did so with stoic fatalism; the endless track to nowhere, in which comradeship dissolved into isolation, and society into mobs of industrial nomads; a history in which the noble bushman, the putative pioneer of civilization, ended as a half-mad swagman on an endless walkabout of exile. It was not simply that an imponderable bush had corroded European civilization; European civilization had destabilized the bush from which Australia sought to derive an identity.

There is a symbolic appropriateness, then, that a poem about a swagman should become a folk anthem. Banjo Patterson's "Waltzing Matilda" tells about a "jolly swagman" traveling from nowhere to nowhere who pauses only long enough to boil his billy. He spies a sheep, shoves the jumbuck into his tucker bag, is pursued by troopers for the theft, and defies them by drowning himself in a billabong. The poem, later set to music, is filled with Aussie slang and references to Australian features, but the swagman is not truly engaged with any of it. He is only passing through and lingers only long enough to set a fire, plunder, and commit suicide. What might have been a cautionary tale skips along on a cheery tune almost grotesquely at odds with the somber lyrics.

So, too, the celebration of the bushman, in all his avatars, seemed skewed when compared to the status of his sustaining bush. Unlike the jolly swagman, bush and bushman could not continue indefinitely what appeared to be a mutual suicide pact. There could be no reform of Australian society without reform of the Australian environment. There could be no new Australia without new Australians.

THE BLACK LEGEND OF THE NINETIES

By the 1880s interest in the question of national character took on some of the traits of an organized movement. Its heyday was a two-decade efflorescence that rather consciously sought a distinctive Australian identity and assembled, out of more or less indigenous materials—stories, songs, legends, images—the intellectual stuff from which a national myth could come and upon which national institutions could rely for legitimation. The Legend of the Nineties, Vance Palmer called it. But this fabled era of cultural nationalism was also an era of environmental crisis. The ripples sent out by European settlement bounced off the tank walls and rebounded to their source. Settlement had its dark side, often painted in the soot, pall, and scorch of bushfires.[4]

The movement had a dramatic debut in 1885, when the Sydney *Bulletin*, the self-styled "Bushman's Bible," began publication. Simultaneously, Tom Roberts, freshly infused with impressionism from Spain, returned to Australia to launch the Heidelberg school of landscape art. A year later, W. G. Spence became secretary of the Australian Shearer's Union. The nationalist movement concludes more impressionistically with a spectrum of events—the participation of Australian soldiers in the Boer War, which helped redefine Australia's place in the empire; the publication of such works as Tom Collins's *Such Is Life* (1903), A. B. Paterson's *The Old Bush Songs* (1905), Bernard O'Dowd's *The Bush* (1912); the Commonwealth Court of Conciliation and Arbitration (1904); the slow recovery from depression and drought that had together devastated the Australian economy and environment. Near its beginning stands the centennial of the First Fleet, celebrated in 1888. Near its end was the act of federation that welded the separate British colonies into a single Commonwealth of Australia on January 1, 1901. The intellectual chorus that accompanied and helped shape these events has become itself a source of cultural mythology.

Its search for a distinctive, justifying identity led inevitably to the bush, what Australia had that no place else possessed. Australian art, literature, science, political and social thought all telescoped on bush themes and bushman icons. The celebrated bushman of the 1880s—literate, endowed with a code of mateship, adapted to an imponderable environment—"looked upon himself as part of an advance-guard that was to shape a new social order." The Noble Bushman was tough, sardonic, independent, and resourceful. But he was also constructive, engaged, capable of collective action, somehow purified by passing through the refiner's fire of bush life. That most Australians lived in cities and that most promulgators of the bushman identity were urbanites mattered as little in Australia as did the promotion of the frontiersman by urban America.[5]

What made the movement ironic was that fin de siècle Australia was devastated by economic and environmental crises. A bank collapse began in 1891, then merged with the global depression of 1893. Within months some 40 percent of Australia's export income went to service its foreign debts. Except for the western goldfields, the ebullient flood of British capital that had watered Australia for four decades dried up. To worsen the scene, the Long Depression correlated almost exactly with the notorious Long Drought. From 1895 to 1903 the southern half of Australia endured rainfall deficits. Not every place suffered every year, but the droughts slowly strangled rural economies over much of the continent. Overextended wheat fields returned to bush. Overstocked ranges culled vast herds and blew away in clouds of dust. The rabbit plague reached catastrophic proportions. The mountains burned. The Red Centre expanded; society retreated. In the years following federation, Australia actually lost population.

Just as Australians began to understand their land, it appeared that they had perhaps damaged it—and themselves—beyond repair. The movement to assess the national character thus included a parallel survey of environmental change as observers began to appreciate the full magnitude of European colonization. In the double-decade-long debate over a national identity, Australians completed a first-order reconnaissance of Australia. Charles Raps discovered the rich deposits at Broken Hill, and others revealed the spangled goldfields of the west. Baldwin Spencer and Francis James Gillen completed their survey of Aboriginal life in the interior, and the great Australian exploring tradition, spearheaded by Douglas Mawson, departed for the Antarctic. At the time Francis Adams compiled his assessment of Australian society, long-time bushmen were reviewing their impact on the land.

The record of environmental deterioration built on facts amassed from every colony. In 1890 A. W. Howitt traced the pervasive effects of pastoralism on the biota of Gippsland. Dating from the earliest flocks to cross the mountains, the influence of settlement had propagated far beyond "lands devoted now to agriculture or pasturage, or by the earlier occupation by a mining population," Howitt concluded. In 1892 Alexander Hamilton presented to the Royal Society of New South Wales a detailed accounting of the "Effect which Settlement in Australia has Produced upon Indigenous Vegetation." While some of the consequences, Hamilton intoned, "are to a great extent capable of being remedied," others were beyond redemption. In Adelaide, Samuel Dixon that same year read before the Royal Society of South Australia a paper with nearly the same title and themes. "It is safe to conclude," Dixon declaimed, "that on the whole cultivation means absolute destruction to the Australian flora." His survey extended to Western Australia, noting that the devastation is "not so conspicious" owing to limitations on livestock and the abeyance, as yet, of rabbits. Richard Helms, ethnographer with the Elder expedition of 1891, reported to the Royal Geographical Society of Australasia of massive changes in the Australian Alps. Squatter curmudgeon Edward Curr detailed the endless deliberate and accidental changes in native biotas. By the 1890s royal commissions began to line library shelves with volumes on the unanticipated consequences of settlement. Collectively, these works stand as an environmental counterpart to the burgeoning literature of cultural nationalism.[6]

The uplifting bushman lived, it seemed, on a subsiding bush. Yet Australians could not, with impunity, destroy the bush they celebrated; they could not build a stable society, much less a national creation myth, on a land in shambles. The degradation of Australia's fantastic bush thus paralleled a deterioration in the character of the bushman into the shiftless cocky farmer, the kangaroo hunter, migratory gangs of ring-barkers and shingle-splitters, the swagman—exploitative, wasteful, ignorant, disengaged. Each brutalized the other, and it was with providential timing that economic disaster coincided with ecological disaster. By the 1890s Australians came to appreciate those costs. The Man from Snowy River saw the Snowy drying up or subjected to gully-gouging floods. The jolly swagman had to stay on his treadmill track because there was little permanent employment in a landscape grazed to nubbin.

Almost universally commentators included fire in their assessment of the environmental revolution—fires that were added by settlers and fires withheld by the elimination of the Aborigines, fires magnified or abolished by changes in fuels, fires kindled out of spite and fires escaped from under innocuous billys, feckless fires sent out into the bush, bushfires that returned to haunt settlement, fires stoked by decades of increased scrub and mountainsides of ring-barked tinder and hoofed flocks that stomped moisture out of compacted soils. The wandering tribes of Europeans left fires at every encounter. "The farmer, the squatter, the miner, and the swagman," Dixon decried, "all cause extensive conflagrations . . . with a recklessness which can only be fittingly described as insane." Constantly-recurring conflagrations, he thought, threatened "the very existence of the indigenous forests." Howitt attributed the deterioration of pastures, the invasion of eucalypts, and the worsening insect infestations to the removal of near-annual fires. Curr asserted that the Aboriginal firestick had induced anthropogenic changes as great as any produced by any people anywhere. Hamilton pondered the profound influence on the native flora of changes in fire practices. Impressive as was the impact of European fire, equally impressive were the consequences of removing Aboriginal fire. "The checking of the fires results in as great an effect in the opposite direction." When the British Association for the Advancement of Science visited Australia in 1914 the tour handbook explained that "one remarkable feature of settlement and of the restriction of the destructive forest fires, which used to burn for weeks without check, is the gradual encroachment of the thick belts of young timber on the lower slopes and foothills of the mountain ranges." Few changes failed to express themselves in fire, and few fire practices failed to propagate throughout whole ecosystems.[7]

European colonization had unleashed a biotic revolution that was fast becoming a reign of terror. While the bushman shared the paradox of all pioneering—destroying the circumstances that made him special—his saga carried a heavier burden for Australians. The shearers' strike that roared out of the bush with such profound social and political consequences witnessed a parallel revolution as the land rebelled against cumulative abuse. But what affected the bush would also affect a redefinition of national character and a recalculation of national legitimacy. Inevitably, when the revolution spilled over, it did so in the form of bushfire. The Black Legend ended in Black Friday.

BLACK FRIDAY

They remain the superlative Australian holocaust.

A week of burning that climaxed on Black Friday—January 13, 1939—sucked 150 years of settlement into a colossal maelstrom of fire. Everything that characterized Australian fires since European colonization was there, and nothing about the burns failed to reach toward hyperbole. Every cause contributed to its extensiveness, every resistance was mounted against its threat, every sentiment and response rallied in reaction. But it all broke down, language no less than institutions. The 1939 fires were a *Götterdämmerung* of European Australia. What the fall of Singapore was to Australian political history, Black Friday was to its environmental history.[8]

While the fires built wholly upon Australian experience, nothing prepared the Australians who experienced them for their scale and ferocity. "Men who had lived their lives in the bush went their ways in the shadow of dread expectancy," intoned a royal commission. But reality exceeded prior experience; accomplished bushmen had, upon reflection, simply "not lived long enough" to understand what might, "and did," happen. The 1939 holocaust signified a systemic breakdown in Australian fire practices and precepts that immediately established itself as the standard for disaster, the worst-case scenario against which every subsequent fire would be measured.[9]

The fires satisfied, then exaggerated, the classic formula for the fire flume. Drought parched the region—streams dried up, small townships saw their reservoirs shrivel into mud cracks, and metropoli instituted water rationing. A heat wave slowly crushed the landscape: temperatures reached a thermometer-shattering 117 degrees Fahrenheit in Adelaide and 114 degrees in Melbourne; they exceeded 120 degrees in rural hinterlands. Even along the coast relative humidity plummeted below 10 percent. As cold fronts brushed over the land, they set up a tidal flow of dry northerlies and cooler southerlies. Intense weather systems unleashed an avalanche of desert air. Fuel loads were nightmarish. Only the grasslands escaped, and that because drought and grazing had made them a desert, dried and eaten into dust. But the forests choked on dense, now desiccated fuels, the living and dead residue of European occupation. Even on reserved forests or protected crown lands, where settlers no longer slashed through the bush, sawmillers took their place, leaving a wide trail of "tops" behind them. Forest litter cracked underfoot. Logs had the moisture content of kiln-dried lumber. Two decades of patient labor by forestry commissions had made only marginal inroads at containing the hazard.

And of course there were ignitions by the fistful. Lightning kindled some fires, but most emanated from a register of casual incendiarists that reads like a roster of rural Australia: settlers, graziers, prospectors, splitters, mineworkers, arsonists, loggers and mill bushmen, hunters looking to drive game, fishermen hoping to open up the scrub around streams, foresters unable to contain controlled burns, bush residents seeking to ward off wildfire by protective fire, travelers and transients of all kinds. Honey gatherers lit smoking fires. Campers burned to facilitate travel through thick scrub. Locomotives threw out sparks along their tracks. A jackeroo tossed lighted matches alongside a track so that his boss would know where he was. Residents hoping to be hired to fight fires set fires. Possibly a third of the documented fires had no known cause. A self-styled bushman shrugged off the multiple sources by explaining to the royal commission that "the whole of the Australian race have a weakness for burning." [10]

Conditions leveraged the fires into monstrous proportions. Fires roared through the fire triangle of South Australia, overran the Australian Capital Territory, and virtually laid siege to Tasmania; every place they appeared they established a new year of record. The worst conflagrations savaged the mountains of Victoria—the "most disastrous forest calamity the State of Victoria has known," Royal Commissioner Judge Leonard E. B. Stretton concluded. It was nothing less than an "invasion" of bushfires, and no one has ever matched Stretton's forceful rendition of its consequences.

Seventy-one lives were lost. Sixty-nine mills were burned. Millions of acres of fine forest, of almost incalculable value, were destroyed or badly damaged. Townships were obliterated in a few minutes. Mills, houses, bridges, tramways, machinery, were burned to the ground; men, cattle, horses, sheep, were devoured by the fires or asphyxiated by the scorching debilitated air. Generally, the numerous fires which during December, in many parts of Victoria, had been burning separately, as they do in any summer, either "under control" as it is falsely and dangerously called, or entirely untended, reached the climax of their intensity and joined forces in a devastating confluence of flame on Friday, the 13th of January. On that day it appeared that the whole State was alight. At midday, in many places, it was dark as night. Men carrying hurricane lamps, worked to make safe their families and belongings. Travellers on the highways were trapped by fires or blazing fallen trees, and perished. Throughout the land there was daytime darkness. At one mill, desperate but futile efforts were made to clear of inflammable scrub the borders of the mill and mill settlement. All but one person, at that mill, were burned to death, many of them while trying to burrow to imagined safety in the sawdust heap. Horses were found, still harnessed, in their stalls, dead, their limbs fantastically contorted. The full story of the killing of this small community is one of unpreparedness, because of apathy and ignorance and perhaps of something worse.

Steel girders and machinery were twisted by heat as if they had been of fine wire. Sleepers of heavy durable timber, set in the soil, their upper surfaces flush with the ground, were burnt through. Other heavy wood work disappeared, leaving no trace. Where the fire was most intense the soil was burnt and destroyed to such a depth that it may be many years before it shall have been restored by the slow chemistry of Nature. Acres upon acres of the soil itself can be retained only by the effort of man in a fight against natural erosive forces.

The speed of the fires was appalling. They leaped from mountain peak to mountain peak, or far out into the lower country, lighting the forests 6 or 7 miles in advance of the main fires. Blown by a wind of great force, they roared as they travelled. Balls of crackling fire sped at a great pace in advance of the fires, consuming with a roaring, explosive noise, all that they touched. Houses of brick were seen and heard to leap into a roar of flame before the fires had reached. Some men of science hold the view that the fires generated and were preceded by inflammable gases which became alight. Great pieces of burning bark were carried by the wind to set in raging flame regions not yet reached by the fires. Such was the force of the wind that, in many places, hundreds of trees of great size were blown clear of the earth, tons of soil, with embedded masses of rock, still adhering to the roots; for mile upon mile the former forest monarchs were laid in confusion, burnt, torn from the earth, and piled one upon another as matches strewn by a giant hand.[11]

These were not the words of panicked survivors or of relief committees trying to rally public sympathy or of tabloid journalists hawking sensationalism. They were the reasoned conclusions of a royal commissioner, a professional juror, following four months of unremitting testimony. Stretton's commission was a stinging indictment of Australian fire practices and the apathy they engendered. If the 1939 fires became the yardstick for future catastrophes, the Stretton report became the reference for future reform.

The savagery of the fires frightened all who had contact with them. After the royal commission released its report, an interstate conference on bushfires convened in Melbourne. Its delegates included the elite of Australian forestry; every state, along with the Commonwealth, sent representatives. Swain, Kessell, G. J. Rodger, S. W. Steane, A. V. Galbraith, Lane-Poole —all were present. Yet more fires followed, and a global war added urgency to the organization of rural fire defense; together they ensured that this fire, unlike its predecessors, would not conclude with a relief committee for the victims, a bureaucratic shudder, the unread reports of constituted officialdom, and a return to fatal apathy. All the states quickly enacted new bushfire acts and organized bushfire brigades, and those in the southeast suite inaugurated major overhauls of their forestry and rural fire programs. Kessell solicited a special report on the 1939 fires and instructed his district foresters to ensure protection for small settlements and sawmills. Victorian foresters traveled to Western Australia for advice. The prospect for a truly national strategy toward bushfire was at hand.

The shock of the fires—their fantastic damage to a country that considered itself civilized—accounts for part of the dramatic reaction. But Stretton, too, deserves praise. His forceful prose brought the matter squarely before the people. The judge showed an unflinching commitment to uncover facts at a time when "the truth was hard to find." Evidence before the commission had been colored by self-interest, much of it had been false, and little unequivocally true. It was as if Australians could not bring themselves to admit the reality of what had occurred or to confess the full complexity of the tragedy or their collective complicity in it. Nothing less than a full reformation of how Australians related to the bush could prevent another catastrophe. Yet that, Stretton knew, was enormously difficult.

The royal commissioner revealed the depth of that task in his rhetoric. Forceful, stentorian, even regal in its perspective, Stretton rendered his account of the Victorian fires—surely the most celebrated expression of that set piece of Australian literature, the bushfire—almost wholly in the passive voice. "These fires were lit by the hand of man." The fires happened to people and to forests. Before such fury everyone was prostrate, and every act futile. The busy but distended and disorganized programs of the Forests Commission proved worthless when confronted with such a holocaust. It was not possible to speak in the active voice or to behave in proactive ways. Yet someone had to do something. European Australia was capable of generating similar conditions again.

Effective reform demanded that programs be in place long before climatic crescendos like Black Friday. Stretton did not wish to banish Australians from their public forests; and he recognized the necessity for anthropogenic fire to make access meaningful. This led him to a keen interest in controlled burning as a compromise. He chastised the Forests Commission of Victoria for failing to practice controlled burning on a scale sufficient to influence major bushfires. Graziers blamed the disaster on foresters who had shut down their routine burning off of the bush, but Stretton went beyond their outbursts of sclf-interest. The Forests Commission, he stated point-blank, had "failed" to recognize "a truth which is universal, namely, that fire prevention must be the paramount consideration of the forester." [12]

Foresters had sought to protect forests from settlement fires, not settlements from forest fires. Instead of active intervention, they had relied on nature to control fuels, "upon the growth of forest canopy to suppress inflammable scrub." That left after-the-fact suppression as a response, and the means at hand were woefully—inevitably—inadequate to control a conflagration. In particular, Stretton charged that the responsible officials had refused "to use burning as a general preventive method," despite substantial evidence that "burning is the only effective safeguard." When Stretton's report appeared, it stuffed page after page with minute recommendations on every aspect of bushfire protection as it argued for a never-idle "protecting hand of man." But it also sanctioned, for the first time from an official source, controlled burning for fuel reduction. [13]

That argument, no less than his passive voice, stemmed from an understanding of what Australia was and how Australians had to relate to it. The issue came out clearly in testimony from Lane-Poole, who confessed like everyone else that the bush was more overgrown and fire-prone than when the first Europeans saw it. It was Lane-Poole's belief that natural succession, if uninterrupted, would purge the understory of woody scrub and bracken; that if Europeans only kept fire out of the bush for a long enough time, it would evolve into a more manageable, less explosive state. "The thickening up of our forests," he explained, "is entirely due to fire and the exclusion of fire will render them less susceptible to fire because it will get rid of an enormous amount of inflammable material." Any fire, from any source, however, would block that succession. [14]

Stretton agreed with the cause but disagreed with the consequence. Settler fires had established a "cycle of destruction" that could not, he admitted, be arrested "in our day." Each degradation had led to more fire. "The scrub grew and flourished, fire was used to clear it, the scrub grew faster and thicker, bushfires, caused by the careless or designing hand of man, ravaged the forests; the canopy was impaired, more scrub grew and prospered, and again the cleansing agent, fire, was used." But where Lane-Poole believed that the exclusion of fire would reverse this trend, Stretton doubted that fire *could* be excluded. Over and again he pressed Lane-Poole for an estimate on how many years such a reversion would require. [15]

The answer, Lane-Poole confessed, "is that we have not done it yet in

Australia. Fires have always come in before we have been able to reach that position . . ." To Stretton's mind, those fires would always come in, and the fire flume would whip even casual ignitions into conflagrations once they entered heavy fuels parched by drought; such fires would quickly incinerate any prospect for control. It was impossible in Australia to keep fire out of the bush long enough for any such hypothetical state as Lane-Poole's to emerge. Whatever its original condition, whatever alternative states the bush might assume, fires would invade it. The Australian reality was fire; the only compromise was to control that fire before it escalated; and the only means of control was, paradoxically, fire.[16]

Ultimately Stretton's dispute with Lane-Poole went beyond conflicting hypotheses about what the unburned bush looked like and how it lived: their quarrel involved differing perceptions about what it meant to be an Australian and about how Australians should live. Lane-Poole—the urbane Englishman with the hyphenated last name, the product of French forestry and British Empire, a man who peppered his lectures at the Australian Forestry School with long quotations in French—argued that Australia could evolve into another Europe. Stretton replied that the Australian bush would never allow that to happen. An Australian, Stretton implied, had to accept Australian conditions. An Australian had to use fire to survive.

"WHO'LL COME A-WALTZING MATILDA WITH ME?"

The debate about the character of the Australian bush was inseparable from the debate about the character of the Australians. As both Lane-Poole and Stretton knew, bushfires existed not only because of Australia's physical climate but because of its climate of opinion. The fires of 1939 had been lit "by the hand of man," and if Australians were to stay them, if Australians were to reconcile themselves with their continent, then they had to stay that contriving hand. Ultimately a fire conscience would arrive only after the emigrants established a commitment to Australia, after they attached themselves permanently to the island continent, remaking it even as they allowed it to remake themselves. The worst pest was not prickly pear or the rabbit but the peripatetic Briton; and he, no less than those other exotics, had to be naturalized. Until the 1939 fires Australian society had treated bushfires with a casualness, with an almost calculated indifference, that typified its own unsettled state. If bushfires were large, there was nothing anyone could do to stop them. If they were not large, then there was no need to do anything. It was a fatalism that could thrive only in a society that regarded itself as helpless or transient or both. No worries, mate.

So, in the end, one comes back to the ambivalent bushman, the Australian Adam. To the competing visions of the Australian bush proposed by

Stretton and Lane-Poole, there were competing images of the Australian bushman—one, the Noble Bushman intent on building a new society, and the other, the Swagman, the colonial as sundowner on an endless walkabout through the outback of empire, living off begged or pilfered scraps of culture. After drought and depression blighted the glowing promise of nationalism, both land and society receded into an uneasy exhaustion.

It is symptomatic of the interwar years that the great achievement in Australian fiction, *The Fortunes of Richard Mahony*, was penned by a Melbourne woman (Mrs. Ethel F. Robertson) writing under a male pseudonym (Henry Handel Richardson) for a London audience about a man who was unable to live in either England or Australia, for whom home was a ceaseless passage between the two. While the Great War forced a reexamination of Australia's relationship to Britain, the postwar era suggested that the new political pieces—now dominions, not colonies—could be reassembled and the empire preserved. Australians could imagine their nation as a province more geographically remote from London than Cornwall or Yorkshire but culturally interchangeable with them. Australian intellectuals told one another that they could survive only by being Englishmen. Alan Moorehead recalled that "as far as possible the local environment was ignored; all things had to be a reflection of life in England"; writers ached with a "yearning to go back to their lost homes on the other side of the world . . ." Britons who cared told them otherwise. George Bernard Shaw scornfully replied that "you Australasians are extraordinary, really. Every year, thousands of you . . . journey to see an inferior country which you persist in calling Home in spite of the fact that its people ignore you and are scarcely aware of your existence." Make Australia your home, he admonished. Stay. Settle.[17]

Slowly, often reluctantly, as much from exhaustion as from design, Australians did just that. They undertook schemes of social and environmental rehabilitation. They installed or recharted forestry commissions. Pastoralism retreated to more manageable populations. Mining paused, burrowing into the earth rather than sprawling across it, converting its accumulated capital to other industries like steel. Despite a few misguided settlement schemes, the domain of farming stabilized. "Sub and super" intensified yields and rebuilt wasted paddocks. Immigration slowed. Australians became naturalized, if not indigenous. Out of the environmental and economic wreckage of the early twentieth century, it seemed to some that Australia could reconstitute its fragmented land into something special, autonomous, and isolated—in fact, special by virtue of its bush and autonomous by virtue of its isolation.

None of this was remote from Australian fire practices. Only a fraction of Australia's founding colonists came as permanent settlers. Most expected to get their ticket-of-leave and return Home, or to make their fortunes and reestablish themselves in British society. Yet, for many reasons, a great majority stayed and were joined by others. Psychological acclimatization lagged, however. That Australia experienced no overt political revolution further deferred a cultural revolution. Environmental deterioration—the mangled scrub, the eruption of conflagrations—reflected that uncertain identity. The mere movement, the ceaseless friction of settlement, kept Australia chronically afire. Many European fire practices were extractive or exclusive: they tended to "mine" the bush like placers or to convert it to approximations of unburnable English fields and gardens. More typically, the European émigré lingered only long enough to boil a billy and leave.

The billy fire, not the hearth fire, was the essential symbol of European colonization. It was everywhere. In its pervasiveness the billy fire replaced the ubiquitous Aboriginal campfire. "Few Australians can be in a forest for long without wanting a taste of the national drug," Hutchins scowled, and he harbored no doubts that "boiling the billy" had "much to do with forest fires in Australia." The casual indifference to lighting billy fires was the sign of an impermanent society uneasy in its surroundings. The bushman was a scleromorph habituated to fire. With his wax match—so flammable, one critic observed, that it practically ignited on casual contact, and packaged "in a box that seems to have been specially designed for the spilling of them"—the bushman trailed fire wherever he went. Burning off was often little more than a billy fire without the billy. The 1939 holocaust was a billy fire that spilled across a state.[18]

Those fire practices had their psychological dimension, too. If Australian expatriates in the interwar years spoke endlessly of a sense of alienation, a "loneliness," so did those who lived in the bush. Certainly the sentiment was strong in the writings of Lawson and White and others who moved beyond reflex chauvinism. The bushman, it seems, was also a kind of internal expatriate. The great charge laid against bush life was its brutalizing sense of loneliness. The supreme terror was the almost palpable presence of the Great Australian Emptiness, as Patrick White termed it. And to this condition bushfires were both contributor and symbol.

Much as there were two perspectives on the bush and two bushmen, so there were two bushfires. The one promoted community, the other pulverized social cohesion into a terrifying isolation. Bushfires were an environmental constant, and fighting them was an act of social solidarity, a tableau of nation building like felling forests and raising towns. But there was that special bushfire, peculiarly Australian, against which action seemed futile. By a kind of psychological pyrolysis, it dissolved social bonds and scattered individuals into its convective firestorm. Such a fire was Black Friday. Its survivors spoke frequently of the overpowering loneliness they felt as the terror approached. That millennial fire illuminated, exaggerated, and blasted a sense of place and being. Some bush folk fled for refuge to dugouts or sawdust mounds where they huddled together. Others took to bush tracks and roads in a "longing for human company." Those who fled were often among the casualties, blinded by smoke, confused and disoriented by noise in a frantic rush for companionship.[19]

Black Friday was a parable of misplaced—unplaced—Australian nationalism. Australians could not abolish bushfires any more than they could abolish the bush, but somehow they had to engage both constructively. Only then could they expunge the great loneliness, which was the expression of an alienating environment produced by an alienated people listening to the ghostly, mocking refrain from the billabong, "Who'll come a-waltzing Matilda with me?" How Australians used and reacted to fire thus encapsulated how they lived in and related to Australia. Reforms in fire practices demanded a reformed bush; a reformed bush demanded, as it would help create, a reformed bushman; a new Australia necessitated a new Australian.

BOOK IV

The
New Australian

17

The Two Fires

In the beginning was the fire;
Out of the death of fire, rock and the waters;
and out of water and rock, the single spark, the divine truth. . . .
The leaves of fallen years, the forest of living days,
have caught like matchwood. Look, the whole world burns.
The ancient kingdom of the fire returns.

> —JUDITH WRIGHT,
> *"The Two Fires" (1955)*

These sons shall be Australia's, only hers;
the firesticks of their minds will soon relight
the scattered camp-fires of Australia's dream.

> —IAN MUDIE, *"All Things Exist*
> *in This Our Country's Scene"*
> *(1943)*

THE 1939 FIRES ANNOUNCED a cascade of new fires that, over a period of fifteen years, pummeled every state. But the fires of Black Friday, awesome as they were, paled before a flame kindled later that year in Europe as Nazi Germany invaded Poland—the onset of a global conflagration that would sweep over all of Australian society. As the Imperial Japanese Army captured Hong Kong and bore down on Singapore in December 1941, Prime Minister John Curtin issued his famous declaration that "without any inhibitions of any kind, I make it quite clear that Australia looks to America, free of any pangs as to our traditional links or kinship with the United Kingdom." In February 1942 Broome and Darwin were bombed and burned in what appeared to foreshadow a Japanese invasion of the Australian continent.[1]

Both events, in their own way, shocked Australians out of their complacency. The realization grew that Britain could no longer sustain Australia.

The military alliance with America foreshadowed a general realignment of Australian political, economic, and social interests, and it announced that the time had come to reassess Australian identity in terms other than as a compliant member of the British Empire. In analogous fashion, Black Friday trumpeted an explosive breakdown in traditional fire practices, a collapse that required new relationships with the bush. The two catastrophes, in curious ways, joined. The war ensured that reforms in bushfire protection would participate in a larger social dynamic, that they had an institutional momentum and nationalistic fervor that could propel them across a generation. Out of the two fires—the Australian and the global—came a New Australia and a new Australian strategy toward fire.

NEW PEOPLES, NEW LANDS:
COLONIZING NEW AUSTRALIA

The reformation began with demographics. In 1945 Australia had a population of 7.3 million, almost exclusively descended from the British Isles. The military implications alone shocked authorities. Acting Prime Minister Francis Forde warned that "history will some day reveal how close Australia was to being overrun . . . We might not be given another chance." Quickly overturned were the White Australia policy, the restrictions on assisted immigration for non-British peoples, and the declining birth rates among native-born Australians. In their place Australia expanded its categories for assisted immigration, accepting large numbers of European refugees; it promoted Asian immigration in acknowledgment of its anomalous political geography; and it saw birth rates soar, as they did in North America. By 1959 the Australian population had climbed to 10 million; by 1972, to 13 million. Not just its total numbers but its relative rate of increase—the sudden reapportioning of age classes and ethnic groups—made that growth explosive. Collectively, postwar demographics created a population of "New Australians," a society who grew up in radically different circumstances than that of their predecessors.[2]

The demographic boom paralleled an economic boom; Australia experienced its greatest economic expansion since the depression of the 1890s. But the prosperity centered largely on metropolitan capitals. This selective enrichment encouraged an internal migration within Australia from the rural landscape to the urban. By the late 1970s some 85 percent of the population lived in the urban penumbra of what were fast becoming city-states. Australia—the land of the bush—became one of the most urbanized nations on the planet. Not even the great mineral discoveries of the 1970s could inspire a reverse migration back to a rural economy. Instead, after a postwar flush, rural economies reached steady state, or faltered. Land for which earlier generations could conceive of no higher use than to foster farms and pastures decayed into marginality.[3]

Soon the New Australians put them to new uses. The metropolitan centers sprawled and leapfrogged into adjacent lands to create an "urban bush." Exurbanites formed a new class of gentry, even claiming moral title (if only by default) from their predecessors who had cut, plowed, shot, burned, and otherwise ravaged indigenous Australia. Under public pressure, authorities reconsidered the automatic leasing of crown lands to pastoralists, and began to reclassify substantial territory as national parks, nature reserves, protected lands of one kind or another. The clearing of the highlands in antipodean Australia swept the countryside of sheep. "Unproductive forests"— mallee, brigalow, red gum, low-grade scleroforest—were felled to make room for exotic plantations, sown pastures, or intensive agriculture. Hobby farmers and recreational landowners flourished. Communes appeared in semiwild bush, a bizarre avatar of traditional programs of group settlement. Aborigines fought to reclaim ancestral lands as permanent reserves. Conservation societies expanded exponentially; bushwalking became a popular pasttime; an inchoate passion to promote "Australian" flora and fauna and to save unravaged remnants of native biotas became widespread, an attempt to green the implacable Red Centre. The tourist replaced the swagman as the archetypal Australian nomad. Australia's environment underwent a massive, largely conscious reconstitution.

The new people sought a new culture by which to define themselves and the interdependence they nurtured with their new lands. Increasingly, this took the form of a binocular vision between Britain and America. Britain never departed completely, and America never claimed all the vacated territory. The decisive blows from Britain probably came when the Common Market replaced the commonwealth as the focus of the British economy; and even then a few knighthoods could seemingly restore the balance of trade. The American "cultural invasion," like the Pax Americana, was short-lived. The Vietnam War too much resembled Gallipoli and the Boer War, other foreign misadventures to which allied empires had dragged Australians; Japan, not America, became the economic dynamo of the Pacific; and American popular culture, while pervasive, remained a playful veneer over more traditional language and mores. While it lasted, however, the American presence was a powerful, polarizing magnet, both attracting and repulsing. In the end, one empire substituted for the other only around the margins. The center belonged to New Australia. Led by Russell Drysdale, artists replaced their Grand Tour of Europe with a sojourn through the Outback; what had been dismissed as a void became an inspiration. As it reinterpreted that Red Centre, New Australia transformed what had seemed a vacuum—the Great Australian Emptiness—into the moral axis of a new society.

The new peoples, the new political and economic alliances, the new landscapes, the tempo of cultural ferment in the arts and sciences—together they amounted to a recolonization of Australia, and collectively they inspired a new query into the Australian identity. The core of the new lands, the least trammeled bush, became the core of that quest. Society sought to preserve the native bush because it was "Australian"; in return, the bush promised to justify and legitimize its preserving society. To encounter the bush, however, was to encounter bushfires.

PASSING THE TORCH

Aftershocks of Black Friday shook Queensland in 1941, and a swarm of new conflagrations invaded the fire flume in 1943–44. In New South Wales massive fires burned through the Blue Mountains and swept hundreds of thousands of hectares in the Western District, in Tasmania they replayed 1939, they tested the newly organized bushfire brigades of the Australian Capital Territory (A.C.T.), and of course they roared through Victoria. Fires claimed ten lives and a score of casualties at Wangaratta, including a brigade unit that was burned over when their truck stalled on an embankment. Bushfires entered Hamilton, where they incinerated over ninety homes, and Yallourn, where they raged through a township under the complete jurisdiction of the State Electricity Commission of Victoria. They sacked Beaumaris, a Melbourne suburb, where they killed at least nineteen persons and leveled sixty-three residences. The Beaumaris blowup came almost five years to the day after Black Friday. The Yallourn debacle inspired another royal commission under the indefatigable Judge Stretton.[4]

The breakdown in fire protection was universal—at Yallourn, by a state commission; at Hamilton, by small towns; at Beaumaris, by suburbanites; in the Western Districts, by rural Australians. The collapse could not be blamed on manpower shortages occasioned by the war. An inquiry into the Beaumaris disaster identified as a major cause of damage the subdivisions that had been allowed "to return to their natural state" and had been stuffed with planted exotics. Stretton's inquiry at Yallourn was a cameo of cause and consequence. The fire originated from a scrub burn by a farmer who had obtained a burning permit from the Forests Commission; but it was impossible, Stretton concluded, to determine what the authorization actually permitted and whether the permission had been lawfully given. The actions of both parties had been imprudent, but not illegal. Likewise, although the means were at hand to protect the township, they lacked any system. "There was no general plan of any real value." Attempting to trace out an organization chart, Stretton threw up his hands in despair because of "vagueness and lack of definition." Volunteers did not even know to whom they could report. Presuppression measures, particularly protective burning, were at best inadequate. Stretton stressed that the failure "to take this ordinary precaution" was a prime cause for the near-demolition of Yallourn and the narrow escape of the exposed coal pits. Areas that had been burned the year previous were "unscathed," he noted—"green oases in a wilderness of destruction." Apart from their scale, except for the context of the war, it was 1939 recycled.[5]

But that context did matter. If the war emergency temporarily denied land agencies the means by which to halt fires, it did confirm for them the proper ends. It nationalized fire consciousness, associated bushfire with enemy invasion, taught something about the power of organization and the value of common action, and stimulated the formation and reformation of bushfire brigades, which could be considered a form of civil defense. Eventually, every state and territory promulgated new bushfire legislation and promoted some form of bushfire brigades. After the 1944 outbreak Victoria hurriedly passed the Country Fire Authority Act, which divided fire responsibilities outside Melbourne between the Forests Commission (for state and crown lands) and the newly constituted Country Fire Authority, which oversaw rural fire brigades. The A.C.T. inaugurated the practice of leasing some 20,000 hectares from New South Wales in order to control illegal fires along a vulnerable border. In 1946 Stretton chaired yet another royal commission, this one focusing on forest grazing. The report merged the debate about appropriate land use with concern over fire practices, and it kept Stretton's convictions about the means and ends of Australian fire protection firmly in the public eye.[6]

Stretton's long service on fire-related royal commissions ensured continuity as well as conviction. The conclusions of one commission he repeated in the next. His stature placed the issue of bushfires beyond the confines of professional forestry no less than outside rural folklore: he criticized all parties even as he empathized with their peculiar problems. Stretton's perspective was fundamentally that of a jurist, mindful of precedent, anxious to eliminate confusion and contradiction. He sought a new codification of fire practices, not their abolition. If he sanctioned controlled fire, he demanded that it and suppression be organized. But with remarkable suddenness after the war, the torch passed to a new generation, and it incited a quiet revolution in Australian fire.

The new men and new means became apparent by 1947 with two seminal publications, one that stated the environmental problem and the other that announced a social solution. J. C. Foley, a climatologist with the Commonwealth Bureau of Meteorology, released his massive *Study of Meteorological Conditions Associated with Bush and Grass Fires and Fire Protection Strategy in Australia* in order to make public "in sufficient detail" the "widespread nature of such calamities," and to lay out the immutable geographic circumstances that make large fires so routine a phenomenon in Australia, conditions that must be accepted by any strategy of bushfire protection. He opened with a long quotation from Stretton's 1939 report; elaborated a text-book summary of fire behavior principles, fire hazard indices, and fire weather forecasts; and concluded with a numbing digest of historic fires for every state. As if in response, that same year R. H. Luke, a young forester, published *An Outline of Forest Fire Control Principles for the Information of New South Wales Foresters*, which he intended to serve as a training manual for the fire-control schools recently inaugurated for field officers. Both men drew heavily upon North American literature and examples.

Already the remarkable realignment of Australia from a wholly British to partially Americanized culture had begun. In 1947 Great Britain hosted the Fifth British Empire Forestry Conference. At the time Britain was reforming its own fire services with new legislation and a national reorganization. The Hill Farming Act (1946) and the Heather and Grass Burning Act (1949) upgraded the regulations regarding controlled burning in England and Wales (Scotland had separate statutes to govern muir burning). The new laws restricted the firing of fodder—grass and heather—to certain seasons and then under the issuance of a license, but anyone could at any time burn waste-lands of gorse, bracken, scrub, or other material. Simultaneously, the Fire Services Act (1947) nationalized fire protection, both urban and rural, by building on the de facto unification of British fire services during the war. British foresters were initially skeptical of their "country" fire services, but the law required the brigades to put out all fires under their jurisdiction—and that included forests. In fact, some rural brigades became "acutely forest-fire conscious" and foresters came to rely on them routinely—an example not lost on Australia, though South Australia felt it most keenly.[7]

The more dramatic reforms, however, were international. The 1947 Empire Forestry Conference was held in Great Britain, but the empire was already breaking up. The keystone, India, gained independence later that year; South Africa quickly followed. Australia and Canada, not the colonies of Greater Gondwana, dominated discussion about fire. For overseas experience and exemplars Australians looked instead to North America. If artists went to the Outback instead of Europe, foresters traveled to Canada and the United States. That firefighting resembled a paramilitary activity made the American ascendancy all that more compelling, for it seemed only natural that a firefighting alliance could complement the military alliance.

The postwar era was, for America, a glorious epoch in fire suppression. Particularly after the Korean War the liberation of surplus war materials allowed firefighting in America to mechanize overnight, most spectacularly with aircraft. While Britain fretted over thatch brooms and uniform hose couplings, American foresters waged a strategic air war on fire. In 1947 the U.S. Forest Service experimented with a "continental unit" that subjected a large chunk of the Rocky Mountains to airborne firefighting—aerial detection, aerial attack by smokejumpers, aerial support by paracargo, even attempts at aerial waterbombing; plans were floated for a force of aerial "shock troops" to sustain campaign fires. Whatever sentimental and ceremonial ties bound Australia to Britain—and they remained remarkably durable—the practical future pointed to North America.

There were, of course, ample precedents for Australian interest in North American fire. Victoria had made imitation a passion. Swain had traveled to America in 1917, and W. D. Muir repeated that tour in 1944. American foresters from time to time visited Australia. *Australian Forestry* routinely reprinted interesting articles from North American journals. As a fellow dominion in the empire, Canada became an increasingly important conduit for all North American ideas. Foley and Luke relied heavily on North American literature as they wrote their *Study* and *Outline,* respectively. When in 1951 the FAO (United Nations' Food and Agriculture Organization) organized its first forest-fire study tour, it traveled to North America, and the entourage included two Australians, Luke and E. R. Torbet, fire control officers for New South Wales and Victoria, respectively.

It was symptomatic that neither remained long enough to attend the next British Commonwealth Forestry Conference, held in Ontario. Luke brought back a small cache of literature—plans for hand tools like the McLeod, a U.S. Forest Service training booklet on water use, model fire plans from Petawawa, Ontario, bushels of published documents, and new ideas for cooperative fire protection. The contrast between Australia and America was startling. Like many American developments, firefighting was an institution of abundance. It was impossible, Luke noted, not to be gluttonous during the lavish American meals, and it was difficult not to remark on the relative disparities in funding available to fire organizations in the two countries. Regardless, "words cannot explain the feeling of inspiration" he derived from his six-week tour. "To try and pass on this feeling to one's fellow Australians—that is the problem." [8]

One means was to upgrade the *Outline;* another was to adapt some institutions. "The idea of co-operative organization," Luke later wrote, was "borrowed from the Americans and wedded to the Australian concept of volunteer bush fire brigades." (The American model of voluntary cooperation contrasted favorably with the more compulsory British model that followed nationalization.) Other Australians also picked up bits and pieces of Americana and tried to adapt them to Australian conditions. Concluding his 1952 description of the Cann Valley, D. M. Thompson even argued for a combination of controlled burning, a method locally sanctioned though "abhorrent to the scientific forester," and aerial fire suppression crews, "as is current practice in America." [9]

There was ferment aplenty, but whether it could lead to fundamental reforms depended on whether the momentum of 1939 and 1944 could continue, and that depended in part on whether large fires persisted. In fact, they did, almost as though they were scripted. On his return from North America, Luke saw bushfires burning across Fiji, "a foretaste," he wrote, "of much worse conditions in N.S.W."—the mammoth fires of 1951–52.[10]

SNOWY RIVER: THE EMERGENCE OF AN AUSTRALIAN SYSTEM

Within a decade after the war the pieces of an Australian system of bushfire protection came together into a coherent whole. The parts gathered from all over Australia, and they forged a *national* strategy. Western Australia reformed its plans and operations to expand dramatically the domain of prescribed fire. The Great Snowy Scheme, a world-class network of dams for water storage and hydroelectric power, inspired an innovative model of fire protection for the Australian Alps. New South Wales rethought the organization and use of volunteer bushfire brigades. The Commonwealth actively entered into bushfire protection through its sponsorship of scientific research and its management of lands in the A.C.T.; the Forestry and Timber Bureau offered, for the first time, a truly national focus to the question of bushfires. And, as though regulated by some climatic thermostat, major bushfires kept the pot boiling.

In 1949, in response to requests from the states, the Director-General of the Forestry and Timber Bureau, G. J. Rodger, convened the All-Australian Conference of Fire Control Officers of State Forest Services. It was a "gratifying" first, *Australian Forestry* editorialized, and a necessary response to "the basic problem of all practising foresters." A second conference followed in 1951, then others on a two-year rotation. Previously fire officers had gathered together only after major disasters, and meetings showed a strong state bias; now they became part of an institutional routine and shared a broadly national perspective. Additional fire conferences sprouted episodically on assorted topics such as rural fire research, bushfire brigades, and the protection of the arid and tropical biotas of the Northern Territory. Building on Foley's legacy, the Bureau of Meteorology sponsored the Fire Weather Conference at Melbourne.[11]

Within a few years the continent came to resemble a giant bar magnet, with one pole in New South Wales and the other in Western Australia. Between them they held the intervening lands within their powerful lines of force. They realigned the parts and pieces of Australian fire practices, converted practices into programs, and transformed local lore into a national strategy. Western Australia brought system, an integrated suite of practices directed toward the intensive management of specific places. New South Wales demonstrated how, through cooperative programs and bushfire brigades, system could be broadcast over large areas. Large fires recharged the magnet.

For New South Wales the reconstruction began in 1951 when a new Bush Fires Act provided the mechanisms for an effective volunteer brigade force. Its first success, interestingly, came when the Snowy Scheme became a national commitment. Without an end to soil erosion, which meant an end to grazing and promiscuous burning, the catchments for the scheme were worthless. Accordingly, in 1950–51, the N.S.W. Forestry Commission surveyed the fire protection needs of the Hume-Snowy watersheds and prepared a plan that called for aggressive protection based on a program of cooperation among the various parties, including the Snowy Mountains Authority, the state departments for soils, forestry, and lands, the Kosciusko Park Trust, and the local shires and scattered bushfire brigades. In the detailed scientific investigations that prepared for the Snowy Scheme, fire planners acquired hard data; in its infrastructure of roads, it discovered a means of access which it quickly mobilized with war surplus trucks and radios; in its level of economic investment and national symbolism, it found a commitment to bushfire protection that had never before existed. Beginning in the spring of 1951, the Hume-Snowy Bush Fire District steadily evolved into a model protection program. Immediately it passed through one of the worst fire seasons in the modern history of New South Wales.

The 1951–52 season caught the entire state in the southeast fire flume. Officials estimated that 2.3 million hectares burned along the coast and mountains, and another 375,00 hectares in the Western Division. With some pride the Forestry Commission noted its relative successes in protecting state forests and the Hume-Snowy Bush Fire District. It was the unprotected crown and private lands that bred fire, it was carelessness and accident that had inspired most of the outbreaks, and it was reckless, disorganized firefighting and panicky backfiring that routed efforts at control. It was apparent, too, that although controlled burning for fuel reduction was a part of commission policy the practice was inadequate to the circumstances. "Too rigid application" of schedules and two years of heavy precipitation had rendered much of the recent burning so ineffective that blow-up fires had raced across those sites as they did all the others. The Hume-Snowy District, however, shone like a beacon of hope, and under Fire Control Officer A. G. McArthur had even repulsed a flank of the monstrous Mangoplah fire. The next year the shires and bushfire brigades met with the Forestry Commission to inaugurate cooperative plans to close the gaps in the unprotected lands in what became known as the South Coast Scheme.[12]

This was the classic strategy at work, the ever-expanding dominion of a fire protectorate. Starved for funds, expansion stalled; but the idea strengthened. Over the next few years the Forestry Commission was able to secure emergency monies to help suppress fires in the region that might otherwise threaten the reserved forests under its protection, and it boldly began planning to extend the principles of the South Coast Scheme elsewhere throughout the tableland and even to the North Coast. Here and there—in typical, incremental New South Wales fashion—pockets of organized firefighting appeared, each more or less autonomous. The South Coast Scheme lacked the national (or even statewide) consensus that the Snowy Scheme claimed, and bushfire protection spread fitfully, much as selectors had once laid claim to the land. Then came the fires of 1957–58.

It was an epic season that retaught mundane lessons. Areas subjected to protection—the state forests, the Hume-Snowy Bush Fire District, townships along the coastal strip outfitted with bushfire brigades—fought the fires to a standstill. The Forestry Commission manned a thousand fires and only endured, all considered, acceptable losses. But on the marginally protected and unprotected lands, the fires burned unchecked. The Blue Mountains suffered most, as local citizens rallied to save separate towns while the flaming front bore down relentlessly from the west. Then a freak fire incinerated Leura. Volunteers had already saved the town from the main fire front when a howling westerly suddenly sprang up and drove another, detached fire through the village center. Within an hour Leura was a flaming ruin.

The public outcry was enormous. The "quiet" planning that had gone on since 1950 now found a receptive political audience—and money. Legislation authorized the sum of £100,000 to be appropriated yearly for each of the coming five years. Additional cooperative schemes were quickly organized in the unguarded South Coast hinterland and along the Victorian border, and over the next couple of decades the program expanded to encompass most of New South Wales. Where there had been no protection the reforms brought some, and where a degree of protection existed it now acquired strength through organization. What might be called the New South Wales Scheme demonstrated how, through the orchestration of existing resources, it was possible to extend first-order bushfire protection over a state.[13]

It remained to Western Australia to examine just what bushfire protection should mean. On the surface a mandate for major reforms was surprising; Westralian foresters had evolved the best-balanced and most-systematic fire organization in Australia, and new bushfire legislation dated from the 1937 fires, not those of 1939, which had spared the southwest. What made the Western Australian reforms fascinating was that the problems they addressed had emerged, like some bush dialectic, out of their own successes. The breakdowns resulted from problems *within* protected areas, not from fires that roared into them from unprotected land outside the reserves. In fact, the greater the protection, the greater the problem.

The perimeter lands were, ironically, safer than the interior because the boundary was routinely burned and the center was not. The breakdowns thus revealed a conceptual flaw in the tripartite program of fire protection endorsed by the Forests Department. Its foresters light burned virgin woodlands, hot burned a huge backlog of accumulated slash, and guarded regenerating forests with *cordons sanitaires* of annually burned buffer strips. On logged areas, they burned both prior to harvesting and afterward. But as freely as foresters accepted broadcast fire, they always considered it a compromise. The time would come, they believed, when intensive silviculture would void the need for intensive fire protection. They control burned as an interim measure to cover that (indefinite) period between the wild and the regulated. In effect, they used fire for a kind of biotic smelting by which to transform the rough ore of wild woods into the refined metal of the regulated forest. Over twenty to twenty-five years, the area of protected—and unburned—forests had steadily expanded. In 1941 Fire Control Officer James O'Donnell announced with some pride that the fire-protection organization of Western Australia was "recognized as probably the most advanced in the Southern Hemisphere." [14]

In 1945, however, unanticipated consequences forced him to reconsider. During the war years the burning program had slackened off and fuels had blossomed dangerously. Broadcast burning became more hazardous, and escapes more common. To better control burn, field officers tended to fire under cooler conditions, which were less effective at fuel reduction. What was especially troubling was that foresters found it increasingly difficult to keep fuelbreak burns from spotting into protected forests and flaring into stubborn, uncontrollable fires. "Breakaway" fires from protective burning increased, lightning kindled fires at unprecedented rates, and serious wildfires proliferated in places that officials assumed they had amply sheltered from it. Extensive fires broke out in 1949 and again in 1950–51, probably the worst season since 1937. The cycle had become self-reinforcing. Factors "generally adverse to successful fire protection," it was agreed, "were snowballing." [15]

In 1953 the Forests Department made a "momentous" decision to inaugurate broadcast burning throughout its protected forests. While Conservator A. C. Harris admitted that "without doubt the greatest and foremost problem of Australian forestry is forest fire control," he exhorted foresters to "rethink their fire control problems and policies" and "honestly assess whether a policy of virtually complete fire protection is practicable and economic." Westralian foresters had discovered that the difficulty, danger, and cost of fire control rose in proportion to the rise in fuels. To a man, officials believed that prior to European settlement the jarrah forests had been burnt over every three years, certainly no less than every five. Something like that prior condition had to be restored. It was no longer sufficient to burn around protected forests: it was essential to burn those forests as well. Foresters, Harris warned, ignored the merits of universal controlled burning "at their peril." [16]

It had been the genius of the first generation of Western Australian foresters to incorporate controlled fire into systematic fire planning, and it was the genius of this second generation to rethink its conceptual and operational complexities. If a backlog of slash had haunted the first generation, a backlog of surface litter in protected forests haunted the second. There was no "immediate solution," they frankly confessed; they anticipated that ten to fifteen years of burning would be necessary to reduce the accumulated hazard to "safe proportions," and accordingly they opted to implement the requisite burning in stages. The proportion of controlled fires rose, overwhelming the acres lost to wildfire. Between 1953 and 1960 some 350 wildfires burned 24,000 hectares of forest annually, while the prescribed fire program put 148,000 hectares to the torch. As a welcome side benefit, they discovered that, as their burning increased, illicit burning by locals decreased. In 1954, too, a new Bush Fires Act granted special status to state foresters as fire officers.[17]

There was symmetry to the reforms that galvanized Western Australia and New South Wales. Westralia advertised a model fire protection system, but one that was restricted to a particular category of lands under the administration of a single agency directed by a common fraternity of professional foresters. Its rigor and completeness also made it exclusive. New South Wales complemented that program by demonstrating a model of cooperative fire protection. The Hume-Snowy Scheme and its successors showed how local brigades and practices would be amalgamated into broad networks that could ensure at least a first-order level of bushfire organization. What such schemes lost in rigor, they gained in breadth. The revolution that became an Australian strategy of fire management followed from the synthesis of those two models. Forest-fire protection became, in fact, the basis for rural fire protection.

THE FORESTER AS FIRE WARDEN:
R. H. LUKE

Harry Luke was a forester. A visitor to his house at Hunter's Hill would be introduced first to the trees. But forestry for Luke's generation began with fire protection, and it was symptomatic of Luke's career that at age sixteen he enrolled at the Victorian School of Forestry (Creswick) just as the 1926 fires raged throughout the southeast. The flames that baked apples on trees through sheer radiant heat also burned into his memory. Through his work on fire he became one of the great figures of Australian forestry.[18]

There were problems at Creswick and Luke stayed in forestry only after he received from the New South Wales Forestry Commission in 1929 a cadetship, a fancy title for a "billy boiler and general dogsbody for a couple of foresters who later became Commissioners." For ten months he learned how life was lived in the blackbutt and blady-grass forests of the North Coast, relishing the open woodlands, absorbing the rich character of the communities, willingly entertained by local "bush philosophers." Then he completed studies at the Australian Forestry School at Canberra (1930–31) before entering forty years of service. In 1938 Commissioner Hudson appointed him fire control officer.

At that time, fighting bushfires, which were frequent, depended largely on "men on horseback armed with rakes, tilting at windmills in the manner of Don Quixote." Controlled burning meant a box of matches and a eucalypt bough. There were few roads, local sentiment favored burning, and what bushfire brigades did exist resisted any effort at organization beyond the most parochial concern; each state forest likewise operated as an independent barony. Then war came to Australia, and Luke served with a Forest Survey Company in New Guinea. When he returned in 1946 he was reappointed fire control officer for the Commission and promptly set to work writing a manual for in-service training. The times were right for reform, and Harry Luke knew how those reforms could come.

The first generation of Australian foresters were empire builders, marcher lords of government bureaus. They fought with everyone. They argued loudly, quarreled among themselves, carved fiefdoms out of the bush, clashed with farmers, loggers, pastoralists, and politicians. But Luke belonged to a second generation, Australian-born, more conciliatory and empathic with local needs. Where Lane-Poole and Swain blustered like the north wind in Aesop's fable, Luke shone like the sun and overcame resistance by the power of gentle, persistent persuasion. In contrast to swashbuckling, he introduced a comparative realism, for while bushfires blanketed the state, forestry controlled only 2 percent of the total lands in need of protection and was hardly in a position to dictate legislation and practice. As a solution he proposed a genuinely cooperative program—an "American style," Luke admitted.

His instincts were syncretic and pragmatic. He tried to work within local mores, to accept local institutions, to bring together the various constituencies, and to accept Australian conditions. His prototype was the Hume-Snowy Bush Fire Protection Scheme, for which, as fire officer for the N.S.W. Forestry Commission, Luke was an overseer. After the scheme demonstrated its power, he became the chief advocate for its proliferation in the form of sister schemes for the North and South coasts and their hinterlands. For several years after the retirement of Lane-Poole, he lectured on fire protection to the Australian Forestry School. In 1951 he joined the FAO study tour to America. Two years later he assembled those lessons into an updated *Fire Control Manual* (1953). Necessarily he relied on American models.

If he deferred to the Americans on matters of fire research, technique, and institution building, he nonetheless disagreed on burning. In 1943— partly under the pressure of the war, partly because of the development of the tractor-plow, partly because of a fuels buildup that was reaching cata-strophic proportions—the U.S. Forest Service had authorized prescribed burning in the southern pine forests. But elsewhere in America burning remained anathema. Luke, however, had no ingrained hostility to fire. From his early years on the North Coast, he had seen folk burners not as improvi-dent destroyers of state forests, but as "blokes trying to make a quid" on a hard land in hard times. He understood the rationale for burning, witnessed firsthand the thickening of eucalypts into impenetrable scrub as fire was withdrawn, and never questioned the value of fuel-reduction burning for fire control. He listened as residents protested over and again that foresters were putting their (the locals') lives and property in danger by not burning enough. And he agreed. He suggested that "fire control" be rechristened "fuel control" in order to "get our thinking straight from the start." Under the Australian climate,

> it just doesn't make sense to attempt to fight fires in heavy fuels under extreme conditions. When the oven door from Hell is open there are never enough fire fighters, bulldozers, tankers, aircraft, radios, heli-copters, women's auxiliaries, police inspectors, rakes, hoes, Section 17 appointees or wet corn sacks to get within Cooee of success unless somebody has had a crack at fuel reduction BEFORE the fire season got underway.

It was not burning per se but its disorganization and cross-purposes that disturbed Luke. One man's controlled fire became a neighbor's wildfire. Too often hazard burning became, as he put it, "hap-hazard burning." [19]

With enormous patience and perseverance, Luke sought to rework and rationalize existing patterns. He helped put controlled burning on a more scientific basis and gave it a social conscience. He promoted local brigades and provided them with professional guidance and a surer institutional con-text. He organized conferences and symposia, building a community of fire specialists. He helped make foresters into good neighbors, not crusaders. With marvelous dexterity, he sorted through the cornucopia of American firefighting techniques for those that suited, or could be made to suit, Aus-tralian conditions. "Anyone concerned with bush fire protection in Australia naturally turns to the U.S.A. for inspiration," he observed. He liked coopera-tive fire programs, backpack pumps, the one-lick method of line construc-tion, and hazard rating sticks; he disliked smokejumpers, thundering fleets of air tankers, and American hostility to fuel-reduction burning. And throughout it all—for nineteen consecutive years as fire officer for the For-estry Commission and across two terms that totaled twenty-seven years on the N.S.W. Bush Fire Committee—he wrote.[20]

He published prolifically for a wide audience and for specialists both. The

Outline of 1947 became a department *Fire Control Manual* in 1953 and expanded into a book, *Bush Fire Control in Australia,* in 1961—the first textbook devoted to Australian fire. Not content to be a chief strategist of the Australian system, he became its chief publicist as well. Much as he orchestrated disparate brigades and landowners into a common cause in New South Wales, so he collated, reorganized, and published the bushfire fighting lore of Australia. He spoke with a national voice, one that was strengthened immeasurably by his collaboration with A. G. McArthur, a friendship that began, as so much of modern Australian fire history does, with the Hume-Snowy Scheme. After McArthur transferred from fire control on the Hume-Snowy to a research position on the Forestry and Timber Bureau of the Commonwealth, he and Luke remained close collaborators. When other nations listened to the Australian experience with fire, it was the syncopated voices of Luke and McArthur that they heard. After Luke retired in 1972, the two combined talents to author a summa to the Australian system and the research that had grown up to sustain it, *Bushfires in Australia,* published finally in 1978. This book was nearly empty of American references.

For their achievements both received N. W. Jolly medals from the Institute of Australian Foresters, reminding everyone of their origins. But Luke, in particular, had quietly changed the character of Australian forestry vis-à-vis fire protection. He insisted that the forester had to be an Australian, that he had to accept Australian conditions, Australian rural mores, Australian institutions, that he had to accept Australian fire. When Luke began, burning was practiced but not really approved, tolerated as an embarrassment of life in the Outback. It stood to European forestry as "Strine" did to English enunciation. By the time he and McArthur completed their careers, controlled burning had become a centerpiece of Australian fire protection and forest management. Luke took immense pride in the volunteer brigades that staffed Australian firelines and in the transfiguration of burning off into prescribed fire; the rural community responded with gratitude. In 1985 Harry Luke received the Order of Australia. The New South Wales forester had become Australia's fire warden. Appropriately, the tree that first greeted visitors to the Luke residence was one that he and Alan McArthur brought back from their investigation of the 1961 fires in Western Australia.

THE GENERAL OPINION IN AUSTRALIAN FORESTRY: THE FIRES OF 1961

By the late 1950s there was progress everywhere, each advance catalyzed by major fires. The 1951–52 fire season had rekindled the concerns voiced by Stretton after 1939; the 1957–58 fires galvanized the emerging trends and models. Even laggards like Tasmania and quiescent Queensland enacted legislation that rewrote prescriptions for fire practices and authorized institutions for rural bushfire protection. The Black Sunday fires (1955) that devastated the Adelaide Hills region swept South Australia into the reformation. Then the 1960–61 fires in Western Australia completed the cycle begun with Black Friday.

The conflagration shocked fire officers who widely regarded Westralia as the paradigm—organized, ruthlessly methodical, dedicated to the use of controlled fire. If bushfire protection was done right anywhere in Australia, it was in the jarrah forests of Western Australia. Yet the 1961 fires roared virtually unchecked. They burned throughout the state: some thirty-three major fires raced across 350,000 hectares in the northwest and central pastoral regions, and another bust, some 1.5 million hectares in the southern pastoral zone. The most frightening fires, however, gutted state forests in the southwest, those paragons of protection, some eight years after the Forests Department had boldly expanded its timetables and geography for burning. One colossal burn steadily advanced southward, spilled over into the coastal plain, and, on January 24, with a howling north wind broke out of confinement and burned down several towns including Dwellingup, where, ironically, the Forests Department had in 1934 established the first fire-weather station in Australia. By the time rains finally extinguished the Dwellingup fire on February 8 it had infected over 145,000 hectares. A royal commission was appointed to inquire into the disaster.[21]

It was possible to interpret the fires as an indictment against the proud reforms of the early 1950s or as a frank admission that holocausts were inevitable in Australia regardless of what measures might be taken. The Commission—packed with a new generation of fire specialists—chose a very different interpretation. The Commissioner, G. J. Rodger, a veteran of the 1939 fires and its interstate conferences, had served as Director-General of the Forestry and Timber Bureau and knew at firsthand the remarkable successes of the southeast. As a technical advisor he chose A. G. McArthur; Harry Luke was among the cadre. The worst fires—the Dwellingup burn among them—the Commission regarded as a freak, the product of marauding electrical storms, a once-in-a-century event beyond the capability (or culpability) of any agency to plan for. The protected sites of the South-West Land Division suffered from probably 110 lightning-kindled fires that accounted for 42 percent of the burned acreage, almost exactly the acreage attributed to escape fires from burning off (43 percent). Simultaneous ignitions on this order simply overwhelmed initial attack units, and after the fires merged, their scale was beyond control by any means the state could muster.

Similarly the Commission deflected criticism away from the suppression effort by deemphasizing the failure to protect lands and accenting the successful protection of lives. No one died—for Australia, a considerable achievement. The failure of fuel reduction to halt fires was, paradoxically, turned to advantage. Where it had been instituted on a regular basis, hazard reduction did achieve some success. The putative "failure" was really one of execution, not design; the Forests Department had simply not burned enough. The Commission went further by praising the Forests Department for its cooperative attitudes, its willingness to accommodate the ideas of local residents within planning. Locals wanted protective burning. But the Commission went further; it announced as the "general opinion in Australian forestry" that programmed fire use was the *only* effective means of fire control. By absolving the Westralian strategy, the Rodger Commission sanctioned the assumptions and components of what was rapidly becoming an Australian strategy of fire protection.[22]

What the Stretton Commission had insisted must be done, the Rodger Commission affirmed was being done. The fires of 1939 had said to Stretton that something was fundamentally rotten; the 1961 fires told Rodger that something was fundamentally sound. What Stretton had proposed by way of controlled burning, the Rodger cadre retested and confirmed as true. The 1961 fires thus complement those of 1939, and between them the two royal commissions bracket the formative era of fire management in New Australia. Before the year was out, Luke wrote *Bush Fire Control in Australia.* The next year McArthur published the conclusions of a decade of research by the Commonwealth and of practice by the Forests Department of Western Australia in a seminal treatise, *Controlled Burning in Eucalypt Forests.*

An Australian strategy had come of age.

18

Antipodean Fire:
The Australian Strategy

If litter concentrations could be permanently reduced, the Australian bush fire problem would be largely solved. This forms the basis of a revolutionary policy of fire protection, which has recently been implemented particularly in Western Australia.

> —DR. R. G. VINES,
> CSIRO Division
> of Applied Chemistry (1968)

Even when the programme of fuel modification burning becomes fully operative throughout Australia—and I must be quite honest on this, no matter what opposition there is to this programme, it will be operative and you will have to accept it as part and parcel of the way of Australian life, because this is the only way we can provide adequate fire protection.

> —A. G. MCARTHUR,
> Symposium Comments (1966)

THE AUSTRALIAN STRATEGY quickly became an Australian revolution. Its components materialized after the war and were shaped into prototypes during the 1950s. Over the next decade those concepts and institutions blossomed into a strategy of fire protection that approximated a national system. When in 1961 the Conservator of Forests for Western Australia announced that "without doubt the greatest and foremost problem of Australian forestry is forest fire control," his purpose was not to recycle a tired lament but to announce a reformation. Its proponents proudly declared a new age.[1]

To their fellow Australians those revolutionaries proposed a solution to catastrophic bushfires. To the rest of the world, particularly to North Americans, they announced a distinctive strategy of bushfire protection that emerged out of indigenous Australiana—the antipodes' unique biota, violent fire weather, and ancient history of burning. Its message went beyond techniques of preparing for and fighting bushfires, for the revolution proposed a new relationship to Australia. Before the 1960s concluded, colleagues were proselytizing that message throughout Australia and beyond.

THE ONLY WAY:
MANIFESTO FOR REVOLUTION

A generation of foresters—native-born Australians all—designed the system around a core of interrelated assumptions, what appeared to them as self-evident propositions. While the sardonic temperament was perhaps too ingrained for them to argue for a former golden age of Aboriginal bliss, it was clear that European settlement had mauled Australia and that the legacy of devastation demanded some restorative measures. Nationalists by choice, idealists by necessity, they sought to define a better past in order to make a better future. As foresters, their vital insight was to turn bushfire against itself, to exploit the peculiar circumstances of Australia to advantage, to revive old fire practices to fashion a new environment. The idea became an ideology of revolution.

The advocates of the Australian strategy believed that Australian climatic conditions made large fires inevitable, for which the fire flume was only the most notorious expression. They believed that the Australian flora, particularly the eucalypts, demonstrated an unparalleled capacity to accommodate fire. Thus, the endemism of fire defined a point of entry for control—poorly managed, the pyrophilia of the eucalypts could erupt into holocausts; manipulated by shrewd humans, it could make low-intensity fire into an environmentally benign tool. Their study of Australian history suggested that Aborigines had disseminated low-grade fires almost universally, that Europeans had distorted those fire practices and magnified the fire hazards of the continent, and that a new generation of Australians could—had to— devise a better, more enduring equilibrium. They recognized, too, that the bush was vast and Australians few. Bushfire protection had to accept limited resources; it had to work within the context of volunteer bushfire brigades and oversight councils cobbled together out of local governments, insurance companies, and representatives from a miscellany of state institutions. A Commonwealth presence would be confined by and large to research and the federal territories. They refused a knee-jerk emulation of North American models of firefighting in the belief that such methods would destroy a sense of Australiana they considered vital, much as American movies had squelched the Australian film industry or as American popular culture had coated Australian society with a raucous layer of teen music, TV sitcoms, and consumer gadgetry. Unlike the Americans they placed controlled burning at the core of bushfire protection.

What offended the principal strategists was not fire use in and of itself but extravagant, promiscuous burning off. They wanted to rationalize rural fire practices, to rebuild the foundations of controlled burning on the basis of scientific information rather than folklore, to break the spiral of random burning and aggravated fuel conditions that had powered a vortex of degradation. Do that and it would be possible to live under modified Australian conditions. The alternatives were to abandon the continent as unlivable or to replace it tree by tree, hummock by hummock with European surrogates.

In 1948 a dismayed journalist wrote that traveling the road from Dwellingup to Pemberton he was "amazed at the number of fires, although the fire weather was classed as 'severe summer.' Farmers, townspeople, and even school children were burning off . . . A farmer with an uncertain grip of the English language and much less of fire-control regulations was reporting his intention of burning off . . . 'Check it? Oh, no! I just light her up, she go to blazes.' " A decade later, however, the Bush Fires Board of Western Australia argued strenuously for massive fuel reduction, urging "that brigades and individuals should organise as much protective burning as possible in the autumn and spring." The burning continued, unabated. Yet something *had* changed: the new enthusiasms for burning had system, support institutions, a foundation in scientific research, even a vision of a new Australia. What changed was the successful promulgation of the Australian strategy that placed the burning into a new cultural context.[2]

By 1968 the revolution elevated systematic fuel reduction by controlled burning into a national creed. "I firmly believe," Alan McArthur wrote, "that the only way to prevent widespread and damaging conflagrations during the heat of summer is to carry out prescribed burning in the spring, autumn and winter in much the same way as the Aborigines did prior to the advent of the white man." The differences were ones of context—the enormous changes wrought by European settlement—and of technology. "Instead of the Aboriginal firestick," McArthur exulted, "we now use aircraft dropping incendiary capsules which light up the country in a grid pattern and produce a mosaic pattern of burnt and unburnt land.[3]

Inevitably the Australian strategy attracted critics. The early advocates of bushfire reform directed their arguments against old-guard foresters and ivory-tower academics, usually British, reluctant to admit controlled fire into their tool caches and libraries. Rural populations sympathized; the increasingly urban population, however, was less easily convinced. As conservation groups and environmental problems proliferated, so did opinions about suitable land-use practices. As demographic shifts reconstituted Australian society, new voices joined a chorus of inchoate criticism. Most skeptics either could not discriminate between controlled burning by foresters and burning off by ruralites or did not want any kind of environmental manipulation and discovered in broadacre burning a useful emblem around which to rally their dissatisfactions.

So long as the strategy remained in state forests, it enjoyed sanctuary. It could be tolerated as a bureaucratic coup that, however passionate among foresters, was effectively quarantined. But it was part of the animating mission of the Australian strategy that it be universal, and it soon invaded other lands. Its aggressive expansion inspired controversy and protest; and its centerpiece, aerial burning, gave its critics a common, polarizing symbol. Increasingly, rigor met rigor, icon opposed icon, organized groups of professionals faced one another across ideological trenches, one concept of Australian identity clashed with another, dialogue became dialectic. Revolution spawned counterrevolution.

STRATEGY BECOMES SYSTEM: INSTITUTIONALIZING THE REVOLUTION

With a determination both inspired and relentless the new generation reworked every dimension of the old order—its folkways, its miscellany of burning practices, its spotty legislation, improvised equipment, and shambles of an infrastructure. The absence of organized protection, they recognized, only encouraged more laissez-faire protective burning. As their rationalizing zeal worked through each component, they transformed the Australian strategy into an Australian system.[4]

They first had to reify their ideas into institutions. Fire control and controlled fire both needed crews, equipment, knowledge, organization. An obvious point of departure was the local brigade. Volunteer fire brigades had sprung up during the nineteenth century along the suburban fringe and more outlying towns. After the 1926 fires in the southeast and the 1936 fires in the southwest, revised statutes improved their legal standing and encouraged local councils to empower them. Their numbers grew. During the war brigades acquired an added urgency as a civil defense measure. But many lands lacked any formal protection, and the proliferation of brigades did not produce an effect greater than (or even equal to) the sum of their parts. Too often brigades flourished immediately after a bad burn, then disappeared, a kind of institutional fireweed. Gazetting new brigades was more like adding marbles to a bag than assembling tiles into a mosaic. They were not only incapable of suppressing large fires, they were incapable of organized presuppression as well—the 1939 and 1944 debacles proved that. Besides, it was impossible to defend settled areas when fires raged out of unsettled lands during extreme conditions. The autonomous brigades employed inadequate means within an inadequate system to achieve inadequate goals. The Australian strategy reformed both means and ends, and gave system to the whole.

Each state and territory has followed a separate evolution, an irregular choreography of bushfires and reforms, the tempo and intensity of change varying with fire load. Each, however, experienced a scaling up of legislation roughly modeled on the Hume-Snowy Scheme that made it possible for local governments to establish brigades and to grant them legal immunity, workman's compensation, and funding for equipment and operations. Most also enjoy control over local fire practices by overseeing permits for burning, by declaring fire bans when conditions warrant, and of course suppressing escape fires. Governing boards typically include representatives from the brigades, the principal landholders, the insurance companies, and affected state agencies. Funding comes from insurance companies, the states, shire councils, and the local brigades themselves.

Big fires and local mores largely governed their separate evolutions. Its vulnerability to holocausts, for example, drove Victoria into a tougher, more singular solution more quickly than its neighbors. Reforms began immediately after the 1944 debacle. The Country Fire Authority Act divided rural fire protection between the Forests Commission, which was given responsibility for most public lands, and the Country Fire Authority (CFA), which assumed responsibility for the remaining rural landscape. The scheme has proved durable, accommodating new levels of organization with new legislation.[5]

New South Wales matured more tentatively, with fresh outbreaks of fire acting incrementally on the Bush Fires Act of 1949, a delayed response to the 1939 holocaust. The act designated responsibilities and established a Bush Fire Committee. After the 1951–52 fires the committee worked with the Forestry Commission to plan for an expansion of fire protection schemes modeled on that developed for the Hume-Snowy. The 1957–58 fires brought in real funds. After large fires in 1965 and 1968, the Bush Fires Act was amended in 1970; this reconstituted the committee into a Bush Fire Council and formally recognized the ten fire prevention schemes that had emerged over the previous two decades. Bits and pieces of every practice in Australia seemed to find their way into the syncretic N.S.W. system, whose strength became, in some respects, its weakness. By 1970 the council had swollen to such proportions that it became necessary to select five members to serve as a coordinating committee.[6]

South Australia built incrementally out of the Bush Fires Act of 1854. After Black Friday a central Bush Fires Advisory Committee appeared to help coordinate activities, and during World War II the Emergency Fire Services organization (a branch of the police department) was established to coordinate civil defense; it survived to oversee bushfire suppression. Soon bushfire brigades ringed Adelaide. In 1949 a compensation act passed, and in 1957, in the wake of the Black Sunday fires, reforms provided for the registration of brigades and for regular financing. Eventually there appeared separate bodies for bushfires equipment subsidies, bushfire research, and the Volunteer Fire Fighters Fund. By the 1970s the proliferating committees needed organization themselves. In 1977 South Australia established a Country Fire Service, roughly comparable to that in Victoria.[7]

Reform in Western Australia began with a new Bush Fires Act in 1937, followed by the establishment of a Bush Fires Advisory Council two years later. A key innovation was the creation of a Bush Fires Board in 1954, coincident with Forests Department reforms in controlled burning. While it did not have direct responsibility for suppression, the board did exercise unusual control over burning practices and oversaw extensive fuelbreak maintenance. Interdistrict associations—amalgamations of brigades on a regional rather than a statewide basis—appeared after the 1960–61 fires. Unlike the other states Westralia provides for a 25 percent reduction in crop insurance if the Bush Fires Board declares a district as of high standards, which indicates not only an efficient brigade but adequate fuel reduction.[8]

Queensland's reformation built on the Rural Fires Act of 1927 which allowed for the creation of rural fire districts and fire wardens. Most of the proclaimed districts clustered around Brisbane. The 1939 fires to the south and local fires during the war years prompted the Rural Fires Act of 1946, which provided for a Rural Fires Board. The act divided fire suppression, a function of brigades, from fire prevention, a duty of wardens who supervised a program of permits for burning; in practice, fire control meant control over burning off. In place of a fire season, Queensland instigated social control by requiring that every applicant for a burning permit poll his neighbors and present their views as part of his request. The state contributed the whole of the program funding, a relatively small sum. Queensland thus presented a system that was strong at local levels and weak beyond it.[9]

Tasmania tried the opposite approach. After the great fires of 1933–34, draconian amendments were added to the Bush Fires Act (1935) that empowered wardens (often foresters) to oversee local burning and to impress local citizens in emergencies as firefighters. The problem was that state officials acted directly on persons; there were no intervening institutions like bushfire brigades or shire councils or oversight boards to buffer the interaction. The system went into immediate overload and collapsed. The Rural Fires Act of 1950 partially rectified this omission by setting up a Rural Fires Board, chaired by the Chief Commissioner of Forests and empowered to appoint wardens to issue burning permits. Curiously there was little motivation for brigades, but this may reflect in part the absence of a dominating metropolis with an extensive fringe of suburbs. The Forestry Department stood practically alone as a bushfire organization. With nothing to intercede between burner and warden, the system was unstable, and the catastrophic Hobart fires of 1967 destroyed it. The Bush Fires Act of 1967 which followed reconstituted the Rural Fires Board, promoted bushfire brigades, designated special fire areas for regions that lacked any significant means of protection, and funded equipment by equal contributions from the state and local councils. Like its bushfire environment, its institutions remained unstable— holocaust fires too infrequent to sustain public enthusiasm, burning too abundant to be contained, and society too diffuse to concentrate resources or reach consensus.[10]

If the Australian Capital Territory shared in the fire traumas of the southeast, it also shared in its triumphs. As advantages it had a small land base, a reasonably restricted population, planned urban development, and a cadre of Commonwealth foresters to mastermind a drive for protection. After the 1939 fires, a Bush Fire Council was established with strong direction from foresters, and after bad fire years in 1943–44 and 1951–52 cooperative programs began with brigades from New South Wales; the Hume-Snowy Scheme provided another source of influence, and the A.C.T. evolved a model program.[11]

By contrast, there was little in the Northern Territory to focus interest. Burning was ubiquitous and annual rather than concentrated into eruptive holocausts, and among a dispersed population there were no real organizations to seize on fire protection. Not until more intensive land use became common in the form of sown pastures, parks, and experimental forestry was there strong enough incentive to undertake formal protection. In 1965 a Bush Fire Control Ordinance inaugurated the process. Essentially it divided the territory into seven fire-control regions for which protection was available and left the remaining lands unprotected. A Bush Fires Council promotes brigades without assistance from local government (restricted in any event to Alice Springs and Darwin). Instead local landowners and government agencies rather than brigades furnish the manpower for protection. The future of protection is very much a function of future land usage; and because the N.T. belongs to the Commonwealth, that decision is a national rather than local one.[12]

By 1965 almost all of Australia in need of organized protection had a statutory mandate to provide it. By 1977 just over half of rural Australia (51 percent) enjoyed some level of protection. The coverage was actually more effective when it is realized that only about 20 percent of the rural landscape requires continuous protection and 31 percent somewhat less regular protection; another 24 percent experiences regular hazards but does not demand regular protection. Most of these unprotected landscapes include those interior wastelands for which fires are infrequent and protection impossible to provide on a consistent basis. Considering that only 2 percent of the continent consisted of public lands like state forests for which rigorous public protection existed, the creation of this infrastructure was an astonishing achievement. Half a century after the 1926 fires goaded a few sluggish rural brigades, Australia could boast of 300,000 volunteers organized into 7,000 brigades. Roughly one rural Australian in ten belonged to a bushfire brigade. These were, as Luke and McArthur exulted, "proportions not paralleled elsewhere in the world."[13]

The creation of an Australian system was inextricably bound up with the creation of the Australian strategy. The belief that it was possible to contain the bushfire menace gave purpose and commitment to institution building, and the appeal to controlled burning instilled an ongoing set of tasks that brigades had to perform year in and year out; they were no longer dependent solely on catastrophic bushfires to rekindle public enthusiasms. The brigades reciprocated by giving substance to strategy. They furnished a relatively reliable pool of manpower, ensured a measure of popular support, and allowed the Australian system to expand exponentially. To appeal to brigades, for example, was to favor broadacre burning not only because it was an adaptation of rural practices but because it was a cheap and nearly universal implement. However vexing might be the problem of orchestrating a score of brigades along the flank of a large fire, the problem was qualitatively different from the specter of cockies and squatters, flushed out like wallabies, wildly setting protective burns around every corner of their lands. Locals traded in their torch for a knapsack; instead of lighting more fires, they attacked the existing ones. The spread of the system rationalized folk fire practices without completely excluding either folk or fire.

AIR SUPPORT

A reliance on volunteer brigades favored practices and procedures that were extensive rather than intensive, and in compensation the Australian strategy searched for means by which to improve efficiency. One solution was to hold biennial fire control conferences to exchange experiences among the states. By publishing the details of the meetings, the conferences established a small reference library of Australian fire literature. Another thrust was to mechanize. The mechanization of the military during World War II was an important exemplar and, after demobilization, often a source of surplus vehicles. The postwar era witnessed the dissemination of improved communications, particularly VHF radio; the proliferation of truck-mounted pumpers, bulldozers, and four-wheel drive vehicles; and, most spectacularly, a revival of interest in aircraft.[14]

The Forests Commission of Victoria and the Royal Australian Air Force had operated a fire reconnaissance service since 1929, and journals and professional contacts constantly reminded Australian foresters of spectacular North American developments in aerial fire control. Within a year after the war the RAAF Aircraft Research and Development Unit at Laverton and the Forests Commission sponsored multiyear experiments in adapting military aircraft, chemicals, and eventually helicopters to bushfire control. In July 1947 Squadron Leader K. V. Robertson traveled to the U.S. Forest Service equipment development center at Arcadia, California, for a close inspection of American trends. The results were technically encouraging—it was possible to scout fires, to "bomb" fires with water and chemical retardants (from a P-51 Mustang), and to move equipment and men across rugged terrain. In March 1950 the only helicopter in Australia, a Sikorsky S-51, flew reconnaissance on a fire bust near Mount Butler. The prospects excited nearly everyone, and the memory of a terrifying war in which air support had figured so prominently added to the conviction that the future of bushfire fighting would include aircraft. "Surely," exulted a participant in the helicopter trials, such glittering examples of applied science would inspire a "revolution."[15]

But the initial euphoria evaporated. The American example stalled until after the Korean War, when it suddenly burst onto the scene in technological splendor. By then the Australians were preoccupied with other aspects of the Australian strategy and skepticism tempered their first thrill. Unlike the Americans, who adapted war-surplus aircraft, Australians did not have a reliable source of cheap planes or helicopters. Inexplicably, Australian statutes expressly prohibited the use of ex-military aircraft for civilian activities. Unlike the Canadians, Australians did not have lakes everywhere to serve as landing sites or sources of water resupply; eucalypts were likely to impale smokejumpers; the mountainous backcountry lacked sufficient landing sites even for helicopters. Moreover, there was the question of funding. Only in the most protected environments could aerial fire control prove cost-effective; even the Forests Commission, with one envious eye always on California, found it difficult to justify a full-blown aerial attack system on state forests.

Perhaps even more tellingly, air attack had to find a place within the evolving Australian strategy. Aircraft was most effective when applied to rapid detection and initial attack, the informing core of the American strategy. Australians, however, needed technologies that could work within a context of limited resources, volunteer brigades, and fire-flume holocausts. There would never be enough money to blanket rural Australia with air tankers and helicopters. Instead the Australian strategy targeted fuel reduction on a huge scale. If aircraft were to succeed as a national tool, they had to participate in broadcast burning. Until that occurred in the mid-1960s, enthusiasts investigated and critics questioned the appropriateness of North American–style air attack.

In 1958 New South Wales experimented with agricultural planes and test fires, though the trials led nowhere. Interest persisted, however, and as the Canadians and Americans scaled up their investment in aerial firefighting, it appeared that Australia might be left in a technological backwater—waving a firestick while their allies flew B-17s and CL-215s in a campaign of strategic bombing. Not surprisingly, the Australians who participated in a 1964 FAO fire-study tour to North America made air attack a major part of the agenda and returned with an inextinguishable ambivalence: they were appalled by the costs of a national program yet admitted the possibility for its selective application under Australian conditions. For the next two years Victorian foresters experimented with light agricultural aircraft as an economic alternative to the converted military bombers that staffed American firefighting fleets; fire officers experimented with cargo dropping, chemical bombing, even cloud seeding. Between 1965 and 1967 a parade of individual Australian fire officers—a group at once dazzled and wary—toured the U.S. If air tankers were problematical, light aircraft increasingly found a place in forestry operations for surveillance and mapping, and as agricultural planes became abundant, their cost put them within reach of foresters.

What liberated aerial fire control was, paradoxically, the development of aerial ignition. Naturally, the breakthrough came in Western Australia. With CSIRO assistance the Westralians developed a technology to deploy incendiary capsules out of planes and ignite areas designated for controlled burning. When the system became operational in 1965, it immediately gave the Australian strategy a countersymbol to North American air tankers. Aerial ignition spread from state to state, from jarrah forest to buttongrass moor to sorghum woodland. Aerial ignition held at bay the fear that air tankers would, like some mechanical virus, take over the apparatus of the Australian system. Almost on cue aircraft usage proliferated. In 1967 Victorian light aircraft dropped chemical retardants on fires, and fixed-wing aircraft and helicopters ferried handcrews to them. Permanent retardant bases were erected. By 1969 the Forests Commission prepared a handbook to guide the use of aircraft in fire control, and the Royal Aeronautical Society sponsored a symposium on the "Application of Aircraft in Bushfire Control."

Nearly every aspect of bushfire protection found a use for aircraft, and nearly every state cultivated some level of air operations. Victoria claimed priority in the use of aircraft for suppression; Western Australia, in its use for controlled burning. But everywhere practitioners labored to keep air attack within the bounds of the Australian strategy, to ensure that a means, however glamorous, did not become an end to itself. Air attack had to complement, not compete with, other forms of fire protection. Even Victoria restricted its early firebombing operations to initial attack on small fires.

Rather, the enormous improvement in suppression efficiency came from more mundane means—from better pumpers and an increase in roads, both of which improved the usefulness of rural brigades; by a better understanding of fire behavior, and better communication on the line; by combining organization with local ingenuity, using the rigor and fervor of the Australian strategy to stiffen existing resources. In remote areas of the interior, for example, it was not a soaring slurry bomber but the lowly Brompton rat, a homegrown grader, that made fire control effective.[16]

THE NECESSARY RESEARCH: BRINGING SCIENCE TO THE AUSTRALIAN STRATEGY

After the 1939 holocaust, *Australian Forestry* editorialized that since all phases of forestry depended on fire protection, "the subject of Fire Control should be regarded as one of the major fields of professional Forestry in Australia, and one which justifies extensive detailed investigation." Like fire practices, however, fire knowledge was oral, empirical, a species of woods lore; excepting Western Australia, there was not even a formal mechanism by which to stimulate scientific inquiry or to transfer its findings from elsewhere. When, after the war, Harry Luke sought out information on which to base his *Outline*, there was almost nothing on the shelves specific to Australia and he deferred to the mountain of literature brought back by Muir from his American tour. Yet the revolution required knowledge and propagandists; it demanded applied science to shape its field operations and intellectuals to justify its assumptions. In return the Australian strategy gave to bushfire research purpose, method, a sense of style, and institutional support. It is no accident that the principal architects of the Australian strategy were also its principal researchers.[17]

Fire research commenced, as so much of the Australian strategy did, in Western Australia. In 1933–34 the Forests Department erected a fire-weather station at Dwellingup, modeled on American experiments in fire-danger rating. For several years after the war, fire officers from South Australia and Tasmania visited the site for training and Westralians lectured at the forestry schools in Canberra and Creswick. With typical thoroughness, Western Australian foresters enlarged their research agenda to include equipment, operations, telecommunications, fire retardants, lightning as an ignition source, and of course fire effects, which merged easily with silviculture. Although Lane-Poole informed the Stretton Commission that Commonwealth forestry "has been making investigations of the fire question as being one of the most important investigations that it has to do," there was almost nothing of practical consequence to emerge. The questions researchers asked were historical, silvicultural, and theoretical, comparing Aboriginal and European fire regimes, for example, or determining the fire susceptibility of species of eucalypts. The real breakthrough came when the postwar generation nationalized fire research and bonded it to the Australian strategy.[18]

In 1953 the Forestry and Timber Bureau established a bushfire research section and appointed A. G. McArthur as "fire research officer" for the Commonwealth. McArthur quickly identified the critical needs—an understanding of fire behavior, the measurement of fire danger, and the publication of practical means by which rural firefighters could translate this knowledge into operations. He took over fire-control lectures at the Australian National Forestry School and sent his students into the field to help conduct hundreds of experimental fires. As much as anyone, McArthur lashed applied science to the Australian strategy until research became as much an indispensable part of bushfire protection as its brigades. Along with Harry Luke and other researchers, McArthur assumed a commanding role in the symposia and conferences that proliferated during the 1960s. When the 1954 fire-control conference recommended that the Forestry and Timber Bureau "undertake the co-ordination of the necessary research work on fire problems," McArthur was prepared to act.[19]

The conferees particularly wanted liaisons with CSIRO. That was slow to come; not until 1956 did the CSIRO Division of Industrial Chemistry agree to commit a researcher. By 1959 enough others had been added to constitute a Bushfire Research Section. Stationed in Melbourne, directed by Dr. A. R. King, the group emphasized laboratory research on combustion and fire behavior, fuels, and chemical retardants. King soon enlarged the scope to include research into fire history and practical protection measures for rural dwellers and firefighters. Somewhat piously, he hoped that "more scientists will enter into research on bushfires; the subject is of great interest, its scope is almost unlimited and practical rewards could be very high."[20]

For whatever reason, other CSIRO units soon followed. The Division of Plant Industry conducted some research into fuelbreaks and fire ecology, and regional range stations included studies on fire effects in pastures. In 1955, too, the Meteorology Act charged the Bureau of Meteorology with issuing fire-weather warnings; this along with Foley's legacy generated an interest in aspects of fire behavior. Immediately two researchers, H. E. Whittingham and G. U. Wilson, were appointed as fire specialists. Within a year they produced a plan for research. In 1958 the bureau convened a large conference on fire weather that brought together most of the research on combustion and fire behavior. Unfortunately, the bureau's enthusiasms then sagged, to be fanned only after major conflagrations.[21]

Meanwhile the base for research broadened. Those states that boasted forestry research redoubled their investments, and those that lacked any formal mechanisms established them. Western Australia continued to lead the way. After the Kongorong fire, South Australia created a Bushfire Research Committee to complement its other fire commissions, and, prodded by Luke, who experimented with a fire-danger index in the mid-1950s, the Forestry Commission of New South Wales inquired into elements of fire research. In Victoria A.P.M. Forests Pty. Ltd. sponsored research into fire effects, the State Electricity Commission investigated aspects relevant to its mission, and eventually the Forests Commission accepted a role as sponsor of fire research. As the use of fire expanded during the 1970s, so did the uses of fire research until every state and territory had a program of some sort and even rural fire authorities had staff officers who specialized in technology transfer, if not original research. The institutional core, however, retained a double nucleus—one in the Forestry and Timber Bureau, headed by McArthur, and the other in the CSIRO Bushfire Section, directed by King.[22]

In a sense, the Australian system built bushfire research as it did bushfire protection, by upgrading and amalgamating local resources. Research committees, analogous to bushfire councils, established their direction. But this left bushfire research as less an enduring institution in its own right than an aggregate of unrelated bodies bound into confederation by a double common cause—a belief in the Australian strategy and a dread of unstoppable wildfires. When, for example, researchers in the early 1960s wanted a journal in which to publish their results in practical form, no single agency could support it. Instead they had to exploit existing publication outlets, scattering their reports through an institutional scrubland. So long as bushfire research remained, as it was initially, the province of a relatively small cadre in broad agreement as to their role and agenda those means were adequate. So long as large fires rekindled the specter of 1939, there was consensus that the purpose of bushfire research was to improve bushfire protection. The Rodger Commission report on the 1961 fires, for which McArthur had served as technical advisor, confirmed that commitment.

By 1962 fire research had become inextricably interconnected with the Australian strategy. The fire control officer conference that year unanimously elected King as chair and McArthur as secretary. King reported that, having inspected North American research firsthand, he felt that "Australia's fire research effort suffered little by comparison." In fact, he considered McArthur's work on fire behavior "far in advance of comparable American research." The Forestry and Timber Bureau assembled an impressive roll call of Australian research; and while the bureau agreed that it was "essential" to monitor overseas trends, a five-month study tour to Europe and North America demonstrated that "Australian forestry fire practice is very sound, realistic and up-to-date." By 1962, that is, both centers of fire research were producing studies vital to their common mission.[23]

The McArthur agenda included experimental field fires to measure fire behavior in grasslands and eucalypt forests, detailed case studies of large fires, and assessments of how fuel loads influenced fire intensity. All of these topics revolved around core precepts—an obsession with the holocaust fire, which McArthur considered the fundamental problem of Australian fire protection; an insistence that fire behavior data had to be packaged into a form usable by fire officers and volunteer brigades; and an unshaken conviction that controlled burning was the only realistic means by which to grapple with Australian fire. McArthur's first fire-danger rating tables appeared in

1958. Within a year he was carrying his methodology for experimental field fires to Western Australia. In 1962 he reprinted his tables in the form of a circular slide rule and published *Control Burning in Eucalypt Forests*, which not only argued the case for prescribed fire but demonstrated how to do it with rigor. When he read his paper to the Eighth British Commonwealth Forestry Conference, he effectively announced the Australian strategy to the world.[24]

The CSIRO group, meanwhile, issued a stream of technical papers on the combustion of Australian fuels, complementing McArthur's open-field experiments with lab-based research. At the same time, they investigated other topics of both theoretical and practical significance. For example, in 1962 they published studies on "Moisture Variation in Forest Fuels" and on "The Efficiency of Rural Firefighters," reported on an improved emergency fire shelter that could protect firefighters from the radiant heat of a flash fire, and prepared for release under King's authorship a historical compendium documenting "The Influence of Colonization on the Forests and the Prevalence of Bushfires in Australia." King even went on Australian television for an interview about how to survive bushfires. In subsequent years the group investigated the chemical and meteorological properties of bushfire smoke.[25]

It was, on the surface, an odd menu, but the program was not omnivorous. It served precisely the needs of an Australian system that relied on volunteer brigades and the imperatives of an Australian strategy that demanded access to controlled burning. It wanted to make possible fire protection by rural brigades. It sought to justify by any and all means at hand—the chemistry of eucalypt leaves, the innocuous attributes of bushfire smoke, the inexorable interdependence between fuel buildup and bushfire intensity, the precedence of Aboriginal burning—the utility and *rightness* of controlled burning in Australia. Bushfire research reached flood stage in 1965 as CSIRO researchers developed the technology for aerial ignition. When that moment came, science merged with symbol.

By the mid-1960s a research agenda was fully established and its findings rapidly disseminated to field operatives. For another decade science flourished, elaborating its methods and data sets, broadening its geographic reach, sharpening the intellectual precepts and the technological apparatus of the Australian strategy. McArthur refined the quantitative database for fire behavior in eucalypt forests and added a drought index to existing meters. The CSIRO section scrutinized long-term patterns of fire in the southeast, so maddeningly close to an eleven- or thirteen-year cycle. In the late-1960s Australia joined Great Britain, Canada, and the United States for a series of experiments on mass fire. Later, with help from the CSIRO Division of Atmospheric Physics, field experiments on the convective and thermal dynamics of very large fires continued as land clearing made fuels available. Its outreach program even extended overseas, as researchers boldly carried the torch to North America, where they celebrated the marvelous adaptations of the eucalypts, chided the Canadians and Americans for their attachment to air tankers, and politely lectured them about the virtues of controlled fire. Not until the mid-1970s, after a roughly twenty-year tenure, did research fall apart.[26]

The achievements and disappointments of bushfire research were indissolvably bound up with the character of the Australian bushfire revolution. The Australian strategy forced Australian science to take bushfires seriously, and it convinced field practitioners that science was mandatory if they wanted to escape from a degrading spiral of laissez-faire burning off. But the context that stimulated bushfire science also retarded it. The research agenda was too closely lashed to the perceived needs of field programs. It waxed and waned with fire seasons. Not scientific curiosity but holocaust fires drove progress, and if those fires disappeared from the scene for a few years, institutional support would likely dry up. If the revolution faltered, if large fires temporarily faded, if the formative personalities retired or its sustaining institutions reorganized, then there was little to sustain the continuity of research.

Its real achievements, however, went beyond fire-danger meters, emergency shelters, and prescriptions for underburning in jarrah and messmate. Perhaps the greatest impact was ideological and psychological. Not surprisingly, researchers became the chief dialecticians of the Australian strategy, challenging equally those who wanted no fire, those who were content with burning off, and those who insisted that catastrophic fires simply had to be suffered along with drought, impauperate soils, and blowflies. Bushfire research, that is, justified and demystified; it attacked folk skeptics and intellectual critics both as it sought a pragmatic middle between the field and the lab.

By helping to legitimize the Australian strategy, it moved arguments over bushfires beyond the realm of folk prejudice, blind intellectualism, and Australian fatalism. It made bushfires into a legitimate topic for scientific inquiry, and ensured that discussions over policy had to accept scientific evidence. Research assured rural brigades that they could fight wildfire and could manage controlled fire, that the one was in fact essential to the other. It allowed rural firefighters to see bushfires as something other than an inevitable catastrophe emanating from an inscrutable bush; it transformed the "red steer" into a line fire propagating at 2,000 kW m^{-1}, sustained by fuel loads of 14 tons/hectare. It aggressively disputed the folk fatalism that said holocausts were inevitable and that made burning off an act of indifferent desperation. Equally, it resisted the intellectual snobbery that insisted Australia could not evolve indigenous solutions to its indigenous problems. To the revolution, it brought the rigor of the intellectual, the values of the practitioner, and the passion of the nationalist.

PILOT IGNITION:
THE ROLE OF CONTROLLED BURNING

The Australian strategy could succeed only if it was part of an Australian system. To reform one part of the Australian fire scene did little good because failures elsewhere would still allow the disaster fire to overwhelm the whole. But there is little doubt that the intellectual and technological core of the Australian strategy, and its emotional essence, were controlled burning for fuel reduction. Fire planning and institution building were characteristic of organized protection everywhere; the special place according controlled fire—with overtones to Australian natural and human history—is what made the strategy *Australian.* More than anything else, it symbolized the revolution.

Foresters had to rationalize burning off as they did other aspects of rural fire; that included their own fire practices. Luke recalled how as a young cadet forester he was given a box of matches and ordered to do some "early burning" without the slightest instructions on how to proceed. Foresters simply engaged in the same kind of ad hoc protective burning as did their rural neighbors. By the mid-1950s that was no longer acceptable. The Australian strategy targeted fuel-reduction burning as the foundation of fire protection, but it demanded that the practice be orderly, integrated, and scientifically based. After a decade of research and planning those requirements were met. At the Coff's Harbor Conference of 1964, Luke announced that the meeting's purpose was to urge foresters to study their fuel problems and to use the principles of fire behavior elucidated by McArthur to conduct a "programme of carefully planned hazard reduction." Within a year aerial ignition burst upon the scene.[27]

Aerial burning did for the Australian strategy what aerial firefighting did for the American strategy. It not only created a practical tool but promised a glamorous symbol that could, it was hoped, carry an overall message to a grateful public. Foresters realized that they had to burn vast areas to be effective and to keep costs within limits. The best technique was a "system of spot fires," each of which grew out to meet others at moderate intensities. This was precisely the range of fire intensities on which McArthur had published his formulas for controlled burning in eucalypts. The breakthrough came when the CSIRO Bushfire Section transferred spot ignition from ground teams to aircraft with the development of special incendiary capsules. Successful field trials followed in Western Australia in 1965, and the leading advocates of the Australian system took the offensive.[28]

If bushfire protection was to succeed, it had to encompass rural lands as well as reserved forests and parks. It needed extensive procedures for extensive lands. It had to constrain burning off in some places, instigate controlled burning in others, and everywhere integrate fire use with fire control. Controlled burning for hazard reduction satisfied all those ambitions, for practically every form of land use had a potential form of fire use. For many sites the Australian strategy actually proposed an *expansion* of burning. It was not enough to burn out fuelbreaks: protection would fail unless burning reduced fuels over much larger areas.

But how large? Advocates like Luke and McArthur candidly recognized the practical limitations of the scheme. There was a tremendous backlog of lands to burn before a cycle of routine maintenance burning could begin. Once a base-level fuel load existed, they estimated for forests that 5–25 percent of the land might require annual burning. Writing prior to aerial ignition, Luke somewhat timidly thought that "1–2% of the forest state" in New South Wales might be adequate. Writing after aerial firebombing appeared, he suggested that 25 percent of the public forests ought to be treated, with 4–5 percent burned annually.

Simultaneously, McArthur explained the variability of need among the states. Granted a five-year rotation, he estimated that New South Wales could get by with perhaps 5 percent of its protected forest burned annually, Victoria with probably 6–7 percent, and Western Australia with 10–25 percent; he implied that Tasmania might need as little as 1–2 percent. Converting these annual quantities to the total forest fraction burned during the whole cycle, he put the figures at 25 percent for New South Wales, 33 percent for Victoria, 50–100 percent for Western Australia, and perhaps 5–10 percent for Tasmania. Thus he thought it "unlikely, and perhaps highly undesirable, that prescribed burning in eastern Australia should ever approach the scale practised in the dry jarrah forests of Western Australia." But his research demonstrated that doubling fuels doubled the rate of spread and quadrupled fire intensity. Fire officers simply had to do something about those fuels.[29]

McArthur emphasized endlessly that aerial ignition was *controlled* burning, not saturation firebombing. This was not a scorched earth policy but a prescribed practice, a way of putting Australian biotas on a fuels diet. Even in the areas treated, because conditions favored low-intensity fires, much of the landscape would not burn. Dry areas—the same areas—would burn over and over, while wet sites would rarely, if ever, burn. McArthur believed that such judicious use of fire could restore the scene to something like what existed prior to European colonization. But he recognized that this variability also meant that controlled burning, by itself, could not eliminate the large fire. Just as American aerial attack worked best when it supplemented rather than replaced initial attack forces, so Australian aerial burning had to complement rather than supersede the rest of the Australian system.

But just as happened with the American system, so in Australia the new technology contained its own dynamic that in the hands of subalterns sometimes swept caution aside. With foresters as principal agents, prescribed burning rapidly diffused throughout Australia. In the early 1950s, for example, Western Australia undertook broadacre burning; Queensland, Victoria, and Tasmania explored the systematic use of fire for regeneration after harvest; and nearly everyone practiced sub-rosa protective burning. Not until the mid-1960s did broadacre burning for fuel reduction become an article of faith, however, and for its spread aerial ignition serves as a convenient tracer.[30]

Western Australia remained the premier practitioner, aspiring to burn on the average 20 percent of its protected jarrah forests annually and other forested lands somewhat less frequently by combining its regeneration burning with its hazard-reduction burning. Aerial ignition came to New South Wales in 1967 as A.C.T. foresters aeroburned their leasehold area; later that year the Forestry Commission carried the program to the rugged South Coast around Bemboka, lands too vast and formidable to ignite by hand and thickly overgrown with coast ash that had sprouted after the 1952 fires. When the Bemboka burn helped halt a major bushfire later that season, the Commission seized on the technique and flew missions not only to other state forests but, under the aegis of the Bush Fires Council, to unoccupied crown lands. Victoria merged aerial ignition with its growing air attack capability—adding helicopters to fixed-wing aircraft as dispensers, experimenting with infrared mapping, and exploiting incendiaries for backfiring as well as presuppression. Tasmania commenced aerial ignition in buttongrass moors in 1969, and later extended it to dry scleroforest, slash, and regeneration sites. Queensland converted from manual to aerial ignition for fuelbreaks, then carried the techniques of helicopter-based ignitions to exotic pine plantations in 1975. The Northern Territory seized on a "Protective Aerial Controlled Burning Programme" to protect the borders of enormous cattle stations. In the interior—for clearing in brigalow, for reducing fuels in mallee, for controlling scrub, for enhancing wildlife habitat, for protecting Mitchell grass—aerial ignition came into vogue throughout the 1970s.[31]

By 1977 prescribed fire was being widely disseminated, with aerial ignition as the technology of choice. To the fire-research working group of the Australian Forestry Council, P. J. Byrne summarized the state of the burning art and V. P. Cleary the status of aerial operations. The overlap was considerable. The great Victorian fires of that year, though confined to grasslands, reminded everyone of the menace that lurked in every season. But the architects of the Australian strategy knew that aerial fire control was meaningless without aerial fire use; fuel reduction, not initial attack, was the logical cornerstone of Australian fire operations. McArthur noted pointedly in 1969 that the value of aerial fire control would depend on the success of aerial burning. "In the case of Western Australia," he insisted, the prevalence of aerial ignition "would preclude any consideration of their [air tankers'] use." That was a parable for all of Australia. Even after Australian researchers were compelled to reexamine North American–style air tankers, their genius continued to find new ways to ignite ground fuels from the air.[32]

Aerial ignition became more than a tool. Controlled burning for fuel reduction claimed the status of a logical verity, part of a catechism of the Australian strategy. Field failures were dismissed as failures of execution, not failures of concept. They indicated burning operations that were too timidly planned or too meager in scale, and that left too many fuels behind for suppression to have a chance at control. Aerial burning promised to solve both limitations. Equally important, however, it became a symbol, an operational icon, around which advocates of the Australian strategy could rally. It confirmed that a great problem demanded a great solution. Nothing short of massive controlled burning could defend rural Australia against invasions like those that swept through the fire flume of the southeast. What the specter of the Munich appeasement was for Cold War politics, the specter of the 1939 fires was for the politics of the Australian strategy. Never again would Australia be left unprotected or dependent on fickle empires, remote, indifferent, and uncomprehending.

But the symbol could also work in reverse. Aerial ignition made the Australian strategy visible to large numbers of Australians. It carried the controversy over fire practices into one environment after another, whether there was an obvious need for it or not. It broadcast the message to one population of Australians after another, not all of whom wanted to hear it. If it appeased ruralites who demanded protective burning, it alarmed urbanites who wanted those lands put to other uses. If it defined an *Australian* strategy vis-à-vis North American styles, it also aggravated the internal dissensions among Australians about the proper place of fire in their natural environment. What was a symbol of national achievement for one group was for the other an emblem of national vandalism. Aerial burning gave to the critics of the Australian strategy, no less than to its advocates, an emotional icon. As aerial burning spread, so did resistance to the strategy it so brazenly announced and rained down like chemical lightning from the sky.

DON'T LET THIS HAPPEN HERE: RESISTING THE AMERICAN INVASION

The Australian strategy was openly nationalistic, and the Australian revolution compelled a redefinition of Australia's place among the world's fire powers. Part of that nationalism was the discovery of an indigenous symbol that could inspire acceptance. The manifold adaptations of gums (which had long been accepted as an emblem of Australia) to fire, the ancient legacy of burning by Aborigines, the folkways of burning off—all communicated the sense that controlled burning for hazard reduction was an exceptionally

Australian practice. The flip side of nationalism was the search for an external challenge, against which partisans of the revolution could react with something like solidarity. Australia's continuing alliance with the United States after World War II served that purpose. The postwar era witnessed spectacular developments in American firefighting, and Australians eagerly exploited the contrast in national styles. Even as the two nations multiplied contacts—an exercise in international mateship—the effect was to reinforce the assumptions each carried to the other.

It was an awkward, unequal relationship. Americans did not fear an Australian cultural invasion as Australians did an American one. The American strategy built on its own internal momentum with scant regard to Australian practices; it did not require a counterexample to define its character. The contrast between national strategies was cultivated by Australians convinced that the American style of fire protection was incapable of addressing Australian problems, that in fact Americans had much to learn from Down Under. Their ultimate triumph would be the export of the Australian revolution to America. If they worried that Australian nationalism might be absorbed into an American leviathan, they fretted equally that the Australian strategy might be ignored altogether.

Exchanges in the form of "fire study tours" continued on both individual and institutional levels. Official tours began in 1951 when the FAO sent Luke and Torbet to America. In 1964 the FAO and the U.S. Agency for International Development sent five Australians (among twenty-two delegates from fourteen countries) to America and Canada. The U.S. did not reciprocate until 1970 under the auspices of the FAO and Australian Forestry Council. That exchange resulted in a formal agreement to send representatives on a six-year cycle. Australian and New Zealand fire officers toured North America in 1971. American and Canadian fire specialists returned the honor in 1975, hosted by the Australian Forestry Council. Three years later the U.S. Forest Service sponsored a tour by eight Australians and one New Zealander. The Americans cycled back to Australia in 1983, and the Australians to North America in 1987. At the same time, individual fire researchers from both nations conducted private tours for which they published reports. The smaller numbers in the Australian fire community meant that over the span of the Australian revolution virtually all the major participants traveled to North American in some official capacity.[33]

It was also an era of international conferences, and through them Australians were able to publicize their accomplishments on a more equal footing. The Tall Timbers Fire Ecology Conferences, which commenced in Florida in 1962, were particularly useful because they had the intention of encouraging more prescribed burning in America and found Australian experiences a useful antidote to American practices. Mass fire experiments conducted through The Technical Cooperative Programme (TTCP) brought

British, American, and Canadian experimenters to Australia for field burns and in 1969 a major symposium. But the deluge followed.

Beginning in the late 1960s, the American fire establishment experienced a major upheaval that saw policy rewritten, prescribed fire accepted, the institutional hegemony of the U.S. Forest Service broken up, and the entire foundation of American fire practices subjected to an intensity of philosophical scrutiny that it had not known for fifty years. Conferences proliferated, and Australians—recognized as skilled practitioners of controlled burning—often participated. By the mid-1970s, the Australian scene acquired added international value as fire ecology flourished and as interest grew in the fire problems of Mediterranean-climate lands. In such forums, Australian research and practice enjoyed a forum of rough parity with that of colleagues in North America—or, indeed, in Europe, Chile, and South Africa. In 1975 the FAO adopted the McArthur meter as the most suitable system for developing countries, a tribute to its practical genius. A year later the Scientific Committee on Problems of the Environment (SCOPE), a subsidiary body of the International Council of Scientific Unions, launched an international program on "The Effects of Fire on Ecological Systems" in which Australians became enthusiastic participants and contributed the program chair, ecologist R. O. Slatyer. In 1978 the Australian Academy of Science sponsored for SCOPE a symposium which became a book, *Fire and the Australian Biota*, Luke and McArthur published *Bushfires in Australia*, and N. P. Cheney completed his *Guideline for Fire Management on Forested Watersheds, Based on Australian Experiences*, a handbook for the FAO that stood alongside the standard text on fire control written after the war by an American. Observers started coming to Australia to learn, not merely to lecture.[34]

Ironically, Australia became an international fire celebrity at a time when the Australian strategy became a pariah to growing numbers of Australians. Once the Americans adopted prescribed fire, the contrast between national strategies lost its punch, and the revolution some of its élan. In fact, among the lands of British Gondwana Australia had proved something of a laggard in adopting early burning. In contrast to a reformed America, Australia's use of controlled burning for fuel reduction seemed single-minded, ideological, even reactionary. By the late 1970s the fundamental quarrel was no longer confined to professional foresters of different nationalities but between foresters and ecologists, and not between Australians and North Americans but among Australians with differing views of their national heritage, identity, and future. It soon became apparent how useful the American analogue had been to the development of the Australian strategy. It had allowed criticism of all kinds to be consolidated into a single "North American" model that could be quickly dismissed as inappropriate to Australia. It had limited the options under discussion to two, the choice between an Australian strategy and an American one.

These contrasts had operated at nearly every level. Australians blinked at the spectacle of American affluence, an abundance that began with the natural environment and continued into the social. To Australian minds, reckless expenditures distorted every aspect of the American fire scene. Americans could afford professional fire crews and outfit them with standard pumpers while Australians had to rely on volunteers. By 1963 the U.S. Forest Service had endowed three dedicated fire laboratories and embarked on a program of sophisticated experimentation and mathematical modeling; Australians like McArthur used students, field burns, and empirical graphs. The American capacity to mobilize thousands of firefighters and ship them across the nation staggered fire officers who had their hands full trying to coordinate brigades from different districts. But nothing focused the contrast as surely as the question of aircraft.

The advocates of the Australian strategy knew that the Australian public identified American firefighting with air tankers and that the public wanted, as a matter of national pride, an iconographic fleet of Australian waterbombers. But understanding the fragility of the Australian system, they worried that air attack was insatiable, that it would gobble up money until nothing was left of Australian firefighting but a tangle of rural brigades barely "making do," leaving Australia as a kind of Third World fire power ostentatiously flashing a few high-tech symbols while failing to address fundamental problems. At a public seminar in 1966 Dr. R. G. Vines of the CSIRO Bushfire Section cited figures about American air attack that "immediately leads us to the conclusion, and I think it is a just one, that this multimillion [dollar] business of chemical fire fighting in the States is a monster that is generated by its own momentum. It doesn't matter, you see, whether it is any good or not. So much money is involved that every one is happy. Don't let this happen here." [35]

Almost to a man the Australian fire community fought to ensure that aerial firefighting on the North American model did not happen in Australia. Air attack had to demonstrate its place in the Australian system *before* it would be admitted. Instead of accepting air tankers and trying to find ways to make them work within the confines of the Australian system, the Australian fire community showed over and again how air attack could not work, how anything other than a commitment to fuel reduction was an expensive frivolity. Instead they proposed an alternative, aerial ignition.

Aerial ignition made an ironic icon, however. It worked wonderfully as a contrapuntal image to North American fire practices, but it served equally well as a rallying point for Australian critics. As "aeroburning" became a symbol of public disapproval, the contrast to blustering America was no longer an adequate argument. As the Americans revised their fire policies and programs to accommodate prescribed fire, the national contrast lost its vitality—or rather turned against the advocates of the Australian strategy, for the Americans did not burn exclusively or even primarily for hazard reduction, but for biocentric purposes, goals that Australian critics quickly turned against Australian practitioners.

But this did not occur until the late 1970s. Until then the contrast had worked to advantage and had held off air tankers long enough for the Australian strategy to mature on its own terms. Until then the dramatic contrast in national styles, the threat of an American "invasion," had confirmed, for the revolutionaries, the rightness of their position and promoted solidarity within the ranks. When the real crisis came it did not emanate from North America but from a reformation in Australian values and land usage, and it took on special power by the simultaneous passage from the scene of the revolutionary generation.

THE ADVOCACY OF ALAN MCARTHUR

The new times brought new men. Like most revolutions the Australian strategy suffered historical amnesia; for its advocates the world originated in the early 1950s when the Hume-Snowy Scheme began to amalgamate brigades into a patchwork quilt, when Western Australia committed to broadacre burning, and when Alan G. McArthur burst upon the scene. McArthur was born for the revolution. It was impossible to imagine McArthur without fire, or Australian fire without McArthur. A native Australian, born to a Western District wheat farmer in 1923, McArthur grew up burning stubble, recalled as a schoolboy the beckoning "night-time glow of large fires in the Cocoparra Range," thrilled to the sights and sounds of bushfires, and made fire a professional passion. The Australian strategy gave an obsessive order to his life, and McArthur reciprocated by becoming its chief dialectician, instilling rigor and voice into its assumptions.[36]

Alan McArthur was a different creature on the Australian fire scene. Proudly nationalistic, a self-proclaimed "ocker," defiantly lowbrow, intensely pragmatic, relentlessly sardonic, a sportsman who detested losing and a gambler who wagered only on solid odds, a public figure who never admitted to error or apologized for mistakes, a tough-hided administrator who insisted on fieldwork and whose personal health suffered through decades of diabetes that culminated in kidney failure and dialysis—McArthur epitomized the Australian as scleromorph. Where Lane-Poole had awed students with visions of empire and French phrases and immersed them in bookishness—an agenda a disgusted Swain had dismissed as "medievalism" —McArthur announced that he was "not a lecturer's arsehole" and sent his students into the field under primitive conditions to conduct hundreds of experimental burns. Where Harry Luke sought to conciliate, McArthur confronted; what Luke communicated with charm McArthur broadcast through a bullhorn of sarcasm. He was biting, impatient, witty, daring—"game as

Ned Kelly," Luke marveled—and not ready to suffer fools, particularly urban critics who knew the bush through Sunday strolls. His passion was for Australia and for rural folk in equal amounts. His vocation was to protect them.

To a phenomenal extent his career reads like a curriculum vitae of the Australian revolution. After graduating from Sydney University with a B.Sc. (Forestry), he joined the New South Wales Forestry Commission and took a diploma in forestry from the Australian Forestry School in 1944. Immediately he encountered the great fires of 1944–45. In 1951 he was appointed fire control officer on the Hume-Snowy Scheme, and within a year found himself battling the conflagrations of 1951–52. A year later he was named fire research officer at the Forestry and Timber Bureau, the first full-time professional fire scientist in Australia. He assumed the lectureship on fire control at the Australian Forestry School, through which he converted a new generation of foresters. Fires were integral to their professional lives, he told them. If they failed to use fire, they would be destroyed by fire. But if they learned from fire, they could fight it. "It can be done and as long as you work systematically, you can wear it down and beat it in the end." [37]

The field data that sustained the Australian strategy over the next two-and-a-half decades came largely from his labors. In the late 1950s, after developing methods for studying experimental fires, he carried the techniques to the broadacre burn blocks of Western Australia. This data he coded into fire-danger meters as guides to brigades. He launched a series of detailed case studies of large fires in different fuel types. He participated in most of the major fire reviews of the era—the principal technical advisor to the Rodger Commission that investigated the 1961 fires; leader of investigations into the 1967 fires that invaded Hobart, the 1974–75 fires that spanned half the continent, and the 1977 fires that raced through western Victoria. He was present at every fire-officer conference and every symposium, always with blunt opinions, a broad accent, and an almost visible anti-intellectual sneer. Along with Luke he ensured that the Australian system extended to the rural landscape, not just to state forests. More than anyone else, he carried the message of the Australian strategy overseas. He lectured about eucalypt plantations to Brazilians and about broadcast burning to Canadians. He saw more of American fire practices—and saw them through greater skepticism—than any other Australian. It was a deeply satisfying moment when the FAO selected his fire-danger meter, not the one that the expensive American labs had labored on for two decades, as its choice for developing nations.

Foresters in particular appreciated his accomplishments; he became director of the Forest Research Institute in 1970, and for a while was acting director of the Forest and Timber Bureau until it was absorbed into CSIRO in 1975. After retirement he collaborated with Harry Luke to summarize the wisdom learned in the three decades since the *Outline;* the result was their magisterial *Bushfires in Australia.* After his death the Institute of Foresters of Australia awarded him, as it did Luke, its highest honor, the N. W. Jolly Award.

McArthur put forth the case for the Australian strategy with characteristic boldness. Without fuel-reduction burning on a massive scale, there was no hope to contain disaster fires, and unless disaster fires were contained, there was little point in protecting lands because the holocaust fire would sweep away years of successful protection. He explained that controlled burning did not translate into a scorched earth policy; in fact because burning created mosaics of fuels it was essential to have adequate fire control forces. "A lot of people think that you can do control burning and that is the whole fire control system," he told an audience of critics, "but this is just as wrong as it could possibly be. Control burning is only a means of making the fire control job a little bit easier . . ." But anyone who thought fire control was possible without extensive presuppression burning was a fool—or worse.[38]

That in fact was the other voice of Alan McArthur, McArthur the moralist. The issue went beyond field operations. The Australian strategy was a matter of national identity, a statement of what Australia was about and how Australians had to relate to their land. It also involved a social compact with those Australians, largely rural, who actually lived under the pall of disaster bushfires and who, in the form of volunteer brigades, manned the firelines. As critics mounted—most of them ecologists not foresters, urbanites interested in wilderness sites not ruralites working the land—McArthur put to them the question of how they proposed to keep fire out of large wilderness sites heavily laden with fuels. How, he asked, can they ask volunteer brigades to risk their lives to suppress wildfires under those circumstances? Had any of them experienced, as he had, that paralyzing moment when "time stands still while you are fighting for your life"? How could they refuse access trails or fuel-reduction burning, and still insist on control? Yet without aggressive protection it was, to McArthur's mind, only a matter of time before any site was incinerated by a large fire—a fire made large by years of successful suppression. There was no technical answer to that question, as he well knew. It was a matter of values.[39]

McArthur's own values were clear. Fire was his life. He trucked his family to fires at the sight of summer smoke. He even had them conduct experimental burns with rudimentary equipment, his wife manning an anemometer, his children marking the fire perimeter with flat rocks identified by lumber crayon. He traveled around Australia and overseas only to study fire. He talked fire, thought fire, lived fire. Fire, he insisted, had to come first. It had priority in Australian forestry; it had priority in fire control. Early on he decided that he would never divert tankers from a fireline to the protection of houses. "The name of the game is to stick by the book, and fight the fire," he lectured, even when it meant, as it once did for him, that he had to watch a breakaway fire race toward the house his family was staying in. And fire had priority in presuppression: only the use of controlled burning could ensure adequate protection against the disaster fire. Those who talked of excluding fire from Australia were fools. Fire was too much an informing principle in Australian natural history.[40]

Australian fire was Alan McArthur's mission. It shaped and animated his life. Friends believed that writing *Bushfires* with Luke literally kept him alive after further systemic failures worsened his health. But that relationship to fire had been reciprocal. What Australian fire gave McArthur, McArthur returned. He endowed the Australian strategy with a distinctive voice, a personality, a vital if sardonic moral tone. He committed Australians to an indissolvable bond with bushfire. If his labors to codify the Australian strategy kept him alive, it is no less true that he kept alive the revolution it inspired. So long as Alan McArthur lived, the Australian strategy thrived.

19

Wild Bush, Urban Bush: Fire Regimes of New Australia

*I love an un*burnt *country.*

—*ENVIRONMENTALIST PUN ON DOROTHY MACKELLAR'S POEM, "I LOVE A SUNBURNT COUNTRY"*

Where Sydney and the Bush meet now,
There is no common ground.

—*LES MURRAY, "Sydney and the Bush"*
(1976)

THE RECONSTITUTION OF AUSTRALIAN SOCIETY after the war paralleled a reconstruction of the Australian environment. The process took several decades before it became evident, slowed at first by the postwar demand for wool, wheat, and basic commodities, then hastened as a service economy matured and "new" Australians became a majority and asserted new values. By the 1970s the reformation was undeniable and probably irreversible. The rural scene—that roughly grazed and farmed landscape that was the legacy of European colonization—broke up into an archipelago of more specialized sites. The artificial unity that agriculture had imposed lost its grip. Farming and forestry disentangled; environments that graziers had crudely homogenized fractionated back into separate identities as distinctive biotas; small rural towns decayed, while the metropolitan centers spread grasping tentacles through an increasingly urbanized bush. Only mining among the rural industries boomed; but it was site-specific, intensely so, quite unlike grazing which had served as an engine of change across such a wide spectrum of environments. To match its self-conscious ethnic pluralism New Australia promoted an environmental pluralism.

The vital bushlands were the wild and the urban. New Australia reclaimed vast dominions of crown lands that it had formerly given over by lease to graziers. Many such areas became parks and nature reserves, or reverted to Aboriginal ownership. In place of exotic flora and fauna, they promoted more indigenous biotas. In place of commodity production, they advanced recreational uses. Instead of the traditional palette of rural Australians, they advertised a new transient through the bush—the sightseer, the scientist, the hobby farmer, the exurbanite. Equally, the great city-states spread into their rural shadows like vines sending out tough tendrils. Sprawling suburbs insinuated themselves into surrounding highlands, their inhabitants less a rural populace crowding into cities than a secondary emigration from urban suburbs into quasi-rural landscapes. The new bushman had different values than his rural predecessor and sought a different "adaptation" to Australia. The new environments went hand-in-glove with a new environmentalism. The new bushman came equipped with different experiences and expectations toward fire.

Old fire practices suffered the same challenges as old landscapes. The Australian strategy had been designed for the rural Australia in which its architects had grown up. It was a broad-brush strategy, ideal for a lightly populated landscape plunked down in a virtual fire flume and for a rural population fanatically confident about the relationship between fuels and fires and familiar with the ritual of burning off. But the decay in traditional rural economies meant a decay in traditional fire lore as well. Routine burning disappeared from places like backblock Tasmania, and no new fires, other than wildfires, took their place. Where traditional burning enjoyed a renaissance, as in the brigalow belt, it occurred outside its familiar sites and context. Even as the advocates of the Australian strategy engineered their ideas into institutions, even as they propelled the system into more and more environments, they met a rising counterforce. Wilderness critics argued that special biotas demanded special fire practices, that burning off was too indiscriminate, that it homogenized what should be segregated. Urban critics protested that burning was an inadequate basis for protection. The wild bush required a miscellany of fire patterns; the urban bush, fire suppression.[1]

What proponents of the Australian strategy saw as a rationalization of rural fire practices, keenly expressive of a resurgent Australian nationalism, rivals saw as continued vandalism in the European vogue—folk medicine unsuitable in environments in which indigenous biotas tottered on the brink of extinction. To a new generation that publicly announced it sought a new relationship to the Australian bush the icons of the Australian strategy seemed misplaced, dubious, perhaps diabolical.

BLACK TUESDAY

Even by the standards of the greater southeast, the Tasmanian fires in 1967 were extraordinary. For an industrialized nation they were also an apparition, like some Pleistocene beast that, exhumed from ice, had come to life in an uncontrollable rampage. The fires represented, in McArthur's plain-spoken prose, "the largest loss of life and property on any single day in the history of the Australian continent." Their fiery perimeter defined the ragged, violent boundary between European Australia and New Australia.[2]

The fires played out according to a classic fire-flume scenario. A wet winter flushed out the grasslands, and a droughty summer parched grass and forest into the dryness of hardwood flooring. Desert winds in advance of a cold front swept from the northwest at record velocities. The fire-danger index soared to 96, challenging the 100-point record of 1939. Rushing winds fanned scores of smoldering fires—sparks cast off from the routine of life in rural Australia—into conflagrations. Some 110 fires burned on Tuesday, February 7, of which 20 accounted for 58 percent of the total burned area. Meager control efforts crumbled before the onslaught. One horrific fire brushed past Hobart, incinerating suburbs as it went. In the space of five hours more than 270,000 hectares, 1,300 houses, and 128 major buildings burned; sixty-two people died.

The fire recalled the great holocausts of European Australia, and they received a classic response. Parliamentary boards of inquiry reconstructed the causes and consequences of the fires. McArthur conducted a thorough study of fire behavior. Academics analyzed the scene from the perspective of public administration and disaster preparedness. Some of the breakdowns reflected familiar failures, generic to most of Australia. But many critical circumstances were peculiar to Tasmania—the absence of a unifying fire program and a reliance on ill-suited wardens, a tolerance toward burning off that bordered on criminal negligence, a pattern of drought, wind, and conflagration that crowded violence into concentrated times and places. Usually damp Tasmania had erupted into one of its roughly fifty-year fires.

The investigating committees freely recognized such idiosyncrasies, but their overall interpretation put the disaster squarely into the context of rural fire practices. Black Tuesday had thrust rural fire at the metropolis. Probably 80 to 88 percent of all fires were the product of unregulated rural burning, and the most damaging fires had roared out of unprotected rural and crown lands, the traditional breeders of wildfire. Accordingly, the boards of inquiry recommended that Tasmania adopt the precepts and programs of the Australian strategy. They urged that Parliament rewrite the Rural Fires Act, that officials reconstitute the Rural Fires Board in order to eliminate a fatal dependence on overly complacent fire wardens, that communities organize for bushfire protection. The Chambers Committee, in particular, recommended adoption of a Lake Country Special Fire Area, modeled on the Hume-Snowy Scheme, as a pilot program.

The committee asserted, too, that "effective hazard reduction or control burning," alongside rudimentary fire prevention measures and the "introduction of organized fire suppression," could "solve most of the existing problems facing control in rural Tasmania today." It went on record to avow "the very firm opinion" that, in keeping with the Australian strategy—then at flood tide—"far more planned hazard reduction work must be undertaken at suitable times and under proper supervision than has ever been done in the past." There was "little doubt" that the severity of the fires stemmed from excess fuels in forest areas "due to the fact that they had not been control burnt for many years." Clearly influenced by McArthur, the committee suggested that Tasmania look into "recent aerial techniques" for burning its scleroforest.[3]

Black Tuesday thus completed a cycle that began with Red Tuesday. The holocaust was a classic European-era conflagration, somewhat modified by a heritage of incremental, inadequate reforms in local fire institutions. Tasmania had not shared as fully in the overall transformation of postwar Australia, and when the fires came they had an anachronistic aura. To their reviewers they sustained the belief that it was possible to solve the problems of New Australia by a rural reformation. While the Chambers report cited the "tremendous area of urban development" around Mount Wellington as a contributing complication, the fires had bubbled out of the common lands of the countryside. Hobart suburbs were, from a fire perspective, less an urban fringe than a rural fringe.

The fires were ideal for proponents of the Australian strategy. They seemed to confirm its tenets, its methods, its viability in New Australia; even remote, anomalous Tasmania could adopt its principles and practices. That McArthur was a primary investigator ensured that Black Tuesday would be interpreted in the shadow of Black Friday, that there would be continuity with the Rodger Commission. Aerial ignition had just flapped its wings, and exhilaration grew among advocates of the Australian strategy that their approach had universal validity. Their interpretation of the fires inspired them to redouble their efforts—to extend the Australian system into other urban fringes, to bring controlled burning to the full spectrum of the Australian biota.

In fact, Tasmania was exceptional, less a harbinger of the future than a throwback to the past. The exquisite timing of the fires inverted their true character. The fundamental problem was less the growth of rural fires into an urban fringe than it was the growth of an urban fringe into rural fire zones. The coming controversies over Tasmanian fire involved the urban and the wild, not the rural, and a strategy of fire protection that sought to protect both ends by an expansion of techniques designed for the rural middle was destined for controversy.

THE BIG SMOKE:
FIRE ON THE URBAN FRINGE

To country folk and Aborigines the European-style cities planted in Australia were often known as the "big smoke." The pressures for close settlement, however, kept the big smoke of chimneys, factories, and debris piles under wraps. City fires stayed in the city. Free-burning fires resided on the frontier, where fire was both an implement of conversion and a hazard inherent in the natural environment. Urban expansion in fact was more or less controlled, the city effectively buffered by a broadening belt of rural landscapes. Fire protection in the city-states grew outward in roughly concentric rings, like medieval cities encircling their enlarged boundaries with new walls. Those who lived outside the walls were especially vulnerable.

New Australia changed this evolution. The metropolitan centers swelled in absolute numbers and in relative proportion to the overall population; and their pattern of expansion altered from one of close settlement to outright sprawl. By the 1980s some 85 percent of Australians resided within the greater metropolitan areas and those areas radiated crazily across the landscape like shrapnel tracks from an exploding bomb. The sprawl scrambled the border between town and country. A variety of urbanlike communities intermingled with a variety of wild and rural lands. A new term emerged to describe the mélange—urban bush.

The phenomenon of exurban migration was not peculiar to Australia: it also typified portions of industrialized Europe and North America in the postwar era. In each case former farmlands or pastures dissolved into a patchwork of subdivisions. In many instances, development thrust exurban fringe areas next to wildlands including parks and forests. Native and exotic flora flourished, particularly on rural sites abandoned but not yet converted, or on lands owned by absentee hobby farmers or around houses bought as holiday homes. The interstitial lands fell through jurisdictional cracks.

For decades it had been the ambition of bushfire protection authorities to eliminate the threat from unprotected lands—the Australian commons, the crown lands loosely leased to transients. The Australian system cultivated by Luke was designed precisely to plug those gaps, but the new settlement melee defied, even reversed that trend. Instead of integrating scattered settlements, instead of imposing standards and a degree of uniformity, the new pattern encouraged diversity. Small remnants and natural refugia, enclaves of housing subdivisions and alternative life-stylers, new influxes of urban tourists and absentee owners—all pushed the environment toward pluralism rather than homogeneity. There was no desire (and no mechanism) to fill in the settlement voids. Corridors of dispersed communities flung out along highways and nestled like scattered birdshot among mountains with no likelihood that the future would replace the intervening bush with town. Fire officers confronted a situation for which they had no precedent, and they stared in disbelief as residents happily encouraged an eruption of flora—volatile fuels all—that would blanch anyone with a memory that dated back to the last holocaust. A different kind of environmental disturbance was again unsettling Australia.

The new landscape reflected changes in social composition and cultural values. The mingling of bush and city that horrified fire officers was in fact one of the prime attractions of the urban bush. Often the higher the proportion of untrammeled bush, the more isolated the site, the looser the pattern of settlement, the greater was its perceived value. There was no desire, and often no provision, to develop systematically those interstitial lands. These sentiments were far from unique to Australia, but the identification of a preserved or resurgent native bush with a New Australia complicated enormously discussions about fire practices. While American exurbanites spilled over New England farmlands, which regrew forests, or splayed across the foothills of Southern California, living cheek by jowl with scleromorphic chaparral, their motives were for a more relaxed life-style, a recreational interest in nature, a distaste for densely urban and populated environments. They used their new affluence to move to that fascinating fringe between the urban and the wild.

All this was no less true for Australians, but there was beneath the surface a shoal of latent nationalism on which public discussions constantly foundered. The environmental legacy of European Australia was an embarrassment to many, not unlike the nation's heritage of Aboriginal relations. New Australia had to do better; New Australians should learn to live in harmony with the bush; they should celebrate it, not despise and seek to replace it; they should evolve new "adaptations" to Australia. A New Australian was one who sought out the indigenous and promoted its unique diversity. Living in dispersed communities surrounded by native flora and fauna was a public declaration of that identity. There was, by contrast, no similar nationalism at work in the exurban fire scene of America or in that of Europe, where developments along the Mediterranean littoral created analogous hazards.

All the city-states watched their urban bush flourish. For Perth and Brisbane fires in the fringe were more nuisance than threat. In the southeastern fire flume, however, any ignition could flame into holocaust during outbreaks of extreme weather. The potential for disaster was greatest where exurbanites thronged to nearby mountains—to the Dandenongs outside

Melbourne, the Blue Mountains beyond Sydney, the Mount Lofty Ranges that fringed Adelaide, Hobart's Mount Wellington. The most desirable sites, those that attracted the most fanatical exurbanites, were also the most hazardous. The urban bush thrust and leapfrogged the metropolis into the realm of rural bushfire. In January 1962 fires broke out in the Dandenongs—small fires by typical Australian standards—and destroyed 454 homes in what might stand as the effective announcement of a new fire regime.[4]

There could be no single response for there was no single provocation. There were many causes, many exurban enclaves, many bushlands. The medium became its own message: the mélange—the mingling—was itself a valued consequence, not simply a means to another end. Foresters had to compete with ecologists and recreational naturalists as authorities on fire. Fire officers had to argue strenuously with residents about the character of the fire hazard and the actions necessary to reduce it. Residents accepted the fire risks but believed that the causes were anthropogenic—the residue of European abuse and rural fire practices—and could be removed. A decade after the 1962 fires 43 percent of Dandenong residents polled thought the bushfire problem could be solved eventually, and another 23 percent were undecided.[5]

All in all exurbanites disliked and distrusted fire. Critics wanted greater specificity to fire practices—specific fuel reduction for specific places at specific times. They saw fire as a powerful agent of biotic change and argued that any use of fire for fuel reduction had fundamental side effects on all of the biota. They protested burning on esthetic grounds. Thus critics argued, from the English model, that it was possible to control fuels through an intensive hand manipulation (a kind of gardening) of the urban bush, and from the American model that it was possible to control new fires at critical times by means of an aggressive suppression organization outfitted with high-tech hardware including air tankers.

Fire officers, particularly foresters, tended to see the fundamental causes as built into the constitution of Australia's natural history. The circumstances for holocaust fires were inexpungable, and only extensive fuel reduction offered a shred of hope for containing the small fraction of fires that did the greatest damage. They accepted their limitations on labor-intensive projects, the boundaries of a system reliant on bushfire brigades. They believed in controlled burning and wanted to see prescribed fire replace burning off. They pointed to Southern California where exurban communities in mountain chaparral were devastated by conflagrations despite a suppression organization that was unparalleled in the world. Along the Angeles Front fuelbreaks, fire stations, and helispots straddled the landscape like an army of occupation; fire suppression had on call a fleet of air tankers larger than the military of many nations; fire agencies in Los Angeles County spent more money each year on fire than Australia did on all of its rural lands—and still fires broke free. No one could garden or bomb fire out of the Australian bush —fire use was the most natural means of fire control.

On virtually every fire issue, debate rapidly polarized. Studies revealed, for example, that firebrands were the principal agent of destruction for houses in the urban bush. To residents this argued against extensive land clearing or broadacre burning for fuel reduction since brands could travel long distances; better to design individual houses to resist wind-driven embers. To fire officers, the same evidence suggested the value of extensive fuel reduction, for such treatment could abate fire intensity and eliminate the firebrands at their source. The one emphasized the source of the brands; the other, their end point. Advocates and critics disagreed about means because they disagreed about ends.

The fundamental questions were not really technical issues. Arguing about the relative costs of hand labor and air tankers or the relative tonnages of eucalypt litter eliminated by various burning schemes did not bring the discussion to closure because the genuine issues went deeper. The recolonization of New Australia had restated the cultural questions raised by the original colonization. Was it possible for European-descended peoples to live in Australia without destroying the bush that made Australia what it was? Could they use the bush as a means of positive identification, as a badge of national character? Could recolonization reestablish a moral order to Australia? The urban bush offered a second chance.

Each side massed technical data that supported its position, and each claimed a nationalist basis. One proposed to evolve fire practices out of past experience; the other to begin anew. One saw Europeans—indeed, humans—struggling against a merciless Australia; the other emphasized an Australia groaning under the reckless acts of a technologically powerful outpost of Western civilization. One located the core problem in rural Australia and the other in urban Australia. One group was prepared to live along the violent, compromised border of the Red Centre. The other wanted to "green" that Centre.

THE GREENING OF THE RED CENTRE

Rural Australia fractured under pressure from the wild as well as the urban. Tourism boomed in the affluence of the postwar era, and membership in conservation societies increased exponentially, swollen by numbers of recreational naturalists, scientists, professional intellectuals, and miscellaneous "greenies." Members were largely affluent urbanites, and they focused considerable attention on remnants of the native biota enmeshed in the urban bush. But these were only tokens; the major thrust involved the preservation of large expanses of Australia as parks and nature preserves. The establishment of the Australian Conservation Foundation in 1965 gave the movement institutional legitimacy, books by Vincent Serventy *(Australia: A Continent in Danger)* and A. J. Marshall *(The Great Extermination)* sounded its alarms to the public, and a report released in 1968 by the Australian Academy of Sciences strengthened its conceptual credibility. The environmental movement became a political force. One by one the states legislated a galaxy of new parks into existence, created a National Parks and Wildlife Service (1967), and officially backed environmental planning. Further legislation in 1974 strengthened the movement. By 1975 Australia had 1.75 acres of parks and protected areas per person, compared to 0.07 acres in America. It was inevitable that fire policy would become a part of the emerging environmental agenda as an expanding Australian strategy encountered an expanding parks system. In 1968, less then a year after their enabling legislation, bushfires pushed against the coastal forests along a fire front virtually unbroken for more than 450 kilometers and threatened to overrun the southeastern parks.[6]

The pressures for parks were varied, and many reflected concerns of what became a transnational movement. Preserves had scientific, recreational, and cultural dimensions. They were genetic banks, warehouses of biodiversity, and unrivaled natural laboratories. They served as playgrounds, gymnasiums and outdoor arenas, and pressure release valves for an urban, industrial society. They were sanctuaries of nature, an act of noblesse oblige by the human stewards of the earth. And they testified to national character, for preserving natural history also preserved human history. Without their strange bush Australians were only Europeans in exile; with it, they had claim to a special identity.

Much as New Australia sought to redefine its political identity among the global commonwealth of nations, so it sought to redefine its relationship to a global environment. Australia's unique biotas and landforms created for it a special niche in the political economy of international environmentalism. If they vanished from Australia such creatures had vanished from the world. "We have gained animals and birds that the whole world has," lamented Eric Rolls, "and have lost and are still losing many species of our own strange, beautiful and distinct creatures." Equally, those biotas and such signatory features as Ayers Rock and the Great Barrier Reef gave Australia talismans with instant power as national symbols. Parks tapped a deep, if inchoate reservoir of Australian nationalism. Preserving nature preserved an irreplaceable part of the Australian experience.[7]

The movement plumbed, too, a reservoir of guilt. Promoting nature reserves, like establishing Aboriginal reserves, was an act of reconciliation, an admission that not all of European colonization had turned out well. Thus preservation often meant restoration, too. If the urban bush offered the chance to recolonize rural Australia, the wild bush proposed a second chance to reenact the European settlement. Bitterly, Judith Wright wrote that Australians "are conquerors and self-poisoners" who will themselves be "ruined by the thing we kill." Nature reserves were an act of atonement, the gesture of people who sought to behave differently than their ancestors. Such overtones gave the parks movement enormous breadth and stamina among the Australian populace.[8]

It came with considerable shock to foresters to learn that they were now numbered among the enemies of the Australian environment. Even as their political status stabilized, they lost the high ground in the emerging moral universe of New Australia. Public forestry in Australia, as elsewhere, became a public incubus. It introduced alien species (like Monterey pine); it sacrificed native forest (even "rainforest") for artificial pine plantations and woodchips to be shipped to that industrial octopus, Japan; it clear-felled woods, purged the indigenous fauna, and burned indiscriminately. Private or public, forestry became identified with the whole complex of European importations and manipulations that had worked so brusquely over the surface of the continent. Foresters had always insisted that good forestry was part of the solution to Australian land abuse; now critics charged that good forestry was not generally practiced, and when done, was an unsuitable—lesser—use of Australian resources.

All this had profound ramifications for Australian fire practices, for the Australian strategy, in particular, had been the special creation of foresters. In fact, the imagery of Australian fire was confusing, often contradictory. It was possible to celebrate a wildfire that raged through the heathlands of the Nadgee Reserve, stimulating a profusion of new growth, yet publish a Geoffrey Allen painting depicting burning off as a condemnatory cover to a popular history of Australian environmental history. The perception of fire as an essential part of native Australia was countered by the image of fire as an agent of destruction, the means by which Europeans had debased Old Australia into an antipodean shadow of Europe. Howard and Mary Alice Evans voiced the sentiments of many ardent environmentalists when they proclaimed that "one thing is certain: to persons interested in plant and animal life, a recently burned forest has little to offer." Particularly for those whose intellectual heritage lay in England, it was unthinkable that fire could serve legitimate uses. (In the 1980s, England actually moved to suppress straw burning as a public nuisance and a degenerative practice.) New data from academic biologists, CSIRO researchers, and others outside mainstream forestry suggested that fire effects were far more complex phenomena than previously believed, and that fire practices had far-ranging implications, not all of which were understood. Controlled burning had consequences that could not be restricted to its impact on fuels.[9]

Policies and position papers sprouted, suffered attack, and regrew in state after state. In 1970 the Australian Conservation Foundation released a reasoned manifesto on "bushfire control and conservation" that encapsulated the sentiments and logic of environmental critics. The foundation recognized that fire in some capacity belonged in landscape, and that barring a technological revolution "we in Australia must lean heavily on control-burning in our fire mitigation policy." But it conveyed powerful reservations. Parks and wildlife reserves should not be managed as commercial forests or wheat fields; controlled burning had become itself a significant source of escape fires, some of which threatened reserves; the full *biological* impact of the fires, beyond their demonstrated effect on fuels, was not known. All this argued for caution in burning, or for alternatives to burning. It was not even obvious that routine controlled fire insulated a site from the holocaust fire, which was the ultimate justification for burning. And fire protection was itself a massive expression of a human presence. It violated the illusion of naturalness by laying down roads, trails, and towers, by terrorizing landscapes with bulldozers and chemicals, and by burning according to human schedules and for human ends.[10]

But what really galvanized the foundation was the specter of aerial ignition and its promise to expand enormously the realm of blackened Australia. Official controlled burning and unofficial burning off together constituted "an ecological assault on our natural environment on an almost frightening scale." The National Parks Association of New South Wales voiced a common sentiment when it argued that "broad area burning for protection reasons alone is an unreasonable protection measure—rather like reducing all lakes to wading ponds in case somebody gets drowned." In state after state, park after park, that scenario repeated itself. The Australian strategy had been forged for rural Australia and against the exemplar of North American firefighting. Now it found itself fighting a fifth column in a kind of Australian civil war over the environment. Its critics did not want to dismantle its institutions or dismiss its research; rather they sought to take over its machinery—to redirect the Australian system to the service of parks and reserves, and to reapply the knowledge of prescribed burning to different, ecological objectives. As the Australian strategy expanded its empire, it faced growing insurgency across the continent. It was clear that, with time, the parks and reserves would command not only public opinion but firefighting resources and, if unchecked, would absorb lands formerly administered directly or as fire protectorates by forestry commissions. Unanswered, the smaller parks agencies could conceivably use the leverage of public opinion to stage a hostile takeover of forestry bureaus.[11]

Park administrators recognized that they needed to propose, not merely dispose. With the facilities and funds at hand, they fashioned an alternative system to that of foresters, a kind of fire establishment in exile. Ecological research supplemented, and at times challenged, forestry research. Sophisticated computer modeling of ecosystems replaced linear graphs of fuels and fire intensity. New concepts of ecological succession after fires supplemented charts of fuel buildup. Richer understanding of fire regimes—how ensembles of fires affected suites of organisms—replaced simplistic assertions that Australian biotas were "adapted to fire," which had become part of a catechism justifying the Australian strategy. Expert systems coded into computer programs knowledge about fire behavior, effects, and management options that, more in theory than in practice, went far beyond the fire-danger meters of McArthur. Field managers sought to apply and withhold fire for a variety of biological purposes—to improve habitat as well as to reduce fuels, to serve quokkas as well as cockies. Much as controlled burning had co-opted burning off, so prescribed fire for ecological purposes threatened to co-opt controlled fire for fuel reduction. Universities and international scientific societies sponsored symposia on Australian fire ecology and broke fire research out of the confines of forestry and fire physics. Conservation agencies formed new institutional alliances—shotgun weddings, really—with established land and forestry agencies. Australian environmentalists even found inspiration in the revolution that began in the late 1960s within the American fire establishment, a movement that challenged the assumption that fire protection was the driving objective of public land administration.

Park fire specialists experimented with an array of fire practices across a full spectrum of Australian environments. Outside the fire flume compromises were possible. Thus, after bushfires ravaged Cooloola National Park in Queensland in the 1960s, officials instigated a program of perimeter burning and fire tracks and by the mid-1970s even inaugurated some aerially ignited interior burns. In Western Australia the Forests Department quickly moved to blunt criticisms and experimented with new practices on parks and faunal reserves, many of which fell under the jurisdiction of foresters. Once again the Westralian style, rigorous and flexible, absorbed the challenges; there was controversy without the polarization that elsewhere made compromise almost impossible. The Forests Department joined a reorganization into a Department of Conservation and Land Management.[12]

In the central deserts there were attempts to reinstate patch burning for habitat restoration and fuel reduction both. Acute overgrazing and the abolition of Aboriginal fire had conspired to render portions of the interior both uninhabitable and vulnerable to large fires; the 1974–75 season burned 80 percent of Uluru National Park. Officials sought to reintroduce fire but not on the metronomic cadence practiced elsewhere, not on the scale made feasible by aerial ignition, and not exclusively for fuel reduction in spinifex. Similar programs began at Sturt National Park in the Western District of New South Wales, at the Tanami Desert Reserve in the Northern Territory, and the Little Desert National Park in Victoria. Mistakes were common—a compound of ignorance, inexperience, understaffing, overzealousness, and the inevitable difficulties that attend any new program as conceptual fault planes, glossed over in written plans, break free under the stress of real-world operations. The Australian strategy, after all, had had its share of break-downs and was, in the mid-1970s, far from infallible.[13]

The major battlegrounds were elsewhere—at Kakadu National Park in Arnhemland, along the perimeters of Tasmanian parks and forests, and at Mount Kosciusko. Lands that had been ignored or abused because they re-sisted European colonization now became valued for precisely those same reasons. Kakadu offered a unique preserve of the wet-dry tropics, Tasmania boasted a temperate rainforest, and Kosciusko, at the summit of the Austra-lian Alps, featured a mosaic of big scleroforest, grasslands, and subalpine biotas. Each had symbolic significance to Australian environmentalism, each posed difficult, unavoidable questions about what kind of fire practices best suited its special biotas. They inscribed a new fire triangle for Australia, their apexes aligned with the political geography of New Australia.

TOP END AND WEST COAST: FIRE AT THE EXTREMES

Scientific interest in Arnhemland fire commenced in the mid-1960s, about equally divided between anthropologists curious about Aboriginal fire prac-tices and foresters concerned with bushfire protection. The prospects of ex-tending aeroburning to the Top End brought discussion to a boil. In 1971 Luke convened for the Bush Fires Council a major conference, "Tropical and Arid Fire Symposium," that surveyed fire in the Northern Territory. The reconnaissance revealed, on one hand, the enormous magnitude of fire that annually visited the Top End and, on the other, a profound ignorance about its ecological role. Subsequently the N.T. Forests Branch and the Forest Re-search Institute undertook a fire ecology project to study the effects of four fire regimes, ranging from fire exclusion to early and late dry season annual burning to biennial fire in the tall open forests and woodlands. A year later another major symposium, this one largely conducted by parks enthusiasts, gathered at Darwin and reviewed fire less from the perspective of bushfire protection than of nature preservation. By the late 1970s Kakadu National Park had become a biotic cognate to Ayers Rock and the Great Barrier Reef as a critical icon of Australia's resolve to preserve its heritage. It is indicative of Kakadu's symbolic power that the movie *Crocodile Dundee*, probably Aus-tralia's best known export of the 1980s, set its bushman hero near Arnhem-land.[14]

The fire scene proved complex, however. There was no prospect for ex-cluding fire over large areas, yet a century of European contact had distorted the region's fire regimes. Early-season fires had become late-season fires, large roaring burns had replaced a patchwork of small burns, exotic invaders like the Cape water buffalo and the South African mimosa were busily restruc-turing fuels, and a resurgent Aboriginal population injected another constituency into already tangled politics. If nothing arrested contemporary trends, portions of the biota would disappear. Clearly the situation called for pluralism—of fire regimes, of fire practices, of fire constituencies.

Two special circumstances encouraged compromise. Aerial ignition was not poised to invade the park itself, and, while fire was ubiquitous, it flourished outside the fire flume. There was urgency without hysteria. There were even calls for protecting some sites from fire indefinitely, if possible—a kind of reinstatement of the sacred groves shielded by Aborigines. Yet it was not obvious just what practices would work, nor who—the park or the bushfire council, Aborigines or graziers, tourists or politicians or ecologists—would determine what practices belonged where. Too little was known. The land showed itself too absorbent, too resilient to a range of fires to compel any single course of action. That combination, however, made Kakadu ideal as a proving ground for new technologies of fire management, and it quickly claimed status as a prototype of the new age. What Western Australia had been to foresters, Kakadu became to park managers.

At the other extreme lay Tasmania. The Chambers Committee charged with investigating the Black Tuesday fires had urged a great expansion in controlled burning for fuel reduction throughout a slate of Tasmanian environments. The committee was obviously mesmerized by McArthur, who sat as a member, and McArthur was clearly enthralled by the prospects of aerial ignition. Tasmania had a pocked history of casual rural burning, interrupted every few decades by spectacular holocausts. The Forestry Department had practiced fuel reduction burning on something like a regular schedule since 1939 in selected locales, and had become more and more dependent on hot slash fires for the regeneration of eucalypts on logged sites. Tasmania's western moorlands and its dry scleroforest, in particular, were ideal targets for broadcast burning; and in 1969 aerial burning of buttongrass moors commenced. By 1975 the program targeted some 10,000 acres for annual firing. As burning escalated, particularly into the West Coast, so did criticism. The West Coast was poorly understood and high-intensity fires—the critical issue —came too infrequently to test theory and practice. Predictably, Tasmania carried its controversies to extremes.

No one disputed the power of fire to shape Tasmanian biotas or the historic evidence that they had done so. But there consensus ended. It was impossible to isolate ancient Aboriginal fire practices with rigor. Portions of the western slopes had been cut, burned, grazed, and gassed to near extinction by smelter fumes during the riotous years of European occupation. Forestry, which had, against the odds, stabilized land use and regularized fire practices, now stood accused of perpetuating old abuses and wantonly torching a dwindling natural phenomenon. Foresters wanted to expand the buffer zones around their reserves; preservationists, the buffers around parks. Increasingly, fire respected neither boundary.

The debate over fire practices merged with unhappiness over woodchipping and forestry in general, with the national controversy over the hydroelectric dams at Lake Pedder, and with the international panic to save remnant rainforest. There appeared to be little semantic difference between burning rainforest in Tasmania and burning it in Brazil. The Australian Conservation Foundation charged in an overheated broadside that "Everyone seems to be lighting fires. Arsonists seem barely distinguishable from authorised users, both in attitude and effect." To critics, the Australian strategy seemed intent on burning holes into Ark Australia. In the absence of real data, theory clashed with theory, speculation with speculation, manifesto with manifesto.[15]

The Forestry Department marshaled its evidence, issued reports and policy declarations, and found in A. B. Mount, a forester in the McArthur mode, an articulate spokesman for burning. Environmentalists countered with alternative evidence, propounded position papers, carried their case to the public with pamphlets, picture books, and symposia, and discovered in W. D. Jackson, an academic botanist, its own champion. Both Mount and Jackson freely admitted the historic significance of anthropogenic fire in shaping the Tasmanian environment, but whereas Mount thought fire natural and contemporary fire practices only the (exaggerated) continuation of trends programmed into the genetic composition of Tasmanian biotas, Jackson interpreted the scene as a massive distortion, a colossal "ecological drift" that had pushed relict rainforest to the brink of extinction. Mount thus argued for controlled burning as mandatory for bushfire protection and essential for biotic health, while Jackson saw fire as a tragic spiral, running down the nutrient reservoir of the wet forests (rainforest and scleroforest both), and believed that a program of fire withdrawal was a mandatory cure for a baleful addiction. Mount believed that the moor-rainforest mosaic was stable; Jackson, that rainforest could reclaim substantial moorlands if fires were removed. There seemed to be no point of compromise between them.[16]

Acre for acre probably more burning occurred in Tasmania than anywhere else in forested Australia. But broadcast fire had been confined and mild, the reburning of grassy openings and the underburning of dry scleroforest. More intense fires accompanied land clearing or regeneration burns, again contained. Only rarely did the bushfire volcano erupt. The infrequency of the holocaust fire and the absence of hard data about fire ecology, when combined with a sense of public urgency, encouraged a kind of scholasticism, a force-fed controversy that drew sustenance from arguments elsewhere.

For environmentalists, the loss of rainforest globally lent their quest a moral legitimacy, an excuse for excess zeal and distortion. They fought, first, to stabilize the boundary of Tasmanian rainforest. Then they advanced outward in a general critique of broadacre and regeneration burning; the more fire they excluded, so they reasoned, the more the rainforest could reclaim lost ground. Fire officers looked elsewhere and came, not surprisingly, to a diametrically opposite conclusion. The success of the Australian strategy on the mainland argued, to their minds, for its natural extension to Tasmania, despite their failure to eliminate the large fire or the growing number of escape fires that faulty technique left in the bush like so much refuse. Each side exaggerated and simplified the claims of the other. Both allowed aerial burning to become the vital symbol of the controversy. Neither side suggested how, in practical terms, either fire exclusion or fire application would cripple the holocaust fire that could ravage even drought-plagued rainforest. They saw fundamentally different histories for Australia and proposed very different futures.

This seemingly irresolvable controversy left factious Tasmania sui generis. It resisted simple analogies drawn from elsewhere yet it was unable to muster the resources to decide its own issues by itself. The controversy polarized and ended, perhaps inevitably, as a political brawl. The great debate would center on mainland Australia. What was needed there was a site that had power as an environment presence and as a public symbol. Mount Kosciusko had both. Here everything converged. The fire practices of New Australia—the Australian strategy itself—came full circle from their mythic origins in the 1939 holocaust.

FIRE SUMMITRY: MOUNT KOSCIUSKO

Mount Kosciusko brought together, as perhaps no other site in Australia could, all the elements and advocates for a full-blown battle over fire policy. The old guard of the Australian strategy still ruled, with Alan McArthur, though ill, a commanding presence. Young Turks—ecologists, environmentalists—believed the time had come to halt what they saw as a misguided, if not mindless, extension of fuel-reduction burning into sensitive biotas. Mount Kosciusko had long served as a nationalist emblem, the summit of the Australian Alps, the core of the Great Snowy Hydroelectric Scheme, a huge state park administered by New South Wales (since 1944), later a popular national park that was relatively close to Sydney and Melbourne and that featured some unusual biology. Not least, its fire problems went to the core of Australian natural and human history.

There were all kinds of fires, and because Kosciusko sits slightly east-of-center of the southeast fire flume it catches from time to time the flanks of the monster conflagrations. Lightning fire has been prominent, even today accounting for 30 percent of annual starts. Less determinate are Aboriginal fire practices. Tribes apparently visited the region seasonally, though there is little direct evidence of broadcast burning according to any routine pattern. More likely is an indirect influence from anthropogenic fires started in lower elevations that subsequently rushed up the slopes during dry spells. The impact of European dislocation is better documented. Herding destroyed fire, then added to it. Pastoral burning disrupted the subalpine biotas. Grazing and fire in combination were fatal to large expanses of snow gum; native grasses deteriorated, rejuvenated only through the application of more fire; shrubby understories spread like an oil slick; intensive postfire grazing led to erosion. When the big fires struck, they did so with devastating effect—the 1926 fire that inspired the great round of forestry reform, the 1939 fire which fundamentally rewrote the ecological mosaic of Kosciusko, the 1952 fire that tested the Hume-Snowy Scheme, the 1965 fires that surged across some 66,000 hectares. The fire history of Mount Kosciusko is a perverse honor roll of Australian holocausts. No fire policy or fire practice could hope to claim national status unless it addressed Mount Kosciusko.

Kosciusko was a conundrum. The Hume-Snowy Scheme fire plan had removed some laissez-faire burning by graziers and substituted controlled burning by foresters. But a century of European usage and, in particular, the aftermath of the 1939 fires had tilted the whole system toward pyrophilia. Snow gums were sensitive to burning and browsing. If browsed, they could not regenerate from lignotubers, and if reburned, they only resprouted, intermingled with flammable pyrophytes, and eventually disappeared. The leguminous *Bossiaea*— flammable as kerosene—blanketed enormous portions of the old burn. In the early 1970s a revised fire plan for the park proposed to expand controlled burning to contain the shrubby fuel load, which it deemed essential if the park was to avoid another conflagration.[17]

This time critics rose from among the intelligentsia. Ecologists such as Malcolm Gill argued that routine, low-intensity burning could commit the park biota to its status quo indefinitely; that, by contrast, a few years of effective fire protection would diminish the shrubs and restore grass; that a systematic manipulation by anthropogenic fire would violate the wilderness values of the park; that, in brief, not enough was known about the biology of burning in this region to accept fuel-reduction fires without scrutiny. It was not good enough to repeat the mantra that "eucalypts are adapted to fire" : what mattered was the effect of fires on snow gums. It was not obvious that controlled burning was the only means to abate the shrub infestation: granted another decade or so without fire, it was possible that natural pressures would eliminate the shrubs and restore grass. Studies after a 1972 fire suggested that, in truth, burning was relatively ineffective in controlling fuels in subalpine biotas. It was not inevitable that Kosciusko had to suffer through another 1939-style holocaust: Australia had changed. Research into fire and fuel loads could not substitute for research into fire ecology. Kosciusko National Park did not exist in order to protect it from bushfire.[18]

The Kosciusko controversy signified a changing of the guard, one greatly assisted by larger social and institutional reforms. The momentum for fire research passed from the Forestry and Timber Bureau to other institutions. The Bureau was itself absorbed into the CSIRO Division of Forestry Research; CSIRO's Division of Plant Industry inaugurated research into fire ecology; Luke and McArthur retired, then McArthur passed away; forestry agencies found themselves reorganized into collaborators with the national parks that seemed to breed like rabbits and to eat away the reserved forests. What the Australian strategy had done to rural burning off, a new generation was doing to the hazard-reduction burning that claimed the symbolic core of the Australian strategy. What the Hume-Snowy Scheme had meant for the Australian strategy, the Kosciusko National Park fire plan meant for its tremulous successor.

But the core fire problems, as distinct from their politics, remained unresolved. Philosophical concepts outraced knowledge, practical experience, and monies. It was no more obvious that the new regime could implement its strategy than could the old. Whatever the logical truth of either proposition, the ultimate truth depended on what could be done in the field. The vegetation of Kosciusko, moreover, contained few biotic relics of ancient Australia; most of its flora dated effectively from the 1939 holocaust. A fire program had to accept the environmental reality, not merely the idea, of Kosciusko. For a biota that had been ravaged by European colonization for so long it was difficult to see how all manipulation could be avoided. For a landscape so young and, because of the enormity of the 1939 fires, so uniform over large areas, it was difficult to see how any single approach could ensure park goals for biodiversity. And it was difficult, too, to decide on what practical basis the park could ensure fire protection.

This last dilemma had two parts, and over both hung the specter of the fire flume. The park had legal and moral obligations to control fires within its boundaries that might threaten neighbors; equally, it had to protect itself from rogue fires that roamed the surrounding landscape. To satisfy these charges it had to rely on volunteer brigades in an uneasy social compact. It was unlikely, however, that the park could afford an American-style suppression organization or that suppression, without fuel reduction, could be effective over the course of many decades. But it was no more likely that the park could afford an extensive burning program or that it could practice burning on the necessary scale without violating park values. It was inevitable that research would be inadequate to the demands placed upon it. Besides, neither side had demonstrated unequivocally that it could prevent the holocaust fire that, within a few hours, could obliterate years if not decades of successful treatment, however defined. It was not even obvious that foresters could halt such fires on their own protected forests.

EXPULSION FROM EDEN

The Kosciusko controversy had perhaps more symbolic than practical significance. A swarm of critics loosely unified by park-related values had chipped
away at the unity of the Australian strategy, but they had not gutted its
infrastructure or proposed an alternative strategy of equal rigor. If stubborn
fire provinces rebelled, controlled burning at least remained secure in its
citadels, the public forests. Advocates of the Australian strategy could—and
did—attribute conceptual failures to the philosophical fanaticism of critics;
and they could dismiss field failures as due to a lack of skill or commitment
by practitioners. That bushfire brigades applied fire too cavalierly, that regeneration burns sometimes escaped, that controlled burning did not abolish
large fires—all such examples they could shunt aside by arguing the need for
more training, more equipment, more systematic burning schedules, more
propaganda. Foresters fought threatening bushfires, as they had for decades,
along the frontier. The homelands were secure.

But the counterrevolutionaries did not restrict their campaign to symbolic outliers. They tapped a deeper reservoir of public angst and hope, and
they carried the fight to the public forests themselves. Critics lambasted
logging as a nutrient drain that would lead already marginal soils to ultimate
impoverishment. They flailed the vastly expanded clear-felling of scleforor-
ests—much of it hauled off as woodchips—as an outrage against indigenous
Australia. They railed against pine plantations as an alien invasive, a biological desert, a dark melanoma on the sunbleached Australian landscape. They
cited unnerving examples of casual, even negligent fire practices by foresters
that were almost indistinguishable from rural burning off. In fact escape fires
from prescribed burns actually did rival escape fires from burning off as a
source of bushfires in some locales. Even within the forestry community,
particularly where strengthened by expatriate Britons, criticism of broadacre
burning grew bolder.[19]

Bushfires even devastated that most contrived of forestry environments,
the pine plantation. While minuscule in total area (about 1 percent of forested Australia), softwood plantations promised to dominate national wood
production by 2010. Often stocked on abandoned farmlands, plantations
offered an alternative to the intensive management of native forests. As
exotics, they were generally free of insects and diseases (excepting those,
like the *Sirex* wasp, that were accidentally introduced). But they were extremely vulnerable to bushfire.

There were regional differences of course. In milder fire climates such as
Queensland's, it was possible to contain fire losses to reasonable numbers by
stalling true blow-up fires. It was possible to plant fire-hardy Southern pines
like slash and loblolly that could accept prescribed underburning, thus abat-
ing fuels that otherwise frustrated any biological decomposition by Austra-

lian microbes. Western Australia found ways to integrate mixed species, grazing, and underburning within its matrix, at least on some sites.

It was a different story, however, in the southeast. Here Monterey pine was by far the preferred species. But *Pinus radiata* was sensitive to grazing in its early years, and to burning as it matured. It was difficult to reduce fuels by livestock, mechanical means, or fire, yet the sites to which pine was planted—the environments most in need of softwoods—crossed the fire flume. Against the worst onslaught of winds and drought, no amount of structural design could by itself halt the spread of a major fire. The solution was to protect the perimeter of the plantation, dissect its interior with fuel-breaks, and rely on rapid initial attack. While controlled burning could lessen fuel hazards around the perimeter, the plantations themselves were, almost by definition, often untreatable.[20]

Thus the peculiar case of the Caroline fire. February 2, 1979, featured classic conflagration weather. Ignitions flared from the scorched landscape like grease popping on a skillet. The new starts overwhelmed initial attack forces even under the automatic-dispatch system adopted by South Australia's Woods and Forests Department. Shortly after one P.M. the Caroline fire flared up, probably in an old windrow surrounded by parched grasses. The fire then raced toward an unthinned pine plantation, and over the next four hours it carved a fingered ellipse some fifteen kilometers long through 3,500 hectares of forest before crossing the border into Victoria and en-gulfing another 3,900 hectares of forest. The fire finally expired from a combination of slackening meteorological conditions and altered fuels outside the plantation proper, including plowed strips, mown grasses, and some pre-scribed-burned native forest. Some 80 percent of the plantation suffered crown fire. Foresters pegged the immediate economic losses at $2 million and noted that their harvest schedule would be disrupted for many years. An official review noted with approval the apparent success of controlled burn-ing outside the plantation and urged its expansion. Unfortunately, the burn-ing had helped retard the fire's spread only *after* it had wreaked havoc, not before.[21]

The pines of course were exotics, so their peculiar fire paradoxes might be isolated from the general debate over what fire practices were appropriate over most of the continent. The Australian strategy had targeted native euca-lypt forests, not imported softwoods unable to cope with the hazards of indigenous Australia. But there was no sidestepping the fire problems associ-ated with the accelerated harvesting and burning of native forests. In the postwar era both state and private forestry had expanded enormously, and both had revised their logging practices from the selective cutting of saw timber for local consumption to clear-felling for an export market in wood-chips. Tasmania had expanded into woodchipping during the 1960s, New South Wales in 1969, Western Australia in 1974. The controversy evoked powerful symbolism, and it focused, in particular, on the scleroforests around Eden, on the South Coast of New South Wales.[22]

Almost from the start the Eden operations drew criticism, like blowflies to a carcass. A select committee in 1972 paired the woodchip industry with exotic plantations as "the two most contentious issues involving forestry controlled areas." To environmentalists, land that might have gone into parks and reserves was being recklessly devastated in the name of crass commercialism. To nationalists, the spectacle of Harris-Daishowa spiriting off indigenous scleroforest to the Japanese, who owned the company, revived bitter memories of the war and reminded Australians how vulnerable they were to economic predation. Much of the activity occurred in state forests and some along the Prince's Highway. That foresters sometimes belittled the low productivity of the scleroforest, that they pursued their single-minded clear-felling with scant regard to public concern, only aggravated the opposition. Both sides, however, seemed unable to come to grips with the fire menace.[23]

Critics saw fire as nothing more than another forestry practice. Many disliked fire of any sort, and others reckoned that fire helped make woodchipping possible by disposing of slash, preparing regeneration, and shielding felled coupes from fires that originated in the checkered native forest. In some respects they were right. The 1967–68 experiments in aerial burning on the South Coast had demonstrated to the Forestry Commission that these otherwise vacant lands—heavily stocked with a near monoculture of coast ash *(E. sieberi)*, the regenerated aftermath of the 1952 fires—could be brought into production. Aeroburned areas around Bemboka had even survived the 1968 wildfires. To critics it appeared that controlled burning and woodchipping had entered into an unholy alliance. When bad fires broke out in 1972, after which the burned trunks were salvage-logged, the spectacle did nothing to quell public fears. One way or another fire led to degradation.

Ironically, foresters also viewed fire suspiciously. The prospects of rampaging bushfires originally frightened them away from the site, particularly granted the prevalent belief that the massive regeneration could not be protected by either suppression or controlled burning. To most foresters wildfire had already degraded the site. But aerial ignition and the aging of the stand rendered fire protection possible, and with it, traditional forestry. Clear-felling proceeded in huge swaths that horrified an uninoculated public. After the 1972 fires, however, pressure mounted to banish the specter, and the Commission compromised by reducing the size of individual coupes and by scattering them in checkered fashion across the hills. And it abolished any broadacre burning.

The felling pattern alone made fuel-reduction burning impossible, not only within the felled coupes but between and around them. Besides, the coastal forests did not require fire for regeneration. At Eden foresters did not burn before logging, did not burn after harvest, did not routinely burn the surrounding forests, and when they disposed of bark and other debris they did so often with poor technique and sometimes flagrant disregard for the fantastic fuel loads heaped like monstrous termite mounds through the forests. Instead they relied, as in pine plantations, on a scheme of initial attack. McArthur howled his protests. The outcome was entirely predictable.

In fact, fire specialists had, almost from the onset, declared Eden "an open invitation to disaster." Periods of transition and geographies of mixed usage always attract disastrous fires, but the architects of Eden had a century of settlement experience behind them and should have known better. After inventorying the fuels within and outside the coupes, A. P. Van Loon cited the history of big fires on the South Coast, which brushed against the fire flume, and pleaded with the Forestry Commission in 1973 to instigate a program of fuel reduction "at the earliest opportunity." At a minimum something had to be done about the postharvest residue. The existing situation was impossible, and Van Loon titled his technical report "Slash— Unlimited." [24]

The growing controversy over woodchipping—over the entire South Coast Project—inspired a cascade of political, economic, and environmental studies, some of which considered bushfire. The CSIRO Division of Land Use Research compiled a history of large fires in the region since 1938 and ticked off conflagrations that appeared with metronomic regularity. In 1978 N. P. Cheney, heir apparent to McArthur, inspected the district and informed the CSIRO Division of Forest Research that he was "horrified with the operation as a whole." From the perspective of fire protection, Eden was indefensible. Meanwhile, the Ashton Committee recommended reforms, including an enlargement of Mimosa Rocks National Park and the establishment of Biamanga Aboriginal Place; the Australian Heritage Commission listed critical sites on the register of the National Estate; public furor escalated, oblivious to bland assurances by industrial foresters that clear-felling could only improve on nature; and the NSW Environmental Planning and Assessment Act gave environmentalist critics further legal muscle. In 1979 the conservator sought to appease environmental critics by promising that there would be no further burning—an easy sacrifice since the Forestry Commission had already miniaturized its fire program to the combustion of residual bark heaps. Even so, escape fires constituted 44 percent of all bushfire ignitions in the project area. Public outrage, as measured by media attention, abated. Soon afterward R. H. Luke emerged from retirement, toured the South Coast by land and air, and prophesied a conflagration at Eden. It materialized a few months later.[25]

The fires broke free on November 18, 1980, and the largest burned to the Pacific Ocean. By Australian standards they were not mammoth—the

Timbillica fire, the biggest, involved 47,000 hectares of forest and another 11,000 hectares of regrowth—but their symbolism was enormous. The Forestry Commission tried to pass off the fires as incendiary. While a review panel convened three months later could not make an unequivocal determination, the weight of evidence, however, indicted slovenly fire practices— long-smoldering bark heaps, an utter indifference to fuel reduction, a misplaced reliance on rapid attack that could never succeed when confronted with a worst-case scenario. It lectured the Commission against encouraging "unfounded rumours of incendiarism," which could be interpreted as a cover-up. The failure belonged with the Forestry Commission. The Conservator ordered a review of fire policy.[26]

The revised fire policies, released in 1983, restored the concept of controlled burning, but confined its goals to the containment of losses in the forests producing for Harris-Daishowa. The compromise restored fire but delimited its domain, and of course satisfied no one. Environmental critics saw fire once again serving the dubious goals of woodchippers, not only making such logging possible but extending manipulation into a broader penumbra defined on one hand by protective burning in the boundary forests and on the other by conflagrations rekindled from inevitable escape fires. Neither foresters nor environmentalists confronted the dilemma of eucalypt regeneration. As logging intensified, it drove more and more of the region into a monoculture of coastal ash regrowth, a species exceptionally prone to reburns and readily damaged by them for probably fifteen years or more. How to use and withhold fire in such an environment was, quite simply, not known.[27]

The revised policies satisfied both parties without solving serious fire problems. Fire specialists noted that the restored burning was still laughably inadequate to the metastasizing fuels. R. J. Sneeuwjagt, a fire researcher from Western Australia, happened to tour the scene ten days before the outbreak and was already preparing a damning contrast to Westralian practices when the fires made their wild rush to the sea. Patiently he explained the choreography of burnings conducted in Westralia, the practice of multiple lightings, the extent to which fire considerations were built into every project from the onset. The Eden fires were, in comparison, an act of hubris, defiance that begged for retribution. Sneeuwjagt despaired that in the southeast hazard-reduction burns "generally fall short of the burn coverage required to be effective for wildfire containment." Western Australian experience called for 60–80 percent coverage in average forests, while Tasmania, Victoria, and New South Wales accepted 30–40 percent. Fire officers worried, too, about their widening rift with forestry. It was apparent that foresters were prepared to sacrifice fire programs to redeem logging and planting programs, and without foresters the Australian strategy lost its professional credibility.[28]

At Eden forestry fell from grace and took the Australian strategy with it.

It was clear that fire protection was impossible without some burning, but it was no less obvious that there could never be enough burning to satisfy the precepts of the Australian strategy. However excessively fuels built up, it was unlikely that controlled burning could reduce them. Whatever the natural order had been, it had long since vanished. All anyone could say was that they could never return to Eden as it had existed before. The entrance was barred with a flaming sword.

20

Dieback

Sometimes I feel dispirited after twenty-five years in the fire game. I think a lot of the tremendous conflict and confusion which exists between foresters and ecologists and other people is due to the fact that people are failing to make a distinction between a wild fire and a controlled fire . . . the National Parks people have got . . . to tell us what they want.

—ALAN G. MCARTHUR, *Symposium Comments (1970)*

I can hear the critics already—you'd rather have wildfire than a few little fires? The way the "little fires" go at present, it's very difficult to distinguish them from wildfire, particularly in respect to their new effect upon natural environments.

—ALLEN A. STROM, *letter to The Living Earth (1969)*

EUROPEANS HAD ASSAULTED *Eucalyptus* from their first landfall. By the 1970s it was estimated that the axe had cleared more than half of Australia's wooded lands. But it was noticed that those trees that had so far survived were dying. Singly and in groves, eucalypts wasted away. In high-elevation Tasmania, in the jarrah forests of Westralia, in the scleroforests of the southeast, in remnant woodland—eucalypts were dying everywhere in rural Australia.

The causes were many. Infectious parasites like the cinnamon fungus, perhaps introduced from Indonesia, increased insect predation, nutrient imbalances, water stresses from salination or overpumping, root damage from trampling, altered microclimates, and distortions among the complex interrelationships between eucalypts and other flora and fauna all contributed to and often interacted with unexpected intensity. Some eucalypts suffered from too few nutrients, a product of soil erosion, plundered water tables, and overgrazing; others from overdoses of "sub and super" that led to toxicity or to increased browsing by insects. Inevitably fire practices were implicated—too much, too little, too routine, too unpredictable, too out of sync. The eucalypt—the very symbol of the Australian bush, a genus whose preservation Samuel Dixon had argued in 1892 was "of the very greatest and most vital importance to the best interests of Australia"—was in universal, perhaps irreversible decline.[1]

Dieback was a complex syndrome with a complicated etiology, but the informing cause was the cumulative trauma of European settlement. Dieback came to stand as a metaphor for rural Australia at large. As the blight spread, as New Australia paused in its postwar economic boom, as it saw its American alliance compromised by the Vietnam War and the Japanese ascendancy, as its vaunted renaissance in the arts looked more like a force-fed silver age, dieback became a handy symbol for a general malaise. The sense grew among many Australians that European colonization, now approaching its bicentenary, had buggered up the island continent, that it had perverted Lifeboat Australia into Hulk Australia, an environmental equivalent of the polluted vessels from which the First Fleet had drafted its human cargo.

As New Australia sought out a novel relationship to the bush, it was not clear that a stable compound of the two was even possible. It was not obvious what corrective actions to take other than declaring as much of native Australia as possible off limits to further manipulation and to restore as much land as possible to presettlement conditions. For some the only solution was a kind of environmental apartheid. Others accepted the inherited complexities and sought to rationalize the points of contact, to ameliorate the worst abuses, to substitute tourist and scientist for swagman.

The Australian strategy, too, showed symptoms of dieback. The pyrophytic eucalypt had justified the arguments for controlled fire; the iconography of the sardonic gum had helped sustain the symbolism of hazard-reduction burning. But what began as a simple equation evolved into a complicated calculus of confused practices and purposes. Whatever its responsibility for eucalypt decline, fire could not by itself restore the eucalypt to health; larger forces of political economics and demographics, the prime movers of rural Australia, shaped both. This a CSIRO research team discovered when it investigated the relationship of fire to grazing. Specifically, the researchers wanted to know if broadcast burning could rejuvenate misused, brush-invaded rangelands. Computer programs simulated the economic consequences of different fire practices and discovered that in all cases, whatever the biological payoffs, the grazier slid into bankruptcy. Either the grazier expanded his land base or he went under. That, in a sense, was a parable of rural Australia. The truest charge against the Australian strategy was not that it was illogical or immoral but that it systematized fire practices for an outmoded landscape—controlled burning could not by itself redeem a rural countryside so long abused.[2]

HAZARD REDUCTION: CONTROLLING THE AUSTRALIAN STRATEGY

With remarkable suddenness, within the span of roughly three years—1976–1978—the old order collapsed. Thirty years had passed since World War II, only a decade longer than the timespan that had defined the heroic era of Australian forestry from the end of World War I to 1939. Even as a new generation proposed to expand controlled burning in the name of hazard reduction, others sought to contain the practice as an even greater hazard. Environmental planning statutes legislated a new legal context for fire use. Air-quality regulations compromised traditional burning along fuel-breaks. Some environmental critics saw routine controlled fire as a more serious biotic threat than wildfire, and some insisted that wilderness *required* uncontrolled bushfires in order to be wild. Incredibly, foresters found themselves arguing with a skeptical public that burning the bush was good and necessary.

Like all logical systems imposed on nature, the Australian strategy suffered internal cracks, and these the strain of controversy widened. Perhaps the most serious fracture was the scientific challenge. The McArthur methodology had emphasized empirical, field-based research, an agenda that worked admirably when the system required practical guidelines over very extensive areas of more or less uniform conditions. It was a means of quickly assimilating large expanses of rural Australia. Experimental fires tested just those fuels and those limited conditions that were most critical to the performance of the system. The Australian strategy promoted research in order to bring scientific analysis to bear on folk practices and to legitimize its axioms.

But the reconstitution of the Australian landscape also restructured the research agenda. The insistence, in the name of biodiversity, that ecosystems experience a variety of fire intensities and frequencies threatened the McArthur model with a methodological crisis. It was impossible to extrapolate existing empirical relationships across the full spectrum of new conditions; and it was unrealistic to subject each fuel array and each fire intensity of potential interest to New Australia to the same kind of field experimentation that McArthur had conducted in designing his fire-danger rating meters for rural Australia. Besides, new questions crowded the agenda.

What had been fringe fire regimes moved to the center. They demanded expertise in fire ecology, not only fire-danger rating; in precise ecological knowledge, not generic fuel loading; in an ensemble of fires applied and withheld in particular environments, not the singular application of scheduled burns on a continental scale. Yet the ruthlessly practical orientation of the McArthur agenda made it difficult for foresters to retool because they lacked a robust core of fundamental fire science. What was needed was something like what American researchers had developed—a fire-behavior model based on analytical principles that could be applied over a wide range of circumstances, subject to modification by selective field and laboratory testing. Once accepted, such a mathematical model could, with computer assistance, simulate real-time fire behavior and effects. Australians, however, had tended to perceive these laboratory-generated models in much the same way they did air tankers, as a kind of North American subversion; they emphasized their flaws rather than their prospects. Ultimately the remorseless practicality of the Australian program rendered its research impractical.

What happened intellectually happened institutionally as well. In 1976 the Scientific Committee on Problems of the Environment (SCOPE) launched a five-year project on "The Effects of Fire on Ecological Systems." The international chair, R. O. Slatyer, was a biologist at the Australian National University who had innovated new concepts of postdisturbance succession. Simultaneously, CSIRO absorbed the Forestry and Timber Bureau and shortly afterward McArthur retired. In 1978 the Australian Academy of Sciences hosted a symposium on "Fire and the Australian Biota" as Australia's contribution to the SCOPE program. Foresters and fire officers participated, as they did in the proliferating symposia sponsored by universities and environmental groups; but it was obvious that the scientific vigor had passed from forestry to ecology, and that, even as a practical measure, field operations had shifted from public forests to new landscapes, the wild bush and the urban bush.

Perhaps nothing so aptly characterizes the transfer of research momentum as the adoption of computer modeling by the National Parks and Wildlife Service (NPWS). In 1978 CSIRO ecologist A. M. Gill invited Stephen Kessell to Australia to explain the elaborate fire ecology software he had developed for Glacier National Park. The New South Wales NPWS contributed funds for Kessell, along with Roger Good, to prepare an analogous program for Kosciusko National Park. Their collaboration led to Preplan (Pristine Environment Planning Language), a prototype that quickly spun off from Kosciusko into other N.S.W. parks and even shires required by statute to evaluate their fire hazards. South Australia planned to adapt a system for the Adelaide Hills. Kakadu National Park combined Preplan software with geographic information systems and expert systems, the one as a source of data, the other as a guide to output. A software package suitable for handheld computers, Fireplan, soon followed.[3]

Initially the programs accepted existing Australian fire behavior models—the McArthur grassfire and forest-fire meters and the empirical tables encoded in Western Australia's "red book." Both were too specific to particular environments to serve as a universal model, however, and eventually the programs switched to the standard American version, the Rothermel fire model. The special promise of the systems was that, by simulating fires, they could allow "experiments" with field operations in advance of managerial decisions; they could "test" fires under different circumstances of weather, fuel, and field practices. Their algorithms also integrated fire behavior with fire ecology. If they were flawed—and their predictions often were—so were the McArthur meters. Whatever their internal integrity, both had to operate in an inexact world. Increasingly, they were tested one against the other.

The bushfire that raged across Morton National Park in January 1983 thus became one of those symbolic events that help redefine an era. If the Dwellingup fires confirmed for the Rodger Commission the value of controlled burning, the Morton fire seemed to validate the power of computer simulation and the legitimacy of a pluralistic fire program. Ignited west of the park, the fire, over the course of four days, burned through private land and state forest, exploded across the park, and finally raced beyond into pine plantations. The National Parks and Wildlife Service exploited its computer program for hour-by-hour forecasts of fire behavior. At subsequent coronial hearings, critics charged that the absence of broadacre hazard-reduction burning had contributed to the losses by making the fire uncontrollable. In response the NPWS submitted its chronicle of computer predictions, which deviated from actual fire perimeters by no more than 25 percent. It then projected bushfire behavior under various conditions of reduced fuels. The putative outcome was that, granted the extreme weather, the abatement in fire intensity and a diminution in the rate of spread was minimal, delaying the conflagration of the pine plantations by seventeen minutes to perhaps four hours. The coroner accordingly ruled out negligence.[4]

If sustained in field and lab, the case gutted the very essence of the Australian strategy. It attacked the conceptual basis of fuel-reduction burning, the ends to which it was put, and the means by which it could be justified. That, at least, is what the proponents of the NPWS fire program argued. But the jury remained undecided. The coroner ruled narrowly, and then on matters of jurisdiction. The arguments from Kessell and Good that prescribed burning as late as 1981 "had no real effect on rate of speed or intensity of the fire" he found surprising and unsubstantiated.

> I do not for one minute suggest that Dr. Kessell and Mr. Good are in any way to be misbelieved but in the light of overwhelming evidence from the other gentlemen . . . and applying common sense to the situation, I do not accept at all that hazard reduction work done in 1980 and 1981 and early 1982 might not have substantially slowed down and moderately reduced the intensity of this bush fire.

The matter was a muddle. Witnesses conflicted, hard evidence was sparse, the park fire plan was incomplete, computer simulation contradicted common sense, and philosophical passions fanned smoldering perceptions into flaming disputations. The coroner ruled but he could not resolve. The disputants took the case to the Australian courts.[5]

Before Preplan could claim supremacy over the McArthur agenda as the new Australian strategy, it had to endure other trials. It was not obvious that computer graphics could substitute for field experience. In the special environments for which it was developed, the McArthur fire-spread model often tested better than the Rothermel. Even in the U.S. fire managers habitually, idiosyncratically introduced fudge factors to make their computer output agree with ground facts. The actual algorithms on which Preplan's predictions were based were never published. The imported computer programs demonstrated a voracious appetite for data that made them costly or, if shortchanged in data, inaccurate. Contrary to claims that they had coded all of Kosciusko Park in a 200-by-200-meter grid, ground surveys had captured only a fraction of the total surface. And if accurate, it was not clear to what ends the new knowledge should be put.

"The effect of fire in forests and nature reserves is so complicated," Eric Rolls despaired, "no one can do anything with the certainty he is right." It was far from obvious that fuel-reduction burning recapitulated Aboriginal fire practices, if only because European settlement had so reordered the Australian landscape that the same techniques could produce different results; the new regimes were assembled out of new materials and obeyed, presumably, a different dynamic. Even if equivalence could be reestablished, not everyone agreed that the Aboriginal era was the best possible model; if not, then what purposes should guide fire practices? A pluralism of ends confounded a pluralism of means. As the battle waned, the two contestants still stood, neither able to finish off the other.[6]

It was possible for advocates of the Australian strategy to dismiss their computer challengers as charlatans and their losses as public relations blunders. More damning for an agenda that had celebrated practicality, however, were the growing numbers of failures in execution. A reliance on volunteer brigades had made it possible to expand bushfire protection quickly over very large areas and had forced residents to assume some responsibility for their own lives. A concourse of volunteer brigades also meant that fire practitioners were amateurs, however enthusiastic; that it would be difficult to adapt brigades established to protect field and town to the special circumstances of nature reserves; that controlled burning sometimes regressed into simple burning off. In many areas controlled burning became a primary cause of wildfire. When a bushfire brigade bumbled its buffer burning at Magnetic Island such that an escaped fire raged through the park it was intended to protect, the incident became a cause célèbre among Australian environmentalists. These were trade-offs that McArthur and his colleagues, looking back to 1939, had willingly accepted; peering into a more hopeful future, a new generation was less forgiving. Critics would accept errors by the new practitioners—including fatalities among park researchers and bushfire brigades—but not breakdowns in hazard-reduction burning. As land use intensified, there was less margin for error. As the ideological issues sharpened, tolerance shrank.[7]

All these objections could be fended off by arguing for better training. What most threatened the Australian strategy was the apparent demonstration that, under the worst weather conditions, fuel-reduction burning failed to make control possible. Here the communiqués were mixed. Outside the fire flume, the evidence for hazard reduction appeared, on the whole, supportive. Western Australia and Queensland confirmed its merits for fire control, and the issue here was less whether prescribed fire worked than whether it should be applied primarily for fuel reduction or for more specific biological ends with fuel reduction a secondary benefit. Within the fire flume the evidence was equivocal. Again and again, the Victorian Forests Commission sought hard data that fuel reduction was effective. What it found were case studies that confirmed that hazard-reduction burning had, in local sites, diminished wildfire and shielded conifer plantations or houses. What it did not discover was a blanket justification for wholesale fuel reduction. Where controlled burning succeeded, it did so in special, intensively managed sites, typically near developments for which brigades could be mustered. Effective fuel reduction was specific to place and time. But within these cases, there were powerful testimonies, including aerial photographs that showed greenish islands within a sea of incinerated scleroforest.

Outside these strategic areas there was little solid validation. It was "impossible to isolate the impact FRB [fuel-reduction burning] has had on the incidence of destructive wildfires in Victoria by an examination of annual fire in statistics." Proponents fell back on arguments that "the theory of fuel-reduction burning has a sound basis in research," the incontestable logic that less fuel meant less fire. The problem was that, in practice, controlled burning affected only a fraction of the land under protection. Actual burning fell short even of planned goals. Between 1972 and 1982, less than 3 percent of state forests were on the average control burned annually; an unknown fraction of that perimeter combusted sufficiently to depress fuel loads to adequate levels. Even with sites targeted along ridgetops and north slopes, this amounted only to a program of enlarged fuelbreaks. These defenses "proved to be inadequate on occasions"—that is, they failed precisely when they were most needed. High-intensity fires could spot across burned traces; under drought conditions, areas not burned during normal operations, and hence heavily loaded with fuels, could flare up uncontrollably; treated areas of reduced fire intensity were effective as end points only to the extent that brigades could be mustered to work them. Nonetheless, the Forests Commission concluded that "of all the fire-prevention and suppression actions available" hazard-reduction burning was "perhaps the most significant and effective." What was needed, it affirmed, was more burning.[8]

Other conclusions were possible, however. Critics argued that precision burning should replace broadacre burning. They exposed the precepts of the Australian strategy as logical truths, not operational truths: the landscape would not be burned on the scale demanded, and anything less would be ineffective. Under these conditions, the burned sites could not prevent an environmental meltdown. The fundamental question was not whether reducing fuels could help control fires but whether under Australian conditions fuels could be reduced sufficiently to provide the desired protection at the desired costs. In the environmental economics of New Australia those costs factored in the ecological consequences—not fully understood—of routine low-intensity burning. Prescribed fire had to serve biological ends, not merely manipulate fuels. In reply, the advocates of the Australian strategy repeated their mantra that fuel reduction was the only means to control bushfire. What began as a bold scientific proposition lapsed into a catechism.

Shortly after CSIRO absorbed the Forestry and Timber Bureau into its Division of Forest Research and abolished the Bushfire Research Unit in Melbourne, McArthur retired and bushfire research went into a tailspin that took the Commonwealth's commitment to fire research down in its smoking spiral. When the Forestry School at the Australian National University sought a lecturer in fire, it appointed an ecologist, not a forester. Professional forestry revealed that, under stress, it was willing to sacrifice bushfire protection in order to spare other programs. State forestry commissions found themselves reorganized into administrative unions with national parks and other conservation programs. In general, while foresters possessed the techniques and field skills to manage fire, the parks people controlled the objectives—when, that is, they could decide on them. Critics acquired an unexpected international ally when the U.S. Forest Service, which had long served the Australian strategy in counterpoint, reformed its policies and accepted prescribed fire for biocentric purposes. Forestry surrendered its research hegemony to a bustle of projects sponsored by the states, the universities, and other CSIRO divisions.

The counterrevolution attacked even the founding myths of the Australian strategy. The specter of the 1939 fires had been the end that justified almost any means; its smoke pall hung over the fire flume for forty years. But to the extent that it equated firefighting with national defense, it had argued for a scorched earth policy, a kind of Brisbane Line born out of Australian weakness. Increasingly, however, critics questioned the dynamics of the conflagration. Contrary to conventional wisdom, S. G. Fawcett noted in a study of regional history that "for a long period prior to 1939, the forests of this area had been regularly and systematically burnt, but the 1939 fires swept through the district almost unchecked. It burnt across areas which had been lightly burnt only a few months earlier." Others challenged the pertinence of Black Friday for a New Australia bent on redefining its domestic and international relations. It was clear that fire hazards had worsened since Black Friday, unclear that controlled burning could dampen them indefinitely, and not obvious that routine burning could be practiced without violating the new land uses to which the region was committed. National defense could not cancel all other national values: bushfire protection could not suppress all other land values. Prescribed fire had to serve other purposes.[9]

THE AUSTRALIAN-AMERICAN ALLIANCE:
PACIFIC PARADOX

By the early 1970s Australia had defined a special status for itself among global fire powers. It proposed a friendly, alternative strategy to that of the Americans, an approach particularly rich with potential for the Third World. Northern Europe had little to offer because of low fire loads; the Mediterranean Basin, little because of feeble fire control. When the FAO recommended that developing nations adopt the McArthur meter, it was a triumph for Australian nationalism as well as for appropriate technology. Australia's peculiar standing—its binocular vision between Britain and America, its status as a European colony in ancient Gondwana—gave it a special mandate and the Australian strategy an additional sanction. Only a fire program that incorporated controlled burning, that co-opted traditional fire uses, could have meaning among developing nations. Its American alliance, however, was vital to the dynamics of the Australian revolution.

In the postwar era America dominated world sciences, wildland fire research among them. Australia had full access to that knowledge. Study tours encouraged an exchange of data, experience, and researchers. The Tall Timbers Fire Ecology Conferences, commencing in 1962, encouraged Australians to describe their achievements in controlled burning. The major players all toured North America. McArthur himself welcomed American research, even as he rejected any direct transfer of models. It was then a matter of exquisite timing that the U.S. Forest Service reformed its policy just as the Australian strategy was dissembling.[10]

The pressures for reform were many. As the American strategy of fire protection expanded, it had compromised. In the South it accepted controlled fire for fuel reduction, officially in 1943, though effective burning on a large scale did not emerge for another couple of decades. In part the move was an act of wartime expediency, and in part a reflection of new technology, the tractor-plow, which promised to keep fires under mechanical control. Those moves tended to disguise the sense that without burning the understory, the famous "rough," control by any means was impossible. Meanwhile, the release of war-surplus equipment powered the mechanization of firefighting almost overnight, and sustained its expansion even into the interior of Alaska in the late 1950s. By 1965 every state had cooperative fire programs with the U.S. Forest Service and interlocking agreements bound the federal agencies together. The Forest Service enjoyed virtual hegemony over every aspect of the American fire establishment.

Then the frontier closed. There were no new lands into which to bring, for the first time, formal fire protection. At least a first-order infrastructure existed everywhere. It was no longer enough to expand into new lands, or to protect existing sites by establishing fire protectorates over adjacent lands. Increasingly critics questioned the purposes to which the fire establishment was put. Nearly every federal land agency had its organic act rewritten, some more than once. The multiplicity of ends demanded a new multiplicity of means. No one agency and no single policy could encompass everything. The Leopold Report (1963) for the National Park Service and the Wilderness Act (1964) for federal lands asserted a special legitimacy to fire in natural areas. The varied liabilities of the American strategy became apparent.

There were social and economic costs, a point of diminishing returns. Pouring more and more money into fire suppression did not lead to a corresponding diminution in burned area; expenditures rose regardless. By the late 1970s even American affluence could no longer tolerate exponential increases in cost. What had been a leaking faucet became a ruptured levee. The American capacity to mobilize enormous logistical campaigns to contain large fires was a wonder of the world, but there were honest doubts that it accomplished much beyond spending money. The American strategy had to return to its founding insights; and to improve initial attack it was necessary to manipulate other components of the fire environment. That meant fuel-reduction programs, often using broadcast fire.

Then there were the environmental costs. Mechanized firefighting frequently inflicted scars on the land; the effectiveness of fire suppression allowed fuels to build up in critical environments, stoking larger fires; and researchers recognized that fires were a natural phenomenon, such that it became difficult philosophically and legally to justify the expulsion of lightning-caused fires from natural areas. The ecological arguments for preserving natural fires merged with powerful ideological currents that swirled around the concept of wilderness. It became apparent that fire control, not fire use, was, in the long scheme of things, the aberration. Forest Service hegemony broke down. Interagency cooperation—from research to fire-control centers —became the norm. A uniform policy became a hydra's head of distinctive but somehow related practices.

The result was a decade of policy reform, replanning, and field experimentation—some painful, some exhilarating. The National Park Service revised its fire policy in 1967–68, leaping its philosophy ahead of its expertise. The Forest Service made some amendments in 1971–72, then issued a wholly revised policy in 1978; but it took the field fully equipped for operations. The outcome was a better balance between fire use and fire control, more a negotiated settlement with fire than a continued campaign for unconditional surrender. The Tall Timbers Research Station concluded its annual conferences in 1974 and published its last proceedings in 1976, confident that the revolution had been won. Prescribed fires became all the rage, a universal antidote to environmental toxins. Natural fires could be reclassified as prescribed fires so long as they burned within preestablished criteria.

But putting those ideas to work in the field was problematic. Since the mid-1970s most of America's disastrous wildland fires have been the result of breakdowns in the execution of prescribed fires. It makes an appalling record. When combined with severe drought, ignorance led to excess, culminating in the Yellowstone fires of 1988 that burned almost 400,000 hectares, or 45 percent of the park. It is indicative of the depth of its conversion to the new philosophy, however, that the fire establishment rushed to defend its reformed policies, convinced that a return to a singular program of suppression was unworkable and environmentally dangerous. Besides, each of the alternatives had its own failures. All the options—massive fuel modifications, prevention, natural fire—brought their own special costs. Prevention was marginally useful in a landscape pounded by lightning and chronically kindled by a mobile, undisciplined population. Fuel-reduction burning never equaled fuel production, pumped prodigious columns of smoke into the sky, and unleashed escape fires with disturbing regularity. Suppression failed often enough for large fires to continue, an irreducible quantum that burned under the worst imaginable conditions.[11]

It became apparent that suppression was not a neutral act. It did not quick-freeze an ecosystem, which changed by having fire withheld as surely as it changed by being burned. There were choices possible, but no escape from the imperative to choose. At the other end of their shovels American firefighters found something that resembled a smoking existentialism. There were good fires and bad fires, good fires that were wrongly suppressed, bad fires that were wrongly allowed to burn, good fires that went wild and became bad fires, and bad fires that, through the wizardry of reclassification, were declared good. The moral geography of wildland fire fragmented into a pluralism of practices and purposes.

America and Australia thus stood as opposites. Whereas Australian critics wanted less fire, American environmentalists wanted more. The American fire establishment appeared to have kept fire out of places that required it; the Australian establishment to have retained fire where it didn't belong. The paradox existed because the two nations defined a "controlled fire" in two ways. For the Australian strategy, prescribed burning meant primarily fuel reduction, with some ancillary biological side effects. For the American strategy, prescribed fire acquired a biocentric purpose, for which fuel reduction was an important epiphenomenon. Implicitly, American foresters believed that their fire establishment was strong enough to contain escape fires, some of which they dismissed as the inevitable cost of large-scale ecological management. By contrast, Australian foresters seemed to believe that fire protection was so difficult that to burn for any reason other than to improve control demanded special justification; and to tolerate free-burning "natural" fires during the height of the fire season was an act of criminal negligence. Increasingly, the two groups talked past each other, each baffled that the other no longer spoke English or comprehended elemental logic.

The American revolution had important consequences for the Australian fire establishment and its critics. The Americans had finally landed. The defenders of the Australian strategy had guarded mightily against such an invasion—an anticipated aerial assault by helicopters, paracargo and smoke-jumpers, air tankers, all the armament of American suppression. Instead the invaders had waded ashore outfitted with professional insouciance, an arsenal of hand-held computers, and concepts like gradient modeling and prescribed natural fire. Perhaps even worse, the Americans at last sanctioned prescribed fire, but in ways that exploited burning as a tool for ecological design rather than primarily for hazard reduction. No longer could the American strategy serve as a counterexample against which the Australian could rally. The straw man had become an effigy that had vanished in happy self-immolation. The Americans, in brief, brought that most powerful of all weapons, an idea whose time had come.

But things had a way of arriving in Australia and being changed. The new American strategy was no more suitable for relocation to Australian conditions than was the old one. The American solution to the urban bush conundrum was to strengthen suppression; their response to the wilderness question was to ignore aboriginal burning and rely, where possible, on "natural" ignitions. Computer simulation often aggravated rather than reduced the disparity between ideals and practice. By contrast, Australians dismissed the prospects for lightning fires and accepted the reality of Aboriginal burning, though they disagreed about what it meant. American wilderness and Australian bush were not interchangeable concepts, and they served cultural nationalism in different ways. But it seemed possible, to Australian critics, to transfer selected elements—computer simulation, biocentric fire planning, even air tankers. That Americans tolerated free-burning fires in wilderness areas staggered nearly all Australian fire specialists. Australia defined its options wholly within the context of anthropogenic fire.

Globally, other regional fire powers emerged to return Australia to isolation. SCOPE organized symposia on fire in Mediterranean-climate lands;

post-Franco Spain became active in fire protection and spread its enthusiasms to Latin America. South Africa added a volume on fire use and control in its ecosystems, biotic cognates of Australia. Western Europe actually organized a fire research group under FAO auspices and, as drought and loosened land use led to outbreaks of wildfire, Europeans held regional conferences. Albert-Ludwigs-Universität at Freiburg sponsored fire ecology conferences on a six-year cycle. More importantly, Britain became an international force in conservation, a refracted legacy of empire. Since Australian intellectuals tended to follow British rather than American fads, the persistent dislike of free-burning fire among the British intelligentsia—the banning of straw burning in the early 1980s being a notorious example—could only harm Australians interested in promoting fire for any purpose.

All this confounded the relationship of fire practices to Australian nationalism. Australia had boldly staked out a policy friendly to but distinct from that of America and Europe. Its distinctive environment had inspired the Australian fire community to pursue distinctive solutions. But they were solutions redolent with universal implications, sparkling with important implications for Mediterranean-type landscapes everywhere, for developing nations eager for fire protection with appropriate technology, and for the major fire powers themselves. Now Australians would not export their revolution. Their practices were probably unique to their unique bush. The environmentalist protest, ironically, reasserted a tyranny of biotic distance. To the extent that Australians solved their own problems, they were unlikely to solve those of others. Distinctiveness yielded to isolation.

POSTMORTEM:
FIRE IN THE WESTERN DISTRICT

There was an uncanny timeliness to the 1977 fires. Only a year before their outbreak N. P. Cheney had summarized bushfire disasters since World War II, and noted that the holocaust fire tended increasingly to develop from a single escape fire and to coincide with a relatively short burst of extreme conditions. The Australia in which low-intensity fires simmered across the landscape constantly ready to flare into conflagrations was, he concluded, being replaced by an Australia staffed with effective firefighting forces and committed to hazard reduction, an Australia calmed by the McArthur method.[12]

There was no denying that acreages burned by wildfire had decreased under the impress of improved fire organization. In theory it was possible to assert that the fire load of Australia would—perhaps should—remain constant, that controlled burning would reclaim acres otherwise lost to wildfire. But the immediate cause was simply more intensive settlement. Sown pastures, cultivated paddocks, intense grazing, a sprawling urban bush, burgeoning bushfire brigades, all brought more land under more thorough control, and proclamations establishing natural preserves did not remove land from fire protection but only transferred fire responsibilities from one institution to another. Fewer and fewer acres fell outside the bushfire jurisdiction of some agency. Although bad fire seasons returned like plagues of grasshoppers, they caused, as it were, fewer famines. In the fire flume bushfires erupted in 1964–65, 1966–67 (Tasmania), and 1968–69, where they ranged along the Great Dividing Range from Victoria to Queensland. Then, for a decade—as if on cue, coincident with the years in which the Australian strategy reached flood tide—conflagrations receded. Big fights in symposia replaced big fires in the bush.

The 1977 fires restored the specter and recalibrated the measurement of bushfire protection. The fires came both early and late, and they returned to areas both familiar and unusual. They scavenged through Queensland in September and October, then lingered into February. The numbers seem modest—273 fires and 118,000 hectares—but many fires invaded coastal conifer plantations, normally considered safe, where they inflicted major economic losses and stunned a complacent bushfire establishment. In New South Wales fires broke out in a great arc around Sydney. There were bad fires in Mulwaree Shire and Morton National Park to the south, in Scone, Murrundi, and Merriwa shires and others along the North Coast, in Sutherland Shire, Royal National Park, and Warringah Shire, where authorities blamed 166 fires on incendiarism, many set at midnight. The most memorable were two terrifying bushfires that raged through the Blue Mountains, revisiting some sites burned in 1968 and 1957.

The fires began on December 16, and brigade units, weary from a three-day battle in the Jamieson Valley, almost immediately called for assistance. Within three hours a Section 41 Emergency was declared under the Bush Fires Act. The entire region mobilized its brigades—more than two hundred tankers and engines, three bulldozers, five military helicopters, and volunteer firefighters to the strength of 1,520 men. Commanders recognized that fire containment was hopeless under the blistering winds. Attack dissolved into a melee of separate actions aimed at saving individual properties. The following day the scene calmed, then the gathering fires returned on December 18 for another run. Containment came the following day around a perimeter of 100,000 hectares. Bushfire destroyed eighty-seven buildings and vehicles, though officials estimated some six hundred properties had been saved.[13]

The fires in Victoria were even more severe, the worst since 1944, the year of reference for the Western District. Actually they were the first of the season, announcing the drought that subsequently spread eastward and northward. On February 12 eleven major bushfires burned more than

100,000 hectares through farm and pasture, inflicting an estimated $20 million in damage. The outbreak was a freakish concatenation of events—late curing of heavy pasture grasses and abnormal loadings of oat and wheat stubble, vicious winds that raced at 50 kilometers per hour or greater and caused failures in powerlines. Arcing and ruptured lines showered tinder with sparks and the outcome was "world-record rates of spread of 16–17 km/hr." Wind blew spots across roads and fuelbreaks. Wooded shelterbelts and remnant woodlands torched and sent firebrands far ahead of the main flaming front. Stony ridges denied access to some eastern fire flanks. Against such conditions brigades were overwhelmed. The multiple starts spread them too thin, and their tendency, in the early hours, to divert their scarce engines to protect houses rather than attack the perimeter of the main fires further diluted their efforts. But they rallied, regrouped, and fought the fires along their flanks. A wind shift with the passage of the forcing cold front broke open the eastern perimeters nearly everywhere and often doubled the final fire size. Diminished winds, concentrated firepower, and dogged perseverance finally corralled the burns.[14]

The 1977 fires burned across a panorama of New Australian environments. The Queensland fires involved scleroforest and conifer plantation. The Blue Mountain fires scorched the urban bush and the wild bush, satellite communities of Sydney and national parks. The Western District fires were profoundly rural, savaging a landscape at once flush with growth and gaunt with "deep [economic] recession."

Each regional outbreak inspired comparisons with the past and each forecast a better future. Queensland searched its records for equivalent years, and discovered some comparison with 1968, 1941, and 1926–27. The Forestry Department quickly experimented with underburning its plantations and signaled a gradual shift in the geography of fire research that made this long-quiescent state the host of important fire symposia. Likewise, the 1977 fires preceded a major reform in Victorian rural bushfire protection, inspired a rash of research programs, and renewed interest in controlled burning for eucalypt forests—those that had been prescribe-burned suffered less than plantations that had not. New South Wales interpreted the fires as a continued evolution of its bushfire protection system. Its year of reference was 1957, when the Leura fire had stunned authorities into the bushfire prevention schemes that, over the course of twenty years, blanketed most of the eastern half of the state. The Leura fires had been a pandemonium of ill-orchestrated firefighting and flight, suppressed only by heavy rains; the Blue Mountain blazes were eventually fought to a standstill by bushfire brigades in often rugged terrain without help from precipitation. The fires confirmed the wisdom no less than the organization of the Australian strategy. Where the 1977 fires had roared into the scenes of the 1957 and 1968 bushfires or into sites of more recent controlled burning, their intensity and rate of

spread diminished. The intensity of the fires was almost directly proportional to the age of the fuels.[15]

Bushfire councils and CSIRO researchers massed testimonials to the efficacy of fuel reduction. "There was no uncertainty on the part of any of the
authorities interviewed as to the benefits that can flow from hazard reduction and of the need for hazard reduction to be undertaken in both the local
and distant areas." The New South Wales Council spoke disparagingly of "a
minority of ill-informed persons" who did not or would not understand the
logic of controlled burning, and its chair, Air Vice-Marshal W. E. Townsend,
challenged the National Parks Association to examine the field evidence for
themselves. They would find that previously burned sites were "the only
green areas which serve as refuges for wildlife and mankind alike and they
should appreciate that mankind is an important species worthy of protection." [16]

But if it won this particular ideological battle, the council was in danger
of losing the fire war: the pertinent agenda was less theoretical than practical. To be effective controlled burning had to expand considerably. It had to
move beyond strategic fuelbreaks and embrace vast bushlands. It had to
suppress sources of firebrands even under extreme weather conditions. A
close reading of the fires' history revealed that effective hazard reduction
had come from very small and very large treatments—from careful house-
cleaning around structures and villages, and from past wildfires, golf courses,
and tended greenbelts. The council singled out as a particular success special
"hazard reduction teams" of full-time employees who supplemented the
volunteer brigades in their controlled burning, but their numbers were small
and their cost high, and it was doubtful that this intensity of hazard reduction could become a norm throughout the region. The areas most in need of
it were typically those that could least afford its cost. To point out, as critics
did, that Los Angeles County committed itself to a budget "almost 100 times
greater" than the Blue Mountains City Council "for a similar area" was
almost gratuitous. Australia would have to operate with the resources at
hand.[17]

If the Blue Mountains fires completed one cycle of Australian fire history,
the fires of the Western District completed another. The Australian strategy
had its genesis in the double fires of 1939 and 1943–44, the one in the
mountains and the other in the grasslands. The mountain scene had become
complicated by the politics of New Australian land use, which made simple
comparisons of historic fires difficult, but the converted grasslands of the
Western District remained profoundly rural. The 1944 fires endured as the
"year of reference." For "twenty years or more," Alan McArthur observed,
"brigade groups and regional officers have trained and planned for another
1944." When it came, despite heavier fuel loads, the fires burned a third as
much territory. They also brought McArthur out of a recent retirement for a

final case study, returning him to the rural landscape of his boyhood for a valedictory report.

With painstaking detail, a labor of love, McArthur worked through the dynamics of each of the eleven major fires, catalogued the record of historic large fires in the region, and spelled out the lessons of '77. Transmission lines had replaced railroads as a source of problem ignition; with almost diabolical cunning the winds that propelled great fires caused powerline failure that resulted in starts under the worst imaginable conditions. That could be fixed with better engineering and better equipment; stronger interbrigade coordination and shrewder tactics could likewise improve actual suppression. Too many starts overwhelmed too few brigades outfitted with too little modern gear. Too often companies failed to attack with sufficient power the eastern perimeter, the flank that the frontal wind shift would tear free. Too often volunteers scrambled to save individual structures, to protect property rather than attack the fire front. But McArthur freely confessed to the limits of suppression under the conditions faced in 1977. The fires burned at velocities never before recorded in Australia, rates probably unparalleled in the world. Upper-scale fireline intensities prevented a frontal attack. Rapid rates of spread in long fingers that shot forward like flamethrowers made close work with engines dangerous and ineffectual. Smoke obscured the field of operations. Vigorous spotting made any closure of the advancing head impossible. No fire control organization on Earth could have blitzed such fires, and for a mob of volunteer brigades to have contained the conflagration so well was little short of phenomenal.

Inevitably, McArthur's analysis turned to fuels. In this, a flat and cultivated landscape, fire behavior conformed closely to variations in fuels and winds. This was no complex of wildland fuels, baffling in its variable moisture contents, transcendental in the complexity of its ecological relationships. These were agricultural fields and paddocks, broken with forested windbreaks and remnant woods. Even so the fuels were only marginally accessible to management and, where treated, of only limited value in the face of extraordinary weather conditions. Heavy rains had yielded profuse pasture and stubble; late curing, then severe fire conditions, had stalled normal buffer burning. It may have mattered little because with or without burning firefighters were helpless in the face of frenetic spotting that spanned fuelbreaks in a heartbeat. The Wallinduc-Cressy fire leaped over a thirty-meter fuelbreak from a heavily grazed paddock. Points of untidiness— rubbish left around structures, overgrown creek beds, wooded strips ripe with forest litter—were critical sources of spotting. During the early hours suppression had "no effect in reducing the area burnt." [18]

It was a classic confrontation, and McArthur relished its study. The worst of Australian bushfires had met the best in Australian bushfire fighting. The Western District boasted an outstanding program of fuelbreaks, the finest homestead protection, and "undoubtedly one of the most efficient volunteer rural fire control organisations in Australia." Here rural Australia had confronted the bushfire menace over several decades, steadily reduced its presence and terror, and posited a pragmatic model for all of New Australia to emulate. The lessons—the heroes—of the fires in the Western District lay in the brigades. "Despite adversity," McArthur concluded with undisguised pride, "the Australian rural community has built up a unique rural volunteer fire control organisation unequalled anywhere in the world." The brigades advertised a model for all of Australian life.[19]

The 1977 fires were Alan McArthur's final study. CSIRO published his report posthumously, a tribute to the rationalizing power of the Australian strategy. It was not obvious to everyone, however, that the Western District was an exemplar for all of Australia. It had no place for the indigenous bush or the urban bush: remnant woodlands were considered a nuisance, pardoned through the penance of prescribed fire; "semi-urban communities" were much in need of rudimentary fire consciousness, to say nothing of responsible self-protection. The Western District was not among the critical landscapes of New Australia. Its fire protection had little meaning to Kakadu, Uluru, Kosciusko, or to the Otways, the Dandenongs, the Adelaide Hills. As a base of comparison, New Australia was less likely to look back on 1944 than ahead to 2010, less concerned about where they had come from than to where they wanted to go. The 1977 complex seemed to many observers, unlike the dying McArthur, as less a paean to the Australian strategy than a kind of postmortem on it.

ONCE YOU ARE HERE, YOU WILL GET USED TO THESE THINGS

Like the Mongols and Manchus in China, fire protection found it had conquered Australia only to be absorbed by its conquests. In the late 1970s the promise of a unified rule had fragmented into a suite of competing fiefdoms, some rife with internal dissent. Critics succeeded by and large in fending off an extension of controlled burning into new landscapes, but they were not always able themselves to defend those lands from bushfire—and a single failure could send decades of successful protection up in smoke. The premier achievement of the Australian strategy had been its assertion that fire practices, and fire regimes, could be shaped consciously, that in the long run something could be done about catastrophic bushfires. Now that legacy, too, fractured into a familiar fatalism. If large fires were not common, they were not a serious problem. If bushfires became large, they were uncontrollable. Either way one simply endured them along with taipans, floods, and other inscrutabilities of antipodean Australia.

The Australia of 1979, however, looked considerably different from the Australia of 1939. Forty years of reform had organized fire institutions, reconstituted fire regimes, redirected many fire practices, and confirmed a fire science. Newly flourishing parks reoriented old fire techniques into biotic restoration and ecological research; pastoralism rediscovered prescribed fire in an attempt to drive back encroaching shrubs and alter grassland composition; scientific inquiry effervesced with experimentation in the biology of bushfires—withholding fire here, applying it there, probing, kindling, swatting out, and suffering an occasional fatality when fires got out of hand. Among its fire provinces, the critical division remained between those that lay within the fire flume and those outside it. Western Australia displayed the greatest stability, accommodating with minimal disruption the demands of new land uses. Late to develop, less hounded by disaster fires, Queensland showed extraordinary vigor, rapidly claiming for itself a special niche in fire use and fire research. The Northern Territory entered the era in the late 1960s under the aegis of the Australian strategy, underwent a review and reorganization in 1977, and concluded a decade later as a prototype for biocentric burning in preserves—in the wet-dry tropics at Kakadu, the central desert at Uluru, the marginal grasslands at Tamani. In the interim it experienced the largest of known Australian fire complexes, the staggering 1974–75 fires that burned an estimated 15 percent of the continent. In an earlier time such fires would have come and gone unnoticed beyond Outback stations.[20]

The *experimentum crucis,* however, remained the southeast. Here everything crowded together, and like the compression that ignites a diesel engine the compaction threatened to kindle its volatile mix of people and land into an explosion. South Australia escaped the worst outbreaks, its most notorious fires confined, it seemed, to remote outposts of pine plantations. Tasmania demonstrated significant improvements after the 1967 debacle, but a coherent fire policy seemed impossible when every expression of fire brought political controversy to a rapid boil. New South Wales appeared content to extend its incremental evolution in the Luke tradition, a program at once diffuse yet concentrated at critical points; failures in the Blue Mountains and Eden were matched by accommodations at Kosciusko park and in the Western District pastoral lands. There were no escape valves, however, for Victoria.[21]

The 1977 fires forced yet another reexamination of the premises and practices of bushfire protection. Premier Malcolm Fraser urged that the fire authorities adopt air tankers, and after he became prime minister and East Gippsland faced a severe fire season in 1980–81, the inquiry went to the CSIRO Division of Forest Research whose chief saw a chance to revive what remained of bushfire research. A proposal from Phil Cheney to review a spectrum of firefighting technologies was refused by CSIRO but somehow

made it to the prime minister who committed funds through a special direc-
tive—at a time of general budget and staff reductions throughout CSIRO.
Meanwhile, Victoria had engineered an experimental program with C-130
Hercules military aircraft outfitted with an overblown American retardant
device known as a Modular Airborne Fire Fighting System (MAFFS) and
Canada applied considerable pressure on Australia to purchase its CL-215 air
tanker, the only aircraft designed specifically for aerial attack. Under
Cheney's direction, and amid considerable resentment from the CSIRO hier-
archy which bridled at its special funding, the project expanded into Project
Aquarius, a three-year program that resuscitated the McArthur agenda.[22]

Aquarius matched field trials with computer simulations, placed both
within a general assessment of fire control technologies available to Australia, and conducted experimental burns in Western Australia to upgrade the
McArthur forest-fire meter. In essence it pitted suppression technologies,
aerial firefighting among them, against fuel reduction. Both the Aquarius
researchers and the Victorian Forests Commission concluded that the value
of American air tankers was marginal and the benefits of Canadian-style
water scoopers almost nil. Victoria recommended continued exploitation of
small, agricultural aircraft, perhaps supplemented by medium-size helicopters. Using a sophisticated simulation program (AIRPRO) developed in Canada, Aquarius demonstrated that a single largish tanker such as a DC6 was
the most economical option but that two medium-size helicopters with additional hand crews or a half dozen Thrush Commanders introduced the greatest economies. All were adamant that aerial attack would not, by itself,
banish bushfires.[23]

But neither, the Forests Commission concluded, would fuel reduction.
Most of the acreage consumed by bushfires resulted from a small fraction of
the total fires, roughly 5 percent, that burned under conditions so extreme
that they made fireline suppression dangerous and long-range spotting probable. In such circumstances fuelbreaks were "obviously pointless" and a fuel-
reduction program had "to create strategic areas of considerable depth" if it
was to lessen spotting as a cause and consequence. The value of such zones
had been demonstrated repeatedly, and the Commission accepted hazard
reduction as the "most critical element in the overall fire protection
scheme": it was the practical creation of large enough areas at the right times
and places that was imponderable. "This difficulty is real," the Commission
affirmed. When one added up all the areas excluded from routine burning,
there was little left, and those were compromised by seasonal fluctuations
that made "it almost impossible for field officers in some areas to achieve any
worthwhile fuel reduction." Successful broadacre burning meant aerial
burning. The Commission thus acknowledged a failure of execution rather
than a failure of philosophy, but to critics it made less and less sense to
distinguish between the two. Bushfire protection was not a sufficient philos-

ophy of fire management; fire management not a sufficient philosophy of land management.[24]

If the fires revived old arguments, they staged the debate within a new context that made the controversies of 1979 different from those of 1939. Whether or not it was possible to fashion a composite fire philosophy depended on whether or not it was possible for a composite Australia to thrive. This too was an old debate in a new context. New Australia argued for— wanted—a stable hybrid of Western civilization and indigenous Australia. It sought to reconcile an Australia profoundly reworked by European colonization with a transplanted European society no less profoundly altered by its experiences in Australia. An expulsion of European influence was impossible, and an environmental apartheid which segregated the wholly indigenous from the wholly Europeanized was distasteful and probably unworkable. New Australia knew that it did not like either indigenous holocausts or the heritage of burning off. Beyond that it was uncertain.

At an early bushfire symposium a man who introduced himself as a " 'New Australian' (an old 'New Australian')" encapsulated those sentiments perfectly.

> I would like to say that one of my first impressions on landing in Australia, in the year 1939, was smoke as far as I could see. When the Customs Officer came on board, we asked him what all the smoke meant, and he told us it was a terrible bush fire along the coast in Victoria and it made a very great impression on us. And he said to us, "Once you are here, you will get used to these things." Well, I've been here for nearly thirty years now, and I'm still not used to it.

The postwar generation as a whole never got used to it. If they could not state exactly what kind of future they wanted, they were confident that it should not resemble what they saw of the past. If there was no going back, however, it was just as difficult to move forward.[25]

The 1977 fires pointed to structural instabilities in Australian settlement. New Australia promoted a composite of peoples and practices and landscapes, and the 1977 fires argued that the mixtures were uncertain and potentially deadly. That the worst ignitions had resulted when desert winds shredded industrial powerlines was an apt symbol of how the natural and the cultural could interact in unexpected and violent ways. Even within the humanized landscape there was friction. Ruralites, exurbanites, environmentalists, foresters, outstation Aborigines—all had different fire needs. There could be no consensus on fire management until there was consensus over land use and over that most elusive of quests, an Australian identity. But with or without consensus, the spinifex cured, the eucalypts shed their bark, droughts parched, winds blew, and bushfires came. It was not obvious—it might never be—whether a composite identity could survive any more than that the competing ecologies of Europe and Australia could coexist in a stable compound or whether, like phosphorus bait sitting under the merciless Australian sun, the amalgamation would eventually, inevitably, erupt into flame.

Epilogue

Ashes to Ashes

Mr. CHYNOWETH—It is very hard for a man to play nature, is it not?
Mr. PACKHAM—Yes.

—PARLIAMENTARY HEARINGS ON THE
ASH WEDNESDAY FIRES (1983)

ASH WEDNESDAY

When dawn broke on February 16, 1983—Ash Wednesday—there were
scores of fires burning throughout the southeast fire flume. Drought—then
in its third, and in some locales fourth year—had leached fuels of moisture.
Powerful cold fronts swept eastward, hurling forth desert winds like parched
tsunamis. Even in November major fires had erupted in eastern Victoria.
Earlier in February a fire at Cann River had burned 100,000 hectares over the
span of twelve days and spread into pine plantations in New South Wales.
But all paled before the spangled holocaust of February 16. On that day a
double cold front intensified, and the Red Centre spilled through the fire
flume. One after another, from the Flinders Range to the Cann River, like an
arc of violent candles lit by some incendiary wind, old flames and new starts
flared into conflagrations. New Australia withered before it.[1]

Bushfires broke out during the morning hours in South Australia.
Country Fire Service brigades caught the fires on the Lower Yorke Peninsula
early. At Port Lincoln, Clare, and the Adelaide Hills a massive, obscuring
dust storm, however, foreshadowed a breakout. One fire mercifully rushed
past the town of Clare before the wind shift drove it eastward, but overall
the complex geography of the hills—human and natural—frustrated control,
and the shifting winds exploded the fire perimeter into a blizzard of flame.
There were fires at Meadows, Tea Tree Gully, Anstey Hill, Gumeracha; fires
swarmed at Hahndorf, Mount Barker, Bridgewater, and Mylor; in the Mount

Lofty region, fires raged through the Mount Crawford and Kuippo Forests; the Mount Osmond and Greenhill fires incinerated Cleland Fauna Park, sparing only the fire lookout and Mount Lofty obelisk. In the southeast, bushfires devastated pine plantations on the Mount Burr, Penola, and Mount Gambier forests. Fires kindled from powerline failures, tractor sparks, incendiarism. Increasing winds and an unstable atmosphere supported massive spotting. Firewhirls proliferated. At Furner, aerial photographs indicated a pillar of flame that towered to 375 meters, probably one of several "fire tornadoes" that danced across the region. Instruments in open fields recorded mean wind velocities of 40–50 km/h^{-1} prior to the front, and 70 km/h^{-1} afterward; gusts exceeded 110 km/h^{-1}. The premier declared a state of emergency. In dozens of communities police ordered evacuations. Brigades rolled, attacked, broke up, regrouped; residents fought and fled. The toll mounted—twenty-six dead, 196 houses burned, 25 to 30 percent of South Australia's conifer plantations devastated in an afternoon. And the holocaust was spreading eastward like a fiery swarm to descend on Victoria. The sheer volume of fires—180 in one day—no less than the vigor with which ignitions escalated into conflagrations overwhelmed the Country Fire Authority and the Forests Commission despite early-season fire restrictions and additional firefighters and aircraft stockpiled in anticipation. Powerline failures ignited fires at Cudgee and Ballangeich in the rural Western District that killed nine persons and destroyed 157 houses. A fire at Mount Macedon, probably electrical in origin, went on a ten-hour rampage that killed seven and leveled 628 houses. Horrendous spotting, heavy fuels, and a landscape immersed in a smoke pall all made orchestrated suppression tenuous. Residents fended for themselves. The noise—a deafening metallic roar—terrified and disoriented, while smoke obscured, isolated, frightened. Fires broke communications, cut off escape routes, and severed the electrical lines that powered water pumps. Particularly after the wind shift, spot fires showered the landscape, seeming to drop fire from nowhere into everywhere. New starts proliferated. A fire of unknown origin erupted near Dean's Marsh and burned southward to the sea until the frontal shift redirected winds to the east and a huge fire front raged through Otway State Forest, swirled around Anglesea, and invaded the rural environs of Geelong, consuming three lives and 782 structures. Another mysteriously started fire—suspected arson—broke free south of Sherbrooke, raced south through Monbulk and Sherbrooke state forests, and sacked Belgrave before the wind shift drove fire toward Beaconsfield, leaving twenty-one fatalities and 238 smoldering structures in its wake. Twelve of the dead were firefighters. The fire was controllable, it was later estimated, only for the first thirty to sixty seconds following its ignition. The state activated its disaster plan. With each hour, however, as wind and flame danced their deadly duet across Victoria, new conflagrations flared. Around 6:30 P.M. another fire, suspected incendiary, invaded Cockatoo, inflicting widespread pandemonium, taking six lives and a handful of houses. A similar fire in rural Branxholme killed one firefighter and destroyed ten buildings. At 7:20 P.M. a fire of "suspicious origin" outside Warburton raced southeast to the outskirts of Powelltown, then swarmed eastward in a melee of spot fires and backburns. The outbreaks continued to the east, but evening brought a change in weather and as fires burned with less voracity brigades had a greater opportunity to cope. Beyond the Cann River, the fire flume ended. Desert winds ceased. The Pacific Ocean rolled a firebreak that even stringybark firebrands could no longer defy. Though mop-up continued until February 18, the Ash Wednesday holocaust concluded, with remarkable suddenness, within twelve hours of the time it began. In succession, following the order in which they had been lit, the candles snuffed out.

Even before the ashes cooled, Australians began comparing Ash Wednesday to Black Friday. The McArthur scale had established Black Friday as its maximum value, 100 points; Ash Wednesday figured at 107. Yet far less acreage had burned in 1983 than in 1939. Of 180 fires unleashed in Victoria on February 16, only 10 had escalated into major holocausts. Rural burning off had not, as it had forty-four years before, kindled the conflagration. New Australia had thrown an incredible armada of machinery and men at the flames—558 brigades, 21,000 firefighters, 15 fixed-wing aircraft, 13 helicopters, numerous earth-moving vehicles, a MAFFS-equipped retardant plane, a FLIR (Forward Looking Infra-Red) mapping scanner. It had activated social, legal, and economic institutions, both private and public. It had declared fire bans and states of emergency. It had tended to fire victims with speed, organization, and compassion. It had virtually mobilized Australian society. None of this had been possible in 1939.

And yet—the losses were greater. Ash Wednesday had claimed seventy-one lives, including those of thirteen firefighters. It destroyed more than 2,300 houses and structures, killed some 350,000 livestock, scorched more than 350,000 hectares of land, including priceless conifer plantations. It burdened Australia with insurance claims likely to exceed $200 million, stimulated state, Commonwealth, and private relief efforts of considerable dimensions, and threw brushfire protection schemes into another bout of introspection. New Australia had less land to trade for bushfires. If there was, as some reviewers concluded, "an unwarranted degree of confidence (complacency may be too strong a word) about the ability to control the fires" before they began, that sense of security vanished immediately after the fires made their runs. Psychiatrists rushed to make studies on the fires' psychological impact on brigade volunteers, on victims, on Australian society. Nearly everyone admitted that Ash Wednesday was only the latest in an interminable succession of Australian holocausts.[2]

There would be more.

EIGHT MONTHS AFTER ASH WEDNESDAY D. R. Douglas, the doyen of South Australian fire, outlined the social ecology of postfire succession. First comes an "elaborate enquiry followed by an excellent report." On occasions some legislative reform follows, typically addressing the need for improved bushfire suppression. Bushfire research flourishes for a few years, then withers away—an ashbed effect. As the years pass there is a "slow, imperfect and steadily declining application in practice of proven measures to mitigate bushfire effects." The status quo ante returns. The drive to integrate or at least coordinate rural fire services falters and evaporates like dew. It was, Douglas concluded, a "sad scenario." And it was completely prophetic of Ash Wednesday's aftermath.[3]

South Australia and Victoria empaneled several inquiries. Tasmania, stung by fires in 1982, reviewed its fire establishment. Always-curious West Australia sponsored inspection tours. New South Wales, still smarting from the Eden debacle and the slopover from the Cann River fire, considered what Ash Wednesday meant for it. The Australian Forestry Council issued a report on the holocaust and sponsored a handbook (and directory) for bushfire research. The many fatalities demanded coroner's inquests, which filled a small library. The Bureau of Meteorology hosted a Fire Weather Service Conference. The Australian Fire Protection Association devoted its Ninth National Conference largely to Ash Wednesday. Symposia blossomed like orchids in the ash. All these investigations were subsumed, however, under a massive inquiry by the House of Representatives Standing Committee on Environment and Conservation. For months the committee held hearings, first in Canberra, then in every state capital. The entire bushfire establishment submitted detailed reports. Conservation organizations, insurance companies, shire councilmen, brigades, professors, graziers, farmers, and private citizens all contributed—the roll call of speakers and submissions constituted a cross section of New Australia. The Hansard report formed a veritable encyclopedia of Australian fire practices and Australian bush life.

The outcome was, as Douglas forecast, modest, if not marginal. The principal initiative was politically the easiest to make: a call for more information, a decision to fund a National Bushfire Research Unit (NBRU) within CSIRO. Instead of expiring in 1984, Project Aquarius was rechartered within the Division of Forest Research. Institutionally, NBRU succeeded in leveraging its funds into a broadly based research program through subcontracts (some begun under Aquarius) to institutions like the National Centre for Rural Fire Research, housed at the Chisholm Institute of Technology, and the Duntroon fire research group, organized within the mathematics department of the Royal Military College. Its chief, N. P. Cheney, proudly declared himself a McArthur protégé, and NBRU revived the McArthur agenda. It sought to upgrade the McArthur meters, to understand through more experimental burning the dynamics of grass fires, to justify hazard-reduction burning, to assist the protection of rural and exurban residents and of brigade volunteers. It sought to exercise a leadership role, suitable for a Commonwealth bureau, among the low-level proliferation of fire-research projects that flowered in the aftermath of February 16.

The task was daunting, and it required a consensus that did not always exist. Other CSIRO divisions investigated fire; state forestry commissions, the National Park and Wildlife Service, and rural fire services explored bushfire topics that interested them; forestry and biology departments in universities, research professors at the Australian National University, the Duntroon mathematics department—all conducted some research into fire, and not all wanted a national agenda or agreed with the revival proposed by the NBRU. The Australian Forestry Council listed scores of research projects, many by part-time fire specialists. Speaking for ecologists, Malcolm Gill outlined an alternative agenda for Western Australia. With or without a Commonwealth commitment, some research would go on. Not even the CSIRO Division of Forest Research, which housed NBRU, really wanted a separate unit. Research funds were too scarce, and NBRU funding came at the expense of other CSIRO projects. By 1980 Australia supported only about 1.5 percent of world science. When funding for research and development was considered relative to gross national product, Australia scored even worse, about 1.01 compared to 2.90 for the United States, 2.65 in Japan, and 2.26 in the United Kingdom. Scientific research was not an Australian priority.[4]

Nor, it became increasingly apparent, was bushfire protection. Ash Wednesday did not shatter the impasse over fire practices. It did not inspire an intellectual or institutional reformation. The interrogation of Ash Wednesday yielded no new breakthroughs in the theory and practice of bushfire protection; rather it confirmed what decades of hard experience had accumulated. Ash Wednesday was less a fact than a specter. It appeared like a recurring nightmare, long forgotten, that suddenly flashed back into consciousness like a scream in the dark. Once its political payoff passed, once the national trauma receded, a marginal program like bushfire research would be hard pressed to survive, and at the end of fiscal year 1988–89, the NBRU was dissolved.

What Ash Wednesday did was to pose before the nation and the world the character of New Australia. It clarified some of the terms by which a new relationship—a new adaptation—to the bush would come. Some answers eerily echoed the past. In the wild bush the solution was nomadism, the transience of the scientist and the tourist. In the urban bush the response was a kind of social scleromorphism. Some institutions weathered the burns, too tough to succumb. Others drew sustenance from national, even international sources, and rebuilt houses, communities, and institutions from the lignotubers and epicormic buds of a global economy. Mostly, things just happened. In this complex recolonization of Australia, as with those that preceded it, the transitional era was the most troubling. A fifty-year bushfire would not roll back settlement. And there was even a macabre suspicion that a fire could rejuvenate as well as destroy.

Among the most intriguing responses to Ash Wednesday was the attempt to analyze the fires in strict economic terms. Only a fraction of the costs and benefits could be converted to an economic calculus, but the scrutiny said much about how New Australians adapted to their land. South Australia and Victoria made good many losses through state funds. The National Disaster Relief Arrangements brought Commonwealth aid in the form of responsibility for meeting three dollars in every four dollars expenditure on "approved measures," grants, interest-free loans, and increased ceilings on state rights to borrow. There were insurance payments. There was a Consolidated Appeal Fund that raised nearly $12 million in voluntary contributions. Very quickly the institutions and residents of the fire zones were compensated. In fact, a South Australian analysis concluded that "a cynic might maintain that fires were good for business." The outpouring of monies dramatically stimulated the regional economy, which suffered an "output loss over all sectors of some $34.8m attributable to the flow-on effect of agricultural and forestry losses" but which found subsequent asset replacement "to the amount of $164m." Other studies suggested that those who had subscribed to fire insurance had suffered, economically, more than those who had not because those who appeared destitute received state and private relief.[5]

Something seemed distorted, unfair. There was little economic punishment or social stigma attached to those who were burned out. Like the rain that falls on the just and the unjust alike, bushfires had burned those who had insured their houses and those who had not; it had destroyed the homes of those who served on brigades and those who hadn't. The immediate response of Australian society was reflexive, humanitarian; only later was it appreciated that it was also paradoxical. By means of public acts the outpouring effectively insulated everyone from private responsibilities. There was little incentive to change attitudes, patterns of behavior, or the design of the urban bush. Urban residents paid the same premiums as bush residents, a considerable inequity in terms of costs. Critics watched aghast as citizens—with more resolution than insight—often rebuilt their houses on the same sites, in the same styles, with the same perception of the bushfire hazard, with at most some marginal improvements in design. Exhortation said one thing; economics another.

But the economics of bushfires was only a part of the explanation. Not everything could be made good with money. The dead were gone, a loss that no fund could replace. This issue was not merely psychological, as social scientists believed, so much as moral. The response to Ash Wednesday demanded something more than basic survival. It questioned the relationships among the different segments of Australian society. It revealed relationships between individual and state. It inscribed, as few other things could, the relationship of the individual New Australian to Australia.

Unlike Black Friday, so quickly followed by world war, the fires of Ash Wednesday had nothing else of sufficient power with which to ally themselves. They burned, yielded a profusion of regrowth—orchids, houses, and commission reports among them—and returned to the status quo. The momentum for reform faltered. Australians tended to overemphasize the bushfire hazard and underestimate their power to control it. They showed a mixture of complacency and fatalism, a psychology of hope more appropriate to a lottery in which, during the next fire, their number would be passed over. They were unwilling to commit to any emphatic course of action. They shunned the two extremes—to convert the land completely to something else or to abandon it to native bush. If the mixture burned, they were prepared to rebuild, to wait out the fire next time, to trust to luck and the state. There were many ways to "live with" bushfires, and tolerating a conflagration, like betting on a roulette wheel, had its economic probabilities. As with the lands, so with the people. There appeared to be an inability to compromise between denial and despondency. The residual medley was one of defiance, indifference, and fatalism.

DAVID PACKHAM HAD TAKEN THE TWO AMERICANS —U.S. Forest Service experts on chemical fire retardants—to the Pink Elephant, an overlook at Upper Beaconsfield. At six P.M. or so, to the west they saw the glow of the bushfire. Packham concluded that the fire was nearly out. Then he saw it, "a big, black cloud—a dust storm." The wind shift had arrived, and the pall foreshadowed it like a squall line. The wind drove toward them, the fire soon to follow. They rushed to their car and managed to flee two hundred meters down the road before the winds struck and shook the car like a leaf. At Packham's house firebrands rained down in a shower. Packham, his wife Helen, and the two Americans, now outfitted with hard hats, made the calculated choice to stay put. No substantial structure would burn in the few minutes that it takes a flaming front to pass through. The house was shelter. It had been designed to withstand bushfire, and even had its own gravity-fed tank to supply water during a power failure. If they survived the thermal pulse, they could probably save the house. With heat and noise, however, came doubts. A tidal wave of flame twenty meters high crashed upon them. "I thought no house could stand it," Packham concluded. "The curtains started to smoulder, windows cracked, the wooden window frames in the study burned through." A bowl of pancake batter on a kitchen table cooked. The small band furiously swatted out tiny fires that ignited and passed buckets of water from a bathtub. The heat was a hundred times greater than the brightest sunlight. Yet they lived. The house endured. And Ash Wednesday experienced one of those epiphanies that transform a story of survival into a moral universe, a world of conscious choice, of acts that express a relationship of humans to the environment around them.[6]

The spectacle has a rough symmetry, an ironic significance. In 1962, as a young scientist, David Packham had signed on to the CSIRO Bushfire Research unit at Melbourne where he assisted with research into fire fundamentals. He found inspiration in Western Australia's controlled-burning program. When George Peet suggested the value of aerial ignition as a means of increasing the safety of hazard-reduction burning, Packham devised the first incendiary capsule. He was involved in nearly every major development in bushfire research—fire behavior, bushfire smoke, large-scale fire behavior and convection. He participated in the debate over air tankers. In 1969 he toured North America, Europe, and South Africa, comparing fire practices. Then CSIRO allowed the Bushfire Research group to decay by natural attrition, and in 1980 Packham joined the Chisholm Institute of Technology where he organized fire research. When Project Aquarius attacted new funds, he assembled a consortium of five fire researchers to work under contract with it. Eventually he severed his ties to Chisholm and set up his own National Centre for Rural Fire Research where his group modeled fire behavior and investigated some technical aspects of aerial suppression by chemicals, which was the reason for hosting the two American specialists. Others at the Centre inquired into the specifics of bushfire survival, the endurance both of persons and of houses. Packham testified forcefully to the parliamentary inquest into Ash Wednesday as the committee's last witness. But Aquarius ended; Packham refused to join the NBRU group at Canberra, took a post as a fire specialist at the Australian Counter-Disaster College, then fell out with colleagues and transferred into the Bureau of Meteorology.

His credentials gave Packham public standing as a scientific authority on fire, and his experience during Ash Wednesday made him, for a time, a bushfire celebrity. He used that visibility to advocate a modernized version of the Australian strategy. "Without doubt," he insisted, "the most effective protection against bushfires is large scale prescribed burning to reduce bush fuels to safer levels." Nothing else was equally effective. Western Australia, he noted, had decided to eliminate large fires and had done so through good technique and firm will. But Packham was no simple ideologue. He cited the pamphlet by the Australian Conservation Foundation as "a very fair and reasonable summation of the pros and cons of fuel reduction burning." Prescribed burning, he informed the Standing Committee on Environment and Conservation, "is a difficult task. It is an expensive task. I believe it costs almost the same as having the disasters, to do it properly. It is very important to do it properly." [7]

He recognized, too, the need for better means of survival in bushfires whether or not residents practiced fuel reduction. Australia needed a "low technology, self-reliant bushfire response," one that provided for survival and put the onus on individual citizens who were, in the end, the responsible agents. His own experiences sustained the general findings. Most destroyed houses burned *after* the flaming front had passed, kindled from radiant heat through glass or firebrands blown into openings. Most fatalities occurred during flight. Evacuation had to come very early or not at all. The best solution was simply to stay put. The house sheltered its occupant against the deadly radiant heat that was the prime killer, and the occupant could protect the house with simple, if exhausting, measures. A reciprocity existed between resident and residence.[8]

In that scenario lay the essence of the Packham proposition and an environmental parable for New Australia. It did no good to reside for a while and then flee, or to flee and then rebuild like eucalypts mindlessly pushing out new sprouts. Survival meant engagement. Survival meant addressing the fundamental question which was, for Packham, "What do we want?" It meant conscious choice, a commitment by citizens and society, the acceptance of responsibility by both individuals and institutions. It meant something between the negligence of the bush larrikin and the naivete of the environmental wowser. While the means proposed by Packham could never serve the ends of all Australia, what was vital was the decision to accept Australia in deliberate ways—to engage it, not merely to endure it or to escape from it.[9]

There was, Packham believed, an irrational fear of bushfires that bred a syndrome of apathy and fatalism. The fear of bushfire belonged with Australians' fear of snakes and of sharks, phobias out of proportion to the facts. They were symptomatic of a reluctance to engage Australia as permanent residents. If bushfire was indigenous and dangerous, it was also necessary and survivable. While there was much that remained mysterious, there was much that was known and much of a practical nature that could be done to reduce their damages. After Ash Wednesday Packham knew, emotionally no less than intellectually, what it took to coexist with bushfires. It required deliberate acts, a constant vigilance, a balance between alarm and caution. The potential for bushfire was always there in the shadow of the gums, in the stir of the wind.

Bold words, these, backed by a gripping trial by fire, but they were words compromised by indifferent acts. If Packham's biography testified to the institutional instability of fire research, it also spoke of a personal restlessness, the intellectual as swagman. His residence was ill-prepared for fire. He refused to burn his own property, tolerating an understory of litter and moribund scrub that brought him into conflict with the local brigades. Instead he estimated that the odds of a major bushfire on his block were sufficiently low to accept the risk. Even his vaunted house, nominally conceived to survive a bushfire, was bloated with hazards: fuelwood was stacked against the walls; the PVC pipe that joined his water tank to his house rested openly, exposed, on heavy fuels; the eucalypt bush, now desiccated into organic dynamite, crowded against the concrete. An expert on fire behavior, he had been sight-seeing when the front arrived and drove the fire to his block. Had he not had the company of two experienced Americans, some colleagues felt he might have perished. No one put forward the philosophical case for actively engaging bushfire so bluntly or gave it such vivid imagery after Ash Wednesday as did Packham. But perhaps the real moral to this environmental fable was the failure to practice what one preached, to treat bushfire as a lottery and to dismiss Australia as a lucky country.[10]

In fact the gap between what was said and what was done was widening. Lawyers quarreled over computer graphics that might or might not have any relationship to real ecosystems. Philosophical disputations raged over matters that could not be translated into field operations. The Red Centre no longer held. But perhaps that mattered little. The real reformation had not come from a single stroke of technology, science, or politics. It had resulted from thousands of individual Australians doing tens of thousands of little acts, a routine of life in the Australian bush, new and old. The heroes of Ash Wednesday were those who had not placed themselves in jeopardy; the real spokespersons were those like Phil Cheney and Malcolm Gill who had, for decades, through good times and bad, as scientists and practitioners, engaged bushfires as a natural phenomenon of Australia and bestowed through their own lives a continuity of knowledge and practical experience that no amount of rhetoric, Sunday-supplement photos, or political posturing could repeal. The dramatic clarity of the choices masked a muddle of practical acts.

But one way or another, the ignorant no less than the wise, the indifferent along with the committed, would have to reconcile the emerging physical geography of New Australia with its emerging moral geography. That moral mosaic would inevitably match the diversity of its environmental mosaic. What it could not dismiss was the presence of fire. Whether they wanted to keep fire out or put it in, Australians could not aspire to a relationship with their bush that denied its reality. If successful, if true to past Australian experience, irony would then replace parody, and the sardonic, the cynical.

ILLUMINATING FIRE

On June 18, 1988, two centuries to the day after the First Fleet made land-fall, the governor-general of Australia ignited a bonfire at Botany Bay. When the flames became visible down the coast, another bonfire was kindled. When that fire flared, there was another. And so it went, one fire after another, throughout the long night, until all of Australia became encircled in a ring of fire. The procession would, Geoffrey Blainey hoped, "celebrate the unity of Australia. It will also honour that most powerful, majestic and frightening force in our history—the force of fire." [11]

To a remarkable extent the unity of Australia and the force of fire had converged in fact and purpose. Since the breakup of Gondwana, fire had progressively insinuated itself into Australian natural history. With isolation and aridity, it had increasingly informed the biotic character of the island continent. Between fire and flora there evolved a fantastic and growing reci-procity. The injection of humans wielding firesticks—inextricable, inextin-guishable—tipped the scale further toward sclerophylly, toward pyrophilia. Anthropogenic fire powered the economics of hunting and foraging, it lit ritual and ceremony, it shaped relationships among people and between Ab-origines and Australia. Europeans subtracted some fires, added new ones, and restructured the fuel complex in fundamental ways. Again, humans dreaded and resisted bushfires even as they advanced behind a covering front of flames, a slow colossal fire drive that eventually burned across a continent. The net effect of this complex colonization was to further accentuate the prevalence of fire. Fire in the bush became pervasive, vital, deadly, appar-ently ineradicable—its geography universal, its history irreversible. The cre-ation myths of Australia were told by firelight. The landscape of Australia became by and large a landscape of fire.

The bicentennial ring of fire was a chain of vestal fires brought from Europe and naturalized in Australia. Its power to shape the natural and human history of Australia was far less ubiquitous than the power of Aborig-inal fire that had preceded it. Settlement, which had so depended on fire during establishment, now circumscribed fire's power to roam. Australia's informing fire had become an illuminating fire, revealing by light what it could no longer shape by the power of continental combustion and the biotic chemistry of a scleromorphic flora.

That once-informing fire illuminated a bond with the bush. To the bush had fled convicts, lordly squatters, hopeful selectors, affluent exurbanites, natural scientists, Heidelberg impressionists. From the bush came the ende-mism that was somehow Australia. The situation was rife with irony that this, the most urbanized of civilizations, should take for its creation myth a symbol from its ineffable Outback. Yet the need was real, and clearly inade-quate was the saga of the First Fleet—of a people who did not want to be there, who did not understand where they were, who considered England "Home" and who viewed this antipodean land of contrarities with misunderstanding, amusement, and contempt. Contact came through the bush. Through the bush came meaning and legitimacy. The Australian was a European naturalized to the bush. But to engage that bush was to engage bushfire, because whatever else it meant, Australia meant fire, and whatever else they did, Australians used fire, and were used by it. Those celebratory bonfires proclaimed a relationship somewhere between the billy fire and the bushfire.

Much had changed: the bush, humans, and fire practices. But in one form or another fire had persisted. That bicentennial ring of fire was an eternal flame that, along with the world sea and the universal sky, bound Australians to a wider world, the fire by which Australia cycled nutrients through a global economy and a global ecology. But it was also the expression of an incompletely domesticated bushfire, a fiery border that segregated city from Outback. It was the campfire ring that warded off the wild beasts and the night terrors. It defined the realm of the habitable and the human. It segregated the wildfire that yet inhabited the continent's Red Centre.

THAT FIRE WAS ALWAYS THERE. It was there in the smothering pall of Henry Lawson's child in the dark and the fear of Judith Wright's snake under the house and the awful sublimity of Henry Kendall's ravenous flames. It brooded over the landscape. It infiltrated the very warp and woof of the Australian biota. It was latent in the desert breeze, the crackle of eucalypt litter, the stiff blades of spinifex. It was the fire of which Patrick White wrote, the fire into which men stared and were changed. It shaped the life of anything and everything that chose to exist or was forced to exist in Australia. It subsumed what was special about the bush—and what was terrible about it. This fire was absorbed into the subconscious. Its smoke haunted memories. Its flames lit nightmares.

It was impossible for humans to live under its tyranny, yet impossible for them to expunge it from the landscape. The bushfire was part of indigenous Australia that would remain forever alien and unassimilable. What mattered was how Australians confronted it. They could fight it, flee it, substitute one fire for another. They could, within limits, transfigure bushfire into bonfire. But whatever course they chose, as they shaped fire, so fire shaped them.

There was Australia; there was the bush—burning, oracular, unconsumed.

Notes

1. The geologic evolution of continental Australia and particularly the history of its soils is described in G. W. Leeper, ed., *The Australian Environment*, 4th ed. (CSIRO, 1973). More detailed surveys of soils is found in J. S. Russell and R. F. Isbell, eds., *Australian Soils. The Human Impact* (University of Queensland Press, 1986); K. H. Northcote et al., eds., *A Description of Australian Soils* (CSIRO, 1975), with atlas; and P. M. Attiwill and G. W. Leeper, *Forest Soils and Nutrient Cycles* (Melbourne University Press, 1987). A popular introduction to physical origins is John Vandenbeld, *Nature of Australia* (Collins Australia, 1988). The importance lies in how such conditions have shaped vegetative history, and most general histories are listed under Note 3. Worth mentioning now, however, are W. R. Barker and P. J. M. Greenslade, eds., *Evolution of the Flora and Fauna of Arid Australia* (Peacock Publications, 1982) and Allen Keast, ed., *Ecological Biogeography of Australia*, 3 vols. (Dr. W. Junk, 1981), both of which contain several good summary articles on the geologic context and the evolution of the Australian climate.

2. Cited in Howard Evans and Mary Alice Evans, *Australia. A Natural History* (Smithsonian Institution Press, 1983), p. 26.

3. For useful summaries of the evolution of the Australian biota, see Keast, ed., *Ecological Biogeography of Australia*, 3 vols.; R. H. Groves, ed., *Australian Vegetation* (Cambridge University Press, 1981); J. M. B. Smith, ed., *A History of Australasian Vegetation* (McGraw-Hill, 1982); W. R. Barker and P. J. M. Greenslade, eds., *Evolution of the Flora and Fauna of Arid Australia*; John Vandenbeld, *Nature of Australia*; B. A. Barlow, "The Australian Flora: Its Origin and Evolution," in Bureau of Flora and Fauna, *Flora of Australia. Volume 1. Introduction* (Australian Government Publishing Service, 1981), pp. 25–76; Helene A. Martin, "Evolution of the Australian Flora and Vegetation

423

through the Tertiary: Evidence from Pollen," *Alcheringa* 2 (1978), pp. 181–202; and the gorgeously illustrated volume by Mary E. White, *The Greening of Gondwana* (Reed Books, 1986). A marvelously distilled version is available in *Australian Natural History* 20, no. 7 (1981), Special Issue on Australia's Flora; in particular, Ross Bradstock, "Our Phoenix Flora," pp. 223–226 and Peter Kershaw, "Climate and Australian Flora," pp. 231–234.

4.   Cited in Vince Palmer, *National Portraits*, 3rd ed. (Melbourne University Press, 1954), p. 94.

5.   For summary fire histories, see Elizabeth M. Kemp, "Pre-Quaternary Fire in Australia" and G. Singh et al., "Quaternary Vegetation and Fire History in Australia," in A. M. Gill et al., *Fire and the Australian Biota* (Australian Academy of Science, 1981), pp. 3–54; Harry F. Recher and Per E. Christensen, "Fire and the Australian Biota," in Keast, ed., *Ecological Biogeography of Australia*, Vol. 1, pp. 137–161; and Henry Nix, "Environmental Determinants of Biogeography and Evolution in Terra Australis," in Barker and Greenslade, eds., *Evolution of the Flora and Fauna of Arid Australia*, pp. 47–66. A succinct encapsulation of Australian fire ecology is given in A. Malcolm Gill, "Fire and the Australian Flora: A Review," *Australian Forestry* 37 (1974), pp. 4–25.

6.   A. B. Edwards, "Fusain in Some Victorian Brown Coals," *Proceedings, Australian Institute of Mining and Metallurgy* 170 (1953), pp. 47–67; J. H. Rattigan, "Phenomena about Burning Mountain, Wingen, New South Wales," *Australian Journal of Science* 30, no. 5 (1967), pp. 183–184.

7.   See Robert L. Stanford, Jr., et al., "Amazon Rain-Forest Fires," *Science* 227 (January 4, 1985), pp. 53–55. They conclude that "it can no longer be assumed that lowland tropical rain forests have been free of fire disturbance." For an introduction to the East Kalimantan coal fires, see J. G. Goldammer and B. Seibert, "Natural Rain Forest Fires in Eastern Borneo During the Pleistocene and Holocene," *Naturwissenschaften* 76 (1989), pp. 518–520.

8.   The statistics on lightning fire are less robust than one might expect. Numbers are lean even in Kemp, "Pre-Quaternary Fire in Australia" and R. H. Luke and A. G. McArthur, *Bushfires in Australia* (Australian Government Publishing Service, 1978). Probably the fullest sources are the annual reports of forestry agencies. Most discussions break down into anecdotal or symbolic references, such as the ones cited: Forests Commission of Victoria, *Fire Protection and Fuel-Reduction Burning in Victoria* (September 1982), Appendix I, p. 3; B. D. Dexter, "From Fire Control to Fire Management," *Victoria's Resources* (March 1975), p. 12; F. R. Moulds, "Effect of Forest Fires and of Forest Policy on Land Use in Victoria," *Forestry Technical Papers No. 19* (Forests Commission, Victoria, 1967), p. 1; A. Hodgson and A. Heislers, "Some Aspects of the Role of Forest Fire in South Eastern Australia," *Bulletin* 21 (Forests Commission, Victoria, 1972), p. 6; Luke and McArthur, *Bushfires in Australia*, p. 256; G. F. Griffin et al., "Wildfires in the Central Australian Rangelands, 1970–1980," *Journal of Environmental Management* 17 (1983), pp. 314–315; R. H. Luke, *Proceedings of the Tropical and Arid Fire Symposium* (Bush Fires Council of the Northern Territory, 1971), p. 14; N. Condon, "Lightning Ignitions in the 1974/75 Bushfire Season," in *Eco-Fire. Proceedings of a Symposium Conducted at the Australian Museum, Sydney* (National Parks Association of New South Wales, 1976), pp. 140–141; "Questions and Comments. Fire Records and History," in A. Heislers et al., eds., *Fire Ecology in Semi-Arid Lands* (CSIRO, 1982); R. A. Anderson and B. G. Muir, "Fire Causes in W.A.

National Parks," *Australian Parks & Recreation* (May 1981), pp. 26–28; G. S. Stocker, "Effects of Fires on Vegetation in the Northern Territory," *Australian Forestry* 30 (1966), p. 225. For Tasmania, always a special case, see J. M. Gilbert, "Fire as a Factor in the Development of Vegetational Types," *Australian Forestry* 27 (1963), pp. 67–76; W. D. Jackson, "Fire, Air, Water and Earth —An Elemental Ecology of Tasmania," *Proceedings of the Ecological Society of Australia* 3 (1968), pp. 9–16; and D.M.J.S. Bowman and W. D. Jackson, "Vegetation Succession in Southwest Tasmania," *Search* 12, no. 10 (1981), pp. 358–362. A misleading analysis of lightning fire is contained in D. R. Horton, "The Burning Question: Aborigines, Fire and Australian Ecosystems," *Mankind* 13, no. 3 (April 1982), pp. 245–246. By comparison, U.S. fire statistics calculate lightning fires as 11 percent of the national total. In remoter, seasonally drier sites such as those in the public lands of the West, lightning contributes 90 percent or more of all starts.

9. The literature on the relationship between fire and rainforest is vast. For Australian summaries, consult D. H. Ashton, "Fire in Tall Open Forests (Wet Sclerophyll Forests)," pp. 339–366, and G. C. Stocker and J. J. Mott, "Fire in the Tropical Forests and Woodlands of Northern Australia," pp. 427–442, both in A. M. Gill et al., eds., *Fire and the Australian Biota.* Also relevant are the still-classic studies, L. J. Webb, "Environmental Relationships of the Structural Types of Australian Rain Forest Vegetation," *Ecology* 49 (1968), pp. 296–311, and W. D. Jackson, "Fire, Air, Water and Earth—An Elemental Ecology of Tasmania." Interesting comparisons are possible with India and South America, but the best summary remains Peter de V. Booysen and Neil M. Tainton, eds., *Ecological Effects of Fire in South African Ecosystems.* Ecological Studies 48 (Springer-Verlag, 1984) and the review essay by Dieter Mueller-Dombois, "Fire in Tropical Ecosystems," in H. A. Mooney et al., eds., *Proceedings of the Conference. Fire Regimes and Ecosystem Properties.* General Technical Report WO-26 (U.S. Forest Service, 1981), pp. 137–176.

1. THE UNIVERSAL AUSTRALIAN

1. For the evolutionary context of *Eucalyptus,* see the entries under note (Prologue, 3). Especially helpful in understanding the enigmatic eucalypt are G. Singh, "Environmental Upheaval," in J.M.B. Smith, ed., *A History of Australasian Vegetation* (McGraw-Hill, 1981), pp. 90–108; L. D. Pryor and L.A.S. Johnson, "Eucalyptus, the Universal Australian" and R. L. Specht, "Evolution of the Australian Flora: Some Generalizations," in Allen Keast, ed., *Ecological Biogeography of Australia,* Vol. 1 (Dr. W. Junk, 1981), pp. 501–536, 785–805; R. G. Florence, "Eucalypt Forests and Woodlands," in Department of Arts, Heritage, and Environment and Institute of Foresters of Australia, *Think Trees, Grow Trees* (Australian Government Publishing Service, 1985), pp. 29–50; R. G. Florence, "The Biology of the Eucalypt Forest," in J. S. Pate and A. J. McComb, eds., *The Biology of Australian Plants* (University of Australia Press, 1981), pp. 147–180; and Mary E. White, *The Greening of Gondwana* (Reed Books, 1986). Useful entries are available in R. H. Groves, ed., *Australian Vegetation* (Cambridge University Press, 1981), N. H. Beadle, *Vegetation of Australia* (Cambridge University Press, 1981), and D. J. Boland et al., *Forest Trees of Australia,* new ed. (Thomas Nelson and CSIRO, 1984). Lindsay D.

Pryor, *The Biology of Eucalypts,* Institute of Biology, Studies in Biology No.

Pryor, *The Biology of Eucalypts,* Institute of Biology, Studies in Biology No. 61 (Edward Arnold, 1976) reconciles popular with technical material.

2. Statistics from White, *The Greening of Gondwana,* p. 204.

3. See J. G. Tracey, "An Ecological Comparison of Vegetation Communities on Each Side of Torres Strait," R. D. Hoogland, "Plant Distribution Patterns Across the Torres Strait," and S.G.M. Carr, "Problems of the Geography of the Tropical Eucalypts," in D. Walker, *Bridge and Barrier: The Natural and Cultural History of the Torres Strait,* Department of Biogeography and Geomorphology BG/3 (Australian National University, 1972), pp. 109–182.

4. See G. Singh et al., "Quaternary Vegetation and Fire History in Australia," in A. M. Gill et al., eds., *Fire and the Australian Biota* (Australian Academy of Science, 1981), pp. 23–54; G. Singh, "Environmental Upheaval," in Smith, ed., *History of Australasian Vegetation,* pp. 90–108. Statistics from R. G. Florence, "Eucalypt Forests and Woodlands," in *Think Trees, Grow Trees,* pp. 31–32 and Robert Zacharin, *Emigrant Eucalypts,* p. 4.

5. Ferdinand von Müller, quoted in Vince Palmer, *National Portraits,* p. 94; Charles Darwin, *Voyage of the Beagle,* ed. Leonard Engel (Anchor Books, 1962), p. 436; Marcus Clarke, "Preface," *Poems of Adam Lindsay Gordon,* 6th ed. (Samuel Mullen, Melbourne, 1890).

6. For a survey of the biotic revolution of the Pleistocene, see Paul S. Martin and Richard G. Klein, eds., *Quaternary Extinctions. A Prehistoric Revolution* (University of Arizona Press, 1984), particularly the essays on Australia, pp. 600–707.

7. See G. Singh et al., "Quaternary Vegetation and Fire History in Australia," in A. M. Gill et al., eds., *Fire and the Australian Biota,* pp. 23–54; Harry F. Recher and Per E. Christensen, "Fire and the Evolution of the Australian Biota," in Allen Keast, ed., *Ecological Biogeography of Australia,* Vol. 1 (Dr. W. Junk, 1981), pp. 137–162; A. Peter Kershaw, "Late Cenozoic Plant Extinctions in Australia," in Martin and Klein, eds., *Quaternary Extinctions,* pp. 691–707. Helpful as an introduction is David G. Green, "Bushfires and Conservation—What Can Pollen and Charcoal Teach Us?," (n.d., photocopy obtained from CSIRO Division of Forest Research library). Still useful as an introduction, though dating rapidly, is A. B. Mount, "Eucalypt Ecology as Related to Fire," *Proceedings, Tall Timbers Fire Ecology Conference* 9 (Tallahassee, 1969), pp. 75–108.

8. Introductions to extratropical eucalypts available in Pryor, *Biology of Eucalypts;* Robert Zacharin, *Emigrant Eucalypts* (Melbourne University Press, 1978); and Carr, "Problems of the Geography of the Tropical Eucalypts," in Walker, ed., *Bridge and Barrier,* pp. 153–182. The overall contrasts between Australia and the Sunda arc are detailed in J. Peter White and James F. O'Connell, *A Prehistory of Australia, New Guinea, and Sahul* (Academic Press, 1982), especially pp. 6–17.

9. My outline follows closely Zacharin, *Emigrant Eucalypts.* For a sample of how *Eucalyptus* is recolonizing Gondwana rainforests, see H. F. Kaiser, "Forest Development in the Congo," *Journal of Forestry* (October 1988), pp. 40–42.

10. See N. P. Cheney and R. R. Richmond, "The Impact of Intensive Forest Management on Fire Protection with Special Regard to Plantations of Eucalypts," paper prepared for Eleventh Commonwealth Forestry Conference (1980). An example of Australian pyrophytes in America is given in Dale Wade et al., *Fire in South Florida Ecosystems,* General Technical Report SE-17 (U.S. Forest Service, 1980).

11. See Stephen Pyne, *Fire in America: A Cultural History of Wildland and Rural Fire* (Princeton, 1982), p. 188. After a severe frost in the 1970s killed many eucalypts above the root collar and induced new sprouting, officials began replacing eucalypts with Monterey pine as a fire-reduction program. For a friendly, if critical assessment, consult A. B. Mount, "An Australian's Impression of North American Attitudes to Fire," *Proceedings, Annual Tall Timbers Fire Ecology Conference* 9, pp. 109–118.

12. The observation that the boundary between rainforest and other subbiotas is sharp and marked by fire is common in the literature, not only for Australia but throughout Greater Gondwana. Sample descriptions are found, for example, in J. E. Granger, "Fire in Forest," in P. de V. Booysen and N. M. Tainton, eds., *Ecological Effects of Fire in South African Ecosystems* (Springer-Verlag, 1984), pp. 177–198; Dieter Mueller-Dombois, "Fire in Tropical Ecosystems," *Proceedings of the Conference, Fire Regimes and Ecosystem Properties,* General Technical Report WO-26 (U.S. Forest Service, 1981), pp. 137–176; and throughout David R. Harris, ed., *Human Ecology in Savanna Environments* (Academic Press, 1980). For a recent Australian assessment, consult A. P. Kershaw, "An Extended Late Quaternary Vegetation Record from Northeastern Queensland and Its Implications for the Seasonal Tropics of Australia" and K. A. Clayton-Greene and J. S. Beard, "The Fire Factor in Vine Thicket and Woodland Vegetation of the Admiralty Gulf Region, Northwest Kimberley, Western Australia," in M. G. Ridpath and L. K. Corbet, eds., *Ecology of the Wet-Dry Tropics,* Proceedings of the Ecological Society of Australia, Vol. 13 (1985), pp. 179–189, 225–230.

2. UNIMAGINABLE FREAKS OF FIRE

1. For bark's influence see A. M. Gill and D. H. Ashton, "The Role of Bark Type in Relative Tolerance to Fire of Three Central Victorian Eucalypts," *Australian Journal of Botany* 16 (1968), pp. 491–498, and A. M. Gill, "Restoration of Bark Thickness After Fire and Mechanical Injury in a Smooth-barked Eucalypt," *Australian Forest Research* 10 (Forestry and Timber Bureau, 1980), pp. 311–319. For a comprehensive summary of the literature on eucalypt fire ecology, see A. Malcolm Gill and I. R. Noble, *Bibliography of Fire Ecology in Australia* (Bushfire Council of New South Wales, 1986). The best summary articles are contained in A. M. Gill et al., eds., *Fire and the Australian Biota* (Australian Academy of Science, 1981), pp. 203–442. Also useful are A. Malcolm Gill, "Fire and the Australian Flora: A Review," *Australian Forestry* 37 (1974), pp. 4–25, and Gill, "Coping With Fire," in J. S. Pate and A. J. McComb, eds., *The Biology of Australian Plants* (University of Western Australia Press, 1981), pp. 65–97; and A. B. Mount, "Eucalypt Ecology as Related to Fire," *Proceedings, Tall Timbers Fire Ecology Conference* 9 (Tallahassee, 1969), pp. 75–108.

2. See A. Malcolm Gill, "Crown Recovery of *Eucalyptus dives* following Wildfire," *Australian Forestry* 41(4) (1978), pp. 207–214.

3. A solid review of ashbed effects under Australian conditions, with a comprehensive bibliography, is F. R. Humphreys and F. G. Craig, "Effects of Fire on Soil Chemical, Structural and Hydrological Properties," in A. M. Gill et al., eds., *Fire and the Australian Biota,* pp. 177–200.

4. Perhaps the best summary expression of the complexity that enshrouds the

concept of "fire adaptations" is A. Malcolm Gill, "Fire. Hazard and Tool," in Christine Haigh, ed., *Heaths in New South Wales* (National Parks and Wildlife, 1981), pp. 50–56.

5.   For grasslands, see R. H. Groves and O. B. Williams, "Natural Grasslands," in R. H. Groves, ed., *Australian Vegetation* (Cambridge University Press, 1981), pp. 293–316; G. N. Harrington et al., eds., *Management of Australia's Rangelands* (CSIRO, 1984); R. H. Specht, "Vegetation," C. M. Donald, "The Pastures of Southern Australia," and W. W. Bryan, "Tropical Pastures," in G. W. Leeper, ed., *The Australian Environment,* 4th ed. (CSIRO, 1970), pp. 44–93; and H. Suijdendorp, "Responses of the Hummock Grasslands of Northwestern Australia to Fire," in Gill et al., eds., *Fire and the Australian Biota,* pp. 417–426.

6.   Grass tree florescence from White, *The Greening of Gondwana,* p. 43. See also Byron B. Lamont and Susan Downes, "The Longevity, Flowering and Fire History of the Grasstrees *Xanthorrhoea preissii* and *Kingia australis,*" *Journal of Applied Ecology* 16 (1979), pp. 893–899.

7.   On heathlands, see R. L. Specht, "Heathlands," in Groves, ed., *Australian Vegetation,* pp. 253–275; Christine Haigh, ed., *Heaths in New South Wales* (National Parks and Wildlife Service, 1981); R. L. Specht, "Responses to Fires of Heathlands and Related Shrublands," in Gill et al., eds., *Fire and the Australian Biota,* pp. 395–416. For a global context, consult R. L. Specht, ed., *Heathlands and Related Shrublands,* Ecosystems of the World, Vol. 9 (Elsevier, 1979).

8.   For descriptions of the supporting scleromorphs, see R. W. Johnson and W. H. Burrows, "*Acacia* Open-forests, Woodlands and Shrublands," and J. H. Leigh, "Chenopod Shrublands," in Groves, ed., *Australian Vegetation,* pp. 198–226, 276–292; K. C. Hodgkinson and G. F. Griffin, "Adaptation of Shrub Species to Fires in the Arid Zone," in W. R. Barker and P.J.M. Greenslade, eds., *Evolution of the Flora and Fauna of Arid Australia* (Peacock Publications, 1982), pp. 145–152. For other trees, see D. J. Boland et al., *Forest Trees of Australia,* 4th ed. (Thomas Nelson, 1984). For she-oaks, consult S. J. Midgley et al., eds., *Casuarina Ecology Management and Utilization* (CSIRO, 1983).

9.   For an overview, see E. V. Komarek, "Fire and Animal Behavior," *Proceedings, Tall Timbers Fire Ecology Conference* 9 (Tallahassee, 1969), pp. 161–207. The best Australian summary is contained in P. C. Catling and A. E. Newsome, "Responses of the Australian Vertebrate Fauna to Fire: an Evolutionary Approach," in Gill et al., eds., *Fire and the Australian Biota,* pp. 273–310.

10.   P.E.S. Christensen, "The Biology of *Bettongia penicillata* (Gray, 1837), and *Macropus eugenii* (Desmarest, 1817) in Relation to Fire," *Bulletin* 91 (Forests Department of Western Australia, 1980).

11.   An outstanding review article on fuels is J. Walker, "Fuel Dynamics in Australian Vegetation," in Gill et al., eds., *Fire and the Australian Biota,* pp. 101–128. The bibliography includes scores of references to studies in particular fuel arrays. A more popular introduction that integrates fuel with fire behavior is available in R. H. Luke and A. G. McArthur, *Bushfires in Australia* (Australian Government Publishing Service, 1978), pp. 31–46, 75–86.

12.   Data on stringybark firebrands from Luke and McArthur, *Bushfires,* pp. 102–103.

13.   Excellent summaries of bushfire behavior are contained in R. G. Vines, "Physics and Chemistry of Rural Fires," and N. P. Cheney, "Fire Behaviour," in Gill et al., eds., *Fire and the Australian Biota,* pp. 129–177, and Luke and McAr-

thur, *Bushfires in Australia,* pp. 23–118, the bibliography of which includes a host of wonderful case studies of large bushfires. Interesting but of lesser interest are articles in the Technical Co-operation Programme, *Mass Fire Symposium. Collected Papers,* Vol. 1 (Defence Standards Laboratories, 1969). Complement these materials with studies on the meteorology of bushfires, for which a good introduction can be found in *Proceedings of Fire Weather Services Conference. Adelaide, May 1985* (Bureau of Meteorology, 1985). See also R. G. Vines, "Air Movements Above Large Bush-fires," *Proceedings, Tall Timbers Fire Ecology Conference* 13 (1969), pp. 295–301; R. J. Taylor et al., *A Meso-meteorological Investigation of Five Forest Fires* (CSIRO Division of Meteorological Physics, Technical Paper No. 18, 1968), and *Some Meteorological Aspects of Three Intense Forest Fires,* CSIRO Division of Meteorological Physics, Technical Paper No. 21 (1971).

14. For a detailed description of an archetypal fire-flume bushfire, see *Report on the Meteorological Aspects of the Ash Wednesday Fires—16 February 1983* (Bureau of Meteorology, 1985).

15. For an introduction to mallee fire ecology, consult R. L. Specht, "Mallee Ecosystems in Southern Australia," in Francesco diCastri et al., eds., *Mediterranean-Type Shrublands. Ecosystems of the World,* Vol. 11 (Elsevier, 1981), pp. 203–231; R. F. Parsons, "*Eucalyptus* Scrubs and Shrublands," in Groves, ed., *Australian Vegetation,* pp. 227–252; J. C. Noble, "Mallee," in Harrington et al., eds., *Management of Australia's Rangelands,* pp. 223–240, and "The Significance of Fire in the Biology and Evolutionary Ecology of Mallee *Eucalyptus* Populations," in W. R. Barker and P.J.M. Greenslade, eds., *Evolution of the Flora and Fauna of Arid Australia* (Peacock Publications, 1982), pp. 153–159, and Noble et al., "Fire in the Mallee Shrublands of Western New South Wales," *Australian Rangeland Journal* 2, no. 1 (1980), pp. 104–141. For a global context, review diCastri et al., eds., *Mediterranean-Type Shrublands* and Jon E. Keeley, "Resilience of Mediterranean Shrub Communities to Fire," in B. Dell et al., eds., *Resilience in Mediterranean-Type Ecosystems* (Dr. W. Junk, 1986), pp. 95–112.

16. For general information on the fire ecology of *Acacia,* see R. W. Johnson and W. H. Burrows, "*Acacia* Open-forests, Woodlands and Shrublands," in Groves, ed., *Australian Vegetation,* pp. 198–226; J. G. Morrissey, "Arid Mulga Woodlands," and B. D. Foran, "Central Arid Woodlands," in Harrington et al., eds., *Management of Australia's Rangelands,* pp. 285–316; and B. R. Maslin and S. D. Hopper, "Phytogeography *Acacia* (Leguminosae: Mimosoideae) in Central Australia," in Barker and Greenslade, eds., *Evolution of the Flora and Fauna,* pp. 301–316.

17. A good summary is A. G. McArthur, "Fire Behaviour in the Brigalow Lands of the Fitzroy Basin," unpublished report (Forestry and Timber Bureau, n.d.), supplemented by A. W. Moore et al., "Dry Matter and Nutrient Content of a Sub-tropical Semi-arid Forest of *Acacia harpophylla* (brigalow)," *Australian Journal of Botany* 15 (1967), pp. 11–24.

3. RED CENTRE

1. An introduction to the fire ecology of *Acacia* is given in R. W. Johnson and W. H. Burrows, "*Acacia* Open-forests, Woodlands and Shrublands," in R. H. Groves, ed., *Australian Vegetation* (Cambridge University Press, 1981), pp.

430   Notes

198–226; J. G. Morrissey, "Arid Mulga Woodlands," G. N. Harrington et al., "Semi-Arid Woodlands," and B. D. Foran, "Central Arid Woodlands," in G. N. Harrington et al., eds., *Management of Australia's Rangelands* (CSIRO, 1984), pp. 189–207, 285–316; and B. R. Maslin and S. D. Hopper, "Phytogeography of *Acacia* (Leguminosae: Mimosoideae) in Central Australia," in W. R. Barker and P.J.M. Greenslade, eds., *Evolution of the Flora and Fauna of Arid Australia* (Peacock Publications, 1982), pp. 301–316.

2. See Harrington et al., "Semi-Arid Woodlands," p. 192; R. H. Luke and A. G. McArthur, *Bushfires in Australia* (Australian Government Publishing Service, 1978), pp. 339–344; Wayne Ralph, "Fire in the Centre," *Ecos* 40 (winter, 1984), pp. 3–10; G. F. Griffin, "The Role of Fire in Arid Lands," in Peter Stansbury, ed., *Bushfires—Their Effect on Australian Life and Landscape* (Macleay Museum, 1981); G. F. Griffin, "Wildfires in the Central Australian Rangelands, 1970–1980," *Journal of Environmental Management* 17 (1983), pp. 311–323; and R. H. Luke, ed., *Tropical and Arid Fire Symposium* (Bush Fires Council of the Northern Territory, 1971). The most recent statistics come from unpublished reports and notes by R. H. Luke, which he generously shared with the author.

3. See R. D. Graetz and A. D. Wilson, "Saltbush and Bluebush," in Harrington et al., eds., *Management of Australia's Rangelands*, pp. 209–222; J. H. Leigh, "Chenopod Shrublands," in Groves, ed., *Australian Vegetation*, pp. 276–292; K. C. Hodgkinson and G. F. Griffin, "Adaptation of Shrub Species to Fires in the Arid Zone," and G. A. Parr-Smith, "Biogeography and Evolution in the Shrubby Australian Species of *Atriplex* (Chenopodiaceae)," in Barker and Greenslade, eds., *Evolution of the Flora and Fauna of Arid Australia*, pp. 145–152, 291–300.

4. For an overview, consult G. F. Griffin, "Hummock Grasslands," in Harrington et al., eds., *Management of Australia's Rangelands*, pp. 271–284; R. H. Groves and O. B. Williams, "Natural Grasslands," in Groves, ed., *Australian Vegetation* (Cambridge University Press, 1981), pp. 293–316; H. Suijdendorp, "Responses of the Hummock Grasslands of Northwestern Australia to Fire," in A. M. Gill et al., eds., *Fire and the Australian Biota* (Australian Academy of Science, 1981), pp. 417–426; S.W.L. Jacobs, "Relationships, Distribution and Evolution of *Triodia* and *Plectrachne* (Gramineae)," in Barker and Greenslade, eds., *Evolution of the Flora and Fauna of Arid Australia*, pp. 285–286. See also references under Note 2 for patterns of fire occurrence.

5. A major overview is available in M. G. Ridpath and L. K. Corbett, eds., *Ecology of the Wet-Dry Tropics*, Proceedings of the Ecological Society of Australia, Vol. 15 (Ecological Society of Australia, 1978), which includes a section on fire ecology. See also R. H. Luke, ed., *Tropical and Arid Fire Symposium*; J.R.L. Hoare et al., "A Report on the Effects of Fire in Tall Open Forest and Woodland with Particular Reference to Fire Management in Kakadu National Park in the Northern Territories," unpublished report (National Parks and Wildlife Service, 1980); G. C. Stocker and J. J. Mott, "Fire in the Tropical Forests and Woodlands of Northern Australia," in Gill et al., eds., *Fire and the Australian Biota*, pp. 425–439; and C. J. Lacey and P. I. Whelan, "Observations on the Ecological Significance of Vegetative Reproduction in the Katherine-Darwin Region of the Northern Territory," *Australian Forestry* 39, no. 2 (1976), pp. 131–139.

6. General discussions of eucalypt forests, grasslands, and the like generally do not distinguish the southwest from the southeast, so the references cited

above apply equally to the southwest enclave. More specialized treatment is given in Julian Ford, ed., *Fire Ecology and Management of Western Australian Ecosystems,* WAIT Environmental Studies Group Report No. 14 (Western Australian Institute of Technology, 1985). Combine with standard review essays in Groves, ed., *Australian Vegetation,* and Gill et al., eds., *Fire and the Australian Biota.*   For an evolutionary perspective, see Mary E. White, *The Greening of Gondwana* (Reed Books, 1986), and Elizabeth M. Kemp, "Tertiary Palaeogeography and the Evolution of Australian Climate," and R. W. Galloway and E. M. Kemp, "Late Cainozoic Environments in Australia," in Allen Keast, ed., *Ecological Biogeography of Australia,* Vol. 1 (Dr. W. Junk, 1981), pp. 33–49, 52–80. For a fire perspective, see Luke and McArthur, *Bushfires in Australia,* pp. 239–246 and N. D. Burrows, "Predicting Blow-up Fires in the Jarrah Forest," Technical Paper 12 (Forests Department of Western Australia, 1984).

7.   W. R. Wallace reported how "the vast extent of the original virgin forest with its carpet of leaf litter and low shrubs presented an ideal fuel bed through which a summer fire could creep for weeks on end, unhindered by anything but a rare shower or an occasional moist gully . . . Even as late as 1925 the writer was able to observe three fires of this nature in unmanaged virgin forest east of Jarrahdale. These fires were alight in December and continued to burn until the following March, increasing in intensity as hot weather developed and waning to a faint smoke on the cooler days, until finally extinguished by steady rain." See "Fire in the Jarrah Forest Environment," *Journal of the Royal Society of Western Australia* 49, part 2 (1965), p. 34.

8.   For case studies of fires whipped to fury by Cyclone Alby, see R. J. Underwood et al., "The Contribution of Prescribed Burning to Forest Fire Control in Western Australia: Case Studies," in Ford, ed., *Fire Ecology and Management,* pp. 160–163.

9.   For lightning statistics outside the archival scrubland of the Forests Department's annual reports, see R. A. Anderson and B. G. Muir, "Fire Causes in W.A. National Parks," *Australian Parks and Recreation* (May 1981), pp. 26–28; Luke and McArthur, *Bushfires,* p. 246; and Wallace, "Fire in the Jarrah Forest," p. 40.

10.   The pattern is described in Luke and McArthur, *Bushfires,* pp. 303–310 and in numerous case studies listed in their bibliography. For a detailed contemporary inquiry of the physics involved, consult *Report on the Meteorological Aspects of the Ash Wednesday Fires—16 February 1983* (Bureau of Meteorology, 1985), and for the overall context, Michael C. R. Edgell and Eric H. Brown, "The Bushfire Environment of Southeastern Australia," *Journal of Environmental Management* 3 (1975), pp. 329–349. The classic depository of information about large fires remains J. C. Foley, *A Study of Meteorological Conditions Associated with Bush and Grass Fires and Fire Protection Strategy in Australia,* Bureau of Meteorology, Bulletin No. 38 (1947). See also Bureau of Meteorology, *Proceedings of Fire Weather Services Conference. Adelaide. May 1985* (Melbourne, 1985).

11.   Quotation from R. G. Vines, "A Survey of Forest Fire Danger in Victoria (1937–1969)," *Australian Forest Research* 4, no. 2, p. 40. Attempts to fit the near-periodic recurrence of large bushfires to some natural cycle can be found in R. G. Vines, *Weather Patterns and Bush-fire Cycles in Southern Australia,* CSIRO Division of Chemical Technology, Technical Paper 2 (1974); R. G. Vines, "Fire and Flood Cycles—Past and Present," and "Features of the Sun-

spot Cycle," in *Proceedings of the Symposium on the Environmental Consequences of Fire and Fuel Management in Mediterranean Ecosystems*, General Technical Report WO-3 (U.S. Forest Service, 1977), pp. 116–131; and A. Malcolm Gill, "Forest Fire and Drought in Eastern Australia," in *Colloquium on the Significance of the Southern Oscillation—El Nino Phenomena and the Need for a Comprehensive Ocean Monitoring System in Australia* (Department of Science and Technology, 1985), pp. 161–184.

12. Lightning statistics outside the raw data of annual reports by the Forests Commission can be found in F. R. Moulds, "Effect of Forest Fire and of Forest Policy on Land Use in Victoria," *Forestry Technical Papers* No. 19, (Forests Commission, Victoria 1967), p. 1; and Forests Commission of Victoria, *Fire Protection and Fuel-Reduction Burning in Victoria* (September 1982), Appendix I, p. 3.

13. Figures from Wallace, "Fire in the Jarrah Forest," pp. 34–36. See also, A. Malcolm Gill, "Patterns and Processes in Open-forests of *Eucalyptus* in Southern Australia," in Groves, ed., *Australian Vegetation*, pp. 152–176.

14. D. H. Ashton, "Fire in Tall Open-forests (Wet Sclerophyll Forests)," in A. M. Gill et al., eds., *Fire and the Australian Biota*, p. 362

15. For general reviews of heathlands, see R. L. Specht, "Heathlands," in Groves, ed., *Australian Vegetation*, pp. 253–275; Christine Haigh, ed., *Heaths in New South Wales* (National Parks and Wildlife Service 1981); R. L. Specht, "Responses to Fires of Heathlands and Related Shrublands," in Gill et al., eds., *Fire and the Australian Biota*, pp. 395–416; and R. L. Specht, ed., *Heathlands and Related Shrublands*, Ecosystems of the World, Vol. 9 (Elsevier, 1979). Specialty studies include J. S. Pate and J. S. Beard, eds., *Kwongan. Plant Life of the Sandplain* (University of Western Australia Press, 1984); J. S. Coaldrake, "The Ecosystem of the Coastal Lowlands ("Wallum") of Southern Queensland," CSIRO Bulletin No. 283 (1961), "The Natural History of Cooloola," *Ecological Society of Australia Proceedings* 9 (1975), pp. 308–313, and "The Climate, Geology, Soils, and Plant Ecology of Portion of the County of Buckingham (Ninety-Mile Plain), South Australia," CSIRO Bulletin No. 266 (1951). For an additional fire perspective, see T. E. Just, "Fire Control Problems of the Wallum with Particular Reference to Cooloola," Technical Paper 3 (Department of Forestry, Queensland, 1977), and A. M. Fox, "The '72 Fire of Nadgee Nature Reserve," *Parks and Wildlife* 2 (1978), pp. 5–24.

16. Summary essays on rainforest include L. J. Webb and J. G. Tracey, "The Rainforests of Northern Australia," in Groves, ed., *Australian Vegetation*, pp. 67–101; L. J. Webb, "Environmental Relationships of the Structural Types of Australian Rain Forest Vegetation," *Ecology* 49, no. 2 (1968), pp. 196–311; and from Ridpath and Corbett, eds., *Ecology of the Wet-Dry Tropics*, A. P. Kershaw, "An Extended Late Quaternary Vegetation Record from Northeastern Queensland and Its Implications for the Seasonal Tropics of Australia," pp. 179–190, J. Russell-Smith, "A Record of Change: Studies of Holocene Vegetation History in the South Alligator River Region, Northern Territory," pp. 191–202, G. L. Unwin et al., "Fire and the Forest Ecotone in the Herberton Highland, North Queensland," pp. 215–224, and K. A. Clayton-Greene and J. S. Beard, "The Fire Factor in Vine Thicket and Woodland Vegetation of the Admiralty Gulf Region, Northwest Kimberley, Western Australia," pp. 225–230. Historically interesting too are Karel Domin, "Queensland's Plant Associations (Some Problems of Queensland's Botanogeography)," *Proceedings*

of the *Royal Society of Queensland XXIII*, part 1 (1911), pp. 63–67; G. C. Stocker and G. L. Unwin, "Fire," in H. T. Clifford and R. L. Specht, eds., *Tropical Plant Communities* (Department of Botany, University of Queensland, 1986), pp. 91–103; W. F. Ridley and A. Gardner, "Fires in Rain Forest," *Australian Journal of Science* 23, no. 7, p. 227; D. A. Herbert, "The Upland Savannahs of the Bunya Mountains, South Queensland," *Proceedings of the Royal Society of Queensland XLIX* (1938), pp. 145–149.

17.   Compare Ashton, "Fire in Tall Open Forests (Wet Sclerophyll Forests)," P. Christensen et al., "Responses to Open Forest to Fire Regimes," and G. C. Stocker and J. J. Mott, "Fire in the Tropical Forests," all in Gill et al., eds., *Fire and the Australian Biota*, pp. 339–395, 425–439, and the various entries in Groves, ed., *Australian Vegetation.* For Tasmania, see Ashton, "Fire in Tall Open Forests"; J. M. Gilbert, "Forest Succession in the Florentine Valley, Tasmania," *Papers of Proceedings of Royal Society of Tasmania* 93 (1959), pp. 129–151; A. B. Mount, "Eucalypt ecology as related to fire," *Proceedings, Tall Timbers Fire Ecology Conference* 9 (Tallahassee, 1969), pp. 166–172; W. D. Jackson, "Fire, Air, Water and Earth—An Elemental Ecology of Tasmania," *Proceedings of the Ecological Society of Australia* 3 (1968), pp. 9–16; D.M.J. Bowman and W. D. Jackson, "Vegetation Succession in Southwest Tasmania," *Search* 12, no. 10 (1981), pp. 358–362; A. B. Mount, "Fire-Cycles or Succession in South-West Tasmania," and Bowman and Jackson, "Reply: Ecological Drift or Fire Cycles in South-West Tasmania," *Search* 13, nos. 7 and 8 (1982), p. 174–175.

4. LAND OF CONTRARITIES

1.   Peron, O'Hara, and Darwin quoted in Geoffrey Serle, *From Deserts the Prophets Come. The Creative Spirit in Australia 1788–1972* (Heinemann, 1973), pp. 14–17; Marcus Clarke, "Preface," Adam Lindsay Gordon, *Poems,* 6th ed. (Samuel Mullen, 1890); poem cited in F. G. Clarke, *The Land of Contrarities. British Attitudes to the Australian Colonies 1828–1855* (Melbourne University Press, 1977), p. 169–170.

2.   Heracleitus, from John Burnet, *Early Greek Philosophers,* 4th ed. (London, 1930), p. 134.

3.   The literature on fire ecology is enormous. For entree, consult Henry A. Wright and Arthur W. Bailey, *Fire Ecology, United States and Canada* (Wiley-Interscience, 1982); Craig Chandler et al., *Fire in Forestry,* Vol. I, Forest Fire Behavior and Effects (Wiley-Interscience, 1983); Stephen J. Pyne, *Introduction to Wildland Fire* (Wiley-Interscience, 1984); and T. T. Kozlowski and C. E. Ahlgren, eds., *Fire and Ecosystems* (Academic Press, 1974), which is dated but still serviceable. To these should be added the *Proceedings, Tall Timbers Fire Ecology Conferences,* Vols. 1–14 (Tallahassee, 1962–1976). Particularly valuable symposia include *Proceedings of the Conference, Fire Regimes and Ecosystem Properties,* General Technical Report WO-26 (1981). Essential for comparative studies are the SCOPE volumes: A. Malcolm Gill et al., eds., *Fire and the Australian Biota* (Australian Academy of Science, 1981); Ross W. Wein and David A. MacLean, eds., *The Role of Fire in Northern Circumpolar Ecosystems,* SCOPE 18 (John Wiley & Sons, 1983); and Peter de V. Booysen and Neil M. Tainton, eds., *Ecological Effects of Fire in South*

African Ecosystems, Ecological Studies 48 (Springer-Verlag, 1984). For the tropics, two particular compendia should be consulted: Robert B. Batchelder and Howard F. Hirt, *Fire in Tropical Forests and Grasslands*, Technical Report 67-41-ES (U.S. Army Natick Laboratories, 1966), and Harley H. Bartlett, *Fire in Relation to Primitive Agriculture and Grazing in the Tropics: Annotated Bibliography*, 3 vols. (University of Michigan Botanical Gardens, 1955, 1957, 1961). An abbreviated version of the massive compendium by Batchelder and Hirt is given in Batchelder, "Spatial and Temporal Patterns of Fire in the Tropical World," *Proceedings, Tall Timbers Fire Ecology Conference* 6 (1969), pp. 171–208. See also, Stephen J. Pyne, *Fire in America: A Cultural History of Wildland and Rural Fire* (Princeton University Press, 1982) for a guide to bibliographies up to 1980.

4. In addition to the literature on savannas and grasslands listed in Note 3, see Daniel Axelrod, "Rise of the Grassland Biome, Central North America," *Botanical Review* 51, no. 2 (1985), pp. 163–201 for a comparison to American savannas.

5. C. O. Sauer, "Man's Dominance by Use of Fire," *Geoscience and Man* 10 (1975), p. 13. The issue contains several articles on grassland fires, including Lee M. Talbot and Richard H. Kesell, "The Tropical Savanna Ecosystem," pp. 15–26, which is of comparative interest to the Australian scene.

6. The human component of savanna fire ecology is ancient, complex, and redolent with a vast literature. Most of the references cited in Note 3 on grassland fires include discussion of anthropogenic fire; those citations are not repeated here. A number of papers and symposia address the issues more directly. See E. V. Komarek, "Fire—and the Ecology of Man," *Proceedings, Tall Timbers Fire Ecology Conference* 6 (Tallahassee, 1967), pp. 143–171, and "Fire Ecology—Grasslands and Man," *Proceedings, Tall Timbers Fire Ecology Conference* 4 (Tallahassee, 1965), pp. 169–220; David Harris, ed., *Human Ecology in Savanna Environments* (Academic Press, 1980), which offers a world survey (refer, in particular, to Rhys Jones, "Hunters in the Australian Coastal Savanna," pp. 107–146); Rhys Jones, "The Fifth Continent: Problems Concerning the Human Colonization of Australia," *Annual Review of Anthropology* 8 (1979), pp. 445–466. Still a classic statement is Carl Sauer, "Grassland Climax, Fire, and Man," *Journal of Range Management* 3 (1950), pp. 49–69. For an interesting discussion of Africa, see Oliver West, "Fire in Vegetation and Its Use in Pasture Management with Special Reference to Tropical and Subtropical Africa," Commonwealth Agricultural Bureaux, Mimeographed Publication No. 1/1965 (1965); "Fire in Africa," *Proceedings, Tall Timbers Fire Ecology Conference* 11 (Tallahassee, 1971); and M. Norton-Griffiths, "The Influence of Grazing, Browsing, and Fire on the Vegetation Dynamics of the Serengeti," in A.R.E. Sinclair and M. Norton-Griffiths, eds., *Serengeti: Dynamics of an Ecosystem* (University of Chicago Press, 1979). For North America—an enormous literature—a good beginning is Roger A. Clouser, "Man's Intervention in the Post-Wisconsin Vegetational Succession of the Great Plains," Occasional Paper No. 4, Department of Geography-Meteorology, University of Kansas (1978); C. T. Moore, "Man and Fire in the Central North American Grassland, 1535–1890: A Documentary Historical Geography," dissertation, University of California at Los Angeles (1972); and Stephen J. Pyne, "These Conflagrated Prairies: A Cultural Fire History of the Grasslands," in Gary K. Clambey and Richard H. Pemble, eds., *The Prairie: Past, Present, and Future. Proceedings of the Ninth North Ameri-*

can Prairie Conference (Tri-College University Center for Environmental Studies, 1986), pp. 131–137.

7.   A good point of departure for Mediterranean environments is Jon K. Keeley, *Bibliographies on Chaparral and the Fire Ecology of Other Mediterranean Systems,* California Water Resources Center, Report No. 58 (1984). Useful symposia volumes include *Proceedings of the Symposium on the Environmental Consequences of Fire and Fuel Management in Mediterranean Ecosystems,* General Technical Report WO-3 (U.S. Forest Service, 1977), *Proceedings of the Symposium on Dynamics and Management of Mediterranean-Type Ecosystems,* General Technical Report PSW-58 (U.S. Forest Service, 1982), and Booysen and Tainton, eds., *Ecological Effects of Fire in South African Ecosystems.* See also Francesco diCastri and Harold Mooney, eds., *Mediterranean-Type Ecosystems. Origin and Structure* (Springer-Verlag, 1973), Francesco diCastri et al., eds., *Mediterranean-Type Shrublands,* Ecosystems of the World, Vol. 11 (Elsevier, 1981), both of which include an orchestration of studies in biological and human history; and Harold A. Mooney, ed., *Convergent Evolution in Chile and California* (Dowden, Hutchinson, and Ross, 1977). A synthesis for Australia is available in M. D. Fox and B. J. Fox, "The Role of Fire in the Scleromorphic Forests and Shrublands of Eastern Australia," in L. Traubaud, ed., *The Role of Fire in Ecological Systems* (SPB Academic Publications, 1987), pp. 23–49.

8.   The major syntheses of Mediterranean terrains include a strong bias of human history. See, for example, Homer Aschman, "Man's Impact on the Several Regions with Mediterranean Climates," pp. 363–371, and Zev Naveh and Joel Dan, "The Human Degradation of Mediterranean Landscapes in Israel," in diCastri and Mooney, eds., *Mediterranean-Type Ecosystems,* pp. 373–390; H. Aschmann and C. Bahre, "Man's Impact on the Wild Landscape," in Mooney, ed., *Convergent Evolution,* pp. 73–84; H. N. LeHeroux, "Impact of Man and His Animals on Mediterranean Vegetation," and L. Trabaud, "Man and Fire: Impacts on Mediterranean Vegetation," in diCastri et al., eds., *Mediterranean-Type Shrublands,* pp. 479–522, 523–538; and Phillipe Boudreau et al., "Influence of Fire on the Stability of Mediterranean Forest Ecosystems," *Ecologica Mediterranea* 12, no. 4 (1987), a special issue devoted to fire. A concise survey of the originating Mediterranean's environmental history is available in J. V. Thirgood, *Man and the Mediterranean Forest* (Academic Press, 1981), which includes considerable references to fire practices.

9.   John Oxley, quoted in Serle, *From Deserts the Prophets Come* (Heinemann, 1973), p. 16. Early British impressions of the Australian scene, more friendly in perception, are surveyed in Helen Proudfoot, "Botany Bay, Kew, and the Picturesque: Early Conceptions of the Australian landscape," *Journal of the Royal Australian Historical Society* 65, part 1 (June 1979), pp. 30–45.

10.   The contrast with New Guinea is a chronic calibration point. See D. Walker, ed., *Bridge and Barrier: The Natural and Cultural History of Torres Strait,* Research School of Pacific Studies, Australian National University, Publication BG/3 (1972); J. Peter White and James F. O'Connell, *A Prehistory of Australia, New Guinea and Sahul* (Academic Press, 1982); and numerous essays by Rhys Jones, including his influential "The Neolithic, Palaeolithic and the Hunting Gardeners: Man and Land in the Antipodes," in R. P. Suggate and M. M. Cresswell, eds., *Quaternary Studies* (Royal Society of New Zealand, 1975), pp. 21–34.

5. FLAMING FRONT

1. See Loren Eiseley, "Man the Fire-Maker," *Scientific American* 191 (1954), p. 57. Understandably the study of fire and early hominids is more speculative than solid, but interesting reviews include John Pfeiffer, "When Homo Erectus Tamed Fires, He Tamed Himself," *The New York Times Magazine* (December 11, 1964), pp. 58, 61, 65–72; Kenneth Oakley, "Fire as Palaeolithic Tool and Weapon," *The Prehistoric Society* 4 (1955), pp. 36–48, and "The Earliest Fire-makers," *Antiquity* 30 (1956), pp. 102–107; E. V. Komarek, "Fire—and the Ecology of Man," *Proceedings, Tall Timbers Fire Ecology Conference* 6 (Tallahassee, 1969), pp. 143–170; Walter Hough, *Fire as an Agent in Human Culture*, U.S. National Museum Bulletin 139 (1926). Of primarily historical interest is Carl O. Sauer, "The Agency of Man on Earth," and Omer Stewart, "Fire as the First Great Force Employed by Man," in William Thomas, ed., *Man's Role in Changing the Face of the Earth* (University of Chicago Press, 1956), pp. 49–69, 115–133, both badly dated, though Sauer's comments have a toughness that renders them yet quotable.   For overviews on human evolution, which include fire references, I relied on John E. Pfeiffer, *The Emergence of Man*, 2nd ed. (Harper and Row, 1972), and David Lambert and the Diagram Group, *The Field Guide to Early Man* (Facts on File Publications, 1987). A fascinating attempt to understand the trilateral relationship between hominids, fire, and large ungulates is Wilhelm Schule, "Landscapes and Climate in Prehistory: Interaction of Wildlife, Man, and Fire," in J. G. Goldammer, ed., *Fire in Tropical Biota* (Springer-Verlag, in press).
2. Lambert and Diagram Group, *Field Guide to Early Man*, p. 82. The dates are constantly revised. Still more recent estimates are given in Richard Kerr, "Modern Human Origins Under Close Scrutiny," *Science* 239 (March 1988), pp. 1240–1241, and C. B. Stringer and P. Andrews, "Genetic and Fossil Evidence for the Origin of Modern Humans," *Science* 239 (March 1988), pp. 1263–1268.
3. See Curt P. Richter, "Discovery of Fire by Man—Its Effects on His 24-hour Clock and Intellectual and Cultural Revolution," *Johns Hopkins Medical Journal* 141 (1977), pp. 41–61.
4. J.A.J. Gowlett et al., "Early Archaeological Sites, Hominid Remains, and Traces of Fire from Chesowanja, Kenya," *Nature* 294 (1981), pp. 125–129. For a critical review, however, see Glynn Isaac, "Early Hominids and Fire at Chesowanja, Kenya," *Nature* 296 (April 1982), p. 870. Pfeiffer, *Emergence of Man*, pp. 136–137.
5. The literature on Aboriginal colonization grows exponentially. Studies that are particularly helpful from the perspective of fire history include Josephine Flood, *Archaeology of the Dreamtime* (Collins, 1983); J. Peter White and James F. O'Connell, *A Prehistory of Australia, New Guinea and Sahul* (Academic Press, 1982); Sylvia J. Hallam, *Fire and Hearth*, Australian Aboriginal Studies No. 58 (Australian Institute of Aboriginal Studies, 1979) and "The History of Aboriginal Firing," in Julian Ford, ed., *Fire Ecology and Management in Western Australian Ecosystems*, WAIT Environmental Studies Group Report No. 14 (Western Australian Institute of Technology, 1985), pp. 7–20. An admirable distillation, intended for secondary schools, is available in Elizabeth Foster, *The Aborigines. From Prehistory to the Present* (Oxford, 1985). Certainly the most readable account—one full of insights and with a special chapter on Aboriginal fire practices—is Geoffrey Blainey, *Triumph of the No-*

mads. *A History of Ancient Australia*, rev. ed. (Sun Books, 1982). Rhys Jones has developed a series of papers on both questions; of particular interest are "The Geographical Background to the Arrival of Man in Australia and Tasmania," *Archaeology & Physical Anthropology in Oceania III*, no. 3 (October 1968), pp. 186–215; "The Neolithic, Palaeolithic and the Hunting Gardeners: Man and Land in the Antipodes," in R. P. Suggate and M. M. Cresswell, eds., *Quaternary Studies* (Royal Society of New Zealand, 1975), pp. 21–34; and "The Fifth Continent: Problems Concerning the Human Colonization of Australia," *Annual Reviews in Anthropology* 8 (1979), pp. 445–466. Volume 3 of Allen Keast, ed., *Ecological Biogeography of Australia* (Dr. W. Junk, 1981) offers a slate of essays on various Aboriginal themes. The most relevant are A. G. Thorne, "The Arrival and Adaptation of Australian Aborigines," pp. 1749–1760; Norman B. Tindale, "Prehistory of the Aborigines: Some Interesting Considerations," pp. 1761–1797; and R. L. Kirk, "Physiological, Demographic, and Genetic Adaptation of Australian Aborigines," pp. 1801–1816. Dense but also fascinating is R. L. Kirk and A. G. Thorne, eds., *The Origin of the Australians*, Human Biology Series No. 6 (Australian Institute of Aboriginal Studies, 1976). See also D. R. Horton, "Water and Woodland: the Peopling of Australia," *Australian Institute of Aboriginal Studies* 16 (1981), pp. 21–27.

6. The impact of Aboriginal fire is discussed in Hallam, *Fire and Hearth* and "The History of Aboriginal Firing"; G. Singh et al., "Quaternary Vegetation and Fire History in Australia," and Phyllis H. Nicholson, "Fire and the Australian Aborigine—an Enigma," in A. M. Gill et al., eds., *Fire and the Australian Biota* (Australian Academy of Science, 1981), pp. 77–128; G. Singh, "Environmental Upheaval," in J.M.B. Smith, *A History of Australasian Vegetation* (McGraw-Hill, 1982), pp. 90–108; Jones, "The Neolithic, Palaeolithic, and the Hunting Gardeners: Man and Land in the Antipodes," and "Fire-stick Farming," *Australian Natural History* 16 (1968–1970), pp. 224–228. An excellent popular survey is given in Geoffrey Blainey, *The Triumph of the Nomads*, rev. ed. (Sun Books, 1983), pp. 67–83.

7. Flood, *Archaeology of the Dreamtime*, pp. 67–83.

8. For recent evidence on Tasmania, see Richard Cosgrove, "Thirty Thousand Years of Human Colonization in Tasmania: New Pleistocene Dates," *Science* 243 (March 1989), pp. 1706–1708. He makes the critical observation that megafaunal fossils are not associated with human remains, suggesting that the megafauna had departed in advance of humans.

9. The Macassans incursion is described in Flood, *Archaeology of the Dreamtime*, pp. 224–225, and Blainey, *The Triumph of the Nomads*, pp. 247–251.

10. C. E. Dortch and B. G. Muir, "Long Range Sightings of Bush Fires as a Possible Incentive for Pleistocene Voyages to Greater Australia," *Western Australian Naturalist* 14, no. 7 (1980), pp. 195–198.

11. Flood, *Archaeology of the Dreamtime*, p. 159. Summary accounts of early perceptions of the Australian scene are available in Helen Proudfoot, "Botany Bay, Kew, and the Picturesque: Early Conceptions of the Australian Landscape," *Journal of the Royal Australian Historical Society* 65, part 1 (June 1979), pp. 30–45, and Geoffrey Serle, *From Deserts the Prophets Come* (Heinemann, 1973), pp. 1–18, but Serle records the commentary through the 1970s.

12. Tindale, "Prehistory of the Aborigines," p. 1763.

13. Another complex subject, without sufficient evidence to force one conclusion or another. An outstanding survey of the question is Paul S. Martin and Rich-

ard G. Klein, eds., *Quaternary Extinctions. A Prehistoric Revolution* (University of Arizona Press, 1984), which commands a global perspective. A special section addresses floral and faunal extinctions in Australia, pp. 600–707. New evidence from Tasmania is reviewed in Richard Cosgrove, "Thirty Thousand Years of Human Colonization in Tasmania: New Pleistocene Dates," *Science* 243 (March 1989), pp. 1706–1708.

14. Flood, *Archaeology of the Dreamtime*, p. 159. The power of Aboriginal fire has been increasingly recognized. In their prehistory of the Sahul, White and O'Connell, ever cautious, still concluded that "within Australia, humanly caused fire seems to have been the most important prehistoric agent" (White and O'Connell, p. 15). With some hyperbole, the archaeologist Flood came to the belief that "directly or indirectly, Aboriginal occupation of the continent had as great an impact on Australian fauna in the Pleistocene as European settlement was to have in recent times" (Flood, *Archaeology*, p. 147). In a review of megafloral extinctions, the paleontologist Peter Kershaw argued that "major vegetation changes, including regional and total plant extinctions within the late Quaternary, can be attributed largely to the influence of fire, and it is no coincidence that changes in fire regimes come within the time when aboriginal man, whose use of fire is widely known, may have been in Australia" (Kershaw, "Late Cenozoic Plant Extinctions in Australia," in Martin and Klein, eds., *Quaternary Extinctions*, p. 701). Anthropogenic fire, like *Homo*, was a qualitatively new condition of life added to prehistoric Australia. How it interacted with other processes is not yet known in detail—may never be known—but its existence is undeniable. Other supporters include P. J. Hughes and M. E. Sullivan, "Aboriginal Burning and Late Holocene Geomorphic Events in Eastern New South Wales," *Search* 12 (1981), pp. 277–278; Duncan Merrilees, "Man the Destroyer: Late Quaternary Changes in the Australian Marsupial Fauna," *Journal of the Royal Society of Western Australia* 51 (1968), pp. 1–24; G. Singh, "Environmental Upheaval: Vegetation of Australasia during the Quaternary," in Smith, *History of Australasian Vegetation*, pp. 90–108; and, with reservations, Hallam, "History of Aboriginal Firing," in Ford, ed., *Fire Ecology and Management*, pp. 7–20. Skeptics reply with D. R. Horton, "The Burning Question: The Aborigines, Fire, and Australian Ecosystems," *Mankind* 13 (1982), pp. 237–257, and "Red Kangaroos: Last of the Australian Megafauna," in Martin and Klein, eds., *Quaternary Extinctions*, pp. 639–680; and Robin Clark, who questions the more grandiloquent conclusions derived from sediment cores with "Pollen and Charcoal Evidence for the Effects of Aboriginal Burning on the Vegetation of Australia," *Archaeology in Oceania* 18 (1983), pp. 32–37, and "The Prehistory of Bushfires," in Peter Stanbury, ed., *Bushfires. Their Effect on Australian Life and Landscape* (Macleay Museum, 1981).

15. G. Singh et al., "Quaternary Vegetation and Fire History in Australia," in Gill et al., eds., *Fire and the Australian Biota*, pp. 34–39; A. P. Kershaw, "Record of Last Interglacial-glacial Cycle from North-eastern Queensland," *Nature* 272 (1978), pp. 159–161, and "Late Cenozoic Plant Extinctions in Australia," in Martin and Klein, eds., *Quaternary Extinctions*, pp. 699–702.

16. G. Singh et al., "Quaternary Vegetation and Fire History in Australia," pp. 26–33; Kershaw, "Late Cenozoic Plant Extinctions in Australia," pp. 696, 701–702.

17. See Notes 6 and 14 for a survey of the critical literature. Between them these references offer a reasonably comprehensive panorama of the secondary litera-

ture and an introduction to the primary sources from explorers, settlers, and others. Blainey, *The Triumph of the Nomads*, p. 31; Hallam, *Fire and Hearth*, p. vii.

18. R. L. Kirk, "Physiological, Demographic and Genetic Adaptation of Australian Aboriginals," in Keast, ed., *Ecological Biogeography of Australia*, pp. 1801–1816; Flood, *Archaeology of the Dreamtime*, p. 68.

19. William Dampier, *A New Voyage Round the World* (Dover Publications, 1968; reprint of 1727 edition), p. 315; Hughes, *The Fatal Shore*, p. 13.

20. See Flood, *Archaeology of the Dreamtime*, pp. 34–39 for a discussion of boating technologies.

6. FIRESTICK FARMER

1. Phyllis H. Nicolson, "Fire and the Australian Aborigine—an Enigma," in A. Malcolm Gill et al., eds., *Fire and the Australian Biota* (Australian Academy of Science, 1981), pp. 61, 70. The major review literature on Aboriginal fire practices is contained in Note 6, Chapter 5. To them should be added Henry T. Lewis, "Why Indians Burned—Specific versus General Reasons," *Proceedings—Symposium and Workshop on Wilderness Fire*, General Technical Report INT-182 (U.S. Forest Service, 1985), pp. 75–80; J. M. Flood, "Fire as an Agent of Change: Aboriginal Use of Fire in New South Wales," *Forest and Timber* (September 1987), pp. 15–18; R. L. Clark, "The Prehistory of Bushfires," in Peter Stanbury, ed., *Bushfires: Their Effect on Australian Life and Landscape* (Macleay Museum, 1981), pp. 61–73; D. R. Harris, "Subsistence Strategies across Torres Strait," in J. Allen et al., eds., *Sunda and Sahul* (1977), pp. 420–463; D. J. Mulvaney and J. Golson, eds., *Aboriginal Man and Environment in Australia* (Australian National University Press, 1971); Mark de Graaf, "The Aboriginal Use of Fire," in R. E. Fox, ed., *Report on the Use of Fire in National Parks and Reserves* (1974), pp. 14–19. Also interesting for their remarkable detail are a series of studies by Boris Sokoloff, "Aborigines and Fire in the Lower Hunter, Part 1: Importance of Fire for the Worimi and Awabakal," and "As It Was in the Past," *Hunter Natural History* (May 1978), pp. 70–84, "Aborigines and Fire in the Lower Hunter, Part 2: Importance of Fire," *Hunter Natural History* (August 1978), pp. 124–133, and "Aborigines and Fire in the Lower Hunter, Part 3: Effects of Aborigines' Use of Fire on the Natural Environment," *Hunter Natural History* (November 1978), pp. 192–197. Most of the symposia included in the bibliographic essay address Aboriginal fire practices in some form. More specifically regional studies are cited in Chapter 8, which summarizes the fire regimes of Aboriginal Australia. Between them these works and those listed above create a fairly comprehensive digest of the known European-based records of Aboriginal fire practices. Most recent insights derive from comparative studies or from ecological evidence, not from the recycling of the known historic observations. A survey of the primary literature up to the early 1970s, actually an annotated bibliography, is available in R. E. Fox, "Summary of Published Work," in Fox, ed., *Report on the Use of Fire*, pp. 1–13. Still useful as a source is A. R. King, *The Influence of Colonization on the Forests and the Prevalence of Bushfires in Australia* (CSIRO Division of Physical Chemistry, n.d.), which can be supplemented by A. G. McArthur, "Historical Aspects of Fire," *Symposium Papers, Second Fire*

Ecology Symposium (Forests Commission, Victoria, and Monash University, 1970).

2. James Backhouse, *A Narrative of a Visit to the Australian Colonies* (London, 1843), p. 99; Robinson quoted in Blainey, *Triumph*, p. 69. The phrase "black lightning" is taken from R. G. Kimber, "Black Lightning: Aborigines and Fire in Central Australia and the Western Desert," *Archaeology in Oceania* 18 (1983), pp. 38–45. See also N.J.B. Plomley, *The Baudin Expedition and the Tasmanian Aborigines 1802* (Hobart, 1983), p. 201, who concludes that "the means by which the Tasmanians made fire has never been ascertained with certainty . . . There is a good deal of evidence that the Tasmanians depended for fire, if they lost it, upon other sources, be those the fire held by their neighbours or that from such natural causes as lightning strikes. They therefore carried fire with them . . ."

3. D. S. Davidson, "Fire-Making in Australia," *American Anthropologist*, n.s. 49 (1947), p. 427.

4. Nicholson, "Fire and the Australian Aborigine," p. 58; Hallam, *Fire and Hearth*, pp. 44–45; Blainey, *Triumph*, pp. 69–70; Davidson, "Fire-Making in Australia," pp. 426–437; Flood, "Fire as an Agent of Change," p. 16; Richard A. Gould, "Uses and Effects of Fire among the Western Desert Aborigines of Australia," *Mankind* 8 (1971), p. 16.

5. Spencer quoted in Nicholson, "Fire and the Australian Aborigine," p. 59; Edward Curr, *Recollections of Squatting in Victoria* (Melbourne, 1883), p. 134.

6. Arthur Phillip to Sydney, May 15, 1788, *Historical Records of Australia*, Vol. I, p. 25; Scott Nind, quoted in Hallam, *Fire and Hearth*, p. 33; Richard Helms, "Anthropology (Scientific Report of the Elder Expedition)," *Transactions of the Royal Society of South Australia* XVI (1892–1896), p. 247; *Tom Petrie's Reminiscences of Early Queensland* (Lloyd O'Neil, 1975), p. 95; N.J.B. Plomley, ed., *Friendly Mission. Tasmanian Journals and Papers of George Augustus Robinson 1829–1834* (Tasmanian Historical Research Association, 1966), passim.

7. Quoted in Blainey, *Triumph*, p. 71.

8. Davidson, "Fire-Making in Australia," p. 427; Spencer, quoted in Nicholson, "Fire and the Australian Aborigine," p. 62; Austin, quoted in Hallam, *Fire and Hearth*, p. 43; James Bonwick, *Daily Life and Origin of the Tasmanians* (London, 1870), p. 21.

9. For Bogong moth harvests, see Flood, *Archaeology of the Dreamtime*, pp. 202–204. Cooking practices are described in Jennifer Isaacs, ed., *Australia Dreaming* (Lansdowne Press, 1980), pp. 194–196, 201. Bonwick, *Daily Life*, p. 18, and Isaacs, ed., *Australian Dreaming*, pp. 194–196. Shell preparation is discussed in Flood, *Archaeology of the Dreamtime*, p. 221.

10. Eyre quoted in Flood, *Archaeology of the Dreamtime*, p. 47 (see also Richard Helms, quoted on page 25); Eyre, quoted in Nicolson, "Fire and the Australian Aborigine," p. 67.

11. Robinson in Plomley, ed., *Friendly Mission*, p. 531. Robinson is the subject of a revisionist biography that, although it questions much of his testimony, accepts the veracity of his particular observations on Aboriginal practices. See Vivienne Rae-Ellis, *Black Robinson* (Melbourne University Press, 1988), p. xvii.

12. Phillip, quoted in King, *Influence of Colonization*, pp. 25–26; Robert Bruce, *Reminiscences of an Old Squatter* (Adelaide, 1902), pp. 66–67; Hallam, *Fire*

and Hearth, p. 24; Dr. John Lhotsky, *A Journey from Sydney to the Australian Alps,* Alan E. J. Andrews, ed. (Hobart, 1979), pp. 85–86. There are numerous references and even drawings that show fire-hollowed trunks and smoking for game; for samples, see John Cobley, *Sydney Cove 1788* (Hodder and Stoughton, 1961), p. 127, and the frontispiece to Charles Sturt, *Two Expeditions into the Interior . . . ,* Vol. 2 (London, 1833).

13.   J. B. Cleland, "Some Aspects of the Ecology of the Aboriginal Inhabitants of Tasmania and Southern Australia," *Papers and Proceedings, Royal Society of Tasmania, 1939* (1940), p. 12; Blainey, *Triumph,* p. 72; Gould, "Uses and Effects of Fire," pp. 16–17.

14.   Dr. Ludwig Leichhardt, *Journal of an Overland Expedition in Australia from Moreton Bay to Port Essington During the Years 1844–45,* Australiana Facsimile Edition No. 16 (Library Board of South Australia, 1964), p. 355; Richard A. Gould, *Yiwara: Foragers of the Australian Desert* (Scribner's, 1969), p. 124; deGraff, "Aboriginal Use of Fire," p. 15; Plomley, ed., *Friendly Mission,* pp. 286, 840, for accounts of mosquito burning; Blainey, *Triumph,* pp. 192–193; Bonwick, *Daily Life,* p. 21. As an example of how explorers relied on smoke for information, see Augustus Charles Gregory and Francis Thomas Gregory, *Journals of Australian Explorations* (Brisbane, 1884; facsimile ed., Hesperian Press, 1981), p. 141.

15.   Blainey, *Triumph,* pp. 192–193; Bonwick, *Daily Life,* p. 21.

16.   Leichhardt, quoted in Sokoloff, "As It Was in the Past," p. 81; "The Native Fires," *Perth Gazette and Western Australian Journal* (February 22, 1833), p. 31; Moore quoted in Hallam, *Fire and Hearth,* p. 45.

17.   J. Logan Jack, *Northmost Australia,* Vol. II (London, 1921), entry for September 9; Louis A. Allen, *Time Before Morning* (Thomas Y. Crowell, 1975), p. 109; Hamelin's report is reproduced in Plomley, *The Baudin Expedition and the Tasmanian Aborigines 1802.*

18.   McLaren quoted in Blainey, *Triumph,* p. 72; A. B. Facey, *A Fortunate Life* (Penguin Books, 1981), p. 162.

19.   Gregory and Gregory, *Journals,* p. 140; Charles Sturt, *Two Expeditions into the Interior of Southern Australia During the Years 1828, 1829, and 1831 . . . ,* Vol. 1 (London, 1833), p. xxix; Plomley, ed., *Friendly Mission,* p. 368.

20.   Blainey, *Triumph,* p. 75; Jones, "The Neolithic, Palaeolithic, and the Hunting Gardeners," p. 26.

21.   Jones, "Fire-stick Farming"; John Hunter, *An Historical Journal of the Transactions at Port Jackson and Norfolk Island . . .* (London, 1795), p. 81; Curr, *Recollections,* p. 88.

22.   Grey and Moore quoted from Hallam, *Fire and Hearth,* pp. 14, 39; Blainey, *Triumph,* p. 164; George F. Angas, *Savage Life and Scenes in Australia and New Zealand* (London, 1847), Vol. 1, p. 232.

23.   Plomley, ed., *Friendly Mission,* p. 366; Jones, "Neolithic, Palaeolithic, and the Hunting Gardeners," p. 26; Flood, *Archaeology of the Dreamtime,* pp. 207, 213–214; Curr, *Recollections,* p. 430; D. A. Herbert, "The Upland Savannahs of the Bunya Mountains, South Queensland," *Proceedings of the Royal Society of Queensland* XLIX (1938), p. 148.

24.   From Flood, *Archaeology of the Dreamtime,* p. 227.

25.   Flood, *Archaeology of the Dreamtime,* pp. 201–202; D. R. Harris, quoted in Nicolson, "Fire and the Australian Aborigine," pp. 68–69; J. M. Beaton, "Fire and Water: Aspects of Australian Aborigine Management," *Archaeology in Oceania* 17 (1982), pp. 51–59.

26. Thompson quoted in Fox, "Summary of Published Work," p. 2; Stokes quoted by Hallam, *Fire and Hearth*, p. 33; Plomley, ed., *Friendly Mission*, p. 210.
27. Jones, "Neolithic, Palaeolithic, and the Hunting Gatherers," p. 25; Haynes, cited by Nicolson, "Fire and the Australian Aborigine," p. 69; Gould, "Uses and Effects of Fire," p. 18.
28. Cunningham quoted in Flood, "Fire as an Agent of Change," pp. 17–18.
29. Hunter, *An Historical Journal*, p. 61; George White, *Journal of a Voyage to New South Wales*, Alec Chisholm, ed. (reprint: Angus and Robertson, 1962), p. 130; Plomley, ed., *Friendly Mission*, p. 837; Angas, *Savage Life and Scenes*, Vol. 1, pp. 112–113. For possum smoking, see the frontispiece to Sturt, *Two Expeditions into the Interior*, Vol. 2.
30. Hallam, *Fire and Hearth*, p. 32; Isaacs, ed., *Australia Dreaming*, p. 167; Gould, "Uses and Effects of Fire," pp. 19–20; G. C. Stocker, "Effects of Fires on Vegetation in the Northern Territory," *Australian Forestry* 30 (1966), p. 225; Plomley, ed., *Friendly Mission*, p. 383; George Moore, *A Diary of Ten Years' Eventful Life of an Early Settler in Western Australia* (University of Western Australia Press, facsimile of 1834 ed.), p. 219.
31. Stokes quoted from Hallam, *Fire and Hearth*, p. 33; Plomley, ed., *Friendly Mission*, p. 210; George Grey, *Journal of Two Expeditions of Discovery in North-West and Western Australia During the Years 1837, 1838, and 1839* (London, 1841), p. 290; Hallam, *Fire and Hearth*, p. 32; Bonwick, *Daily Life*, p. 14; Sturt, *Two Expeditions*, p. 113; Reverend John Wollaston, *Wollaston's Picton Journal*, Vol. 1 of *Journals and Diaries of Archdeacon of Western Australia*, Vol. 1 (Perth, 1948), p. 11; Hallam, *Fire and Hearth*, p. 32; Moore, *Diary of Ten Years*, p. 259.
32. Hunter, *Historical Journal*, p. 43; Dale and Nind quoted in Hallam, *Fire and Hearth*, pp. 28, 32. See also, Bonwick, *Daily Life*, p. 14; Barrallier cited in *Eco-Fire. Proceedings of a Symposium Conducted at the Australian Museum, 1976* (National Parks Association of New South Wales, 1976), p. 137; Caley cited in P. H. Edwards, "Historical and Cultural Background to the Fire Problem on the Blue Mountains," *The Living Earth* (March 1974), p. 7.
33. Hedley H. Finlayson, *The Red Centre. Man and Beast in the Heart of Australia* (Angus and Robertson, 1936), pp. 63–67. See also deGraff, "Aboriginal Use of Fire," pp. 16–17.
34. L. Stokes, *Discoveries in Australia—Voyage of HMS Beagle During 1837–43* (London, 1846), p. 228; D. F. Thompson, "Arnhem Land: Explorations Among an Unknown People, Part II," *Geographic Journal* 113 (1949), p. 7; the Daisy Utemara story is reported in Isaacs, ed., *Australian Dreaming*, p. 200.
35. John Wedge, *The Diaries of John Wilder Wedge 1824–1835* (Royal Society of Tasmania, 1962), entry for September 8, 1827; R. W. Ellis, "The Aboriginal Inhabitants and Their Environment," in C. R. Twidale et al., eds., *Natural History of the Adelaide Region* (Royal Society of South Australia, 1976), p. 113; Hunter, *Historical Journal*, p. 81; Richard Gould, *Living Archaeology* (Cambridge University Press, 1980), p. 81.
36. T. L. Mitchell, *Journal of An Expedition into the Interior of Tropical Australia* (London, 1848), p. 306; Leichhardt, "Journal of an Overland Expedition," p. 355.
37. Mitchell, *Journal of an Expedition*, pp. 412–413.
38. Cook from Captain W.J.L. Wharton, ed., *Captain Cook's Journal, 1768–71*, Australiana Facsimile Editions No. 188 (Libraries Board of South Australia,

1968), p. 312; Philip P. King, *Narrative of a Survey of the Intertropical and Western Coasts of Australia,* Vol. 1 (London, 1827), p. 383; Phillip cited in Cobley, *Sydney Cove 1788,* p. 201; Governor Philip to Viscount Sydney, May 15, 1788, *Historical Records of Australia* (Sydney, 1914), Vol. 1, p. 31; White, *Journal of a Voyage,* p. 129.

39. DeNyptang in R. H. Major, ed., *Early Voyages to Terra Australia* (Adelaide, 1963), p. 122; Governor Phillip to Viscount Sydney, *Historical Records,* p. 31; Peron cited from Jones, "Fire-stick Farming," p. 225; Parry cited in Sokoloff, "Aborigines and Fire in the Lower Hunter, Part III," pp. 192–193; Jones, "Fire-stick Farming," p. 226; Plomley, ed., *Friendly Mission,* p. 252; Menzies and Vancouver quoted in Hallam, *Fire and Hearth,* p. 17–18; Wollaston, *Journals and Diaries,* p. 41.

40. Sturt, *Two Expeditions,* p. xxviii–xxix, xxx; Curr, *Recollections,* p. 88.

41. Rhys Jones, "Cleaning Up the Country," *BHP Journal* 1 (1980), pp. 10–15; C. D. Haynes, "The Pattern and Ecology of *Munwag:* Traditional Aboriginal Fire Regimes in North-Central Arnhemland," in M. G. Ridpath and L. K. Corbett, eds., *Ecology of the Wet-Dry Tropics,* Proceedings Ecological Society of Australia 13 (1985), p. 210.

7. FIRES OF THE DREAMING

1. General works that address Aboriginal mythology include W. Ramsay Smith, *Myths and Legends of the Australian Aboriginals* (Johnson Reprint Corp., 1970); Jennifer Isaacs, ed., *Australian Dreaming. 40,000 Years of Aboriginal History* (Landsdowne Press, 1980); A. W. Reed, *Aboriginal Myths* (Reed, 1978), *Aboriginal Legends* (Reed, 1978), and *Myths and Legends of Australia* (New York, 1973); Roland Robinson, *Aboriginal Myths and Legends* (New York, 1969); A. P. Elkin, *The Australian Aborigines,* 3rd ed. (1954); Louis A. Allen, *Time Before Morning. Art and Myth of the Australian Aborigine* (Thomas Y. Crowell, 1975); Melva Jean Roberts and Ainslie Roberts, *Dreamtime Heritage* (Rigby, 1975); and a series of wonderfully illustrated books by Charles P. Mountford and Ainslie Roberts. A study that arrived after I completed my research, which synthesizes the art and mythology and should prove indispensable is Peter Sutton, ed., *Dreamings: The Art of Aboriginal Australia* (George Braziller, 1988). For references that analyze fire mythology more specifically, see Sylvia A. Hallam, *Fire and Hearth* (Australian Institute of Aboriginal Studies, 1979), and Kenneth Maddock, "Myths of the Acquisition of Fire in Northern and Eastern Australia," Ronald M. Berndt, ed., *Australian Aboriginal Anthropology* (University of Western Australia Press, 1970). To place Australian lore in a global context, consult the unbelievably dull but essential James Frazer, *Myths of the Origin of Fire* (Hacker Art Books, 1974). For a philosophical reverie on fire mythmaking, see Gaston Bachelard, *The Psychoanalysis of Fire* (Beacon Press, 1964).

2. Bachelard, *Psychoanalysis of Fire,* p. 55.

3. Roberts and Roberts, *Dreamtime Heritage,* p. 32.

4. Isaacs, ed., *Australian Dreaming,* p. 21–24; Richard Kimber, "Black Lightning: Aborigines and Fire in Central Australia and the Western Desert," *Archaeology in Oceania* 18 (1983), pp. 38–45; Isaacs, ed., *Australian Dreaming,* p. 92; Charles P. Mountford and Ainslie Roberts, *The Dreamtime Book* (Prentice-

Hall, 1973), pp. 54–55; Isaacs, ed., *Australian Dreaming*, pp. 158, 42; Mountford and Roberts, *Dreamtime Book*, p. 28; Smith, *Myths and Legends*, p. 276.

5.　See Frazer, *Myths*, pp. 5–24 passim.

6.　Allen, *Time Before Morning*, pp. 109–113.

7.　"The Burning Anthill," in Roberts and Roberts, *Dreamtime Heritage*, pp. 30–31, 28–29; Frazer, *Myths*, pp. 15–16; Charles P. Mountford and Ainslie Roberts, *The Dawn of Time* (Rigby, 1969), pp. 42–43.

8.　Mountford and Roberts, *The Dawn of Time*, pp. 52–53; Allen, *Time Before Morning*, pp. 81–85 (see also, Maddock, "Myths," p. 186); Roberts and Roberts, *Dreamtime Heritage*, pp. 28–29.

9.　Grey quoted in Hallam, *Fire and Hearth*, p. 44; Mountford and Roberts, *Dreamtime Book*, pp. 48–49, 174–175; George F. Angas, *Savage Life and Scenes in Australia and New Zealand* (London, 1847), Vol. 2, p. 232; Richard A. Gould, "Uses and Effects of Fire Among the Western Desert Aborigines of Australia," *Mankind* 8 (1971), p. 17.

10.　Mountford and Roberts, *Dreamtime Book*, pp. 164–165; Mountford and Roberts, *The Dawn of Time*, p. 70–71; Roberts and Roberts, *Dreamtime Heritage*, p. 34–35; Isaacs, ed., *Australian Dreaming*, p. 158 (see also, Mountford and Roberts, *The Dawn of Time*, pp. 34–35, Frazer, *Myths*, pp. 16–17, and Isaacs, ed., *Australian Dreaming*, pp. 255–258); Frazer, *Myths*, pp. 20, 3–4; Mountford and Roberts, *Dreamtime Book*, pp. 94–95; N.J.B. Plomley, ed., *Friendly Mission. Tasmanian Journals and Papers of George Augustus Robinson 1829–1834* (Tasmanian Historical Research Association, 1966), p. 837; Isaacs, ed., *Australian Dreaming*, p. 143.

11.　Isaacs, ed., *Australian Dreaming*, pp. 255–258.

12.　Maddock, "Myths of the Acquisition of Fire in Northern and Eastern Australia," in Ronald M. Berndt, ed., *Australian Aboriginal Anthropology* (University of Western Australia Press, 1970), p. 176.

13.　Robinson in Plomley, ed., *Friendly Mission*, p. 765.

14.　Frazer, *Myths*, pp. 16–17.

15.　Allen, *Time Before Morning*, pp. 70, 109

16.　See Allen, *Time Before Morning*, pp. 248, 109, 180–185; Gould, "Uses and Effects of Fire," pp. 17–18; W. Lloyd Warner, *A Black Civilization*, rev. ed., especially pp. 278–279.　An interesting legend to accompany ritual purification comes from the Gunwinggu tribe. It tells of Luma Luma, a giant with magical powers, who finally, after attacks, agrees to initiate humans into the great mysteries. Taking a carved figurine of the Rainbow Serpent, he holds it over a steaming fire, with the words, "I purify this totem, for it is the strongest and most sacred. It will watch over you and cause your numbers to increase and prosper." Cited in Allen, *Time Before Morning*, p. 19.

17.　Allen, *Time Before Morning*, p. 19; Smith, *Myths and Legends*, p. 212.

18.　Allen, *Time Before Morning*, p. 109.; Warner, *Black Civilization*, pp. 300, 318–319; Gould, "Uses and Effects of Fire," p. 17; Warner, *Black Civilization*, pp. 313–314, 321, 342, 349, 261–262; Smith, *Myths and Legends*, p. 412.　Smith records an ancient legend in which a fire drive is employed to contain and destroy the Evil One. As each creature tries to flee the encircling fire, he is attacked and thrown back. Though the Evil One can change form he, too, is kept within the fire and his material manifestation is destroyed. Neither, because they had also passed through the fires, could the Evil One reoccupy the form of any animal. He exists only as a spirit, and he can claim only humans because they alone stood outside the great ring of fire (pp. 292–294).

19.   Baldwin Spencer, *Wanderings in Wild Australia*, Vol. 1 (Macmillan, 1928), pp. 447–455

20.   Mountford and Roberts, *Dreamtime Book*, pp. 168–169 (also Hallam, *Fire and Hearth*, pp. 81–84); quoted in Hallam, *Fire and Hearth*, p. 81; Gould, "Uses and Effects of Fire," p. 17.

21.   Allen, *Time Before Morning*, pp. 104–108.

22.   Warner, *Black Civilization*, p. 406. For smoke as prophylactic against body reinvasion, see Isaacs, p. 221.

23.   John Morgan, *The Life and Adventures of William Buckley . . .* (Caliban Books, 1979; from 1852 ed.), p. 52; Warner, *Black Civilization*, pp. 407, 412; D. F. Thompson, "Arnhem Land: Explorations Among an Unknown People, Part II," *Geographic Journal* 113 (1949), p. 5; Isaacs, ed., *Australian Dreaming*, p. 224.

24.   Angas, *Savage Life and Scenes*, Vol. 2, pp. 97, 227; James Backhouse, *A Narrative of a Visit to the Australian Colonies* (London, 1843), p. 105; James Bonwick, *Daily Life and Origin of the Tasmanians* (Sampson, Low, Son, and Marston, 1870), pp. 91–92; Josephine Flood, *Archaeology of the Dreamtime* (Collins, 1983), p. 44.

25.   See Flood, *Archaeology of the Dreamtime*, pp. 44–52.

26.   Hallam, *Fire and Hearth*, p. 94.

27.   Allen, *Time Before Morning*, pp. 80–85. I have followed closely this account with quotation and paraphrase, abbreviating only the story.

8. SMOKES BY DAY, FIRES BY NIGHT

1.   Perhaps the principal exception is Cleland, who concluded that "any alteration in the appearance of the vegetation from this cause [fire] is as nothing compared with the effects of clearing the land and grazing produced by Europeans" (from "Some Aspects of the Ecology of the Aboriginal Inhabitants of Tasmania and Southern Australia," *Papers and Proceedings, Royal Society of Tasmania 1939* (1940), p. 15). Cleland was writing from the 1930s, not the 1850s, however, and it is clear that his concern is with highlighting the enormous biotic revolution wrought by the European. His position has been recapitulated by recent critics, particularly those interested in nature preserves. See, for example, Joan Bradley, "Aborigines and Fire," *Eco-Fire*. Proceedings of a Symposium Conducted at the Australian Museum, Sydney (National Parks Association of New South Wales, 1976), pp. 117–135. By contrast most early observers were more inclined to agree with Curr, and most contemporary critics would echo Rhys Jones who emphasized that "as an anthropologist, I can state that at the time of ethnographic contact with the Aborigines, and probably for tens of thousands of years before, fires were systematically lit by Aborigines and were an integral part of their economy" ("Fire-Stick Farming," *Australian Natural History* (September 1969), p. 228).

2.   Basic studies of Aboriginal fire practices around Arnhemland include A. Chase and P. Sutton, "Hunter-Gatherers in a Rich Environment: Aboriginal Coastal Exploitation in Cape York Peninsula," in Allen Keast, ed., *Ecological Biogeog-*

raphy of Australia, Vol. 3 (Dr. W. Junk, 1981), pp. 1817–1852; C. D. Haynes, "The Pattern and Ecology of *Munwag:* Traditional Aboriginal Fire Regimes in North-Central Arnhemland," in M. G. Ridpath and L. K. Corbett, eds., *Ecology of the Wet-Dry Tropics*. Proceedings of the Ecological Society of Australia, Vol. 13 (1985), pp. 203–215; J. Russell-Smith, "A Record of Change: Studies of Holocene Vegetation History in the South Alligator River Region, Northern Territory," in Ridpath and Corbett, eds., *Ecology of the Wet-Dry Tropics*, pp. 191–202; Rhys Jones, "Hunters in the Australian Coastal Savanna," in D. R. Harris, ed., *Human Ecology in Savanna Environments* (Academic Press, 1980), pp. 107–146; R. Jones and J. Bowler, "Struggle for the Savannah: Northern Australia in Ecological and Prehistoric Perspective," in Rhys Jones, ed., *Northern Australia: Options and Implications* (Research School of Pacific Studies, Australian National University, 1980), pp. 3–31; C. D. Haynes, "Land, Trees, and Man," *Commonwealth Forestry Review* 57 (1978), pp. 99–106; and Henry T. Lewis, "Burning the 'Top End': Kangaroos and Cattle," in Julian Ford, ed., *Fire Ecology and Management in Western Australian Ecosystems*, WAIT Environmental Studies Group Report No. 14 (Western Australian Institute of Technology, 1985), pp. 21–31. A good (but dated) survey of the literature is R. E. Fox, "Summary of Published Work," in R. E. Fox, ed., *Report on the Use of Fire in National Parks and Reserves* (Darwin, 1974), pp. 1–10. A distilled overview of resulting fire ecology is given in G. C. Stocker and G. L. Unwin, "Fire," in H. T. Clifford and R. L. Specht, eds., *Tropical Plant Communities* (Department of Botany, University of Queensland, 1986), pp. 91–103.

3.   Jones, "Neolithic, Palaeolithic, and the Hunting Gardeners," p. 25.

4.   Lewis, "Burning the 'Top End'," p. 25.

5.   Lewis, "Burning the 'Top End'," p. 28.

6.   Basic sources for Aboriginal fire practices in the central and western deserts include Norman B. Tindale, "Desert Aborigines and Southern Coastal Peoples: Some Comparisons," in Keast, ed., *Ecological Biogeography,* Vol. 3, pp. 1853–1889; Andrew Burbidge, "Fire and Mammals in Hummock Grasslands of the Arid Zone," in Ford, ed., *Fire Ecology*, pp. 91–94; G. F. Griffin, "The Role of Fire in Arid Lands," in Peter Stanbury, ed., *Bushfires: Their Effect on Australian Life and Landscape* (Macleay Museum, 1981); Wayne Ralph, "Fire in the Centre," *Ecos* 4 (winter, 1984), pp. 3–10; P. K. Latz and G. F. Griffin, "Changes in Aboriginal Land Management in Relation to Fire and to Food Plants in Central Australia," in B. S. Hetzel and H. J. Frith, eds., *The Nutrition of Aborigines in Relation to the Ecosystem of Central Australia* (CSIRO, 1978), pp. 77–85; G. F. Griffin et al., "Wildfires in the Central Australian Rangelands, 1970–1980," *Journal of Environmental Management* 17 (1983), pp. 311–323; Graham Griffin and Grant Allan, "Fire and the Management of Aboriginal Owned Lands in Central Australia," section 2.6 in Barney Foran and Bruce Walker, eds., *Science and Technology for Aboriginal Development* (CSIRO and Centre for Appropriate Technology, n.d.); G. F. Griffin, "Hummock Grasslands," and K. C. Hodgkinson et al., "Management of Vegetation with Fire," in G. N. Harrington et al., eds., *Management of Australia's Rangelands* (CSIRO, 1984), pp. 271–284, 141–156.

7.   For a good introduction to ever-controversial Tasmania, see W. D. Jackson, "Fire, Air, Water and Earth—An Elemental Ecology of Tasmania," *Symposium on Physiological Aspects of Plant and Animal Management*, Proceedings, Ecological Society of Australia, Vol. 3 (1965), pp. 9–16; D.M.J.S. Bowman and

M. J. Brown, "Bushfires in Tasmania: A Botanical Approach to Anthropological Questions," *Archaeology in Oceania* 21 (1986), pp. 166–171; Jim Stockton, "Fires by the Seaside: Historic Vegetation Changes in Northwestern Tasmania," *Papers and Proceedings of the Royal Society of Tasmania* 116 (1982), pp. 53–63; A. B. Mount, "Fire-Cycles or Succession in South-West Tasmania," and W. D. Jackson and D.M.J.S. Bowman, "Reply: Ecological Drift or Fire Cycles in South-West Tasmania," *Search* 13 nos. 7 and 8 (August–September 1982), pp. 174–175; Rhys Jones, "The Neolithic, Palaeolithic and the Hunting Gardeners: Man and Land in the Antipodes," in R. P. Suggate and M. M. Cresswell, eds., *Quaternary Studies* (Royal Society of New Zealand, 1975), pp. 21–34, and "The Geographical Background to the Arrival of Man in Australia and Tasmania," *Archaeology and Physical Anthropology in Oceania* III, no. 3 (October 1968), pp. 186–215. Jennifer Read and Robert S. Hill, "Rainforest Invasion onto Tasmanian Old-fields," *Australian Journal of Ecology* 8 (1983), pp. 149–161; and R. C. Ellis, "Aboriginal Influences on Vegetation in the Northeast Highlands," *Tasmanian Naturalist* (January 1984), pp. 7–8. Quotation from Jackson and Bowman, "Reply," p. 175.

8.   Explorer quotes mostly from Jones, "Geographical Background," p. 206. I have followed Jones closely in reconstructing the Tasmanian scene. Furneaux quoted in James Bonwick, *The Last of the Tasmanians* (London, 1870), p. 4. For an important compendium of early reports, see N.J.B. Plomley, *The Baudin Expedition and the Tasmanian Aborigines 1802* (Hobart, 1983), especially pp. 202–203.

9.   Jones, "Neolithic, Palaeolithic, and the Hunting Gardeners," p. 26; Stockton, "Fires by the Seaside," pp. 53–63; Jones, "Geographical Background," p. 207, 210; Walker quoted in Ellis, "Aboriginal Influences on Vegetation," p. 7; Jackson and Bowman, "Reply."

10.   Lieutenant Bunbury quoted in Vincent Serventy, ". . . They Saw a Large Smoak," in *Environments to Order?*, Proceedings of a Symposium at the Australian Museum (National Parks Association of New South Wales, 1970), p. 43.

11.   C.W.M. Hart and Arnold R. Pilling, *The Tiwi of North Australia* (Holt Rinehart and Winston, 1960), p. 42; Matthew Flinders, *A Voyage to Terra Australis . . .*, Vol. 1, Australiana Facsimile Editions No. 37 (Libraries Board of South Australia, 1960), p. clxxx.

12.   G. Singh et al., "Quaternary Vegetation and Fire History in Australia," in A. M. Gill et al., eds., *Fire and Australian Biota* (Australian Academy of Science, 1981), pp. 39–44; Josephine Flood, *Archaeology of the Dreamtime* (Collins, 1983), pp. 111–117.

13.   Arthur S. Weston, "Fire—and Persistence of the Flora on Middle Island, a Southwestern Australian Offshore Island," in Ford, ed., *Fire Ecology and Management in Western Australia*, pp. 111–118. See also Flinders, *Voyage*, Vol. II, p. 171. Neighboring Mondrain Island was "set on fire" by Captain King's party, though it is also true that they found evidence of native fireplaces (see Sylvia J. Hallam, *Fire and Hearth* [Australian Institute for Aboriginal Studies, 1979], p. 22).

14.   Alison M. Baird, "Notes on the Regeneration of Vegetation of Garden Island after the 1956 Fire," *Journal of the Royal Society of Western Australia* 41 (1958), pp. 102–107. For an interesting comparison to the mainland, see A. M. Baird, "Regeneration After Fire in King's Park, Perth, Western Australia," *Journal of the Royal Society of Western Australia* 60, part 1 (1977), pp. 1–22.

15. Hallam, *Fire and Hearth*, p. 50.
16. Eric Rolls put the matter succinctly when he wrote, "For varying periods of Australia there was no more regular burning"—*A Million Wild Acres* (Penguin Books, 1984), p. 246. The particular examples cited come from Karel Domin, "Queensland's Plant Associations," *Proceedings of the Royal Society of Queensland* XXIII, part I (1911), pp. 63–67; D. N. Jeans, *An Historical Geography of New South Wales to 1901* (Reed Education, 1972), p. 64; Samuel Dixon, "The Effects of Settlement and Pastoral Occupation in Australia upon the Indigenous Vegetation," *Transactions and Proceedings and Report of the Royal Society of South Australia* XV (1982), p. 200; Stokes and Bunbury quoted in Hallam, *Fire and Hearth*, pp. 48, 47; Helen Baker Proudfoot, "Botany Bay, Kew, and the Picturesque: Early Conceptions of the Australian Landscape," *Journal of the Royal Australian Historical Society* 65, part 1 (June 1979), p. 41; T. L. Mitchell, *Journal of an Expedition into the Interior of Tropical Australia* (London, 1848), p. 413; R. J. Lampert and Frances Sanders, "Plants and Men on the Beecroft Peninsula, New South Wales," *Mankind* (1973), p. 102; D. A. Herbert, "The Upland Savannahs of the Bunya Mountains, South Queensland," *Proceedings of Royal Society of Queensland* XLIX (1938), p. 148.
17. See B. Meehan and R. Jones, "The Outstation Movement and Hints of a White Backlash," in Jones, ed., *Northern Australia*, pp. 131–157, and Graham Griffin and Grant Allan, "Fire and the Management of Aboriginal Owned Lands in Central Australia," in Barney Foran and Bruce Walker, eds., *Science and Technology for Aboriginal Development* (CSIRO and Centre for Appropriate Technology, n.d.), Chapter 2.6.
18. See E. C. Saxon, ed., *Anticipating the Inevitable: A Patch-burn Strategy for Fire Management in Uluru (Ayers Rock–Mt. Olga) National Park* (CSIRO, 1984). A good summary of the Kakadu scene is Henry T. Lewis, "Traditional vs. Contemporary Ecological Knowledge: Aborigine, Ranger, and Fire," unpublished paper presented to Canadian Ethnological Society, Annual Meeting, Saskatoon, Sasketchewan (1988).
19. A. W. Howitt, "The Eucalypts of Gippsland," *Transactions of the Royal Society of Victoria* II, part I (1890), p. 111.

9. THIS WONDERFUL DEPOSITORY OF FIRE

1. Eric Rolls, *A Million Wild Acres* (Penguin Books, 1984), p. 248; Cook, quoted in A. Malcolm Gill, "Fire Ecology in Australia: A Short Bibliographic History" (unpublished report, 1981), p. 1; Captain W.J.L. Wharton, ed., *Captain Cook's Journal During his First Voyage Round the World . . .* (London, 1893; facsimile ed., Libraries Board of South Australia, 1968), p. 263.
2. Josephine Flood, *Archaeology of the Dreamtime* (Collins, 1983), p. 18; Geoffrey Blainey, *Triumph of the Nomads*, rev. ed. (Sun Books, 1983), p. 83.
3. Captain W.J.L. Wharton, ed., *Captain Cook's Journal During his First Voyage Round the World . . .* (London, 1893; facsimile ed., Libraries Board of South Australia, 1968), p. 238.
4. G. H. Kenihan, ed., *The Journal of Abel Janszoon Tasman, 1642* (Adelaide, n.d.), p. 29.
5. J. C. Beaglehole, ed., *The Endeavour Journal of Joseph Banks 1768–1771*, Vol. II, second ed. (Public Library of New South Wales, 1963), pp. 49–132, esp. 51,

52–56, 72, 82; Wharton, ed., *Captain Cook's Journal*, pp. 138–317 passim, especially p. 251.

6. Beaglehole, ed., *Endeavour Journal*, p. 132.

7. Beaglehole, ed., *Endeavour Journal*, p. 82.

8. Beaglehole, ed., *Endeavour Journal*, pp. 132, 131.

9. Beaglehole, ed., *Endeavour Journal*, p. 55; quoted in Harley H. Bartlett, *Fire in Relation to Primitive Agriculture and Grazing in the Tropics: Annotated Bibliography*, Vol. 3 (University of Michigan, Department of Botany, 1961), pp. 173–175.

10. Cook, quoted in Bartlett, *Fire*, Vol. 3, pp. 173–175.

11. Beaglehole, ed., *Endeavour Journal*, p. 50.

12. Various evidence points to a probable origin in Southeast Asia. The Polynesian word for fire, *afi*, is clearly cognate with the Old Malayan expression for fire, *api*. Bartlett attempts, with mixed success, to trace similar etymologies for words that describe swidden. See Harley H. Bartlett, *Fire*, Vol. 2 (1957), p. 799.

13. For an excellent summary of the processes involved, see Dieter Mueller-Dombois, "Fire in Tropical Ecosystems," in *Proceedings of the Conference, Fire Regimes and Ecosystem Properties*, General Technical Report WO-26 (U.S. Forest Service, 1981), pp. 137–176.

14. John Horne, *A Year in Fiji* (Edward Stanford, 1881), pp. 7, 20; Bartlett, *Fire*, Vol. 1, pp. 453–454; George Brown, *Melanesians and Polynesians* (London, 1910), p. 321; Bartlett, *Fire*, Vol. 2, p. 106. Bartlett's three volumes are the outstanding reference document. For a distillation, see H. H. Bartlett, "Fire, Primitive Agriculture, and Grazing in the Tropics," in William L. Thomas, Jr., ed., *Man's Role in Changing the Face of the Earth*, Vol. 2 (University of Chicago Press, 1956), pp. 692–720. An updated panorama, equipped with extensive maps, is available in Robert B. Batchelder and Howard F. Hirt, *Fire in Tropical Forests and Grasslands*, Technical Report 67-41-ES, U.S. Army Natick Laboratories (1966), and in abbreviated form, as Robert Batchelder, "Spatial and Temporal Patterns of Fire in the Tropical World," *Proceedings, Tall Timbers Fire Ecology Conference* 6 (Tallahassee, 1967), pp. 171–207. To supplement with the other lands of Greater Gondwana, see George P. Murdock, "Human Influences on the Ecosystems of High Islands of the Tropical Pacific," and Kenneth B. Cumberland, "Man's Role in Modifying Island Environments in the Southwest Pacific: with Special Reference to New Zealand," in F. R. Fosberg, ed., *Man's Place in the Island Ecosystem. A Symposium* (Bishop Museum Press, 1963), pp. 145–152, 187–205, for an introduction to the Pacific Islands. J. Peter White and James F. O'Connell, *A Prehistory of Australia, New Guinea, and Sahul* (Academic Press, 1982) surveys the New Guinea records. An excellent cross-cultural panorama comes from David R. Harris, ed., *Human Ecology in Savanna Environments* (Academic Press, 1980), which includes South America, Africa, India, Southeast Asia, and New Caledonia as well as Australia. For southern Africa, see J. D. Scott, "An Historical Review of Research on Fire in South Africa," in P. deV. Booysen and N. M. Tainton, eds., *Ecological Effects of Fire in South African Ecosystems* (Springer-Verlag, 1984), pp. 53–66. Modern surveys of Southeast Asia include Peter Kunstadter et al., eds., *Farmers in the Forest* (University of Hawaii Press, 1978). For Madagascar, see R. Battistini and P. Verin, "Man and the Environment in Madagascar," in R. Battistini and G. Richard-Vindard, eds., *Biogeography and Ecology in Madagascar* (Dr. W. Junk, 1972), pp. 311–337. Also in-

valuable is Paul S. Martin and Richard G. Klein, eds., *Quaternary Extinctions.*
A Prehistoric Revolution (University of Arizona Press, 1984), particularly
Robert E. Dewar, "Extinctions in Madagascar: the Loss of the Subfossil Fauna,"
pp. 574–599, Michael M. Trotter and Beverley McCuilloch, "Moas, Men, and
Middens," pp. 708–727, and Richard Cassels, "Faunal Extinction and Prehis-
toric Man in New Zealand and the Pacific Islands," pp. 768–784. Useful for
contextualizing the Australian scene is Rhys Jones, "The Geographical Background to the Arrival of Man in Australia and Tasmania," *Archaeology and
Physical Anthropology in Oceania* 3, no. 3 (1968), pp. 186–215. A fascinating study—obtained from Professor Lewis after I had drafted my analysis of
Aboriginal fire geography—is Henry T. Lewis and Theresa A. Ferguson, "Yards,
Corridors, and Mosaics: How to Burn a Boreal Forest," *Human Ecology* 16, no.
1 (1988), pp. 57–77. The analogy to Tasmania is particularly strong. I appreciate Professor Lewis's sharing of these insights with me.

15.   J. P. Harrington, "Tobacco Among the Karok Indians of California" Bureau of
American Ethnology Bulletin No. 94 (1932), p. 63.   Invaluable for my understanding of California Indian fire practices is a small depository of research
documents, some published and some unpublished, from Omer C. Stewart.
The notes include detailed accountings of what tribes used fire to what purposes. I am grateful for the loan of the many materials Dr. Stewart has collected over the course of several decades.   Among published surveys of fire
practices among California aborigines are Henry T. Lewis, *Patterns of Indian
Burning in California: Ecology and Ethnohistory,* Ballena Press Anthropological Papers No. 1 (Ballena Press, 1973); C. Kristina Rover Wickstrom, *Issues
Concerning Native American Use of Fire: A Literature Review,* Publications
in Anthropology No. 6, Yosemite Research Center (Yosemite National Park,
1987); John L. Vankat, "Fire and Man in Sequoia National Park," *Annals of
the Association of American Geographers* 67, no. 1 (March 1977), pp. 17–27;
Richard A. Minnich, *The Biogeography of Fire in the San Bernardino Mountains of California. A Historical Study,* University of California Publications
in Geography Vol. 28 (1988); Jan Timbrook et al., "Vegetation Burning by the
Chumash," *Journal of California and Great Basin Anthropology,* no. 2
(1982), pp. 163–186; Omer Stewart, "The Forgotten Side of Ethnography," in
R. F. Spencer, ed., *Method and Perspective in Anthropology* (University of
Minnesota Press, 1954), pp. 221–248; L. T. Burcham, "Fire and Chaparral
before European Settlement," in Murray Rosenthal, ed., *Symposium on Living
with the Chaparral, Proceedings* (Sierra Club, 1974), pp. 101–120. Other citations come from typed notes in the Stewart collection. To put fire practices
into the context of Indian daily life, see Heizer and Elsasser, *Natural World of
the California Indians,* supplemented by Theodora Kroeber et al., *Drawn
From Life: California Indians in Pen and Brush* (Ballena Press, 1977). Behind
them stands Robert Heizer, ed., *Handbook of North American Indians,* Vol. 8
—California (Smithsonian Institution, 1978). Other sources are summarized
in Stephen J. Pyne, *Fire in America: A Cultural History of Wildland and
Rural Fire* (Princeton University Press, 1982), pp. 413–423.   Surveys of the
ecological context can be found in Notes 7 and 8, Chapter 4. To them should
be added Timothy Plumb, ed., *Proceedings of the Symposium on the Ecology,
Management, and Utilization of California Oaks,* General Technical Report
PSW-44 (US Forest Service, 1980), especially Randall S. Rossi, "History of
Cultural Influences on the Distribution and Reproduction of Oaks in Califor-
nia," pp. 7–18.

16. See Lowell John Bean and Harry W. Lawton, "Some Explanations for the Rise of Cultural Complexity in Native California with Comments on Proto-Agriculture and Agriculture," in Lewis, *Patterns of Indian Burning*, Introduction.
17. Quoted in Lewis, *Patterns of Indian Burning*, p. xx.
18. Belcher and Jepson, quoted in Rossi, "History of Cultural Influences," p. 9; W. L. Jepson, *The Silva of California* (University of California Press, 1910), Vol. 2, pp. 11–12.
19. See Rossi, "History of Cultural Influences," p. 9.
20. See Minnich, *Biogeography of Fire*; Roger Byrne et al., "Fossil Charcoal as a Measure of Wildfire Frequency in Southern California: A Preliminary Analysis," *Proceedings of the Symposium on the Environmental Consequences of Fire and Fuel Management in Mediterranean Ecosystems*, General Technical Report WO-3 (1977), pp. 361–367.
21. Cabrillo and Vizcaíno quoted in Lewis, *Patterns of Indian Burning*, p. xix; Vancouver quoted in Louis Barrett, "Record of Forest and Field Fires in California from the Early Explorers to the Creation of the Forest Reserves" (U.S. Forest Service, 1935), pp. 52–53; DeMofras, from Minnich, *Biogeography of Fire*, p. 15.
22. Moncada and Arrillaga, from Raymond Clar, *California Government and Forestry*, Vol. 1 (California Division of Forestry, 1959), pp. 7–9. For the conflict between aboriginal and Spanish practices, see also Albert Hurtado, *Indian Survival on the California Frontier* (Yale University Press, 1988), p. 130.
23. These early voyages are described in Blainey, *Triumph of the Nomads*, pp. 247–251.
24. From Jennifer Isaacs, ed., *Australian Dreaming* (Lansdowne Press, 1980), p. 263.
25. Matthew Flinders, *A Voyage to Terra Australis* . . . , Vol. 2 (London, 1814), p. 7; Sydney Parkinson, *A Journal of a Voyage to the South Seas* (London, 1773), p. 133.
26. Banks in Beaglehole, ed., *Endeavour Journal*, Vol. 2, pp. 96–97; Wharton, ed., *Captain Cook's Journal*, p. 289.
27. Beaglehole, ed., *Endeavour Journal*, pp. 96–97.

10. ENTWINING FIRE

1. Patrick White, *The Tree of Man* (Penguin Books, 1955), p. 9.
2. George William Evans, "Assistant-Surveyor Evans's Journal, 1813–1814," in George Mackaness, ed., *Fourteen Journeys over the Blue Mountains of New South Wales, 1813–1841* (Sydney, 1965), p. 30; T. L. Mitchell, *Three Expeditions into the Interior of Eastern Australia*, 2nd ed. (London, 1838), p. 53.
3. Evans, "Assistant-Surveyor Evans's Journal," p. 30; William Hardman, ed., *The Journals of John McDouall Stuart During the Years 1858, 1859, 1860, 1861, and 1862*, 2nd ed., Australiana Facsimile Editions No. 198 (Libraries Board of South Australia, 1975), p. 348; Philip King, *Narrative of a Survey of the Intertropical and Western Coasts of Australia*, Vol. 1 (London, 1827), p. 371.
4. Captain W.J.L. Wharton, ed., *Captain Cook's Journal During his First Voyage Round the World* . . . , Australiana Facsimile Editions No. 188 (Libraries Board of South Australia, 1968), pp. 244–245; J. C. Beaglehole, ed., *The En-*

deavour Journal of Joseph Banks 1768–1771, Vol. II, 2nd ed. (Public Library of New South Wales, 1963), pp. 57–60. British landscape history is a vast and detailed field, of which my essay represents little more than a sketch. Useful introductory works include W. G. Hoskins, *The Making of the English Landscape* (Penguin, 1955); Ian Simmons and Michael Tooley, eds., *The Environment in British Prehistory* (Duckworth, 1981); W. G. Hoskins and H.P.R. Finberg, *Common Lands of England and Wales* (Collins, 1963); H. C. Darby, *An Historical Geography of England Before A.D. 1800* (Cambridge University Press, 1951); and Leonard Cantor, *The Changing English Countryside 1400–1700* (London, 1987), among many others. From the ecological perspective, see Harry Godwin, *The History of the British Flora,* 2nd ed. (Cambridge University Press, 1975); A. G. Tanley, *The British Islands and Their Vegetation* (Cambridge University Press, 1939); and for a very concise précis, Winifred Pennington, *The History of British Vegetation* (London, 1969). Also interesting is Oliver Rackham, *The History of the Countryside* (London, 1986). Rackham conveys well the skepticism of the British intellectual toward fire, arguing that fire had little place in the British past and less in its future.   To place the British experience into a European context, consider William A. Watts, "Europe," Brian Huntley, "Europe," and Karl-Ernst Behre, "The Role of Man in European Vegetation History," in B. Huntley and T. Webb III, eds., *Vegetation History* (Kluwer Academic Publishers, 1988), pp. 155–192, 341–384, 633–672.

5.   J. J. Wymer, "The Palaeolithic," in Simmons and Tooley, eds., *Environment in British Prehistory,* pp. 77–78.

6.   I. G. Simmons et al., "The Mesolithic," in Simmons and Tooley, eds., *Environment in British Prehistory,* p. 106. See also Simmons, "Evidence for Vegetation Changes Associated with Mesolithic Man in Britain," in Peter J. Ucko and G. W. Dimbleby, eds., *The Domestication and Exploitation of Plants and Animals* (Chicago, 1968), pp. 111–119; G. W. Dimbleby, "The Ancient Forest of Blackamore," *Antiquity* 35 (1961), pp. 123–128; and for an excellent discussion of peat formation, Peter D. Moore, "Origin of Blanket Mires," *Nature* 256 (July 1975), pp. 267–269.

7.   For the elm decline, see A. G. Smith et al., "The Neolithic," in Simmons and Tooley, eds., *Environment in British Prehistory,* pp. 152–170; and the classic papers of J. Iversen, of which the last (in English) is "The Development of Denmark's Nature since the Last Glacial," *Danmarks Geologiske Undersgelse* Series 5, No. 7-C (1973), pp. 1–126.

8.   On forests, see Charles Cox, *The Royal Forests of England* (London, 1905); Charles R. Young, *The Royal Forests of Medieval England* (University of Pennsylvania Press, 1979); N.D.G. James, *A History of English Forestry* (Basic Blackwood, 1981); and Mark Anderson, *A History of Scottish Forestry,* 2 vols. (Nelson, 1967). Most of the forests have separate histories, of various purposes and value. Useful studies of forest lands by Oliver Rackham include *Ancient Woodland. Its History, Vegetation and Uses in England* (Edward Arnold, 1980), *Hayley Wood. Its History and Ecology* (Naturalists' Trust, 1975), and *The History of the Countryside* (London, 1986). Better for fire references are Colin R. Tubbs, *The New Forest: An Ecological History* (David & Charles, 1968) and *The New Forest* (Collins, 1986).   On rabbits and other faunal pests, see James Ritchie, *The Influence of Man on Animal Life in Scotland* (Cambridge University Press, 1920).

9.   Quoted in W. G. East, "England in the Eighteenth Century," in Darby, ed.,

An Historical Geography of England Before A.D. 1800 (1951), p. 477. For overviews on the Second Reclamation, see Eric Kerridge, *The Agricultural Revolution* (George Allen and Unwin, 1967), and J. D. Chambers and G. E. Mingay, *The Agricultural Revolution 1750–1880* (Schocken Books, 1966).

10. East, "England," p. 477.

11. In the twentieth century drought and fire have caused problems for foresters in 1929, 1933, 1955, and 1976; but it is sufficient for fires to have dry spells before or after the main summer growing period. For moorland fires see J. Radley, "Significance of Major Moorland Fires," *Nature* 205 (1965), pp. 1254–1259; A. J. Kayll, "Some Characteristics of Heath Fires in North-East Scotland," *Journal of Applied Ecology* 3 (1966), pp. 29–40, and "Moor Burning in Scotland," *Proceedings, Tall Timbers Fire Ecology Conferences*, Vol. 6 (Tallahassee, 1967), pp. 41–46; A. J. Kayll and C. H. Gimingham, "Vegetative Regeneration of *Calluna vulgaris* after Fire," *Journal of Ecology* 53 (1965): pp. 729–734; C. H. Gimingham, "British Heathland Ecosystems: The Outcome of Many Years of Management by Fire," *Proceedings, Tall Timbers Fire Ecology Conferences*, Vol. 10 (Tallahasee, 1970), pp. 293–321, "Fire on the Hills," *Journal of the Forestry Commission* 25 (1956), pp. 148–150, and *Ecology of Heathlands* (London, 1972). A rather full analysis of fire ecology in the British context is contained in Tubbs, *The New Forest* (1968), particularly pp. 185–188, 224–229. For understanding pastoralism, too, see R. F. Hunter, "The Grazing of Hill Pasture Sward Types," *Journal of the British Grassland Society* 9 (1954), pp. 195–208. A cautious overview of fire and fauna is given in G. R. Miller and Adam Watson, "Some Effects of Fire on Vertebrate Herbivores in the Scottish Highlands," *Tall Timbers Fire Ecology Conference* 13 (Tallahassee, 1973), pp. 39–64. Rackham, in his *History of the Countryside*, questions whether fire had much place in British history and refuses to grant it any positive value. Historic fires mentioned are cited in Anderson, *Scottish Forestry*, Vol. 1, pp. 507, 659, and "58th Annual Excursion—Northumberland," *Scottish Forestry* 9 (1955), p. 120. Several outbreaks of lightning fire have been recorded in recent decades; see for example Donald A. Thompson, "Lightning Fires in Galloway, June 1970," *Scottish Forestry* 25 (1971), pp. 51–52. A dry lightning storm ignited twenty-three fires; and as more land is returned to conifer, the number of lightning fires will continue to rise.

12. I. G. Simmons et al., "The Mesolithic," in Simmons and Tooley, eds., *Environment in British Prehistory*, p. 124.

13. For examples see Frederick Pottle, ed., *Boswell's Journal of a Tour to the Hebrides with Samuel Johnson, 1773* (McGraw-Hill, 1961), p. 155; Edward T. MacDermot, *The History of the Forest of Exmoor* (Barnicott & Pearce, Taunton, 1911), p. 252.

14. See Anderson, *Scottish Forestry*, Vol. 1, pp. 135–136.

15. See A. G. Tansley, *The British Islands and Their Vegetation* (Cambridge University Press, 1939), p. 145; Radley, "Significance of Major Moorland Fires," p. 1259.

16. Frank Elgee, *The Moorlands of North-eastern Yorkshire* (London, 1912), pp. 33–35, 44–46.

17. Reverend Arthur Young, *General View of the Agriculture of the County of Sussex* (London, 1813; reprint, New York, 1970), pp. 471, 208; Anderson, *History of Scottish Forestry*, Vol. 1, p. 343.

18. William Marshall, *Rural Economy of the West of England*, 2 vols. (Reprint of 1796 edition; New York, 1970), pp. 145–152; H. C. Darby, "The Draining of

the Fens, A.D. 1600–1800," in Darby, ed., *An Historical Geography*, p. 455; Young, *General View*, pp. 197–199, 208–209, 218.

19. Anderson, *Scottish Forestry*, p. 507; John Prebble, *The Highland Clearances* (Penguin, 1963), p. 77; Ritchie, *Influence of Man*, p. 323; Anderson, *Scottish Forestry*, p. 347.

20. Rackham, *Ancient Woodland*, p. 88; MacDermot, *The History of the Forest of Exmoor*, pp. 274–275; *Manwood's Treatise of the Forest Law*, 4th ed. (London, 1717).

21. Radley, "Significance of Major Moorland Fires," p. 1255; Anderson, *Scottish Forestry*, Vol. 1, pp. 239, 349; G. R. Miller, "The Management of Heather Moors," *Advancement of Science* 21 (1961), p. 164.

22. Anderson, *Scottish Forestry*, Vol. 1, pp. 493, 659, 507–508; W. R. Fisher, *Dr. Schlich's Manual of Forestry*, Vol. IV, Forest Protection (London, 1907), p. 645; Staffordshire quote from L. Rymer, "The History and Ethnobotany of Bracken," *Botanical Journal of the Linnaean Society* 73 (1976), p. 172; Gilbert White, *The Natural History of Selborne* (London, 1924), p. 32.

23. Anderson, *Scottish Forestry*, Vol. 2, pp. 228–229, 48x.

24. Anderson, *Scottish Forestry*, Vol. 2, p. 351; White, *Natural History*, p. 31.

25. Anderson, *Scottish Forestry*, p. 307.

26. See Carl Sauer, *Northern Mists* (University of California Press, 1968), p. 96 for examples of real and symbolic burning in Iceland. H. C. Darby, "The Economic Geography of England, A.D. 1000–1250," in Darby, *An Historical Geography*, p. 167; Anderson, *Scottish Forestry*, pp. 143–144, 510.

27. Quoted in E.G.R. Taylor, "Camden's England," in Darby, *An Historical Geography*, p. 377.

28. See Young, *General View*, p. 481 for examples of how potential fuels were utilized to other ends.

29. Quoted in Anderson, *Scottish Forestry*, p. 342.

30. See Kayll, "Moor Burning in Scotland," pp. 29–40; Tubbs, *The New Forest*, pp. 139–140. Miller, "Management of Heather Moors," pp. 163–169. The classic account—one of the most fascinating documents in British fire history—is Lord Lovat, "Heather Burning," in Committee of Inquiry on Grouse Disease, *The Grouse in Health and Disease* (London, 1911), Vol. 1, pp. 392–413.

31. For the controversy over straw burning, see R.T.R. Pierce, "Why Farmers Burn Straw," *Span* (February 25, 1982), p. 65; B. Wilton, "Straw: Burn or Incorporate?," *Span* (January 28, 1985); Ministry of Agriculture, Fisheries and Food, *Straw Disposal and Utilisation. A Review of Knowledge* (July 1984); and E. R. Bullen, "Burning Cereal Crop Residues in England," *Tall Timbers Fire Ecology Conference* 13 (Tallahassee, 1973), pp. 223–235.

32. See forestry periodicals such as the *Journal of the Forestry Commission, Forestry, Scottish Forestry*, and Forestry Commission Bulletin No. 14, *Forestry Practice* (many editions), and Forestry Commission, "Forest Fires," Leaflet No. 9; *Journal of the Forestry Commission* 13 (March 1934), pp. 9–29; "58th Annual Excursion—Northumberland," *Scottish Forestry* 9 (1955), p. 120; Sir Alexander Rodger, "Recent Forest Fires," *Journal of the Forestry Commission* 14 (March 1935), p. 20; Mr. Long, *Proceedings, Fourth British Empire Forestry Conference* (Pretoria, 1936), p. 195.

33. See Rymer, "History and Ethnobotany of Bracken," p. 173, and Edward Salisbury, *Weeds and Aliens* (London, 1961), passim.

34. James Frazer is the principal source for European fire myths and rituals: *The

Golden Bough (Macmillan, 1923), pp. 609–657, and *Myths of the Origin of Fire* (Hacker Art Books, 1974).

35. Frazer, *The Golden Bough*, p. 622.

36. Frazer, *The Golden Bough*, pp. 641–642.

37. Quotes from Gaston Bachelard, *Psychoanalysis of Fire*, translated by Alan C. M. Ross (Beacon Press, 1964), p. 60. A wonderful source of quotations from early modern fire science, but otherwise a fatuous book.

38. See Alfred Crosby, *Ecological Imperialism. The Biological Expansion of Europe, 900–1900* (Cambridge University Press, 1986), p. 270.

39. From Robert Hughes, *The Fatal Shore* (Alfred Knopf, 1986), p. 96; Phillip and Miller cited in John Cobley, *Sydney Cove 1788—the First Year of the Settlement of Australia* (Hodder and Stoughton, 1962), pp. 232, 154.

40. "Here, Nature Is Reversed," in Alec H. Chisholm, ed., *Land of Wonder. The Best Australian Nature Writing* (Angus and Robertson, 1964), p. 3.

41. For language, see *The Macquarie Dictionary;* Sidney J. Baker, *The Australian Language,* rev. ed. (Sun Books, 1981); G. A. Wilkes, *A Dictionary of Australian Colloquialisms* (Fontana/Collins, 1978).

42. Stirling quoted in Sylvia J. Hallam, *Fire and Hearth* (Australian Institute of Aboriginal Studies, 1979), p. vii; Wentworth quoted in Robin Bromby, *The Farming of Australia* (Doubleday, 1986), p. 28.

43. From Hughes, *The Fatal Shore,* p. 577; Phillip quoted in John Cobley, ed., *Sydney Cove 1788—the First Year of the Settlement of Australia* (Hodder and Stoughton, 1962), p. 142; Captain William Bligh, *A Voyage to the South Sea* (London, 1792), p. 49.

44. E.H.F. Swain, "Rural Fires," *Australian Forestry Journal* (March 15, 1927), pp. 69–73.

45. Charles Sturt, *Two Expeditions into the Interior of Southern Australia . . . ,* Vol. 1 (London, 1833), p. 29; Louisa Anne Meredith, "A Lady's Journey to Bathurst in 1839," in Mackaness, ed., *Fourteen Journeys,* p. 4. D. H. Lawrence, *Kangaroo* 2 (Penguin, 1950), p. 18. For samples of pioneer stories see E. E. Morris, ed., *Cassell's Picturesque Australia* (Cassell, 1890), Vol. 2, p. 287, and Vol. 3, pp. 46–53.

46. René Lesson, "Journey Across the Blue Mountains, 1824," in Mackaness, ed., *Fourteen Journeys,* p. 152; Mrs. Sophia Stanger, "A Journey from Sydney over the Blue Mountains to Bathurst Forty Years Ago," in Mackaness, ed., *Fourteen Journeys,* p. 260; J. M. Whitfeld, *The Spirit of the Bush Fire* (Sydney, 1898).

47. Reverend R. Collie, "The Influence of Bush Fires on the Distribution of Species," *Transactions, Royal Society N.S.W.* 21 (1887), pp. 103, 105.

48. White, *Tree of Man,* pp. 163–183.

11. RECONNAISSANCE BY FIRE

1. Charles Sturt, *Two Expeditions Into the Interior of Southern Australia . . . ,* Vol. 2 (London, 1833), p. 163.

2. Cited in R. W. Ellis, "The Aboriginal Inhabitants and their Environment," in C. R. Twidale et al., eds., *Natural History of the Adelaide Region* (Royal Society of South Australia, 1976), p. 113, and Derek Whitelock, *Conquest to Conservation* (Wakefield Press, 1985), p. 29.

3. Alfred Searcy, "The Last Voyage of S. S. Ellengowan," in C. C. Macknight, ed., *The Farthest Coast* (Melbourne University Press, 1969), pp. 169, 173; Matthew Flinders, *A Voyage to Terra Australis* . . . (London, 1814), p. 4.

4. G. E. Brockway, "Fire Control Organisation and Fire Fighting Operations in Mundaring District, Conference of Western Australian Foresters," *Australian Forestry Journal* (October 1923), p. 261.

5. Quoted in D. M. Whittaker, *Wangaratta* (City of Wangaratta, 1963), p. 147.

6. "Allan Cunningham's Journal. Botanizing at Parramatta, March, 1817," from photocopies in McArthur collection, source book unidentified, pp. 170–295.

7. James C. Hawker, *Early Experiences in South Australia* (E. S. Wigg and Son, 1899), p. 37.

8. George Cayley, *Reflections on the Colony of New South Wales* (Landsdowne Press, 1966), J.E.B. Cumey, ed., p. 112; Ernest Giles, *Australia Twice Traversed*, Vol. 1 (London, 1889), pp. 215–216.

9. Reverend John Lhotsky, *A Journey from Sydney to the Australian Alps*, Alan E. J. Andrews, ed., (Blubber Head Press, Hobart, 1979), pp. 149–150.

10. James Backhouse, *A Narrative of a Visit to the Australian Colonies* (London, 1843), p. 128.

11. John J. Shillinglow, ed., *Historical Records of Port Phillip. The First Annals of the Colony of Victoria,* new edition, C. E. Sayers, ed., Pioneer Series edition (William Heinemann, Australia, 1972), p. 24; James Fleming, "The Voyage of His Majesty's Colonial Schooner 'Cumberland,' from Sydney to King Island and Port Phillip in 1802–03," idem, p. 24.

12. Domeny de Rienzi, quoted by James Bonwick, *The Last of the Tasmanians* (London, 1870), p. 3. See N.J.B. Plomley, *The Baudin Expedition and the Tasmanian Aborigines 1802* (Hobart, 1983), especially pp. 202–203, for a composite of early fire references.

13. Quoted in McArthur, "Historical Place of Fire in the Australian Environment," *Symposium Papers Presented at the Second Fire Ecology Symposium, Monash University* (Forests Commission—Victoria and Monash University, 1970), p. 7; T. L. Mitchell, *Journal of an Expedition into the Interior of Tropical Australia* (London, 1848), pp. 298–299; Baudin cited in C. W. MacFarlane and L. A. Triebee, *French Explorers in Tasmania and in Southern Seas* (Sydney, 1937), p. 18.

14. Captain Charles Sturt, *Expedition Down the Murrumbidgee and Murray Rivers in 1829, 1830, and 1831,* Vol. II (London, 1833), p. 43; Sturt, *Two Expeditions,* Vol. I, p. 44; Ludwig Leichhardt, *Journal of an Overland Expedition in Australia* . . . (London, 1847), p. 321; Augustus Charles Gregory and Francis Thomas Gregory, *Journals of Australian Explorations* (Brisbane, 1884), p. 143; Giles, *Australia Twice Traversed,* Vol. 1, pp. 314–315; William Carron, *Narrative of an Expedition Undertaken Under the Direction of the Late Mr. Assistant Surveyor E. B. Kennedy* . . . (Sydney, 1849), p. 52; F. Howard and R. H. Edmunds, "McKinlay's Expedition from Escape Cliffs," in Macknight, ed., *The Farthest Coast,* p. 150; Mary Stuart Webster, *John McDouall Stuart* (Melbourne University Press, 1958), pp. 205–206; William Hardman, ed., *The Journals of John McDouall Stuart During the Years 1858, 1859, 1860, 1861, and 1862,* Australiana Facsimile Editions No. 198 (Libraries Board of South Australia, 1975), pp. 416, 451.

15. Hugh Anderson, *The Flowers of the Field, Together with Mrs. Kirkland's Life in the Bush* (Melbourne, 1969), p. 181; Gilmore quoted in Vincent Serventy, *A Continent in Danger* (Andre Deutsch, 1966), p. 170; Marie Bassett, *The*

Hentys (Melbourne University Press, 1962), pp. 405–406; Dr. Leigh cited in J. S. Cumpston, *Kangaroo Island 1800–1836* (Canberra, 1970), p. 107.

16. Examples all from Henry Reynolds, *The Other Side of the Frontier* (Penguin Books, 1982), pp. 108–109, 105–106, 109; Phillip, in *Historical Records of Australia* (Sydney, 1911), Vol. 1, p. 77.

17. James Bonwick, *The Last of the Tasmanians* (London, 1870), pp. 179–180.

18. A good sampling is found in James Bonwick, *The Last of the Tasmanians*, Australiana Facsimile Editions No. 87 (Libraries Board of South Australia, 1969), pp. 51, 117, 122, 119, 107, 141, 179–180. See also N.J.B. Plomley, ed., *Friendly Mission. Tasmanian Journals and Papers of George Augustus Robinson 1829–1834* (Tasmanian Historical Research Association, 1966), p. 508 and passim; Geoffrey Blainey, *Triumph of the Nomads*, rev. ed. (Sun Books, 1982), p. 108; *The Diaries of John Helder Wedge 1824–1835* (Royal Society of Tasmania, 1962), note for December 4, 1827; Reynolds, *Other Side*, p. 94.

19. Collins, quoted in John Cobley, ed., *Sydney Cove—1792* (Hodder and Stoughton, 1962), entry for December 5.

20. From Cobley, ed., *Sydney Cove—1792*, entries for December 3 to December 7.

21. Peter Taylor, *Australia. The First Twelve Years* (George Allen & Unwin, 1982), p. 173.

22. Taylor, *Australia*, p. 173; Governor Hunter to duke of Portland, June 10, 1797, *Historical Records of Australia*, Series 1, Vol. II, pp. 19–20, Orders August 20, 1798, pp. 206–207, Governor Hunter to duke of Portland, September 18, 1798, p. 228, Governor Hunter to duke of Portland, May 1, 1799, p. 351; John Lang, "On the Conflagration of the Forest Around Sydney—November 26th, 1826," *Poems: Sacred and Secular* (Sydney, 1873), p. 104.

23. James C. Hawker, *Early Experiences in South Australia* (Adelaide, 1899), p. 35; Michael Williams, *The Making of the South Australian Landscape* (Academic Press, 1974), p. 138.

24. George J. Webb, "The Bush Fire," *The Swan River News, and Western Australian Chronicle*, No. 43 (July 1, 1847), pp. 151–152. Episode occurred in 1841.

25. *Tasmanian Mail*, January 8, 1898 (p. 12).

26. William Howitt, *Land, Labor and Gold*, Vol. 2 (Boston, 1855), p. 156.

27. Geoffrey Blainey, *The Rush That Never Ended*, 3rd ed. (Melbourne University Press, 1981), p. 106; Geoffrey Blainey, *The Peaks of Lyell*, 4th ed. (Melbourne University Press, 1979), pp. 6–7.

28. Müller, quoted in King, *Influence of Colonization*, pp. 19–20; Howitt, *Land, Labor and Gold*, Vol. 2, p. 153; S. G. Fawcett, "Report on the Ecology of the Hume Catchment," unpublished report for Soil Conservation Authority, Victoria, pp. 1, 10; Howitt, *Land, Labor and Gold*, Vol. 2, p. 190; George S. Perrin, "Forests of Tasmania: Their Conservation and Future Management," Parliamentary Papers No. 48 (1898), p. 13; M. R. Banks and J. B. Kirkpatrick, eds., *Landscape and Man. The Intraction Between Man and Environment in Western Tasmania*, Proceedings of a Symposium Organized by the Royal Society of Tasmania (1977), p. 153; "The Fire at Port Arthur," *The Tasmanian Mail* (January 8, 1898), p. 12.

29. Blainey, *Peaks of Lyell*, p. 100.

12. RED STEERS AND GREEN PICK

1. W.H.L. Ranken, *The Dominion of Australia* (London, 1874), p. 53.   Pastoralism is one of the oldest and most complicated activities of European Australia. Useful introductions include D. N. Jeans, *An Historical Geography of New South Wales to 1901* (Reed Education, 1972); A. Grenfell Price, *Island Continent* (Angus and Robertson, 1972); Stephen H. Roberts, *History of Australian Land Settlement 1788–1920* (Johnson Reprint Corporation, 1964); *The Squatting Age in Australia 1835–1847* (Melbourne University Press, 1964); and Alan Barnard, ed., *The Simple Fleece* (Melbourne University Press, 1962), especially R. M. Moore, "Effects of the Sheep Industry on Australian Vegetation," pp. 170–183. The best summary is G. N. Harrington et al., eds., *Management of Australia's Rangelands* (CSIRO, 1984).

2. Lang quoted in A.G.L. Shaw, "History and Development of Australian Agriculture," in D. B. Williams, ed., *Agriculture in the Australian Economy* (Sydney University Press, 1967), p. 4.

3. Ludwig Leichhardt, *Journal of an Overland Expedition in Australia . . .* (London, 1847), pp. 354–355; T. L. Mitchell, *Journal of an Expedition into the Interior of Tropical Australia* (London, 1848), p. 413; Peter Cunningham, *Two Years in New South Wales,* Australiana Facsimile Editions (Library Board of South Australia, 1966), Vol. 1, p. 24; Harvey Blanks, *The Story of Yea Shire* (Hawthorn Press, 1973), p. 53; Curr, *Recollections of Squatting in Victoria* (Melbourne University Press, 1965; reprint), p. 62; P. L. Brown, ed., *The Narrative of George Russell of Golf Hill . . .* (Oxford University Press, 1935), p. 187.

4. Joan Austin Palmer, ed., *William Moodie, A Pioneer of Western Victoria* (Maryborough, n.d.), pp. 4, 62.

5. Curr, *Recollections,* pp. 160–161.

6. Rogers letters cited in N. A. Wakefield, "Bushfire Frequency and Vegetational Change in South-eastern Australian Forests," *The Victorian Naturalist* 87, no. 6 (June 1970), pp. 153, 157–158.

7. Reverend John Ramsden Wollaston, *Journals and Diaries of Archdeacon of Western Australia, Rev. John Ramsden Wollaston* (Perth, 1948), pub. February 1843; A. W. Howitt, "The Eucalypts of Gippsland," *Transactions, Royal Society of Victoria II,* part I (1890), p. 109; Alex. G. Hamilton, "On the Effect which Settlement in Australia has Produced upon Indigenous Vegetation," *Transactions, Royal Society of New South Wales* (1892), p. 200.

8. E. E. Moore, ed., *Cassell's Picturesque Australia* (London, 1890), Vol. 2, "Murndal"; Rolf Boldrewood, *Old Melbourne Memories* (William Heinemann, 1969; reprint of 1884 ed.), p. 94.

9. James Bonwick, *Western Victoria. Its Geography, Geology and Social Condition* (Geelong, 1858; William Heinemann, 1972), C. E. Sayers, ed., pp. 4–5; Samuel Shumack, *An Autobiography or Tales and Legends of Canberra Pioneers* (Australian National University Press, 1967), p. 8; Reverend James S. Hassall, *In Old Australia* (Brisbane, 1902), p. 50; John Bull, *Early Experiences of Life in South Australia and an Extended Colonial History* (London, 1884), p. 132; Anthony Trollope, *Harry Heathcote of Gangoil* (reprint: Dover Books, 1987), pp. 115, 19.

10. Grazier quoted in R. L. Heathcote, *Back of Bourke* (Melbourne University Press, 1965), p. 16.

11. Blanks, *Yea Shire,* p. 33. For more recent examples of what a bad bushfire

means to pastoralists, see Department of Agriculture, New South Wales, "After the Bush Fires" (Mudgee, Government Printer, 1980), and R. L. Willson, "Assessment of Bush Fire Damage to Stock," *Australian Veterinary Journal* 42 (March 1965), pp. 101–103.

12. Wainwright quoted in Jim Stockton, "Fires by the Seaside: Historic Vegetation Changes in Northwestern Tasmania," *Papers and Proceedings of the Royal Society of Tasmania* 116 (1982), p. 60.

13. Stephen Kessell, "Development of Forest Practice and Management in Western Australia" (Forests Department of Western Australia, n.d.), p. 16; G. E. Brockway, "Conference of Western Australian Foresters," *Australian Forestry Journal* (October 15, 1923), p. 260.

14. A. V. Galbraith, "Forest Fires: Cause and Effect," reprint from *The Gum Tree* (1926), pp. 1–2.

15. *Report of the Royal Commission to Enquire into Forest Grazing* (Victoria, 1946), pp. 12–17, 8.

16. *Report of Royal Commission,* Chapter II.

17. D. M. Thompson, "Forest Fire Prevention and Control in the Cann Valley Forest District" Thesis, University of Melbourne (1952), pp. 2, 3, 25, passim. My account is by and large a series of running paraphrases and glosses on Thompson's thesis.

18. Overviews of settlement and the ecology of tropical pastoralism are contained in B. R. Davidson, *The Northern Myth,* 3rd ed. (University of Melbourne Press, 1972); Alan Powell, *Far Country. A Short History of the Northern Territory* (Melbourne University Press, 1982); Alex Kerr, *Australia's North-West,* rev. ed. (University of Western Australia Press, 1975); Price, *Island Continent,* especially pp. 162–174; F. H. Bauer, *Historical Geography of White Settlement in Part of Northern Australia,* Part 1. Introduction and the Eastern Gulf Region (Divisional Report No. 59/2), Part 2. The Katherine-Darwin Region (Divisional Report No. 64/1) (CSIRO, 1959, 1964); G. C. Stocker and J. J. Mott, "Fire in the Tropical Forests and Woodlands of Northern Australia," in A. M. Gill et al., eds., *Fire and the Australian Biota* (Australian Academy of Science, 1981), pp. 427–442.

19. Bauer, *Historical Geography,* Part 2, p. 96.

20. R. A. Perry, *Pasture Lands of the Northern Territory, Australia,* Land Research Series No. 5 (CSIRO, 1960), p. 41; Charles M. Davis, "Fire as a Land-Use Tool in Northeastern Australia," *Geographical Review* XLIX (1959), p. 552.

21. Davis, "Fire as a Land-Use Tool," pp. 557–558 (close paraphrase); P. Anning, "Pastures for Cape York Peninsula," *Queensland Agricultural Journal* (March–April 1980), p. 161.

22. Davis, "Fire as a Land-Use Tool," pp. 558–559 (again, a close paraphrase).

23. Henry T. Lewis, "Burning the Top End: Kangaroos and Cattle," in Julian Ford, ed., *Fire Ecology and Management in Western Australian Ecosystems.* WAIT No. 14 (Western Australian Institute of Technology, 1985), pp. 21–32.

24. Lewis, "Burning the 'Top End'," p. 28.

25. See, for example, P. Anning, "Pastures for Cape York Peninsula," pp. 148–171. Scientific and trade journals document many examples. As samples, see J. C. Tothill, "A Review of Fire in the Management of Native Pasture with Particular Reference to North-Eastern Australia," *Tropical Grasslands* 5, no. 1 (March 1971), pp. 1–10; R. F. Isbell, "The Distribution of Black Spear Grass (*Heteropogon contortus*) in Tropical Grasslands," *Tropical Grasslands* 3, no.

1 (June 1969), pp. 35–41; and John D. Sturtz, "The Use of Fire in Northern Territory Pasture Establishment," *The Pastoral Review* (July 17, 1970), pp. 563–565.

26. For an overview, see W. K. Hancock, *Discovering Monaro. A Study of Man's Impact on His Environment* (Cambridge University Press, 1972); N. D. Jeans, *Historical Geography of New South Wales to 1901;* H.W.H. King, "Transhumant Grazing in the Snow Belt of New South Wales," *The Australian Geographer* VII (1957–1960), pp. 129–140; and S. G. Fawcett, "Report on the Ecology of the Hume Catchment," unpublished report (Soil Conservation Authority and University of Melbourne, n.d.). Irreplaceable as a source is B. U. Byles, "Report on a Reconnaissance of the Mountainous Park of the River Murray Catchment in New South Wales," Commonwealth Forestry Bureau Bulletin 13 (mimeographed copy, 1932). Supplement these historical surveys with scientific studies, most of which incorporate historical summaries of grazing and burning. The most active researcher, A. B. Costin, consolidated his research into "Alpine and Sub-Alpine Vegetation," in R. H. Groves, ed., *Australian Vegetation* (Cambridge University Press, 1981), pp. 361–377 and "Vegetation of the High Mountains in Australia," in Allen Keast, ed., *Ecological Biogeography of Australia,* Vol. 1 (Dr. W. Junk, 1981); and Stella G. M. Carr and J. S. Turner, "The Ecology of the Bogong High Plains," *Australian Journal of Botany* 7 (1959), pp. 12–33. Perhaps the richest data come from a series of studies published in the *Journal of the Soil Conservation Service of New South Wales* in the 1950s: J. C. Newman, "Burning on Sub-Alpine Pastures," Vol. 10 (1954), pp. 135–140, and "Tumut Catchment Area—Survey of Vegetation and Erosion," Vol. 11 (1955), pp. 95–111; R. T. Morland, "Erosion Survey of the Hume Catchment Area," Vol. 15 (1959), pp. 66–78, 208, 225, 293–297; L. J. Durham, "Indicators of Land Deterioration in Snowy Mountains Catchments," Vol. 15 (1959), pp. 333–350. More recent updates include W. G. Bryant, "Grazing, Burning, and Regeneration of Tree Seedlings in Eucalyptus Pauciflora Woodlands," *Journal of the Soil Conservation Service of New South Wales* 27, no. 2 (1971), pp. 121–135, and "The Effect of Grazing and Burning on a Mountain Grassland, Snowy Mountains, New South Wales," *Journal of the Soil Conservation Service of New South Wales* 29, no. 1 (1973), pp. 29–44.

27. Citations from Fawcett. I follow closely his arguments.

28. Supplement Fawcett and Hancock with Josephine Flood, *Archaeology of the Dreamtime* (Collins, 1983), pp. 202–204 for insight into the highland economy of Aboriginal moth harvesters.

29. Fawcett, "Report on Ecology," p. 11.

30. Byles, "Report on a Reconnaissance," p. 28.

31. Fawcett, "Report on Ecology," p. 13.

32. Statistics from R. H. Anderson, "Presidential Address," *Proceedings of the Linnaean Society of New South Wales* LXVI (1941), p. vii; Mark Twain, *Following the Equator* (New York, 1897), Vol. 1, p. 167; Eric Rolls, *They All Ran Wild. The Story of Pests on the Land of Australia* (Angus and Robertson, 1969), p. 210. For an overview, see P. W. Michael, "Alien Plants," in Groves, ed., *Australian Vegetation,* pp. 44–64. Brief but interesting discussions are available in Geoffrey Bolton, *Spoils and Spoilers. Australians Make Their Environment 1788–1980* (George Allen and Unwin, 1981), and Geoffrey Blainey, *A Land Half Won* (Sun Books, 1983), pp. 300–304.

33. Rolls, *A Million Wild Acres* (Penguin, 1983), pp. 28–29; R. H. Groves and

O. B. Williams, "Natural Grasslands," in Groves, ed., *Australian Vegetation,* pp. 298–299; Rolls, *Million,* pp. 111–114. Examples of how fire interacted with new and old species are found in C. J. Gardener, "Tolerance of Perennating Stylosanthes Plants to Fire," *Australian Journal of Experimental Agriculture and Animal Husbandry* 20 (1980), pp. 587–593; R. T. Parrott and C. M. Donald, "Effect of Length of Season and of Defoliation on the Growth, Water Content and Desiccation of Annual Pastures," *Australian Journal of Experimental Agriculture and Animal Husbandry* 10 (1970), pp. 67–75; M. H. Campbell, "Burning Aids in the Control of Serrated Tussock," *Agricultural Gazette* (June 1961), pp. 311–313; R. Wesley-Smith, "Townsville stylo . . . Effects of Burning," pp. 25–27. Curr, *Recollections,* p. 86.

34.   Rolls, *Million,* pp. 182–183, 246–248.

35.   Rolls, *Million,* p. 1.

36.   Rolls, *Million,* p. 84.

37.   Parrott and Donald, "Effect of Length of Season . . . ," p. 67; Wilshire quoted in Reverend R. Collie, "The Influence of Bush Fires on the Distribution of Species," *Transactions, Royal Society of New South Wales* 21 (1887), p. 107; E. Halpern and C. P. Gabel, "The Fire Hazard in Tasmania," *Tasmanian Journal of Agriculture* (May 1975), pp. 117–119.

38.   Quoted in Eric Rolls, *They All Went Wild,* p. 215.

39.   My account of the rabbit invasion follows Rolls closely. A popular version is in Blainey, *A Land Half Won,* pp. 300–315. For the antecedents, see James Ritchie, *The Influence of Man on Animal Life in Scotland* (Cambridge University Press, 1920), pp. 247–254. Ritchie is worth quoting on livestock as well. "No influence has been more potent in changing the surface features of Scotland and in altering the relationships of the wild life of the country than this forethought bred of the care of domesticated animals" (p. 27).

40.   H. Suijdendorp, "Responses of the Hummock Grasslands of Northwestern Australia to Fire," pp. 417–426, in A. Malcolm Gill et al., eds., *Fire and the Australian Biota* (Australian Academy of Sciences, 1981); E.H.M. Ealey, "Ecology of the Euro in N. W. Australia, I. Environment and Change in Euro and Sheep Populations," *CSIRO Wildlife Research* 12 (1967), pp. 9–25; E.H.M. Ealey and T. M. Richardson, "A Successful Campaign Against the Euro," *Journal of Agriculture of Western Australia* 1 (1960), pp. 757–769; H. Suijendorp, "Pastoral Development and Research in the Pilbara Region of Western Australia," *Australian Rangeland Journal,* 2, no. 1 (1980), pp. 115–123.

41.   James Fenton, *Bush Life in Tasmania Fifty Years Ago* (Hazell, Watson, & Niveny, n.d.), pp. 79–81. The other fundamental sources on the 1851 fires are: Henry Gyles Turner, *A History of the Colony of Victoria* (London, 1904), Vol. 1, pp. 331–334; William Howitt, *Land, Labor and Gold* (Boston, 1855), Vol. 1, pp. 74–75, Vol. 2, pp. 190–191; James Bonwick, *Western Victoria—Its Geography, Geology and Social Condition,* C. E. Sayers, ed., (William Heinemann, 1972); Margaret Kiddle, *Men of Yesterday* (Melbourne University Press, 1962), pp. 182–183; *Fire-Protection in Country Districts,* Eleventh Progress Report of the Royal Commission on State Forests and Timber Reserves (Victoria, 1900), Appendix, pp. 23–24; J. H. Kerr, "Glimpses of Life in Victoria by a Resident," in James Grant and Geoffrey Serle, *The Melbourne Scene 1803–1956* (Melbourne University Press, 1957), pp. 66–67; Boldrewood, *Old Melbourne Memories,* pp. 100–102; John Bull, *Early Experiences of Life in*

South Australia (London, 1884), pp. 311–312; "Victoria's 1851 Bushfire," *Parade* (August 1969), pp. 28–29; and newspaper notices collected by A. G. McArthur, held by the CSIRO Division of Forest Research.

42. Boldrewood, *Old Melbourne Memories*, p. 118; Garryowen [pseudonym] quoted in *Fire-Protection in Country Districts*, Appendix, pp. 23–24; Turner, *History of the Colony*, p. 333; Reverend J.H.L. Zillman, *Past and Present Australian Life* (London, 1889), p. 39; Howitt, *Land, Labor, and Gold*, Vol. 2, pp. 190–191.

43. Bonwick, *Western Victoria*, pp. 2–3.

44. Bonwick, *Western Victoria*, pp. 2–3; Turner, *History of Colony*, p. 333.

45. Boldrewood, *Old Melbourne Memories*, p. 121; *Melbourne Argus* (February 12, 1981).

46. T. L. Mitchell, *Journal of an Expedition into the Interior of Tropical Australia* (London, 1848), p. 413.

47. Mitchell, *Journal*, p. 413; Legge quoted in Stockton, "Fires by the Seaside," p. 57; Mitchell, *Journal*, p. 413.

48. S. R. Morton and M. H. Andrew, "Ecological Impact and Management of Fire in Northern Australia," *Search* 17 (1986), pp. 77–82.

13. BEYOND THE BLACK STUMP

1. Quoted in A.G.L. Shaw, "History and Development of Australian Agriculture," in D. B. Williams, ed., *Agriculture in the Australian Economy* (Sydney University Press, 1967), p. 1.

2. Ludwig Leichhardt, *Journal of an Overland Expedition in Australia from Moreton Bay to Port Essington . . .* (London, 1847), p. 122. For an introduction to Australian agriculture apart from pastoralism, see Shaw, "History and Development of Australian Agriculture"; Robin Bromby, *The Farming of Australia* (Doubleday, 1986); A. Grenfell Price, *Island Continent* (Angus and Robertson, 1972); Geoffrey Blainey, *A Land Half Won*, rev. ed. (Sun Books, 1982). Most regional histories describe agricultural settlement, and I found the following particularly helpful: Michael Williams, *The Making of the South Australian Landscape* (Academic Press, 1974); J.M.R. Cameron, *Ambition's Fire. The Agricultural Colonization of Pre-Convict Western Australia* (University of Western Australia Press, 1981); N. D. Jeans, *An Historical Geography of New South Wales to 1901* (Reed Educational, 1972). Of special interest to fire historians are R. W. Johnson and R. W. Purdie, "The Role of Fire in the Establishment and Management of Agricultural Systems," in A. M. Gill et al., eds., *Fire and the Australian Biota* (Australian Academy of Sciences, 1981), pp. 497–528; R. R. Green, "The Ecological Effects of Fire with Special Reference to its Use in Agriculture," B.Sc. thesis (University of New England, 1971); and John R. Hardison, "Fire and Flame for Plant Disease Control," *Annual Review of Phytopathology* 14 (1976), pp. 355–379. An interesting discussion of fire protection on the farm c. 1900 is R. W. Peacock, "Precautions Against Fires," *Agricultural Gazette of New South Wales* XII (1901), pp. 529–530. More recent surveys include "The Farmer and Fire," *Journal Department of Agriculture Victoria* 67 (1969), pp. 259–265; and David F. Smith, "Fire and Farm Management," *Farm Management* (1971), pp. 76–80. Most recently concerns have shifted from farms per se to the environment of the urban bush, described in Chapter 19.

3.   Geoffrey Bolton, *Spoils and Spoilers* (George Allen & Unwin, 1981), p. 135.
4.   Reverend John Wollaston, *Wollaston's Picton Journal*, Vol. 1, *Journals and Diaries of Archdeacon of Western Australia, Rev. John Ramsden Wollaston* (Perth, 1948), p. 116; Governor King to Hobart, January 11, 1804, *Historical Records of Australia*, Series 1, Vol. V, pp. 74, 277; Williams, *Making the South Australian Landscape*, p. 138.
5.   Quoted in Vincent Serventy, *A Continent in Danger* (Andre Deutsch, 1966), p. 16; James Bonwick, *The Last of the Tasmanians*, Australiana Facsimile Editions No. 87 (Library Board of South Australia, 1969), p. 67; James Backhouse, *A Narrative of a Visit to the Australian Colonies* (London, 1843), p. 181.
6.   James Fenton, *Bush Life in Tasmania Fifty Years Ago* (London, n.d.), p. 108; Wollaston, *Picton Journal*, p. 151.
7.   Alexander Harris, *An Emigrant Family* (London, 1849), p. 402n; "An Emigrant Mechanic," *Settlers and Convicts* (reprint: Melbourne University Press, 1969), p. 16; Wollaston, *Picton Journal*, p. 152; George Mackaness, ed., *The Correspondence of John Cotton, Victorian Pioneer 1842–1849*, Part II (Sydney, 1953), Letter No. 4, Melbourne, October 1843; George Angas, *Savage Life and Scenes in Australia and New Zealand*, 2nd ed., Vol. I (London, 1847), p. 119.
8.   Adelaide reports from Russell Smith, *1850—A Very Good Year in the Colony of South Australia* (Sydney, 1973), p. 10; T. W. Dunn, "Notes on the Dunn Family of Oura, 1850–1923," *Wagga Wagga and District Historical Society Newsletter* (October 1970), p. 5; Wollaston, *Picton Journal*, pp. 151, 56, 4.
9.   Ruse quoted in Robert Hughes, *The Fatal Shore* (Alfred Knopf, 1986), p. 106; James Atkinson, *An Account of the State of Agriculture and Grazing in New South Wales*, facsimile ed. (Sydney University Press, 1975), p. 28.
10.   See George Moore, *A Diary of Ten Years' Eventful Life of an Early Settler in Western Australia* (University of Western Australia Press, facsimile ed.), p. 232; Williams, *Making of the South Australian Landscape*, p. 150; Atkinson, *Account*, pp. 30–31, 21.
11.   Atkinson, *Account*, p. 91.
12.   Fenton, *Bush Life*, p. 108; G. Ross Cochrane et al., "Land Use and Forest Fires in the Mount Lofty Ranges, South Australia," *The Australian Geographer* VIII, no. 4 (March 1962), p. 154; John Slee, *Cala Munnda* ("Shire of Kalamunda", 1979), p. 134; *Report of Conference on Bush and Forest Fires Held at Sydney, 30th March to 1st April, 1926* (New South Wales, 1926), p. 252.
13.   G. J. Rodger, *Report of the Royal Commission Appointed to Enquire into and Report upon the Bush Fires of December, 1960 and January, February and March, 1961 in Western Australia* (Western Australia, 1961), p. 8.
14.   See, for example, Geoffrey Bolton, *A Fine Country to Starve In* (University of Western Australia Press, 1972) for expressions of this attitude well into the twentieth century; quotation from Michael Williams, *The Making of the South Australian Landscape* (Academic Press, 1974), p. 124.
15.   Quoted in Robert Hughes, *The Fatal Shore*, p. 318.
16.   James Backhouse, *A Narrative of a Visit to the Australian Colonies* (London, 1843), p. 114; Fenton, *Bush Life*, p. 53.
17.   E. E. Morris, ed., *Cassell's Picturesque Australia* (London, 1890), Vol. 2, p. 263.
18.   Cameron, *Ambition's Fire*, p. 121; Samuel Shumack, *An Autobiography or*

Tales and Legends of Canberra Pioneers, J. E. and Samuel Shumack, eds. (Australian National University Press, 1967), p. 51; Francis Ratcliffe, *Flying Fox and Drifting Sand* (New York, 1938), p. 65; Cameron, *Ambition's Fire*, p. 121. Good, detailed descriptions of pioneering, including burning off, can be found in Morris, ed., *Cassell's Picturesque Australia*, Vol. 2, pp. 272–278.

19. A. B. Facey, *A Fortunate Life* (Penguin Books, 1981), pp. 195–197; 68–69.

20. W.H.C. Holmes, "Picking Up," in Committee of South Gippsland Pioneer's Association, *Land of the Lyre Bird* (Gordon and Gotch, 1920), pp. 79–133.

21. Edward S. Sorensen, *Life in the Australian Backblocks* (London, 1911), p. 174; *Report on Conference on Bush and Forest Fires*, p. 174.

22. Sorensen, *Life*, pp. 193–194.

23. Williams, *Making of the South Australian Landscape*, p. 144; Sir Hal Colebatch, ed., *A Story of a Hundred Years. Western Australia 1829–1929* (Perth, 1929), pp. 235–236; Williams, *Making of the South Australian Landscape*, p. 150.

24. For a description of brigalow burning, see R. W. Johnson, *Ecology and Control of Brigalow in Queensland* (Queensland Department of Primary Industries, 1964), pp. 34–56, 74–75; Johnson, "Relationship between Burning and Spraying in the Control of Brigalow *(Acacia harpophylla)* Regrowth, Part I. Burning as a Pre-Spraying Treatment," and "Part II. Burning as a Post-Spraying Treatment," *Queensland Journal of Agricultural and Animal Sciences* 34, no. 2 (1977), pp. 179–196; Johnson and P. V. Back, "Influence of Environment on Methods Used to Control Brigalow *(Acacia harpophylla),*" *Queensland Journal of Agricultural and Animal Sciences* 30, no. 3 (1973), pp. 199–211.

25. René Lesson, "Journey Across the Blue Mountains, 1824," in George Mackaness, ed., *Fourteen Journeys Across the Blue Mountains of New South Wales 1813–1841* (Sydney, 1965), p. 160.

26. N. R. McKeown and R. N. McCulloch, "The Effect of Burning and Cultivating Residual Wheat Stubble on the Yield of Oats and Associated Plants," *Australian Journal of Experimental Agriculture and Animal Husbandry* 1, no. 1 (May 1961), pp. 197–203; Soil Conservation Service of New South Wales, *The Environmental Impact of Bushfires*, submission to House of Representatives Standing Committee on Environment and Conservation (July 1983), Appendix p. 13; M. G. Mason et al., "Stubble Burning Helps Control Wimmera Rye Grass," *Journal of the Department of Agriculture, Western Australia* 9, no. 12 (December 1968), pp. 582–583.

27. A. G. McArthur, "Rural Fire Protection," in *Growing Trees on Australian Farms* (Forestry and Timber Bureau, 1968), p. 293.

28. For a synoptic history of sugar cane in Australia see Jeans, *Historical Geography of NSW*, pp. 239–249, and Bromby, *Farming of Australia*, pp. 97–113.

29. "Burning Cane Before Cutting," *The Australian Sugar Journal* 2 (April 7, 1910), pp. 31–32; "Burnt Cane Problems," *The Australian Sugar Journal* 4 (March 6, 1913), pp. 329–330.

30. See J. Wright, "Pre-Harvest Burning of Flooded Cane," *Queensland Bulletin* 36, no. 1, pp. 32–33; and N. P. Cheney and T. E. Just, *The Behaviour and Application of Fire in Sugar Cane in Queensland*, Leaflet No. 115, Forestry and Timber Bureau (Australian Government Publishing Service, 1974). Also interesting is Norman J. King et al., *Manual of Cane-Growing* (American Elsevier, 1965).

31. The primary documentation resides among the many recollections contained in Committee of the South Gippsland Pioneers' Association, *The Land of the*

Lyre Bird. Quotations from T. J. Coverdale, "Recollections and Personal Experiences of the Great Fires of February, 1898," p. 361; George S. Perrin, "Forests of Tasmania: Their Conservation and Future Management," *Parliamentary Papers No. 48* (Hobart, 1898), p. 14.

32. A. W. Elms, "A Fiery Summer," *Land of the Lyre Bird*, p. 307.

33. W.H.C. Holmes, "Recollections and Experiences," *Land of the Lyre Bird*, p. 177–178; J. Western, "Recollections and Experiences," *Land of the Lyre Bird*, p. 276; Elms, "Fiery Summer," p. 309.

34. Elms, "Fiery Summer," p. 309; Holmes, "Recollections and Experiences," pp. 177–178.

35. Elms, "Fiery Summer," p. 311; J. Tainsh, "Bush Fires in Victoria," unpublished report, Forests Commission Victoria (1952), p. 3.

36. Elms, "Fiery Summer," p. 309.

37. W. J. Williams, "Recollections and Experiences," *Land of the Lyre Bird*, p. 298; Elms, "Fiery Summer," p. 308.

38. Western, "Recollections and Experiences," p. 277; Coverdale, "Recollections and Experiences," p. 133; *Fire-Protection in Country Districts*, Eleventh Progress Report of the Royal Commission on State Forests and Timber Reserves (Victoria, 1900), p. 14.

39. Henry Lawson, "Crime in the Bush," Brian Kiernan, ed., *Henry Lawson* (University of Queensland Press, 1976), pp. 212–213.

14. FIRE CONSERVANCY

1. Phillip, quoted in L. E. Carron, *A History of Forestry in Australia* (Australian National University Press, 1985), p. 2; Baron Ferdinand von Müller, *General Information Respecting the Present Condition of the Forests and Timber Trade of the Southern Part of the Colony* (Perth, 1882), p. 23.

2. George S. Perrin, "Forests of Tasmania: Their Conservation and Future Management," Parliamentary Papers No. 48 (Hobart, 1898), p. 4; S. L. Kessell, "The Development of Forest Practice and Management in Western Australia," Forests Department Bulletin No. 43 (Perth, 1939), p. 16; Frederick D'A. Vincent, *Notes and Suggestions on Forest Conservancy in Victoria* (Victoria, 1887), p. 27; *Report of the Conservator of Forests for the Year Ending 30th June, 1890* (Victoria, 1890), p. 15; S. L. Kessell, "Discussion," *Fourth British Empire Forestry Conference. Proceedings* (Union of South Africa, 1936), p. 194.

3. The principal sources for Australian forestry are Carron, *History of Forestry in Australia;* D. E. Hutchins, *A Discussion of Australian Forestry* (Perth, 1916); royal commission on forest questions; the annual reports and other special studies from the forest departments themselves; and ongoing conferences on fire and other questions by the Institute of Foresters of Australia and other professional bodies. An essential periodical is *Australian Forestry* (formerly, *Australian Forestry Journal*). A fundamental chronology of bushfires and institution building is given in R. H. Luke and A. G. McArthur, *Bushfires in Australia* (Australian Government Publishing Service, 1978). Largely anecdotal but useful is Athol Meyer, *The Foresters* (Institute of Foresters of Australia, 1985). The British Empire Forestry Conferences furnish an important political and international context for Australian programs. Other articles of

interest, particularly from the perspective of fire, include: R. H. Luke, "The Role of Foresters in Rural Fire Protection in Australia," *Conferences of the Institute of Foresters of Australia* (Canberra, 1958), pp. 1–2; M. R. Jacobs, "History of the Use and Abuse of Wooded Lands in Australia," *Report of the Thirty-Second Congress, Dunedin*, Australia and New Zealand Societies for the Advancement of Science (January 1957), pp. P132–P139; H. R. Gray, "State Forests of the Empire: Australia," *Empire Forestry Journal* 14, no. 1 (1935), pp. 27–36, 235–249; R. J. Slinn (compiler), *Forest Authorities and Related Legislation in Australia* (Forestry and Timber Bureau, 1964); M. R. Jacobs, "The Development of Forest Policy in Australia," in J. A. Sinden, ed., *The Natural Resources of Australia* (Angus and Robertson, 1972), pp. 244–260; A. G. McArthur, "Fire as an Ecological Tool in Conserving Natural Studies," *Riverina Conference Papers No. 2* (Institute of Riverina Studies, 1969), and "Historical Place of Fire in the Australian Environment," *Symposium Papers Presented at the Second Fire Ecology Symposium* (Monash University, 1970).

4. Owen Jones, "Australia," *Second British Empire Forestry Conference, Proceedings and Resolutions* (Ottawa, 1927), p. 174; Hutchins, *Discussion*, pp. 42–44, 111, 364.

5. Kessell, "Development of Forest Practice," p. 16; *Report of the Conservator of Forests for the Year Ending 30th June, 1890* (Victoria, 1890), p. 15.

6. Hutchins, *Discussion*, pp. 383, 20; M. R. Jacobs, "The Primary and Secondary Leaf-Bearing System of the Eucalyptus," Commonwealth Forestry Bureau Bulletin No. 18 (n.d.), p. 65.

7. J. E. Brown, *Practical Treatise on Tree Culture in South Australia* (Adelaide, 1881), p. 48; Swain, quoted in Carron, *History of Forestry*, p. 101.

8. L. D. Pryor, "Ash Bed Growth Response as a Key to Plantation Establishment on Poor Soils," *Proceedings, Institute of Foresters of Australia, Third General Conference* (1962), p. 2. See also R. N. Cromer, "The Significance of the 'Ashbed effect' in *Pinus Radiata* Plantations," *Appita* 20, no. 4 (1967), pp. 104–112. Considerable controversy attends the role of ash, particularly in wet scleroforest; see Note 20, Chapter 19.

9. H. A. Lindsay, *The Red Bull* (Robert Hale, Ltd., 1959), pp. 36, 66–67.

10. Hutchins, *Discussion*, p. 74.

11. Hutchins, *Discussion*, p. 142.

12. Hutchins, *Discussion*, p. 43; A. V. Gailbraith, "Forest Fires: Cause and Effect," *The Gum Tree* (1926), reprint—no pagination.

13. E. Maxwell, *Afforestation in Southern Lands* (Auckland, 1931), p. 146; S. L. Kessell, "Fire Control" (Perth, n.d.), p. 6.

14. Hutchins, *Discussion*, pp. 24, 53.

15. Jones, "Australia," p. 175; G. E. Brockway, "Fire Control Organisation and Fire Fighting Operations in Mundaring District, Conference of Western Australian Foresters," *Australian Forestry Journal* (October 15, 1923), pp. 261–262.

16. Jones, "Australia," p. 175.

17. Hutchins, *Discussion*, p. 28.

18. Hutchins, *Discussion*, p. 20.

19. E. O. Shebbeare, "Fire Protection and Fire Control in India," *Third British Empire Forestry Conference* (Canberra, 1928), p. 1; B. Ribbentrop, *Forestry in British India* (Calcutta, 1900), pp. 149–150. Shebbeare's is an excellent summary, though it necessarily loses much of the year-by-year richness of the controversy. Complement it with M. P. Ray, "Fire Conservancy in North Ben-

gal," *West Bengal Forests* (Government of West Bengal, 1964), pp. 123–128. For surveys of forestry and fire in British India, see E. P. Stebbing, *The Forests of India*, 3 vols. (London, 1923); Bernhard E. Fernow, *A Brief History of Forestry* (University of Toronto Press, 1907); Ribbentrop, *Forestry in British India*. To appreciate how the ecological context was understood, see R. S. Troup, *The Silviculture of Indian Trees*, 2 vols. (Oxford, 1921). The entire controversy exfoliates nicely within the pages of *The Indian Forester* and of course the annual reports and inspection tours of the various reserved forests, both indispensable sources. An early survey of the problem is contained in D. Brandis and A. Smythies, eds., *Report of the Proceedings of the Forest Conference Held At Simla, October 1875* (Calcutta, 1876), pp. 3–23. Other documents and conference proceedings are housed at the Commonwealth Forestry Institute, Oxford University, England. The Indian Institute Library has a complementary, and with a few exceptions fuller, register of materials, including printed copies of all the working plans for each working circle. Less useful because of its enormity and density were the India Office Records in London.

20. Pearson, quoted in Shebbeare, "Fire Protection," p. 1; Stebbing, *Forests of India*, Vol. 2, p. 542; Pearson, in Shebbeare, "Fire Protection," p. 1.

21. Ribbentrop, quoted in Stebbing, *Forests of India*, Vol. 2, p. 542. An interesting summary of fire protection in the eastern lands is contained in H. P. Smith and C. Purkayastha, *A Short History of the Assam Forest Service 1850–1945* (Assam Government Press, 1946), pp. 21–22.

22. Shebbeare, "Fire Protection," p. 5–6.

23. See Fernow, *A Brief History of Forestry*, p. 345.

24. E.H.F. Swain, *An Australian Study of American Forestry* (Department of Public Lands, Queensland, 1918), p. 5.

25. Bernhard Fernow, *A Brief History of Forestry*, p. 399; Fernow quoted in Andrew Rogers III, *Bernhard Eduard Fernow* (New York, 1968), p. 167. The best summary of the American fire scene is Stephen J. Pyne, *Fire in America: A Cultural History of Wildland and Rural Fire* (Princeton University Press, 1982), pp. 184–198. An abbreviated, but dating version is available in "Fire Policy and Fire Research in the U.S. Forest Service," *Journal of Forest History* 25, no. 2 (April 1981), pp. 64–77.

26. From Plumas Boundary Report of 1904, quoted in Louis Barrett, "A Record of Forest and Field Fires in California from the Days of the Early Explorers to the Creation of the Forest Reserves" (U.S. Forest Service, 1935), p. 48.

27. Elers Koch, "Region One in the Pre-regional Office Days," in *Early Days in the Forest Service*, Vol. 1 (Missoula, Montana, 1944), p. 102; Inman Eldridge, quoted in Elwood R. Maunder, ed., *Voices From the South: Recollections of Four Foresters* (Forest History Society, 1977), p. 17–18; Coert duBois, *Trailblazers* (Stonington, Connecticut, 1957), p. x.

28. The best interpretation of the 1910 fires comes from Pyne, *Fire in America*, pp. 239–252. For a physical description, see Pyne and Philip N. Omi, *Wildland Fires and Nuclear Winters: Selected Reconstructions of Historic Large Fires* (Defense Documentation Center, DNA-TR-85-396, 1986).

29. For the light-burning controversy, see Pyne, *Fire in America*, pp. 100–122.

30. Gifford Pinchot, "Study of Forest Fires and Wood Protection in Southern New Jersey," *Annual Report of Geological Survey of New Jersey* (Trenton, 1898), Appendix, p. 11; Henry Graves, *Report of the Forester for 1913* (Washington, DC, 1914), p. 16; William Greeley, *Forests and Men* (Arno Press, 1972; reprint), and "Foreword," in Stewart Holbrook, *Burning an Empire: The Story*

of American Forest Fires (Macmillan, 1943); E. Deckert, "Forest Fires in North America: A German View," *American Forests* 17 (May 1911), pp. 275, 279.

31. See Coert duBois, *Systematic Fire Protection in the California Forests* (U.S. Forest Service, 1914) and "Organization of Forest Fire Control Forces," *Society of American Forestry Proceedings* 9 (1914), pp. 512–521.

32. S. L. Kessell, "The Damage Caused by Creeping Fires in the Forest," Forests Department Bulletin No. 33 (Perth, 1924), p. 3.

33. *British Empire Forestry Conference, Summary Report and Resolutions* (Ottawa, 1923), Appendix C, Forest Fire Protection, p. 16; *Third British Empire Forestry Conference, Proceedings* (Canberra, 1928) pp. 134–135.

34. Ribbentrop quoted in Owen Jones, "Forestry in Victoria," *Empire Forestry Journal* 5, no. 1 (1926), p. 96. The *Indian Forester* 12, no. 12, reported in 1887 that "the progress of forestry in Australia will be watched with interest in India . . . The question of cheap fire-conservancy in a hot, dry climate, where workmen's wages vary between six and eight shillings a day is a case in point" ("The Forest Question in Australia," p. 574); Swain, *Australian Study,* pp. 5, 61; "Fires in Forests," Forests Department leaflet (Perth, 1921).

35. Jones, "Australia," p. 175; Kessell, "Fire Control," p. 1.

36. Lane-Poole, *Notes on the Forests,* p. 111.

37. Kessell, "Damage Caused by Creeping Fires," p. 4; S. L. Kessell, "Fire Control in Australia," *Third British Empire Forestry Conference, 1928,* pp. 741–748.

38. Kessell, "Damage Caused by Creeping Fires," p. 4.

39. W. R. Wallace, "Fire in the Jarrah Forest Environment," *Journal of the Royal Society of Western Australia* 49, part 2 (1965), pp. 36–38.

40. Harris quoted by R. J. Vines, "The Forest Fire Problem in Australia—A Survey of Past Attitudes and Modern Practice," *Australian Science Teachers' Journal* (November 1968—CSIRO reprint), p. 1; A. C. Harris, "Fire—Master or Servant," paper prepared for Australia and New Zealand Association for the Advancement of Science meeting, 1961 (unpublished copy in Forests Department files), pp. 2–3.

41. Jacobs, "Primary and Secondary Leaf-Bearing Systems of the Eucalypt," p. 67.

42. The principal sources for the 1926 fires include *Report of the Royal Commission of Enquiry on Bush Fires in the State of New South Wales* (Sydney, 1927); *Report of the Advisory Committee on Bush Fires Appointed by the Hon. T. Dunstan, Minister for Lands* (Brisbane, 1927); *Report of Conference on Bush and Forest Fires Held at Sydney, 30th March to 1st April, 1926; Report of Bush Fire Conference* (Forests Commission, Victoria, 1926). Consult, too, the annual reports of the forestry commissions. A summary is contained in Luke and McArthur, *Bushfires in Australia,* pp. 307–308.

43. See major reports plus J. Tainsh, "Bush Fires in Victoria," unpublished report (Forests Commission of Victoria, 1952), pp. 6–7.

44. *Report of the Conference on Bush and Forest Fires Held at Sydney, 30th March to 1st April, 1926,* p. 1.

45. *Report of Conference,* p. 1.

46. *Fire-Protection in Country Districts,* Eleventh Progress Report of the Royal Commission on State Forests and Timber Reserves (Victoria, 1900).

47. Quoted in Meyer, *Foresters,* p. 46; Kessell, "Damage Caused by Creeping Fires," p. 4.

48. Kessell, *Development of Forest Practice,* pp. 16–17. See also M. R. Jacobs, *Growth Habits of the Eucalypts* (Forestry and Timber Bureau, 1955), p. 180.

15. BURNING OFF

1.   The best synthesis is R. H. Luke and A. G. McArthur, *Bushfires in Australia* (Australian Government Publishing Service, 1978), which summarizes each state and territory. Sources for each province are listed with the subchapter that details its history. The annual reports of forestry commissions are the most consistent mines of information, with some help from bushfire councils as they are established. The monumental J. C. Foley, *A Study of Meteorological Conditions Associated with Bush and Grass Fires and Fire Protection Strategy in Australia,* Bulletin No. 38 (Bureau of Meteorology, 1947) remains a fundamental authority for the record of large fires.

2.   Forestry Commission, "Forest Fire Prevention in New South Wales by the Forestry Commission 1916–1966," unpublished report (1967), p. 1.   Reflecting its evolution, there is no systematic study of fire in New South Wales, only a composite of sources. Luke and McArthur, *Bushfires in Australia,* pp. 289–302, and the annual reports of the Forestry Commission are the best single references. See also J. A. Duggin, *Bushfire History of the South Coast Study Area,* CSIRO Division of Land Use Research, Technical Memorandum 76–13 (1976).

3.   S. L. Kessell, "Fire Control in Australia," *Third British Empire Forestry Conference, 1928* (Canberra, 1928), p. 741.

4.   Forestry Commission, "Forest Fire Prevention," p. 1; Patterson cited by R. H. Luke, "Keynote Address," *Proceedings of the Tropical and Arid Fire Symposium* (Darwin, 1971), no separate pagination.

5.   Forestry Commission, *Report for the Year Ended 31st December, 1929,* p. 12; S. L. Kessell, *Forestry in New South Wales. A Report* (Sydney, 1934).

6.   Mr. Hudson, "Discussion," *Fourth British Empire Forestry Conference, Proceedings* (Union of South Africa, 1936), p. 193.

7.   Forestry Commission of New South Wales, *Report for Period 1st July, 1936, to 30th June, 1937,* p. 5.

8.   Attempts to correlate their arrival with sunspots or the southern oscillation have been routinely frustrated. For example, see A. Malcolm Gill, "Forest Fire and Drought in Eastern Australia," pp. 161–186, in Australian Marine Sciences and Technologies Advisory Committee, *Colloquium on the Significance of the Southern Oscillation—El Nino Phenomena and the Need for a Comprehensive Ocean Monitoring System in Australia* (Department of Science and Technology, c. 1985); R. G. Vines, "A Survey of Fire Danger in Victoria (1939–1969)," *Australian Forest Research* 4 (1969), pp. 39–44; R. G. Vines, "Weather Patterns and Bush-fire Cycles in Southern Australia," *CSIRO Division of Chemical Technology Technical Paper* 2 (1974).   Helpful documents for unraveling Victoria's history of fire and bushfire protection include *Victoria's Volunteers against Fire* (Country Fire Authority, n.d.); F. R. Moulds, "Effect of Forest Fires and of Forest Policy on Land Use in Victoria," *Forestry Technical Papers No. 19* (Forests Commission, 1967), pp. 1–11; "Fire Protection," *Handbook of Forestry in Victoria* (Forests Commission, 1928); M. Carver, "Forestry in Victoria (1838–1919)," Volume E (Forests Commission), especially pp. 76–93; R. J. Ritchie, "Bushfire Perspective and Legislation Since 1918," *Victoria's Resources* 13, no. 4 (1972), pp. 6–9; "Brief History of the Country Fire Authority," unpublished report (Country Fire Authority, n.d.); Lieutenant-Colonel T. S. Marshall, *The Victorian Country Fire Service* (Country Fire Brigades Board, 1930).

9.   Charles F. Chapman, Forester to W. E. Ivey, May 4, 1875, quoted in A. R. King, *The Influence of Colonization on the Forests and the Prevalence of Bushfires in Australia* (CSIRO, n.d.), p. 41; Foley, *Study of Meteorological Conditions*, p. 66; other citations from M. Carver, *Forestry in Victoria (1838–1919)*, p. 4.

10.   Quoted in Owen Jones, "Forestry in Victoria," *Empire Forestry Journal* 5, no. 1 (1926), p. 91; Frederick D'A. Vincent, *Notes and Suggestions on Forest Conservancy in Victoria* (Melbourne, 1887), p. 27; *Report of the Conservator of Forests for the Year Ending 30th June, 1890* (Victoria, 1890), p. 14–16.

11.   B. Ribbentrop, *Report on the State Forests of Victoria* (Melbourne, 1896), p. 1; *Fire-Protection in Country Districts*, Eleventh Report of the Royal Commission (Victoria, 1900); Crook, *Report of Acting Conservator of Forests for 1905*, p. 3; H. Mackay, *State Forests Department Report for the Year Ended 30th June, 1914*; D. E. Hutchins, *A Discussion of Australian Forestry* (Perth, 1916), pp. 318–319; Carron, *History of Forestry*, pp. 180–185.

12.   J. Tainsh, "Bush Fires in Victoria," unpublished ms. (Forests Commission, 1949), p. 4; Forests Commission of Victoria, *First Annual Report. Financial Year 1919–1920*.

13.   Foley, *Study of Meteorological Conditions*, p. 80.

14.   Forests Commission of Victoria, *Eighth Annual Report. Financial Year 1926–1927; Statement of Past Fire Protection Policy and Recommendations for Development of Future Policy*, evidence presented to royal commission by Forests Commission of Victoria (1939), p. 26. On aircraft patrols, see "Use of the Aeroplane in Forest Ranging," *Australian Forestry Journal* (April 15, 1921), p. 101; Conrad Wood, "Getting up in the Air about Trees," *Forest and Timber* 10, no. 3, pp. 1–2; Galbraith, "Discussion," *Fourth British Empire Forestry Conference* (Union of South Africa, 1936), p. 195.

15.   Forests Commission of Victoria, *Handbook of Forestry in Victoria* (Melbourne, 1928), p. 52.

16.   Marshall, *Victorian Country Fire Service*, p. 7.

17.   Forests Commission of Victoria, *Eighth Annual Report. Financial Year 1926–1927*.

18.   Quoted in Carron, *History of Forestry*, p. 201.

19.   *Statement of Past Fire Protection Policy and Recommendations for Development of Future Policy*, evidence presented to royal commission by Forests Commission of Victoria (1939), p. 42.

20.   On Victoria's endless comparison with California, Richard White cites comments in the *Age* on the occasion of the founding of the Melbourne Public Library: "Victoria should not be content to be a single step behind America" *(Inventing Australia* [George Allen and Unwin, 1981], p. 61).

21.   Quoted in James R. Hancock, "The Foresters—The Community and Fire," *Eighth Triennial Conference, Institute of Foresters of Australia*, Vol. 1—Session Papers (Adelaide, 1977), p. 5. Basic sources for South Australian bushfire protection history include "Brief History of the Country Fire Authority," unpublished report (Country Fire Authority, n.d.); N. B. Lewis, *A Hundred Years of State Forestry. South Australia: 1875–1975* (Woods and Forests Department, 1975); G. Ross Cochrane et al., "Land Use and Forest Fires in the Mount Lofty Ranges, South Australia," *The Australian Geographer* VIII, no. 4 (March 1962), pp. 143–160; Michael Paige, *Muscle and Pluck Forever! The South Australian Fire Services 1840–1982* (South Australian Metropolitan Fire Service, 1983); and, for insight into the general history of clearing and

settlement, Michael Williams, *The Making of the South Australian Landscape* (Academic Press, 1972).

22. For examples of plantings and grazing, see *Annual Progress Report upon State Forest Administration in South Australia for the Year 1926–27* (Adelaide, 1927), p. 7; *Annual Progress Report upon State Forest Administration in South Australia for the Year 1915–16* (Adelaide, 1916).

23. *Forests Board Annual Report and Financial Statement for 1878–79* (Adelaide, 1879), p. 36; *Annual Progress Report upon State Forest Administration in South Australia for the Year 1890–91* (Adelaide, 1891), p. 9.

24. *Annual Progress Report upon State Forest Administration in South Australia for the Year 1926–27* (Adelaide, 1927), p. 7; Hancock, "The Forester—The Community and Fire," p. 9. For the record of major fires see Foley, *Study of Meteorological Conditions,* pp. 151–160, and Luke and McArthur, *Bushfires in Australia,* pp. 275–288. *Annual Report of the Woods and Forests Department for the Year 1933–34* (Adelaide, 1934), p. 9.

25. A. Ingles, "Fire," Working Paper 2, *Environmental Impact Statement on Tasmanian Woodchip Exports Beyond 1988* (Tasmanian Forestry Commission, n.d.), p. 22. Studies that present historical overviews of Tasmanian fires include Jim Stockton, "Fires by the Seaside: Historical Vegetation Changes in Northwestern Tasmania," *Papers and Proceedings of the Royal Society of Tasmania* 116 (1982), pp. 53–63; D. M. Chambers and C. G. Brettingham-Moore, *The Bush Fire Disaster of 7th February, 1967* (Tasmania, 1967); D. M. Chambers et al., *Fire Prevention and Suppression* (Tasmania, 1967).

26. Matthew Flinders, *A Voyage to Terra Australis . . . ,* 2 vols. (London, 1814), Vol. 1, p. clv.

27. Mary Nicholls, ed., *Traveller Under Concern. The Quaker Journals of Frederick Mackie on his Tour of the Australasian Colonies 1852–1855* (Launceston, 1973), pp. 2, 4–5.

28. James Fenton, *Bush Life in Tasmania Fifty Years Ago* (London, n.d.), pp. 108–109; James Backhouse, *A Narrative of a Visit to the Australian Colonies* (London, 1843), p. 114; Ingles, "Fire," pp. 20–23.

29. Most of the published records take the form of newspaper reports; I relied on those gathered by the late A. G. McArthur and those stored in the files of the Tasmanian Forestry Commission. See also the general accounts of the 1898 fires in Gippsland, Note 30, Chapter 13; stories of 1897 fires derived from excerpts of the "Mercury" saved in the files of the Forestry Commission; some repeated in Hutchins, *Discussion,* p. 32. Hutchins is especially vitriolic—and interesting—about the Tasmanian fire scene.

30. Excerpts from "Mercury," p. 11 of composite files; Hutchins, *Discussion,* pp. 32–33, 335–339.

31. Hutchins, *Discussion,* p. 339; *Report of the Forestry Department for the Year Ended 30th June, 1932* (Tasmania, 1932); excerpts from "Mercury" for 1927, unpublished files in Forestry Commission.

32. *Report of the Forestry Department for the Year Ended 30th June, 1934* (Tasmania, 1934), pp. 5–6.

33. S. L. Kessell, *Report on the Forests and Forestry Administration of Tasmania* (Tasmania, 1945), pp. 5, 13.

34. Francis Ratcliffe, *Flying Fox and Drifting Sand* (McBride, 1938), p. 65; E.H.F. Swain, "Rural Fires," *Australian Forestry Journal* (March 15, 1927), pp. 70–71.

35. Anthony Trollope, *Harry Heathcote of Gangoil* (Dover Publications, 1987;
     reprint), p. 107.
36. E.H.F. Swain, *An Australian Study of American Forestry* (Brisbane, 1918), p.
     3; Hutchins, *Discussion*, p. 297.
37. *Annual Report of the Director of Forests for the Year Ended 30th June, 1920*
     (Queensland Forest Service), p. 31.
38. *Annual Report of the Director of Forests for the Year Ended 30th June, 1920*,
     p. 31.
39. *Report of the Advisory Committee on Bush Fires* (Brisbane, 1927), pp. 2,
     5, 12.
40. *Report of the Director of Forests for the Year Ended 30th June, 1937.*
41. Swain, "Rural Fires," pp. 72–73.
42. See R. J. Underwood and P.E.S. Christensen, *Forest Fire Management in West-
     ern Australia*, Special Focus No. 1 (Forests Department of Western Australia,
     1981), pp. 12–13; W. R. Wallace, "Fire in the Jarrah Forest Environment,"
     Journal of the Royal Society of Western Australia 49, part 2 (1965), p.
     34.   The literature on Western Australian fire protection is exceptionally rich.
     Luke and McArthur, *Bushfires in Australia*, pp. 239–250, captures a fraction.
     Consult, in addition, "Bush Fires Board of Western Australia. Historical Back-
     ground," unpublished manuscript (Bush Fires Board, 1982); D.W.R. Stewart,
     Forest Administration in Western Australia 1929–1969 (unpublished ms.,
     Forests Department, 1973); W. R. Wallace, "Fire in the Jarrah Forest Environ-
     ment," *Journal of the Royal Society of Western Australia* 49, part 2 (1965),
     pp. 33–44; Forests Department, *Fifty Years of Forestry in Western Australia*,
     supplement to 1968–69 annual report; J. R. Robertson "The Origins of Forestry
     Administration in Western Australia: 1829–1929," (unpublished ms., Forests
     Department, 1959); G. J. Rodger, *Report of the Royal Commission . . .*
     (Western Australia, 1961); Roger Underwood, ed., *Leaves From the Forest.
     Stories from the Lives of West Australian Foresters* (Perth, 1987); S. L. Kes-
     sell, "The Development of Forest Practice and Management in Western Austra-
     lia," Forests Department Bulletin No. 43 (1928); James O'Donnell, "Forest
     Fire Control in Western Australia," *Australian Forestry* IV, no. 1 (reprint, no
     pagination). Match these studies with general political and environmental his-
     tories of the region such as G. C. Bolton, *A Fine Country to Starve In* (Univer-
     sity of Western Australia Press, 1972); C. T. Stannage, ed., *A New History of
     Western Australia* (University of Western Australia Press, 1981); and Brian
     DeGaris, et al., *European Impact on the West Australian Environment 1829–
     1979* (University of Western Australia Press, 1979). Not to be overlooked is
     A. B. Facey, *A Fortunate Life* (Penguin Books, 1981), with its detailed depic-
     tions of frontier life.
43. Scott Nind, "Description of the Natives of King George's Sound (Swan River
     Colony) and Adjoining Country," *Royal Geographical Society* 1 (1831), p.
     28; G. C. Bolton and D. Hutchinson, "European Man in Southwestern Austra-
     lia," *Journal of the Royal Society of Western Australia* 56, parts 1 and 2
     (1973), p. 59.
44. Baron Ferdinand von Müller, *Report on the Forest Resources of Western Aus-
     tralia* (London, 1879), p. 22, and *General Information Respecting the Present
     Condition of the Forests and Timber Trade of the Southern Part of the
     Colony* (Perth, 1882), p. 24; S. L. Kessell, "The Development of Forest Prac-
     tice and Management in Western Australia," Bulletin No. 43 (1939),
     p. 16.

45. Hutchins, *Discussion*, p. 107.

46. S. L. Kessell, "Fire Control" (Forests Department, n.d.), p. 1; S. L. Kessell, "Fire Control in Australia," *Third British Empire Forestry Conference, 1928*, p. 741.

47. *Annual Report of the Woods and Forests Department for the Year Ended 31st December, 1917.*

48. *Annual Report of the Woods and Forests Department for the Year Ended 31st December, 1916*, p. 4; *Report of the Forests Department for the Year Ended 30th June, 1924*, p. 11.

49. *Report on the Operations of the Forests Department for the Year Ended 30th June, 1927*, p. 26.

50. See *Bush Fires*, Bulletin No. 52 (Forests Department, c. 1938–1939).

51. Carron, quoted in Meyer, *The Foresters*, p. 55.

16. WHEN THE BILLY BOILED

1. J. A. Froude, *Oceana* (1886), quoted in Geoffrey Sherington, *Australia's Immigrants* (George Allen and Unwin, 1980), p. 58.

2. Henry Mayhew, quoted in M. B. and C. B. Schedvin, "The Nomadic Tribes of Urban Britain: A Prelude to Botany Bay," in John Carroll, ed., *Intruders in the Bush. The Australian Quest for Identity* (Oxford University Press, 1985), p. 82.

3. Francis Adams, *The Australians. A Social Sketch* (London, 1893), p. 165. For American literary and cultural uses of the frontier, see Henry Nash Smith, *Virgin Land* (1950), and Roderick Nash, *Wilderness and the American Mind*, 3rd ed. (Yale University Press, 1983).

4. See Richard White, *Inventing Australia* (George Allen and Unwin, 1981); Vance Palmer, *The Legend of the Nineties* (Melbourne University Press, 1963); John Carroll, ed., *Intruders in the Bush. The Australian Quest for Identity* (Oxford University Press, 1982); Geoffrey Serle, *From Deserts the Prophets Come. The Creative Spirit in Australia 1788–1972* (William Heinemann, 1973).

5. Palmer, *The Legend of the Nineties*, p. 50.

6. A. W. Howitt, "The Eucalypts of Gippsland," *Transactions, Royal Society of Victoria* II, part 1 (1890), pp. 109–113; Alexander G. Hamilton, "On the Effect Which Settlement in Australia Has Produced upon Indigenous Vegetation," *Journal and Proceedings of the Royal Society of New South Wales* XXVI (1892), pp. 178–233; Samuel Dixon, "The Effects of Settlement and Pastoral Occupation in Australia upon the Indigenous Vegetation," *Transactions and Proceedings and Report of the Royal Society of South Australia* XV (1892), pp. 195–206; Richard Helms, "The Australian Alps, or Snowy Mountains," *Journal of the Royal Geographical Society of Australasia* VI, no. 4 (1896), pp. 75–96.

7. Dixon, "Effects of Settlement," pp. 197, 205; Edward Curr, *Recollections of Squatting in Victoria* (Melbourne University Press, 1965; reprint), p. 88; Hamilton, "On the Effect," p. 203; A. M. Laughton and T. S. Hall, *Handbook to Victoria*, British Association for the Advancement of Science, Australian Meeting (Melbourne, 1914), p. 312.

8. The starting point for any review of the 1939 fires remains Leonard E. B. Stretton, *Report of the Royal Commission . . .* Useful materials to amplify

points or extend them into related areas include W. S. Noble, *Ordeal by Fire. The Week a State Burned Up* (Hawthorn Press, 1977); A. V. Galbraith, *Statement of Past Fire Protection Policy and Recommendations for Development of Future Policy* (Forests Commission of Victoria, 1939); C. E. Lane-Poole, "Transcript of Evidence Given before Royal Commission . . . 1 April 1939"; A. V. Galbraith, "Proceedings of the Victorian Bush Fire Conference, August, 1939," *Australian Forestry* IV (1939), pp. 79–81; S. L. Kessell, letter to D. R. Moore, May 26, 1939 (copy in Forests Department files); A. C. Shedley, "Forest Areas in Victoria," unpublished report, Forests Department of Western Australia (1939); Bush Fire Control Committee, "Bush Fire Control: Australian Capital Territory," March 16, 1939, and "Report on the Forest Fires. 11–15th January, 1939," unpublished ms.; Queanbeyan Branch of the Graziers' Association of New South Wales and Australian Capital Territory Rural Lessees' Association, "Bush Fire Fighting Organization," unpublished ms. (1939); "Note on the 1939 Bush Fires," Forestry Commission of Tasmania, unpublished ms. (1939); "Bush Fire Legislation, 1939," *Victorian Forester* 2, no. 4 (1940), pp. 13–15; J. H. Chinner, "Some Meteorological Observations Relating to the Bush Fire Season 1938–39," *Victorian Forester* 2, no. 4 (1940), pp. 15–19; "Hills Fire Relief Fund. 1939 Fires Report," unpublished ms. (copy, 1953), South Australia; "Interstate Conference . . . to Discuss Methods for the Prevention of Bush Fires and for the Protection of Lives in Forest Areas," agenda for meeting (1939). The annual reports of the forestry commissions are, of course, invaluable. For the obsessed a multivolume set of coroner reports is housed in the Victoria Forests Commission library, Melbourne.

9.   Stretton, *Report*, p. 5.
10. Noble, *Ordeal by Fire*, p. 10.
11. Stretton, *Report*, p. 5.
12. Stretton, *Report*, p. 15. For the opinion of graziers, see Tor Holth with Jane Barnaby, *Cattlemen of the High Country* (Rigby, 1980), p. 99, and Queanbeyan Branch of the Graziers' Association of New South Wales and Australian Capital Territory Rural Lessees' Association, "Bush Fire Fighting Organization," attached to letter from J. G. Thomas, Feb 17, 1939, to Bush Fire Council of A.C.T. (in Bush Fire Council files).
13. Stretton, *Report*, p. 14.
14. C. E. Lane-Poole, "Transcript of Evidence Given before Royal Commission . . . 1 April 1939," p. 2382.
15. Stretton, *Report*, p. 11.
16. Lane-Poole, "Transcript," p. 2383.
17. Quoted in Serle, *From Deserts*, pp. 125, 135.
18. D. E. Hutchins, *A Discussion of Australian Forestry* (Perth, 1916), p. 24; W. Russell Grimwade, "Discussion," *Proceedings, Third British Empire Forestry Conference, 1928* (Canberra, 1928), p. 136.
19. Noble, *Ordeal*, p. 31; Stretton, *Report*, p. 11.

17. THE TWO FIRES

1.   Curtin quoted in Norman Harper, *A Great and Powerful Friend. A Study of Australian American Relations Between 1900 and 1975* (University of Queensland Press, 1987), p. 105.

2. Forde quoted in Geoffrey Sherington, *Australia's Immigrants 1788–1978* (George Allen and Unwin, 1980), p. 127.

3. For studies on recent demographics of relevance to land use and bushfires, see I. H. Burnley, ed., *Urbanization in Australia. The Post-War Experience* (Cambridge University Press, 1974), and *Population, Society and Environment in Australia* (Shillington House, 1982).

4. Sources for the fires contained in newspaper clippings collected by A. G. McArthur, now on file with the CSIRO Division of Forest Research, and O. M. Whittaker, *Wangaratta* (Council of City of Wangaratta, 1963), pp. 147–148; *Hamilton Spectator* (Saturday, January 15, 1944), p. 5. See also State Electricity Commission of Victoria, *Report of the Yallourn Bush Fire Protection Committee* (December 1944); "The 1944 Bush and Grass Fires," *S.E.C. Magazine* (March 1944), reprint with *First and Interim Report on Bush Fire at Yallourn on 14th February, 1944, with Particular Reference to Report of Royal Commission of Inquiry—March, 1944.* The fires that raged in the mountains are recalled in Midgley Ogden, "My Life in the Forests of Victoria and the Timber Industry (1914–1976)," unpublished ms., Forests Commission of Victoria, pp. 127–130. See also the annual report of the Forests Commission.

5. See *Melbourne Argus*, notes collected by A. G. McArthur, filed with CSIRO Division of Forest Research; G. J. Barrow, "A Survey of Houses Affected in the Beaumaris Fire, January 14, 1944," *CSIR Journal* 18 (1945), pp. 27–28; Leonard E. B. Stretton, *Report of the Royal Commission to Enquire into the Place of Origin and the Causes of the Fires Which Commenced at Yallourn on the 14th Day of February, 1944 . . .* (Melbourne, 1944), pp. 5, 8.

6. The best summary of the institutional reorganization that followed the war is R. H. Luke and A. G. McArthur, *Bushfires in Australia* (Australian Government Publishing Service, 1978). For Stretton's sequel, see Leonard E. B. Stretton, *Report of the Royal Commission to Enquire into Forest Grazing* (Victoria, 1946).

7. Mr. Ryle, "Discussion," *Proceedings, Seventh British Commonwealth Forestry Conference, 1957,* pp. 231–232.

8. R. H. Luke, "Report of Forest Fire Control Training Program in U.S.A. during 1951," unpublished ms., Forests Commission of New South Wales. For an interesting illustration of how British and Australian opinions were diverging, see C. A. Connell, "American Commentary," *Journal of the Forestry Commission* 22 (1951), pp. 4–11, which reported to the British Forestry Commission on the same tour.

9. R. H. Luke, "Recent Fire Protection Developments in N.S.W.," (undated ms.), p. 18; O. M. Thompson, "Forest Fire Prevention and Control in the Cann Valley Forest District" (University of Melbourne, thesis, September 1952), pp. 68–69.

10. Luke, "Report of Forest Fire Control Training Program," p. 40 (end of Part 1).

11. "Fire Control Conference," *Australian Forestry* 13 (1949), pp. 1–2. For a summary of how the conferences developed, see R. H. Luke, "Keynote Address," *Proceedings of the Tropical and Arid Fire Symposium* (Darwin, 1971). A full list of those conferences for which I have located published proceedings is given in the Bibliographic Essay.

12. Forests Commission, *Report on Forest Fire Protection in New South Wales During the 1951–52 Fire Season,* supplement to annual report (Sydney, 1952), pp. 6–9. See also *Report of the Forestry Commission on Fire Protection of the Hume-Snowy Group of Catchment Areas* (1951).

13. General summaries of these years can be found in R. H. Luke, "Fire Plan for Unprotected Areas in North Eastern N.S.W." (unpublished ms., 1961) and "Recent Fire Protection Developments in N.S.W." (unpublished ms., n.d.). A concise overview is available in Luke and McArthur, *Bushfires in Australia,* pp. 297–302. Also useful is R. H. Luke, "A Brief History of the N.S.W. Bush Fire Committee," *Bush Fire Bulletin* (winter 1970), pp. 13–24. For a local brigade's experiences of the Leura catastrophe, see *A History of the Blaxland Volunteer Bushfire Brigade,* the years of 1957–58.

14. James O'Donnell, "Bush Fire Prevention and Suppression in Western Australia," (unpublished ms., 1941), p. 1. For postwar developments in Western Australia, see also James O'Donnell, "Forest Fire Control in Western Australia," *Australian Forestry* 4, no. 1 (1951), pp. 15–21; A. B. Hatch, "The Effect of Frequent Burning on the Jarrah (Eucalyptus marginata) Forest Soils of Western Australia" *Journal of the Royal Society of Western Australia,* 42 part 4 (1959), pp. 97–100; D.W.R. Stewart, "Some Aspects of Fire Control in Western Australia," *Australian Forestry* (1951), pp. 172–178; W. R. Wallace, "Fire in the Jarrah Forest Environment," *Journal of the Royal Society of Western Australia* 49, part 2 (1965); A. C. Harris and W. R. Wallace, "Controlled Burning in Western Australian Forest Practice," (unpublished ms., n.d.); O.W.R. Stewart, "Forest Administration in Western Australia 1929–1969," unpublished ms. (Forests Department); G. J. Rodger, *Report of the Royal Commission Appointed to Enquire into the Report upon the Bush Fires of December, 1960 and January, February, and March, 1961 in Western Australia* (Western Australia, 1961).

15. Wallace, "Fire in the Jarrah Forest," p. 40.

16. Harris, "Fire—Master or Servant," p. 1.

17. Harris, "Fire—Master or Servant," p. 5.

18. My sources of biographical information on Luke include "N. W. Jolly Medal, 1980 Award: Robert Henry Luke," *Australian Forestry* 44, no. 2 (1981), R. H. Luke, "Sixty Years of Forestry," unpublished address (1988), and two delightful days as a guest of Harry Luke at his house.

19. R. H. Luke, "Recent Fire Protection Developments in N.S.W.," unpublished report (Forestry Commission of N.S.W., n.d.), p. 14; R. H. Luke, "Fuel Reduction," unpublished report (n.d.), pp. 2, 1.

20. R. H. Luke, "The Bush Fire Problem in Australia," unpublished ms., prepared for A. R. King (n.d.), p. 5.

21. For descriptions of the fires, see Rodger, *Report of the Royal Commission,* and Luke and McArthur, *Bushfires in Australia,* pp. 245–246; and for an analysis of their damages, see G. B. Peet and A. J. Williamson, "An Assessment of Forest Damage from the Dwellingup Fires in Western Australia," *I.F.A. 5th Conference* (Perth, 1968).

22. Rodger, *Report of the Royal Commission,* pp. 7, 59.

18. ANTIPODEAN FIRE

1. A. C. Harris, "Fire—Master or Servant," prepared for Australia and New Zealand Association for the Advancement of Science annual meeting (1961), pp. 1, 6.

2. Ray Bean, "Fire Control in Western Australian Forests," *Walkabout* (July 1, 1948), p. 13.

3.   "Mayanup fire," *W.A. Firefighter* (May 1958), p. 11; A. G. McArthur, "Plotting Ecological Change," in David Dufty et al., eds., *Historians at Work. Investigating and Recreating the Past* (Hicks Smith and Sons, 1973), p. 44.

4.   Again, the best (and most concise) source for this eruption of institution building is R. H. Luke and A. G. McArthur, *Bushfires in Australia* (Australian Government Publishing Service, 1978). Necessary supplements are the annual reports of forestry commissions, bushfire councils, and country fire services. Also informative is *The Bushfire Problem in Public Lands. Proceedings of a Seminar Conducted at Leura, NSW* (National Trust of Australia, 1966). For the role of foresters, consult R. H. Luke, "Role of Foresters in Fire Protection in Australia," in *Conference of the Institute of Foresters of Australia* (Canberra, 1958), pp. 1–2; R. H. Luke, "Fire and the Conservation of Natural Resources in New South Wales," *Journal of the Soil Conservation Service of New South Wales* 19 (1963), pp. 37–45; W. E. Hurditch, "The Influence of Foresters on Bush Fire Control in New South Wales," *Seventh Triennial Conference*, Institute of Foresters of Australia (Caloundra, 1974), Vol. 1, pp. 354–364; James R. Hancock, "The Foresters—The Community and Fire," *Eighth Triennial Conference*, Institute of Foresters of Australia (Adelaide, 1977), Vol. 1, pp. 1–29.

5.   Special articles relevant to Victorian fire protection include *Victoria's Volunteers against Fire* (Country Fire Authority, n.d.); "Brief History of the Country Fire Authority," unpublished report (C.F.A., n.d.); A. G. Pitfield, "The Country Fire Authority and Fire Control," *Victoria's Resources* 12, no. 2 (June–August 1970), pp. 12–16; P. S. Lang, *From Beater and Knapsack . . . History of the Lismore Rural Fire Brigades' Group 1944–1985* (Lismore, Victoria, 1987).

6.   Useful addenda to the fire history of New South Wales, apart from annual reports of the principal institutions, include *Bungaree Rural Fire Brigade, 1942–1982* (Bungaree, 1982); *History of Blaxland Volunteer Bushfire Brigade* (n.d.); R. H. Luke, "History of N.S.W. Bush Fire Committee," *Bush Fire Bulletin* 8, no. 2 (June 1970), pp. 13–23; R. H. Luke, "Fire Plan for Unprotected Areas in North Eastern N.S.W.," report to Forestry Commission (1961); R. W. Raue, "Bushfire Fighting Organization in New South Wales," in Royal Aeronautical Society, *Application of Aircraft in Bushfire Control* (1969), 13 pp; Co-ordinating Committee, Bush Fire Council of N.S.W., *A Guide to Planning Co-operative Bush Fire Suppression* (n.d.).

7.   Special materials for South Australian bushfire protection include Michael Page, *Muscle and Pluck Forever! The South Australian Fire Services 1840–1982* (South Australian Metropolitan Fire Service, 1983) and *Report of the Working Party . . . Proposed Re-organization of Country Fire Services in the State*, Parliamentary Paper 106 (Adelaide, 1973).

8.   The major documents for Western Australia have been described in Note 14, Chapter 17. Two additional guides to the annual reports literature are "Bush Fire Control Organization in Western Australia" (January 1986) and "Bush Fires Board of Western Australia, Historical Background" (December 1982), both published by the Bush Fires Board.

9.   Helpful in understanding the postwar developments in Queensland is "The Rural Fires Act 1946–1977" (Rural Fires Board, n.d.), 14 pp.

10.   Most of the pertinent reviews follow the 1967 Hobart fires and are listed under that rubric, Note 2, Chapter 19. A subsequent analysis of some interest, however, is Board of Inquiry, *Fire Protection Arrangements in the State of Tasmania* (Hobart, 1977).

11. For the origins of A.C.T.'s Bush Fire Council, see L. D. Pryor, "The Bush Fire Problem in the Australian Capital Territory," *Australian Forestry* 4, no. 1 (1939), pp. 33–38; D. W. Shoobidge, "Fire Control in the Australian Capital Territory," *Australian Forestry* 13, no. 1 (1949), pp. 8–14; and the early minutes of the council, preserved in its files. A more recent survey is contained in Phillip Shepherd, "The Adequacy of Fire Protection in the Australian Capital Territory," B.Sc. (Forestry) thesis (Australian National University, 1972).

12. For the Northern Territories, see R. H. Luke, ed., *Tropical and Arid Fire Symposium* (Darwin, 1972); R. J. Hooper, "Fire Control in the Northern Territory," *Turnoff* 1 (1969), pp. 47–50; P. E. Leske, "Bushfire Control at Roper River," Working Paper 65/689 (Bureau of Meteorology, 1966).

13. Luke and McArthur, *Bushfires in Australia*, pp. 20, 22.

14. Survey histories and basic documents on aerial firefighting include Royal Aeronautical Society, *Application of Aircraft in Bushfire Control* (1969); R. H. Luke, "Report on an Investigation into the Use of Aerial Tankers during the Winter of 1958," unpublished report (Forestry Commission of N.S.W.); R. Rawson and B. Rees, *A Review of Firebombing Operations in Victoria* (Forests Commission, Victoria, 1983); Conrad H. Wood, "Air Attack on Bushfires—Australia, Canada and United States of America," *Fourth Australian National Conference on Fire* (1973, reprint); V. P. Cleary, "Air Operations for Fire Control," Position Paper for the Meeting of Research Working Group No. 6, *Fire Management Research* (1977); A. Hodgson, "An Air Attack System for Forest Fires in Victoria," *Australian Forestry* 32, no. 4 (November 1968), pp. 226–232 and "Applying Perspective to Air Attack on Fires," *Aircraft* 48, no. 7 (1969), pp. 20–21; E. L. Ellwood, "Notes on the Suppression of Bushfires from Aircraft," *Australian Forestry* 12 (1948), pp. 127–133; V. P. Cleary, "Aerial Attack on Rural Fires: Chemicals and Bentonites," unpublished report; Conrad Wood, "Plane Forestry," *Victoria's Resources* (March 1975), pp. 26–29; Alan Don, "A Study of the Use of Agricultural Aircraft and Fire Retardants in Australian Fire Control," B.Sc (Forestry) thesis (Australian National University, 1972). Only a tiny historical review is contained in I. T. Loane and J. S. Gould, *Aerial Suppression of Bushfires. Cost-Benefit Study for Victoria* (CSIRO National Bushfire Research Unit, 1986).

15. See Flight Lieutenant H.R.W. Archer and Flight Lieutenant R. W. Saunders, "Bush Fire Control" (Aircraft Research and Development Unit, Laverton, 1948); Squadron Leader K. V. Robertson and Flight Lieutenant K. Busby, "Sikorsky S-51 Helicopter Type Trials, Part 2—Initial Flying Trials in Heavily Timbered Mountainous Country (in Conjunction with the Forests Commission of Victoria)" (Aircraft Research and Development Unit, Laverton, 1949); Robertson, "Report on Investigation of Possible Uses of the Sikorsky S-51 Helicopter in Combating Forest Fires" (American trip); J. C. Westcott and V. P. Cleary, "An Account of the Use of the Helicopter in Fire Suppression Work in the Victorian Mountain Forests," *Australian Forestry* 13, no. 1 (1950), pp. 11–16.

16. See S. Wedd, "Bush Fire Prevention with the 'Brompton Rat,'" *Agriculture Gazette* (December 1978), pp. 42–43; R. W. Condon, "The Brompton Fire Rat. Application in Control of Bush Fires in Western Division," unpublished report, Western Lands Division, New South Wales.

17. "The Fire Problem," *Australian Forestry* IV (1939), p. 2.

18. T. N. Stoate, *Report on Research Activities on the Forests Department to December, 1953* (unpublished ms., n.d.), Chapter 2, Section 3. See also W. R.

Wallace, "Forest Fire Weather Research in Western Australia," *Australian Forestry* 1, no. 1 (1936), pp. 17–24; C. E. Lane-Poole, *Transcript of Evidence Given before the Royal Commission . . . Saturday, 1st April, 1939*, pp. 2375–2377.

19. *Recommendations of the Fourth Australian Fire Control Conference Held at Canberra, 24–28th May, 1954*, p. 1.

20. A. R. King, "Bushfire Research," *The Royal Australian Chemical Institute, Proceedings* (June 1960), p. 250; memo of April 24, 1956 quoted in "Action on 1954 Conference Recommendations," *Recommendations of the Fourth Australian Fire Control Conference, 1954*, p. 2.

21. J. C. Foley, "Fire Weather Warning Service," address given to a regional officers' school of Country Fire Authority (Ballarat, 1955); H. E. Whittingham, "A Review of Fire Weather Investigations in Australia," *Australian Meteorological Magazine* 35 (December 1961), pp. 10–14; "Report on Organisation and Present Development of Fire Weather Service," *Fifth Australian Fire Control Conference, Maryborough, Queensland, 1956*, p. 2; *Proceedings of the Fire Weather Conference* (Bureau of Meteorology, 1958).

22. For South Australia, see L. T. Jacobs, "A Summary of Bushfire Research, 1964–1974, Conducted under the Guidance of the Bushfire Research Committee," Report No. 56, and D. R. Douglas and B.J.T. Graham, eds., *Bushfire Protection in South Australia for the 1970s*. Among reports see D. R. Douglas, "Forest Fire Weather Studies in South Australia," Bulletin No. 9 (Woods and Forests Department, 1957). Western Australian research is summarized in Neil Burrows, "Summary of Fire Research in Western Australia," unpublished report (Forests Department, 1985). In Victoria, see Reg Oakley, "The Role of the Committee. Inaugural Meeting of the VRFBA Research Committee," unpublished report. For early work in New South Wales, see *Effects of Fire on Forest Conditions* (Forestry Commission, 1966). The year-to-year research by the states and Commonwealth are summarized in their annual reports.

23. King quoted in *Meeting of Fire Control Officers, Scottsdale, 1962*, p. 10; Fire Research Section, Forestry and Timber Bureau, *Fire Control Research in Australia* (Canberra, 1962), p. 5.

24. A. G. McArthur, "The Preparation and Use of Fire Danger Tables," *Proceedings of the Fire Weather Conference* (Bureau of Meteorology, 1958), and "Report on Fire Behaviour Studies in Jarrah Fuel Types. Dwellingup, Western Australia, April, 1959," unpublished report (Forestry and Timber Bureau, 1959); A. R. King, *The Efficiency of Rural Firefighters*. CSIRO Chemical Research Laboratories Technical Paper No. 4 (Melbourne, 1962); A. R. King, *A Survival Tent for Rural Firefighters*. CSIRO Division of Physical Chemistry (Melbourne, 1962); and A. R. King, *The Influence of Colonisation on the Forests and the Prevalence of Bushfires in Australia* (CSIRO Division of Physical Chemistry, n.d.)

25. Transcript of "Television Interview of 20th January 1962" (unpublished ms., NBRU files). On smoke studies, see D. G. Reid and R. G. Vines, "A Radar Study of the Smoke Plume from a Forest Fire," Division of Applied Chemistry Technical Paper No. 2 (CSIRO, 1972); A. J. Eccleston et al., "The Scattering Coefficient and Mass Concentration of Smoke from Some Australian Forest Fires," *Air Pollution Control Association Journal* 24, no. 11 (1974), pp. 1047–1050; L. F. Evans et al., "Further Studies on the Nature of Bushfire Smoke," Division of Applied Organic Chemistry Technical Paper No. 2 (CSIRO, 1976); "Looking into Smoke," *Ecos* 9 (August 1976), pp. 10–14; R. J.

Taylor et al., "A Meso-Meteorological Investigation of Five Forest Fires," Division of Meteorological Physics Technical Paper No. 18 (CSIRO, 1968).

26.   Fire behavior studies center on A. G. McArthur, "Fire Behavior in Eucalypt Forests," Leaflet No. 107 (Forestry and Timber Bureau, 1967), "The Application of a Drought Index System to Australian Fire Control" (Forestry and Timber Bureau, 1966), and "The Fire Resistance of Eucalypts," *Proceedings, Ecological Society of Australia* 3 (1966), pp. 83–90. A fuller bibliography is contained in Luke and McArthur, *Bushfires in Australia.* For recurrence patterns in extreme weather, see R. G. Vines, "Weather Patterns and Bush-fire Cycles in Southern Australia," Division of Chemical Technology Technical Paper No. 2 (CSIRO, 1974), and "A Survey of Forest Fire Danger in Victoria (1937–69), *Australian Forest Research* 4 (1969), pp. 25, 39–44.   The international connection is described in The Technical Co-operation Programme, *Mass Fire Symposium,* 2 vols. (Defence Standards Laboratory, 1969). A summary was prepared by K. Felton, "Report on Mass Fire Symposium, Canberra, February 1962," unpublished ms., CSIRO files.   For status reports and samplings of the international scene, see R. G. Vines, "Bushfire Research in CSIRO," *Search* 6, no. 3 (March 1975), pp. 74–79; "The Bushfire Problem in Australia," *Rural Research in CSIRO 69,* pp. 8–13; A. Hodgson, "Fire Management in Eucalypt Forest," *Proceedings, Tall Timbers Fire Ecology Conferences* 6 (Tallahassee, 1967), pp. 97–111; A. B. Mount, "Eucalypt Ecology Related to Fire," and "An Australian's Impression of North American Attitudes to Fire," *Proceedings, Tall Timbers Fire Ecology Conference* 9 (Tallahassee, 1969), pp. 75–118. Most of the international symposia on fire ecology, particularly those targeting Mediterranean-climate regions, included Australian participants.

27.   R. H. Luke, conversations with author; R. H. Luke, "N.S.W. Forestry Commission—Hazard Reduction Policy and Planning," in R. H. Luke et al., eds., *Fire Control Symposium, Coff's Harbour* (Forestry Commission, 1964), p. 4.

28.   W. R. Wallace, "Fire in the Jarrah Forest Environment," *Journal of the Royal Society of Wstern Australia* 49, part 2 (1965), p. 42; Luke, "N.S.W. Forestry Commission—Hazard Reduction Policy and Planning," p. 4.

29.   R. H. Luke, comments in *The Bushfire Problem in Public Lands* (National Trust of Australia, 1966), p. 26; A. G. McArthur, "Prescribed Burning in Australian Fire Control," *Australian Forestry* 30 (1966), p. 8; J. R. Baxter et al., *Control Burning from Aircraft* (CSIRO, 1965).

30.   The literature on the expansion of controlled fire is large and fugitive, perhaps best captured in the succession of conferences, symposia, and so on that proliferated during the period. The critical document was clearly McArthur's *Controlled Burning in Eucalypt Forests* (1962), but there were regional variations. An interesting version concerns intense burning for regeneration (forestry's equivalent to the "good burn" of land-clearing settlers). In Victoria, after some notorious escapes, this led to a committee of inquiry which submitted its report in June 1964. The Tasmanian scene heated more intensely, spilling over into an environmental controversy about logging as well as fire.

31.   See Forests Department, Western Australia, *Focus on Controlled Burning for Forest Conservation* (1970).   For a survey in the late 1970s, see P. J. Byrne, "Prescribed Burning in Australia—The State of the Art," presented to Australian Forestry Council, Research Working Group No. 6—Fire Management, Fifth Research Meeting (1977). On aerial ignition in New South Wales, consult Bob Richmond, "Development of Aerial Burning Technique," *Forest and Timber* 10, no. 3 (October 1974), pp. 9–10, and "Aerial Prescribed Burning,"

Forest and Timber 9 (spring 1973), pp. 8–91; R. H. Luke, "Aerial Hazard Reduction in Eastern N.S.W.," *Bush Fire Bulletin* (winter 1979), pp. 19–24; annual reports of the Forstry Commission and the Co-ordinating Committee of the Bush Fire Council of New South Wales. For Victoria, see Conrad H. Wood, "Forest Fuel Reduction—an Air Craft Down Under," paper presented to 3rd International Aerospace Symposium, *Special Aviation Services to Conservation of the Environment* (Vancouver, 1973), pp. 5–14; Athol Hodgson and N. P. Cheney, "Aerial Ignition for Backburning," *Australian Forestry* 33, no. 4 (May 1970), pp. 268–274. For Tasmania, see Jim Hickman, "The Policy of the Forestry Commission Relating to Fire Management in State Forests," paper for *Fire and Forestry Management* (Tasmanian Conservation Trust, 1981); Evan R. Rolley, "Hazard Reduction Burning," Forest Fire Control Conference—Campbell Town (1979); and A. Ingles, "Fire," Working Paper 2, *Environmental Impact Statement on Tasmanian Woodchip Exports Beyond 1988* (Forestry Commission of Tasmania, n.d.). For Queensland, see N. B. Henry, "Complete Protection versus Prescribed Burning in the Maryborough Hardwoods," Research Notes No. 13 (Queensland Forest Service, 1961); T. E. Just, "Plantation Establishment Burns in the Hoop Pine Plantation Areas of South East Queensland," unpublished report (Queensland Forest Service); J. Walker, "Use of Aerial Incendiaries to Establish Linear Fire Breaks," report (1978); P. J. Byrne, "Prescribed Burning in Queensland Exotic Pine Plantations," prepared for *Eleventh Commonwealth Forestry Conference* (Queensland Forest Service, 1980); P. J. Byrne and T. E. Just, "Exotic Pine Plantation Prescribed Burning Using a Helicopter," Technical Paper No. 28 (Department of Forestry, Queensland, 1982); and, most comprehensively, *Fire Conference—Gympie* (Department of Forestry, 1980), Topic 2. For a description of the Northern Territory program, see H. T. Lewis, "Burning the 'Top End': Kangaroos and Cattle," in Julian Ford, ed., *Fire Ecology and Management in Western Australian Ecosystems* (1985), p. 26. For controversy over interior fire programs, see J. C. Noble, "Prescribed Fire in Mallee Rangelands and the Potential Role of Aerial Ignition," *Australian Rangeland Journal* 8, no. 2 (1986), pp. 118–130.

32. V. P. Cleary, "Air Operations for Fire Control," Position Paper for Meeting of Research Working Group No. 6—Fire Management Research (1977), and P. J. Byrne, "Prescribed Burning in Australia—The State of the Art," from Australian Forestry Council, Research Working Group No. 6—Fire Management Research (1977); A. G. McArthur, "The Role of Waterbombing Aircraft in the Suppression of Forest Fires," in Royal Aeronautical Society, *Application of Aircraft in Bushfire Control* (1969), p. 22; N. Gellie, "Evaluation of Ignition and Field Operation of Laser Ignition Device," unpublished report (Forestry Commission of Tasmania, 1983); Michael D. Waterworth, "Laser Ignition Device and Its Application to Forestry, Fire, and Land Management," *Proceedings of the Symposium on Wildland Fire 2000*, General Technical Report PSW-101 (U.S. Forest Service, 1987).

33. A history of the tours is encapsulated in N. P. Cheney et al., "Fire Management Study Tour of the United States. 21 July–26 August 1978," report submitted to Standing Committee of Australian Forestry Council (1979), p. 10. In brief, Luke and Torbet—Australians—traveled with an FAO tour to the U.S. in 1951. A second tour of Australians (and others) to the U.S. and Canada followed in 1964. American foresters toured Australia in 1970, Australian and New Zealand foresters went to the U.S. in 1971, Americans returned to Australia in 1975, and Australians recycled to North America in 1978. The Ameri-

cans returned in 1983 (for which a formal report has never been written). Australians visited North America again in 1985 and 1989. Reports include R. H. Luke, "Report of Forest Fire Control Training Program in U.S.A. during 1951"; "Final Report on the Forest Fire Control Study Tour, Australia 1970" (U.S. Forest Service, 1970); D. R. Douglas, "Report of Fire Study Tour of the United States and Canada, July–August 1964"; N. P. Cheney et al., "Fire Management Study Tour of the United States"; "Australian Forest Fire Study Tour of USA and Canada. 16 July–16 August 1985," report to Standing Committee of Australian Forestry Council (1986).   Individual tour reports include T. Ryan, "A Report on Australian and New Zealand Fire Study Tour of United States" (1978); G. B. Peet, "U.S.A. Fire Management Tour Report 1978"; F. Campbell, "Report on Fire Control Operations' Tour of California and Georgia, U.S.A." (1972); D. R. Packham, "Report on Fire Study Tour of Northern America, Europe and Southern Africa. May–September 1969"; C. E. Van Wagner, "Impressions of Forest Fire and Forestry in Australia" (December 1975); and, with reservations, Stephen J. Pyne, "Report on Ad Hoc Fire Study Tour of Australia, 2 June–2 August, 1986," revised (February 1987).   For an interesting context, see Richard White, " 'Combating Cultural Aggression': Australian Opposition to Americanisation," *Meanjin* 39, no. 3 (October 1980), pp. 275–289.

34.   For the SCOPE contribution, see A. Malcolm Gill et al., eds., *Fire and the Australian Biota* (Australian Academy of Science, 1981), p. iii.
35.   R. G. Vines, commentary in *The Bushfire Problem in Public Lands* (National Trust of Australia, 1966), p. 28.
36.   A. G. McArthur, untitled lecture (c. 1977), p. 2 (copy courtesy of N. P. Cheney).
37.   For biographical information, see "Alan G. McArthur," *Australian Forestry* 41, no. 4 (1978), pp. 189–190; "N. W. Jolly Medal, 1978 Award: Alan G. McArthur," *Australian Forestry* 42, pp. 57–58; "McArthur, A. G.," *Growing Trees on Australian Farms* (Forestry and Timber Bureau, 1968), p. x; N. P. Cheney, "A Short Biography of Alan McArthur," letter to author, July 3, 1989. A good summary of McArthur's ideas is contained in "Scourge of the Bushfire," *Hemisphere* 13, no. 3 (1969), pp. 2–11.
38.   McArthur, comments in *Environments to Order?* Proceedings of a Symposium (Australian Museum, 1970), p. 2.
39.   See McArthur, comments in *The Bushfire Problem on Public Lands* (National Trust of Australia, 1966), p. 36.
40.   A. G. McArthur, untitled lecture (c. 1977), p. 4 (copy courtesy of N. P. Cheney).

19. WILD BUSH, URBAN BUSH

1.   The Tasmanian example comes from A. Ingles, "Fire," Working Paper 2, *Environmental Impact Statement on Tasmanian Woodchip Exports Beyond 1988* (Forestry Commission of Tasmania, n.d.), p. 12. As graziers deserted bush paddocks, no other group dedicated to routine burning took their place.
2.   A. G. McArthur, "The Tasmanian Bushfires of 7th February, 1967, and Associated Fire Behaviour Characteristics," *Second Australian National Conference*

on Fire (Australian Fire Protection Association, 1968), p. 25.   The literature on the 1967 fires is exceptionally dense and comprehensive. The fundamental documents include D. M. Chambers et al., *Fire Prevention and Suppression. Bush Fire Disaster of February 1967* (Hobart, 1967); D. M. Chambers and C. G. Brettingham-Moore, *The Bush Fire Disaster of 7th February, 1967. Report and Summary of Evidence* (Excluding Appendices) (Tasmania, 1967); R. G. Cox, *Fire Protection Arrangements in the State of Tasmania: Report of Board of Enquiry* (Parliament of Tasmania, 1977); A. B. Mount, "7th February 1967—A Day of Extreme Fire Weather" (unpublished report, Forestry Commission of Tasmania, 1981; revised, 1983); A. G. McArthur and N. P. Cheney, "Preliminary Report on the Southern Tasmanian Fires of 7th February, 1967" (Forest Research Institute, 1967); H. G. Bond et al., *Report on the Meteorological Aspects of the Catastrophic Bushfires in South-Eastern Tasmania on 7 February 1967* (Commonwealth Bureau of Meteorology, 1967); R. G. Vines, "Hobart Fire Investigation (March 7–9, 1967)," Appendix C to *Parliamentary Paper No. 16* (1967). The institutional response is thoroughly reviewed in R. L. Wettenhall, *Bushfire Disaster. An Australian Community in Crisis* (Angus and Robertson, 1975), which subsumes two earlier studies: R. L. Wettenhall, and J. M. Power, "Bureaucracy and Disaster," *Public Administration* XXVIII (1969), pp. 273–277, and "Bureaucracy and Disaster II," *Public Administration* XXIX (1970), pp. 165–188.

3.   Chambers et al., *Fire Prevention and Suppression*, pp. 24, 28–29.

4.   The urban bush is too immense a subject to do more than sample relative to bushfire concerns. Most of the recent fire symposia include the urban bush among their topics (see Bibliographic Essay for a listing). Of special interest are B. R. Roberts, ed., *Queensland Fire Research Workshop* (Darling Downs Institute of Advanced Education, 1980); Susan A. Moore, ed., *The Management of Small Bush Areas in the Perth Metropolitan Region* (Department of Fisheries and Wildlife, 1983); Roger Fenwick and David C. Everall, "Fire Management in Urban Grasslands," *Australian Parks & Recreation* (November 1975), pp. 25–29; Mark W. Fleeton, "Public and Private Adjustment to the Bush Fire Hazard in Australia: Empirical Evidence from New South Wales," *Australian Geographer* 14 (1980), pp. 350–359; *Urban Bushland Management Symposium* (Willoughby Municipal Council, 1983); Bushfire Research Committee of South Australia, *Fire in the Hills: Bushfire and the Environment* (1971); G. Ross Cochrane et al., "Land Use and Forest Fires in the Mount Lofty Ranges, South Australia," *Australian Geographer* 8, no. 4 (1962), pp. 143–160; Brian Page, "Wild Fire Hazard in the Environs of Hobart," M.Sc. thesis (University of Tasmania, 1976); Michael C. R. Edgell and Eric H. Brown, "The Bushfire Environment of Southeastern Australia," *Journal of Environmental Management* 3 (1975), pp. 329–349. Pertinent to Greater Sydney is P. T. Hutchings, "Fire Frequency in the Blue Mountains and the 1968 and 1977 Wildfires in Retrospect," unpublished report (CSIRO National Bushfire Research Unit, n.d.). A special review of the Melbourne perimeter is available in "The Dandenongs," in Alan Gilpin, *The Australian Environment. 12 Controversial Issues* (Sun Books, 1980).

5.   See Michael C. R. Edgell and Eric H. Brown, "Bushfires in the Dandenong Ranges. The Attitudes of Residents," *Victoria's Resources* (December 1971–February 1972), pp. 10–14; H. E. Whittingham, "Meteorological Conditions Associated with the Dandenong Bush Fires of 14–16 January, 1962," *Austra-*

lian *Meteorological Magazine* (1964), pp. 10–37; M.C.R. Edgell, "Nature and Perception of the Bushfire Hazard in Southeastern Australia" (Department of Geography, Monash University, 1973), p. 35.

6. Australian Academy of Science, "National Parks and Reserves in Australia" (1968); Howard Evans and Mary Alice Evans, *Australia. A Natural History* (Smithsonian Institution Press, 1983), p. 195. See also Geoffrey Bolton, *Spoils and Spoilers. Australians Make Their Environment 1788–1980* (George Allen and Unwin, 1981), especially pp. 159–160, and Alan Gilpin, *Environment Policy in Australia* (University of Queensland Press, 1980), pp. 147–185. On the impact of the 1968 fires, see E. G. Weir, "Development of a Fire Policy," *Parks and Wildlife* 2, no. 2 (1978), pp. 25–28. On fire policy, in general, each of the state National Parks and Wildlife Service agencies has issued particular policies, as have the state forest commissions and conservation associations. A helpful (if dated) summary for the southeast can be found in B. D. Dexter, "Fire Management in National Parks in South Eastern Australian Sclerophyll Forests," *Seventh Triennial Conference*, Institute of Foresters of Australia, Vol. 1—Working Papers, pp. 313–337. An essential starting point is R. B. Good, "The Role of Fire in Conservation Reserves," in A. M. Gill et al., eds., *Fire and the Australian Biota* (Australian Academy of Science, 1981), pp. 529–550. On the 1968 fires, Phil Cheney has written: ". . . despite the introduction of aerial burning which we had just demonstrated to be effective in containing parts of these fires, the Forestry Commission withdrew their support for fire suppression activities in these areas and contracted back to the State forests on the coast . . . The aero-burns that we did in 1967 near Moruya and in May 1968 near Bemboka both withstood the onslaught of the '68 coastal fires and were held up as a prime example of the efficacy of prescribed burning" (letter to author, February 3, 1990).

7. Eric Rolls, *They All Went Wild* (Angus and Robertson, 1969), p. 209.

8. Judith Wright, "Australia 1970," *Collected Poems 1942–1970* (Angus and Robertson, 1971), p. 292.

9. On the Nadgee fire, see Roger Good, "Heathland Fire Management," in Christine Haigh, ed., *Heaths in New South Wales* (National Parks and Wildlife Service, 1981), pp. 57–64; A. M. Fox, "The '72 Fire of Nadgee Nature Reserve," *Parks and Wildlife* 2 (1978), pp. 5–24; Heimo G. Posamentier et al., "Succession Following Wildfire in Coastal Heathland (Nadgee Nature Reserve, N.S.W.)," *Australian Journal of Ecology* 6 (1982), pp. 165–175; Harry F. Recher et al., "A Grand Natural Experiment. The Nadgee Wildfire," *Australian Natural History* 18, no. 5 (1975), pp. 154–163. An Allen painting graces the cover of Bolton, *Spoils and Spoilers*. Evans and Evans, *Australia*, p. 49. On British straw burning as a controversy, see Note 31, Chapter 10.

10. Australian Conservation Foundation, "Bushfire Control and Conservation," Viewpoint Series No. 5 (November 1970), p. 1.

11. Australian Conservation Foundation, "Bushfire Control and Conservation," p. 12; National Parks Association of New South Wales, "Policy Statement on Fire Management in Natural Areas" (December 1980), p. 6.

12. See Queensland Department of Forests, "Plan for Fire Management of Cooloola, Including the Como Scarp"; C. Sandercoe, "Fire Management at Cooloola National Park," in Brian Roberts, ed., *Third Queensland Fire Research Workshop* (Darling Downs Institute of Advanced Education, 1987), pp. 139–158. For the southwest, see R. J. Underwood and P.E.S. Christensen, *For-*

est Fire Management in Western Australia, Special Focus No. 1 (Perth, 1981) and Per Christensen, "Using Prescribed Fire to Manage Forest Fauna," *Forest Focus* 25 (August 1983, reprint), pp. 8–21.

13.   See Wayne Ralph, "Fire in the Centre," *Ecos* 40 (winter 1984), pp. 3–10; G. F. Griffin, "The Role of Fire in Arid Lands," in Peter Stanbury, ed., *Bushfires— Their Effect on Australian Life and Landscape* (Macleay Museum, 1981); and Ken C. Hodgkinson, "Influence of Fire on Arid Land Vegetation and Some Implications for Management," CSIRO Division of Wildlife and Rangelands (reprint), 3 pp.; G. F. Griffin, "Hummock Grasslands," in G. N. Harrington et al., eds., *Management of Australia's Rangelands* (CSIRO, 1984), pp. 271–284; W. E. Mulham, "Vegetation Changes after Fire on Two Land Systems in Arid North-West New South Wales," *Australian Rangeland Journal* 7, no. 2 (1985), pp. 80–87.

14.   R. H. Luke (chair), *Proceedings of the Tropical and Arid Fire Symposium* (Bush Fires Council of the Northern Territory, 1971); J.R.L. Hoare et al., *A Report on the Effects of Fire in Tall Open Forest and Woodland with Particular Reference to Fire Management in Kakadu National Park in the Northern Territory,* interim report to Australian National Parks and Wildlife Service (March 1980); R. E. Fox, *Report on the Use of Fire in National Parks and Reserves* (Darwin, November 28–29, 1974); C. D. Haynes, "Land, Trees, and Man," *Commonwealth Forestry Review* 57 (1978), pp. 99–106; S. R. and M. H. Andrew, "Ecological Impact and Management of Fire in Northern Australia," *Search* 18, no. 2 (March–April 1987), pp. 77–82; Andrew Bell, "Fire Damages Top-End Forests," *Ecos* 30 (1977), pp. 12–17. See also entries in Note 2, Chapter 8.

15.   Australian Conservation Foundation, "The Burning Question! A Discussion Paper on the Problem of Fire in Tasmania" (n.d.).

16.   The intellectual gridlock is well inscribed in Andrew Bell, "Fire and Rainforest in Tasmania," *Ecos* 37 (1983), pp. 3–8. The basic documents include J. B. Kirkpatrick, et al., "Fire in the South-West," and W. D. Jackson, " 'Ecological Drift.' An Argument against the Continued Practice of Hazard Reduction Burning," in Helen Gee and Janet Fenton, eds., *The South West Book* (Australian Conservation Foundation, 1978), pp. 93–101; D.M.J.S. Bowman and W. D. Jackson, "Slash-burning in the Regeneration of Dry Eucalypt Forests," *Australian Forestry* 44, no. 2 (1981), pp. 118–124; W. D. Jackson and D.M.J.S. Bowman, "Comments," *Australian Forestry* 45, no. 1 (1982), pp. 63–66; W. D. Jackson and D.M.J.S. Bowman, "Reply: Ecological Drift or Fire Cycles in South-West Tasmania," *Search* 13, nos. 7 and 8 (August–September 1982), pp. 175–176; *Symposium—Role of Fire in the Management of Tasmanian National Parks and the South-West Area* (1976); Sean Cadman, *Fire and Forest Management. Impact and Alternatives* (1984); J. B. Kirkpatrick, ed., *Fire and Forest Management in Tasmania* (Tasmanian Environment Centre, 1982); A. B. Mount, "Natural Regeneration Processes in Tasmanian Forests," *Search* 10, no. 5 (1979), pp. 181–186, "Eucalypt Ecology as Related to Fire," *Proceedings, Tall Timbers Fire Ecology Conference* 9 (Tallahassee, 1969), pp. 75–108, "Natural Regeneration Processes in Tasmanian Forests," paper Presented at 27th ANZAAS Congress (1976; revised, 1977), and "Fire-Cycles or Succession in South-West Tasmania," *Search* 13, nos. 7 and 8 (August–September 1982), p. 174; Forestry Commission of Tasmania, "Analysis of the Tasmanian Fire Pattern" (unpublished, n.d.), and "Suggested Principles Con-

cerning Use of Fire in Native Eucalypt Forests," in *The Planned Burning Course, 1985* (Forestry Commission). Additional materials of relevance include N.J.H. Gellie, "Fire Ecology of Buttongrass Moorlands," Bulletin No. 6, Forestry Commission of Tasmania (1980); Nic Gellie, and Evan Rolley, *A Report on Aerial Burning 1978–79* (Forestry Commission of Tasmania, 1979); "A Report to the Honourable the Premier by a Committee Formed to Review Various Aspects of Hazard Reduction Burning" (Tasmania, c. 1972). The most concise summary of fire practices remains Ingles, "Fire," Working Paper 2.

17.   The story can be worked out through the following documents: A. M. Gill et al., "Fire in Kosciusko National Park," *CSIRO Division of Plant Industry Annual Report*, 1975, pp. 38–44; "Burning Question in the Snowy," *Ecos* 20 (1977), pp. 12–17; W. G. Bryant, "The Effect of Grazing and Burning on a Mountain Grassland, Snowy Mountains, New South Wales," *Journal of the Soil Conservation Service of New South Wales* 29 (1973), pp. 29–42; W. G. Bryant, "Grazing, Burning and Regeneration of Tree Seedlings in *Eucalyptus pauciflora* Woodlands," *Journal of the Soil Conservation Service of New South Wales* 27, no. 2 (1971), pp. 121–134; R. B. Good, "A Preliminary Assessment of Erosion Following Wildfires in Kosciusko National Park, N.S.W., in 1973," *Journal of the Soil Conservation Service of New South Wales* 29 (1973), pp. 191–199.

18.   For an outstanding critique of simple hazard-reduction burning, see A. Malcolm Gill, "Management of Fire-Prone Vegetation for Conservation," *Search* 8, nos. 1 and 2 (1977), pp. 20–26. Although Gill served as its most eloquent spokesman, he conveyed the ideas of a group that dated back to the pioneering studies of A. B. Costin.

19.   Important criticisms include R. and V. Routley, *The Fight for the Forests*, 3rd ed. (Research School for the Social Sciences, Australian National University (1975); Sean Cadman, "Fire and Forest Management—Impacts and Alternatives" (Forest Action Network, 1984); Gilpin, *Environment Policy in Australia*, pp. 169–185; and virtually all the fire ecology symposia held during the 1970s and 1980s. For a summary of the nutrient controversy, see Mary Lou Considine, "Prescribed Burning and Forest Nutrition," *Ecos* 42 (summer 1984–85), pp. 12; R. J. Raison, "A Review of the Role of Fire in Nutrient Cycling in Australian Native Forests, and of Methodology for Studying the Fire-Nutrient Intraction," *Australian Journal of Ecology* 5 (1980), pp. 15–21; R. C. Ellis and A. M. Graley, "Gains and Losses in Soil Nutrients Associated with Harvesting and Burning Eucalypt Rainforest," *Plant and Soil* 73 (1983), pp. 437–450; and P. M. Attiwell and G. W. Leeper, *Forest Soils and Nutrient Cycles* (Melbourne University Press, 1987).

20.   For plantation fire protection, see D. R. Douglas, "Plantation Fires," unpublished manuscript, South Australia Woods and Forests Department (c. 1986), "Some Characteristics of Major Fires in Coniferous Plantations" (1963), "Characteristics of Major Fires in Coniferous Plantations" (1964); "The Effectiveness of Fire Protection Systems in *Pinus pinaster*," (unpublished ms., Forests Department, Western Australia); Mark Dawson, "High Intensity Fires in Plantations of *Pinus radiata*. Report to the Fire Research Working Group, October 1982"; P. J. Byrne, "Prescribed Burning in Queensland Exotic Pine Plantations," prepared for *Eleventh Commonwealth Forestry Conference* (1980).

21.   See D. J. Geddes and E. R. Pfeiffer, *The Caroline Forest Fire, 2nd February, 1979.* Bulletin 26, Woods and Forests Department, South Australia (December 1981).

22. For general information about woodchipping, consult Routley and Routley, *The Fight for the Forests;* Daniel Lunney and Chris Moon, "The Eden Woodchip Debate (1969–86)," *Search* 18, no. 1 (1987), pp. 15–20; and L. T. Carron, *A History of Forestry in Australia* (Australian National University Press, 1985), pp. 42–48, 50, 79–89, 196, 167–169.

23. Cited in L. T. Carron, *A History of Forestry in Australia* (Australian National University Press, 1985), p. 44.

24. A. P. Van Loon, "Slash—Unlimited. A Commentary on the Slash Problem of the Eden Woodchip Operations," unpublished report, Forestry Commission of New South Wales (October 1973), pp. 7, 14. In addition to published documents, an incomplete sampling for such a controversial story, I have relied on comments communicated by Phil Cheney to me in a letter dated February 3, 1990, prodded by an early draft of my manuscript.

25. J. A. Duggin, *Bushfire History of the South Coast Study Area.* CSIRO Division of Land Use Research, Technical Memorandum 76/13 (1976); N. P. Cheney, "Memorandum to Mr A. G. Brown, Assistant Chief. 26 October 1978," files of CSIRO National Bushfire Research Unit, p. 1.

26. N. P. Cheney, "An Investigation of the Cause of the Timbillica Fire and Other Fires in the Eden Area, 1980–1981," A report to the Forestry Commission of New South Wales (April 1981), pp. 9–10.

27. See Lunney and Moon, "The Eden Woodchip Debate," pp. 17–18; "Fuel Management Plan," *Annual Report for 1987.* Information on Luke's visit from conversations. Cheney's investigation demonstrated that "that 8-year regrowth which had regenerated on areas burnt in the 1972 fires, suffered considerably less damage (and in some cases didn't burn at all) than regrowth established amongst the heads without burning. . . . The potention to burn 15-year old forests was now a possibility again as it was in 1968 at Bemboka" (letter to author, February 3, 1990).

28. R. J. Sneeuwjagt, "The Eden Fire and Its Implications for Fire Protection," *Institute of Foresters of Australia Newsletter* 22, no. 4 (December 1981), pp. 8–14.

20. DIEBACK

1. Samuel Dixon, "The Effects of Settlement and Pastoral Occupation in Australia upon the Indigenous Vegetation," *Transactions and Proceedings and Report of the Royal Society of South Australia* XV (1892), p. 199. On the dieback phenomenon, see K. M. Old et al., eds., *Eucalypt Dieback in Forests and Woodlands* (CSIRO, 1981); R. C. Ellis et al., "Recovery of *Eucalyptus delegatensis* from High Altitude Dieback after Felling and Burning the Understory," *Australian Forestry* 43, no. 1 (1980) pp. 29–35; T. Bird et al., "The Eucalypt Crown Diebacks—A Growing Problem for Forest Managers," *Australian Forestry* 37 (1975), pp. 173–187; G. A. Kile, "What's Wrong with That Tree?," in *Think Trees, Grow Trees* (Australian Government Publishing Service, 1985), pp. 131–142; S. R. Shea et al., "A New Perspective on Jarrah Dieback," *Forest Focus* 31, no. 4 (1984), pp. 3–11.

2. Andrew Bell, "Fire v. Shrubs in the Semi-Arid Rangelands," *Ecos* 46 (summer 1985–86), p. 7.

3. See Stephen R. Kessell, and Roger G. Good, "Technological Advances in Bushfire Management and Planning," in *Natural Disasters in Australia,* pp. 3–

22; Stephen R. Kessell et al., *Computer Modelling in Natural Area Management.* Special Publication 9 (Australian National Parks and Wildlife Service, 1982); S. R. Kessell et al., "Implementation of Two New Resource Management Information Systems in Australia," *Environmental Management* 8 (1984), pp. 251–270. For an example of the extension service, see L. A. Love and S. Ferrier, "Application of a Computer Base Fire Management System in Yuraygir National Park," pp. 69–89, in Brian Roberts, ed., *Third Queensland Fire Research Workshop* (1986). For Kakadu, see Andrew Bell, "A Computer 'Expert' Helps out at Kakadu," *Ecos* 55 (autumn 1988), pp. 3–8; J. R. Davis et al., "Developing a Fire Management Expert System for Kakadu National Park, Australia," *Journal of Environmental Management* 22 (1986), pp. 215–227; J. Walker et al., eds., "Towards an Expert System for Fire Management at Kakadu National Park," *CSIRO Division of Water and Land Resources Technical Memorandum* No. 85/2 (1985); J.R.L. Hoare et al., "The FIRES Expert System Knowledge Base," *CSIRO Division of Water and Land Resources Technical Memorandum* No. 86/19 (1986). See also Michael J. Crock, "A Brief History of Fire Behaviour Modelling and Its Future Prospects in Australia," in Roberts, ed., *Third Queensland Fire Research Workshop,* pp. 33–52.

4.   Kessell and Good, "Technological Advances in Bushfire Management and Planning," pp. 11–19. For an overview of the new agenda of bushfire research goals, see A. Malcolm Gill, "Research for the Fire Management of Western Australian State Forests and Conservation Reserves" (Department of Conservation and Land Management, 1986).

5.   See testimony from J. L. McMahon, "Finding of the Coronial Enquiry into the Bushfire in the Bundanoon/Morton National Park/Kangaroo Valley Areas on 8 January 1983 and Subsequent Days" (1984). I am indebted to a feisty critique by Phil Cheney of an early draft of the manuscript for bringing this exact testimony to my attention rather than receiving it through second parties.

6.   Eric Rolls, *A Million Wild Acres* (Penguin Books, 1981), p. 404.

7.   G. E. Heinsohn, "The Magnetic Island Bushfire—1972," *Wildlife in Australia* 10, no. 4 (1973), pp. 136–139.

8.   J. B. Johnston et al., *Fire Protection and Fuel-Reduction Burning in Victoria.* A Report to the Minister of Forests (1982), p. 29; R. Rawson et al., "Effectiveness of Fuel-Reduction Burning," Fire Protection Branch, Research Report No. 25, Conservation Forests and Lands, Victoria (1985), p. 10 (see also P. Billing, "The Effectiveness of Fuel Reduction Burning. Five Case Histories," Fire Research Branch Report No. 10 (1981)); R. Rawson et al., "Effectiveness of Fuel-Reduction Burning," p. 10; Johnston et al., *Fire Protection and Fuel-Reduction Burning in Victoria,* p. 55.

9.   S. G. Fawcett, "Report on the Ecology of the Hume Catchment," unpublished report, Soil Conservation Authority of New South Wales, p. 38.

10. For a summary of the American revolution in fire policy and practice, see Stephen J. Pyne, *Fire in America: A Cultural History of Wildland and Rural Fire* (Princeton University Press, 1988, paperback ed.).

11. See Pyne, "Vestal Fires and Virgin Lands: A Historical Perspective on Fire and Wilderness," in James Lotan et al., *Proceedings—Symposium and Workshop on Wilderness Fire,* General Technical Report INT-182 (U.S. Forest Service, 1985), pp. 254–262; "Letting Wild Fire Loose: The Fires of '88," *Montana. The Magazine of Western History* 39, no. 3 (summer 1989), pp. 76–79; and "The Summer We Let Wild Fire Loose," *Natural History* (August 1989), pp. 31–39.

12.   N. P. Cheney, "Bushfire Disasters in Australia, 1945–1975," *Australian Forestry 39*, no. 4 (1976), pp. 245–168.

13.   See L. S. Hawkes, *Fire Protection for Queensland Coastal Plantations, as Highlighted by the 1977 Fire Season* (October 1979); Bush Fires Council of N.S.W., *The Need for Improved Publicity on Bush Fires and Their Effects* (1978) summarizes and interprets the fires.   A closer view of the firefighting is given in assorted articles in *Sitrep* 3, no. 2 (autumn 1978), pp. 2–10; J. R. Colquhoun, "Meteorological Aspects of the December 1977 Blue Mountains Bushfires," Meteorological Note 116, Bureau of Meteorology (July 1981); P. T. Hutchings, "Fire Frequency in the Blue Mountains and the 1968 and 1977 Wildfires in Retrospect," unpublished ms., NBRU (August 1978); Blue Mountains Bush Fire Prevention Association, "Report on Various Aspects Relating to Property Damage; 16th, 17th, 18 December 1977. Blue Mountains Bush Fires" (1978; copy with R. H. Luke); James Lumbers, "Our Changing Bushfire Scene," *Rural Research* 105 (1979), pp. 8–13; E.H.E. Barber, *Report of the Board of Enquiry into the Occurrence of Bush and Grass Fires in Victoria* (Melbourne, 1977). Official damage reports all vary in their estimates of losses.

14.   A. G. McArthur et al., *The Fires of 12 February 1977 in the Western District of Victoria.* (CSIRO Division of Forest Research and Country Fire Authority, Victoria, 1982), p. 10.

15.   McArthur et al., *The Fires of 12 February 1977*, p. 72; L. S. Hawkes, *Fire Protection for Queensland Coastal Plantations* (Queensland Department of Forestry, 1979); Hutchings, "Fire Frequency in the Blue Mountains," passim.

16.   Bush Fire Council of N.S.W., *The Need for Improved Publicity on Bush Fires and Their Effects*, pp. 8, 10; W. E. Townsend, "Chairman Answers Criticism on Prescribed Controlled Burning," *Sitrep* 3, no. 2 (autumn 1978), p. 10.

17.   Hutchings, "Fire Frequency in the Blue Mountains," p. 18.

18.   McArthur, *The Fires of 12 February 1977*, p. 61.

19.   McArthur, *The Fires of 12 February 1977*, p. 72.

20.   On the 1974–75 fires see R. H. Luke and A. G. McArthur, *Bushfires in Australia* (Australian Government Printing Service, 1978), pp. 339–344; R. W. Condon, "Report on Bushfires in the Western Division of New South Wales. November, 1974 to March, 1975," and R. W. Condon, "Fire Behaviour and Fire Fighting in Relation to Landscape Types in the Western Division of N.S.W." (1981).   On reading a manuscript draft, Roger Underwood argued strenuously for the reconciliation of fire interests, with special attention to Western Australia. Whether the debate was as torrid or divisive as I have presented it depends on the sources consulted. Clearly Western Australia was again exceptional, its fire officers absorbing a new fire mission within the existing institutional framework.

21.   See Forestry Commission of New South Wales, "Forestry Commission Fire Policy" (July 26, 1974).

22.   A descriptive summary of personnel and programs is given in "National Bushfire Research Unit," leaflet (1986).

23.   I. T. Loane and J. S. Gould, *Aerial Suppression of Bushfires. Cost-Benefit Study for Victoria* (National Bushfire Research Unit, 1986) and "Aerial Suppression of Bushfires. Cost-Benefit Study for Victoria. Summary and Conclusions" (National Bushfire Research Unit, 1985); R. Rawson and B. Rees, "A Review of Firebombing Operations in Victoria" (Forests Commission of Victoria, 1983); R. Rawson, "Project MAFFS/Hercules. The Modular Airborne Fire

Fighting System in Victoria," Fire Research Branch, Report No. 15 (Forests Commission of Victoria, 1982); N. P. Cheney et al., "Aerial Suppression of Bushfires. Assessment of MAFFS/Hercules Operations. Victoria, January–March, 1982" (CSIRO Division of Forest Research, 1982).

24.   See Dr. F. R. Moulds, "Submission by the Forests Commission to the Board of Inquiry into the Occurrence of Bush and Grass Fires in Victoria" (June 1977), pp. 26–28. See also H. G. Brown, "Report on Fuel Reduction Study Tour in Western Australia. 21 November to 14 December 1983" (1984), and *Fire Protection and Fuel-Reduction Burning in Victoria*. Report to the Minister of Forests (Forests Commission, 1982).

25.   F. Vanry, comments in *The Bushfire Problem in Public Lands* (National Trust of Australia, 1966), p. 24.

EPILOGUE: ASHES TO ASHES

1.   Many accounts of the Ash Wednesday fires exist, not all of them in agreement even as to the number and nature of the casualties. My recounting follows: A. Keeves and D. R. Douglas, "Forest Fires in South Australia on 16 February 1983 and Consequent Future Forest Management Aims," *Australian Forestry* 46, no. 3 (1983), pp. 148–162; K. L. Bardsley et al., "The Second Ash Wednesday: 16 February 1983," *Australian Geographical Studies* (April 21, 1983), pp. 129–141; M. E. Voice and F. J. Gauntlett, "The Ash Wednesday Fires in Australia," *Monthly Weather Review* 112 (1984), pp. 584–590; "A Natural Disaster Evolves—Ash Wednesday II," *The Volunteer* 17 (autumn–winter, 1983), whole issue; "Coroner's Inquest—Findings—1983 Ash Wednesday II Bushfires," *The Volunteer* 20 (autumn–winter, 1984), pp. 6–9; Derrick J. Pounder, "The 1983 South Australian Bushfire Disaster," *The American Journal of Forensic Medicine and Pathology* 6, no. 1 (March 1985), pp. 77–92; Dr. A. C. McFarlane, "Ash Wednesday and C.F.S. Fire Fighters," *The Volunteer* 20 (autumn–winter, 1984), pp. 8–9; "The Major Fires Originating 16th February, 1983" (Country Fire Authority Victoria, 1983); *Report on the Meteorological Aspects of the Ash Wednesday Fires—16 February 1983* (Bureau of Meteorology, 1984); Phil Ackman, "Fire Power," *Penthouse* (1984), pp. 37–39; P. Billing, "Otways Fire No. 22—1982/83. Aspects of Fire Behaviour," Fire Research Branch, Report No. 20 (1983); Australian Forestry Council, *The 1982/83 Bushfires*; Edward Mundie, *Cockatoo. Ash Wednesday 1983. The People's Story* (Hylund House, 1983); D. T. Healey et al., eds., *The Economics of Bushfires: The South Australian Experience* (Centre for South Australian Economic Studies and Oxford University Press, 1985); House of Representatives Standing Committee on Environment and Conservation, *Bushfires and the Australian Environment*; Hansard Report, Hearings before Standing Committee on Environment and Conservation, 1983; "What We Learned from Ash Wednesday," *Forest and Timber* 20 (1984), pp. 16–18; N. P. Cheney, "Forest Fire Management in Australia," pp. 75–83, in D. E. Dube (compiler), *Proceedings of the Intermountain Fire Council 1983 Fire Management Workshop*. Information Report NOR-X-271 (Northern Forest Research Centre, Canadian Forestry Service, 1985); R. A. Orchard, "The Disastrous Fires of 1983 and the Lessons Learnt," in Australian Fire Protection Association, *Proceedings of the Ninth National Conference* (1983)

2. J. Oliver et al., *The Ash Wednesday Bushfires in Victoria.* Disaster Investigation Report No. 7 (Centre for Disaster Studies, James Cook University of North Queensland, February 1984), p. 22.

3. D. R. Douglas, "Bushfire Disasters—Findings from the Past, and Pointers to Future Research and Development," *ANZAAS Symposium* (October 1983), p. 2.

4. Australian Forestry Council, *Australian Bushfire Research. Background, Guidelines and Directory* (1987); A. Malcolm Gill, *Research for Fire Management of Western Australia State Forests and Conservation Reserves* (Conservation and Land Management, 1986). See also Roger Underwood, "Research for Forest Fire Operations in Australia" reprint by Department of Conservation and Land Management (Western Australia); David R. Packham, "Bushfire Research in Australia. A Summary," unpublished statement (courtesy of author); B. R. Roberts, "Identification of Research Needs," pp. 287–291, in B. R. Roberts, ed., *Third Queensland Fire Research Workshop* (Darling Downs Institute of Advanced Education, 1986). For Australia's support for science at large, see David Widdup, "Science and Technology Expenditure and Lobbying Activity," *Search* 19, no. 2 (1988), pp. 58–64.

5. D. T. Healey et al., eds., *The Economics of Bushfires: The South Australian Experience*, p. 5.

6. Quoted in Phil Ackman, "Fire Power," *Penthouse* (1983), pp. 36–39, and "The House That Beat the Blaze," *Trees and Victoria's Resources* 25, no. 3 (1983), p. 11.

7. D. R. Packham, "Survival in Bushfires: A General Discussion," *Australian Fire Protection Conference* (1983), p. 1; National Centre for Rural Fire Research, "Environmental Impact of Bushfires," submission to Standing Committee on Environment and Conservation (April 5, 1984), pp. 2069, 2103, Official Hansard Report.

8. Packham, "Environmental Impact of Bushfires," p. 2103; Andrew A. G. Wilson and Ian S. Ferguson, "Fight or Flee?—A Case Study of the Mount Macedon Bushfire," *Australian Forestry* 47, no. 4 (1985), pp. 230–236.

9. Conversations with Chuck George, one of the Americans with Packham, and correspondence with Phil Cheney, letter dated February 3, 1990. The two Americans helped cover up the PVC pipe with dirt as the fire approached.

10. See Packham, "Survival in Bushfires," p. 1. Analogies to sharks and so forth from conversation with author.

11. Geoffrey Blainey, "Birthday Beacons Shed Light on the Fire of Our History," *The Australian* (June 4, 1988).

Bibliographic Essay

Most of my sources I have inserted into the notes, with the first note of every subchapter typically surveying the principal references for the topic at hand. For the most part these consist of articles, books, and unpublished reports, supplemented by interviews, primarily fire-related documents generated by scientists, public agencies, explorers and settlers. General works in Australian history have helped frame these observations. What follows is a description of where I got those materials and a summary of major documents, both published and unpublished, relevant to Australian fire history.

In my travels, I collected in the libraries of each of the state forestry agencies, a few of the state agricultural libraries, several university libraries, and three state libraries—the Mitchell Library in New South Wales, the Battye Library in Western Australia, and the State Library of the Northern Territory at Darwin. Of special value was the wonderful CSIRO Division of Forest Research Library and the extensive holdings of the CSIRO National Bushfire Research Unit (NBRU, since dissolved), both in Canberra. In addition, each of the state forestry agencies and several of the bushfire councils and country fire authorities graciously made available published and unpublished reports, photographs, and other materials, and, not least of all, themselves for interviews. In addition, N. P. Cheney, then head of NBRU, opened his files to inspection; these included several hundred pages of notes and photocopies gathered by the late A. G. McArthur that related to the history of fire, mostly citations drawn from explorers' journals. The references had to be verified, but the collection was an extraordinary cache of materials that helped jump start my research into a new (for me) field of history. R. R. Richmond also very generously revealed his historical researches on early fire occurrence. Later, I was able to supplement these records with research at the Oxford Forestry Institute and India Institute Library (Bodleian Library), Oxford University. After I completed most of my collecting, Malcolm Gill sent me a copy of his just-published bibliography on Australian fire ecology; it proved helpful in identifying missing publications.

GENERAL SOURCES,
AUSTRALIANA AND FIRE

Among very general or synthetic works that provide, in effect, running bibliographies of fire and Australiana three works must be consulted: A. Malcolm Gill et al., eds., *Fire and the Australian Biota* (Australian Academy of Science, 1981); A. Malcolm Gill and I. R. Noble, *Bibliography of Fire Ecology in Australia* (Bushfire Council of New South Wales, 1986); and R. H. Luke and A. G. McArthur, *Bushfires in Australia* (Australian Government Publishing Service, 1978), which is both a working manual and a compendium of major fires and fire protection organizations. The bibliography by Gill and Noble largely supersedes the earlier annotated compendium by Charles F. Cooper, *An Annotated Bibliography of the Effects of Fire on Australian Vegetation* (Soil Conservation Authority of Victoria, 1963) and other compilations.

A popular, thoughtful introduction is found in Peter Stanbury, ed., *Bushfires: Their Effect on Australian Life and Landscape* (Macleay Museum, 1981). No better point of departure exists for Aboriginal fire history than Sylvia J. Hallam, *Fire and Hearth*. Australian Aboriginal Studies No. 58 (Australian Institute of Aboriginal Studies, 1979), though its conclusions should be supplemented by more recent work, including that by the author (see notes to chapters 5 to 9). Although dating rapidly, still useful is A. R. King, *The Influence of Colonization on the Forests and the Prevalence of Bushfire in Australia* (CSIRO, n.d.). Two books on bushfire protection that include some historical material (and illustrations) are Ted Foster, *Bushfire. History, Prevention, Control* (A. H. and A. W. Reed, 1976) and Joan Webster, *The Complete Australian Bushfire Book* (Thomas Nelson, 1986). Monumental, if somewhat unwieldy, the Hansard Report of the Select Committee on the Environment's inquiry into the Ash Wednesday fires is the major repository of information about Australian fire in the early 1980s.

Many books deserve mention as introductions to large areas of Australiana relevant to fire history. Since so much evidence derives from early encounters, consult Michael Cannon, *The Exploration of Australia* (Reader's Digest, 1987) for a wonderfully illustrated tour of European exploring expeditions and a helpful bibliography. (Supplement it with Ian Wynd and Joyce Wood, *A Map History of Australia*, 3rd ed. [Oxford University Press, 1978.]) Josephine Flood, *Archaeology of the Dreamtime* (Collins, 1983) is a popular but thorough survey of Aboriginal history as revealed by archaeology. L. T. Carron, *A History of Forestry in Australia* (Australian National University Press, 1985) plods year by year and state by state, but it is helpful on politics and sources. A good introduction to the ecology of the natural scene is *Think Trees, Grow Trees* (Australian Government Publishing Service, 1985), whose breadth far exceeds its parochial title. To it should be added G. N. Harrington et al., eds., *Management of Australia's Rangelands* (CSIRO, 1984); R. H. Groves, ed., *Australian Vegetation* (Cambridge University Press, 1981); G. W. Leeper, ed., *The Australian Environment*, 4th ed. (CSIRO, 1970); and J.M.B. Smith, ed., *A History of Australasian Vegetation* (McGraw-Hill, 1982).

Americans unfamiliar with Australiana will find, as I did, that I. Kepars, *Australia*, World Bibliographical Series Vol. 46 (Clio Press, 1984) is reliable and reasonably comprehensive. That multivolume testimony to Australian scholarship, *Australians. A Historical Library*, arrived too late in North America to shape my research, but anyone working in Australian history will discover in it a monumental panorama, itself a rich nugget of the Australian experience.

For Americans, I would recommend as introductions to Australian history Manning Clark, *A Short History of Australia,* 2nd rev. ed. (New American Library, 1980) and Donald Horne, *The Story of the Australian People* (Reader's Digest, 1985), which includes wonderful illustrations to accompany its cultural and social history. For more traditional political narratives, see Frank Crowley, ed., *A New History of Australia* (William Heinemann, 1974) and C. Hartley Grattan, *The Southwest Pacific since 1900,* 2 vols. (University of Michigan Press, 1963). State histories are an apparent growth industry; of particular weight is C. T. Stannage, ed., *A New History of Western Australia* (University of Western Australia Press, 1981). On Australia's origins, see A.G.L. Shaw, *Convicts and the Colonies* (Melbourne University Press, 1978) and Robert Hughes, *The Fatal Shore* (Alfred Knopf, 1987). An excellent, condensed introduction to demographics is available in Geoffrey Sherrington, *Australia's Immigrants* (George Allen and Unwin, 1981).

Beginning surveys of environmental history should include Geoffrey Bolton, *Spoils and Spoilers* (George Allen and Unwin, 1981) and A. Grenfell Price, *Island Continent* (Angus and Robertson, 1972). These should be joined by somewhat smaller-scale studies: Michael Williams, *The Making of the South Australian Landscape* (Academic Press, 1972); D. N. Jeans, *An Historical Geography of New South Wales to 1901* (Reed Education, 1972); and W. K. Hancock, *Discovering Monaro* (Cambridge University Press, 1972). Above all Geoffrey Blainey's major books—*The Tyranny of Distance,* rev. ed. (Sun Books, 1983), *Triumph of the Nomads,* rev. ed. (Sun Books, 1983), *A Land Half Won,* rev. ed. (Sun Books, 1981), and *The Rush That Never Ended,* 3rd ed. (Melbourne University Press, 1978)—are not be missed, probably the most graceful and fascinating entree imaginable into Australian history.

On Australian cultural history, I found particularly helpful Richard White, *Inventing Australia* (George Allen and Unwin, 1981) and Geoffrey Serle, *From Deserts the Prophets Come* (William Heinemann, 1973), each of which surpasses equivalent American cultural history surveys. (Supplement White's book with his fascinating essay, " 'Combating Cultural Aggression': Australian Opposition to Americanisation," *Meanjin* 39, no. 3 (October 1980), pp. 275–289.) An essential collection of essays is John Carroll, ed., *Intruders in the Bush. The Australian Quest for Identity* (Oxford University Press, 1982). On more special topics, see Vance Palmer, *The Legend of the Nineties* (Melbourne University Press, 1963) for a seminal interpretation of a critical era of Australian cultural nationalism; Russell Ward, *The Australian Legend,* 3rd ed. (Oxford University Press, 1978); Geoffrey Dutton, ed., *The Literature of Australia,* rev. ed. (Penguin Books, 1976); and the many volumes by Bernard Smith on Australian art. Two critical studies, both now dating but not before their vocabulary entered popular discourse, are Donald Horne, *The Lucky Country* (Penguin Books, 1964) and Robin Boyd, *The Australian Ugliness,* rev. ed. (Penguin Books, 1963). In the category of essential references, I would place Sidney J. Baker, *The Australian Language,* rev. ed. (Sun Books, 1981); G. A. Wilkes, *A Dictionary of Australian Colloquialisms* (Fontana, 1980); and *The Macquarie Dictionary,* rev. ed. (Macquarie Library, 1981).

Norman Bartlett, *1776–1976. Australia and America Through 200 Years* (Ure Smith, 1976) traces out the surprising interconnections between the two nations and demonstrates how likeness confuses as well as illuminates. A diplomatic history, but one with breadth, is Norman Harper, *A Great and Powerful Friend. A Study of Australian American Relations Between 1900 and 1975* (University of Queensland Press, 1987). Angrier and less supple is Michael Dunn, *Australia and the Empire* (Fontana, 1984). That no comparable study exists from the American perspective speaks volumes about the nature of the relationship.

SPECIFIC SOURCES,
PUBLISHED AND UNPUBLISHED

Another special category embraces those published or internally published symposia, conference proceedings, minutes of meetings, etc., that are invaluable, even if not mined for quotations and thereby not included among the sources cited in separate chapters. A list of those I consulted follows, arranged in alphabetical order:

ANZAAS Symposium on Bushfires: Minimising Their Number and Effects (1983)
Australian Academy of Sciences, *Proceedings of Rural Fire Conference* (Canberra, 1969)
Australian Arid Zone Research Conference (Kalgoorlie, 1976)
Australian Counter Disaster College, *Bushfire Seminar* (1978)
Australian Fire Protection Association, *First Australian National Conference on Fire* (Sydney, 1965)
———, *Ninth National Conference on Fire* (Sydney, 1983)
Australian Forestry Council, "Bushfire Research Conference" (Adelaide, 1966)
———, "Bushfire Research. Working Group No. 6, Report of 2nd Meeting" (Canberra, 1971)
———, "Bushfire Research. Working Group No. 6, Report of 3rd Meeting" (Adelaide, 1972)
———, "Bushfire Research. Working Group No. 6, Report of 4th Meeting" (Canberra, 1975)
———, "Fire Management Research. Working Group No. 6, Report of 6th Meeting" (Gympie, Queensland, 1980)
———, "Fire Management Research. Working Group No. 6, Report of 7th Meeting" (Bunbury, W.A., 1982)
———, "Fire Management Research. Working Group No. 6, Report of 8th Meeting" (Tasmania, 1984)
———, "Fire Management Research. Working Group No. 6, Report of 9th Meeting" (Eden, N.S.W., 1986)
Bevan, C. R., ed., *National Conference on Arson* (Australian Institute of Criminology, 1983)
Bureau of Meteorology, *Fire Weather Conference* (Melbourne, 1958)
———, *Proceedings of Fire Weather Services Conference* (Adelaide, 1985)
"Conference of Rural Fire Service Chiefs" (Canberra, 1960)
Conservation Council of Victoria and Environmental Studies Association of Victoria, *Fire Seminar* (Melbourne, 1983)
"Current Fire Control Research and Operational Developments. Report of Working Group No. 6, Bushfire Research" (1971)
Ealey, E.H.M., ed., *Fighting Fire With Fire. Proceedings of Symposium on Fuel Reduction Burning* (Monash University, Conservation Council of Victoria, Forests Commission of Victoria, Melbourne, 1983)
Eco-Fire. Proceedings of a Symposium Conducted at the Australian Museum (National Parks Association of New South Wales, Sydney, 1976)
Environments To Order? Proceedings of a Symposium Held at the Australian Museum (Australian Museum and National Parks Association of New South Wales, Sydney, 1970)
Fire Conference. Gympie. February 1980 (Department of Forestry, Queensland, 1980)
"Fire Control Conference, Fifth" (Maryborough, Queensland, 1956)

"Fire Control Conference, Ninth" (Como, Western Australia, 1968)
"Fire Control Conference, Campbell Town" (1979)
"Fire Control Research in Australia" (Forestry and Timber Bureau, Canberra, 1962)
Fire Ecology Symposium (Monash University, Melbourne, 1969)
Fire in the Forest Environment. A Fire Ecology Seminar (Forests Commission of Victoria and Monash University, 1974)
Fire in the Hills: Bushfire and the Environment (Adelaide, 1971)
Ford, Julian, ed., *Fire Ecology and Management in Western Australian Eco-systems.* WAIT Environmental Studies Group Report No. 14 (Western Australian Institute of Technology, 1985)
"Forest Fire Control Officers, 8th Meeting" (Sydney, 1965)
Forestry Commission, N.S.W., *Coff's Harbour Conference* (Sydney, 1953)
Forests Commission, Victoria, *Fire Protection Conference, Marysville* (1963)
Forestry Commission, N.S.W., "Advanced Fire Control Study Course" (1965)
"Fourth Fire Control Conference" (Canberra, 1954)
Fox, R. E., ed., *Fire Management in Top End Conservation Reserves.* Parks and Wildlife Technical Bulletin Number One (Conservation Commission of the Northern Territory, Darwin, 1980)
Heislers, A., et al., eds., *Fire Ecology in Semi-Arid Lands. Proceedings of a Workshop Held at Muldura, Victoria* (Council of Nature Conservation Ministsers, 1981)
Institute of Foresters of Australia, *Third General Conference* (Melbourne, 1962)
"Interstate Conference of Rural Forest Fire Authorities" (Sydney, 1955)
Luke, R. H., ed., *Proceedings of Tropical and Arid Fire Symposium* (Bush Fires Council of the Northern Territory, Darwin, 1971)
"Meeting of Fire Control Officers, Launceston" (Tasmania, 1962)
"Meeting on Forest Fire Research. Minutes and Proceedings" (Melbourne, 1959)
Moore, Susan A., ed., *The Management of Small Bush Areas in the Perth Metropolitan Area* (Perth: Department of Fisheries and Wildlife, 1984)
Roberts, B. R., ed., *Second Queensland Fire Research Workshop* (Darling Downs Institute of Advanced Education, Gympie, 1983)
———, *Third Queensland Fire Research Workshop* (Darling Downs Institute of Advanced Education, Gympie, 1986)
South Australian Bushfire Research Committee, *National Bushfire Prevention Conference* (Adelaide, 1972)
Towards Maximum Ability to Control Wildfire (Canberra, 1967)
Western Branch Grasslands Society, *Fire Strategies. Before—During—After* (1977)
Willoughby Municipal Council, *Urban Bushland Management Symposium* (Willoughby, N.S.W., 1983)
Woods and Forests Department, S.A., "Forest Owners—Fire Control Officers Workshop" (Mount Gambier, 1984)

Index